Encyclopedia of 20th-Century American Humor

Encyclopedia of
20th-Century
American Humor

Alleen Pace Nilsen
and
Don L. F. Nilsen

Oryx Press

2000

The rare Arabian Oryx is believed to have inspired the myth of the unicorn. This desert antelope became virtually extinct in the early 1960s. At that time, several groups of international conservationists arranged to have nine animals sent to the Phoenix Zoo to be the nucleus of a captive breeding herd. Today, the Oryx population is over 1,000, and over 500 have been returned to the Middle East.

© 2000 by Alleen Pace Nilsen and Don L. F. Nilsen
Published by The Oryx Press
4041 North Central at Indian School Road
Phoenix, Arizona 85012-3397
www.oryxpress.com

Published simultaneously in Canada
Printed and bound in the United States of America

∞ The paper used in this publication meets the minimum requirements of American National Standard for Information Science—Permanence of Paper for Printed Library Materials, ANSI Z39.48, 1984.

Library of Congress Cataloging-in-Publication Data

Nilsen, Alleen Pace.
  Encyclopedia of 20th-century American humor/Alleen Pace Nilsen and Don L.F. Nilsen.
    p. cm.
  Includes bibliographical references (p.) and index.
  ISBN 1-57356-218-1 (alk. paper)
    1. American wit and humor—20th century—Encyclopedias. I. Title: Encyclopedia of twentieth century American humor. II. Nilsen, Alleen Pace. III. Title.
PS438.N55   2000
817'.503—dc21   99-047257
                                                                              CIP

CONTENTS

PREFACE

We were pleased and challenged when Oryx editors suggested that we write an encyclopedia of humor. When we shared the good news with friends and colleagues, they responded with opposite sets of assumptions. One group asked such questions as "How can you find out about all those sitcoms?" and "With the turnover in stand-up comedians, won't it be obsolete before you're done?" The other group smiled skeptically as if the concepts of humor and encyclopedia were incompatible; surely there isn't enough information about jokes to fill an encyclopedia.

To the friends who expected us to focus only on comedy performers, we explained that would be like writing an encyclopedia about food and commenting only on what chefs prepared and served. And to those who didn't think there was enough information for an encyclopedia, we said, "Wait and see!"

During the 25 years that we have been working with humor studies, we have found that, while most people think humor is important, they each have their own relatively narrow definition. For example, as English teachers, we were attracted to humor studies because we wanted to make our grammar lessons more interesting. We suspected that students could learn as much about language by working with deviant as with standardized sentences, and so, to us, humor meant language play. In 1982, when we invited the public to come to our first April Fools' Day humor conference at Arizona State University, we expected the participants to be people who worked with language in departments of communication, English, and perhaps drama and theater. We were pleasantly surprised when, in addition to language scholars, people came from medicine, art, business, philosophy, anthropology, history, political science, social work, sociology, education, performance, and the physical sciences.

Since then, we have been learning that humor means different things to different people. Many disagreements over the purpose of humor, its appropriateness, its effectiveness, and even what humor is, can be traced to people's differing definitions and expectations. By pulling together an overview of humor studies and treating a wide range of humor-related subjects, we hope to show that humor cuts across many aspects of life, and it is to be expected that architects, for example, will view humor differently from lawyers, or children, or stand-up comedians. It is also to be expected that circumstantial and individual experiences and differences will influence the way individuals respond to various kinds of humor. We recently heard about a group of citizens suing the National Science Foundation and a researcher for wasting taxpayers' dollars. The researcher had been awarded a grant to study psychological underpinnings of laughter. If the individuals who instigated the lawsuit had read this encyclopedia, we think they wouldn't have been so quick to assume that the researcher was on a fool's errand.

As we have worked in humor studies, we've felt like those tourists who come to Arizona and start hiking down into the Grand Canyon. The further into it they get, the bigger it seems to grow. We hope something similar will happen to our readers, whom we envision as intellectually curious people wanting to get more pleasure and understanding from their listening to, and reading of, public media, as well as from interacting with friends, neighbors, and colleagues. We also hope it will aid those who communicate with the public (journalists, humor consultants, public speakers, writers, advertisers, comedy performers, and health care workers) to reach a fuller understanding of their respective crafts. And because we want to encourage a new generation of humor scholars, we hope that our encyclopedia will find its way into high school and college libraries and will inspire students to write research papers on humor-related topics as alternatives to such grim subjects as abortion, capital punishment, drug abuse, and environmental problems.

Organization

Organizing our materials to illustrate the broad scope of humor studies while still tying related information together was challenging, and we made many arbitrary decisions. The 98 entries that we settled on could have been divided into as few as 80 or as many as 1,000. As readers will see, subtopics are included within many of the entries such as those on particular genres and particular kinds of writers or performers. We do not have separate entries for individuals and specific works because that kind of information can be found on the Internet and in encyclopedias and dictionaries already in print. Also, the grouping of various kinds of performers and creators proved to be efficient because the individual cases illustrate the patterns and the trends and connections that have significance beyond the individual examples. This means that readers looking for information about specific individuals, events, genres, and theories will need to use the subject index.

The overall focus of the *Encyclopedia* is on 20th-century American humor, with historical and international information being included only when it resonates in contemporary America. In literature, for example, we did not feel it appropriate to ignore Mark Twain, while the entries on humor in classical music and art, genres that are worldwide in nature, would have been woefully incomplete if we had looked only at Americans. We tried to begin each entry with a definition and then to include the standard information about the subject, followed by descriptions of controversies and recent theories and ideas. The books listed under "Further reading" were chosen for their currency as well as for their contents. Since we restricted ourselves to only two or three suggestions, readers wanting to do research on a particular topic would be well advised to skim through the bibliography on pages 311–331, which lists books about humor. Examples of actual humor in books and other media are not included in the bibliography because we include such information within the entries.

Over the last two years, we have collected information specifically for this encyclopedia by reading books written by our colleagues in humor studies; other encyclopedias and guide books; and journals, magazines, and newspapers. We also performed Internet searches, made telephone calls, and interviewed specialists. But in reality, we have been collecting the information in this encyclopedia from the time we began our college teaching careers in the 1970s. Since its founding in the early 1980s, Don has been executive secretary of the International Society for Humor Studies. As part of his job, he has served as a clearinghouse on humor studies and has provided bibliographies to members and others on over 100 different areas of humor scholarship. Since 1988, Alleen has been the organization's quarterly newsletter editor, and in that capacity has kept her finger on the pulse of humor developments in both academic and popular culture settings.

Acknowledgments

With many encyclopedias, different experts are asked to write each piece. We decided against this approach because we thought readers would be more comfortable with a similar writing style throughout the book. Also, we wanted to control against the overlapping of information from one entry to the next. To get the expert knowledge we needed, we frequently turned to our colleagues at Arizona State University. Willis Buckingham helped us with poetry; Elizabeth McNeil with American Indian Humor; Ken Donelson with radio, drama, and literature; D. G. Kehl with literature and laughter; Jim Koncz with comedian authors; Gene Valentine with art and pop-up books; David Stocker and Dale Dreyfoos with music; and Sandra Luehrson and Marilyn Miller with architecture. Our ASU department chair Nancy Gutierrez and secretary Mary Jones were helpful and supportive, as were our editors at Oryx, Henry Rasof and Jennifer Ashley. We are especially grateful to members of the International Society for Humor Studies who over the past 10 years have sent us articles and news clippings to consider for the ISHS Newsletter. Many of the citations throughout this encyclopedia come from materials clipped and forwarded by ISHS members, most notably, Don Hauptman, but also Salvatore Attardo, Ed Callary, Amy Carrell, Christie Davies, Peter Derks, Emil Draitser, Martin Lampert, Joel Goodman, Paul and Robin Grawe, Lyman and Patricia Hagen, M. Thomas Inge, Paul Lewis, Larry Mintz, John Morreall, Ofra Nevo, Victor Raskin, Mary Ann Rishel, Elaine Safer, Joyce Saltman, Patty Wooten, Anat Zajdman, and others.

And lastly we need to thank our three grown children: Kelvin, Sean, and Nicolette. They provided encouragement and solid information from their respective fields: computers, law, and international tourism. They, their spouses, and their children have also provided us with a living laboratory so we could observe at close range the tremendous variation among individual senses of humor.

Encyclopedia of 20th-Century American Humor

A

Academic Study of Humor

"THERE ARE ESSENTIALLY FOUR BASIC FORMS FOR A JOKE — THE CONCEALING OF KNOWLEDGE LATER REVEALED, THE SUBSTITUTION OF ONE CONCEPT FOR ANOTHER, AN UNEXPECTED CONCLUSION TO A LOGICAL PROGRESSION AND SLIPPING ON A BANANA PEEL."

©1999 by Sydney Harris

The academic study of humor cuts across many disciplines as scholars explore the nature of one of the few traits that is common to humans across both time and distance. Among the questions being asked are: Why do we have humor? What is its social purpose? How does it differ among individuals and among groups? How is it created? What does it do for individuals? and What does it do for society?

The fact that the study of humor is interdisciplinary in nature is both an advantage and a disadvantage. It is a disadvantage in that most scholars are forced to give their primary allegiance to some other academic field, which means that people do not earn a Ph.D. in Humor Studies. However, students at the University of Reading in England can earn a Master of Arts in Humor, and many students in various fields write theses and dissertations on humor in relation to other academic disciplines.

The interdisciplinary nature of humor is advantageous in that it encourages creative approaches to study, as when the 1992 spring semester at the University of Michigan was designated the "Comedy Semester" with a wide group of courses being offered so that what students learned in one class would be reinforced and further developed in other classes. Over 600 students enrolled in English department courses, with many others taking humor-related courses in history, communication, art history, and romance languages, and courses in the School of Music and the Program in Film and Video Studies. The UM Museum of Art participated with lectures and an exhibit of historic French caricatures and comic works. Planners wanted to provide students with a sense of how ideas travel across the arts and how humor runs from certain forms of parody and satire to the romantic and the sentimental. Professor Ejner J. Jensen explained that while comedy sometimes separates people, it also pulls people together by showing how human we are and how we share ways of looking at the world.

In April of 1998, the annual student conference sponsored by the Department of English at SUNY-Buffalo had as its theme "(In)finite Jests." In the call for papers, student organizers Adam Sills and Kevin Costa wrote:

> From Aristophanes to Woody Allen, from Dante to Sandra Bernhardt, comedy and ideas of the comic have occupied a central place in history. Unfortunately, comedy just as frequently has been berated and ignored by scholars because of its alleged inferiority to tragedy and other sanctioned genres and fields of scholarly inquiry.

The students were hoping their conference would be a small step toward balancing the scales of scholarship.

One of the first scholars to study literary humor seriously was Walter Blair (1900–1992), a University of Chicago professor of English. He wrote and edited more than 30 books on subjects ranging from the mythical characters of Paul Bunyan and Davy Crockett to those in Garry Trudeau's *Doonesbury* cartoons. He was considered the world's foremost authority on Mark Twain. Saul Bellow and Philip Roth both took classes from him, along with four other Pulitzer Prize winners.

Evan Esar (1890–1995), another pioneer of humor studies, worked at classifying humor and at studying its nature and evolution as "a man of science." His books include *Esar's Comic Dictionary* (1943), *Esar's Joke Dictionary* (1945), *The Dictionary of Humorous Quotations* (1949), and *The Comic Encyclopedia* (1978).

Virtually all English departments have courses that deal with literary humor, just as schools of art offer classes in cartooning and art history, while schools of telecommunication offer classes in advertising and scriptwriting. Faculty members in many departments of psychology explore connections between humor, emotions, intelligence, and creativity, while health care professionals are beginning to investigate connections between health and healing.

Some of the more unusual college classes currently being offered include an annual summer seminar sponsored by the University of Central Oklahoma College of Liberal Arts. It is under the direction of English professor Amy Carrell, with half of the time being devoted to the study of humor and health, while the other half is devoted to the specialty of the year's guest instructor.

Mel Helitzer, a retired advertising executive, has taught classes in humor writing and performing at Ohio University in Athens. Mary Ann Rishel in the communications program at Ithaca College in upstate New York also teaches humor writing, but her focus is less on performance than on writing. Her philosophy is that students will be better all-around writers when they have mastered such humor techniques as being succinct, writing vivid descriptions, recognizing ironies, and picking out the significant details.

Gila Safran Naveh, a teacher of Judaic Studies at the University of Cincinnati, teaches a course in Jewish/Women's Humor in which students study the complexity of humor and laughter, the catharsis experienced through laughter, and the specific ways in which humor reveals the cultural identity of a people, a country, or an ethnic group.

For over a decade, Leon Rappoport, a professor of psychology at Kansas State University in Manhattan, has taught a course in ethnic humor. He says that in spite of warning students that some of the material may be offensive and promising that he will give a passing withdrawal up to the very last day, he must remain on his toes, ready to step in and ameliorate situations when students or visiting speakers make remarks that offend some class members. He tries to avoid the question of whether ethnic humor is harmful or helpful because "it can't be answered and will take you out in the desert where you'll never get back."

In the mid-1990s, Mel Gordon, a professor of dramatic arts at the University of California, Berkeley, offered a class called "The History of Offensive Humor: From the Mudheads to Howard Stern." The first reference in the course title is to a kind of clown in Southwest American Indian tribes, while the reference to Howard Stern opens the door to studying the *Badkhn*, a 17th-century Yiddish term for "insult artist." According to Gordon, the *Badkhn* and Howard Stern have the same philosophy, "The worse the world, the better our jokes!"

Law school students study not only the legal ramifications of humor being used as a tool for harassment, but also some of the ways that humor can be used in negotiating conflicts and in getting clients to question their assumptions. In the state of California, where attorneys are required to take continuing education courses, approved classes in humor have been accepted since the mid-1990s.

Emil Draitser, professor of Russian and Slavic languages at Hunter College in New York, teaches a continuing education course for New York University under the heading "What's So Funny Comrade? Contemporary Russian Humor." Topics include political humor, ethnic humor, and sexual folk humor. Each summer, Joyce Saltman, a professor of education at the University of Southern Connecticut, conducts a week-long continuing education course for 300 teachers where they learn about using humor for their and their students' psychological and intellectual well-being.

Examples of academic organizations founded to encourage the study of humor include the American Humor Studies Association, which publishes a journal, *Studies in American Humor*, edited by Karen L. Kilcup from the University of North Carolina–Greensboro, and also a *To Wit* newsletter, edited by Cameron Nickels from James Madison University in Harrisonburg, Virginia. Members are mostly professors of literature who meet annually in conjunction with the Modern Language Association. Of the hundreds of presentations made at the annual December meeting of MLA, usually between 50 and 70 relate to literary or linguistic humor.

The International Society for Humor Studies (ISHS) welcomes scholars from all fields. It publishes *Humor: International Journal of Humor Research* (edited at the University of Maryland by Lawrence Mintz) and holds annual conferences alternating between the United States and other countries. Don Nilsen from Arizona State University in Tempe is the executive secretary.

In the early 1990s, art professors Walter Askin at California State University in Los Angeles and Gerald G. Purdy at the University of Southern California founded The Visual Humor Project to coordinate exhibitions and publications involving artists using visual humor. The Association for the Therapeutic Study of Humor was founded by nurses, counselors, doctors, and consultants who want to encourage the use of laughter both for patients and for care givers. It meets annually and sponsors a variety of workshops and publications.

As interest in the formal study of humor has increased, so has the interest of scholarly publishers. Wayne State University Press in Detroit has a Humor in Life and Letters series with nearly a dozen books in print, including Emil Draitser's 1998 *Taking Penguins to the Movies: Ethnic Humor in Russia*, Elaine Safer's 1988 *The Contemporary American Comic Epic: The Novels of Barth, Pynchon, Gaddis, and Kesey*, and Lawrence Clayton and Kenneth Davis's 1991 *Horsing Around: Contemporary Cowboy Humor*. Gordon and Breach Publishers have a Studies in Humor and Gender series, which includes such books as Gail Finney's 1994 *Look Who's Laughing: Gender and Comedy* and Barbara Levy's 1997 *Ladies Laughing: Wit as Control in Contemporary American Women Writers*. Mouton deGruyter sponsors a Humor Research series in cooperation with the International Society for Humor Studies. Titles include Christie Davies's 1998 *Jokes and Their Relation to Society*, Salvatore Attardo's 1994 *Linguistic Theories of Humor*, and Robert L. Latta's 1998 *The Basic Humor Process: A Cognitive-Shift Theory and the Case against Incongruity*. In the early 1990s, Garland Press published several humor titles, including the 1993 *Black Humor: Critical Essays* edited by Alan R. Pratt and the 1994 *American Women Humorists: Critical Essays* edited by Linda A. Morris.

University presses regularly publish humor-related titles; for example, many of the books published as part of the Studies in Popular Culture series for the University of

Mississippi Press relate to humor. Examples of humor titles from other academic presses include Gregg Camfield's 1994 *Sentimental Twain, Samuel Clemens in the Maze of Moral Philosophy*, from the University of Pennsylvania Press; Barbara Bennett's 1998 *Comic Visions Female Voices: Contemporary Women Novelists and Southern Humor*, from the Louisiana State University Press in Baton Rouge; Steven Weisenberger's 1995 *Fables of Subversion/Satire and the American Novel: 1930–1980*, from the University of Georgia Press in Athens; and Neil Grauer's 1995 *Remember Laughter, A Life of James Thurber*, from the University of Nebraska Press.

Independent scholarly journals include *Thalia: Studies in Literary Humor*, edited by Jacqueline Tavernier-Courbin at the University of Ottawa in Canada; *Metaphor and Symbol: A Quarterly Journal,* edited by John M. Kennedy at the University of Toronto, Canada; *Studies in Contemporary Satire*, edited by C. Darrel Sheraw at Clarion State College in Pennsylvania; *Satire*, edited by Larry Logan from Hancock, Maryland; and *Journal of Play Theory & Research*, edited by Margaret Carlisle Duncan at the University of Wisconsin–Milwaukee.

Brief descriptions of some of today's leading scholars (in alphabetical order) will further illustrate the variety of humor-related work being done in academic institutions. This list is intended only as a sampling with the work of many other scholars being described throughout this encyclopedia.

Mahadev L. Apte is an anthropologist at Duke University. His *Humor and Laughter: An Anthropological Approach* (1985) compares and contrasts smiling across cultures and explores how various kinds of inequalities (sex, age, group identity, etc.) affect joking relationships. In 1987, he edited *Language and Humor*, a special issue of the *International Journal of the Sociology of Language*.

Regina Barecca teaches in the English department at the University of Connecticut. Her 1988 *Last Laughs: Perspectives on Women and Comedy* contains articles on the humor and irony of writers including Aphra Behn, Jane Austen, Virginia Woolf, and Muriel Sparks. Her 1992 *New Perspectives on Women and Comedy* discusses the wit and the sexual politics of Roseanne, Helen Keller, Louise Erdrich, Maxine Hong Kingston, Alice Walker, and Flannery O'Connor. Other titles include *Untamed and Unabashed* (1994), *They Used to Call Me Snow White . . . But I Drifted* (1991), and *Perfect Husbands (& Other Fairy Tales): Demystifying Marriage, Men, and Romance* (1993).

Arthur Asa Berger is professor emeritus of communication at San Francisco State University. Because of his accessible writing style, his books are read by the general public as well as by academics. Titles include *An Anatomy of Humor* (1993), *Li'l Abner: A Study in American Satire* (1994), *Blind Men and Elephants: Perspectives on Humor* (1995), *The Genius of the Jewish Joke* (1997), and *The Art of Comedy Writing* (1997).

Joseph Boskin teaches history at Boston University. In *The Humor Prism in 20th Century America* and *Rebellious Laughter* (both 1997), he develops the point that jokes of the people provide a barometer of society's concerns and anxieties prior to becoming grist for stand-up comics. His *Sambo: The Rise and Demise of an American Jester* (1986) traces the development of an African American stereotype that began almost playfully but ended as racist.

Sarah Blacher Cohen teaches in the English department of the State University of New York in Albany. Her books include *Comic Relief: Humor in Contemporary American Literature* (1978), *From Hester Street to Hollywood: The Jewish-American Stage and Screen* (1986), *Jewish Wry: Essays on Jewish Humor* (1987), and *Cynthia Ozick's Comic Art: From Levity to Liturgy* (1994). She is the editor of a Wayne State University Press series on Humor in Life and Letters.

Christie Davies teaches in the Department of Sociology at the University of Reading in England. His 1980 *Ethnic Humor around the World: A Comparative Analysis* (1990) illustrates how most ethnic jokes pin an undesirable quality, often developed to a ludicrous extent, on a particular group. His 1998 *Jokes* *and Their Relation to Society* is a further exploration of jokes from around the world and what they say about the joke tellers.

Alan Dundes is an anthropologist, focusing on contemporary culture, at the University of California, Berkeley. He and **Jan Harold Brunvand**, now at the University of Utah, were fellow students of folklore at the University of Indiana in Bloomington, and the two of them have been instrumental in educating the general public about urban legends. Dundes has written over 150 articles for popular and scholarly magazines. Besides his books on urban legends, he has written (with Alison Dundes Rentein) *Folk Law: Essays in the Theory and Practice of Lex Non Scripta* (1994), *The Cockfight: A Casebook* (1994), and *The Blood Libel Legend: A Casebook in Anti-Semitic Folklore* (1991).

William F. Fry Jr. is professor emeritus in the Department of Medicine at Stanford University. He has written many articles reporting on connections between humor and body changes. His *Sweet Madness: A Study of Humor* (1963) and his *Make 'Em Laugh: Live Studies of Comedy Writers* (1975) (with Melanie Allen) reflect his interest in studying how the implicit and the unconscious are used in humor.

Stephen H. Gale teaches at Kentucky State University in Frankfort. He is an unusually productive writer and editor. In 1988, he edited the *Encyclopedia of American Humorists*. He also compiled *Critical Essays on Harold Pinter* (1990) and *S. J. Perelman: An Annotated Bibliography* (1985), and wrote *S. J. Perelman: A Critical Study* (1987).

Henry Louis Gates Jr. does not claim to be a humor scholar, but his *The Signifying Monkey: A Theory of African-American Literary Criticism* (1988) nevertheless makes a contribution to the study of humor by showing that when African Americans were slaves, they were denied the use of normal and private communication. This forced them to develop double-entendre Trickster signifiers. Speakers would say something that meant one thing to whites and another to Blacks. The humor comes from the realization that simultaneous messages are being communicated and that the authority figures (usually whites) are understanding only one message while the other participants comprehend both.

M. Thomas Inge is Distinguished Blackwell Professor of Humanities at Randolph-Macon College. In 1974, he was a founding member of the American Humor Studies Association, and with Larry Mintz, from the University of Maryland, established the organization's first publication, *American Humor, An Interdisciplinary Newsletter*. He is editor for the Studies in Popular Culture series produced by the University of Mississippi Press. Well-received books that he has either edited or written include his 1995 *Anything Can Happen in a Comic Strip: Centennial Reflections on an American Art Form*, his 1994 *Perspectives on American Culture, Essays on Humor, Literature, and the Popular Arts*, his 1993 *Dark Laughter: The Satiric Art of Oliver W. Harrington*, his 1990 *Comics as Culture*, and his 1989 *Handbook of American Popular Literature*.

Paul E. McGhee is now a humor consultant living in Montclair, New Jersey, while **Jeffrey H. Goldstein** teaches in the Department of Organizational Psychology at the University of Utrecht in the Netherlands. Earlier when they were both U.S. academics (McGhee at Texas Tech University in Lubbock and Goldstein at Temple University in Philadelphia), they pioneered in the study of humor and psychology. In 1972 they published *The Psychology of Humor*, while in 1983 they published *The Handbook of Humor Research, Volume I: Basic Issues* and *Handbook of Humor Research, Volume II: Applied Studies*. These handbooks contain summaries of empirical research on various theories of humor as well as on sense of humor, psychopathology, psychotherapy, and contrasts between smiling and laughing.

Victor Raskin is a linguist at Purdue University and is best known for his work on script model grammar in relation to structures of humor as explained in his 1985 *Semantic Mechanisms of Humor*. In 1987, he was founding editor for *Humor: International Journal of Humor Research*. With Willibald Ruch, a psychologist from the University of

Dusseldorf in Germany, Raskin edits the Humor Research series of scholarly books published by Mouton de Gruyter.

David E. E. Sloane, a professor of English at the University of New Haven in Connecticut, is executive director for the American Humor Studies Association. In 1979 he published *Mark Twain as a Literary Comedian*, in 1983 *The Literary Humor of the Urban Northeast 1830–1890*, in 1987 *American Humor Magazines and Comic Periodicals*, and in 1998 *New Directions in American Humor*.

Nancy Walker is a professor of literature at Vanderbilt University, where among her other classes she teaches seminars in American humor. With Regina Barreca, she is editor of the Gordon and Breach Studies in Humor and Gender series. She is the author of the 1990 *Feminist Alternatives: Irony and Fantasy in the Contemporary Novel by Women* and the 1995 *The Disobedient Writer: Women and Narrative Tradition*. In 1998, she edited *What's So Funny? Humor in American Culture*.

Internet sites likely to provide helpful information on the academic study of humor include the following:

American Humor Studies Association
  http://www.newhaven.edu/UNH/Special/
  AHSA/AHSAHomePage.htm

The Art Gliner Center for Humor Studies
  http://www.otal.umd.edu/amst/
  humorcenter/

Humor: International Journal of Humor Research
  http://www.uniduesseldorf.de/WWW/
  MathNat/Ruch/SecretaryPage.html

The International Society for Luso-Hispanic Humor Studies
  http://acad.ursinus.edu/~pseaver/
  main.htm

Laughingly Referred To (Humor Research)
  http://les.man.ac.uk/cric/Jason_Rutter/
  HumorResearch/search.htm

See also BUSINESS HUMOR, HEALTH AND HEALING, LEGAL HUMOR, SCHOOL HUMOR

Further reading: Don L. F. Nilsen, *Humor Scholarship: A Research Bibliography* (1993). David E. E. Sloane (ed.), *New Directions in American Humor* (1998).

Accidental Humor

Accidental or unintentional humor comes in two basic types: one is physical, while the other is linguistic. Accidental linguistic humor comes from misspellings, mispronunciations, errors in logic, and the kinds of speaker confusions called *Freudian slips*, *malapropisms*, and *spoonerisms*. Physical humor is the slipping-on-a-banana-peel type, which obviously contains the essential element of surprise. The creators of slapstick and screwball comedy work hard to make funny incidents appear accidental; however, audiences know that the situations are contrived and that to get full enjoyment they must engage in a willing suspension of disbelief.

Because such suspension is not necessary with "authentic" shows, audiences laugh freely at television specials made from bloopers and outtakes, at police shows about criminals whose best-laid plans have gone awry, and at the incidents shown on *The World's Funniest Videos*; for example, the baseball player who catches a fly ball and in the process loses his pants, the bridegroom who during the wedding ceremony methodically pulls out a small container and sprays his mouth before kissing his bride, and the three-year-old at an Easter egg hunt who searches for eggs only in the baskets of other children who are busy searching in bushes and behind rocks. The success of *Candid Camera*, which from 1960 to 1962 was among the 10 most watched television shows, was due at least partly to its accidental humor. Even though the situations were contrived with the perpetrators and usually the viewers knowing what was going on, the "victims" were genuinely surprised.

Newspapers regularly print stories about surprising events as in this Associated Press story from Niagara Falls, Ontario:

> ***This Auto Has Suicidal Tendencies***
> Tourists enjoying a sunny day here found their attention diverted from the grandeur of the cataracts yesterday.

An unoccupied car, parked near the Horseshoe Falls, turned its lights on. Then the lenses shattered.

Then the horn began to blow.

The engine started.

The car burst into flames and the windshield exploded.

Firemen blamed the activity on a short circuit.

Phoenix Gazette, Apr. 10, 1973

An equally surprising United Press International story from Sheridan, California, told about a farm goose flying along and exploding in mid-air. A sheriff's deputy explained that the goose must have swallowed a blasting cap, which was somehow set off.

Other news stories recount events or situations that the participants view as straightforward but that reporters and readers view as ironic or funny; for example, a United Press International story about 87-year-old Andrija Artukovic, who in 1987 was sentenced to death by a Yugoslav court because during World War II he had ordered more than 1,000 Croatian deaths. However, a medical review determined that the man was in no condition to be executed, but "plans would resume if and when his health improved."

The hard-to-follow directions on these signs are examples of accidental linguistic humor:

On a northern Arizona ski slope: *Out of control skiers yield right-of-way.*

On a West Coast bridge during World War II: *In case of bombing attack, drive directly off the bridge.*

The "Marginalia" column in the *Chronicle of Higher Education* reprints mistakes from academic communications, while "The Lower Case" in each issue of the *Columbia Journalism Review* prints a dozen or so newspaper bloopers chosen from the approximately 300 clippings sent in by readers from around the world; for example, this announcement from the *Salt Lake Tribune*:

The Salt Lake City Track Club's All-Women's 10,000-meter race is scheduled Saturday at 8 a.m. at Sugarhouse Park. The entry fee is $4 with shirt or $1 without.

Headline writers are especially apt to create unintended humor because they are trying to attract attention and communicate a whole story in only a few words as shown in these examples reprinted by the *Columbia Journalism Review*:

- Dr. Ruth Talks about Sex with Newspaper Editors
- Red Tape Holds Up New Bridge
- Defendant's Speech Ends in Long Sentence
- Blind Woman Gets New Kidney from Dad She Hasn't Seen in Years

Because people now rely on computers to check spellings, new kinds of spelling errors frequently get into print. Before computers, spelling errors were usually reversals or nonsense words, but computer software will ignore a word that is spelled correctly, even if it is the wrong word. For example, an educational journal had an article about *rapping* instead of *tapping* teacher potential, teachers facing *their own worst tears* instead of *their own worst fears*, and a lead-in that read, *"It is worth nothing that . . . ,"* instead of *"It is worth noting that . . . ".*

When children are faced with language that is above their level of experience, they change words into something that sounds familiar, hence they play *chest* instead of *chess* and they translate the old church hymn, "Gladly the Cross I'd Bear" into "Gladly the Cross-Eyed Bear."

Richard Lederer's *Anguished English* is filled with children's mistakes, many of which he put together and supplemented with his own creativity for an essay, "The World According to Student Bloopers." This essay is so often reprinted and distributed electronically that readers may recognize this excerpt:

Queen Elizabeth was the "Virgin Queen." As a queen she was a success. When Elizabeth exposed herself before her troops, they all shouted "hurrah." Then her navy went out and defeated the Spanish Armadillo.

It was an age of great inventions and discoveries. Gutenberg invented the Bible. Another important invention was the circulation of blood. Sir Walter Raleigh is a historical figure because he invented cigarettes and started smoking. And Sir Francis Drake circumcised the world with a 100-foot clipper.

Lederer also reprinted mistakes from parents who wrote these excuses for their children's absences at school:

- Carlos was absent yesterday because he was playing football. He was hurt in the growing part.
- Mary could not come to school because she has been bothered by very close veins.
- Please excuse Jimmy for being. It was his father's fault.
- Teacher, please excuse Mary for being absent. She was sick and I had her shot.

Such blunders are funny because they involve the reader or listener in mentally drawing together two scripts—the one that was said and the one that was intended. And as serendipity, the pleasure is increased by a feeling of superiority over the person who made the mistake.

Nonnative speakers of English who are wooing American dollars in international tourism are notorious for the signs they put up, as with these examples reprinted in an Ann Landers column:

- From a Norwegian cocktail lounge: *Ladies are requested not to have children in the bar.*
- From an Acapulco hotel: *The manager has personally passed all the water served here.*
- From a Japanese hotel: *Cold and Heat. If you want to condition the warm in your room, please control yourself.*
- From a Hong Kong tailor shop: *Ladies may have a fit upstairs.*

Well-educated adults often make slips of the tongue because they are nervous or distracted; for example, someone talking about World War II might talk about *Pearl Island* instead of *Pearl Harbor*, while someone else might refer to *neon stockings* instead of *nylon stockings*. Such slips of the tongue are called *malapropisms* from the character name of the befuddled Mrs. Malaprop in Richard Brinsley Sheridan's 1773 play *The Rivals*.

In his *Introductory Lectures on Psychoanalysis*, Sigmund Freud described slips of the tongue as evidence of people's subconscious desires, as when the president of the Lower House of Parliament opened a meeting by saying, "Gentlemen, I take notice that a full quorum of members is present and herewith declare the meeting closed." Freud explained that "it is clear that he wanted to open the sitting (that is, the conscious intention), but it is equally clear that he also wanted to close it (that is, the disturbing intention)."

In real life, so-called "Freudian slips" sometimes reveal a person's subconscious desires, but at other times they are simply pronunciation or spelling errors. However, when creative writers put Freudian slips into the mouths of their characters, the intention is clearly to communicate something about the speaker's personality or desires. In an essay on "Bunkerisms," Alfred Rosa and Paul Eschholz in their 1982 *Language Awareness* show how Archie Bunker's linguistic mistakes on television's *All in the Family* (1971–1979) were created to reveal his character. When Michael called Archie prejudiced while he was singing "God Bless America," Archie responded that he was singing a song by a well-known and respected Jewish guy, Milton Berlin. Archie was, in fact, revealing his narrowness by bringing together the only two Jewish people he knew of: the comedian Milton Berle and the composer Irving Berlin. Most of Archie's confusions pointed to his lack of education and his xenophobic tendencies as when he confounded such expressions as *Morgan David wine, Blackberry Finn, pushy imported ricans,* a *regular Marco Polish, Englebum Humperdunk, welfare incipients, the immaculate connection, Dun and Broadstreet,* a *groinocologist,* and "Don't take everything so liberally."

Comedian Norm Crosby, who in the 1970s starred in Las Vegas and from 1978 to 1983 hosted television's *The Comedy Shop,* was billed as "Mr. Malaprop." He presented lectures based on *hysterical truths* for which he loved to receive *standing ovulations*. Crosby is partially deaf, and in 1979 became national chairman for the Council for Better Hearing and Speech, and in 1988 became their public information ambassador.

Other comedians who have relied heavily on malaprop humor include Jimmy Durante in both movies and stand-up routines, Leo Gorcey in *The Bowery Boys*, Goldie Hawn on *Laugh-In*, Gilda Radner on *Saturday Night Live*, Don Knotts on the *Andy Griffith* show, and Lou Costello in the *Abbott and Costello* routines.

Spoonerisms are a distinctive kind of speech error in which the initial sounds of two or more words are transposed as in "tons of soil" for "sons of toil." They are named after British clergyman William A. Spooner, who as the warden of New College, Oxford, frequently made such mistakes in Sunday morning services. Once he got the reputation, he was credited with many more spoonerisms than can actually be documented, including "Three cheers for our queer old dean" (referring to Queen Victoria), "Is it kistomary to cuss the bride?" and "Stop hissing all my mystery lectures." Once a prominent person gets a reputation for blunders (as did Vice President Dan Quayle), then his or her persona will be used as a hook on which to hang similar jokes, as when people say that "Reverend Spooner started out to be a bird watcher, but ended up a word botcher."

Samuel Goldwyn was proud of the fact that he grew rich and famous without a formal education and so he cultivated a talent for making statements that would cause listeners to shake their heads as they tried to figure out his paradoxical statements:

- A verbal contract isn't worth the paper it's written on.
- Every Tom, Dick, and Harry is named William.
- For your information, I would like to ask a question.
- Now, gentlemen, listen slowly.

Baseball manager Casey Stengel is credited with saying, "I guess I'll have to start from scraps," and "Everybody line up alphabetically according to your height." Another baseball manager, Yogi Berra, offered such gems of wisdom as "That restaurant is so crowded, nobody ever goes there anymore," "I want to win 100 or 105 games this year—whichever comes first," "It's *deja vu* all over again," and "It ain't over 'til it's over." When Mack McGinnis, editor of *Speaker's and Speechwriter's Guide* asked Berra if he was actually responsible for all of the quotes attributed to him, Berra responded, "I really didn't say everything I said." *See also* AMBIGUITY, PUNS, SCREWBALL COMEDIES

Further reading: Gloria Cooper, *Red Tape Holds Up New Bridge: And More Flubs from the Nation's Press* (1987). Jane Goodsell, *Not a Good Word about Anybody: A Wicked and Wonderful Collection of Other People's Mishaps, Blunders, and Inexcusable Behavior* (1988). Richard Lederer, *Anguished English: An Anthology of Accidental Assaults upon Our Language* (1987).

Acquisition of a Sense of Humor

Acquisition of a sense of humor has two aspects; one is the understanding and appreciation of humor, while the other is the creation and performance of humor. Acquisition begins early and may continue throughout life. Studying children's acquisition of humor appreciation is more complex than studying their acquisition of speech because, as also happens with laughing adults, it isn't always possible to know whether they have caught onto a joke or whether they are laughing just because other people are laughing.

Psychologists and educators used to believe that young children did not have a sense of humor. They came to this conclusion as a result of testing children's comprehension and appreciation of such humor techniques as allusion and wordplay, but as scholars developed broader definitions of humor and began observing children engaged in natural play they found that even babies have a sense of humor. Those who laugh when playing peek-a-boo are showing an appreciation of surprise and the breaking of expectations.

Toddlers watching *Sesame Street* smile at the incongruity and the exaggeration of Big Bird; three-year-olds who pull funny faces to tease other children and four-year-olds who memorize insulting chants are illustrating the enjoyment of hostility and superiority, while five-year-olds who develop a repertoire of knock-knock jokes and riddles are learning the art of performance.

According to Swiss psychologist Jean Piaget (1896–1980), it isn't until about the age of 12 that children's brains develop the "formal operational" stage of thinking. This has important implications for humor because it is this stage that gives young people the power to imagine actions and their results even when there is no way to actually try them out. Only after children's minds develop to this stage do they have the ability to hold two different ideas about the same thing. This is crucial for the understanding of sophisticated jokes, and is probably the reason that early psychologists thought young children did not have a sense of humor.

In *It's a Funny Thing, Humour,* edited by Antony Chapman, Alice Sheppard outlined levels of humor appreciation as developed by children between birth and late adolescence:

LEVEL 1: IDIOSYNCRATIC. Involves amusement related to a young child's individual experience as with a surprise, a physical sensation, or a response to someone else's smile or laughter.

LEVEL 2: NORMATIVE. Involves a generalization that implies a rule, or a convention.

LEVEL 3A: NORMATIVE. Involves not only a generalization, a rule or a convention, but also its violation.

LEVEL 3B: EXPECTATION. Involves a reference to the unusualness or the improbability of an event.

LEVEL 4: RELATIONAL. Involves concern for inner motives related to a situation, relations among events, and multiple aspects of the situation.

LEVEL 5: EXTRA-CONTEXTUAL. Involves context beyond the situation implied in the notion of parody, take-off, irony, or satire. It also involves the distinction between appearance and reality; the humor

is revealed as contingent upon subtle aspects of events.

LEVEL 6: PHILOSOPHICAL. Involves the ability to see what is ridiculous in the nature of things and to generalize an outlook from humor examples.

Contemporary psychologist Paul McGhee, who specializes in humor studies, does not advise waiting for children to develop their cognitive skills before using humor with them. Instead, he says that adults who use humor with children in a playful and stress-free environment give children a head start in their cognitive development. For example, playing peek-a-boo with a baby helps the baby develop what Piaget called "sensorimotor" intelligence, which is the ability to construct a mental picture of a world of objects existing independently from the child. Similarly, playing simple games of hide-and-seek helps babies develop a sense of object permanence. McGhee found that children who had recently mastered what Piaget labeled "Conservation" were the ones most appreciative of a joke that depended on the understanding that the mass of something is the same even though it is fitted into different containers or its shape is changed. He told children of different ages a joke about a man going to a pizza parlor and asking the server to cut his pizza into four pieces because he wasn't hungry enough to eat six pieces. First-graders didn't find the joke funny at all because they hadn't yet mastered the concept of conservation and so didn't see the story as a joke. Neither did eighth graders find the joke funny because they had mastered conservation so long ago that there was no tension. The children who were amused by the joke were those in the middle grades. They experienced pleasure because they were at the cognitive level where they could take pride in the fact that they were able to figure out that the amount of pizza was the same regardless of how many pieces it was cut into.

Folklore collector Alvin Schwartz has explained the popularity of children's vulgar or crude jokes by saying that because matters of the toilet are of considerable concern, there is nothing so funny and so reassuring to children of six and seven as such jokes and rhymes as

> I see London; I see France.
> I see Betsy's underpants.
> They aren't green, they aren't blue,
> They're just filled with number two.

From matters of the toilet, children go on to joke about secret parts of the body as in

> Mary had a little bear,
> The best that she could find.
> And everywhere that Mary went,
> There was her bare behind.

As they grow older, children get increasingly brave as shown by the line in the 1982 Steven Spielberg movie *ET: The Extraterrestrial* when the boy called his brother "Penis Breath." From 12- and 13-year-olds, Schwartz collected such parodies as

> Jack and Jill went up the hill
> To fetch a pail of water.
> Jill forgot to take the pill
> And now she's got a daughter.

Schwartz says that by the teen years, today's children know pretty much all there is to know about the body and sexuality and that their jokes begin to resemble those of adults.

Many four- and five-year-olds confuse the punch lines of jokes because learning a joke format is easier than catching onto the dual meanings of words. And children don't have to understand every nuance of a riddle to appreciate it. Alison Lurie gives the example of the riddle "Why did the Little Moron throw the clock out the window? . . . Because he wanted to see time fly." The teller of the riddle might be claiming superiority by showing an understanding of the "time flying" metaphor, but listeners might just be enjoying "the vicarious expression of forbidden impulse . . . the rage children feel when some adult points to the clock as a reason for going to bed, or not having lunch. 'No, dear; see, the clock says it's not time yet.' No wonder the child wants to throw the clock out the window, to make time fly."

In another example, children are amused by recognizing their own emotions and those of their friends in *Sesame Street*'s Oscar the Grouch, but it may be years—or never—before they connect *Sesame Street*'s Oscar the Grouch to *The Odd Couple*'s grouchy Oscar Madison. Likewise, it may take years of watching television commercials before they catch on that "brought to you by the letter A," for example, is a parody.

Because of inexperience and a lack of practice in covering up their emotions, children often do and say things that strike adults as funny. Also, young speakers are refreshingly honest in the explanations they give and in the metaphors they create when they can't think of a standard "adult" way to state what they wish to communicate. Such accidental humor is soon outgrown, although some clever individuals learn to capitalize on their ability to make people laugh and so purposely repeat what started out as accidental. For example, at age 10, when Red Skelton was trying out for a job as a salesman in a medicine show, he accidentally fell off the stage and broke several bottles of medicine. People laughed so hard that he began falling on purpose and experimenting with other humorous body movements. *See also* ANTIAUTHORITY HUMOR, CHILDREN'S LITERATURE, CHILDREN'S TELEVISION

Further reading: Sheila Hanly, *Peek-A-Boo! 101 Ways to Make a Baby Smile* (1998). Susan M. Hoyle and Carolyn Temple Adger, *Kids Talk: Strategic Language Use in Later Childhood* (1998). Paul E. McGhee, *Humor and Children's Development: A Guide to Practical Applications* (1989).

Adaptation

Adaptation is a kind of language play in which a well-known word, name, or phrase is recycled into a new usage. Oftentimes small changes are made, but if the changes are so great that listeners or readers are not reminded of the original, at least on a subconscious level, then some of the effect will have been lost.

Although most adaptations aren't laugh-out-loud funny, many have elements of surprise and incongruity that bring smiles, while at the same time making the new usages memorable. For example, in 1997, Dolly, the cloned sheep, was featured in news stories

...all around the world, whereas earlier clonings, even of chimpanzees, which are much closer in structure to humans than are sheep, were written about only in scientific journals. A major difference was that Dolly had been cloned from an adult sheep while previous clonings had been accomplished during conception. However, another difference in the speed with which the story caught the public fancy was that Dolly had been given an easy-to-say and easy-to-remember name. Because of having been cloned from a mammary gland, she was named "in honor" of the buxom Dolly Parton, a fact that disappeared from the story as it gained momentum and commentators began debating serious scientific and moral issues.

Businesses look for names that will bring a smile of recognition as when a shoe manufacturer names its shoes *Aerosoles* to imply that wearing the shoes will be like walking on air, or when another manufacturer names its shoes *Hush Puppies* to imply that they will soothe "tired dogs." *V-8* juice sounds strong and healthy because of its association with a V-8 engine, while Yves Saint Laurent's *Champagne* perfume sounds luxurious, even though wine makers successfully sued to keep it from being sold in France. The logo of the Circle-K convenience stores is a subconscious reminder of *OK*, the most widely known phrase in the world, while the *7-Eleven* logo has positive connotations because of being a lucky roll of the dice in a game of craps. (It originally also communicated the store's hours.)

Some businesses seem satisfied with adapted names even when there is no clear-cut semantic relationship. The Paper Mate company named a line of ball point pens *Write Bros.*, apparently in honor of Orville and Wilbur Wright, inventors of the airplane. A bank that launched an ad campaign for automatic teller machines under the slogan "Simon, the Simple Teller" ignored the last lines of the old nursery rhyme where the pie man says to Simple Simon, "Show me first your penny," and Simple Simon responds, "Indeed I haven't any." The company that makes *Amelia Earhart* luggage probably doesn't want customers to think too deeply

about what happened to Earhart's luggage, nor does the company that in an *if-you-can't-beat-them-join-them* attitude chose *Duck* as its trademark for duct tape want customers to think about feathers and quacks.

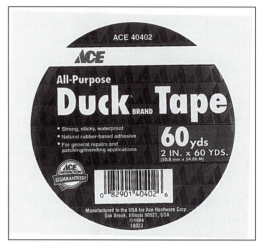

The Ace Hardware Corporation was either making a joke or saying "If you can't beat them, join them" when they named their duct tape "Duck Brand Tape."

Purists argue against the name of the *Buffalo Bills* football team because the name of western showman William Frederick Cody, popularly known as *Buffalo Bill,* refers to Wild West associations, not Buffalo, New York. However, most people simply appreciate the name's familiar ring and its strong masculine connotations. In a similar way, magician David Copperfield's name is easy to say and to remember because of the Charles Dickens character.

The changing of place names into people's names has a proven history in making names memorable. Rock Hudson's name alludes to the *Rock* of Gibraltar and the *Hudson* River. When Janet Reno's father was a young newspaper reporter, he grew tired of people not remembering, or misspelling, his surname of Rasmussen and so he looked on a map until he found a short name that started with *R* and would be impossible to misspell. A generation later, his choice helped his daughter's name become a household word. Other memorable place-name adaptations include *River Phoenix, John Denver, Tennessee Williams, Minnesota Fats, Chevy Chase, Indiana*

Jones, and the thousands of children who have been given such newly fashionable names as *Dakota, Tex, Cody,* and *Montana.*

Entertainers have a head start in the game of name recognition if their name is already familiar to a large number of speakers. However, they run a risk in taking someone else's name because if the name is too famous, the new owner may not be able to wrest ownership away from the original. When in the mid-1990s, a young football player changed his name to that of basketball star Kareem Abdul-Jabbar (with a slight difference in spelling), Jabbar expressed his doubts by saying that the young athlete would probably have been wiser to try to make a name for himself, both literally and figuratively. At the 1994 meeting of the American Name Society, a researcher told about interviewing pop singer Madonna, who expressed surprise that anyone still thought of the mother of Jesus when hearing the name *Madonna.*

Baby Ruth candy bars are not named for the baseball player, but for the daughter of Grover Cleveland, who as a White House baby at the time of George Herman Ruth's birth in 1895 was as famous in her time as were Caroline and John-John during the Kennedy administration. Herman's name was a play on *Baby Ruth,* and in fact, is the name that Herman himself used even though fans and the plaque in Baseball's Hall of Fame use *Babe.*

Cloud Nine Promotions Inc. of Alpharetta, Georgia, was taken to court for distributing *Tushie Rolls* toilet paper packaged in a brown cover with red-orange stripes. In filing its successful suit, a Tootsie Rolls spokesman cited a policy against permitting use of the company trademark "for scandalous, immoral, obscene, scatological, unwholesome, or distasteful purposes."

The maxim "Just do it" was already in popular culture before Nike claimed ownership of it through an extensive advertising campaign that included a stylized check mark (a "swoosh") reinforcing the idea of checking off items on a "to do" list. The Nike slogan became such a part of popular culture that after his surprise wedding John F. Kennedy Jr. got a laugh when he told a group of advertisers that his decision had been influenced by looking out the window of his New York apartment and seeing a large billboard message from a famous shoe company.

Among dozens of parodies, Nike itself has marketed sweat shirts decorated with "Just Brew It!" and during the 1997 controversies over working conditions in overseas factories protestors made their own "Just Don't Do It!" sweat shirts. Such overuse of the slogan influenced Nike advertisers to look for something new so that in 1998 they began an advertising campaign centered around "I Can," again a phrase already part of the popular culture.

Humorous adaptations by the general public often incorporate a kind of escalating competitiveness as when graffiti artists incorporate the taggings of rival groups into their own designs and when on the night before football games college students try to paint their own colors on the rival school's sacred icons. Fundamentalist Christians, who place the outline of a small fish on their cars, sometimes filled with the Greek initials for "Jesus Christ King of the Jews," are teased by believers in evolution: they sport a similarly shaped fish, this one with legs (as if it's evolving), which is filled with the letters, *D-A-R-W-I-N.* Another example are the parents who top their neighbors' "My child is an honor student at . . . School" bumper sticker with "My Kid Beat Up Your Honor Student!"

An international example of such playful competitiveness is the postage stamp that the country of Abkhazia released to celebrate its independence from the former Soviet Union. It created a best-selling stamp honoring Lennon and Marx, with the fun being that the honorees are John Lennon and Groucho Marx. *See also* LANGUAGE PLAY, PARODY, PUNS, STAGE NAMES.

Further reading: Henri Charmasson, *The Name Is the Game: How to Name a Company or Product* (1988). Leslie Dunkling, *The Guinness Book of Names,* 6th ed. (1993).

African American Humor

African American entertainers have a unique history related to the fact that before the Civil War most African immigrants to the United States were brought in as slaves. In West Africa, the original home of more than 50 percent of American slaves, sociologists have found cultures with many of the same characteristics that African Americans rely on for their humor: extensive wordplay and punning, signifying (verbal put-downs), the mocking of an enemy's relatives, the chanting and singing of ridicule verses, bent-knee dancing, an admiration for the Trickster, and aggressive joking that demands verbal quickness and wit.

African American slaves were forced to rely for their humor on folk culture because they were forbidden education. There are few records of the humor that slaves used amongst themselves, although slave narratives as well as other writings mention the rich laughter of slaves and the fact that a slave who could sing or perform was more valuable. Pre–Civil War references have been found to a New Orleans street vendor, Signor Corneali, or "Old Corn Meal," who entertained potential customers in both a rich baritone and a high falsetto voice; to John "Picayune" Butler, a "French darky banjo player," who traveled as a musician and a clown; and to William Henry "Juba" Lane, who may be the father of tap dancing because of the way he combined European and African jigs to "beat time with his feet."

Although they never achieved the success or earned the money of white minstrelsy troupes, even before emancipation there were troupes of Black performers, including an 1855 group that toured Massachusetts and New York as "SEVEN SLAVES just from Alabama, who are EARNING THEIR FREEDOM by giving concerts under the guidance of their Northern friends." After the Civil War ended in 1865, African American Charles "Barney" Hicks directed the Georgia Minstrels (a mostly white group) touring in the Northeast. Hicks worked for 40 years as both performer and manager, taking troupes to Canada, Europe, Australia, New Zealand, and Java.

Because of the heavy costuming and the similarity of most minstrel shows, it was hard for performers to gain star status, especially if they were African American; however, dancer and comedian Billy Kersands (1842–1915) was an exception. He had an exceedingly large mouth, which he used to full comic advantage, once telling Queen Victoria that if God had wanted his mouth any bigger, he would have to have found a new place for his ears. Kersands epitomized a problem that still troubles African American performers, which is whether they should build on or downplay the exaggerated and burlesqued traits that white minstrels were using in their caricatures of Blacks. People who, like W. E. B. Du Bois, wanted to raise the image of Blacks by presenting the most "talented tenth" of the Black race, were offended by Kersands. Mel Watkins has said that "Ernest Hogan, 'Pigmeat' Markham, Stepin Fetchit, Willie Best, Mantan Moreland, nearly the entire cast of the *Amos 'n' Andy* television show, and more recently, Richard Pryor, Eddie Murphy, and the TV variety show *In Living Color* have faced a similar dilemma."

Despite the offensive stereotyping, in the late 1800s and early 1900s, many African Americans went to see minstrel shows, especially those that were Black owned or that featured Black actors. Kersands, along with Sam Lucas, Tom McIntosh, and Tom Fletcher, were celebrities who gave hope to poor blacks. Sam Lucas witnessed tremendous changes during his lifetime from 1850 to 1916. As a teenager he was a singing barber, then after the Civil War, he entertained on Ohio River boats. In 1890, he was the endman in *The Creole Show*, which with its chorus line of female dancers foreshadowed the kind of urban variety shows still seen today. A year before his death in 1916, he starred in a film version of *Uncle Tom's Cabin*.

In the 1920s, African American influence on the broader culture was widely felt although not always recognized. Jazz and ragtime music and such popular dances as the Charleston, the Lindy, and the Cake Walk spread throughout America from their origins in Harlem. The acceptance of African American verbal humor was slower because of the problem of dialect and a feeling on the part of white Americans that verbal humor was an intellectual pursuit and whites weren't ready to play intellectual games with Blacks.

Bert Williams (1876–1922), who along with George Walker, had made the Cake Walk famous, was probably the first Black comedian to have his singing preserved for posterity by Victor Recordings. He was also one of the few early comedians booked into white theaters, including the *Ziegfeld Follies*, where he starred for several years.

Lincoln Perry (1896–1985), universally known as *Stepin Fetchit*, was a Jamaican comedian who perfected the comic role of an inept and inarticulate shuffler. In a circular fashion, his name is still used as a derogatory descriptor. He was the first Black American to work with major studios in Hollywood and to become a millionaire. However, his popularity waned after World War II when Black leaders were eager to reject the old stereotypes. In his disappointment, he complained about not getting the credit he deserved for setting up the thrones that Bill Cosby and Sidney Poitier later occupied.

Jackie "Moms" Mabley (1897–1975) was the most successful woman comic to perform in Black theaters. She would come on stage in oversized clodhoppers, a raggedy dress, and an oddball hat and immediately take the audience into her confidence with the comforting line, "Moms knows hows it is." As a ribald "granny," she created dozens of variations on her running joke, "An old man can't do nothin' for me except to bring me a message from a young man." She was nearly 70 before she played for white audiences, her debut being at the Playboy Club in Chicago. Her first television appearance was on Harry Belafonte's 1967 *A Time for Laughter*, with later guest appearances with Bill Cosby, the Smothers Brothers, and Flip Wilson. One of her irreverent jokes played with the cliched advice that you shouldn't say anything about someone who had died unless it was good: "He's dead; that's good!"

The raucous Pigmeat Markham (1904–1981) starred in dozens of burlesque sketches, including one in which he played the world's funkiest judge. When he entered the courtroom, everyone on stage would say, "Here come de Judge," a line later popularized by Sammy Davis Jr. and Flip Wilson.

During the 1930s, the radio show *Amos 'n' Andy*, starring white actors doing the radio equivalent of blackface comedy, was the most popular of all radio shows. On week nights, one-third of the nation turned in from 7:00 to 7:15 to listen to hustling Amos, slow-witted Andy, scheming Kingfish, and nagging Sapphire. When the show moved to television in 1951, African Americans were hired as the performers, including Alvin Childress, Spencer Williams Jr., Tim Moore, Jane Adams, Ernestine Wade, Amanda Randolph, Lillian Randolph, Johnny Lee, and Nick O'Demus. Flournoy Miller, who with Aubrey Lyles, had been a prominent Black writer and performer in vaudeville, was one of the writers who is praised for getting some genuine Black humor into the show. However, the controversial show was cancelled in 1953 partly because it had lost its old zing as the producers tried to put together a politically correct version. While everyone agrees that, by today's standards, the show was racist and stereotyped, critic Joe Franklin says that it was never as bad as the protesters thought it was, and that safely fictional Blacks may have prepared "the ground for the acceptance of real blacks in the American cultural mainstream."

The 1950s was a transitional period in which Black comedians broke out of the "chitlin' circuit" to perform before primarily white audiences. Primary figures were Timmie Rogers with his "Ohh . . . yeah!"; Slappy White, who was known as "father of the integrated joke"; Nipsey Russell, who because of his funny rhymes, was known as the "poet laureate of comedy"; and George Kirby, who was mainly a song-and-dance man but also did masterful impersonations.

Eddie Anderson (1905–1977) played Rochester in the popular *Jack Benny Program* (1932–1965). Besides his dialect, one of Anderson's comic assets was a foghorn voice (damaged when as a child he hawked newspapers). As Jack Benny's servant and constant companion, Rochester's role on the program was to point out Benny's stinginess.

The audience laughed at the boss more than at the servant; nevertheless, activists of the 1950s criticized Rochester's role as being stereotyped. In his autobiography, Benny wrote that the show consistently received more complaints from viewers upset at Rochester's sassiness than at his stereotyping.

Rochester's role foreshadowed the roles that Robert Guillaume would play as Benson DuBois on ABC's *Soap* (1977–1981) and *Benson* (1979–1986). In the first show, Benson was butler to the wealthy Tate family, while in the spinoff, Benson was loaned to a cousin running for governor. As the series progressed, Benson was promoted from domestic helper, to budget director, then to the executive secretary, and finally to lieutenant governor.

John Sanford (1922–1991), who adopted the stage name of Redd Foxx (spelled with a double *d* and a double *x* so he "wouldn't be a color or an animal"), was popular with Black audiences long before he starred on television's *Sanford and Son* (1972–1977) as a lovable, cantankerous, and devious junk dealer with attitude.

Dick Gregory (1932–) is one of the first comedians who entered mainstream comedy without learning his profession by performing before primarily Black audiences. Gregory studied Nipsey Russell's performances in front of both Black and white audiences and was convinced that whites were so nervous listening to a Black performer that his first job was to put the audience at ease. This is why he started his performances with non-racial references, "I bought a suit with two pairs of pants and burned a hole in the jacket." Only when he was sure the audience thought of him as a funny man who happened to be Black, rather than a Black man who happened to be funny, would he start talking about America being the only country in the world where a man can grow up in a ghetto, go to really bad schools, be forced to ride in the back of the bus, and then get paid $5,000 a week to tell people about it.

Godfrey Cambridge (1933–1976) was on his way to true star status when during the filming of a television movie, *Victory at Entebbe*, he suffered a fatal heart attack.

Cambridge's parents were from British Guiana, and it was not until he was in college that Cambridge decided he needed to find out what it meant to be a Negro. He was drawn to comedy even though he had never seen a Black comedian because the only places they performed were nightclubs, a setting off-limits to his religious family. He was influenced by such radio and TV comedians as Jack Benny, Fred Allen, and Jack Carter, so that when he went on stage he projected a friendly, nonethnic image similar to Bill Cosby's. But once he had established rapport, Cambridge would do comic scenes similar to Dick Gregory's, as when he explained that the town of Yuma, Arizona, was named after a Black man who had been shot by a white sheriff, and had uttered as his last dying words, "You mu—."

Early in his career, Clerow "Flip" Wilson (1933–1998) boosted the spirits of military personnel throughout the Pacific by waxing eloquent on "the Sex Habits of the Coconut Crab." Wilson's ascent to stardom was so rapid that *Time* magazine called him "TV's first black superstar." Between 1970 and 1974, the *Flip Wilson Show* was one of television's highest-rated variety shows; in the 1990s it was syndicated for reruns. Wilson developed a cast of characters including the Reverend Leroy, the playboy Freddie Johnson, and the irrepressible Geraldine. These stock, humorous characters out of the Black tradition differed from earlier exaggerated stereotypes in that Wilson gave them an underlying dignity, and by playing the role of both sophisticated and funny narrator and the stock characters, he made it clear that they were humorous inventions rather than real-life portrayals.

In the mid-1960s, Bill Cosby was the first Black performer to be recruited from stand-up comedy to star in a dramatic TV series, *I Spy*. Cosby, who after entering show business earned a doctorate in education, created the Fat Albert character for the CBS cartoon show *Fat Albert and the Cosby Kids*. He also was instrumental in developing *The Electric Company* for National Educational Television. In 1968, he starred on the *Bill Cosby Show* as Chet Kincaid, a school teacher in a contemporay Black community. In 1972, he did a CBS comedy and variety show, and from 1984 to 1992, he starred in *The Cosby Show*, about the upwardly mobile Huxtable family. For most of its eight years, the show was number one in the ratings. Cosby, who in 1997 resurrected Art Linkletter's *Kids Say the Darndest Things*, has sometimes been criticized for not being "Black enough," but Redd Foxx is among those who praised him for showing "that being Black is no different from being white or brown or whatever color."

In the late 1970s, the controversial Richard Pryor (1940–) fused different schools of comedy. Like Pigmeat Markham he would speak in Black dialect, like Lenny Bruce he dealt unflinchingly with racial and sexual tensions, and like Bill Cosby and George Carlin he transformed himself into a clown. The more controversial Pryor's acts became, the greater was his stardom. Some people said he was a genius, while others quoted the title of one of his comedy albums, "That Nigger's Crazy." Pryor acted in nearly 40 movies and wrote the scripts for 10. For two months in 1977, he had his own television show, which NBC canceled because it thought mainstream audiences were more comfortable with such sitcoms as *What's Happening* (ABC 1976–1979), *The Jeffersons* (CBS 1975–1985), and *Good Times* (CBS 1974–1979). However, the 1979 success of *Wanted: Richard Pryor Live in Concert*, the first filmed concert to be distributed in theaters, and its follow-up, *Live on the Sunset Strip*, showed that the public indeed was ready for authentic African American humor. Playwright Neil Simon said that Pryor was "the most brilliant comic in America. There's no one funnier or more perceptive," while in 1997 critic Laurie Stone wrote, "Although by the mid-eighties, Pryor has already leaked his genius into drugs, self-loathing, and limp movies, his influence on comic performance—his combination of rage, vulnerability, and ironic detachment—can't be overstated."

In the 1970s and 1980s, tall and skinny Jimmy Walker starred in *Good Times*, *B.A.D. Cats*, *At Ease*, and *Bustin' Loose*. Fred MacDonald described Walker with his broad

Richard Pryor is considered by many to be one of the most influential comedians of our time. *Columbia Pictures/Archive Photos*

smile and his signature expression, "DYN-O-MITE!" as "the coon character, the rascalish, loud, pushing and conniving stereotype." However, a difference from the old days was that in the 1970s and 1980s, the "coon" character wasn't the only African image in the media. Also Walker would lull an audience by his silliness and then ask such a question as, "When was the last time you seen a Black embezzler—or a Black man getting busted for juggling the bankbooks? I mean, what's the use of having a Black brother on the Supreme Court if none of us can commit a crime classy enough to get it tried there?"

Whoopi Goldberg has a talent for mimicking anyone from a Valley Girl to a down-and-out bum. But unlike many comedians, Goldberg's imitations have strong pathos and a streetwise edge. For example, she makes audiences laugh as she recounts the sexual experiences of a naive surfer chick, but suddenly the audience realizes that the monologue isn't funny any more because Goldberg is describing how her character used a coat hanger to abort her pregnancy: "I'm not gonna be able to have kids. . . . You can't drag babies around. . . . Besides, I'm turning 14 next week. I've got my whole life ahead of me." Over two decades, Goldberg's fame has increased so that she is admired not only as an entertainer but as a cultural figure, rather like Madonna has become.

In the 1990s, Whoopi Goldberg's talent for ad lib and for making a stage sparkle with power was showcased in her role as host of the Academy Awards. *Reuters/Gary Hershorn/Archive Photos*

During the 1980s and 1990s, the smiling and boyish-looking Eddie Murphy, who had been a star on *Saturday Night Live*, became one of the hottest comics in America. He demonstrated his street smarts in *Trading Places* (1983), and in *Beverly Hills Cop* (1984), *Beverly Hills Cop II* (1987), and *Beverly Hills Cop III* (1984). Popular Eddie Murphy movies of the 1990s included *The Nutty Professor* (1996) and *Life* (1999), where he co-starred with Martin Lawrence. Part of his appeal is the twinkle in his eye and an uncanny ability to cross over from innocence to hustle, a trait also honed by Will Smith for his role in the 1998 *Men in Black*.

Between 1990 and 1992, Marsha Warfield (1955–), the stocky five-foot-eleven Black bailiff on television's long-running *Night Court*, starred in her own *Marsha Warfield Show*. Also in the early 1990s, Arsenio Hall began hosting his own late-night comedy show. When his show was moved to 11:30

to challenge Johnny Carson, he quipped that he was not "going after Johnny's crowd"; instead he was after the children of Johnny's viewers.

In the late 1990s, stand-up comedian Chris Rock got his own weekly HBO talk show, which was unusually successful in attracting a wide range of viewers. Listed on the show's Web site as the "Best Monologue Jokes" of the 1998 season were "What Monica Won't Do for Free," "Viagra Unveils Its Own Ad Slogan," and "Clinton Really Does Deserve Credit for the Economy." Among the "Best Guest Highlights" were Rosie Perez talking about sexual harassment before and after Monica, Lisa Nicole Carson talking about fan mail from the brothers in lockdown, Magic Johnson on what's up with the NBA strike, Johnnie Cochran offering legal advice, Jerry Springer talking about his favorite episode, and Larry Elder debating Rock on the Clinton scandal.

Similar to how in the 1970s the Osmonds and the Jacksons were dominant families in popular music, in the 1990s the Wayans family became dominant figures in comedy. The family grew up in New York with 10 children. According to Shawn, second to the youngest, their father worked about six jobs while their mother took care of the family and gave each child as much attention as she could. Out of necessity they all helped each other out, a practice that still continues.

The older brothers (Keenen and Damon) and sister Kim were successful, along with Jim Carrey, Kelly Coffield, Tommy Davidson, David Alan Grier, and T'keyeh "Crystal" Keymah, in helping to launch the 1990 television show *In Living Color*. This popular variety show ran for five years. Some of the most memorable satirical sketches were the "Homeboy Shopping Network," in which Keenen and Damon played two homeboys trying to sell obviously stolen items on cable TV. In "The Brothers Brothers," the two who were both named Tom were often mistaken for being Black, a charge that they would counter by warning people not to be fooled by appearances. In "Les and Wes," they played Siamese twins. Because Wes seemed to get all the luck in life, the two were more or less estranged and acted as though they seldom saw each other. In "Men on . . ." two gay men (Damon Wayans and David Alan Grier) would review movies and other "stuff." Damon, who has been criticized for the vitriol of his anti-gay humor, grew up with a club foot, which he now acknowledges had some benefit in keeping him out of gang activities.

Shawn Wayans worked first as a disc jockey, but in 1991 was given a regular spot in the *In Living Color* cast. In 1995, he began starring with younger brother Marlon in *The Wayans Bros*, a sitcom on the WB network. Shawn describes it as *The Odd Couple*

Shawn Wayans, along with sister Kim and brothers Keenan, Damon, and Marlon, relies on a refreshing mix of old and new comedy techniques. *Albert Ferrier/Globe Photos Inc.*

meeting *The Honeymooners* in the *Good Times* apartment.

In conclusion, what has happened to African American comedy in the hundred years between 1900 and 2000 is that both the number and the range of Black comedians, writers, producers, and performers has increased so that it is impossible in this kind of a brief review to describe them all. Among those that we have not written about are Thea Vidal,

George Wallace, Sinbad, Martin Lawrence, Joseph Papp, Russell Simmon, Dael Orlandersmith, and Angela Scott. That we don't have space for everyone illustrates the point that Mel Watkins makes at the end of *On the Real Side* where he writes that the variety and the force with which African American humor has arrived in mainstream America means that at last white America is no longer laughing at, but with, Black America. The fame of many African American entertainers is not based so much on the fact that they are Black as on some other aspect of their personalities. This is further illustrated by the number of African Americans mentioned in other entries throughout this encyclopedia. *See also* BLACKFACE COMEDY, ETHNIC HUMOR, RADIO

Further reading: M. Fred MacDonald, *Black and White TV: Afro-Americans in Television since 1948* (1983). Laurie Stone, *Laughing in the Dark: A Decade of Subversive Comedy* (1997). Mel Watkins, *On the Real Side: Laughing, Lying, and Signifying* (1994).

Aging and Humor

Humor in relation to aging has at least three distinctive aspects. The first is the kind of humor the general population creates about older people, the second is the humor that older people create and enjoy about themselves or other seniors, while the third relates not so much to different kinds of humor as to the role that humor plays in the lives of people as they grow old.

A comparison of the humor created about the elderly as opposed to that created by the elderly illustrates differences in points of view. A Scripps Howard news story (Nov. 15, 1997) told about a free speech controversy at the University of Memphis where student Kevin Murphy used the university's computer system to create an "Old Folks' Home Page," in which he referred to the elderly as "geezers" and "wrinklies," and said that attempts to cure Alzheimer's disease were only prolonging death. When challenged by the AARP (American Association of Retired Persons), Murphy defended the material as "new, alternative, well-written, and funny." He believes most of what he writes, but overstates it for the sake of humor. In his opinion, the exaggeration distinguishes his Web page from those put out by hate groups. "True hate speech," he says, "is much more restrained."

At the opposite end of the spectrum is an anecdote, probably an urban legend, about a young college kid in a sports car who whips into a parking lot and sees an older man maneuvering to turn his Cadillac around so he can get into the only space available. The young man deftly slips his little car around the bulky Cadillac and into the space. He jumps out and laughingly says, "See what you can do if you're young and quick!" The older man, who by now has his car in position to drive into the space, puts the Cadillac in low gear and accompanied by sounds of breaking glass and crunching metal drives forward. As he climbs out of his newly parked car, he triumphantly says, "See what you can do if you're old and rich!"

With these extreme examples, it is easy to see whose viewpoint is being represented, but with many other examples even well-intentioned people including politicians, comedians, and advertisers who are trying to amuse older people often end up insulting them. Psychologist Lucille Nahemow says that when people feel a pressure to laugh at insulting jokes then they are being doubly punished. Because it is "only a joke," they are denied a chance to respond directly to the insult, and being forced to "swallow" the insult is likely to generate self-hatred.

Some older people have gotten this message and are no longer willing to pretend to enjoy humor that targets them. For example, when a comedian was booked to do a 30-minute warm-up show for singer Vicki Carr at the Sundome Auditorium in Arizona, he knew his audience would be elderly people because the auditorium is shared by the retirement communities of Sun City and Sun City West in suburban Phoenix. Tailoring his material to the audience, he chose the majority of his jokes to be about aging. The audience laughed good naturedly when he talked about prune juice and Geritol, but then he began talking about sex. He said the night before he had been the master of ceremonies

at a golden wedding anniversary party held in a grand old San Diego hotel. The couple was coming back to relive their wedding night of 50 years before. After the party, they went upstairs and got ready for bed. Among the reminiscing and the fond exclamations, the wife remembered a poignant detail. She turned to her husband and said, "Oh, darling, bite me on the shoulder like you used to." When she cuddled over expectantly, her husband jumped out of bed. "Where are you going?" she asked. "To get my teeth," he replied.

While some in the audience laughed, the general feeling was one of discomfort. The comedian tried to win back the audience by telling about a woman being raped, or as the newspaper put it, "violated." Her former husband had quipped to reporters that he was sure it hadn't been "a moving violation." The audience, typical of older groups, included twice as many women as men, and they let the comedian know that they were not going to laugh at something they considered cruel.

Older women have long been the butt of jokes about a lack of attractiveness and of sexual interest as shown by a content analysis of "oldster" jokes conducted by Erdman B. Palmore in 1977 and reported in *Humor and Aging*. He analyzed 264 jokes about aging or the aged collected from 10 popular joke books. Overall, he found that 25 percent of the jokes presented a positive view of aging. However, these positive jokes were more than twice as likely to be about men than about women. Women, especially if unmarried, were nearly always presented in a negative light. However, there were jokes portraying women as more capable than expected, as in the story of the 80-year-old woman who went to her doctor to report that she was losing her sexual desires. When asked by her doctor when she first noticed this, she replied, "Last night and then again this morning."

Other research findings reported in *Humor and Aging* include the following:

- The top five topics for jokes about the elderly were age or longevity, physical ability or appearance, being old fashioned, losing sexual ability or interest, and concealing one's age. Palmore suggested a correlation between this frequency chart and the topics that consistently worry people.

- Two content analyses of birthday cards showed that of those that focused on age (between one-third and one-half), the majority portrayed getting older as shameful. Over half dealt with physical or mental loss and one-fourth were about concealing one's age. Only 10 percent implied that things get better with age or that aging is just a mental attitude.

- A study of 144 "oldster" jokes told by people between the ages of 60 and 90 differed from collections of "oldster" jokes told by the general public in that there were no jokes about people concealing their ages. The researchers did not know whether this meant that in spite of the stereotype older people do not really conceal their age or whether they do but don't like to joke about it. The other major difference was that few of the jokes were about the loss of attractiveness. Again, the researchers were unsure as to whether the elderly do not worry about their appearance or whether they worry about it so much that it is not a joking matter.

- One-third of these jokes told by older people dealt with sex. Forty-three percent of the jokes told by males were sexual in nature as contrasted to only 20 percent of those told by females. Themes that were treated included an awareness of decline coupled with an ability to laugh at oneself; an affirmation that while there's life, there's sex; an association of sex with virility and fertility; and a vicarious identification with the sexual activities of the young.

- As a result of an analysis of the findings of the Harvard University Longitudinal Grant Study, psychiatrist George Vaillant designated humor as one of the five mature coping mechanisms available to humans for successfully dealing with disadvantageous circumstances.

Predicting how people, especially elderly people, will react to jokes about aging is difficult because while the specter of death used to be spread through all age groups, today's advances in medicine and accident prevention mean that people associate death with old age. And because people are afraid of death, they experience varying degrees of emotional interference when they hear jokes about the elderly. Also, the older people are, the more individualized—the more set in their ways—they have become. With normal five-year-olds researchers can predict what they will find funny, but with people who have had 70 or 80 years of unique experiences, there will naturally be great variations in their attitudes and their reactions to people's stories. Related to this issue of individuality is the wide age range considered to be "old." Few people expect 20-year-olds to have much in common with those who are 40 or 50, but in industrialized America, once people have retired from their jobs, they are lumped together as "senior citizens," and 60-year-olds are treated as if they were the same as 90-year-olds.

Older people who feel secure enough to create self-deprecating jokes about their frailties and fears are probably genuinely amused, at least when they are in the playful mood that goes along with creating jokes, but when these same jokes are generalized to all senior citizens, many individuals are likely to resent the implication that the joke is true of them. In reference to the fine line between humor and ridicule, writer Max Shulman has said that if he told a joke that would make listeners say, "Ah ha, I know someone like that," he would get a laugh. But if he told a joke that made listeners say, "Oh no, that's me," he would get silence or worse.

Popular humor writers Dave Barry and Bill Geist, both of whom grew up as part of the baby boomers' generation with its slogan of "Never trust anyone over 30," have written books about such traumas as turning 50, having a last child go off to college, losing one's teeth, growing hair in one's nose, and, worst of all, receiving a welcoming letter from AARP. Their books can be light-hearted and funny because, to most people, age 50 isn't really very scary, nor are the traumas nearly as real as getting cancer or Alzheimer's, becoming impotent, losing one's income, or being abandoned by one's spouse or one's children.

Lucille Nahemow suggests that the humor used by older people, even though it "is hard to classify, difficult to categorize, and impossible to pin down," is a vital part of the aging process and that gerontologists could benefit from studying it and from using it in their work. For example, she cites the lengthy discussions that gerontologists have had over a definition of aging only to conclude that it is relative. "How much easier," she says, "to quote the proverb, 'An old maid who gets married becomes a young wife.'"

A second example that she cites as providing insights into the elderly is the story of an 83-year-old woman visiting her doctor. After he examined her, he sympathetically confided, "There are some things not even modern medicine can cure. . . .You know, my dear, I can't make you any younger." "Who asked you to make me younger?" she replied. "I want you to make me *older*."

An anecdote that on the surface seems similar, in fact, carries the opposite message. An 80-year-old man is being examined by a young and energetic doctor who declares with enthusiasm, "You're in excellent health; you'll live 'til your 80!" "I'm already 80," says the man. The doctor responds, "See, what did I tell you!"

Humor as created and used by elderly people in their social interactions probably plays a bigger part in the everyday lives of elderly people than do canned jokes. However, comic performances, such as those arranged in the early 1990s when the city of New York Department of Cultural Affairs paid minimum wages to nine elderly comedians to perform at senior citizen centers and retirement homes, may set the mood and encourage older people to view their lives from a flip side. In *Humor and Aging* (1986), Nahemow tells about an unforgettable experience that she had in a nursing home when she visited residents during their crafts class.

> An old woman, looking grim, was hemming a square of cloth. I sat down to talk with her and made the mistake of admiring her stitches. She looked at me with an unexpected clarity and said, "I am a tailor. For sixty years I am a tailor." We both looked down at the pathetic cloth with new understanding. I was appalled and my expression must have reflected my feelings. She looked at me kindly and turned tragedy into humor by laughing suddenly and saying, "She don't know. I let her teach me. She's a nice lady. I make her happy." I started to giggle, then to laugh, and finally we both roared.

This incident from real life has the same kind of tragic-comedy that Herb Gardner captured in his prize-winning play *I'm Not Rappaport* (1984). The play is about two old men who meet regularly in a New York park. Midge is a Black ex-prize fighter who for years has been the night custodian at an apartment house that is being modernized and turned into condos. He is going to lose his job because they are replacing the old furnace that only he knows how to run. Nat is a Jewish man whose daughter wants him to come and live with her in the suburbs or move into a retirement home or at least go to the senior citizen center for a hot meal and an afternoon of activities. As Nat explains to Midge, "We got three possibilities; we got exile in Great Neck, we got Devil's Island, and we got kindergarten. All rejected." Toward the end of the play, Nat is a little more humble and has agreed to his daughter's demand that he go to the senior citizen center, but he still has his cynicism to help him feel in control as he explains to Midge, "The day begins at noon there. I must be prompt. At 12, guest speaker Jerome Cooper will lecture on 'Timely Issues for the Aging': refreshments will be served to anyone who's alive at the end."

The title of the play comes from a vaudeville skit that Willy Howard used to do. When Nat tries to do the skit with his daughter, it doesn't work because she isn't in the same playful mood as are Nat and Midge in this pivotal scene showing their mutual respect and enjoyment of each other:

NAT: Hello, Rappaport!

MIDGE: I'm not Rappaport.

NAT: Hey. Rappaport, what happened to you? You used to be a tall, fat guy; now you're a short, skinny guy.

MIDGE: I'm not Rappaport.

NAT: You used to be a young fellah with a beard; now you're an old guy without a beard! What happened to you?

MIDGE: I'm not Rappaport.

NAT: What happened, Rappaport? You used to dress up nice; now you got old dirty clothes!

MIDGE: I'm not Rappaport. I'm Midge!

NAT: And you changed your *name* too.

See also CHILDREN'S LITERATURE, ETHNIC HUMOR, HEALTH AND HEALING

Further reading: Dave Barry, *Dave Barry Turns Fifty* (1998). William Geist, *The Big Five-O!* (1997). Lucile Nahemow, Kathleen A. McCluskey-Fawcett, and Paul E. McGhee (eds.) *Humor and Aging* (1986).

Allusion

An allusion is an implied or indirect reference. The noun form of the word *allude* comes from Latin *ad* plus *ludere*, which means "to play," and this is exactly what people do when using humorous allusions. Because allusions are concentrated food for thought, they make for efficient communication as when the mention of a name or the use of a particular phrase triggers a reader's or a listener's mind to puff up a story and fill in the details. This is especially important when time or space is limited, as is the case with commercials, cartoons, headlines, and bumper stickers.

The challenge in using allusion comes in finding references that will communicate the same idea to a wide audience. One solution is to make allusions to the stories and the nursery rhymes that most Americans hear in their childhood. For example, a happy wife is shown standing with her husband in the family's new den. In an allusion to "This is the house that Jack built," she is proudly saying, "This is the room that Herb panelled." In an allusion to the story about Chicken Little, an ad for using diet salad dressing as barbecue sauce reads, "The calories are falling." The 1997 movie title, *Kiss the Girls*, was planned to make viewers think of

Georgie Porgie, Puddin' and Pie,
Kissed the girls and made them cry. . . .

However, some young moviegoers did not catch on to the allusion because that particular nursery rhyme is now viewed as sexist and so was left out of many collections now used in preschool and kindergarten.

In a boxed feature labeled "Pinocchio Index," the editors of *Time* magazine used to print a quote that they judged to be less than honest. Above the statement was a head shot of the speaker enhanced by a Pinocchio-like nose. Jiminy Cricket from the Walt Disney version of *Pinocchio* is almost as famous as Pinocchio, and provides a good illustration of how complex allusions can be. In the Walt Disney movie, Jiminy Cricket plays the role of Pinocchio's conscience. However, in the original Italian story by C. Collodi, there is no mention of a Jiminy Cricket; instead there is a "Talking Cricket" who appears on fewer than a dozen pages out of the 310-page book, and in chapter four is killed when Pinocchio throws a hammer at him. Somewhere between the original Italian story and the Walt Disney movie, a creative mind connected the "Talking Cricket" with a slang term that was already part of popular culture. This term evolved out of *Gemini*, which had long been used as a swear word with the implication being that the speaker was swearing double (*Gemini* is the name of the constellation created when the twin sons of Zeus and Leda were placed in the sky). By the 1830s Americans had simplified the spelling to *Jiminy*, and by the middle of the century were using *Jiminy Crickets*, followed a few decades later, by the alterant form, *Jiminy Christmas*. Because of the similarity in beginning sounds to *Jesus*

Christ, the phrase gradually changed from being a swear word alluding to the twins of Greek and Roman mythology, to being a euphemistic slang term for *Jesus Christ*. For a naughty little boy's conscience, there could hardly be a better name than this veiled and playful reference to deity.

Well-known adult literature is another popular source for allusions. The newspaper headline "My Boss, Big Brother," appeared on a story about a newly passed Illinois law permitting employers to listen in on workers' phones. "Texas caught in Catch-22" was on a story about a prisoner on death row who refused to take his anti-psychotic medicine. The complication was that Texas laws prohibit executing anyone who is insane. "Great Expectations" drew attention to a story about the hoped-for jobs of those who successfully worked for President Clinton's second-term election. Many readers may have missed the connection between the popular movie title *Sleepless in Seattle* and the news headline "Clueless in Washington." However, this wouldn't have kept them from understanding the story, which asked why the United States wasn't warned that Mexico's top drug fighter was being arrested for corruption.

Allusions based on current events make timely joke subjects for late-night television because there is nearly always someone in the studio audience who will recognize the allusion and start the laughter. However, with print media where messages go to individuals, many allusions are missed because the news of the world provides more grounding for allusions than people can organize in their minds. Also, there is such a turnover that by the time someone makes a humorous allusion, many people will have forgotten the original story. For example, the bumper sticker, "So many stupid people . . . So few Comets," will probably outlast the general public's interest in the 1997 Heaven's Gate suicides connected to the Hale-Bopp comet. Another bumper sticker from the same period, "Jack Kevorkian for White House Physician," may also lose its timeliness, but because the controversial Michigan doctor and his campaign of assisted suicide were

repeatedly in the news for a longer period of time, this bumper sticker has longer lasting communicative powers than does the one about the comet.

A different kind of humor comes from playing with mistaken or confused allusions—those the listener has to think about twice—as in this George Burns and Gracie Allen skit:

> GEORGE: If you keep saying funny things, people are going to laugh at you.
>
> GRACIE: That's OK. Look at Joan of Arc. People laughed at her, but she went ahead and built it anyway.

One of the objects that comedian Michael Davis juggled was an ax that he claimed was the original one that George Washington had used to chop down the cherry tree: "However," he confesses, "I did have to replace the handle . . .(after a long pause) . . . and the head."

Since scholars have cast doubt on the original story about the cherry tree, Davis's allusion is probably as true as the story. Besides, allusions are made to the thoughts in people's heads rather than to the actual items as shown by how often people allude to nonexistent magic elixirs, goblins, wood nymphs, satyrs, griffins, unicorns, gorgons, elves, gremlins, phoenix birds, cyclops, and Minotaurs. People in a playful mood also allude to skyhooks, pole stretchers, and left-handed monkey wrenches, along with Santa Claus, the Easter Bunny, the Tooth Fairy, Old Father Time, the Sand Man, and the Boogie Man.

Just for fun, people create variations on these established mythologies as when in the mid-1980s, 1,200 fans in 35 states belonged to the "Rula Lenska Fan Club." At the time, Lenska was a little known actress who pushed hair products. While she was relatively unknown, the commercials were made as though she were a true celebrity. This difference caught the fancy of some creative individuals who invited the public to join in celebrating Rula Lenska Day by either choosing a "special activity to do nonstop for 14 hours, by using a whole can of hair spray for one 'do,' or by leaving their headlights on for 24 hours."

A similar kind of fascination went along with the bit of graffiti, "Who is John Galt?" which appeared all over the United States and was worked into the plot of Ayn Rand's novel *Atlas Shrugged*. With today's Internet, it should be easier for playful people to create such imaginary folk heroes, but without the communication challenge it may not be as much fun. *See also* IMPLICATION, LANGUAGE PLAY, METAPHORS, POSTMODERNISM

Further reading: Stuart Berg Flexner, *I Hear America Talking: An Illustrated Treasury of American Words and Phrases* (1976). Richard Lederer, *Pun and Games* (1996).

Ambiguity

Ambiguity occurs when something can be understood in two or more senses or ways. It is a key component in the kind of humor where a situation is established so that the mind of a listener or a reader moves forward filling in details and making what seems to be a clear picture. Then something clicks, and there is a sudden, often laughable, realization that the mind had been going in the wrong direction. An excellent illustration of ambiguity occurs in this mildly risque story that in 1960 was censored by Jack Paar's network, causing him to walk off his show for a week.

The joke is in the form of a letter from a Swiss schoolmaster who had misunderstood a British visitor's request for information about the "W.C." The schoolmaster thought the woman was asking about the "Wayside Chapel," when in fact she was asking about the availability of a water closet (British for toilet). The schoolmaster wrote:

> The W.C. is situated nine miles from the house. It is capable of holding 229 people and is open on Sunday and Thursday only. I would suggest that you come early, although there is plenty of standing room as a rule. A good number of people bring their lunch and make a day of it. It may interest you to know that my daughter was married in the W.C., and it was there that she met her husband. I can remember the rush there was for seats. There were 10 people to a seat usually occupied by one.

The fun of this story relates to the multitude of dual meanings that developed out of the initial confusion over "Wayside Chapel" vs. "water closet." Lexical ambiguity, which is caused by the same word, in this case the same set of initials, having two different meanings is the easiest kind of ambiguity to create because many words in English have more than one meaning. Advertisers use ambiguous language in hopes of enticing readers or listeners to spend more time with a company's message and thereby become convinced of its efficacy, as with these examples:

> Sign on a garbage truck: "Our business is picking up."
>
> Advertisement for cheese: "Cheese can make you a hero this weekend."
>
> Sign on a drapery shop: "After 35 years, we've finally got the hang of it."
>
> An optometrist's sign: "There's more to a vision examination than meets the eye."
>
> Advertisement for aspirin: "We go to a lot of pains."
>
> Slogan for a pizza parlor: "We roll our own."

For the mind to experience the sharp surprise that is at the root of humor based on ambiguity, the number of possibilities must be limited probably to two, or occasionally three, definite interpretations. For instance, a 1940s Helen Hokinson cartoon for *The New Yorker* shows one of her "girls" calling from a police station, "Albert, I did something wrong on the George Washington Bridge." The amusement in this droll cartoon does not come from ambiguity, because there are literally hundreds of things the woman could have done wrong. Instead the humor comes from Hokinson's drawing and from the fact that the addle-headed woman upsets expectations by being so vague.

Syntactic ambiguity is more complex than lexical or word-based ambiguity because it develops through the grammar of a sentence as in this story about an older man and his alligator. The man goes into a restaurant dragging along a 10-foot alligator. With considerable effort, he manages to get the alligator stuffed under a table in the corner, where he sits down wearily. When the waitress approaches, he asks her if they serve senior citizens here. "Of course," she smiles sweetly. "Good," he says. "Give my alligator a senior citizen and I'll have a cheeseburger."

The ambiguity in this story circles around the question of whether the restaurant serves *something* to senior citizens, or whether the restaurant serves *senior citizens* to something or someone? Other examples of syntactic ambiguity (which may include lexical ambiguity) are Stan Kenton's song title, "Celery Stalks at Midnight," and Charles H. Ulrich's riddle:

Q: Do you know what good clean fun is?
A: No. What good is it?

In a *Frank and Ernest* comic strip, Frank, who is talking to a real estate agent, says, "Sure, we'd like to see a model home. . . . What time does she get off work?" In Bud Blake's *Tiger* comic strip, when a little boy reports, "I'm gonna be in the school play." His mother asks, "What part?" and he responds, "All of me!"

These sentences have been used in various linguistic textbooks to illustrate different kinds of syntactic ambiguity:

- The governor is a dirty street fighter.
- Did you ever see a horse fly?
- I cannot recommend him too highly.
- Could this be the invisible man's hair tonic?
- He gave her dog biscuits.
- It's the world's largest war surplus store.
- Cynthia left directions for her Dad to follow.

Syntactic ambiguity often occurs accidentally because people fail to make clear just what a phrase in a sentence is modifying as in these examples collected by Norman Stageberg:

- Sign outside a dance hall: *Clean and decent dancing every night except Monday.*
- Questionnaire sent to law schools: *How many faculty members do you have, broken down by sex?*
- Statement in a speech at an educator's conference: . . . *I have discussed the high cost of living with several women.*
- Sign in a diner in Chillicothe, Ohio: *Wanted: Man to scrub floor and two waitresses.*

See also LANGUAGE PLAY, PUNS

Further reading: Delia Chiaro. *The Language of Jokes: Analyzing Verbal Play* (1992).

American Indian Humor

To refer to "American Indian (or Native American) humor" as if it were one type of humor is to overgeneralize because when Europeans first came to the American continent some 500 years ago, there were hundreds of distinct nations speaking close to 1,000 different languages. These peoples had lived side by side for generations, but had chosen to keep their tribal beliefs, languages, and customs separate. In the years that followed, many clans joined together as all Native Americans experienced losing their lands, moving to reservations, and adapting their beliefs and lifestyles to technological, and in some cases urban, societies. However, there are still major differences among tribes, and when members are asked whether they want to be called *Native Americans* or *American Indians*, many will say they want to be known by their tribal names. The term *pan-Indian* has been coined to refer to interests and characteristics held in common among tribes.

Native American writers Louise Erdrich and Michael Dorris made this point on the Public Broadcasting System when Bill Moyers interviewed them in relation to their forthcoming 1991 book *The Crown of Columbus*. When Moyers asked Erdrich about the humor in her poems and short stories and in her 1984 *Love Medicine*, 1986 *The Beet Queen*, and 1988 *Tracks*, Erdrich conjectured that creating and enjoying ironic survival humor, often at the expense of white oppressors, may be one of the few universal characteristics shared by all U.S. Indian tribes. As an example of a pan-Indian joke, she cited Vine Deloria Jr.'s observation that when the first missionaries came they had only the Bible and Indians had all the land; now "they" have all the land and Indians have only the Bible.

In both his speaking and his writing, Deloria has campaigned against the stereotype of the stoic Indian, a caricature that he says has made it difficult for whites to understand how humor permeates virtually every area of Native American life. Very little, he says, is accomplished in Indian national affairs without humor. Humor is used not only for entertainment but also for education and for spurring people to action. Deloria took the name of his 1988 book *Custer Died for Your Sins* from a bumper sticker designed to tease missionaries on the Sioux reservation.

Kenneth Lincoln explains that "not only do Indians bond and revitalize, scapegoat and survive through laughter, but they draw on millennia-old traditions of Trickster gods and holy fools, comic romance and epic boast." Among the pieces of evidence he presents for the importance of humor in Indian life is the fact that the Hopi word for *clowning* means "to make a point." In the Navajo culture, the first time an infant laughs, the family holds a celebration in which the child symbolically provides bread and salt to family members and guests, signifying that he or she is now a part of the tribe.

Lincoln cites speech patterns that N. Scott Momaday uses in his 1968 *House Made of Dawn* to illustrate how a pan-Indian English is developing as "the native grammar (and humor) of lived situations." This language is quite separate "from the mainstream schoolings, European origins, and class proprieties of America," and is all the more interesting because it is a "cross-tribal red English." In *House Made of Dawn*, Momaday writes about southwestern, California, and northern and southern plains Indians whose native languages include Navajo with its 13 distinct tenses and Hopi, which has no verb

tenses. As an example of interesting code switching, framing, and mixing of references, Lincoln quotes this welcoming speech given by one of Momaday's characters:

> Good evening, blood brothers and sisters, and welcome, welcome. Gracious me, I see lots of new faces out there tonight. *Gracious me!* May the Great Spirit—can we knock off that talking in the back there?—be with you always.

Paula Gunn Allen in her 1987 "Autobiography of a Confluence" (*I Tell You Now: Autobiographical Essays by Native American Writers,* edited by Brian Swann and Arnold Krupat) talked about what she called "an odd brand of English . . . a punning, cunning language" that is "mostly local, mostly half-breed spoken by the people around me, filled with elegance and vulgarity side by side, small jokes that are language jokes and family jokes and area jokes. . . ."

Humor develops on the edges of social change, which is why the blending of European and Native American cultures is a common source of humor. Will Rogers, who was born in Claremore, Oologah Indian Territory in Oklahoma, got laughs by telling people he had just enough white blood to make his honesty questionable. Singer and comedian Cher, whose name was originally Cherilyn Sarkisian, says that her name honors her Cherokee ancestors and jokes that, like about one-half of the people in the United States, she has a Cherokee grandmother. At Barry Goldwater's May 1998 funeral, Bruce Babbitt said there were only two Arizonans whose names were recognized worldwide: Barry Goldwater and Geronimo.

Probably the strongest book to present dark humor from a Native American perspective is Thomas Berger's 1964 *Little Big Man.* Berger based his novel on *Black Elk Speaks; Being the Life Story of a Holy Man of the Oglala Sioux, as Told through John G. Neihardt (Flaming Rainbow),* illustrated by Standing Bear, published by the University of Nebraska Press in 1961. Black Elk, who survived the Battle of Little Big Horn in which General Custer and his soldiers were killed, lived from 1863 to 1950 and told his story to

Neihardt, who died in 1973. The *New York Times Book Review* praised Berger for "expertly flinging mud at the more solemn and self-important national myths." However, some critics worried that the popular 1970 movie starring Dustin Hoffman as Little Big Man obscured the subtleties of the book.

The dark irony in the story centers around opposites and the breaking of expectations. The young Black Elk's family is massacred by Pawnee Indians, but he is found and adopted by Cherokees. Years later he is again "found" and re-adopted by a preacher, but the preacher's wife turns out to be a whore. Wild Bill Hickok wanders into the picture and is killed not by a desperado but by a boy whose father Hickok had killed. Little Big Man's red-headed wife is stolen by Indians and he spends years searching for her, but when he finds her she doesn't recognize him and he decides to leave well enough alone. Little Big Man advises the arrogant General Custer not to attack the Indians gathered at Little Big Horn, but Custer suspects a trick and so does the opposite and is totally defeated. In the battle, Little Big Man is severely wounded, but an Indian brave whose life had once been saved by Little Big Man rescues him, only to announce that they are now even and the next time he sees Little Big Man he will feel free to kill him.

One of the funniest parts is the appearance of a contrary clown who arrives riding backwards on a horse with his body painted in motley colors. He says "Goodbye" for "Hello," "I'm glad I did it!" for "I'm sorry," cleans himself with sand, and then strides off walking through the river.

The modus operandi for contrary clowns, who appear in many tribes, is to do the opposite of what is expected. In the summer, a contrary might pretend to feel cold and so dress in buffalo robes, while in winter he pretends to be warm and so stands naked in the snow. Arapaho contraries groan loudly when they lift light objects and pretend not to notice when lifting truly heavy objects. Koshari contraries talk backwards and know how to babble total nonsense, while Mayan contraries pretend to be afraid of inconsequential

events and fall to the ground when confronted by small obstacles.

One purpose of traditional Native American clowns is to demonstrate the humiliation that must be suffered when social and cultural codes are violated. During certain religious ceremonies, Tohono O'odham (Papago) clowns use squeaks and signs to beg food from the audience, while Hopi clowns are beaten and forced to undergo mock castrations by their fellow dancers. These ritual clowns serve as a counterbalance on solemn occasions and are authorized to ridicule, burlesque, and defile even sacred religious traditions and sexual mores. Clowns in Pueblo communities dress in rags and masks and mock the serious Kachina dancers by stumbling, falling down, throwing and sometimes miming eating excrement, and worshiping fake gods in an exaggerated manner. Occasionally the sacred and the profane become indistinguishable as when a shaman provokes laughter during a magical performance. In Zuni, Ojibwa, Lakota, and Canadian Dakota cultures, clowning and exaggerating are deemed to be therapeutic.

Sherman Alexie's 1998 movie *Smoke Signals* earned critical acclaim for being a major movie directed by a Native American and presented from a Native American perspective. The movie, which is based on a short story from Alexie's 1993 book *The Lone Ranger and Tonto Fistfight in Heaven*, is set on the Coeur d'Alene Indian Reservation in northern Idaho. While the story does not shy away from such serious problems as alcoholism, alienation, and broken dreams, the wry humor made both whites and Indians laugh at such parodies as a T-shirt advertising "Fry Bread Power" and "The Miracle of the Fry Bread," when Victor's mother magically feeds a crowd that is twice as big as she had expected by raising her arms heavenward and solemnly ripping each piece of fry bread in half, and the KREZ radio station with its traffic reporter who every day reports on the two or three cars he sees from atop his broken-down Volkswagen van. While both groups appreciated the enthusiastic announcer who sounds like Robin Williams when he shouts,

"It's a great day to be indigenous!" Indian viewers seemed more amused by Victor telling Thomas to shut off the television, "There's only one thing more pathetic than Indians on TV and that's Indians watching Indians on TV."

Indian viewers also laughed uninhibitedly at the two gum-chewing, soda-drinking sisters who sat sideways facing each other in the front seat of their old car as they listened to rock music and drove backwards. While white viewers were troubled by such practical questions as "Can't they afford to get it fixed?" Indian viewers appeared to accept the women as genuinely funny versions of contrary clowns.

While authorized clowns may be free to make fun of sacred items and rituals, those outside tribal culture are not, which has been vividly demonstrated by Native Americans protesting against the name of the Washington Redskins football team, the "tomahawk chop" of the Kansas City Chiefs, and the use of a fictional Indian, Chief Illiniwek, as the "honored symbol" of the University of Illinois. In reference to this latter controversy, Charlene Teters, a Native American graduate student at the University of Illinois, was featured in a documentary, *American Indian Mascots in Sports*, shown on the PBS *Point of View* series, 15 July 1997. In a public debate with the student who that year had been chosen to portray the chief, Teters said, "You keep referring to your dance, your eagle feathers, your outfit or whatever you want to call it, as ceremony, as religion. Why is the university involved with some kind of religious ceremony at half-time?" The documentary shows a sampling of Chief Illiniwek cartoon caricatures produced by local businesses and appearing on buildings, signs, and clothing sanctioned by the university. It then returns to Teters saying, "These images should have gone by the wayside along with little Black Sambo and the Frito Bandito."

During the late 1960s and 1970s, Native American groups began asking schools to "Play Ball, Not Indians," and in the decades that have followed, many high schools and colleges have changed team names that related in some way to Native Americans. Also, in elementary schools, fewer children sing the old nursery favorite "Ten Little Indians," just as fewer are presented with "cutesy" stories glorifying whites in a paternalistic relationship to Indians or trivializing Native customs connected with such matters as the meanings of personal names and rites of passage.

While Sherman Alexie's 1998 movie *Smoke Signals*, set on the Coeur d'Alene Indian Reservation in northern Idaho, treats many serious problems, it also has moments of laugh-out-loud hilarity. *Fotos International/Archive Photos*

The widespread criticism of the "poor history" in the 1995 animated Disney film *Pocahontas* illustrates an increase in the level of general awareness about the complications inherent in presenting accurate portrayals of Native Americans.

Although Indian critics are undoubtedly discouraged at how slowly things move, some authentic Native American stories are being brought into schools and into the literature of both young and old. One of the ways this is being done is through Native American Trickster stories. The Trickster figure is ubiquitous throughout both oral and written literature, and while the Trickster is nearly always shown in the form of an animal, his real significance is his human characteristics, and storytellers do not quibble about what these "people in fur" can do. For example, in Leslie Marmon Silko's *Storyteller*, Coyote rides a bus to the Hopi Second Mesa. Northwest Indians often showed the Trickster as a Raven with the ability to shoot arrows and carve out canoes. Eastern tribes favored the Rabbit as a Trickster, while Southwestern and Plains tribes favored the Coyote. The Deer, the Spider, the Jay, the Wolverine, and the "Old Man" Nanaboyho also play the Trickster role.

In 1996, the University of Nebraska Press reproduced two volumes of Frank B. Linderman's *Indian Why Stories (Sparks from War Eagle's Lodge-Fire* and *More Sparks from War Eagle's Lodge-fire)*. Sidney Larson wrote the introductions to these books, which were originally published in 1915 and contain Linderman's renderings of the "Old-man's" droll stories about Creek and Blackfeet Tricksters and braves with supernatural powers.

In Andrew Wiget's 1994 *Dictionary of Native American Literature*, Barbara Babcock lists several features commonly associated with the peripatetic and scatological Trickster. Tricksters demonstrate a breakdown of the distinction between reality and reflection, which means they are freed from the ordinary demands of the social code. In addition, they tend to

- exhibit an independence from ordinary temporal and spatial boundaries, sometimes being situated half in this world and half in the other world.

- be creative, destructive, and amusing, often in scatological ways.

- play both hero and villain roles and sometimes be a shape shifter or appear in disguise. The different roles occur episodically and contribute to the tribal knowledge of the Trickster as a fully rounded character.

- be either mentally and/or physically abnormal.

- have enlarged sexual qualities and enormous libidos and be more concerned with sex than with procreation.

- serve as a symbol of extremes between young and old, good and evil, and life and death.

- sometimes appear as a human with animal qualities or as an animal with human qualities.

- have their most endearing female relationships with their mothers or grandmothers even though they are always trying to copulate with others.

Although many of the Trickster stories may be considered scatological, they are nevertheless told to Indian children, because they are considered to be instructive as well as entertaining. The stories target the Trickster's excesses and serve as cautionary tales while also releasing psychic tension by permitting taboo fantasies. In stories written for non-Native adults, these excesses are presented in their full form, but in stories written for non-Native children the sexual and excretory indiscretions are ignored or translated into less specific offenses. When a third- or fourth-grade teacher reads aloud some of the newly published Trickster stories, listeners may get a sense of *deja vu* because they have already met the Trickster archetype and his friends through such television cartoon characters as Wile E. Coyote, Roadrunner, and Elmer

Fudd's "wascally wabbit," Bugs Bunny. *See also* CLOWNS, ETHNIC HUMOR, SATIRE

Further reading: William J. Hynes and William G. Doty (eds.), *Mythical Trickster Figures: Contours, Contexts, and Criticisms* (1993). Kenneth Lincoln, *Indi'n Humor: Bicultural Play in Native America* (1993). *Native American Authors Online*, http://hanksville.org/storytellers (Nov. 1999). Scott B. Vickers, *Native American Identities: From Stereotype to Archetype in Art and Literature* (1998).

Anachronism

Anachronism comes from the Greek prefix *ana* meaning "against" and the morpheme *chronos* meaning "time," so an anachronism is something that goes against time, as when a person or an event is chronologically misplaced. Teachers of serious historical writing stress the importance of avoiding anachronisms, while humorists are constantly looking for new ways of mixing past, present, and future, as when in a parody of the Oedipus myth Steve Katz has the protagonist put out his eyes with a *Py-Co-Pay* toothbrush.

Prototypical examples of comic anachronisms are Washington Irving's short story, "Rip Van Winkle," about a crusty New England settler who falls asleep for 20 years and awakens to find everything different, and Mark Twain's *A Connecticut Yankee in King Arthur's Court*, about an early American having to deal with the social customs of the Middle Ages.

Science fiction and its concept of time travel has opened the door to a whole new kind of anachronistic comedy as in the 1985 Steven Spielberg and Robert Zemeckis film *Back to the Future*. Christopher Lloyd plays the part of a wacky scientist who sets the story in motion, while Michael J. Fox plays the part of a teenager of the 1980s who is whisked back to the 1950s where he must arrange for his mismatched parents to meet. If he doesn't succeed, then he can't be born. Part of the fun in time-travel stories are these kinds of brain teasers, while another part is the special effects that can by created by mixing current technology with either past or future lifestyles and customs. The *Back to the Future* movie was followed by two sequels and

an animated TV series. In the concluding movie, Fox goes back to the Wild West of the 1880s where he tries to find Lloyd and change history.

The Monty Python group, especially in its 1979 *Life of Brian* movie and its 1983 *The Meaning of Life*, treats history with an outrageous irreverence, and so does Mel Brooks, who first came to widespread attention in 1960 when his LP "The 2,000-Year-Old Man" became a sensation.

Less dramatic examples of anachronistic humor are worked into comedy acts, as in a Bob Newhart sketch, when the audience hears the reaction of the head of the West Indies Company in London when Sir Walter Raleigh telephones:

What is it this time, Walt? You got another winner for us do you? Tobacco? What's tobacco, Walt? It's a kind of a leaf and you bought 80 tons of it? . . . You take a pinch of tobacco and shove it up your nose and it makes you sneeze. I imagine it would, Walt. . . . You're going to have a tough time telling people to stick burning leaves in their mouths.

In one of Bill Cosby's memorable skits, he plays the role of a surprised Noah when God tells him to start building an ark. Steve Allen and his wife, Jayne Meadows, performed funny "Meeting of Minds" skits in which Meadows would be interviewed from the current day's perspective while she played the roles of famous women in history from Cleopatra to Marie Antoinette.

An especially intriguing kind of time play occurs when people refer to events in the time period before such events occurred. For example, in William Gibson's Christmas play *Butterfingers Angel*, Joseph asks Mary when the baby is due and she replies, "Around Christmas." In structure, this joke is similar to the story about the Jewish fortune teller who was called before Hitler because the Fuhrer had heard that the man was foretelling his death. When Hitler asked, "When am I going to die?" the man responded, "On a Jewish holiday." When questioned a bit further as to just which holiday, the man explained, "It doesn't matter; whatever day you

die will be a Jewish holiday!" *See also* ALLU-
SION, LANGUAGE PLAY

Animation

The literal meaning of *animation* is the giving of life to something. An animated cartoon is a motion picture made from a series
of individual hand-drawn sketches in which
the positions or gestures of the figures are
varied slightly from one sketch to another.
When the pictures are projected on a screen,
the figures appear to be moving. Besides being used with drawings, this stop-frame process might also be used with either
three-dimensional or flat puppets that are
moved slightly between each frame, with dia-
grams, silhouettes, or any number of objects,
including humans.

From its beginnings, one of the challenges
in animation has been reducing the work required. With the first cartoons, totally new
pictures were drawn for each frame, but
within a short time, artists figured out that
they could use the same background and
change only the characters in front. They began putting their pictures on see-through
celluloid (called *cels*) so that layers could be
moved and photographed in various combinations. The cels were perforated at the top
and fastened to hooks for stabilization, and
multiplane cameras were invented to give
depth by taking pictures at various levels.
Studios hired inkers and colorists to fill in
the drawings of their best artists, while many
American producers worked with studios in
countries where the pay scales were lower.
The most recent innovation has been to use
computer-aided pictures, but still expenses
are tremendous. Adding both the production
and advertising costs, Disney's 1998 *Mulan*
cost $95 million to make.

From its beginnings, animation has been
associated with humor because of the possibilities for surprise, exaggeration, and fantasy. While the milestones described below
are not a complete history, they give an indication of the way the art has changed over
the course of the 20th century. Animation
started by providing two- or three-minute
novelty items to be shown in burlesque halls
and went on to become an integral part of
American life. Characters that have been
brought to life through cartoons are seen on
products ranging from key chains to
children's underwear, while animation techniques are used to produce entertainment
ranging from interactive video games to humorous television commercials and popular
full-length movies and television programs.

1914: Winsor McCay, the great comic strip
artist and creator of *Little Nemo in
Slumberland*, animated *Gertie the Dinosaur*.
This was not the first animated film, but it
was the first to catch the public's fancy because viewers knew that it could not have
been made from pictures of a real dinosaur.
McCay did 10,000 drawings for the film (16
for each second of action), which portrayed
Gertie as a playful and overgrown child interacting with him and finally carrying him
off.

1924: In Kansas City, Fritz Freleng, fresh
out of high school, took a handful of drawings and answered an ad for "an office boy
who could draw" at the United Film Ad Company. This Kansas City firm is now called
"the cradle of film animation" because of
having been the first place that Freleng, Ub
Iwerks, Hugh Harman, and Walt Disney
worked. Freleng learned to do animation by
trial and error, and in 1927 was lured away
by Walt Disney, who by then had moved to
California and established his own studios.
In Hollywood, Freleng began to feel that he
was Disney's whipping boy and in 1930
moved to Warner Brothers where he became
head animator for *Looney Tunes*, a director
of *Merrie Melodies*, and the artist for Bugs
Bunny, Daffy Duck, Porky Pig, Tweety,
Speedy Gonzales, Yosemite Sam, and
Sylvester and Tweety Pie. Later, he created
The Pink Panther, for which he won one of
his five Academy Awards. Freleng combined
live-action and animation in the film *You
Ought to Be in Pictures*. After the animation
studio at Warner Brothers closed, he established Depatie-Freleng Enterprises where he
made television and theatrical-short films.

When he died in 1995, he was called "The Last of the Great Animation Pioneers."

1928: Walt Disney, in his first job in Kansas City at the United Film Ad Company had created an *Oswald the Rabbit* cartoon. When he sought a new contract and money to improve the product, Oswald was taken from him because the character was copyrighted under the name of its New York film distributor and backer. Early in 1928, Disney, now in his mid-20s, was traveling by train back to Los Angeles from his disappointing visit in New York. As he mulled over losing Oswald, he decided to create a new character based on one of the mice that used to scamper around his drawing board in the Kansas City studio. He spent the hours on the train sketching this mouse, which he named Mortimer. When he got home, Disney's wife, Lillian, suggested that *Mortimer* was too pompous; it didn't ring right, and so they settled on *Mickey Mouse*. Disney immediately put his small studio to work on Mickey Mouse. They did *Plane Crazy,* inspired by the Lindbergh flight to Paris, and *Gallopin' Groucho,* neither of which he could sell because the public now wanted "talkies" after Al Jolson's *The Jazz Singer.* Refusing to give up on Mickey, Disney tried again, this time creating an accompanying sound track. The result was *Steamboat Willie,* which was booked into the Colony Theatre in New York on 18 November. Audiences loved it, especially Mickey's high, squeaky voice, which Disney himself had provided. Based on the success of *Steamboat Willie,* Disney added sound to *Gallopin' Groucho* and *Plane Crazy* and successfully offered them as a package of three shorts.

1928: Myron "Grim" Natwick, an artist with classical training, was asked by Max and Dave Fleischer to design a girl character for the "Boop-Boop-a-Doop" song, which had been made popular by singer Helen Kane. At the end of "I wanna be loved by you, by you and nobody else but you," Kane improvised a timid little "boop-boop-a-doop," which became a sensation. Natwick created the enduring character of Betty Boop, whose popularity he attributed to "a suggestion you could spell in three letters: s-e-x." Mae Questel, who did the voices of Olive Oyl, Little Audrey, Winky Dink, Casper the Friendly Ghost, and later some of the characters in the 1988 *Who Framed Roger Rabbit,* provided Betty Boop's voice.

1937: Walt Disney's *Snow White and the Seven Dwarfs* premiered as the first feature-length animated film. It was made from 250,000 separate drawings and won a special Academy Award. In 1998, The U.S. Postal Service issued a *Snow White* stamp honoring the film as one of the significant events of the 1930s. Only nine months after *Snow White,* Disney released his second full-length film, *Pinocchio,* to be followed over the years by *Fantasia,* which some people still consider his best, and such other films as *Song of the South, 101 Dalmatians,* and *Dumbo.* After Disney's death, Disney Studios produced *Aladdin, The Little Mermaid, The Lion King,* and *Mulan.*

1949: *Crusader Rabbit* was launched as the first cartoon series made especially for television. Television cartoons differed from those made for big screens in that an uncluttered look was needed for small screens showing only black and white. *Crusader Rabbit* laid the groundwork for hundreds of television series and for the streamlined animation that was to come later in Hanna and Barbera's *Flintstones* and *The Jetsons,* and even later in Matt Groening's *The Simpsons* and in Scott Adams's *Dilbert.*

1955: As the climax to Walt Disney's career, his scrupulously planned and executed Disneyland theme park opened in California, where it has served as a model for theme parks worldwide. This gave Disney a chance to do three-dimensional re-creations of his most popular cartoon characters and to present them to the world in a controlled environment. While the Disney characters have been translated from paper and cels to breathing human beings, the illusion of them being fantasy characters is carefully maintained. It would be unthinkable for the human actor inside the Mickey Mouse costume to be seen walking down the street carrying his head.

Mid-1950s: A group of artists broke away from Disney because they were tired of drawing "cute" animals. So that they could experiment with lines and colors, they developed Mr. Magoo, a nearsighted curmudgeon with a bulbous nose, who, as Lisa Bannon observed in *The Wall Street Journal* (Jul. 31, 1997), "could do no wrong. The year was 1957, and Mr. Magoo was about to win his second Academy Award. The U.S. Treasury Department used him to sell bonds, the Navy to recruit men, and General Electric to sell light bulbs." In 1997, the Disney Studios released a Mr. Magoo movie with live actors (Leslie Nielsen starred as Magoo) and ran into protests from the National Federation of the Blind. Bannon wrote that "Disney executives are doing verbal somersaults to make sure their Mr. Magoo is politically correct." Contributing to the protest was not only 40 years of changing social attitudes, but also the fact that the movie characters were played by real people. Viewers seem able to accept as fantasy actions and situations in cartoons that they find troubling when photographed from real life.

1960s: From the beginning, animated cartoons with their reliance on classical music, sophisticated allusions to world events and personalities, shapely and sexy women, and parodies of famous literature have been designed for adult enjoyment. Mickey Mouse originally smoked and drank, while early versions of Bugs Bunny have been censored because of his risque comments. *The Flintstones*, which premiered on prime-time television to an adult audience in 1960, was set in the stone age but modeled after Jackie Gleason's adult sitcom *The Honeymooners*. This transferring of ordinary sitcom families to extra-ordinary settings through animation continued with the futuristic *The Jetsons* and demonstrated how a distinctive look can breathe new life into daily human interactions.

1965: The first animated *Peanuts* special, *A Charlie Brown Christmas*, was shown on 9 December. The program, which is regularly run every December, drew more than 50 percent of the viewing audience and won both an Emmy and a George Foster Peabody Award. Several other animated *Peanuts* specials have followed including *It's the Great Pumpkin, Charlie Brown,* and *Be My Valentine, Charlie Brown.* The narration is done by co-producer Bill Melendez, while the other voices are those of young children. To keep their voices from sounding too mature, a new group of readers is chosen every two years.

1968: Gene Deitch, the New York animator who created the NBC color peacock and made the *Tom Terrific* series shown on *Captain Kangaroo* for 25 years, settled in as director at an animation studio in Prague, Czechoslovakia. He worked on contract to Morton Schindel, head of Weston Woods Studios in Connecticut, and animated many of the best American picture books. Libraries and schools bought the high-quality films, never realizing they were produced behind the Iron Curtain. In the 1985 film, *Gene Deitch: The Picture Book Animated*, Deitch shows how the studio worked on and off for five years before feeling satisfied with their 10-minute rendition of Maurice Sendak's *Where the Wild Things Are.* The high quality work, which remained faithful to the original art in each book, introduced millions of children to art styles and kinds of animation far different from what they usually saw on Saturday-morning television.

1970s: As technology improved and more cartoons were shown on television, the bright colors, the music, and the magical movements proved attractive to children as well as adults. When producers and product sponsors saw how much children liked cartoons, they dusted off old shorts and cranked up their production of new cartoons to be used as Saturday-morning fillers on television. One result was that people began to think of cartoons as being for children. On the negative side, this discouraged theater managers from going to the extra expense of showing cartoons before feature films, while on the positive side, it raised a generation of individuals with wide experience in viewing cartoons.

1980s: Children in the 1970s and 1980s were more familiar with the voice of Mel Blanc (1908–1989) than with that of any other performer. During his long career, Blanc provided the voices of Daffy Duck, Foghorn Leghorn, Pepe le Pew, Porky Pig, the Road Runner, Sylvester the Cat, Tweety Pie, Woody Woodpecker, Yosemite Sam, and both Dino and Barney Rubble in *The Flintstones*. His most famous voice was the Bronx wise-guy accent of Bugs Bunny. Among his catch phrases were Tweety Pie's "I tawt I taw a Puddy Tat!" Sylvester's "Thufferin' Thuccotash!" Daffy Duck's "You're dethpicable!" and Porky Pig's "Th-th-th-that's all, folks." When Blanc died in 1989, he was buried in Hollywood Memorial Park under a tombstone reading, "That's All, Folks."

1986: Computer whiz Steve Jobs acquired Pixar with its six employees. By 1998, the computer animation company had 400 employees and 12 Academy Awards. Two of the awards went to John Lasseter, the animator behind *Toy Story* and *A Bug's Life*. Even though Lasseter helped to create Pixar's RenderMan technology, he likes to focus his efforts on creating memorable characters. He appreciates computer animation not because it saves money—it doesn't—but because he can get unusual three-dimensional effects. The Pixar system was used not only for *Toy Story* and *A Bug's Life*, but also to create the dinosaurs in *Jurassic Park*.

1989: Matt Groening's *The Simpsons* began its unusually long run as an animated sitcom. Nine years later, critic David Owen, writing in a special issue of *TV Guide* (Jan. 3–9, 1998) identifying the 12 best episodes, said that it was the only show his family watches "without simultaneously talking, reading, or fighting. They don't want to miss anything." Noting that *Leave It to Beaver* declined irretrievably when Jerry Mathers hit puberty, Owen said that "Bart, in contrast, will never have to graduate from fourth grade." Other advantages of animated shows are that even though they are relatively expensive to make, management does not have to arrange pay raises and weeks off for the stars, nor do they have to worry about child labor laws, the expense of having four airplanes fly overhead, or arranging celebrity appearances.

The Simpsons is the longest-running animated sitcom in television history. *20th Century Fox/Archive Photos*

1997: Because of the positive and playful connotations connected to cartoon art, many in-print advertisements are designed to resemble cartoons, while cartoon characters are used as the models for hundreds of products. A deal between Warner Brothers and the U.S. Post Office resulted, for the first time, in more money changing hands in relation to Warner's Bugs Bunny than to Disney's Mickey Mouse. The Post Office sold not only stamps, but ties, caps, toys, and T-shirts featuring such Looney Tunes characters as Bugs Bunny, Tweety Bird, Sylvester, Daffy Duck, and Taz.

1998: "I don't know of any big network that isn't looking to anchor its schedule with some form of adult animation," said David Pritchard, president of a Hollywood animation studio. Popular animated shows in prime-time include MTV's *Beavis and Butthead* and its spinoff *Daria*, Comedy Central's *South Park, Bob and Margaret*, and *Dr. Katz*, Fox's *King of the Hill*, and *The PJs*. Caryn James writing in *The New York Times* (Jun. 22, 1998) gave one reason for the trend, "With so little realism on the surface, animated characters can sneak up and irreverently hit plenty of nerves. The dunderheaded fathers of *The Simpsons* or *King of the Hill*, much less the boys of *South Park*, would never get on the air if they were breathing actors." Other critics pointed out that the present generation of creative young leaders in entertainment grew up watching cartoons and so find it a natural medium. Mike Judge, the creator of *Beavis and Butt-head,* confided to *New York Times* writer Andy Meisler (Feb. 22–28, 1998) that he is "old enough to remember when comedy writers were only trying to hook up with a hot comedian or a live sitcom. Now a lot of times they come up to me and say, 'Can you hook me up with a good animator?'"

Bill Plympton is one of the most famous independent producers of adult animation and is fierce about being a one-man operation. According to *The New York Times* (Aug. 23, 1998) when his *I Married a Strange Person* was scheduled for a showing, along with his *Sex and Violence* and *The Exciting Life of a Tree*, at the American Museum of the Moving Image in New York, Plympton went around Manhattan putting up his own posters. "It's a real independent kind of thing, a one-man show, and that's how I survive," he told the *Times*. Plympton spends about $200,000 to do a single film as compared to the millions that go into commercial films.

1999: The news at the turn of the century is the way animation is being returned as a medium for adults. The January issue of *Animation Magazine* devoted its cover and five pages to DreamWorks' newly released *Prince of Egypt*, the story of Moses. The sell-line on the cover and the inside lead were both devoted to the news that the company was reaching "for a new animation audience—one that's a little older, a little more sophisticated and not dominated by children and licensed product." Another article by Peter Chung told about his part in designing an erotic 13-part fantasy adventure, *Alexander the Great*. The epic is being produced by *Madhouse*, Japan's top producer of cutting-edge animation. The film will probably be shown in animation festivals and in art theaters. Festival winners are sometimes gathered into such films as the annual *Spike and Mike's. . . Festival of Animation*, which for 1998 included short pieces as different as *Underwear Stories*, a collection of 15-second films, and *Geri's Game* about an old man cheating himself at chess. This film made by Pixar Studios won an Oscar for Best Animated Short Film and was shown in theaters preceding *A Bug's Life*. See also ART, CARTOONS, COMIC BOOKS, HUMOROUS ICONS

Further reading: Giannalberto Bendazzi, *Cartoons, One-Hundred Years of Cinema Animation* (1995). Karl F. Cohen, *Forbidden Animation: Censored Cartoons and Blacklisted Animators in America* (1997). Jayne Pilling and J. Libbey (eds.), *A Reader in Animation Studies* (1998). Kevin S. Sandler (ed.), *Reading the Rabbit: Explorations in Warner Bros. Animation* (1998).

Antiauthority Humor

Antiauthority humor illustrates the theory that people use humor to relieve stress by making fun of situations where they feel put upon. For example, children use antiauthority humor against adults, teenagers against "the establishment," workers against bosses, enlisted men against officers, and the general public against government officials.

Children's folklore is filled with examples of youngsters bonding against the adult world as in

> Row, row, row your boat
> Gently down the stream.
> Throw your teacher overboard,
> And you will hear her scream.

Children in San Francisco end their version with

> Throw your teacher in the bay,
> The sharks will eat today.

During the 1960s and 1970s when graffiti was a popular form of protest, much of it expressed antiauthority sentiments just as do today's commercialized graffiti of bumper stickers and T-shirts with such messages as "Question Authority!" and "Don't Blame Me! I Voted for _____!"

In offices, antiauthority humor is circulated on e-mail or through photocopy humor, some of it openly and some underground, for example:

Rule No. 1
The boss is always right!
Rule No. 2
If the boss is wrong, see rule No. 1.

One of the reasons there is controversy over whether employers have the right to read the e-mail of their employees is that people who have been reprimanded or fired for sending witticisms or snide notes about their bosses are objecting that their rights to privacy and free speech have been violated.

Alan Dundes and Carl R. Pagter named one of their collections *Work Hard and You Shall Be Rewarded* after a cartoon showing a disgruntled worker with a big screw through his belly. On the cover and inside the book, they reprinted six versions of the cartoon and observed that those who passed it on to others seemed to get satisfaction from redrawing the "original," and adding to the cutline ironic references to such qualities as loyalty, integrity, diligence, honesty, kindness, and being good-natured instead of simply photocopying whatever version they'd received.

In May of 1996, *Business Week* reported that Scott Adams's latest book, *The Dilbert Principle,* was at the top of their bestseller list, "a roster customarily dominated by such titles as *The Death of Competition.*" They described the book as "part comic collection, part management-book parody, and all antiboss," and went on to write that compared with Dilbert's world, *Blondie's* comic strip husband, Dagwood Bumstead, has it lucky.

Adams was the first cartoonist to go online, and every day he gets hundreds of messages from people who in their work have had "some hideous experience." He manages to turn about one in 100 into a cartoon, but he says they all help him understand what people are feeling. And even though his strip is aimed at corporate America, many of the people who share ideas with him are hospital workers, military personnel, and clergy, professions that are hierarchically structured, and in which individual workers are likely to suffer frustration.

Much of the comedy in the 1953 movie *Stalag 17* and in the 1960s television sitcom *Hogan's Heroes*, both about American soldiers in German POW camps, was antiauthority, as the prisoners succeeded in outsmarting the officers. For this kind of humor to work, it is not always necessary for the officers to come from the opposing camp, as shown by Mort Walker's *Beetle Bailey* comic strip and by the trials and tribulations suffered by Bill Mauldin's beleaguered WW II foot soldiers Willie and Joe. Antiauthority humor is also at the heart of three of the greatest satirical novels in modern literature: Ken Kesey's *One Flew over the Cuckoo's Nest* (1962), Kurt Vonnegut's *Slaughterhouse-Five* (1972), and Joseph Heller's *Catch-22* (1961).

The desire to make fun of authority is so strong that it often overrides other values, such as in an anecdote that Lawrence Van Gelder printed in his "On the Job" column in *The New York Times* (Jul. 7, 1996). The anecdote was about a police officer staking out a particularly rowdy bar for possible violations of driving-under-the-influence laws.

Scott Adams's *Dilbert* targets corporate America with its antiauthority humor. *Dilbert reprinted by permission of United Feature Syndicate Inc.*

While he was watching from his squad car, he saw a man stumble out the door, trip on the curb, and try 14 cars before finding his own and promptly falling asleep in the front seat. As the hours went by, he continued sleeping while all the other car owners came out and drove away. Finally, the sleeping man woke up, fumbled for his keys and drove away. The police officer immediately went into action, signaling the man to pull over. He administered a Breathalyzer test and was amazed when the results showed a 0.0 blood-alcohol level. The puzzled officer asked how this could be. The driver replied, "Tonight, I'm the designated decoy."

Although people laugh at the joke, they also empathize with the angry person who wrote a letter of complaint saying that the joke seemed to condone drinking and driving: "Considering the educational efforts of organizations like Mothers Against Drunk Driving and Students Against Driving Drunk, I would think we had come further on this issue."

While Americans worry about getting this kind of criticism for their antiauthority humor, people in totalitarian countries worry at a different level. A *New York Times* article (Jan. 31, 1997) about Ali Farzat, Syrian cartoonist and head of the Society of Arab Cartoonists, said that Mr. Farzat creates healthy doses of antiauthority humor, but is careful to aim his satire at mid-level government bureaucrats. For example, one of his cartoons shows a customs official, who, after looking inside a man's suitcase, lifts the top of the man's head to peek at what's inside. Farzat says he models his work after the French master Honore Daumier and the American caricaturist Pat Oliphant, but he is extremely careful not to include any identifying marks such as license plates or signs that would point readers to specific individuals. As careful as he is, Farzat has nevertheless been barred from entering Jordan, deported from Abu Dhabi, and threatened on the radio and by anonymous callers in Syria. He says his goal is to help free his fellow countrymen from many of their irrational fears. The article concluded that Farzat "has learned to draw within narrow lines, mocking without pointing, criticizing without naming, skewering without ever being specific in a way that has made him the most admired caricaturist in the Arab world from a country that does not have much of a reputation for humor."

Sociologist Christie Davies from the University of Reading in England has talked and written about how in Eastern Europe before the breakup of the Soviet Union, people avoided making jokes against top party leaders, but instead took out their frustrations by joking about anonymous, mid-level authorities including soldiers and police officers. For example, *Question*: "Why do Russian officers have three stripes on the sleeves of their uniforms?" *Answer*: "So they can tell where to bend their elbows!" and *Question*: "Why do their soldiers always go around in threes?" *Answer*: "Because one can read and one can write, and the other one has to keep track of the intellectuals."

When Yuri Nikulin, the 75-year-old comedian known as the "Russian Charlie Chaplin" died in August 1997, his *New York Times* obituary said that in the years after World War II Nikulin began to despise the political repression of the Communist party. He gradually began tweaking authorities with political jokes, but for his own protection would record nonpolitical versions in his journals. Also, to stay out of trouble while telling antiauthority jokes, he sometimes skipped over Soviet officials and told jokes about Americans and God. One of his most popular was about an American actor who railed against his fancy New York tailor, "God needed only seven days to create the universe and it took you 30 days to make me pair of trousers." "Yes," answered the tailor, but "Look at the world and then look at the trousers." *See also* BLACK HUMOR, CENSORSHIP, CHILDREN'S LITERATURE, SUPERIORITY AND HOSTILITY

Further reading: Scott Adams, *The Dilbert Principle: A Cubicle's-Eye View of Bosses, Meetings, Management Fads and Other Workplace Afflictions* (1996). Alan Dundes and Carl R. Pagter, *Sometimes the Dragon Wins: Yet More Urban Folklore from the Paperwork Empire* (1996). Steve

Lipman, *Laughter in Hell: The Use of Humor during the Holocaust* (1993).

Architecture

Humor related to architecture is of two basic kinds. One is humor about the profession and its practitioners, while the other is humor applied to the design and building of actual structures. Architects are proud to point out that theirs is a joyful profession. People call doctors when they are sick and lawyers when they are in trouble, but they call architects when they have money and a dream and are hoping to make that dream come true. This optimistic view of their profession, along with the fact that architects are creative and artistic, is reflected in such books as Louis Hellman's 1992 *Archi-Tetes*, which contains 24 postcard-size portraits of prominent architects. Each one is drawn so as to illustrate the architect's major contribution. For example, the top of Buckminster Fuller's head is part of a geodesic dome, which he developed, while Frank Lloyd Wright peers out from the "face" of Taliesin West.

Charles Knevitt's 1986 collection, *Perspectives: An Anthology of 1001 Architectural Quotations*, contains a fair portion of witty and humorous thoughts, while *The Architect* by Loup (1977) is a colorful, surrealistic collection of large, double-page paintings done in cartoon style. It illustrates the architectural nightmares of being locked in mortal combat with a tree, construction equipment, big-city streets, and traffic jams. One picture illustrates a remodeling job where the building has taken on the mystifying characteristics of a geometrically distorted M.C. Escher drawing.

Forrest Wilson's 1974 *A History of Architecture on the Disparative Method: With Apologies to Sir Banister Fletcher (All Eighteen Editions)* is a spoof of a serious textbook. In it Wilson offers such explanations as "We know from histories other than those of architecture that the gleesome fleasome medieval mason carved obscene sculptures on lofty cathedral capitals to plague his client, the stilted churchman, who was too timid to climb the scaffolding," and about

England's Stonehenge, "The structure was assuredly religious. The type of hoisting tackle then available would have been totally ineffective without the power of prayer."

Artist David Macaulay's 1978 *Great Moments in Architecture* is another spoof, but one that relies more heavily on drawings than on words. Plate VIII, "The Great and Lesser Walls of China," shows two mismatched walls creeping toward each other. A note in parentheses explains, "This plate was formerly believed to represent the meeting of English and Metric." Plate XI shows several sets of old-fashioned architects, engineers, and diggers with picks and shovels spread across a rocky prairie. The title is "Early Work on the Grand Canyon." Another Macaulay spoof is his 1980 *Unbuilding,* which "documents" the taking apart of the Empire State Building in preparation for moving it across the ocean to be rebuilt for a wealthy Middle East oil magnate. The story was probably inspired by the taking apart of the London Bridge and the rebuilding of it in Lake Havasu, Arizona, where it has become the fourth most popular tourist site in the state.

A different kind of humorous book about architecture is Tom Wolfe's 1981 *From Bauhaus to Our House*. It is "factual," but filled with such sarcastic observations as "every child goes to school in a building that looks like a duplicating-machine replacement-parts wholesale distribution warehouse. Not even the school commissioners, who commissioned it and approved the plans, can figure out how it happened." Under a photo of Walter Gropius, the founder of the Bauhaus School in Weimar, Germany, Wolfe identifies Gropius as "the Silver Prince, White God No. 1." Then he explains that "young architects went to study at his feet. Some, like Philip Johnson, didn't get up until decades later." Wolfe says that the eagle shape of Eero Saarinen's TWA terminal in New York City and the winged roof he put on the Dulles International Airport in Washington, DC, "infuriated modernists" because "originality in design had become a cardinal sin." In support of this claim, he says that John Portman, the designer of the Hyatt Regency hotels with "their 30-story atriums and hanging gardens and crystal elevators," is not so much attacked as ignored by the establishment. "He is invisible. He takes on the uncertain contours of the folk architect. He becomes a highly commercial (and therefore unredeemable) version of Simon Rodia, who built the Watts Towers" (folk art towers made from scrap metal and other found objects in Watts, a section of Los Angeles).

Wolfe is pointing to the challenge that architects face if they want to be truly original, much less humorous. Frank Lloyd Wright scoffed at the plans that Jorn Utzon drew for the Sydney Opera House, declaring, "The circus tent is not architecture." This illustrates the fine line that architects have to walk between being considered creative and being judged to have surrendered to kitsch. In English, this German word for "trash" has come to mean "garish, sentimental, pretentious, or vulgar art." Understandably, such institutions as financial centers, research foundations, universities, governmental agencies, churches, and hospitals want to stay away from kitsch because they feel that to be trusted they must communicate an air of seriousness and responsibility, as well as careful management of taxpayers' and investors' funds. But on the other hand, many institutions also want to communicate that they are creative and look beyond traditional architectural solutions, which was the intent of the city of Tempe, Arizona, when it built its city hall in the shape of an upside-down pyramid.

A compromise that some institutions have come up with is to separate business and humor by placing artistic "jokes" outside their buildings, as with the giant baseball bat that Claes Oldenburg created for the city of Chicago. The Team Disney building in Burbank, California, built in 1990, is decorated with a fresco of the Seven Dwarfs, while the nearby Feature Animation Building (1994), in which the animators actually work, has a roof line made to look like a reel of film. The portico over the entrance is a huge replica of the hat worn by the Sorcerer's Apprentice.

In the entertainment and tourism industries, architectural humor is integral. When people go out to dinner many choose restaurants as much for their "character" as for their menu offerings. During the 1960s, as part of urban renewal, many old buildings were remodeled to become restaurants, and now even new buildings are being designed to resemble old breweries, train stations, carriage houses, waterworks, boats, ships, lighthouses, barns, and homes from different places and different times. People also enjoy being surprised and amused by staying in hotels with "atmosphere," whether it comes from entering the dining room by walking under a waterfall and through a jungle in Hawaii; or watching the parade of ducks being brought for their twice-daily swim in the lobby fountain of the Peabody Hotel in Memphis, Tennessee.

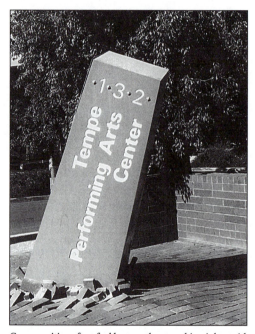

Communities often feel braver about making jokes with sidewalk art than with million-dollar buildings. Here a sign for the Tempe, Arizona, Performing Arts Center is made to look as if it has just burst through the sidewalk. *Photo by A.P. Nilsen*

Such bits of local color are appreciated as authentic because hotel guests see how they fit into each hotel's uniqueness and into the overall history and setting of the geographical region. The city of Las Vegas, on the other hand, suffers from its own success and is accused of kitsch, because unlike a single hotel or a theme park that has an overall concept and planning board, Las Vegas is made up of hundreds of independently owned casinos, hotels, resorts, and restaurants all competing to attract tourists. There is such a mishmash of ideas that many visitors feel overwhelmed rather than amused. For example, on the travel pages of newspapers targeting potential visitors to Las Vegas, the humorous ads for the three biggest hotels end up competing with one another. The *Luxor*, which is modeled after the Egyptian Sphinx and nearby pyramids, proclaims, "The Egyptians built pyramids to link heaven and earth. You need only a telephone." The *Excalibur* ad shows a departing dragon's tail and a knight's armor lying nearby. Their cutline is, "Need a room? We just had a check-out," while the *New York New York* advertises itself as "The Greatest City in Las Vegas." When *Time* magazine did its 1997 year-end summary of the "best" and the "worst" of the year's accomplishments it devoted a half-page to a twilight photo of the *New York New York* with this commentary:

> O.K., it's a hoot, a building that's made to look like a jumble of buildings. This massive Las Vegas hotel with a "Central Park-themed" casino takes as its silhouette the Manhattan skyline and for good measure crams in Grant's Tomb, Ellis Island and the Statue of Liberty. Did we mention the Coney Island roller coaster? Tasteless, you say? We say, beyond tasteless. Hey man, you got a problem with that?

An even more surprising structure is the WonderWorks building adjacent to the Orlando Convention Center in Florida. It is made to look as if a tornado had lifted up a large, white neoclassical building complete with its nearby street lights and palm trees, flipped it upside down, and planted it at an angle on top of a red brick warehouse from the 1930s. Inside the startling structure are several restaurants and an interactive entertainment center that will allow visitors to experience simulated hurricanes and earthquakes. *See also* ART, GOTHIC HUMOR

Further reading: Karal Ann Marling (ed.), *Designing Disney's Theme Parks: The Architecture of Reassurance* (1997). Celeste Olalquiaga, *The Artificial Kingdom: The Experience of Kitsch* (1998). Dell Upton, *Architecture in the United States* (1998).

Art

The word *art* comes from the Latin word *ars,* meaning "skill." In this entry it refers to the skill displayed by artisans of sculpture and painting. Humorous art has been created in even the most primitive cultures, but when looked at from today's perspective it is often unclear which parts of the humor are in the eyes of beholders and which in the eyes of creators. For example, most ancient cultures made masks for ritual dances and ceremonies, and while some are realistic, many others are stylized and made to resemble animals or fantasy creatures. It is likely that some of these were intended as humorous, just as it is likely that some humorous stories have been told through the decorations put on pottery and in the sculptured friezes and mosaics with which Egyptians, Greeks, and Romans decorated their buildings. The artist, who before volcanic ash covered Pompeii, made the famous mosaic of the god Priapus weighing his extended penis on a balancing scale must have enjoyed at least a sense of exaggeration, if not of humor. Even with contemporary art, it is not always possible to know the degree to which humor was intended, but clues are easier to figure out for something from one's own culture.

By the beginning of the 20th century in America, photography was so well established that the general public no longer viewed sculpture and painting as the best means of preserving realistic images, and already the world had grown small enough that art transcended national boundaries. Rather than being valued for their drawing skills, artists began to be valued for their creativity; for how different—how shocking—they could be. In 1913, the Armory Show (named for the building where it was set up, in New York, to be followed by an exhibit in Chicago) introduced the American public to the new worlds of Impressionist and Cubist art. The pieces on display incorporated such characteristics of humor as surprise, incongruity, and exaggeration. Viewers were forced to become emotionally involved; as with a joke, they couldn't appreciate what they were viewing if they did not expend intellectual energy to come up with their own insights.

In the years that followed, experimentation became so much the norm that artists began to worry that there would no longer be standards by which to judge "great" art. Dada came in as a kind of anti-art or parody of art. So too did Pop art, which relies for its effectiveness on new ways of displaying icons, especially commercialized ones, from the mass culture. With this new emphasis on creativity and the downplaying of drawing skills, ordinary people, not just those who had formal training as artists, were inspired to try their hand at creating "art." Among these new "artists" were photographers. While some people thought that photography was destroying art, photographers viewed it as a new kind of art and began experimenting with more unusual forms of their craft.

Because of this increased interest and accessibility, playful community art is now thriving in America. City councils have increased funding for public arts projects and put out calls to local artisans to build new and unusual bus stops, parking racks for bicycles, adornments along freeways, entrances to public buildings, decorations for airports, and unusual seating areas in public spaces.

Professional artists are also involving communities in creating conceptual art. In 1970, Robert Smithson's creation of *Spiral Jetty* required the moving of more than six thousand tons of rock and earth to create an artificial spiral on the northern shore of Great Salt Lake in Utah. In 1983, Bulgarian artist Christo used help from 430 workers in Florida to create his *Surrounded Islands*, a two-week event in which great circles of pink fabric were floated in Florida's Biscayne Bay. Christo has hung a one-quarter-mile-long orange curtain across a Colorado valley and continues to create other such highly publicized artworks.

Especially in the southwestern United States, artists make playful use of such traditional American Indian figures as Kokopelli (the flute-playing, humpbacked trickster), coyotes, rabbits, snakes, birds, and clowns, as in these wall decorations created by John Nelson in Tempe, Arizona. *Photo by A.P. Nilsen.*

Below are brief descriptions of a sampling of well-known 20th-century artists whose work included humor as one of its elements. They are listed chronologically by year of birth. The variety in their methods, their goals, and the materials they use illustrates that visual humor has as many variations as does verbal humor.

Pablo Picasso (1881–1973) was the first artist to have a mass audience during his own lifetime. Although he is not generally thought of as a humorist, his work was so creative that it opened the door for experimentation and play as when he juxtaposed a bicycle seat and handlebars to make a stylized sculpture of a bull's head. In the early 1900s, he worked with Georges Braque in the development of Cubism. They fragmented forms to show simultaneous multiple views of what was being depicted rather than to portray realistic representations. He inspired modern sculpture and collage by putting together unrelated items in surprising combinations that opened the door to Pop art. Picasso also experimented with displacement, explaining that he would "put eyes between the legs, or sex organs on the face. To contradict. Nature does many things the way I do, but she hides them! My painting is a series of cock-and-bull stories."

Marcel Duchamp (1887–1968) was the star of the 1913 Armory Show. Crowds gathered on a daily basis to stare at his *Nude Descending a Staircase No. 2.* There was no nude at all, but rather something that looked like multiple exposures of a shapely robot. The colors and the various rectangular shapes gave rise to its description as an "explosion in a shingle factory." Based on this one painting, Duchamp became one of the best known French artists of the day. In 1917, he again shocked the art world, this time with a piece of Dada or anti-art. He took a porcelain urinal and transformed it into art by giving it an artist's signature and the title of *Fountain*.

Marc Chagall (1887–1985) in 1911 painted *I and the Village*, considered to be one of the first examples of surrealism. Many of his works have a whimsical but dreamlike quality; his figures, often upside down, are distributed on his canvases in an arbitrary fashion that sometimes resembles a film montage. Chagall was Russian, and his work has been described as a combination Yiddish joke, Russian fairy tale, and visual vaudeville act as when in *The Fiddler* he paints a violinist sitting on a roof.

Joan Miro (1893–1983) was one of Spain's foremost exponents of surrealist fantasy. He painted in an aggressive but playful style even when he was using his work for social criticism. *The Reaper,* painted during the Spanish Civil War, is an example. While some of his paintings make people smile, others inspire a kind of quasi-religious meditation. Miro also had an interest in Dadaism and Minimalism. Dating from the mid-1960s, Minimalism is a kind of abstract art characterized by few elements and simple geometric forms, and executed in an impersonal style.

Rene Magritte (1898–1968) was a Belgian painter who specialized in surrealism as he explored the subconscious and the world of dreams. He painted fish with human legs, a man with a bird cage for his torso, and a mermaid with the head of a fish but the body of a human. He loved doing dislocations of space, time, and scale. His *Attempting the Impossible* is a picture of himself painting a nude; he is not painting a picture of the nude on a traditional canvas but rather is using his brush to make the nude come into reality from empty space. His *Perspective II: Manet's Balcony* is a 1950 parody of Edouard Manet's 1869 *The Balcony*. In Magritte's parody, the three figures have been replaced by three coffins, one of them in a sitting position. In *Golconda*, middle-class men in bowler hats are falling like rain toward a street lined with houses, while *The Two Mysteries* suggests that a pictorial representation of a pipe really "is not a pipe." Included in the painting are the words, "Ceci n'est pas une pipe."

M.C. Escher (1898–1972) was a Dutch graphic artist specializing in what are called *trompe l'oeil*; literally, "to deceive the eye." His work is often reproduced on T-shirts and posters. Escher did lithographs of waterfalls that function as their own source, stairs that continue going up (and down) forever, and foregrounds that turn into backgrounds and vice versa. Nearly all of his images represent curious points of view, whether they show elegantly designed Mobius strips, people walking up walls and on ceilings, hands drawing themselves, or objects leaving the paintings and entering the real world. He transforms triangles into birds, black-on-white into white-on-black, and ceilings and walls into floors. His flatly drawn reptiles appear to change into three-dimensional living and crawling reptiles.

Alexander Calder (1898–1976) was one of the sculptors, along with Alberto Giacometti, Jean Arp, Jacques Lipchitz, Henry Moore, Barbara Hepworth, Picasso, and Julio Gonzalez, credited with developing the sculpture of fantasy between 1920 and 1945. These artists tried to incorporate visions, hallucinations, reverie, and memory into their sculptures. Calder is generally credited with being the creator of the mobile. He also worked with the element of surprise in children's toys and created a cast of wire figures that he placed in a vast miniature circus.

Salvador Dali (1904–1989) is the world's best known surreal artist. To bring up images from his subconscious mind, he practiced hallucinatory states that he called "paranoiac critical." He depicted dream worlds in which commonplace objects were juxtaposed, deformed, or metamorphosed into bizarre and irrational distortions. At the same time he was distorting the objects, Dali was filling them with realistic details and placing them into bleak, sunlit landscapes reminiscent of his Catalonian homeland. His most famous enigmatic image is *The Persistence of Memory* in which limp, melting watches rest in an eerily calm landscape.

Jackson Pollock (1912–1956) was born in Cody, Wyoming, and studied at the Art Students' League in New York under the direction of Thomas Hart Benton. In 1947, Pollock developed his "drip" method of painting, which earned him a place among such abstract expressionists as Barnet Newman, Franz Kline, Clyfford Still, Mark Rothko, and Willem de Koonig. Pollock would lay out large canvases on which he would fling and dribble paint in energetic swirls and lines. Pollock's goal was not humor but expression. However, many people in the general public suspected a joke and dubbed Pollock "Jack the Dripper."

Roy Lichtenstein's (1923–1997) paintings became a featured attraction in 1963 when the Solomon R. Guggenheim Museum in New York City staged its first show of Pop art. Lichtenstein was quoted in news stories about the event, saying that he found modern art despicable with some artists thinking they could get away with "hanging a wet paint rag." Lichtenstein was an Abstract Expressionist, but in 1960 when he painted a picture of Walt Disney's Mickey Mouse as a present for his children he became interested in reproducing comic-strip figures and images from romance magazines. He had his characters speak in balloons, and he used a metal screen as a stencil to produce a "pointillistic" look in imitation of enlarged dots from newsprint photos. The visual impact was increased by the way he outlined his brilliant, flat colors in black.

George Segal (1924–) is an artist whose work has inspired imitation. In the 1960s, he began wrapping models in a light coating of gauze and then pouring plaster of paris casts of them. One of his first models was his father standing in the window of his butcher shop. From the plaster casts, Segal made life-size bronze figures to be placed in settings where they might actually appear; for example at bus stops, sitting on benches in public parks, or standing on the platform of a train station. In the late 1960s, Segal began painting some of his casts in vivid colors as joking metaphors for "a rosy disposition," "a blue funk," and a "black mood." He has gone on to use his method for such solemn public monuments as his 1982 *The Holocaust* in San Francisco and his 1980 *Gay Liberation* in New York. Moreover, other artists around the world are using the method he developed to create public art; for example, we have seen the bronze figure of a teenage girl standing in the doorway of a McDonalds in Bergen,

Norway, and a group of children running across the lawn of an office building in downtown Phoenix, Arizona.

Claes Oldenburg (1925–) is a Swedish-born American artist, who along with Lichtenstein and Warhol, and such other artists as Tom Wesselman, James Rosenquist, and Robert Indiana, pioneered the Pop art movement. Oldenburg is best known for his large, soft plastic sculptures of such ordinary items as bathroom fixtures, hamburgers, typewriters, and a spiral notebook in disrepair with pages fluttering in the "wind." At the same time that Oldenburg's drooping objects surprise and amuse viewers, they express a kind of social criticism about what cultures value. Oldenburg has also done "hard" sculptures as with a giant baseball bat created for the city of Chicago. Oldenburg's work has been a source of inspiration for community artists around the country.

Robert Rauschenburg (1925–) is best known for his collages or "combined paintings" in which he blends the found objects of Dada with the painterly style of the Abstract Expressionists. Rauschenburg's *Retroactive 1* (1964) has a photo of a youthful President Kennedy surrounded by such images as an astronaut and a shelf of produce in a grocery store fused in a surrealistic manner. When viewed as a collage, the pictures make a powerful statement about the mixing of the grand and the commonplace and the ephemeral nature of modern life.

Andy Warhol (1928–1987) studied the art of being a celebrity and is probably remembered as much for his observation that "in the future everyone will be world famous for 15 minutes" as for the Pop art that he created. During the 1960s, Warhol surprised the art world with his open worship of commercialization. He took objects and people from daily life and from newspaper headlines—Campbell's Soup cans, the electric chair at Sing Sing, Elvis Presley, and Marilyn Monroe—and gave them new lives through brightly colored silk-screened prints. In 1998, his *Orange Marilyn, 1964* was sold by Sotheby's for $17.3 million. Warhol's work opened the door for a new generation of Pop artists including Julian Schnabel, David Salle, Cindy Sherman, Sherrie Levine, Jeff Koons, and Damien Hirst. *See also* ARCHITECTURE, CARTOONS, POP-UP BOOKS

Further reading: Heinz K. Henisch and Bridget A. Henisch, *Positive Pleasures: Early Photography and Humor* (1998). Robert Hughes, *American Visions: The Epic History of Art in America* (1997). Wendy Wick Reaves, *Celebrity Caricature in America* (1998).

B

Black Humor

Black humor (sometimes called dark humor) relies for its comic effect on morbidity, absurdity, and anarchy. Black humor mixes humor with anger and bitterness; this mixture is as important as the grotesque and morbid situations that reveal the suffering and anxiety, usually connected to death that black humor portrays. Terms used in reference to black humor include *gallows humor*, the *American absurd novel, Yankee existentialism*, the *anti-novel, theater of the absurd*, and *film noir*. Critic Douglas Davis says that black humor "laughs at the absurd tragedy which has trapped us all: man, woman, child, self." He considers it to be part of broader movements that include neo-Dada and Pop art, along with electronic poetry, computer music, and "the happening," which are all artistic protests against science and technology.

A characteristic of black humor is that the line between fantasy and reality is flickering or nonexistent, and readers of a novel, for example, are unsure about the point at which realism fades into fantasy. For example, in Terry Southern's 1960 *The Magic Christian* (1969 movie), Guy Grand buys a huge newspaper company and converts the newspaper entirely to readers' opinions. Is this a joke or simply a forerunner of talk radio?

In Joseph Heller's 1961 *Catch-22* (1970 movie), Yossarian protests the brutality of war by sitting naked in a tree, while in John Barth's 1967 *The Floating Opera*, Todd Andrews contemplates his own suicide as he works out a puzzle involving $3 million and 129 pickle jars filled with excrement. Thomas Pynchon in his 1972 *Gravity's Rainbow* tells a joke about a boy born with a golden screw in his navel. The boy devotes his life to consulting with specialists about how to get rid of his golden screw. A voodoo doctor finally gives him a potion that sends him into a wild dream, and when he wakes up, the golden screw is gone. In ecstasy, he jumps out of bed and his bottom falls off. Other highly respected black humor novels include William Gaddis's 1955 *The Recognitions* and James Donleavy's 1958 *The Ginger Man*.

The American public at large has appreciated black humor mostly through movies. Alfred Hitchcock's 1955 *The Trouble with Harry* is a fairly early example of black comedy based on mis-identification. While the movie revolves around death and frustration, it does not have the political concerns that later movies had. Harry Rogers is an apparent murder victim whose body is found over and over again, buried, exhumed, and reburied. A whole cast of characters is suspected of killing him; however, by the end of the movie, the entire story proves to be much ado about nothing because Harry Rogers had died from a heart attack. Hitchcock's 1976 *Family Plot* and 1948 *Rope* are also considered to be interesting examples of black humor.

Terry Southern and Stanley Kubrick's 1964 film *Dr. Strangelove, or: How I Learned to Stop Worrying and Love the Bomb* satirizes war. At one point, a fight breaks out between the characters and the group is severely admonished, "You can't fight in here; this is the war room." As in Aldous Huxley's *Brave New World*, people are to be chosen for living in the deep mine shafts after the war on the basis of how they will contribute to a "perfect" society. The missile complex is named *Laputa*, an allusion to Jonathan Swift's *Gulliver's Travels*, while the hydrogen bombs that are being prepared for Operation Drop Kick are named *Hi There* and *Dear John. POE* is an acronym for both "Peace on Earth" and "Purity of Essence." Closing of the Doomsday Gap is seen as a deterrent to war.

The 1965 movie *The Loved One*, from Evelyn Waugh's 1948 novel, satirizes the commercialization of death by showing how the California funeral industry turns burials into Hollywood extravaganzas. At Whispering Glades, caskets come in three grades: waterproof, moisture proof, and dampness proof. The park is divided into zones, each having its own work of art. The "Poet's Corner" for example has "Xanadu Falls" and is dedicated to Homer. The movie becomes darker as it focuses on Aimee Thanatogenous, who thinks a connected pet cemetery makes a "mockery out of death." The Guru Brahman sarcastically tells her to go to the 14th floor, his office, and jump out of the window. She goes to the 14th floor, and in the manner of Cleopatra, who clasped poison adders to her breasts, Aimee commits suicide by injecting herself with embalming fluid.

Terry Southern's 1969 film *The Magic Christian* targets capitalism, war, violence, and gender roles. Peter Sellers plays Sir Guy Grand, the Richest Man in the World; Ringo Starr plays a homeless person who becomes Youngman Grand, Sir Guy's son and heir. The movie is filled with incongruous absurdities. Heavy artillery is used for the hunting of pheasants, and during scenes of riots and police brutality, Sellers and Starr calmly play a harp and a recorder. During the war games in the living room, all the furnishings get blown up. To demonstrate Sir Guy's richness, a restaurant episode shows the waiters ignor-

ing all the other patrons while giving full attention to Sir Guy. Sir Guy is equipped with a wet suit and safety belts, and after a lusty battle with a caviar meatball, has to be hosed down. In a boxing match, the fighters end up kissing each other, and the announcer says that the crowd seems to be sickened by the sight of no blood.

The 1975 *Monty Python and the Holy Grail*, featuring Graham Chapman, John Cleese, Terry Gilliam, Eric Idle, Terry Jones, and Michael Palin, is a satire about the romances, the wars, and the quests of the Middle Ages. When King Arthur fights the Black Knight, he cuts off the knight's arms and both of his legs, but the Black Knight still taunts King Arthur and wants to continue the fight. The presentation of the story is episodic and includes the tale of Sir Robin the Not-So-Brave, the tale of Sir Galahad the Chaste, and the tale of Sir Lancelot. During their adventures, the knights have to cross the bridge of death, where three questions are asked: "What is your name?" "What is your quest?" and "What is your favorite color?" Much of the humor comes from how difficult these questions become for some of the knights. The violence, killing, and bloodshed are all justified in the name of Christianity. In an anachronistic ending, the police arrive, dressed in modern British uniforms, and load King Arthur and the others into a paddy wagon.

The 1979 *Monty Python's The Life of Brian* features the same set of actors as *Holy Grail*. Character names include *Nautius Maximus, Biggus Dickus,* and *Incontinentia Buttocks*. The movie takes place in Bethlehem during the time of Christ—or more specifically, on Saturday afternoon at tea time during the time of Christ. The film satirically targets religion, ritual, and blind faith. When Brian of Nazareth is asked if he is the Messiah, he says, "No," and the villagers respond, "Only the *true* Messiah denies his divinity." Brian becomes a sacred icon, along with his sandal and his gourd. When the Christians ask, "What have the Romans ever done for us?" the response is "aqueducts, sanitation, roads, irrigation, medicine, education, wine, public baths, peace." There is confusion over whether Myrrh is a "balm" or a "bomb." The Israelites are referred to as the "Red Sea pedestrians." When the Christians write on the walls of the palace, "Romans eunt domus," meaning "Romans go home," the Romans who see the graffiti are totally oblivious to the meaning as they go about correcting the grammar. The movie ends with Brian and other Christians hanging from crosses, but doggedly singing, "Always Look on the Bright Side of Life."

Woody Allen's 1971 *Bananas* makes fun of the military solutions that the United States invokes on third-world countries. In parody form, the movie contains Howard Cosell's play-by-play announcement of the assassination of "El Presidente" (Woody Allen), and his introduction of the New Dictator, General Emilio Elena Vargas. As a parody of a parody, the movie also contains Howard Cosell's play-by-play description, as though on *Wide World of Sports*, of the consummation of the marriage of Fielding Melish and Norma, an ingenue devoting her life to third-world causes. Other Woody Allen movies that include black humor are *Love and Death* (1975), *Annie Hall* (1977), *Zelig* (1983), *Crimes and Misdemeanors* (1989), and *Deconstructing Harry* (1997).

In the 1982 movie version of John Irving's 1978 *The World According to Garp*, Robin Williams plays the role of T. S. Garp, while Glenn Close plays the role of Garp's mother, Jenny. Jenny was a nurse who got herself pregnant by taking advantage of an injured and dying soldier, Technical Sergeant Garp, who had been brought in from his downed airplane with a permanent erection. After Garp is born, Jenny works as the school nurse in exclusive prep schools where Garp grows up. He is such a determined boy that when a dog bites him, Garp bites back and takes off part of the dog's ear.

Some of the funniest parts of the movie circle around Jenny's detached attitude towards all things sexual. She tries to have an open mind, and she conducts an asexual interview with a puzzled prostitute. When she writes a book that becomes a feminist bestseller, she uses the profits to found a shelter for abused women—and one man—a transvestite named Roberta (played by John Lithgow). Roberta used to be a wide receiver for the Philadelphia Eagles, and some of the humor comes from the inevitable confusions surrounding this. That Roberta appears to be the most "normal" person in the shelter reflects the zaniness of the cast.

When people ask Garp what his name means, he tells them that the *T. S.* used to stand for "Terribly Sad," but now it stands for "Terribly Sexy." Garp's heritage as the son of a pilot is a motif that runs throughout the movie. It opens with a happy scene of Baby Garp being tossed again and again into the air. During his childhood, Garp tries to fly by jumping off a building. When he gets married and he and his wife are out with the real estate agent looking at a house to buy and a small plane crashes into the roof, Garp knows this is the home for them because of the infinitesimal chances of the same house being hit twice by an airplane.

Quentin Tarantino's 1994 *Pulp Fiction* is a parody targeting pulp fiction, religion, and the criminal world. The setting is Los Angeles, some of it at Jack Rabbit Slim's place—"a wax museum with a pulse." Among those playing major roles are Uma Thurman, John Travolta, Samuel L. Jackson, and Bruce Willis, who plays Butch, a boxer who refuses to throw a fight. Four interlocking stories circle around a cast of bumbling robbers, real gangsters, the Boss, and the Boss's wife, whose hairdo and dress are perfect for the cover of a sleazy novel. In all the episodes, Marsellus, the Boss, watches jealously over Mia, his wife. A man who gives her a foot massage is later pushed from the roof of a building. Mia is so passive and ineffectual that viewers don't know whether the phrase "taking care of the Boss's wife," means killing her, protecting her, or providing her with sex.

In a memorable scene, two gangsters go over a speed bump, causing a gun to go off in the face of a man they were guarding in the back seat of the car. Almost as shocking is the history of Butch's gold watch. His father, who during the war was captured and

Quentin Tarantino's 1994 *Pulp Fiction* extended the boundaries for dark humor in mainstream movies. *Archive Photos*

held as a POW, hid the precious gold watch in his anus for five years. Just before being executed, he passed it on to another POW who also hid it in his anus for a number of years. At last, the watch makes its way home and the grateful and loving Butch keeps it on his bedside table.

The violence of *Pulp Fiction* is almost like the violence in a *Tom-and-Jerry* cartoon. In one scene, bullets whiz back and forth, but through what looks like divine intervention, Vince and Jules remain alive and unharmed. Also right out of a cartoon is the scene where Butch is looking for a weapon. First, he finds a hammer, then a bat, then a chainsaw, and finally a sword.

Other movies that make use of black humor are the 1970 movie *Little Big Man,* based on Thomas Berger's 1964 novel; the 1972 *Slaughterhouse-Five,* based on Kurt Vonnegut's 1969 novel; the 1975 *One Flew over the Cuckoo's Nest,* based on Ken Kesey's 1962 novel; the 1979 *Being There,* based on Jerzy Kosinski's 1970 novel; the 1988 *Milagro Beanfield War,* based on John Nichols's 1974 novel; the 1991 *Naked Lunch,* based loosely on William Burroughs's 1959 novel; and the 1998 *Lolita,* based on Vladimir Nabokov's 1955 novel. From a deconstructionist point of view, black humor

illustrates the futility of looking for easy and neat answers to the tragedies of life. Black humor is nevertheless consoling because of the way it demonstrates that in spite of bewilderment, death, and chaos, people can laugh. *See also* ANTIAUTHORITY HUMOR, GOTHIC HUMOR, POSTMODERNISM, SUPERIORITY AND HOSTILITY

Further reading: William Keough, *Punchlines: The Violence of American Humor* (1990). Lance Olsen, *Circus of the Mind in Motion: Postmodernism and the Comic Vision* (1990). Alan R. Pratt (ed.), *Black Humor: Critical Essays* (1993).

Blackface Comedy

Blackface comedy, in which singers, dancers, and actors darkened their faces, dressed in exaggerated clothing, and spoke with heavy accents, was a primary form of American entertainment through the 19th and well into the 20th centuries. Blackface performers developed the concept of the minstrel show, which in some parts of the early United States brought African Americans out of a state of near-invisibility and paved the way for African Americans to perform before white audiences.

Historian Joseph Boskin says that minstrelsy disseminated the image of the Black man as "the natural performer, the comedian par excellence," while allowing whites to "peer into black culture without much anxiety, subject their stereotypes to some skepticism, cope with ambivalent racial feelings, and appreciate the nuances of the black experience." But at the same time, blackface and minstrelsy created and taught the stereotypes that Blacks are musical and nimble of foot, intellectually weak but athletically strong, happy and childlike, sexually coarse, and incapable of speaking standard English. Minstrelsy also popularized such terms as *Sambo, Nigger, Jim Crow,* and *Coon,* and by establishing a stage role that African American performers were forced to fit into, it guaranteed a long life for these stereotypes.

Boskin says that blackface entertainment was based on the *Sambo* archetype, an "enduring comic image" that had its beginnings in mirth and merriment, much like the jester role in European stories, but that between 1820 and 1960 gave way to a stereotype that was wholly demeaning and "reinforced the viciousness of unrestrained racism."

The war of 1812 engendered a patriotic desire for "authentic" Americana. Evenings at the theater had typically consisted of a full-length play supplemented by such variety acts as trained animals, jugglers, acrobats, dancers, and singers. Many specialty performers were from Jamaica or the West Indies, but the new sense of "Americanism" caused theatergoers in the 1820s to reject these "foreigners" in favor of white actors dressed in "Black" clothing and makeup and prancing "in a jolly and comic style," as they sang such pieces as "The Bonja Song":

> Me sing all day, me sleep all night
> Me have no care, me sleep is light
> Me tink no what tomorrow bring
> Me happy so me sing.

The heavy stereotyping began in 1827 when George Washington Dixon and others smeared on blackface and donned exaggerated costumes and sang "Coal Black Rose" and "My Long Tailed Blue." These two songs presented the flip sides of the stereotyped comic Black. One was the plantation "darky,"

the country cousin; while the other was the city "dandy."

In 1828, Thomas D. Rice began entertaining audiences by jumping and dancing to a popular English ditty adapted to his version of African American style:

> Wheel about, turn about,
> Do jis so,
> An' ebery time I wheel about
> I jump Jim Crow.

Rice "authenticated" his dance by saying that he had seen a Black stable groom (some stories say the man was crippled) singing and doing the dance as he performed his work. However, audiences didn't care whether the dance was authentic; they just enjoyed the lively music and the quick steps. In another act, Rice came on stage carrying a gunny sack and singing "Me and My Shadow." When he put the sack down, a child, also in blackface, climbed out and imitated Rice's every move. Rice inspired hundreds of imitators, all white Northerners, who for the most part had never observed actual African Americans at play. Many imitators were recent immigrants who "translated" German and English melodies to slave style while adding their personal anecdotes and immigrant messages.

According to author Mel Watkins, by the mid-1830s, "*Jim Crow,* the unkempt, ignorant plantation slave had displaced the backwoods or frontier caricature; and *Zip Coon* or *Jim Dandy,* the bombastic, dandified city slicker, replaced the Yankee character as America's central comic figures." The caricatures began with a kernel of truth that was so overstated that it was more representative of the imagination of Northern whites than of the actual lives of African Americans. Appearance was exaggerated by costumes looking either richer or poorer than in real life. Bright red lipstick was used to draw huge lips, while white circles were drawn around the eyes. The reason for the white circles was to protect the eyes from the soot or burnt cork, which was used for blacking, but the result was a bug-eyed look. Actions were just as exaggerated. While it's true that drums, and hence rhythm, played a more important part in African than in European music, and that African religious practices encouraged a more physical participation, the real differences between people of African and European ancestry were not nearly as extreme as were the stage differences. Also, African Americans were purposely kept from learning standard English and from being taught to read, so most of them spoke nonstandard English, but not the extreme dialects portrayed by blackface performers. And while African Americans made fun of "the fools" in their midst, these "fools" were identified as particular individuals. They were the exception, similar to the way white Americans later made fun of The Three Stooges or Laurel and Hardy. However, when blackface comedians told African American fool stories, they overgeneralized and assigned the characteristics of the fool to a whole race. They also tended to ignore the stories that slaves told amongst themselves where "the fool" turned out to be a wise fool or a Trickster.

The first full-length minstrel show was established in 1842. The nation was still reeling from the financial panic of 1837, which had been particularly hard on the theatrical scene, and four unemployed actors, all of whom had done some work in blackface, met in a New York hotel to figure out a future for themselves. Dan Emmett, who is said to have borrowed his performance almost in its entirety from Rice, came up with the idea of forming a troupe and concentrating exclusively on blackface mimicry. The men (Billy Whitlock, Frank Brower, Frank Pelham, and Emmett) opened their show, the Virginia Minstrels, at the Bowery Ampitheatre in New York as part of the Olympic Circus. Their next performance was at the Masonic Temple in Boston where fliers promised they would perform the "oddities, peculiarities, eccentricities, and comicalities of the Sable Genus of Humanity." The show was a sensation, and within a year the group had departed for a successful tour in England leaving behind dozens of imitators who made blackface minstrelsy America's most popular form of entertainment.

Contributing to their instant popularity was the way they integrated the raucous and irreverent style of Yankee and frontier humor with audiences' curiosity about African Americans in light of the increasing tensions over slavery. Also white actors in blackface seemed to be freed from their own inhibitions which, contributed to a heightening of excitement and to the frenetic pace. Robert C. Toll has written that once on stage, minstrel actors "could not stay still for an instant. Even while sitting, they contorted their bodies, cocked their heads, rolled their eyes, and twisted their outstretched legs . . . their wild hollering and their bobbing seemingly compulsive movements charged the entire performance with excitement."

While on their English tour the Virginia Minstrels disbanded, but back home their place was taken by the Ethiopian Serenaders, who were so popular that in 1844 they were invited to perform at the White House for President John Tyler, whose family were aristocratic southern tobacco growers. When the Serenaders departed for an overseas tour in 1846, E. P. Christy and his Christy Minstrels became the most famous group partly because they were fortunate in having Stephen Foster, who as a teenager had done amateur blackface performances, as a songwriter. Traveling performance groups came together throughout the United States, including the South and the far West. Among the most famous were the African Melodists, the Congo Minstrels, the Buckley Serenaders, the Ethiopian Mountain Singers, and Bryant's Minstrels.

A typical performance, consisting of three acts, opened with a walk-around, where all the performers strutted their stuff, sometimes doing the Cake-Walk dance. After the parade, members of the troupe arranged themselves on stage in a semicircle. Comic songs and jokes alternated with popular dances and love ballads. The master of ceremonies (the interlocutor) sat in the middle and directed a kind of improv by calling on the endmen— Mr. Bones and Mr. Tambo (named for their musical instruments)—to engage in two-person skits or in banter with the interlocutor, much like the rapid-fire puns and gags still seen in today's stand-up comedy. The act ended with a rousing song and dance number.

The second act was an *olio,* or variety segment, which often included a stump speaker doing a satirical parody of a speech on emancipation, or women's suffrage, or education. Watkins says that "Malaprop reigned supreme; although important issues were often addressed, the focus here was purely on humor . . . not only were serious issues lampooned, but blacks' abilities to understand or interpret sophisticated ideas were ridiculed and mocked."

The last act was usually a plantation skit featuring songs and dances. In the beginning, these minstrel shows were romanticized views of plantation life filled with frenetic action, slapstick, and malapropisms. Watkins says that after the 1850s, farcical versions of serious dramas such as Shakespeare's *Macbeth* became fashionable with the intent being to portray "free blacks as bombastic fools or helpless incompetents . . . obviously misplaced in any serious context." While early blackface performances had allowed at least a glimpse into African American life, as tensions leading up to the Civil War increased, minstrel shows became increasingly hostile toward African Americans. Satirical parodies of Harriet Beecher Stowe's 1852 *Uncle Tom's Cabin* became popular. Some of the shows changed to focus on the suffering of white, Northern soldiers and their families, while after the war, others turned to lampooning the participation of Blacks in political affairs.

Constance Rourke explained in her 1931 *American Humor: A Study of the National Character* that blackface comedy became increasingly popular during the 1800s because "to the primitive comic sense, to be black was to be funny." Blackface comedy appealed to the same vulgar curiosity as did circus exhibits of bearded ladies, conjoined twins, and "Jo-Jo, the dog-faced boy." Also, the scripts fit with the writings of Joel Chandler Harris, Seba Smith, James Russell Lowell, Artemus Ward, and Mark Twain, who were amusing readers by having their uneducated characters speak in heavy dialect.

When African Americans in large numbers began to actually participate in American life, the minstrel shows lost their sense of the exotic. They suffered another blow when, in the late 1800s, women singers and dancers moved away from their association with saloon entertainment and began to be included in variety shows. There was no way that minstrel shows could incorporate this new kind of woman performer because they had always portrayed both male and female African Americans as asexual buffoons. By the mid-1890s, vaudeville was the people's preferred entertainment, soon to be replaced by silent movies and later by "the talkies."

By 1920, Al G. Field, one of the last owners of a minstrel show, said that there were only three first-class minstrel shows still touring. Field closed his company in 1928 and Carl Wittke wrote that with Field's closing, "the final curtain was wrung down on what, at one time, was America's most successful form of entertainment."

Long after vaudeville supplanted minstrelsy, white performers still "corked up" to impersonate Blacks and rework some of the old minstrel bits. Al Jolson is the most famous, but other whites who performed in blackface include Buster Keaton, Eddie Cantor, Eddie Leonard, Moran and Mack (played by George Searcy and Charles Sellers and sometimes Jack Swor), Freeman Gosden, and Charles Correll. Black performers who participated in vaudeville wearing blackface include Bert Williams, George Walker, Irvin C. Miller, Flournoy E. Miller, Ernest Hogan, and Butterbeans and Susie. Watkins says that even after blackface was no longer required, some African Americans kept using it as though "comedy and burnt cork were inseparable." The most famous African American blackface performer was Pigmeat Markham, who worked in blackface until after World War II. "When audiences and critics demanded that the burnt-cork performances end, they were astonished to find that he was actually darker than the makeup he had used."

In spite of having received praise from Mark Twain and Charles Dickens, blackface and minstrelsy were, in general, lowbrow entertainment, and many Americans never saw a blackface performance. However, virtually everyone experienced ripple effects as exaggerated blackface illustrations and idiom were used to sell postcards, sheet music, food products, props for gags, joke books, and scripts for amateur productions. In the 1930s, the WPA (Works Progress Administration) produced minstrel shows (including marionette shows) through the Federal Theater project, and in 1938 the project distributed a book of songs and scripts, *56 Minstrels*, for community productions by youth groups. Included with the comedy scripts, all given in heavy dialect, were musical arrangements for "The Coon-Town Thirteen Club," "The Darktown Follies," "Watermelon Minstrel," and "Plantation Days with the Snowflake Family." Only in the 1960s did the Philadelphia Mummers change from blackface to goldface for their New Year's Day parade, and only in the 1970s did the Rotarians in Traverse City, Michigan, give up their two-day minstrel show and community sing. *See also* AFRICAN AMERICAN HUMOR, RADIO, TELEVISION, VAUDEVILLE AND BURLESQUE

Further reading: Joseph Boskin, *Sambo: The Rise and Demise of an American Jester* (1986). W. T. Lhamon, *Raising Cain: Blackface Performance from Jim Crow to Hip Hop* (1998). Eric Lott, *Love and Theft: Blackface Minstrelsy and the American Working Class* (1993). Mel Watkins, *On the Real Side* (1994).

Body Humor

Body humor is related both to the shape of a performer's body and to what a performer does with that body. In the 1940s and early 1950s the importance of body humor was vividly demonstrated as hundreds of radio performers tried to move to television. Many failed because they knew only how to stand in front of a microphone and throw their energy into their voices, while the success stories—Milton Berle, Red Skelton, Groucho Marx, and Lucille Ball and Desi Arnaz—had come to radio via vaudeville and variety shows in which they had worked in front of live audiences. These performers made quick movements, contorting their bodies and putting their hands and feet to work while mugging

the cameras and "making eyes" at their audiences.

Deformed bodies have long been associated with humor as shown by European customs in the Middle Ages of using dwarves or hunchbacks as court jesters, clowns, and fools. Small stature and deformities were meant to guarantee that performers could do and say funny things without becoming genuine threats to the ruler. A connection between comedy and smallness is also shown through the "little people" of folk literature: gremlins, trolls, hobgoblins, leprechauns, elves, fairies, gnomes, and brownies. The creators of modern stories have furthered the association with J. R. R. Tolkien's hobbits, television's Smurfs and Muppets, the Munchkins in the 1939 *Wizard of Oz*, Artoo Detoo in the *Star Wars* movies, and the title character in the 1982 *ET: The Extraterrestrial*.

Some of the world's most famous comedians, Charlie Chaplin, Buster Keaton, and Mickey Rooney, have been unusually short. They set an example for an entire group of comedians who capitalizes on their diminutiveness with such quips as "In a heavy rain, I'll be the last to get wet, but the first to drown." Five-foot-two Rick Moranis was the smallest member of the team in the 1984 *Ghostbusters* and the 1989 *Ghostbusters II*. He played Dark Helmet, the intergalactic menace, in Mel Brooks's 1987 *Spaceballs*, while in the 1986 *Little Shop of Horrors* he played the doofus who accidentally raises a man-eating plant, and in the 1989 *Honey I Shrunk the Kids!* and its sequel *Honey, I Blew Up the Kid,* he played a "genius" father experimenting on his own children.

Tim Conway, who in the 1960s played Ensign Charles Parker on *McHale's Navy*, created a super-short character named Dorf, who gave pompous, and hilarious, lectures on sports. For the role, Conway would stand in a hole and put shoes on his knees so that he could wear bermuda shorts as full-length pants. He kept his balance by tipping forwards and backwards while his knuckles dragged on the ground.

A secret to Red Skelton's success was his "plastic" face demonstrated by stock characters he played on his 1950s and 1960s television show. ©*Globe Photos Inc.*

Buddy Hackett, at five-foot-six, has a teddy-bear body that has been described as "a baked potato out for a stroll." He played the role of Lou Costello in the television film *Bud and Lou*. Dudley Moore, in the 1979 movie *10*, had to look up to Bo Derek, while in the 1981 *Arthur* and the 1988 *Arthur 2*, his lack of stature made him seem all the more like his nickname, "Cuddly Dudley."

Five-foot Danny DeVito had a prominent role in television's *Taxi* (1978–1983), and since then has been a favorite to play the role of a comic villain in such movies as *Romancing the Stone* (1984), *Ruthless People* (1986), *Throw Momma from the Train* (1987), *Other People's Money* (1991), and *Batman Returns* (1992), and his height was used for comedy in his roles in *The Jewel of the Nile* (1985) and *Get Shorty* (1995).

Woody Allen's diminutive body frame is set off by his large spectacles. Neil Schmitz in his 1983 book *Of Huck and Alice: Humorous Writing in American Literature* has observed that Allen projects a "disheveled boyishness, which generates without the aid of funny lines its own droll melancholy." Schmitz explains that the wistful appeal has

been both helpful and hazardous to Allen's acting because while he looks like such an innocent, Allen's humorous writing has become more complex, and there is also a need for him to appear mature and thoughtful. Audiences find it hard to believe that any "significant harm can ever befall . . . this childish fellow, because he is too innocent to be wrong."

Schmitz's observation illustrates how viewers have almost subconscious expectations connected with body types. Skinny comedians—Jerry Lewis, Pee-Wee Herman, and Emo Philips—are expected to be jerky and frenetic in their thinking as well as in the way they move their bodies. John Cleese is so tall that he dominated the Monty Python troupe and is remembered as the "Minister of Silly Walks."

Six-foot-five-inch Fred Gwynne illustrates the power of being both tall and heavy. In the early 1960s, he played Officer Francis Muldoon on television's *Car 54, Where Are You?* where his height contrasted with Joe E. Ross playing Officer Gunther Toody. As Herman Munster in the mid-1960's *The Munsters*, Gwynne had a hearty laugh, nervously fluttering fingers, a silly wide smile, and bright eyes that jutted out from under his monster brows. His flat, nasal, timid, and whining voice was all the funnier in contrast to his imposing and muscular body.

When overweight comedian Chris Farley died in December 1997 of an accidental drug overdose and the Cook County medical examiner announced that a narrowing of the arteries supplying the heart muscle contributed to his death, media discussions centered on the role of fatness in getting laughs. Los Angeles psychologist Harvey Mindess noted that laughter is provoked whenever someone's physical build is "nowhere near the norm, is eccentric, or peculiar." He related the idea to the superiority theory, saying that we are predisposed to laugh at fat or awkward people because "compared to them, we're pretty good."

Funny fat men have a long history going back to Shakespeare's Falstaff, and in more recent times to Oliver Hardy, Roscoe "Fatty" Arbuckle, Lou Costello, Buddy Hackett, John Candy, John Belushi, Louie Anderson, and Drew Carey. When Jackie Gleason became an adult he ballooned to 285 pounds and earned the nickname *The Great One*, an allusion to both his size and his talent. Zero Mostel was given the stage name of *Zero* partly because of his shape and partly as an ironic prediction of his future success. He was a huge clown but surprised audiences by having a Chaplinesque kind of control over his massive body. During the 1960s, Mostel had memorable performances in the Broadway production of *Fiddler on the Roof* in the role of Tevye; the Mel Brooks film *The Producers;* and both stage and screen versions of *A Funny Thing Happened on the Way to the Forum* and *Rhinoceros*.

Audiences hesitate to laugh at overweight comedians before the comedian has reassured them through telling fat jokes or self-deprecating anecdotes. Because society is more comfortable with large men than with large women, very few overweight women have succeeded in communicating that audiences are free to laugh rather than to feel sorry for them.

Moms Mabley carried a few extra pounds and so did Sophie Tucker. They both exuded good-natured, mature sexuality, with Tucker billing herself as "the last of the Red Hot Mamas." In the next generation, Totie Fields created a similar image, joking about how hard it was to "squeeze fat Jewish feet into thin Italian shoes." In the 1980s, Roseanne in her stand-up routines broke the fat barrier for women but was still ridiculed and encouraged to go through the public dieting rituals.

It is common practice for women to make self-deprecating jokes about their bodies; their thighs are too fat, their breasts too small, and their hips too broad. Sandra Bernhard tells about growing up feeling like a loser because of her big nose, thick lips, and the gap between her front teeth. Phyllis Diller, who started her career with such jokes as "my Playtex Living Bra died—of starvation," and "Lloyds of London refused to insure my face. They told me—what the hell more could happen to it," was the first performer to surprise her audiences with comic routines about all the plastic surgery she has endured. Of the new generation of comedians, Mo'Nique is the most shocking by coming on stage and yelling, "Y'all give it up for my fat ass!"

Many successful comedians (Lucille Ball, Jackie Gleason, Buddy Hackett, Oliver Hardy, Buster Keaton, Stan Laurel, Jerry Lewis, Eddie Murphy, Red Skelton, and Lily Tomlin) have what are called "elastic" or "plastic" faces. Their faces are not dependent on any one particular feature, but on how all the features relate to each other and whether any one feature is distinctive. Eddie Cantor was known for his "banjo eyes," Fred Allen for the bags under his eyes, and Rodney Dangerfield for his "bug eyes." Marty Feldman was called a visual sight gag, continuing in the tradition of Ben Turpin from silent film. Feldman had jutting ears, a hooked nose, and bulging eyes. He could make audiences laugh just by putting on a sly smile, a fiendish grin, or a blank look of innocence. In Mel Brooks's 1974 *Young Frankenstein*, he played the role of the grotesque Igor (which he pronounced "eye-gore"), the hunchbacked assistant to Dr. Frankenstein.

Ears only occasionally come into comedy, although Carol Burnett did end each of her shows by tugging on an ear to tell her grandmother at home that everything was okay. When H. Ross Perot ran for president in the 1990s, his protruding ears were caricatured by hundreds of cartoonists, some of whom compared him to Walt Disney's animated Dumbo, the little elephant whose ears were so big he could use them as wings.

Big noses are also fodder for caricature. W. C. Fields was famous for his nose, which was only slightly smaller and less red than a clown's rubber nose. Jimmy Durante was known as "Schnozzola" or simply "de schnoz." His nose was insured with Lloyds of London, listed in *Who's Who*, and pressed into the concrete at Grauman's Chinese Theater in Hollywood. Bob Hope made jokes about his ski-lift nose, saying that after his birth his mother took one look at his nose and cried in alarm that the doctor had "taken the baby and left the stork." William Bendix was a 200-pound hulk with a large oval face and a huge broken nose. He also had a small mouth, which enhanced his quizzical expression when he played "dumb-ape" roles.

The mouth is the most expressive feature on the face, with human lips having some 180 muscles, none of which are anchored to bone. This means that speakers can move their lips into a wide variety of positions, ranging from snarls to smiles; from frowns to grins; and from open-mouthed wonder to quick pecks or long, sexy kisses. In the days of blackface comedy, mouths were always made bigger with bright red grease paint, while today some actresses get silicone injections to make their lips look larger and most wear lipstick. Joe E. Brown had a mammoth mouth from which he could emit an alarm-like shriek that would put his audiences into an uproar. Penny Marshall has said that she never enjoys watching her own performances because she is "all nose and teeth." Both David Letterman and the British comedian Terry-Thomas have prominent gaps between their front teeth. Thomas put the hyphen between his two names as a reminder of his tooth gap. He played stereotypically silly Englishmen and

dastardly amusing villains, made all the funnier by his gleaming, malicious smile.

Many men accent their mouths by wearing mustaches, none more famous than Charlie Chaplin's toothbrush-sized one. It was originally created from a clipping of Mack Swain's larger mustache that had been left on Swain's dressing table. Chaplin's mustache was imitated by Groucho Marx, who when he moved to television's *You Bet Your Life* was forced to grow his own. Chester Conklin was a little man with a drooping, walrus-like mustache. He was kicked, pushed, and shoved by the Keystone Kops, abused by W. C. Fields, and mangled in machinery in Charlie Chaplin's 1936 *Modern Times*. He played his role so well that after one of these disasters, he could elicit laughs simply by peering dolefully at the audience from over his hangdog mustache. *See also* COMEDY TEAMS, EXAGGERATION, MIMES, SILENT FILMS, STAND-UP COMEDY

Business Humor

Business humor concerns the role that humor plays in businesses and workplaces not connected to entertainment. While some critics and scholars simply make observations about the effects of humor in business, others have become consultants who work with companies to develop a playful, nonthreatening atmosphere under the philosophy that happy workers will be better workers. The services offered by humor consultants range from creating jokes or writing limericks for particular professions or events to becoming semipermanent members of a company's management team, consulting on matters ranging from office layouts to assembly-line assignments. In between are the suggestions for "dress-down" or "dress-up" days, free cookies on Fridays, checking out potential employees for their senses of humor, and starting weekly sales meetings by honoring top performers with clever posters or new words sung to popular tunes.

Southwest Airlines and Ben & Jerry's ice cream company are famous for having turned smiles into dollars, but such companies as IBM, Kodak, Monsanto, Deloitte & Touche,

Honda, and even the Internal Revenue Service, have hired consultants to give them lessons on "lightening up." In 1977, Joel Goodman in upstate New York established the HUMOR Project <http://www. humorproject.com>, with a goal of providing services, programs, and resources focusing on the positive power of humor and creativity. Each summer, the HUMOR Project sponsors a week-long workshop attended by over 1,000 managers, business people, health care workers, educators, and other professionals interested in learning how humor can help relieve stress and improve working conditions. The project also sponsors a speakers' bureau, a quarterly publication *Laughing Matters*, and a *HUMOResources* mail-order bookstore. In 1997, Goodman said that he received 20 requests a day to provide humor consultants. Many come from corporations that are downsizing or for some other reason have morale problems. They call Goodman hoping that an infusion of humor will help employees feel better. Goodman says he lets the companies know that while he may have lots of "inspirational" one-liners, he has "no desire to cover up a company's real problems with a Band-Aid." Goodman's suggestions for making workplaces less intimidating and more fun range from photocopying cartoons onto memos to dressing in superhero costumes complete with capes and tights for important sales meetings.

One of the most famous consultants is John Cleese, who was featured in a *Fortune* interview (Jul. 6, 1998) talking about his role with the Monty Python comedy group and how he is now the "maker of the world's best-selling business videos, on confidence vs. fear, where creativity comes from, and more." When Cleese first started making his films through the Chicago- and London-based Video Arts, people would ask him, "How can you use humor in these films? Don't you consider training to be a serious thing?" He says it took him a long time to come up with the answer that "there is all the difference in the world between being serious and being solemn." He went on to explain that while people are talking about something very se-

rious such as their children's education they can still be laughing. He got a great lesson in this when he had the good fortune to interview the Dalai Lama and to ask him why in Tibetan Buddhism people laugh so much. "And he said to me, very seriously, that laughter is very helpful to him in teaching and indeed in political negotiations, because when people laugh, it is easier for them to admit new ideas to their minds."

Consultant John Morreall in his 1997 book *Humor Works* says that people do their best in an atmosphere where they have control over their work and feel like valued members of a team. Humor is effective in so far as it

- helps reduce the psychological distance between management and non-management

- minimizes formality and makes it easy and comfortable for people to communicate across levels

- fosters camaraderie and team spirit

- is used as positive rather than negative reinforcement

- encourages people to take risks and try new things

Esther Blumenfeld and Lynne Alpern in their 1994 *Humor at Work* say that humor can provide perspective and balance, help people cope with problems, serve as a safety valve for anger, enhance communication, and make work fun. In one of their better examples of humor used as a corrective, they tell about a group of women who noticed that at meetings a male colleague kept dropping his pen so that he could bend down and look at their legs. Before the next meeting, they got ready for him by printing on their knees "HI RALPH!" one letter per kneecap.

Gregory F. Farrell's 1996 *A Funny Thing Happened at the Interview: Wit, Wisdom and War Stories from the Job Hunt* will either make job applicants laugh or cry. It contains 119 humorous accounts of garbled resumes and interviews gone awry. Scattered throughout are such statements as Robert Frost's, "By working faithfully eight hours a day, you may eventually get to be a boss and work twelve hours a day." C. W. Metcalf put his 1994 *Lighten Up: The Amazing Power of Grace under Pressure* on four cassette tapes, while Ed Kittrell offers his ideas through a *Funny Business* newsletter. Subscribers also get his *1998 Funny Business Almanac* as a bonus.

In 1997, the University of Chicago M.B.A. (Master of Business Administration) program brought in Brett Scott, a director, writer, and actor affiliated with Chicago's Second City acting troupe, to help students improvise comic situations. Earlier in the year, business students at Vanderbilt had gone through a similar experience. In relation to this kind of training, C. Thomas Howard, director of the M.B.A. program at the University of Denver, explained to a *New York Times* reporter (Feb. 12, 1997), "It's interesting that hard skills are considered better than soft, but when people go into management, it's the soft skills that . . . make the difference in career success."

Many businesses and service groups go a step further by extending their use of humor to customers. In the 1980s, the San Francisco Police Department hired humor consultants Mike Iapoce and Karen Warner to revise their plans for Neighborhood Crime Prevention meetings after they learned that their workshops left people feeling more— rather than less—traumatized about crime. The humor consultants added a light touch with such quips as "under daylight savings time, you'll be glad to know our officers will respond to calls a full hour earlier." While several of the jokes that the consultants suggested were censored by someone in the police chain of command, the department was nevertheless satisfied because people were less alarmed and more attentive. They went away better informed and therefore safer. The same humor consultants also worked with AT&T to create such jokes as "First, the bad news: rates are going up! Now the good news: the continents are drifting closer together!" and "One of the reasons we put zip code maps in phone books is so that if your call doesn't go through, you can write."

During the 1993 presidential campaign, Eric Stromquist, owner of a Chinese restaurant in Oregon was featured on a National Public Radio interview because of the messages he was putting in his fortune cookies, including

- You're no Jack Kennedy!
- Your dental work will be wrong and you will have to return!
- This town isn't big enough for the both of you.

Stromquist said he didn't expect big laughs, just smirks. Occasionally a customer was offended, but more often they came back and brought their friends to get their own "unfortunes." Stromquist laughingly said that more important than making his restaurant stand out from other Asian restaurants is the fact that he views thinking up the predictions as a hobby, which keeps him amused and happy while he's cooking.

In California, as well as in many other states, first-time traffic offenders have the option of attending school rather than having the ticket go on their permanent record. Offenders are free to choose from a wide variety of state-approved schools. One of the largest is the Lettuce Amuse U traffic school founded in 1985 by Ray and Linda Regan. When the Regans operated a more traditional traffic school, they found that their most successful teachers were the funny ones. They decided to make all their classes funny, but then faced the dilemma of hiring police officers and training them to be funny or hiring comedians and training them in the intricacies of good driving. They opted for the latter approach so that offenders are now given an extra reason for keeping their babies safe in a backward-facing car seat: "If you get rear-ended, you've got a witness." And when another instructor tells how most car accidents happen within 10 miles of home, she adds, "The last time I mentioned that, a guy jumped up in the back of the class and said, 'That's it. I'm moving!'"

Humorous advertising also communicates a laid-back and friendly posture. And as British author Jean-Louis Barsoux points out in his 1993 *Funny Business: Humour, Management and Business Culture,* it has three other benefits. First, both humor and advertising require brevity; second, it opens people's minds so they are ready to consider a new viewpoint; and third, because the audience has to get involved to understand the joke, they will process the message and remember the ad longer. For example, Volkswagen successfully introduced the Rabbit into the United States with a 10-second TV commercial showing two rabbits looking into the camera with a solemn voice stating, "In 1956, there were only two VWs in America."

Some critics think the humor in business movement is simply a fad that will soon fade away. One of the most virulent critics of humor consultants is Scott Adams, the creator of the *Dilbert* comic strip and author of *The Dilbert Principle: A Cubicle's-Eye View of Bosses, Meetings, Management Fads, and Other Workplace Afflictions* (1996). He says, "It's been my experience that when things are well-managed and people aren't under a lot of stress, there's plenty of laughter and creativity." He implies that consultants are confusing cause and effect by trying to insert humor artificially at the wrong end of the process. His belief is that humor comes naturally "after you've done everything else right." The difference in the humor that Adams creates with his anti-boss humor and that which the consultants create is that Adams is coming from the outside and making fun of the failures in business. This is easy to do because businesses portray themselves as struc-

tured and rational enterprises and so deviations are surprising and, depending on one's viewpoint, either maddening or funny. One of the examples Adams gives in his book is the company that bought laptop computers for its traveling employees. To keep them from getting stolen, they permanently attached them to employee desks. Another is a company that simultaneously started two new programs: a random drug-testing program and an "Individual Dignity Enhancement" program.

John Morreall points to the widespread acceptance of Scott Adams's cynicism as a warning sign that things are very wrong. Morreall says that American business will be in deep trouble if everyone follows Adams's "Dinosaur Strategy," which advises "ignoring all new management directives while lumbering along doing things the same way you've always done them." Adams explains that the average life of an organization chart is only six months, which means that you can safely ignore any order that will take six months to complete because "if you wait long enough, any bad idea will become extinct." *See also* ANTIAUTHORITY HUMOR, LEGAL HUMOR, SCHOOL HUMOR

Further reading: Jean-Louis Barsoux, *Funny Business: Humor, Management, and Business Culture* (1993). Malcolm Kushner, *The Light Touch: How to Use Humor for Business Success* (1990). John Morreall, *Humor Works* (1997).

C

Cartoons

Cartoons are drawings intended as caricature, satire, or humor. They differ from comic strips in that they usually contain only a single panel, which, according to gag writer Harald Bakken, means their creators have less than seven seconds to make someone laugh. The word *cartoon* came into existence during the Middle Ages when it was used to describe the life-sized sketches that artists drew on leaves of paper or on cardboard in preparation for making frescos and stained-glass windows. Since the colonization of America, cartoons, with their present-day meaning of a caricature or a humorous drawing, have played a part in public life. In 1754, rumors of a possible war with France inspired Benjamin Franklin to draw a picture of a snake cut into parts. He labeled the head "New England" and put the initials of the other colonies on the various parts. The caption, "Unite or Die," became a rallying cry for those wanting a federal government as opposed to independent colonies.

As the country's first postmaster general, Franklin founded a system that enabled publishers to distribute their magazines and newspapers, and many of these entrepreneurs followed his example of including both written and visual humor. Throughout the 18th and 19th centuries, cartoons were published in almanacs and in satirical newspapers such as *Leslie's Illustrated Weekly* and *Harper's Weekly*. Following the Civil War, political cartoons became such an established part of newspapers that they were credited with swinging the 1884 presidential election toward Grover Cleveland.

Thomas Nast was the most famous cartoonist of the 1800s and is responsible for the American image of Santa Claus and the Republican party's elephant logo. His 1871 cartoons about Boss Tweed and the Tammany Hall corruption in New York City so infuriated Tweed that he ordered, "Stop them damn pictures! I don't care so much what papers write about me. My constituents can't read. But, damn it, they can see the pictures!" Tweed is said to have offered Nast a half million dollars to "study art in Europe." Ironically, Nast chose to stay in the United States, while Tweed fled to Europe only to be arrested and brought back for trial when a Spanish official recognized him from one of Nast's drawings.

As political cartoons gained in popularity, so did nonpolitical cartoons that commented on social relationships, family values, and human psychology. In 1863, Frank Leslie immigrated to the United States from England and established the first American graphic humor magazines: *Budget of Fun*, *Comic Monthly*, and *Phunny Phellow*. The *San Francisco Wasp* and *Wild Oats* were soon competing. *Puck* was founded in 1877 by Joseph Keppler, an immigrant from Vienna. *Life* was founded in 1883, *Judge* in 1885, and the *Chap-Book* in 1894. These publications, along with companies such as Currier and Ives, which printed comic lithographs, provided a medium for such artists as A. B. Frost, C. Jay Taylor, Palmer Cox, E. W. Kemble, T. S. Sullivant, Walt Kuhn, S. D. Erhart, Walt McDougall, James Montgomery Flagg, and Charles Dana Gibson. Out of such works came the "gag" cartoons that now enliven the pages of magazines ranging from *The New Yorker* to *MAD Magazine* to *Parade*. More than any other venue, *The New Yorker*, founded in 1925, has influenced and refined the genre of gag cartoons. Gag cartoons in newspapers may be printed on the same page as comic strips, but they are usually separated from the editorial cartoons.

Cartoon techniques are as individualistic as their creators. Roger Price invented "droodles"—four squares: two black and two white labeled "Chessboard for Beginners," and a black circle with two white triangles spaced across from each other and labeled, "Outside World as Seen by Very Small Man Living in a Beer Can." Shel Silverstein divided his time between writing and illustrating irreverent poetry for kids and making risque cartoons for *Playboy*, while John Callahan, who is a recovering alcoholic with a severed spine, divides his time between developing a reputation as "the high master of rude cartooning" and being a politician in Oregon. In 1996 he ran for the Oregon state legislature saying he "wanted to be Oregon's first 'openly quadriplegic' state legislator."

Cartoonists often hit a sympathetic chord when they go against current trends. Around the time of the World War II when society was beginning to worship technology, Rube Goldberg (1883–1970) became known as "the world's top inefficiency expert." He drew pictures and gave careful instructions for using levers, gears, trap doors, locomotives, moon rockets, safety pins, matches, and occasionally trained fleas for such simple actions as boiling an egg or removing cotton from the top of an aspirin bottle. His name is in today's dictionaries for "a Rube Goldberg contraption," and also appears on the Reuben Award given to the Outstanding Cartoonist of the Year as selected by other cartoonists.

Goldberg was hired as staff cartoonist for the *New York Sun* in 1938 and was awarded the Pulitzer Prize in 1948.

A history book about World War II is hardly complete if it does not contain a "Willie and Joe" cartoon drawn by Bill Mauldin. Mauldin, a regular soldier, first drew Willie and Joe to amuse his barracks mates. But when the woeful pair came to the attention of editors of the army's *Stars and Stripes* newspaper, Mauldin was offered a full-time job as a cartoonist. As Sergeant Bill Mauldin, he was awarded the 1945 Pulitzer Prize, and was again honored as a civilian in 1959 when working for the *St. Louis Post-Dispatch*.

Starting in 1922, a Pulitzer Prize for editorial cartooning has been given every year except 1923, 1936, 1960, 1965, and 1973. At first the award was given for a specific cartoon, but was gradually changed to honor cartoons from the previous year, or more recently, cartoons relating to one subject or the entire body of a cartoonist's work. When Richard Nixon was vice president, he canceled his subscription to the *Washington Post* because he didn't want his daughters to see how the 1979 winner, Herblock, portrayed him. Paul Conrad, the 1971 and 1984 winner, was also on Nixon's "enemies list."

In 1992, Signe Wilkinson, the first, and so far the only, woman to win a Pulitzer for cartoons, responded to an interviewer's question about why there were so few women in political cartooning: "It is a rough game, and women are raised to be nice. . . . You have to take rejection, rejection, and rejection. . . . I get a lot of 'critical' mail. I have been accused of being anti-semitic, anti-Catholic, anti-religion, unfair, and even having arrived at a 'new low.'"

Jules Feiffer, who won in 1986, is quoted as saying that "cartoons are more likely to be effective when the artist's attitude is hostile, to be even better when his attitude is rage, and when he gets to hate he can really get going." Jeff MacNelly, who won in 1972, 1978, and 1985, remarked that he knows "many great cartoonists who if they couldn't draw would be hired assassins."

Because of this hostility, and also because cartoons leave so much room for personal interpretation, they are especially prone to complaints about offensiveness. Editors will often pull a potentially offending cartoon before publication, or if it is published, the cartoonist may be asked to issue an apology or to resign from the publication. Garry Trudeau wrote an op-ed piece for *The New York Times* (Jul. 10, 1994) in which he cited several international incidents of cartoonists, or in some cases their editors, being beaten and jailed. Among the disasters he reported on were the assassination of Palestinian Naji Salim el-Ali, reportedly by the Palestine Liberation Organization, and the suicide in Japan of the target of a political cartoon. Cartoonists say that with all the economic and political pressures that newspapers currently face, editors are loathe to chance offending readers.

This was one of the issues discussed by Rona March in the *Manhattan Spirit* (Jun. 11, 1997) in a two-page cover story, "The Last Laugh," inquiring whether New York's political cartoonists were practicing a dying art. The story was inspired by the salary dispute that resulted in Jules Feiffer's departure after 40 years from *The Village Voice*. The *Voice* had decided to take Feiffer off his $75,000 per year salary and purchase his cartoons through syndication, a practice that many newspapers have resorted to because the cost to a mid-size daily paper for the option of running a syndicated cartoon is about $25 a week, obviously a major savings compared to paying an artist's salary and benefits. The downside for the public is that fewer newspapers have their own cartoonists focusing on local issues, while for cartoonists the downside is that more of them are being forced out of the business. Even when cartoonists independently syndicate their work, their income is doubtful because syndication rates were originally established under the assumption that cartoonists also had a basic salary from a home newspaper.

According to March, at the turn of the century there were 1,000 professional, political cartoonists, but today there are only some 200. The number is even smaller if being a professional is defined as earning at least half of one's income from cartooning. According to a 1997 newsletter published by the Association of American Editorial Cartoonists, in 1980 there were 180 such cartoonists while in 1997 there were only 60. Signe Wilkinson has compared the disappearance of three or four jobs every year to a disheartening game of musical chairs.

At the School of Visual Arts in Manhattan, Jack Endewelt, chair of the Department of Illustration and Cartooning, says his school is the only one in the country that has a cartooning department. However, students "have all but deserted the courses on humor, considered the backbone of any great cartoon" (*New York Times*, Jun. 9, 1997). Instead of looking at cartoons, they are looking at science-fiction or adventure themes or graphic novels. There simply are not enough magazines that carry cartoons to make young people think that either editorial or gag cartooning will be a viable way to earn a living.

For the 1995 annual meeting of the Association of American Editorial Cartoonists, Rob Rogers drew five cartoons illustrating current frustrations. In one, an editor explains to a puzzled cartoonist, "No, 'downsizing' does *not* mean drawing smaller," and in one, a cartoonist explains to his publisher, "I may be expensive but I'm indispensable to the newspaper." The publisher responds: "Is your name *newsprint*?" Under the heading of "Play by the Rules" a cartoonist reads a sign, "No swearing, No nudity, No religious icons, No ethnic caricatures, No racial stereotypes, No sexism, No non-PC humor, No horseplay," and mutters, "Well . . . that leaves weather cartoons." From his editor's office comes a voice, "Careful not to offend God!"

In July and August of 1991, the National Archives in Washington celebrated the 200th anniversary of the Bill of Rights with a display entitled "Draw! Political Cartoons from Left to Right." The 135 cartoons on display were mostly borrowed from collections at the country's eight presidential libraries. Featured cartoonists included Thomas Nast, Bill Mauldin, Herbert Block (Herblock), Pat Oliphant, Jeff MacNelly, and Garry Trudeau.

Also located in Washington, DC, is the National Gallery of Caricature and Cartoon Art, which owns original cartoons by 3,000 artists with a total of 45,000 pieces dating back to 1747.

It is unclear exactly how displays of the future will differ from these current exhibits, but there will undoubtedly be changes related to internationalism. With so much information immediately available through television, e-mail, and the Internet, cartoonists will make more jokes about events outside the boundaries of their own countries. And as worldwide communication increases, more questions will arise about intellectual property rights and plagiarism. On its "Letters" page, the editors of *Witty World: International Cartoon Magazine*, founded in 1978, regularly run complaints and evidence of borrowing and adaptation. This troublesome issue is probably going to worsen because of the ease of photocopying, scanning, and downloading from the Internet. Aspiring cartoonists in the farthest corners of the world now have access to the creative thoughts as well as the actual drawings of their colleagues in every other part of the world.

Creative artists are also likely to think of many new ways to take advantage of computer-assisted drawing, which is already being used to turn photographs into caricatures. Also, how distribution will be affected by the Internet is unclear because several new marketing techniques are being explored. For example, *The New Yorker* now owns *The Cartoon Bank*, which contains a data base of tens of thousands of cartoons, which can be searched through a variety of cross-indexes. The cartoons, only some of which have appeared in *The New Yorker*, are being offered for sale to be used in advertisements, books, direct mail, magazines, newsletters, presentations, product development, and Web pages.

While techniques and distribution methods may change, cartoonists' goals will probably remain much the same because as political issues become more complex and special interest groups become more assertive with their calls for censorship, the com-

"I don't know. George got it somewhere."

This cartoon by James Thurber is one of the thousands offered for sale by the *New Yorker* through its Web-based Cartoon Bank. ©*The New Yorker Collection, 1932, James Thurber, from Cartoonbank.com. All rights reserved.*

munications role of cartoonists may become more important. Because of the ambiguity in their art, cartoonists can often imply things that editorial writers cannot say.

Cartoonists who as of 1998 had been elected to the Hall of Fame of the International Museum of Cartoon Art in Boca Raton, Florida, include

- Peter Arno (1904–1968) for his work with *The New Yorker* as illustrated in his 1945 book *Man in the Shower*.

- Charles Dana Gibson (1867–1944) for his "Gibson girl" drawings and his satirical illustrations for *Life* and *Collier's* magazines.

- Rube Goldberg (1883–1970) for his *Boob McNutt, Foolish Questions, Mike and Ike, I'm the Guy, Lalapalooza,* and *Foolish Inventions* and for founding the National Cartoonists Society.

- Thomas Nast (1840–1902) for being the "father of American political cartooning."

- Frederick Opper (1857–1937) for being the chief political cartoonist for *Puck*, for providing a daily political cartoon for the Hearst papers, and for creating Happy Hooligan, Alphonse and Gaston, and Maud the Mule.

See also ANIMATION, ART, CENSORSHIP, COMIC BOOKS, COMIC STRIPS, MAGAZINES

Further reading: *International Journal of Comic Art* (quarterly). John A. Lent (comp.), *Animation, Caricature, and Gag and Political Cartoons in the United States and Canada* (1994). Wendy Wick Reaves, *Celebrity Caricature in America* (1998). *Witty World: International Cartoon Magazine* (quarterly).

Censorship

Censorship is the examination of materials by someone in authority for the purpose of removing parts that are considered objectionable or harmful or for forbidding an artist, writer, photographer, or performer from making his or her work public. Censorship has a long history, going back to early Rome where two government magistrates, one who counted the people and one who examined and assessed morals and conduct, were called *censors*. Governmental authority and the assessment of morals and conduct are still tied to the concept of censorship; however, the authority to censor is not limited to government officials. In their own realms of authority, school personnel, religious leaders, business executives, and parents all practice censorship as they decide what books, magazines, music, movies, computer games, television shows, and Internet sites they wish to withhold from children.

People in authority in the United States get their power from the public, which means that to some extent their values will reflect the values of the culture. Nevertheless, there are often disagreements over what gets censored because the meanings of such concepts as free speech, selection, appropriateness, taste, kindness, respect, sensitivity, and tolerance differ from one individual to another. And often the people with the power to censor something are not the people who have thought the most about such concepts.

Humor is often censored because people joke about their basic fears connected to sex, religion, politics, ethnic differences, disasters, job security, and status. Even when smiles counterbalance worries, these subjects can make people uncomfortable. Over 2,000 years ago, Plato, in his *Republic*, wrote that amusement caused people to lose control of their rational selves. He advised against abandoning oneself to laughter and wanted all references to laughing gods and heroes to be removed before the stories were presented to young people.

While the United States has no formal body charged with protecting the morals of the country, various agencies have the authority to engage in limited kinds of censorship. After the Civil War, a postal censorship law was enacted that gave authorities permission to inspect reduced-rate mail. The goal was to control political mail, but by the late 1870s, due largely to Anthony Comstock's campaigns for morality, the law was extended to include punishment for using the mails to distribute obscene matter. It was partly because of the threat of this law that U.S. publishers of comic books devised their own self-censorship code.

In 1915, the U.S. Supreme Court ruled that films were basically commercial entertainment rather than political expression; hence, they could be subjected to prior or prerelease censorship. Local boards were established to view films and decide on their suitability for particular communities. Many such committees would recommend deletions before films were shown. To cut down on such disruptions, the 17 major film producers agreed to follow guidelines established by the Hays Office, later renamed the Motion Picture Production Code Administration. For several years, theaters refused to show films that did not follow these guidelines, but then in the 1950s and 1960s foreign films with fewer restrictions began to compete with American films. United Artists chose to back out of the code, antitrust laws made the control of distribution much harder, and other court cases gave support to the idea that movies had free-speech protection. Local censorship boards charged with preapproving movies became a thing of the past; however, police vice squads still make arrests if specific complaints about child pornography or about a film being a danger to society are judged viable. In an attempt to avoid complaints, the majority of American movie makers submit their films for labeling based on age appropriateness, with "mature" and "adult" being used to identify either sexual or violent content and/or language.

The FCC (Federal Communications Commission), established by statute in 1934, was specifically forbidden to engage in censorship but was charged with the responsibility of renewing broadcasters' licenses every three years. Decisions were to be based on whether a competing applicant would provide better service to the general public. Because of limitations on the number of licenses that can be granted, broadcasters have engaged in self-censorship lest they be judged to be harmful to the general public and thereby be in danger of having their license given to someone else.

In the days of vaudeville, government agents often arrested performers under local anti-obscenity laws. Mae West developed her coyness and her skill in innuendo as a way of outwitting government censors sitting in the audience. Belle Barth achieved a similar effect by slipping into Yiddish, something Lenny Bruce also did in the late 1950s and 1960s. However, Bruce was more interested in changing public attitudes toward censorship than in staying out of jail, and so each time he was arrested he used the experience as fodder for future rantings and ravings.

While Bruce was arrested on the basis of his language, people were equally offended at the irreverence of his observations, for example, just after the assassination of President Kennedy he asked if when the shots were fired Jacqueline Kennedy was running for cover or going for help. Bruce's language and observations are not shocking when compared to those of such 1990s stars as Andrew Dice Clay, Eddie Murphy, and Howard Stern, but he was saying such things at a time when the Smothers Brothers lost their comedy show for making mildly critical remarks about the Vietnam War and when Jack Paar walked off his show to protest his network's censorship of an amusing British story in which there was confusion over whether W.C. stood for Wayside Chapel or water closet.

When on 3 August 1966, Bruce was found dead in his bathroom with a needle in his arm, his electric typewriter was still running. It was stopped midway in the sentence, "Conspiracy to interfere with the fourth amendment const . . ." Later comedians, most notably George Carlin, who for years ended his act by shouting out the seven words not allowed on television, carried on Bruce's campaign of making fun of the arbitrariness of censorship.

The United States government generally takes a hands-off approach to humorous criticism of religious matters whether the criticism is offered by cartoonists, comedians, or writers. Because of this, Americans are surprised at the tactics used by other governments as when in 1994 the publication of the two-panel Johnny Hart *B.C.* strip, shown on page 66, in *The Arab News* resulted in lashings, fines, and prison terms for the newspaper's feature editor and editor-in-chief, who had failed to see the blasphemy in Hart's cartoon.

American officials are more concerned with obscenity, especially in protecting young people and those who have not made a conscious choice to see an X-rated movie, buy a pornographic magazine, or log onto a sexually explicit Internet site. An example of the difficulties involved in adapting old laws to new technologies and customs is the way that various states are reacting to the humorous and scatological messages being put on license plates and bumper stickers. Because these are under the control of the individual states, a variety of approaches are being tried. The state of California has compiled a listing of 50,000 number and letter combinations that it judges as possibly obscene and so will not allow on vanity license plates. A Georgia law, now declared unconstitutional, read, "No person owning, operating, or using a motor vehicle in this state shall knowingly affix or attach to any part of such motor vehicle any sticker, decal, emblem, or other device containing profane or lewd words concerning sexual acts, excretory functions, or parts of the human body." The law was rescinded when challenged by a man who was arrested for a "Shit Happens" bumper sticker.

The idea that young people need to be protected from bad role models is the cornerstone of PG-13 and NC-17 age restrictions on movies, the difference between prime-time and late-night television, the

B.C. by johnny hart

GOD, IF YOU'RE UP THERE, GIVE ME A SIGN.

WELL, WE KNOW TWO THINGS:

HE'S UP THERE; AND HE'S GOT A SENSE OF HUMOR.

When this Johnny Hart strip was run in *The Arab News*, both the feature editor and the editor-in-chief were sentenced to lashings and prison terms for failing to recognize the blasphemy. Their sentences were reduced after the incident caused an international furor. *By permission of Johnny Hart and Creators Syndicate Inc.*

"carding" of young people for entrance to comedy clubs, and the many disagreements over what materials should be in school libraries or in the youth sections of public libraries. Among the humorous children's books that have been the subject of school censorship cases are Shel Silverstein's poetry books *Where the Sidewalk Ends* and *The Light in the Attic*; Jerry Spinelli's *Space Station Seventh Grade*; Judy Blume's *Are You There, God, It's Me Margaret?*; Alvin Schwartz's *Scary Stories to Tell in the Dark, More Scary Stories to Tell in the Dark,* and *Scary Stories 3: More Tales to Chill Your Bones*. R. L. Stine's *Goosebumps* books are enormously popular as well as controversial. People who take them seriously are asking that they be censored, while those who recognize the author as the same "Jovial Bob Stine" who writes joke books for kids, are more likely to see the books as humorous, pseudo-scary spoofs of Gothic novels.

The American Library Association publishes a bimonthly *Newsletter on Intellectual Freedom*, which reports on cases of school and library censorship. The general media also report on school censorship cases, such as when singer Barry Louis Polisar's books, videos, and sound recordings were banned from the 70 schools in Anne Arundel County, Maryland, because he uses such words as *doo-doo, pee-pee,* and *poo-poo*. Polisar, who has written over 140 children's songs and recorded for *Sesame Street*, put a warning label on his "Naughty Songs for Boys and Girls": "The songs on this recording have been known to offend some adults. Children are advised to use discretion when exposing grownups to this material." Among his song titles are "A Sick Song (I Got Snot)"; "Don't Put Your Finger Up Your Nose"; "Mom and Dad Aren't Always Right"; and "I've Got a Teacher, She's So Mean." The music committee was not amused at such pandering to children's yen for grossness and their anti-adult sentiments.

In high schools, censorship cases are increasingly focused on students' own writing for school publications and on their productions of video tapes or messages put on the Internet while using school equipment. However, the publishers of school textbooks also practice censorship in hopes of protecting their sales. In a letter to the editor of *English Journal* (Apr. 1997), junior high school teacher John Oster told about reading Ray Bradbury's novel, *Fahrenheit 451*, with his eighth graders. The focus of the book is the ridiculousness of censorship and book burning (farenheit 451 is the temperature at which paper will burst into flames). Oster had a hardback edition, while the students had paperbacks. "When we came to a passage with *damn* in it, the student did not say the word. I assumed he felt uncomfortable swearing, so I said nothing." After the same thing happened again, the teacher took a turn reading. His passage contained *damn, hell,* and *bastard*. A student asked, "Mr. Oster, where are you getting these words? They aren't in our book." When Oster looked at the students' books, "sure enough, they had been omitted." After he got over his embarrassment about the students thinking he had inserted the swear words "to enliven the text," he explained that the paperback publisher probably deleted the swear words so as not to lose sales to a school whose selection committee might disapprove of swear words. Then he told his students that if they ever forgot the meaning of irony, they could "just think back to this situation."

Organizations that work with schools and libraries in support of free speech include

- The American Civil Liberties Union, 132 W. 43rd St., New York, NY 10036
- The Freedom to Read Foundation (affiliated with the American Library Association), 50 E. Huron St., Chicago, IL 60611
- The National Coalition Against Censorship, 2 W. 64th St., New York, NY 10023
- People for the American Way, 2000 M St. NW, Washington, DC 20036
- SLATE (Support for the Learning and Teaching of English) and The Standing Committee on Censorship, National Council of Teachers of English, 1111 Kenyon Rd., Urbana, IL 61801.

See also LEGAL ISSUES, SCATOLOGY AND OBSCENITY

Further reading: Jean E. Brown (ed.), *Preserving Intellectual Freedom: Fighting Censorship in Our Schools* (1994). Herbert N. Foerstel, *Banned in the U.S.A.: A Reference Guide to Book Censorship in Schools and Public Libraries* (1994). Nat Hentoff, *Free Speech for Me—But Not for Thee: How the American Left and Right Relentlessly Censor Each Other* (1992).

Children's Literature

Humor in children's literature occurs in virtually every genre including picture books, poetry, fantasy, biographies, realistic stories, and informational books. Of the thousand titles recommended in the *New York Times Parent's Guide to the Best Books for Children*, nearly one-third are identified as humorous. This fairly representative list contains twice as many humorous books for young children as for preteens. Contributing factors to this difference are that many picture books are built around extended jokes, and even in those that are not, the illustrations may be cartoon style. Also, the humor in books for older children is more subtle and therefore less likely to be identified as the main focus of a book.

While the authors of children's books use many of the same techniques as other authors, the roles that children play in life and their different levels of intellectual maturity mean that a collection of humorous children's books will be quite different from a collection of humorous adult books. One of the ways that children's humor differs from adult humor is that it is more exaggerated. Opportunities abound for humor when things are too big or too little or there are too many or too much. Both Wanda Gag's *Millions of Cats* (1928) and Dr. Seuss's *The 500 Hats of Bartholomew Cubbins* (1938) are stories of too many. In the latter, every time Bartholomew removes his hat to bow to the king, a new one appears in its place. Seuss's first book *And to Think That I Saw It on Mulberry Street* (1937) is a story of too much as Marco exaggerates what he sees on his way home from school.

Sorche Nic Leodhas's *Always Room for One More* (1965), illustrated by Nonny Hogrogian, is about a generous host who welcomes everyone in until his house bursts. It is similar to Jan Brett's retelling of the old Ukrainian tale, *The Mitten* (1989), in which too many forest animals squeeze inside a mitten they find lying in the snow.

Hugeness is the appealing feature of Oliver Butterworth's *The Enormous Egg* (1958), of Glen Rounds' *Ol' Paul, the Mighty Logger* (1949), and of Steven Kellogg's *Paul Bunyan* (1984). Smallness is at the heart of the humor in Mary Norton's *The Borrowers* series (1953–), and in Florence Parry Heide's *The Shrinking of Treehorn* (1971–), and its wistfully comic sequels about a little boy who is getting littler all the time with no one seeming to notice or care.

William Pene du Bois's 1947 *The Twenty-One Balloons* is a classic story of an exaggerated adventure. Professor William

Waterman Sherman sets out from San Francisco in 1883 in a hot-air balloon and three weeks later is found in the Atlantic Ocean with a fantastic story that he won't share until he gets back to make a formal report to his Explorers' Club. The exaggeration in Richard and Florence Atwater's 1938 *Mr. Popper's Penguins*, illustrated by Robert Lawson, is lower key but is just as funny.

While exaggeration runs through virtually all humorous literature for children, authors' other techniques can be divided into four basic, but intermingling, types: antiauthority humor; comedies of manners; intellectual play, which includes fantasy and wordplay; and finally the humor of surprise and incongruity developed through scary, shocking, or verboten references.

Because children are at the mercy of an adult world, they enjoy making fun of adults. When popular author Roald Dahl died in 1990, *Time* magazine quoted him as saying that because "parents and school teachers are the enemy," conspiring with children against adults is "the path to their affections." In *Matilda* (1988), which is one of his most popular books, he portrays the parents as abusive and neglectful. They think of their daughter Matilda as "nothing more than a scab, something you have to put up with until the time comes when you can pick it off and flick it away." When Matilda is old enough to go to school, it is her misfortune to be sent to Crunchem Hall, run by Miss Trunchbull, a diabolical headmistress with a face like a boiled ham, fingers like salamis, and calf muscles as big as grapefruits. The two evil aunts in Dahl's *James and the Giant Peach* (1961) are equally negative representatives of the adult world.

Dr. Seuss is much gentler in his treatment of adults; nevertheless, the plot of *The Cat in the Hat* (1957) revolves around the mischief that the cat leads Sally and her brother into while their mother is away. The mother never knows what happens because the Cat in the Hat miraculously restores order just as she opens the front door. Chris Van Allsburg's *Jumanji* (1981), which was made into a popular 1995 movie starring Robin Williams, has a similar, but more intense, plot.

Much of the appeal of Astrid Lindgren's irrepressible *Pippi Longstocking* (1950) is that Pippi lives on her own and is able to outsmart, and even outmuscle, the grownups who are foolish enough to think they can turn her into an ordinary and pleasant little girl. The hero in Jerry Spinelli's 1991 Newbery Award–winning *Maniac Magee* is similar to Pippi, although tempered by "modern realism."

The conflict between children and authority figures doesn't have to be direct or mean, it can be sympathetic and funny as in Peggy Rathman's 1996 Caldecott Award–winning *Officer Buckle and Gloria*. When Officer Buckle goes with his police dog, Gloria, to give safety lectures to school children, the dog stands behind her unknowing master and performs tricks that make the audience laugh and cheer.

Because children are so often the underdogs, they especially enjoy humor that makes them feel superior or that much closer to adulthood. Beverly Cleary devised her *Ramona* (1968–) books to make 10- and 11-year-old readers feel superior as they laugh at the kinds of mistakes they *used* to make as when on the first day of school Ramona's kindergarten teacher tells her to "sit here for the present," and poor Ramona sits and waits all day for her present.

Alison Lurie in her 1990 *Don't Tell the Grown-Ups: Why Kids Love the Books They Do* conjectures that one of the reasons children love the *Winnie the Pooh* books is that they identify with Christopher Robin, who gets to be an all-powerful, beneficent dictator, or at least the parent figure, for Pooh, Tigger, Eeyore, Kanga, Baby Roo, Owl, and Rabbit.

The greedy children who get their just desserts in Roald Dahl's *Charlie and the Chocolate Factory* (1964) make readers feel superior as the characters do in Harry Allard and James Marshall's *The Stupids Have a Ball* (1971), *The Stupids Step Out* (1978), and *The Stupids Die* (1981). These humorous exaggerations of stupidity are what more than a century ago made Lucretia Hales's *The Peterkin Papers* (1880) so popular.

Humorous mystery and detective stories also fall into this category because readers identify with the smart young detectives who figure out what's going on. It is fun to understand more than do the characters as when readers of James Marshall and Harry Allard's *Miss Nelson is Missing* (1971) catch on that the dreadful Miss Viola Swamp was really the dear Miss Nelson in disguise.

Children identify with the young and the innocent and cheer when they triumph in stories as varied as William Steig's *Doctor De Soto* (1982), Arthur Ransome and Uri Shulevitz's *The Fool of the World and the Flying Ship* (1968), and various versions of *Jack and the Beanstalk*.

While comedies of manners for adults satirically portray the manners and fashions of a particular set of society, those for children show protagonists with lives more interesting than the readers' but whose experiences are close enough to real life that young readers can imagine themselves or their friends in their place. In reaction to the didacticism that was fashionable in books for children during the 1800s, today's authors and publishers say that they do not want to preach to children, but in reality most people who work with children are interested in helping them develop skills and attitudes likely to make for a satisfying life. This means that while the writers of contemporary comedies of manners have entertainment as their primary goal, they also want to show children how *not* to act. At the same time that they are warning children about the wide range of behavior they are likely to meet in the world, they are also helping children develop the ability to cope through laughing at themselves as well as at others.

One of the most entertaining comedies of manners is Barbara Robinson's *The Best Christmas Pageant Ever* (1972) in which the worst kids in town, the Herdmans, who have even been known to smoke cigars and to steal stuff from the Sunday School cupboard, are assigned the best parts in the church Christmas program. Lois Lowry's *Anastasia Krupnik* (1979) and Claudia Mills's *Dynamite Dinah* (1992) also present feisty and funny girls whose antics are real and filled with humor.

Mary Rodgers's *Freaky Friday* (1972) and *Summer Switch* (1982) are comedies of manners exploring a new point of view. The child protagonists wake up in the bodies of their parents and have a whole new world to cope with. Thomas Rockwell's *How to Eat Fried Worms* (1973) is about a boy brave enough to carry through on a ridiculous bet, while John Fitzgerald's *Great Brain* (1967) series is set in frontier Utah and told by "the Great Brain's" little brother. Helen Cresswell is a British writer whose six novels in the *Bagthorpe Saga* (1977–1989) make children feel like apologizing for the ordinariness of their own families.

One of Judy Blume's strengths in such books as *Are You There, God? It's Me, Margaret* (1970) and *Tales of a Fourth Grade Nothing* (1972) is the witty dialogue of her characters. Her fictional children say the things that many readers wish they were articulate enough to verbalize. A book such as Judith Viorst's 1972 *Alexander and the Terrible, Horrible, No Good, Very Bad Day* makes readers laugh at Alexander's frustrations while at the same time lending reassurance that people do survive bad days.

Marc Brown's numerous stories about *Arthur* (1984–) have been made into animated television shows that treat the traumas of childhood (new glasses, a bully in school, losing a tooth, being frightened at Halloween, etc.) in a light way that reassures young children at the same time it makes them smile.

The vicissitudes of friendship are made funnier because of such animals as the huge and awkward hippos in the *George and Martha* (1972–) books by James Marshall and Harry Allard, the petulant innocence of the little badger in the *Frances* (1964–) books by Russell and Lillian Hoban, and the prickly but loving relationship between the two leads in Arnold Lobel's *Frog and Toad Are Friends* (1970–) series.

Beverly Cleary's *The Mouse and the Motorcycle* (1965) and *Runaway Ralph* (1970) appeal to middle-grade children who enjoy the relationship between a human boy and a personified mouse. This is the age group that also loves E. B. White's *Charlotte's Web* (1952) and *Stuart Little* (1945). *Charlotte's Web* is saved from being maudlin by Templeton the Rat, a classic comic villain.

Books that are appealing because of their intellectual play include humorous fantasy that builds on and continues the kind of imaginative play that seems to come naturally to young children. Toys are brought to life in such all-time favorites as A. A. Milne's *Winnie the Pooh* (1926), C. Collodi's *Pinocchio* (1925), and Michael Bond's *A Bear Called Paddington* (1960–). Many fantasy tales are really comedies of manners with the added element of the characters being personified animals as in Kenneth Grahame's *The Wind in the Willows* (1908), Jean De Brunhoff's *Babar* books (1933–), H. A. Rey's *Curious George* (1941–) books, and Else Holmelund Minarik's *Little Bear* (1957–) books. Part of the charm of the *Little Bear* books are the illustrations by Maurice Sendak, who has created such imaginative books as *Where the Wild Things Are* (1963) and *In the Night Kitchen* (1970). Sendak's dream sequences are as creative as the ones in Lewis Carroll's *Alice in Wonderland* (1865) and *Through the Looking Glass* (1871), and as a bonus they are accessible to much younger children.

William Steig's entertaining stories about animals with human sensibilities include *The Amazing Bone* (1976), in which heroine Pearl (a piglet) finds a talking bone that has fallen out of a witch's basket; *Abel's Island* (1976), in which a gentleman mouse impulsively chases his wife's scarf during a storm and is carried off by the elements, not to return for a whole year; and *Sylvester and the Magic Pebble* (1969) whose winning of the Caldecott Award was controversial because the officers of the law are portrayed as pigs— and not very bright pigs at that.

Walter Redfern, in his 1984 book *Puns*, says that children play with words much like they do with toys, and that without humor, they would lack practice in the art of thinking—the most complex and powerful survival tool that humans have. As children fool around, dislocating and reassembling words, they are learning about their language. They appreciate the absurd because it is a way of playing with unusual combinations of ideas, which leads to creative thinking, inventions, and discoveries. Norton Juster's *The Phantom Tollbooth* (1961), illustrated by Jules Feiffer, is a classic example of humor that leads middle-grade children into intellectual games. Milo, the hero, drives his little car through what looks like a regular tollbooth but instead emerges into a mysterious land of science, logic, and wordplay.

The puns and double meanings in nursery rhymes and nonsense verse get children ready for the double meanings of words in the 11 *Amelia Bedelia* (1963–) books by Peggy Parish, illustrated by Fritz Seibel. Amelia is a housemaid who takes everything literally. When she is told to "put out the lights," she hangs the light bulbs outside on the clothesline; when she is told to "dress the chicken," she puts ruffles and a skirt on it; and when she is told to "draw the drapes," she gets out a sketch pad and makes a picture.

Pour quoi folk tales, those that answer "why," stimulate intellectual pleasure, as with Rudyard Kipling's *Just So Stories* (1902). In his retellings of the legends of India, Kipling uses solemn language to provide wildly improbable explanations for how the whale got its throat, the elephant its trunk, and the camel its hump.

Parodies are also mind stretchers because children are expected to remember the original and then savor the changes. In actuality, today the process is reversed for many children who encounter the parodies either in books or on television before they encounter the original. Nevertheless, the best-done parodies, as in Jon Scieszka and Lane Smith's *The True Story of the 3 Little Pigs* (1989), Scieszka and Steve Johnson's *The Frog Prince Continued* (1991), and Scieszka and Smith's *The Stinky Cheese Man: And Other Fairly Stupid Tales* (1992), work for both experienced and inexperienced readers. Scieszka and Lane took a different approach to intellectual humor in their postmodern *Math Curse* (1995).

While no one has been able to give an airtight definition of humor, everyone agrees that it has to include an element of surprise or incongruity. Dr. Seuss provides children with early lessons in incongruity in *Green Eggs and Ham* (1960), as well as in *Horton Hatches the Egg* (1940). In the latter book, Horton the elephant sits for a whole year on lazy Mayzie's nest and hatches her baby bird, which turns out to look as much like an elephant as a bird. With P. D. Eastman's easy-to-read *Are You My Mother?* (1960), kids giggle at how the little bird who hatches while his mother is running an errand sets out to find his mother by questioning a steam shovel, an old car, and whatever else he happens to meet. In Robert McCloskey's *Make Way for Ducklings* (1941), the incongruity of Boston city traffic having to stop while a mother duck leads her babies across the street is so amusing that cities around the country have put up similar duckling signs near their public parks. Trina Hakes Noble and Steven Kellogg's *The Day Jimmy's Boa Ate the Wash* (1980) is about an ill-fated school field trip, while Judi and Ron Barrett's *Cloudy with a Chance of Meatballs* (1978) is a fantastically illustrated story about the magical land of Chewandswallow where meals come from the sky. Their *Animals Should Definitely Not Wear Clothing* (1980) presents equally incongruous ideas and illustrations. Incongruity is also at the heart of Eve Merriam's poems in *You Be Good and I'll Be Night* (1988) and in many of the funny poems in Shel Silverstein's *Where the Sidewalk Ends* (1974), *The Light in the Attic* (1981), and *Falling Up* (1996).

The fun of being surprised is sometimes related to being frightened, but if a story is truly scary, children won't be amused. However, moderately scary stories can be therapeutic because children enjoy getting a little scared and then laughing at their fears. This is part of the reason for the incredible popularity in the 1990s of R. L. Stine's Goosebumps books, along with his Fear Street books for older readers.

A generation ago, the success of Maurice Sendak's *Where the Wild Things Are* (1963) made lovable or misidentified monsters a popular subject as in Roald Dahl's *BFG* (*Big Friendly Giant*) (1968), Mercer Mayer's *There's a Nightmare in My Closet* (1968), and Jack Prelutsky's poetry collections *Nightmares: Poems to Trouble Your Sleep* (1976), *The Mean Old Mean Hyena* (1978), and *Something BIG Has Been Here* (1990).

Alvin Schwartz's and Stephen Gammill's *Scary Stories to Tell in the Dark: Collected from American Folklore* (1981), *More Scary Stories to Tell in the Dark* (1983), and *Scary Stories III* (1991) are junior versions of urban legends. *Bunnicula: A Rabbit Tale of Mystery* (1983) by Deborah and James Howe is a creative spoof on Dracula. A family brings home a bunny that was left in a shoe box at the local theater. An early clue that there is something different about him is that he drains the juice from their vegetables.

Natalie Babbitt's *The Devil's Storybook* (1974) and *The Devil's Other Storybook* (1987) portray the devil as a supernatural Trickster who relieves his boredom by coming to earth and playing jokes on gullible individuals. Other good Trickster stories are *Raven: A Trickster Tale from the Pacific Northwest* (1993) by Gerald McDermott and *Why Mosquitoes Buzz in People's Ears* (1975) by Verna Aardema, illustrated by Leo and Diane Dillon.

Young children can be shocked by very simple allusions. For example, kindergartners' eyes grow big when they imagine Hans Christian Andersen's Emperor without his clothes, and they giggle at the sight of holey socks, boxer shorts, garter belts, and bras in Karla Kuskin and Marc Simont's *The Philharmonic Gets Dressed* (1982). Slightly older children are equally amused when in Harve and Margot Zemach's *Duffy and the Devil* (1973), a Cornish version of *Rumpelstiltskin*, a frustrated devil turns Squire Lovel's newly knit clothes to ashes leaving the squire out on the moor naked except for his boots and the hat he clutches in front of his genitals.

Shel Silverstein's poetry appeals to kids' prurient interests by mentioning such forbidden topics as group baths and various kinds of underwear, including a brassiere for a camel. Roald Dahl is probably the "bravest" author in writing about his Big Friendly Giant who thinks "whizzpopping [farting] is a sign of happiness . . . music to our ears." In Dahl's *The Twits* (1980), Mr. and Mrs. Twit are two of the grossest characters in all of children's literature. Mr. Twit is repulsive and hairy and has a disgusting beard that is a smorgasbord of moldy, rotten, leftover bits of food stuck to his whiskers. Mrs. Twit is ugly mainly because she is filled with "ugly thoughts." In one scene she drops her glass eye into Mr. Twit's beer so that when he gets to the bottom of the glass he is amazed to see it staring up at him. "'I told you I was watching you,' cackled Mrs. Twit. 'I've got eyes everywhere so you better be careful.'"

In conclusion, there is just as much humor (in fact, the percentage may be higher) in children's literature as in literature for adults. The main technique that authors of children's literature use is exaggeration as they develop humor that targets authority figures, puts child characters in comedies of manners, stimulates intellectual play, and amuses children through surprising them with scary, shocking, or verboten references. *See also* ACQUISITION OF A SENSE OF HUMOR, ANTIAUTHORITY HUMOR, CHILDREN'S TELEVISION, GOTHIC HUMOR, LANGUAGE PLAY, POETRY

Further reading: Michael Cart, *What's So Funny? Wit and Humor in American Children's Literature* (1995). Charlotte S. Huck, Susan Hepler, and Janet Hickman, *Children's Literature in the Elementary School,* 5th ed. (1993).

Children's Television

Television humor for children under the age of 12 has been created through many of the same techniques that are used for general audience humor, but there is always a child-oriented slant. Instead of late-night hosts, there are early-morning and after-school hosts, and on most shows designed for children there is an underlying desire to teach children about the world around them. The humor is often used as a bribe not only to keep children watching, but also to turn them into consumers of sponsors' products.

The first three Emmy Awards for children's television (given in 1949, 1950, and 1952) went to station KTLA's *Time for*

Beany, a puppet adventure show later adapted into the *Beany and Cecil* cartoons that played on ABC between 1963 and 1988. The fourth Emmy for children's television, given in 1953, went to NBC's puppet show *Kukla, Fran and Ollie.*

As the years went on, more than 50 percent of the Emmys honoring children's programming went to shows that were mainly or partially humorous; for example, an NBC version of *Jack and the Beanstalk* and several CBS Charlie Brown cartoons. In the late 1960s, NET (National Educational Television), which was soon changed to PBS (Public Broadcasting System), won two Emmys for *Mr. Rogers' Neighborhood,* a show in which a kindly man teaches life lessons to visiting children. In 1970, *Sesame Street,* the now-famous program for preschoolers won its first Emmy, an accomplishment to be repeated at least 10 more times. In the mid-1970s, ABC's special, *Marlo Thomas and Friends in Free to Be . . . You and Me,* was honored along with the new educational programs *Zoom* and *The Electric Company.* Other prize-winning educational programs included CBS's long-running *Captain Kangaroo,* the syndicated *Big Blue Marble,* CBS's *Razzmatazz,* ABC's *Science Rock,* ABC's *Schoolhouse Rock,* and PBS's *Reading Rainbow,* all of which incorporated healthy doses of humor. ABC produced prize-winning animations of Dr. Seuss books as well as *Winnie the Pooh* stories, while in 1983, NBC created *The Smurfs.*

Although not prize winners, shows in which local children would come to a television studio and interact with a host are often popular. Gabby Hayes had such a show between 1950 and 1956, but his popularity came nowhere near that of *The Howdy Doody Show,* hosted by "Buffalo" Bob Smith. Each show had a "peanut gallery" of 40 to 50 child visitors. Bob Keeshon, who at the time was working as a page assigned to keep the audience quiet, was drafted to serve as Clarabell the Clown. Keeshon acted the clown role for four years before leaving and eventually starring as the host of *Captain Kangaroo,* a show that also had child participation, but on a smaller scale. *Howdy Doody* ran for 12 years, until sponsors began moving over to *The Shari Lewis Show* and ABC decided to compete by airing its more lavish *Mickey Mouse Club* in the same time slot.

The Mickey Mouse Club was produced only between 1955 and 1959, but generations are familiar with the show because of reruns and two remakes, one in the 1970s and one in the 1990s. The child participants were not just ordinary kids but performers themselves who belonged to the Mouseketeers. The show started with 27 Mouseketeers (Annette Funicello was the most famous), but the number was cut down to 12 or so in the last two seasons. The Mouseketeers wore Mickey Mouse hats, talked and joked with hosts Jimmie Dodd and Roy Williams, and sang the club song, "Who's the leader of the club that's made for you and me? M-I-C- - K-E-Y, M-O-U-S-E!" The daily format included a "What I Want to Be" interview, a Jiminy Cricket lesson on safety, a Mickey Mouse newsreel, a Mickey Mouse cartoon taken from the Disney vault, and then a theme for the day that might relate to a guest star, a musical performance, a talent round-up, or a surprise.

Some participation shows, for example, *Romper Room* and *Bozo the Clown*, were franchised. Cartoons, films, props, costumes, and suggestions for stories and activities were provided, along with professional training for the hosts. *Romper Room* was a kindergarten of the air that ran in various forms from 1953 to 1991. Standard props included a smiling Jack-in-the-Box, a *Mr. Do Bee* puppet who taught behavior lessons, and a "magic mirror" through which the hostess teacher would pretend to see viewers at home, "I see Susie and Brad, and, oh yes, there's Jennifer too."

In total number of viewers, *Romper Room* is second only to the *Bozo the Clown* programs, which still air in some areas. In 1956, Larry Harmon obtained the television rights for Bozo the Clown, although Pinto Colvig had earlier starred in a year-long program and had made bestselling records. The franchise idea was Harmon's, and during the 1960s he trained 100 Bozo clowns in the United States, plus several in Germany,

France, and Japan. Willard Scott, who went on to become weatherman for the *Today* show, was one of Harmon's Bozo trainees.

In 1984, when the Federal Communication Commission softened its requirements for children's television, many stations no longer felt as motivated to work with children's programming and so they began relying more heavily on network or syndicated productions, including made-for-television cartoons. Although these were expensive to produce, they were affordable because local stations had to pay for only a fraction of the production costs.

Nationally broadcast children's variety shows included the *Soupy Sales Show*, which relied on slapstick and on obvious puns: "Show me a bathing beauty, and I'll show you a girl worth wading for." Before he left children's television to appear on *Hollywood Squares* and in miscellaneous comedy acts, Soupy Sales had been hit in the face with 20,000 pies.

Pee-Wee Herman (Paul Reubens) was host of the innovative *Pee-Wee's Playhouse*, which ran on CBS from 1986 to 1991. He attracted a cult following and was featured in *Rolling Stone* magazine. One viewer survey found that one out of three viewers was over the age of 18. While Pee-Wee was clearly an adult, he dressed and acted like a spoiled child, chanting such lines as, "I'm rubber and you're glue; everything you say bounces off me and sticks to you!"

On today's television, children's humorous programming is aimed at basically three age groups as shown by the language used, the ages of the characters, and the commercials shown between segments. First are the programs for toddlers and preschoolers, next are programs for young school-aged children from ages five through eight, and finally programs for older children from ages nine through 11.

Contemporary programs for toddlers and preschoolers are filled with light-hearted music, happy or silly characters, soothing voices, familiar settings and situations, and theme songs promoting the feeling that every child is loved and the world is a happy place. In such shows as *Barney*, *Teletubbies*, *Bananas in Pajamas* (an Australian import), *Mr. Rogers' Neighborhood*, and *Sesame Street*, the humor is mostly based on surprise, exaggeration, and incongruity. Children giggle at the surprise of a small, stuffed dinosaur changing into the big goofy Barney, while on *Sesame Street* they laugh at the exaggerated size of Big Bird and the incongruity of a Muppet prancing with a professional ballet dancer.

In 1998, PBS brought *Teletubbies* from England to America with high hopes that the Teletubbies would soon be as famous as Barney. The four characters named Tinky Winky, Dipsy, Laa-Laa, and Po are space-age kewpie dolls designed to entertain children who don't yet talk, walk, or even sit up straight. A simultaneous marketing campaign makes it possible for babies to hold one of the dolls while watching the show. Low camera angles give a toddler's view, there is endless repetition, and the dolls use baby talk and play such simple games as peek-a-boo. While some critics have said that the show is a "dumbing down" of children's television, others say that children need time to mellow out, minus the pressure of learning numbers or letters. The show has developed a cult following of adults, who have created their own humor. For example, almost a year before Jerry Falwell announced that Tinky Winky was gay, *Entertainment Weekly* magazine (Apr. 17, 1998) asked, "All right, we've seen the *Teletubbies*. Now what's the deal with the purple one and his purse?" Among those answering the question was *Village Voice* columnist Michael Musto, who said, "Tinky Winky is out and proud. It's a great message to kids—not only that it's okay to be gay, but the importance of being well accessorized." This kind of play is similar to the way that adults have made *Barney* and the gentle Mr. Rogers the butt of jokes and satires.

One of the reasons for the success of *Sesame Street* is its wide range of humor, including allusion and satire. Adult viewers vi-

Few critics have anything but praise for *Sesame Street*, which by now has influenced the sense of humor for at least two generations of American children. *Archive Photos*

sualize the second level of an amusing parody or are reminded of a clever joke. *Sesame Street* also brings in celebrities to interact with puppets and with the children on the show. Young viewers see a straightforward interaction, while older viewers are amused at seeing celebrities in different contexts.

Producers who provide laugh tracks and live audiences know that laughter is contagious. This same contagion occurs during family viewing of television, which provides children with opportunities to develop a mature sense of humor because when they hear their parents and older children laugh, they are stimulated to figure out what is funny.

Children who have started school are attracted to shows like *Arthur*, a PBS animated version of Marc Brown's books about a very "human" aardvark, and *The Magic School Bus*, another PBS animated series in which Ms. Frizzle, an unorthodox teacher whose voice is provided by Lily Tomlin, directs kids in madcap, scholarly adventures. When Ms. Frizzle remarks, "As my cousin Bea always says, 'Pollen's got to travel for its wonders to unravel,'" young children laugh at the rhyme, while older children feel superior because they understand the allusion to bees. Both younger and older children can relate to Ms. Frizzle's funny clothes including her earrings that look like bologna sandwiches and her shoes decorated with miniature beehives. They can also relate to the surprise of suddenly shrinking down to see the inside of someone's stomach or the inside of an electrical wire. Young children, however, enjoy these adventures as fantasy, while older children understand them as simulations of real science.

Such television shows as *Arthur* and much of Disney's *One Saturday Morning* on ABC, which includes *New Doug, Recess, Pepper Ann, Jungle Cubs, Winnie the Pooh*, and *Science Court*, feature characters coping with such real-life predicaments as facing the class bully, falling in love, dealing with show-offs, getting the meanest teacher in school, sleeping away from home, having a divorced parent miss an important event, or experiencing a status change, for example, going from popular to unpopular or vice-versa. Because the solutions to these problems are often not the expected ones, children are amused. They also laugh out of relief that the problem is someone else's and not theirs, and they are comforted to see that such problems can be overcome. Parents identify with the shows because they remember facing such problems when they were children, and they appreciate using the shows as conversation starters with their children. Because they are talking about characters on a television show, they can discuss real-life problems in a light-hearted manner.

Children in the upper grades of elementary school who are approaching puberty and looking forward to becoming teenagers are interested in such issues as friendships, family relations, the value of money, boyfriends and girlfriends, and problems relating to drugs and gangs. Advertisers are pushing for more programming aimed at these children, who are old enough to have their own money and to make their own purchasing decisions. ABC's *Sabrina: The Teenage Witch* is an attempt to reach this age group, but even here the producers have included elements such as Sabrina's magic tricks and her talking cat, which are amusing to children much too young to understand the plot line. Another attempt to please this age group is the programming on the Nickelodeon channel. When in 1996, Nickelodeon held national auditions to find seven child comedians to perform in a kids' version of *Saturday Night Live*, over 2,000 children came for the tryouts. Starting in January of 1999, Nickelodeon and the Children's Television Workshop, the producers of *Sesame Street*, joined forces in a new network called Noggin, which has as its goal helping children feel good about being smart. Initial programming was first directed at preschoolers with a plan to gradually move upwards.

As children grow older, many of them are attracted to the same types of sitcoms, talk shows, soap operas, and variety programs that adults watch. In some families, adults who are uncomfortable about the frankness and sexual references in today's sitcoms have turned to cable television and other sources of reruns so they and their children can watch the "innocent" shows they loved when they were young. *The Andy Griffith Show, My Three Sons, Bewitched, The Beverly Hillbillies, Petticoat Junction, I Love Lucy, The Brady Bunch*, and *The Munsters* work as nostalgia for parents but as fresh comedy for children. *See also* ACQUISITION OF A SENSE OF HUMOR, ANIMATION, CHILDREN'S LITERATURE, PUPPETS AND PUPPETEERS

Further reading: Cary Bazalgette and David Buckingham, *In Front of the Children: Screen Entertainment and Young Audiences* (1995). Wesley Hyatt, *The Encyclopedia of Daytime Television* (1997). Lawrence Jarvik, *PBS: Behind the Screen* (1997). *People's Magazine Entertainment Almanac* (annual).

Clowns

Clowns are costumed characters whose work is to make people laugh in circuses, vaudeville shows, and in many other settings. The word began appearing in English during the 12th and 13th centuries where it was adapted from *cloun* or *cloyn*, meaning "lump" or "clod."

Although the word for *clowns* is fairly recent, the concept has a long history. Many cultures, including some Native American communities, have ritual clowns and contraries whose job it is to demonstrate what respectable people are *not* to do. This kind of comic clown is a Trickster, a jester, a sacred fool with license to break taboos. During the time he is on stage, the clown represents the world turned upside down, the world of Saturnalia, Mardi Gras, or carnival. The clown's mockery, parody, and even blasphemy is not only tolerated, but officially sanctioned.

In ancient Egyptian art going back to 2400 B.C., clowns along with acrobats, jugglers, and animal acts are pictured entertaining nobles and citizens, especially in parade settings. In ancient Greece, clowns had shaved heads and wore padded costumes as they presided at dramas and mime exhibitions. They entertained and distracted audiences, sometimes throwing nuts to the crowds, much as today's clowns throw candies. Their Roman counterparts, who wore ragged patchwork robes and pointed hats, parodied the more serious

actors and served as the targets of jokes played by the actors.

Then, as now, the clown's primary job was to interact personally with audience members and to give them something to watch while performers changed costumes or scenery and made other necessary preparations. Clowns have always had to be flexible and skilled at improvisation because they are traditionally assigned to replace missing performers, cover up accidents, and handle "technical" difficulties.

Throughout Europe during the Middle Ages, probably because life was so miserable and demanding, clowns and the laughter they inspired were found in every royal castle and at every festival and celebration. English medieval mystery plays often contained a buffoon or prankster, one who might even be clever enough to deceive Satan himself. Agrarian audiences were delighted to see rustic, ignorant dolts outwit their "superiors." The court jesters and fools of the time were easily recognized by their distinctive costumes and exaggerated and far-from-normal behavior. Only the jester was allowed to poke fun at the king or express popular opinions through discussions with his alter ego, the miniature kingly scepter he always carried. A wise jester would cleverly do this without inciting the king's anger, and a wise king would pay close attention to the parodies, wit, and satire of his jester. By the late Middle Ages, traveling entertainers began to imitate these court jesters.

During the 15th and 16th centuries in Italy, as the world-famous commedia dell'arte was developed, three basic categories of clowns began to evolve: the Harlequin, the Auguste, and the character clown. In the latter half of the 16th century, the *Arlecchino* (Harlequin) clown started out as a foolish servant and then developed into a more sophisticated, acrobatic prankster. He carried a large stick that was split so that abrupt movements would make the separated parts hit against each other with a loud noise. The dramatic effect of this *slapstick* occurred with little or no harm coming to the person or the thing that was "struck." Harlequin clowns had elegant, patched costumes with symmetrical patterns and a black domino mask covering half of their faces. Today's Harlequin clowns (including mimes) still wear precise, neatly detailed makeup, and a sophisticated demeanor of being "in charge." Their aura of control is sometimes heightened by the contrast of having a "fool" companion, a practice dating back to the late 1600s. This is when Pierrot, a French clown with a bald head, a flour-whitened face, and an always-gullible demeanor, began appearing as the fool for Harlequin straight men.

By this time, the role of clowns in public dramas was well established, and clowns began to appear elsewhere. In the 18th century, Philip Astley became the "Father of the Modern Circus," setting up his burlesque equestrian shows to entertain throughout Britain and Europe. He used clowns to distract the audience while acts were prepared and the animals were calmed down and moved into and out of the performing ring.

Because circus arenas were so large, clowns relied on exaggerated makeup and costumes and used large-scale physical humor (riding, juggling, and tumbling) to be more easily seen and appreciated. But today such technology as film, television, and advanced sound systems makes it possible for some clowns to return to the satire and lyricism of the early court jesters. In Russia, clowns generally did not engage in buffoonery nor wear makeup or costumes, but instead emphasized takeoffs of famous people, facial expressions, and wordplay. Oleg Popov (1930–), a highly admired clown who debuted with the Moscow Circus in 1949, was called the highest-paid "ambassador" the Soviet circus ever had because his political satire both supported and ridiculed the government.

In 1805, Joseph Grimaldi of England first appeared as *Joey* and is given credit as being the first true circus clown. He specialized in classical physical tricks including pratfalls, slapstick beatings, and acrobatics. In the 1860s, a low-comedy buffoon began performing in baggy clothes, oversized shoes, and a big nose under the name of *Auguste*, possibly from a German nickname for someone who is clumsy. By this time, the Harlequin clown had adopted the whiteface makeup of Pierrot, so to be different Auguste clowns wore a light-colored makeup with white used only to highlight the eyes and mouth. Auguste clowns are the ones with the big red noses, baggy clothes, and floppy clown shoes. They do clumsy acrobatics and often play the fool for Harlequin or whiteface clowns. Lou Jacobs (1903–1992) is probably the most famous American example of an Auguste clown and contortionist. He performed for the Ringling Brothers and Barnum and Bailey Circus for more than 60 years. His picture was used in the circus's souvenir literature so that generations of circus-goers are familiar with his classic too-tall face topped with a tiny hat.

At the turn of the century, character clowns were becoming popular. They had such identifiable personalities as tramps, scarecrows, grandmothers, out-of-work gentlemen, and many others. Dan Rice (1823–1900), who wore little makeup with his chin whiskers, top hat, and striped leotard costume, is considered America's first great character clown. He was memorable because of his singing and his skills as a strongman and an animal trainer. Cartoonist Thomas Nast drew a caricature of him, which became the foundation for the "Uncle Sam" image.

In the 1920s, the Fratellini Brothers incorporated all three categories of clowns into their act. Francois was the Harlequin whiteface clown; Albert was the Auguste clown with a nose shaped like a potato; and Paul was the character clown dressed as a lawyer with a top hat, black suit, and monocle. The trio was idolized in France, where they performed for years.

The advent of moving pictures, where the intimate nature of the camera made exaggerated makeup, clothing, and actions unnecessary, helped dignify and popularize the image of the character clown. Charlie Chaplin, the Marx Brothers, and The Three Stooges were all character clowns whose personalities are still loved and imitated. Emmett Kelly's *Weary*

Willie and Red Skelton's *Freddie the Free-loader* were both influenced by Chaplin's "little tramp" image, while Jerry Lewis and Rowan Atkinson (*Mr. Bean*) are popular 20th-century character clowns in their own right.

Historically, circus clowns began as acrobats, aerialists, jugglers, animal trainers, or musicians. They became clowns only after failing at their chosen careers, but they used their already developed skills to make their acts more varied and memorable. Many of today's specialized clowns have similar background skills; for example, rodeo clowns have to know how to manage animals, while the clowns at ice shows have to be superb skaters. To avoid injury, stunt men, especially those who perform before live audiences, must be highly disciplined athletes, race car drivers, and acrobats.

Clown training, in and of itself, has also become more formalized. Only 30 out of every 1,000 applicants are accepted to the Ringling Brothers and Barnum & Bailey Clown College, where for eight weeks they work from 8 A.M. until 10 P.M. with only Sundays off. They practice doing makeup, acrobatics, juggling, prop building, and gag development. For graduation, they are required to do an individual two-and-a-half-hour presentation in front of judges. Organizations working to support the training and professionalization of clowns include Clowns of America International, the International Shrine Clown Association, the World Clown Association, and Clown Camp Inc. A Clown Hall of Fame is located in Delavan, Wisconsin, while clowns are also honored in the Circus Hall of Fame in Peru, Indiana, and in the circus performers' Ring of Fame in Sarasota, Florida.

Clowns' faces must be unique, with each one being a protected trademark that may not be exactly copied. One of the universally accepted "guidelines" is that it is unacceptable for clowns to be seen doing "normal" things like shopping or eating meals while in character, or to appear in public partially out of costume. In keeping with this, when she is on official duty as a nurse, Patty Wooten, creator of the Nancy Nurse character clown, wears an unadorned formica badge reading "Clown: Plainclothes Division."

True clowns protested when one Halloween in Paulsboro, New Jersey, a police officer dressed up as a clown and managed to arrest 12 individuals, most of whom were wanted for routine traffic offenses. He explained that instead of getting the usual "he isn't home" response the clown costume allowed him to go into homes unsuspected. When during a campaign speech, Bob Dole referred to President Clinton as a *Bozo*, Larry Harmon, the creator of the franchised *Bozo* television program, let national news services know that he was not amused to have his name used as an insult.

Most good-sized towns have a cadre of people working as part-time clowns. Street mimes use their bodies and their faces as props, while volunteer clowns visit hospitals and other care centers or take particular programs into schools. They capture children's interest by interacting on a personal level, while they fascinate adults by performing magic tricks and twisting balloons into giveaway souvenirs. Clowns who work commercially host children's birthday parties, hire out to community celebrations, welcome visitors to theme parks, and play such already structured roles as Ronald McDonald for the fast food restaurant chain or Bozo for the syndicated television show.

The newest commercial role for clowns is that of sports mascots. Among the most famous are Paws for the Detroit Tigers, Billy for the Florida Marlins, and the San Diego Chicken for the Padres. Because of the size of sports arenas and fields, these clowns are much like early circus clowns in wearing oversized, one-of-a-kind costumes; practicing exaggerated pantomimes; doing acrobatics; and using huge props. Philly Phanatic rides around on his own dune buggy, while the Phoenix Suns Gorilla makes baskets with the help of a trampoline. These clowns not only work as unofficial cheerleaders, they fill in dead time with their antics, provide photo opportunities, give young children someone to relate to, and work as genuine clowns at community events where they represent the team. *See also* AMERICAN INDIAN HUMOR,

CHILDREN'S TELEVISION, MIMES, PUPPETS AND PUPPETEERS

Further reading: Linda Granfield, *Circus: An Album* (1998).Tristan Remy (trans.), Bernard Sahlins, *Clown Scenes* (1996).

Comedian Authors

One of the publishing phenomena of the 1980s and 1990s was the development of a cadre of authors whose chief qualification to write a book was that they had name recognition. In the trade, these are known as "celebrity authors." While comedians have been among the most successful, not everyone is comfortable with the idea of having celebrity authors as shown by these news summaries:

- In July of 1996, Russell Baker devoted one of his columns to a court case between Random House publishers and television star Joan Collins. Random House had paid her a million or so dollars to write some steamy novels. Now they were asking for the money back and "heaping contumely on her authorial reputation." Russell surmised that the reason they didn't hire a "book doctor" was that Collins had lost her celebritude. He cheered the ruling that went against Random House because "somebody should have to pay for turning literature into sausage."

- Charles Barkley and O. J. Simpson, both "claimed to have been misquoted in their ghostwritten autobiographies—thus inviting jeers, catcalls and obloquy" (*New York Times Book Review*, Jan. 5, 1997).

- Writer Elizabeth Koehler-Pentacoff expressed her frustrations in a funny article she wrote for the *San Francisco Examiner* (Jun. 29, 1997). She had just learned that some marketing departments won't let editors buy a book until they had viewed the author's video clip. Since Koehler-Pentacoff doesn't look like Christie Brinkley, and can't get on *Jerry Springer* because she hasn't had "an affair with a transsexual cross-dressing escaped convict," she was advertising for the reverse of a ghostwriter: someone "22, skinny and sexy. She can spend her time at the gym and the salon, while I slave away at the computer. She'll star in my video clip. After my book hits the shelves, she'll hit the road for the book tours. Meanwhile, I'll be in my old blue bathrobe, writing chapter seven of my next novel."

One reason that comedians have been more successful authors than some other celebrities is that the entertainment industry has always been fluid. Funny writers have been lured to Hollywood and to Broadway both to write for other performers and to become personalities in their own right as with S. J. Perelman and Dorothy Parker. More people knew Will Rogers through his newspaper columns than through his performances, and long before Woody Allen became a performer, movie director, and writer, he wrote jokes. Dave Barry's humorous writing "inspired" the television show *Dave's World,* while Calvin Trillin has been invited to share his humorous writings on television and in one-man shows (*Calvin Trillin's Uncle Sam* [1988] and *Calvin's Trillin's Words, No Music* [1990]) at New York's American Place Theatre. Comedians, who long before the advent of celebrity publishing, increased their incomes and their fame through publishing books include Fred Allen, Steve Allen, Milton Berle, George Burns, Bob Hope, Jack Paar, Richard Pryor, Mort Sahl, and Jonathan Winters.

Another reason for the success of comedians as authors is that they are culture watchers accustomed to looking for interesting and amusing happenings. However, there is a difference between being a comedian and an author because authors are limited to words while performers have help from timing, inflection, and body language, and writers toil in relative isolation, while performers are able to get immediate feedback and to adjust accordingly.

And perhaps most important, comedians are accustomed to working with writers and other team members, and so with a kind of good-natured cynicism they aren't ashamed to admit that as a celebritiy writer they had help. In his *No Shirt, No Shoes . . . No Problem!* (1996), Jeff Foxworthy begins his "Special Thanks" page with "I don't possess adequate words to thank David Rensin for the talent and effort he brought to this project. Without him, you would be reading a pamphlet, not a book." Cartoonist John Callahan wrote on the acknowledgments page of his *Don't Worry, He Won't Get Far on Foot* (1989): "Finally, David Kelly, working from hundreds of hours of my tapes, drafted each chapter and then rewrote it again and again and again and *again* until no trace of his own voice remained. 'We're not going to have one of those goddam *as-told-to* books,' he would snarl. And we don't."

In the big business atmosphere of today's publishing world, some comedians also have a business advantage. The publisher of their book might be affiliated with the owner of their television show and so provides assistance and encouragement because a successful book will aid in the popularity of the TV show. For example, in the introduction to Tim Allen's *Don't Stand Too Close to a Naked Man* (1994), Allen wrote that he really didn't want to write the book because he already felt stretched between television, movies, and the stage, but

> The publisher finally took some drastic measures, which convinced me that being an author would be a wise addition to my resume. Here's what changed my mind about doing the book. Hyperion [his publisher] is owned by Disney, which also owns my television show. Disney owns Disneyland and Disney World. Disney also owns Euro-Disney, Tokyo-Disney, and a Disney store in every city, town, and hamlet in the world. *They also have my cat.*

He ended his introductory chapter with "and if all goes well and you buy lots and lots of copies, maybe Disney will give me back my cat."

In 1998, Jim Koncz, a doctoral student at Arizona State University, studied 10 popular books written by comedians who had also starred in their own television shows. Among his findings were that the books differed considerably in genre and style ranging from the crudeness of Drew Carey's *Dirty Jokes and Beer: Stories of the Unrefined* (1997) to the light and humorous essays in Ellen DeGeneres's *My Point . . . And I Do Have*

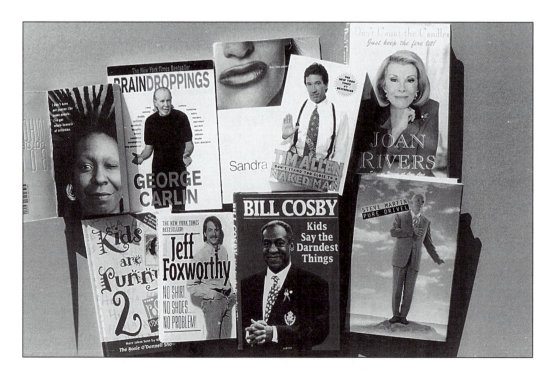

One (1995). He found that the books that sold best were closely tied to the performer's onstage personalities. Koncz agreed with Maureen Golden, a Barnes & Noble executive, who said that "people fall in love with the character; that's who they want to read about." An example is Jerry Seinfeld's 1993 *Seinlanguage,* which stayed on *The New York Times* bestseller list for 33 weeks and was made mostly from revisions of the two- or three-minute monologues that Seinfeld used to set the stage for the events that would follow in his sitcom.

The New York Times "Book Notes" (May 12, 1994) credited the success of Seinfeld's book with encouraging publishers to make book deals with other comedians including Paul Reiser, a star of *Mad about You,* and Brett Butler, star of *Grace under Fire.* When Butler's book *Knee Deep in Paradise* (1996) came out, the sales were somewhat disappointing even though Koncz judged the book to be the best written and to provide genuine information and insights into Butler's real life. Koncz concluded that some buyers may not care as much about the real person as about the comedy character. The only book that had fewer sales among the 10 that Koncz studied was Roseanne Arnold's second book *My Lives* (1994). Her first book written under the name of Roseanne Barr, *My Life as a Woman* (1989), had sold over 450,000 copies in hardcover before going into paperback. Koncz thought the appeal of the 1989 book was that it showed a woman "straddling the edge between brilliance and insanity," much like her comic character. But five years later, Roseanne had slipped over into vitriol and much of the humor was gone. Nevertheless, even the second book made it to 15th place for one week on the *Publishers Weekly* bestseller list.

The potential for financial gain is illustrated by the fact that for three years in a row, the nonfiction division of Bantam Books made its highest profits on comedians' books: Seinfeld's *Seinlanguage* in 1993, Paul Reiser's *Couplehood* in 1994, and Ellen DeGeneres's *My Point . . . And I Do Have One* in 1995.

This annotated list of the books in the photo on p. 80 is intended simply to illustrate how the books one might find on the humor shelves of a local bookstore differ in size, subject matter, genre, tone, and style.

- *Book* by Whoopi Goldberg. Avon paperback, 1998, 286 pp. In keeping with her bare bones title, Goldberg's chapters are such one-word titles as "Fate," "Cost," "Flock," "Love," "Race," "Sex," "Need," "Dick," and "Taste." She promises, "It'll make you laugh—maybe not out loud, but in that place deep down where you know a good joke when you hear one." The hardback version from William Morrow published in 1997 was entitled *Whoopi.*

- *Brain Droppings* by George Carlin. Hyperion, 1997, 258 pp. Carlin's book got lots of free publicity when in August of 1998, Mike Barnicle, a popular columnist for *The Boston Globe,* was fired for using eight of Carlin's jokes without giving credit. The book is a collection of Carlin jokes, lists, observations, riddles, and monologues.

- *Don't Count the Candles: Just Keep the Fire Lit!* by Joan Rivers. HarperCollins, 1999, 194 pp. Rivers dedicates her book "to all the innovative plastic surgeons of tomorrow: Hurray!!!" She uses her typically breezy and self-confident style to advise other women on staying youthful looking. Earlier Rivers books include *Having a Baby Can Be a Scream* (Avon, 1978), *Still Talking* (Avon, 1992), and *Bouncing Back: How to Survive Anything . . . & I Mean Anything* (with Ralph Schoenstein, HarperCollins, 1994).

- *Don't Stand Too Close to a Naked Man* by Tim Allen. Hyperion, 1994, 254 pp. Allen, the star of television's *Home Improvement,* wrote a combination autobiography and sex education manual for adults. It made it to the number one spot on *The New York*

Times bestseller list. His follow-up book, *I'm Not Really Here* (Hyperion, 1996), did not sell as well perhaps because bubbling up from underneath were mid-life frustrations.

- *Kids Are Punny 2: More Jokes Sent by Kids to the Rosie O'Donnell Show.* Warner Books, 1998. The book is copyrighted by the For All Kids Foundation, which receives the profits. It is a result of O'Donnell throwing out an invitation on her daytime talk show asking kids to send in their favorite jokes. Many of them sent along drawings, which are included.

- *Kids Say the Darndest Things* by Bill Cosby. Bantam, 1998, 163 pp. Photos from Cosby's new television show are on the jacket of this book of transcriptions from his conversations with kids. The introduction pays tribute to Art Linkletter, who had the original *Kids Say the Darndest Things* television show. Earlier Cosby books include *Fatherhood* (Berkley, 1987), *Time Flies* (Bantam, 1988), and *Love and Marriage* (Bantam, 1990),

- *May I Kiss You on the Lips, Miss Sandra?* by Sandra Bernhard. Rob Weisbach Books/William and Morrow, 1998, 209 pp. In keeping with Bernhard's name recognition, the title of the book is printed on the cover one-eighth the size of her name and almost small enough to fit in the crack between her luscious lips. Inside, there's lots of white space and room for contemplation between her musings, essays, poems, favorite quotes, and one-liners.

- *No Shirt, No Shoes, No Problem!* by Jeff Foxworthy. Hyperion, 1996, 366 pp. Foxworthy had written seven books before this one, but while they were spin-offs from his stand-up comedy act, this one is more of an autobiography and is filled with anecdotes and joking observations on his image as a southerner.

- *Pure Drivel* by Steve Martin. Hyperion, 1998, 104 pp. Martin took three years off from acting and while vowing to do "nothing and leave myself alone about it," he wrote two screenplays and a handful of fresh and sophisticated sketches, most of which were published in *The New Yorker* before being gathered in *Pure Drivel*. Sample titles include "Taping My Friends," "The Paparazzi of Plato," "How I Joined Mensa," and "In Search of the Wily Filipino."

See also SITCOMS, STAND-UP COMEDY, TELEVISION

Comedy Teams

Comedy teams are made up of two or more performers who work together under a group name that has either been purposely coined or has developed in the manner of a nickname. Forty-three out of the approximately 500 entries in Ronald L. Smith's *Who's Who in Comedy* (1992) are about comedy teams. Teams have the following advantages over individual performers:

- Teams are often more recognized and more memorable than are the individuals who make up the teams.

- Good "chemistry" enhances creativity and enjoyment.

- Through interacting with each other, team members can revitalize old gags.

- Differing appearances, personalities, and voices provide for contrast and for the efficient creation of stock characters.

- With teams, audiences can enjoy both surprise and anticipation because while teams do new material they usually have a style that carries over from one performance to another.

Since the 1600s, clowns have performed in teams, but the teams were based more on types than on individuals, such as when a Harlequin clown would work with a tramp or a fool clown. In vaudeville and burlesque, most partnerships were also based on types as when a comic villain was paired with a young innocent, a bossy wife with a picked-on husband, a sexy young woman with a gullible old man, and so forth. But as publicity became more important in recruiting audiences and permanent records were made of performances, first through sound recordings, then on radio and on film, successful partnerships became a way for individuals to gain fame and stand out from the competition.

No standard pattern exists for comedy teams, and their creation, organization, management, and reputations are as varied as the individuals who make them up.

Savoy and Brennan (Bert Savoy [stage name of Everett McKenzie] and Jay Brennan) got together in 1913 to do campy performances in which McKenzie was a bold and forward female impersonator. Mae West is thought to have imitated Savoy's exaggerated mannerisms and to have adapted his signature line, "You *must* come over!" **Moran and Mack** (played by George Searchy, Charles Sellers, and sometimes Jack Swor), also known as the Two Black Crows, competed with dozens of whites performing in blackface. Their first hit was in the 1917 Broadway show, *Over the Top*. They continued performing and making comedy records through the 1920s. **Miller and Lyles** (Flournoy E. Miller and Aubrey Lyles) were a popular African American comedy team who in the 1920s were both praised for their mainstream humor and criticized for not being "black enough." They hoped to get their own radio show but were turned down by WGN in Chicago, which later produced the *Amos 'n' Andy* show featuring white performers (Charles Correll and Freeman Gosden) pretending to be Black. **Duffy and Sweeney** (Jimmy Duffy and Fred Sweeney) also worked in the tough world of 1920s vaudeville where they played and lived the parts of heavy-drinking, hard-fighting roustabouts.

In the early days of film, group style was demonstrated by Mack Sennett's **Keystone Kops**, played by Charles Avery, Bobby Dunn, George Jesky, Edgar Kennedy, Hank Mann, Mack Riley, and Slim Summerville, plus, on occasion, Fatty Arbuckle, Bobby Vernon, and

Eddie Sutherland. In the 1940s, the **East Side Kids,** a grown-up street gang, made comedies for Monogram Studios. Tough-guy stars Leo Gorcey and Huntz Hall were masters at mangling the English language; other members included Bennie Bartlett, William Benedict, Stanley Clements, Gabriel Dell, David Gorcey, Billy Halop, Bobby Jordan, Bernard Punsly, and Ernest "Sammy" Morrison.

When radio broadcasters found that different voices were needed to keep an audience listening, male and female teams had a natural advantage. Between 1933 and 1949, the **Easy Aces** (Goodman Ace and Jane Ace) teamed up as a smart husband and a dumb wife. When Goodman said he didn't want his wife to work, she countered that he was giving her an "interior complex" and that she had worked her "head to the bone" and "desecrated" her life to him.

The Aces' humor was similar to that of **Burns and Allen** (George Burns and Gracie Allen), but Burns and Allen had something special that made them one of the most beloved husband-and-wife teams in the history of comedy. They teamed up in vaudeville and then went on to succeed in both radio and television where George was only one of the millions who fell in love with Gracie. When

George Burns and Gracie Allen were so famous as a team that after Gracie retired in 1958, few people imagined that George Burns would ever again be a star, and, in fact, it took him two decades to rebuild a career. *CBS Photo Archive/Archive Photos*

she retired in 1958, her picture was on the cover of *Life* magazine, and her 1964 death was featured on the news display board at the World's Fair.

The development of radio and film also increased the need for more humor. In vaudeville, performers could work for years using the same basic set of jokes and gags because each night they worked in front of a different audience. With radio, new jokes were needed on a daily basis, and one way to bring in variety and surprise was to replace the telling of jokes by a single person with their presentation in the form of skits and dialogues.

In 1931, **Lum and Abner** (Lum Edwards played by Chester Lauck and Abner Peabody played by Norris Goff) began broadcasting from a local Arkansas radio station. Lum ran the Jot-Em-Down Store in the fictional town of Pine Ridge, Arkansas, where Abner and such other townspeople as Doc Miller, Squire Skimp, and Cedric Wehunt (played with different voices by Lum and Abner) would drop in. The show stayed on the air for 23 years, serving as a model for the kind of rural humor later seen on television's *Green Acres* and the *Andy Griffith Show*. To take advantage of the fame of what was arguably the most famous town in Arkansas, the town of Waters, Arkansas, changed its name to Pine Ridge.

In movies, **Stan Laurel and Oliver Hardy** were living proof that incidents were funnier when acted out than when told as anecdotes. They began working together when Laurel was asked to replace an injured Hardy in a 1926 movie; their continued association grew from this venture. Their first masterpiece was the 1927 *Battle of the Century*, famous for its pie fight. Their trademark was reciprocal violence, beautifully illustrated in the 1929 movie *Big Business* in which they sell Christmas trees and happen to get the top of a tree caught in a prospective customer's door. When they ring the doorbell to ask the homeowner to release the tip of their tree, the homeowner clips it off. Laurel and Hardy respond by cutting off the man's tie. In the 20-minute film, Laurel and Hardy demolish the man's house brick-by-brick, while the man takes their delivery truck apart and reduces their trees to kindling.

Another aspect of teaming that Laurel and Hardy illustrate is the value of contrast. Laurel was British and would blink his eyes and look bewildered, then scratch the top of his head, and when all else failed, dissolve into infantile weeping. Hardy was short and fat with a cherubic face and a small mustache. His specialty was changing whatever situation the two were in from bad to worse; after which he would look at Laurel and say, "Well, here's another nice mess you've gotten us into." In a parody of this signature line, a *New York Times* headline read, "For Fans, A Nice Mess of a Convention to Get Into." The story was about the 1994 international convention of the Sons of the Desert being held in Tarrytown, New York. The organization was founded in 1964 as a Laurel and Hardy fraternal appreciation society and was named after the team's 1933 feature film in which Laurel and Hardy sneak off without their wives to a Shriners-like convention.

As the pace of Laurel and Hardy's work slowed, **Abbott and Costello** (Bud Abbott and Lou Costello) took their place with quick moving comedy routines perfected through a decade of work in vaudeville. They succeeded in transforming burlesque routines into successful radio performances, and from there they went into the movies. Their wordplay, along with Costello's amazing pratfalls, made them the most popular comedy team of the 1940s. Their "Who's on First?" routine always sounded fresh because while they had to remember that *Who* is on first base, *What* is on second base, *I Don't Know* is on third base, and *I Don't Give a Damn* is the shortstop, they varied the other details thereby forcing each other to concentrate. They would sometimes add new characters and create names for a catcher, a pitcher, and three outfielders. Besides their work on stage and radio, they made 34 films in 16 years and in 1952–1953 had a television show.

Names play a surprisingly important role in the success of comedy teams. Some teams, in fact, are little more than a name as when journalists led the public to call Frank Sinatra, Dean Martin, Sammy Davis Jr., Peter Lawford, and Joey Bishop the **Rat Pack**, based on their Las Vegas clowning both on-

and off-stage during the early 1960s. Lauren Bacall had coined the name for husband Humphrey Bogart's drinking gang, which included Frank Sinatra. After Bogart's death, Sinatra kept the name alive by founding his own circle of well-known buddies.

Between 1946 and 1956, **Dean Martin** had been phenomenally successful in a 10-year comedy partnership with **Jerry Lewis**. The two met when Lewis was the master of ceremonies at a club where Martin was appearing as a new singer. Lewis got laughs by breaking into Martin's songs, and Martin, although not thrilled, adjusted good naturedly to the interruptions. Later when Martin accepted an invitation from Lewis to perform at the Club 500 in Atlantic City, the audience response was so enthusiastic that Martin and Lewis became a team and replaced Bud Abbott and Lou Costello as America's favorite comedians. However, Martin never liked playing the straight man to Lewis, and when in 1956 they announced they had played their last date together, the public was disappointed but not surprised. Both men went on to individual careers undoubtedly made more successful by the fame they had achieved as a team.

Robert Elliott and Raymond Goulding, under the team name of **Bob and Ray,** had a career that spanned 40 years. Their first show was the 1946 *Matinee with Bob and Ray* on Boston radio station WHDH. They specialized in role-playing and parodies, which simultaneously glorified and made fun of life's everyday dreariness as when they portrayed a man who was proud of his ability to imitate vegetables, did a commercial for "The House of Toast," visited a pair of "nonidentical Siamese twins," reported on the Slow Talkers of America, and interviewed a champion low-jumper. As their fame increased, Bob and Ray took movie parts, created a successful advertising agency, starred on Broadway in a two-man show, and parodied such celebrities as Walter Cronkite (Walter Chronic) and Arthur Godfrey (Arthur Lordly). When Ray died of kidney failure in 1990, Bob said, "I think the main reason we worked well together was that we really appreciated each other, as opposed to some comedy teams. We had no rivalry, just great mutual respect."

Mike Nichols and Elaine May, who performed together for only four years, are another example of the importance of "good chemistry." The two had the ability to slip into and out of a large repertory of characters, changing their voices, language, and body movements with incredible precision. They were the comedians chosen to perform at the Madison Square Garden birthday party for President John F. Kennedy where Marilyn Monroe sang "Happy Birthday." When brought together for a 1996 PBS *American Masters* special, Mike Nichols reminisced on the casual way they had decided not to do a sitcom that Desi Arnaz and Lucille Ball had offered them. He said they were probably just too young to appreciate the success they had. They both continued with careers in show business working more behind the scenes as writers and directors. Susan Lacy, executive producer of the *American Masters* special said about Nichols and May that "in their own way, they were a watershed. There isn't a working comedian today, from Woody Allen to Robin Williams, who doesn't say that Nichols and May opened their eyes. Whenever there's creative work that lasts, it's because it has an essential humanity that does not age."

When teams break up, there are so many variables that it is hard to determine how much of their later success is based on the name recognition of the team. For example, when **Cheech and Chong** (Richard Marin and Tommy Chong), who were described as the Bob and Ray of the scruffy drug culture, broke up in 1985, Tommy Chong did not seem to be particularly advantaged over Richard Marin. The *I Love Lucy* show made Lucille Ball's name a household word, but because in the show Lucille went by her real name while her husband Desi Arnaz went by the fictional name of Ricky Ricardo, many people thought of **Lucy** and **Ricky** as the comedy team. However, this was somewhat counterbalanced by the couple choosing *Desilu* as the name of their production company.

In the 1960s, the name **The Smothers Brothers** helped people remember Tom and Dick Smothers's signature act, which consisted of variations on the theme of sibling rivalry, but later on, it worked against their branching out as individual performers and also against their changing the nature of their act. **The Marx Brothers** did not suffer from any such restrictions partly because there were five of them and partly because from the beginning they stressed their differences. Their names (Chico, Harpo, Gummo, Zeppo, and Groucho) were cleverly chosen to be a set while still communicating individuality. Harpo had his demented faces and his magical sight gags, while Groucho had his zany singing and dancing and his punchy one-liners. Zeppo played the straight man to Groucho, while Chico had his amusing piano playing, his outrageous Italian accent, and his bad puns. Between 1929 and 1949, the Marx Brothers made 13 films, several of which became classics. Groucho used his fame with the group as the foundation for his own television career as the host of *You Bet Your Life*, where for 10 years he entertained a new generation.

How difficult it is to connect the names of performers whose team name differed from the individuals' names is illustrated by how many people remember famous team names, but not the performers' names from old time radio. For example, almost everyone has heard of **Fibber McGee and Molly** and perhaps Molly's signature line, "T'ain't funny, McGee," but few people remember the names of Jim Jordan and Marian Driscoll. **Vic and Sade** were praised by poet Edgar Lee Masters for providing "the best American humor of its day," but few people know that Art Van Harvey and Bernardine Flynn played the roles.

However, comedy teams with neutral names have a kind of flexibility not allowed those named after specific individuals. For example, dozens of children were members of the **Our Gang** movie team, whose name was changed to **The Little Rascals** when it moved to television. The best known were Scotty Beckett, Darla Hood, Spanky McFarland, Frederic "Sunshine Sammy" Morrison, Billy "Buckwheat" Thomas, Alfalfa Switzer, and of course, Petey, the dog with the circle around one eye. The series began

as short films in 1922 and continued in one form or another until 1944. This long life meant that individual children outgrew their roles and had to be replaced. Something similar happened to **The Three Stooges**, who made some 200 short films for Columbia from 1934 to 1958. As the group aged and had health problems, they brought in substitutes for one or the other of the original team. The basic group consisted of brothers Moe and Curly Howard, and a friend Larry Fine. Alternates included Shemp Howard, Joe Besser, and Joe DeRita.

A team that illustrates modern approaches to naming is the 1970s British group called **Monty Python's Flying Circus**. Members included Graham Chapman, John Cleese, Terry Gilliam, Eric Idle, Terry Jones, and Michael Palin. When they received their first contract to do 13 shows for BBC, the question of a name came up. During months of discussions, they considered Owl Stretching Time, Gwen Dibley's Flying Circus, and Bum, Wackett, Buzzard, Stubble and Boot. When the BBC asked for "something sensible," John Cleese said, "How about something slimy, like a python?" Eric Idle thought the name "Monty" sounded like a slimy music hall agent and the group agreed: they had found their name. Between 1969 and the early 1980s, when they went their separate ways, the group was phenomenally successful. At a 1998 reunion in Aspen, Colorado, attended by all but Graham Chapman, who died in 1989, Eric Idle complained, "We'll be ex-Pythons even after we're dead." *See also* BLACKFACE COMEDY, CLOWNS, MOVIES, PUT-DOWNS AND REJOINDERS, RADIO

Comic Books

Comic books, in the usual sense, are newsprint booklets telling visual stories in comic-strip format. They vary in size from tiny miniatures to oversize pages, but most of them are in the neighborhood of 8 by 10 inches with between 16 and 64 pages. They developed as an extension of the comic strips that since the 1890s have been popular features in newspapers. By the turn of the century, enterprising newspapers were reprinting their recent comic strips, binding them together, and selling them through newsstands on a monthly, bimonthly, or quarterly basis. Because they were dated and sold regularly, the term *comic magazine* was also used.

Comic books with original material and with a whole book focusing on a single strip did not appear until the 1930s. The first one, *Funnies on Parade* (1933), was distributed as an advertising giveaway by Proctor and Gamble. The next year, Max Charles Gaines, a salesman for the Eastern Color Printing Co., repackaged comic strips into a book called *Famous Funnies*, which he sold for 10 cents. The success of this commercial venture inspired competition, and in February of 1935 *New Fun Comics* was published, consisting solely of original material. The name was eventually changed to Adventure Comics, which today continues to publish both *Superman* and *Batman*. In 1936, Popular Comics came out with *Dick Tracy, Terry and the Pirates*, and *Little Orphan Annie*. King Comics (1936) developed *Flash Gordon, Mandrake the Magician*, and *Popeye*, while Ace Comics (1938) developed *The Phantom*. This costumed hero was imitated by dozens of others because creators knew that readers liked to be able to imagine themselves as the real people behind the masks and the exotic clothing.

The terms *comic strips* and *comic books* became so firmly entrenched that they continued to be used even when creators moved away from the kinds of humorous events and jokes that had been the norm in such "innocent" strips as *Mutt and Jeff, The Yellow Kid*, and *Krazy Kat*. Today *comic strip* is more a description of format than of editorial content. This change in meaning was furthered by the development of comic books. When strips ran only in newspapers, the daily interruptions and the limited number of frames discouraged creators from working with complex plots. Comic books provided both an opportunity and an obligation for writers and artists to create fuller characters and to tell more complex stories complete with introductions, conflicts, resolutions, and denouements.

By the end of the 1930s, not only humor but adventure, magic, fantasy, detective, and Wild West stories were all being expressed pictorially through comic books. Decreased economic and health standards and the disheartening effects of the Depression made readers long for happy romance stories, while rising inner-city crime and the violence of World War II encouraged readers to turn to crime and horror stories, counterbalanced by adventure comics and patriotic stories such as Jack Kirby's *Captain America* and *Fighting American*. An increased interest in technology, chemical warfare, and outer space encouraged the development of science fiction comics and superheroes, some of whom had been radioactively mutated.

How fast the industry grew is shown by the fact that the number of comic books being published rose from 60 in 1940 to 168 in 1941. At United States army posts, 10 times as many comic books were sold as the combined totals of such standard magazines as *Reader's Digest, Saturday Evening Post*, and *Life* magazine. This period between 1938 and 1945 is generally considered to be the "Golden Age" of comic books.

In 1938, Joe Shuster and Jerry Siegel introduced **Superman**, who is considered to be the first comic superhero and the model for every superhero since. Readers were attracted by the action and the fantasy more than by the dialogue, which was somewhat stilted. Because of Superman's success, in 1940, Will Eisner was asked to create a costumed superhero. He agreed to draw a mask and gloves, but refused to "dumb down" his new creation, *The Spirit*, which was launched as a 16-page syndicated newspaper insert that became a classic. To appeal to the whole family, Eisner used adult humor and subtlety with allusions to movies, literature, and philosophy. Steve Ditko gave his **Amazing Spider-Man** (1962) superhero a sense of humor. Shy teenager Peter Parker gets his magical powers when he is bitten by a radioactive spider. He is guilt ridden because of failing to stop a fugitive who later kills his uncle. He consequently decides to devote his life to fighting crime, but quickly learns that with supernatural power comes supernatural responsibili-

The Amazing Spider-Man was an awkward and unsure teenager whose power came from being bitten by a radioactive spider. *Spider-Man: ™* and © *1999 Marvel Characters Inc.* Used with permission.

ties. Even though he was a hero, as a forerunner to the *Archie* comics, he was besieged by the kinds of problems teenagers could relate to; for example, "If this doesn't take the cake!! I can't go out in public as Spider-Man until my mask is sewn up, and when it comes to sewing, I'm all thumbs!" *The Hero Defined: MAGE* and *The Tick* are contemporary satires of superhero comic books. While *The Tick* has the attention span and the interests of an eight-year-old, he also has superpowers and the intellectual help of his sidekick, Arthur, the Moth-Man.

Early comic books, as well as current ones, rely on situation humor. Carl Barks, who in 1940 created **Donald Duck** and his nephews Huey, Dewey, and Louie, along with Uncle Scrooge McDuck, for *Walt Disney Comics and Stories*, at first relied on sight gags, pratfalls, and muggings, but as the characters developed, he put them in exotic situations calling for creative solutions to bizarre predicaments. For authenticity of settings, he researched encyclopedias as well as *National Geographic* and *Scientific American* magazines.

A less obvious type of comic-book humor is autobiographical, in which the creators exaggerate their own past experiences, observations, fantasies, and desires. Readers identify with the characters because they have had similar experiences, as with the overeating that was the impetus for the surrealistic dreams in Winsor McCay *Dreams of the Rarebit Fiend* (1905). Today, adult collectors and historians get an extra measure of pleasure from being able to associate incidents in a strip with the life of a particular artist or writer. Many comic books are created by teams rather than by individuals, and in the early days, when comic books were considered neither great art nor respectable literature, many creators hid behind pseudonyms or worked anonymously. Historians are now going back to search for running gags and idiosyncrasies that will allow them to know just which artist or writer was responsible for a particular drawing or story line. In addition to the individuals mentioned elsewhere in this entry, early contributors to the development of the comic book include C. C. Beck, Milt Caniff, Jack Cole, Bernard Krigstein, Harvey Kurtzman, Alex Toth, Basil Wolverton, and Wallace Wood.

By the 1950s, comic books were being designed for and read by war veterans and young married couples in addition to average 12-year-old children—mostly boys. Concerned parents created a demand for censorship, the British Parliament outlawed the importing of American comic books, and the U.S. Senate appointed a Subcommittee to Investigate Juvenile Delinquency as encouraged by comic books. Parents and teachers were especially concerned about such books as William Gaines's *Crypt of Terror*, *The Vault of Horror*, and *The Haunt of Fear*. In 1954, partly to protect themselves from outside censorship and from lawsuits, comic-book publishers formed an association and established the Comic Authority Code, which continues to monitor the editorial content and advertising allowed in comic books. As a result, the number of devoted comic-book readers declined sharply and the industry of underground comics was born.

Underground comics are created and published by individuals or small companies that choose to bypass industry standards and mainline marketing. In underground comics (or *comix* from co-mix of image and words) such topics as drugs, sex, violence, racism, elitism, blasphemy, risque music, bodily functions, and crude language are made light of rather than preached against. For example, Robert Crumb, known to many as "the Father of Underground Comix" from his work in the late 1960s, puts himself in many of his comics as a neurotic recluse obsessed with taking sexual advantage of large women, a topic offbeat enough to surprise and either amuse or offend readers. His most famous characters, the "Keep on Truckin" guys (who have come to represent a laid-back, hang-in-there feeling) and "Mr. Natural" (the good conscience we all have that sometimes goes astray), are more socially acceptable and more universally appreciated. Crumb's "Keep on Truckin" image with its shrunken head and enlarged feet came from his L.S.D.-distorted view of people in general. According to Crumb, he was simply drawing what he saw, and his fans made an icon out of it. Two other crudely amusing Crumb characters are Fritz the Cat and Devil Girl.

Gilbert Shelton is another drug-inspired underground comics writer of the 1960s whose *Fabulous Furry Freak Brothers* featured three dope- and sex-hunting heroes. It was a well-received parody of the 1960s hippie culture, designed to entertain, not preach. Shelton also created *Wonder Wart-Hog* as a parody of superhero comics. In some circles, the term *alternative* is replacing *underground*, and people are talking about *serious comic art* in reference to such comics as *Acme Novelty Company, Artbabe, Berlin, Black Hole, Bone, Dirty Plotte, Eightball, Jimbo, Love and Rockets, Minimum Wage, Palestine, Palookaville,* and *Yummy Fur.*

In 1994, *The New York Times* "Arts & Leisure" section (Nov. 20, 1994) devoted most of three pages to a feature on how women cartoonists are transforming the underground comic universe. An example is Diane DiMassa's *Hothead Paisan, Homicidal Lesbian Terrorist.* In one strip, Hothead is sitting on a park bench and a man sitting next to her carelessly lets his leg touch hers. She quickly whips out an ax and chops off the man's leg.

The contentious issues that were brought up about comic books in the 1950s are still discussed today; however, they are discussed without so much fervor because comic books no longer play such a dominant role in children's entertainment. While most children still know and talk about characters from comic strips and comic books, chances are they met these characters through television, movies, or toys rather than through comic books. One of the defenses mounted for comic books in the 1950s was that they taught children to read. The pictures and the balloons coming from characters' mouths helped children comprehend more complicated stories than the ones they read in straight type. Because of these aids to reading comprehension, many organizations produce comic books filled with persuasive or educational messages. While teaching at the School of Visual Arts in New York, Will Eisner worked on the side for 25 years creating educational and promotional comics. Subjects for such "comic" books range from maintenance instructions for new cars, to prevention of sexually transmitted diseases, to messages against smoking, drinking, and drugs. Over the last 40 years, Californian Jack Chick has drawn and published a series of religious tracts in the form of comic booklets about the size of baseball cards. These books have been translated into 43 languages, and while their production cost is 13 cents per booklet they are distributed free by church members who tuck them away at highway rest stops and leave them in motels, on buses, at pay phones, and even in rental bowling shoes. Each cover has a startling drawing and a dramatic title; for example, "Gomez Is Coming," "Doom Town," "Somebody Goofed," and "The Death Cookie." Popular culture authority M. Thomas Inge suggests that the appeal of the tracts lies in "the seeming paradox: the idea that comics are subversive contrasted with the message of good contained within."

At the opposite end of the spectrum from these comic booklets are coffee table books in the form of beautifully printed, bound collections of comic strips. They usually have introductory and explanatory comments by the creators as in *Pluperfect Pogo* by Walt Kelly (1987), *The Calvin and Hobbes Tenth Anniversary Book* by Bill Watterson (1995), *Bloom County Babylon: Five Years of Basic Naughtiness* by Berkeley Breathed (1986), and *Bugs Bunny: Fifty Years and Only One Grey Hare* by Joe Adamson (Holt, 1990). These books are so far removed from the penny dreadfuls, the chap ("cheap") books, the dime novels, and other pulp fiction that are the ancestors of today's comic books that few people even think to call them comic books.

Books halfway between cheap giveaways and the coffee-table extravaganzas are the medium-sized collections printed in both hard and soft bindings such as Charles Schulz's various collections of *Peanuts* strips including *Happiness Is a Warm Puppy, Home Is on Top of a Dog House, I Need All the Friends I Can Get*, and *Security Is a Thumb and a Blanket*. Scott Adams's *Dilbert*, which in the mid-1990s was "arguably the country's hottest comic strip" has also been collected and marketed under various titles. The *Wall Street Journal* (Sep. 17, 1996) described the best-selling collection *The Dilbert Principle* (1996), as "part comic collection, part management-book parody, and all anti-boss." It was used as a textbook in business classes at the University of Chicago and was described by the director of Emory University's CEO College as "being talked about more than any single management book."

While the dubious heritage of comic books and the confusion over whether "comic" is describing content or format have in some cases enticed readers to consider messages they might have initially rejected, they have also worked against the full-fledged acceptance of what publishers call *graphic novels*. Many people were shocked when Art Spiegelman won a Pulitzer Prize for his 1986 *Maus*, in which he used a comic-book for-

mat to retell his father's Holocaust memories through humanized mice. Spiegelman's success encouraged mainstream publishers to take a new look at the genre and to publish other graphic novels. However, sales were disappointing so that the publication of graphic novels (also called serious comics) reverted to such speciality publishers as Fantagraphics Books, Kitchen Sink Press, and Drawn & Quarterly Publications. In 1998, Tom DeHaven, a professor at Virginia Commonwealth University who teaches a course in the graphic novel, complained in an article for *New York Times Book Review* (May 31, 1998) that "while commercially this is comics' Great Depression, creatively it's one of the most fertile periods in decades." DeHaven had to work hard to cut down the list of graphic novels that he wanted to teach. Among the dozen-plus that he settled on were Howard Cruse's *Stuck Rubber Baby*, Jason Lutes's *Jar of Fools*, Chester Brown's *I Never Liked You*, and Gilbert Hernandez's *It's a Good Life if You Don't Weaken*. DeHaven described the term *comics* as "an unfortunate, as well as an ineradicable name" that has come to be as much of an umbrella term as *movies*. Today's comics encompass "everything from *Beetle Bailey* and *Spider-Man* to Robert Crumb's nakedly autobiographical rants and Harvey Pekar and Joyce Brabner's memoir, *Our Cancer Year*." *See also* ART, CARTOONS, COMIC STRIPS, GOTHIC HUMOR, MAGAZINES

Further reading: M. Thomas Inge, *Comics as Culture* (1990). John A. Lent (ed.), *Comic Books and Comic Strips in the United States: An International Bibliography* (1994). Richard Reynolds, *Super Heroes: A Modern Mythology* (1992).

Comic Strips

Comic strips are open-ended dramatic narratives told through a series of drawings about a recurring set of characters. Although they are now enjoyed around the world, they were invented in America a little over a century ago. Much of the action is shown through character dialogue printed in all-capital letters set in balloon outlines and occasionally supplemented by narrative text. Beginning in the late 1890s, comic strips, also called "the funnies," were printed serially in newspapers, but today some of them appear first on the Internet or in mass market comic books or in the publications of special interest groups.

While the exact date that a humorous drawing was turned into a "comic strip" is disputed, most people agree that the first successful comic strip was *Hogan's Alley* (soon called *The Yellow Kid*) by Richard F. Outcault (1863–1928). Outcault had worked as a scientific and technical illustrator for Thomas Edison's laboratories, but wanted to combine his drafting skills with his keen observation to create comic art. In April of 1895, Joseph Pulitzer's *The World* agreed to carry his one-panel work, *Hogan's Alley*.

Outcault's timing was fortunate because *The World* had just purchased a color press with the intention of reproducing great art pieces. However, the color separations were not fine enough for art and so the decision was made to use the new technology for humor. One of the characters in *Hogan's Alley* was a buck-toothed street urchin with protruding ears and a shaved head, a typical practice used to protect slum children from head lice. His name was Mickey Dugan, but because a pressman took it upon himself to color his oversized shirt yellow, he was called *The Yellow Kid*. Outcault printed The Kid's statements on the front of his shirt and below the drawings. Bill Blackbeard, who wrote the text for the 1995 centennial book *R. F. Outcault's The Yellow Kid*, described The Kid as "the first great newspaper comic character" and the "lucrative predecessor to Maggie and Jiggs, Popeye, Blondie, the Gumps, Dick Tracy, Flash Gordon, Buck Rogers, and Charlie Brown and Snoopy."

Many of the first comic strip characters were naive innocents placed by their creators in amusing situations. Besides *The Yellow Kid*, Rudolph Dirk's *The Katzenjammer Kids* and James Swinnerton's *Little Bears and Tigers* featured "ignorant" children or animals that were able to outsmart adults and other "intelligent" characters. The writers used nonstandard English to represent the foreign accents, dialects, or uneducated speech patterns of their characters. This use of innocents, as depicted by their language, amused new immigrants because they recognized familiar speech patterns and variations on their own struggles to learn a new culture, and they cheered when the innocents put one over on their unsuspecting victims. More sophisticated Americans were amused because they could laugh at the ignorant ways of children, foreigners, and the uneducated even though the "sophisticates" were the ones being duped in the end.

This tradition was continued in the 1930s and 1940s by such great comic strips as Jack Coles's *Home in the Ozarks* and Al Capp's *Li'l Abner*, two strips about offbeat hillbilly families; in the 1950s by *Our Gang*, featuring kids who sometimes outwitted smart animals and always outwitted dumb adults; and by Walt Kelly's *Pogo Possum*, a surprisingly astute observation of American politics and social situations.

When the 100th anniversary of the comic strip was celebrated in 1995, *The New York Times*, which is one of the few newspapers that does not carry comic strips, saluted comics "from a distance." An editorial writer pointed out how in the 1930s such storytelling was banned in Italy by Mussolini, while in the 1950s comic books were investigated by U.S. Senator Estes Kefauver of Tennessee. When radio arrived, comics were counted for dead, again their demise was predicted when movies started to talk, and then again when television programming was developed. But from all appearances, they are alive and well with 86 million adults and 27 million kids being regular readers.

A problem for today's artists is shrinking space. In the 1930s, a typical Sunday comic page would be divided into five rows with either three or four boxes in each row. Today's pages are more likely to have eight strips with between three and six boxes in a strip. Daily papers are even more condensed with some using a split-page format so that a single page might contain over 20 strips. One reason is that most of the cities that used to have two or more competing newspapers now have just one. People no longer decide which paper they will buy based on their comic strip preferences; instead, editors try to include as many as possible so as to please different constituencies as with Greg Howard's *Sally Forth* for feminists, Rick Kirkman and Jerry Scott's *Baby Blues* for new parents, and Jerry Scott and Jim Borgman's *Zits* for teenagers.

Artists, including Berkeley Breathed and Bill Watterson, who retired while their comic strips were still highly popular, mentioned the small panels as a contributing factor to their decision to quit, while Charles Schulz has laughingly said the reason he never puts adults in *Peanuts* is that they would bump their heads.

In comparison to the first generation of comic strips, today's cartoonists are disadvantaged in having no room for the kinds of complicated details that went into *Rube Goldberg's Inventions*, the beautiful dream-like drawings that Winsor McCay prepared for *Little Nemo in Slumberland*, the crowded scenes and dialogue in Rudolph Dirks's *The Katzenjammer Kids*, the conflicts and insults in Bud Fisher's *Mutt and Jeff*, the full cast of characters in George McManus's *Bringing up Father*, and the stark and eerie landscapes that set the stage for George Herriman's *Krazy Kat*, which has been described as America's contribution to Dada art.

Nor do today's artists have the space to develop the kind of suspenseful drama that went into the next generation of cartoons, which in the 1920s and 1930s moved away from slapstick comedy into adventure; for

Today's comic strips are so squeezed for space that few characters get to be as wordy as were *Mutt and Jeff* in 1919 (this five-panel strip has been divided into two rows for this illustration). *Mutt and Jeff by Bud Fisher.*

example, Roy Crane's *Wash Tubbs*, Richard W. Calkins and Phil Nowlan's *Buck Rogers*, Vincent Hamlin's *Alley Oop*, Chester Gould's *Dick Tracy*, Milton Caniff's *Terry and the Pirates* and *Steve Canyon*, Harold Gray's *Little Orphan Annie*, Harold Foster's *Prince Valiant*, Alfred Andriola's *Charlie Chan* and *Kerry Drake*, and Harold Foster and Burne Hogarth's comic strip adaptation of Edgar Rice Burroughs's *Tarzan*. The kind of human interest stories now mostly enjoyed through television soap operas came into the comics through Allen Saunders and Dale Connor's *Mary Worth*, Dahlia Messick's *Brenda Starr Reporter*, Stanley Drake's *The Heart of Juliet Jones*, and Nicholas Dallis's *Rex Morgan, M.D.*, *Judge Parker*, and *Apartment 3-G*. In 1942, Jerry Siegel and Joe Schuster created *Superman*, soon to be followed by *Batman*, *Captain Marvel*, and *Spider-Man*, all superhuman heroes who fit into the American penchant for such real life exaggerations as Davy Crockett, Wild Bill Hickok, Buffalo Bill, and John Henry.

In the 1950s, Chic Young's *Blondie* was the most popular comic strip in the world, and is said to have been the model for television's family-oriented sitcoms. Al Capp satirized American foibles through his hillbilly comedy of *Li'l Abner*; Walt Kelly's *Pogo* set new standards for art work and intellectual stimulation; while Mort Walker's *Beetle Bailey*, Johnny Hart's *B.C.*, Hart and Brant Parker's *The Wizard of Id*, and Dik Browne's *Hagar the Horrible* proved there was no end to imaginative settings. More recently, personified animals have been the chosen characters for Jeff MacNelly's *Shoe*, Jim Davis's *Garfield*, Berkeley Breathed's *Bloom County*, and Bill Watterson's *Calvin and Hobbes*.

In March of 1996 when the International Museum of Cartoon Art opened in Boca Raton, Florida, some of the creators whose comic strips were being featured were interviewed by the *Miami Herald* (Mar. 3, 1996). Jim Davis, creator of *Garfield*, said, "If you found a newspaper in an archaeological dig 100 years from now, I don't know if the headlines would tell us as much about what made us tick as the comics. They cut through the

rhetoric, the jargon, and get right to the subject matter. . . . They're brutally honest." Jerry Robinson, who drew *Batman* in its early years and created the character of The Joker, said that "comics are part of American history, American journalism. They've permeated our culture—from Broadway plays and songs to TV and film. *Annie* and *Li'l Abner* on Broadway. Movies based on *Dick Tracy*, *Superman*, and *Batman*. They all started as comics." Stan Lee, co-creator of *Spider-Man*, said, "There's virtually nobody who hasn't read a comic strip," while Cathy Guisewite, creator of *Cathy*, said, "It isn't that this museum elevates comic strips—they're elevated already. They're important. But this museum gives them the credit they should have."

In the summer of 1997 when the Pathfinder landed on Mars, NASA scientists named specific rocks *Casper*, *Scooby-Doo*, and *Yogi*. These comic names join other words from the cartoon world that have been adapted into American English: a *Dagwood* sandwich, a *Mickey Mouse* college course, a *Rube Goldberg* contraption, a *Buster Brown* haircut and *Buster Brown* shoes, and most recently, a *Dilbert* situation. Cartoonists have also created a whole vocabulary of onomatopoeic words including *Zap! Ka-platz! Smak! Boinggg! Pow! Klank! Pam!* and *Kazaam!* They also popularized the use of specific words and phrases ranging from Billy DeBeck's 1920s Barney Google sayings, "Heebie Jeebies," "horse feathers," and "Sweet Momma"; to Al Capp's 1950s "Sadie Hawkins Day" and "Kickapoo Joy Juice"; to Walt Kelly's 1971 Pogo statement, "Yep, son, we have met the enemy and he is us."

Garry Trudeau has his *Doonesbury* characters reach through comic borders and touch real life. In January of 1992, when he lampooned President Bush for adopting Texas, which has no state income tax, as his home, over 10,000 readers applied to the state of Texas for "out-of-state residency." State Comptroller John Sharp responded with a humorous "certificate of citizenship" in an envelope marked, "For state income tax purposes only (And then only if you can get away with it)." The message invited those who

Garry Trudeau is well known for addressing controversial subjects in *Doonesbury*. *Doonesbury* ©1986 Garry Trudeau. Reprinted with permission from Universal Press Syndicate. All rights reserved.

couldn't "get away with it," to "kiss Aunt Tillie goodbye and move on down here to God's own country, where the grass grows tall and the wind blows free and anyone who says 'income tax' gets his mouth washed out with soap." In October of 1996, California's Attorney General Dan Lundgren did not respond so good-naturedly when Trudeau's Zonker Harris made fun of the way a San Francisco emporium selling marijuana to chronically ill people was shut down.

Because comic strips both reflect and shape culture, it is to be expected that they will be influenced by many of the same social factors that are affecting society at large. In the 1980s, Mort Walker's *Beetle Bailey* came under fire from feminist critics who thought his presentation of Miss Buxley was sexist, while in 1991 Dean Young (son of the founding artist Chic Young) decided that it was time for Blondie to join the 61 percent of American mothers who hold jobs outside the home. "Popeye Falls Off His Pedestal" was a 1995 *Wall Street Journal* headline on a story about Popeye's waning popularity in America. Karal Ann Marling, a University of Minnesota art historian, explained that Popeye with his "I yam what I yam an' that's all that I yam!" is "the Mike Tyson of cartoon characters—a brute." His image doesn't fit with current American sensibilities, even though he's still selling eyeglasses in Italy, spinach soup in Brazil, toilet paper in Australia, and skateboards and youth magazines in Japan.

Other recent changes have made the world of cartooning more inclusive. "Blondie, meet Herb and Marcy" was the headline on a 1992 *Time* magazine story about how African American cartoonists are tickling the public fancy in newspapers across the country. Recently syndicated are Ray Billingsley with his *Curtis* strip, Stephen Bentley with *Herb & Jamaal*, Rob Armstrong with *Jump Start*, and Barbara Brandon with *Where I'm Coming From*. The cartoonists sketch situations that affect people of any race, but with a distinctively Black sensibility not always appreciated by editors. Morrie Turner, who for years has drawn *Wee Pals*, complained that editors don't really "want a black strip. They want a *Peanuts* in Coppertone."

In the first days of comic strips, artists were overwhelmingly all men. Early on, Dahlia Messick, the creator of *Brenda Starr Reporter* changed her name to Dale Messick because she thought women were not welcome as cartoonists. There are still many more male than female comic strip artists, but women are being published and, in the process, are bringing changes to the field as shown in the 1993 publication of *A Century of Women Cartoonists* by Trina Robbins and two 1994 New York shows: *Comic Power* at Exit Art and *Bad Girls* at the New Museum of Contemporary Art. Nicole Hollander, who draws *Sylvia*, told a *New York Times* reporter that she adores "relationships like a political cartoonist adores politicians when they make grievous mistakes." While she realizes that most of her readers are women, she nevertheless fantasizes about the *Pinedale Roundup* in Wyoming, the smallest of the 60 papers that run her cartoon. She likes to imagine "all these cowboys sitting around reading *Sylvia*."

Comic strip creators who as of 1998 had been elected to the Hall of Fame of the International Museum of Cartoon Art include

- Dik Browne (1917–1989) *Hi and Lois* and *Hagar the Horrible*
- Milton Caniff (1907–1988) *Terry and the Pirates* and *Steve Canyon*
- Al Capp (1909–1979) *L'il Abner*
- Roy Crane (1901–1977) *Wash Tubbs*, *Captain Easy*, and *Buzz Sawyer*
- Billy DeBeck (1890–1942) *Barney Google*
- Rudolph Dirks (1877–1968) *The Katzenjammer Kids* and *The Captain and the Kids*
- Budd Fisher (1885–1954) *Mutt and Jeff*
- Harold Foster (1892–1982) *Tarzan* and *Prince Valiant*
- Chester Gould (1900–1985) *Dick Tracy*
- Harold Gray (1894–1968) *Little Orphan Annie*
- George Herriman (1880–1944) *Krazy Kat*
- Walt Kelly (1913–1973) *Pogo*
- Winsor McCay (1869–1934) *Little Nemo in Slumberland*
- George McManus (1884–1954) *Bringing up Father* (Maggie and Jiggs)
- Richard Outcault (1863–1928) *The Yellow Kid* and *Buster Brown*
- Alex Raymond (1909–1956) *Flash Gordon, Jungle Jim, Secret Agent X-9*, and *Rip Kirby*
- Charles Schulz (1922–) *Peanuts*
- Elzie Segar (1894–1938) *Thimble Theater* and *Popeye*
- Jimmie Swinnerton (1875–1974) *Little Bears, Mr. Jack*, and *Canyon Kiddies*
- Mort Walker (1923–) *Beetle Bailey, Hi and Lois, Boner's Ark*
- Chic Young (1901–1973) *Blondie*

See also CARTOONS, COMIC BOOKS, HUMOROUS ICONS, INTERNET INFLUENCES, MAGAZINES

Further reading: Bill Blackbeard (ed.), (introduction) *R. F. Outcault's The Yellow Kid: A Centennial Celebration of the Kid Who Started the Comics* (1995). Robert C. Harvey, *The Art of the Funnies: An Aesthetic History* (1994). Alice Kominsky-Crumb and Diane Noomin (eds.), *Twisted Sisters* (1990).

Comic Zeitgeists

Comic zeitgeists are the jokes that reveal the spirit of a particular time. (*Zeit* is the German word for "time" while *geist* means "ghost" or "spirit.") While one of the values of humor is that much of it transcends time and place to reveal the universality of the human experience, there are also connections between the humor that a society creates and cherishes and what is occurring at the moment to affect living conditions and the cultural beliefs and values of the society. For example, America's tall tales from the 1800s were unique to frontier conditions, just as today's urban legends are unique to a high-tech society where most people find themselves living in cities among people who for the most part are strangers.

In his book *Cracking Jokes*, anthropologist Alan Dundes explains that there is "no more direct and accurate way" of discovering a people's collective mind "than by paying attention to precisely what is making the people laugh." Among the zeitgeists of the 1970s and 1980s were the social laws attributed to both mythical and real wise men. The most famous was Murphy's law, "If anything can go wrong, it will," which was extended to "When left to themselves, things always go from bad to worse," and "If anything can go wrong, it will, and even if it can't it might." O'Toole, another of the mythical wise men, offered the commentary, "Murphy was an optimist," to which Damon Runyon added, "In all human affairs, the odds are always six to five against."

People enjoyed these witty, compact, and unequivocal laws, which were declared with such confidence that they inspired both belief and imitation. They parodied C. Northcote Parkinson's 1957 *Parkinson's Law* and 1960 *The Law and the Profits* and J. Lawrence Peter and Raymond Hall's 1969 *The Peter Principle: Why Things Always Go Wrong*. Although, "the Peter Principle" was too complex to fit into one pithy sentence, many people were familiar with the basic idea that in every hierarchy—government, business, or whatever—each employee tends to rise to a level of incompetence. That is, as long as people are doing well, they will be promoted, which means that workers are constantly being put in new jobs for which they feel only marginally prepared. They therefore find comfort in such "laws" as Marshall's Generalized Iceberg Theorem, "Seven-eighths of *everything* can't be seen," and in Paul Herbig's Principle of Bureaucratic Tinkertoys, "If it can be understood, it's not finished yet."

In *The Humor Prism in 20th Century America*, Mac E. Barrick writes about Helen Keller jokes as a comic zeitgeist that began in the 1960s, but that peaked after the 14 October 1979 NBC presentation of William Gibson's play *The Miracle Worker,* starring Melissa Gilbert and Patty Duke Astin. Gibson's play about Helen Keller was first produced on the CBS *Playhouse* in 1957 and on Broadway during the 1957 and 1958 seasons, while the movie opened in 1962 and was shown sporadically on television. Throughout this time, there were some Helen Keller jokes, but according to Barrick, the real popularity came when the 1979 production of the play coincided with the passing of Public Law 94–142, the Education for All Handicapped Children Act, which mandated that crippled, blind, and deaf children were to be "mainstreamed" into public schools. Having disabled children in regular classrooms was a change that affected virtually all children in America, and it is to be expected that discomforts and tensions would be relived through the making of jokes. Barrick thinks that "lacking a well-known public figure of an amputee or wheel-chair rider . . . , students seized on Helen Keller to provide a universally recognizable focus for their physical-disability humor." Because she was multiply handicapped and had lived among ordinary people, she was an ideal subject. The jokes fell into two categories. Those about blindness included references to Helen Keller's new book, *Around the Block in 80 Days,* and to how she burned her face while "answering the iron." References to her deafness and the use of sign language included

What did Helen Keller's parents do when they caught her swearing?
They washed her hands with soap.

Why did Helen Keller fall out of a tree?
She was yelling for help.

Barrick concluded that the Helen Keller jokes helped to erase the pity normally felt toward disabled people, and hence contributed to the success of the Handicapped Children Act, because "how can you hate someone who makes you laugh?"

Historian Joseph Boskin concludes his 1997 book, *Rebellious Laughter,* with a "Tattered Dreams" chapter where he discusses today's version of the Frankenstein story, in which "the roseate years of expansion" that followed World War II collided with such scientific and technological failures as the near meltdown at the Three-Mile Island nuclear plant in Pennsylvania; the radioactive explosion at the Chernobyl plant in Russia; the contamination of the town of Love Canal near Niagara Falls in New York; the explosion of the *Challenger* space shuttle and subsequent NASA failures; the Union Carbide chemical leak, which killed thousands in Bhopal, India; innumerable oil spills including the massive one from the *Exxon Valdez* in Prince William Sound, Alaska; famines in Ethiopia and other places, and the dangers of deteriorating infrastructures in big cities, railroads, highways, bridges, and dams. Added to these technologically related problems were such social disasters as drug problems, sex problems, suicides, murders, and economic misfortunes.

Boskin quotes a multitude of jokes relating to these catastrophes that "overwhelmed sensibilities from the late 1970s into the 1990s." The jokes are proportionately as extreme as were the disasters, as they offered "the specter of a totally irrational universe," where the only defense was to engage in what Gunter Grass has labeled "a hellish laughter." For example:

What is the weather forecast in Kiev?
Overcast and 7000 degrees.

What does an Ethiopian call his dog?
Dinner.

Did you hear the good news/bad news about drinking water in the year 2000?

> *The bad news is that in the year 2000 the only drinking water will be recycled sewage. The good news is that there won't be enough to go around.*

What were Christa McAuliffe's last words to her husband?

> *You feed the dog and I'll feed the fish.*

What do you call a guy who has syphilis, herpes, AIDS, and gonorrhea?

> *A hopeless romantic!*

These jokes are obviously tied to time, place, and mood, even though many of them are adaptations of earlier jokes and will probably be readapted to fit future events. Other popular kinds of jokes that have been identified as comic zeitgeists include the racial riddles and "Polack" jokes that were popular from the 1950s through the 1980s, the JAP (Jewish American Princess) and JAM (Jewish American Mother) jokes, and the ubiquitous *How many . . . does it take to screw in a light bulb?* jokes. While the form of light bulb jokes will also be discussed under "Joke Patterns," Daniel Harris, writing in *The New York Times Magazine* (Mar. 23, 1997) under the title "How Many Light-Bulb Jokes Does It Take to Chart an Era?" made the point that light-bulb jokes reflect U.S. political history of the last half of the century. He said that the light-bulb joke "mirrors our ambivalent attitudes toward technology" while at the same time being "the epitaph for an obsolete class of household slaves and the patriotic battle hymn of the bedraggled housewife and the diligent handyman." Harris started with the old joke of the 1950s:

> How many Polacks does it take to screw in a light bulb?
>
> > *Five—one to stand on a table and hold the bulb in the socket and four to rotate the table.*

His use of the word *Polack* earned him a protest letter from the Anti-Bigotry Committee of the Polish American Congress in Brooklyn. After this example, he went on to the 1960s with the joke about "How many psychiatrists. . . ? Only one, but the light bulb has to really *want* to change." From the 1970s, "How many feminists . . . ? One, and that's not funny!" From the 1980s, "How many Reagan aides . . . ? None—they like to keep him in the dark." From the early 1990s, "How many baby boomers . . . ? Ten—six to talk about how great it is that they've all come together to do this, one to screw it in, one to film it for the news, one to plan a marketing strategy based on it, and one to reminisce about mass naked bulb-screwing in the 60s." From the late 1990s, "How many computer hardware engineers. . . ? Thirty—but of course just five years ago all it took was a couple of kids in a garage in Palo Alto."

Harris concluded that "the fact that a single joke is used to belittle the supposed deficiencies of minorities and the esoteric skills of the intelligentsia suggests that, in some sense, we equate the tensions caused by ethnic conflicts with the tensions caused by the new hierarchies of knowledge." *See also* DISABILITIES AND HUMOR, ETHNIC HUMOR, GENDER AND HUMOR, JOKE PATTERNS, URBAN LEGENDS

Further reading: Joseph Boskin, *Rebellious Laughter* (1997). ——— (ed.), *The Humor Prism in 20th Century America* (1997). Christie Davies, *Jokes and Their Relation to Society* (1998). Barry Sanders, *Sudden Glory: Laughter as Subversive History* (1995).

Computer Humor

Computer humor comes in two categories. One is humor about computers, while the other is the "humor" that is being programmed into computers by some of the brightest minds in the world. These scientists are not interested in equipping robots with stand-up comedy routines; instead, they are using humor as a tool for creating and testing artificial intelligence. Humor is among the most sophisticated forms of everyday language, and understanding even the simplest of jokes requires a computer to be programmed with a myriad of cultural references and expectations along with the ability to simultaneously test dozens of possible interpretations before settling on the one that is intended to be funny. It is even more challenging to program a computer to create a joke.

In 1996 the computer science department at the University of Twente in the Netherlands devoted its annual Workshop on Language Technology to an international conference on Automatic Interpretation and Generation of Verbal Humor. Titles of some of the presentations give an indication of the kind of work being done: "Why Do People Use Irony?—The Pragmatics of Irony Usage," "Password Swordfish: Verbal Humour in the Interface," "Computer Implementation of the General Theory of Verbal Humor," "Humor Theory beyond Jokes: The Treatment of Humorous Texts at Large," "Speculations on Story Puns," "Relevance Theory and Humorous Interpretations," "What Sort of a Speech Act Is the Joke," "A Neural Resolution of the Incongruity-Resolution and Incongruity Theories of Humor," "Humorous Analogy: Modeling the *Devil's Dictionary*," "Why Is a Riddle Not Like a Metaphor?" and "An Attempt at Natural Humor from a Natural Language Robot."

The second kind of humor is the humor that people create about computers. However, some of this is insider humor that the general public either doesn't understand or doesn't appreciate. Alan H. Schoenfeld, a math professor at the University of California, Berkeley, gives the example of arriving at a conference in Sydney, Australia, and being handed the key to his room, number 1024. "Wow!" he laughingly said as he showed the key to his wife. She looked blank. He showed it to two other attendees; one looked blank while the other one brightened up, smiled, and offered congratulations. Schoenfeld was amused that he had discovered a way to find out who was at the conference as a computer person and who was there for some other reason. The number 1024 has special meaning for computer experts because it is 2^{10}, which in computer language equals a megabyte. Most English speakers are so accustomed to working with a base-10 system, that the base-2 system of computer language simply does not register as meaningful.

In the 1980s, when computers were making the big leap from corporate to personal use, people used jokes to vent their frustrations over working with a technology that they didn't quite understand or control. For example, the computer building at Stanford University is named the Margaret Jacks Hall, but students refer to it as the *Marginal Hacks Hall*. Frustrated users gave the IBM 360 the name of *Three-Sickly*, while they referred to Macintosh computers as *Mackintoy* or *Mackintrash*, and to programs coming from the University of California at Berkeley as *Berzerkeley*.

Such book titles as *Windows for Dummies* and *A Nerd's Introduction to the Internet* turn this kind of frustration into self-deprecating humor. Users struggling to master the intricacies of a new software program or to find some specific information on the Internet are comforted to learn they aren't the only ones feeling challenged by new technology. This underlying sense of insecurity probably contributed to the public's enjoyment of jokes about the 1994 discovery that, when working with high numbers, the Intel Corporation's Pentium computer chip made mistakes. Jokes coming out of the highly publicized recall included

> What do you get when you cross a Pentium personal computer with a research grant?
> *A mad scientist.*

> Why didn't Intel call the Pentium the 586?
> *Because they added 486 and 100 on the first Pentium and got 585-999983605.*

Rich Tennant is a cartoonist who does cartoons for *Computerworld* and *Federal Computer Week*. His cartoon that has proven the most popular shows a typical office with two "geeks" working at their computers with a frustrated-looking repairman standing in the middle with his tools and a boxy-looking something. The cutline reads, "In a display of perverse brilliance, Carl the repairman mistakes a room humidifier for a mid-range computer but manages to tie it into the network anyway."

Long before the general public began making jokes about computers, inventors, developers, and programmers were searching for names to communicate about new concepts and items. Many of the names these early computer geniuses adapted to their needs reflect a playful creativity as well as a fondness for science fiction and fantasy, especially that popularized in movies and television. They called huge network packets or those broadcast widely *Godzillagrams* after the monster of 1950s Japanese movies. They called aspiring teenage hackers *Munchkins*, based on the little people in *The Wizard of Oz*, while those who mischievously program something to keep repeating itself were dubbed *Wabbits* from cartoon character Elmer Fudd's "You Wascawwy wabbit!" A program that accidentally repeats itself is said to be in *Sorcerer's Apprentice* mode, a reference to Walt Disney's *Fantasia*.

From *Star Wars* comes *UTSL*, for "Use the Source, Luke!" which is a play on "Use the Force, Luke!" It's a polite way of telling someone to read the manual before asking for help. An *Obi-Wan error*, taken from the name of Obi-Wan Kenobi, refers to any computation that is *off-by-one*, as when a programmer starts counting a particular quantity at 1 instead of 0. By analogy, an Obi-Wan alphabetical code uses letters that are one off so that *HAL*, for example, might stand for *IBM* as many viewers thought it did in the 1968 movie *2001: A Space Odyssey*.

In the original *Star Trek* television series, a *Vulcan nerve pinch* was used to paralyze people. In computer talk, it describes the keyboard action of simultaneously pressing the "control," "alt," and "delete" keys to reboot one's system. *Droid,* from *android,* is used to imply that someone is acting mindlessly, as though programmed. *Marketdroids, trendroids*, and *sales droids* promise customers things that can't be delivered or that are essentially useless. *Code police* and *net police*, named after the *thought police* in George Orwell's *1984*, take upon themselves the responsibility of enforcing programming and Internet etiquette standards.

Spell-check programs can be a source of humor unique to computers as when *Time* magazine (Dec. 20, 1993) published a letter to the editor referring to a feature on Sigmund Freud: "Whenever I write the name *Freud*, my computer spell-check system thinks at first I meant to spell *fraud*. Do you think its subconsicous is revealing a long-suppressed and painful truth?"

Computer language has so many acronyms that programmers make fun of themselves by having acronyms for acronyms. *TLA* stands for *Three Letter Acronym* while *YABA* stands for *Yet Another Bloody Acronym*. When companies choose new names they check to make sure they are "YABA compatible," meaning the initials can be pronounced easily and won't make a suggestive or unpleasant word.

Initial-based computer slang, which is used to save time and space in e-mail, is an extension from the technical acronyms, for example:

AFAIK = As far as I know
BCNU = Be seeing you
BTW = By the way
CUL or CUL8R = See you later
GIGO = Garbage In Garbage Out
GFR = Grim File Reaper
LOL = Lots of laughs
OIC = Oh, I See
ROTF = Rolling on the Floor
ROTFLMAO = Rolling on the Floor Laughing My Ass Off
RUOK = Are you okay?
TIA = Thanks in Advance
WYSIWYG = What you See Is What You Get

Books and articles introducing people to the "proper" use of e-mail often advise against using humor. This overgeneralization warns users that what they may think is a private message can with the click of a few keys be forwarded to other readers, maybe even thousands of them. Also, legal guidelines have not been clearly established on whether supervisors and company owners have a right to read e-mail messages sent on work time and on company- or government-owned computers. Newspaper stories regularly document incidents in which an employee is being chastised for sending out racist or hostile jokes or for making snide remarks about fellow employees or supervisors.

In spite of such risks and warnings, virtually everyone who uses e-mail on a regular basis either sends or receives some humor.

Much of it is no different from what finds its way into ordinary correspondence; for example, joking about the weather, politics, or current events; sharing personal experiences; telling anecdotes about mutual acquaintances; and teasing each other. In some ways, e-mail contains more humor than does handwritten correspondence; users don't even need to retype amusing messages before forwarding them to others.

Also, some people add favorite quotes or witticisms to their signatures so they go out to all correspondents. Polish professor Robert Lew uses a variety of signature statements related to computers; for example, "Smash forehead on keyboard to continue," and "11th commandment: Covet not thy neighbour's Pentium II." Other people create visual humor for their signatures by using regular keyboard symbols to draw self-portraits or cartoon characters; seasonal icons such as jack o'lanterns, snowballs, Christmas trees, or Easter bunnies; or professional representations such as a cow for a dairy farmer, a pencil for a writer, and a car for a mechanic.

The most often used symbols are *emoticons* made from pictures of sideways faces. As more people learn to interpret them, their popularity is growing because they are an efficient way to hint at the tone intended by the sender, as with these examples:

:-) or :-)))))) = smiling or really smiling
:-{ or :-{{{{{{ = frowning or really frowning
;-) = winking
:-* = kissing
I-0 = yawning
:-& = tongue-tied
:'-{ = crying
:-/ = undecided
:-II = angry

See also INTERNET INFLUENCES, LANGUAGE PLAY, METAPHORS

For further reading: J. Hulstijn and A. Nijholt (eds.), *Twente Workshop on Language Technology 12: Automatic Interpretation and Generation of Verbal Humor* (1996). Eric S. Raymond, *The New Hacker's Dictionary*, 2nd ed. (1993). *Webster's New World Dictionary of Computer Terms*, 4th ed. (1992).

D

Dialect Humor

Dialect humor is language play based on group differences in vocabulary, pronunciation, or grammar as used by speakers from different geographical areas. For example, in this joke about two men in Central Park, one of them says, "Gee look at the boids!" The other one says, "Those aren't *boids*, they're *birds*." "That's funny," says the first, "they chirp like boids."

Dialectal differences are usually based on geographical location, such as those shown by how differently English is spoken by people in London as opposed to those in Delhi, India, as well as by Bostonians as opposed to Texans. However, dialects might also be influenced by a person's ethnic group. For example, within a 10-mile radius there could be speakers using the English language quite differently, depending on whether they grew up in a Pennsylvania Dutch, an African American, an Asian American, a Jewish, or a Hispanic family. Immigrants, visitors, and others who are nonnative speakers of English are also said to be dialectal speakers because of accents as well as grammatical structures they may have carried over from their first languages.

Writers and performers frequently use dialectical differences when developing humorous characters and in creating plots. A basic appeal of dialect humor is that many readers, listeners, and viewers feel superior to those they perceive as speaking nonstandard English. Because of the history of the United States, dialect humor has been consistently popular as new waves of immigrants have sought to make themselves feel better about their own struggles to learn standard English. In 1936, Max Eastman offered the explanation that "when we smile at misused language, what amuses us is the ignorance, or pretended ignorance, of the character using it." American writers during the 1800s who created dialect humor through comic misspellings and malapropisms include Joel Chandler Harris, Marietta Holley, James Russell Lowell, James Kirke Paulding, Henry Wheeler Shaw, and Seba Smith. While Artemus Ward and Mark Twain are the most famous of the many writers who used this technique, they were less extreme, which may be one of the reasons that their stories are still read while the others are incomprehensible to many readers.

The general acceptance of dialect humor was advanced in vaudeville and minstrel shows where, especially after the Civil War, white entertainers, along with some African Americans, dressed in blackface and performed songs and dances loosely borrowed from slave entertainment. The verbal humor in these shows relied heavily on exaggerated dialects and linguistic mistakes.

When in the 1920s performers from vaudeville and from blackface began moving to radio, some of them brought along their skills with dialect humor. Since radio relies totally on sound, and it soon became apparent that listeners wanted a variety of voices and sounds, dialect humor became a main staple of radio. While the *Amos 'n' Andy* (1929–1954) show done in Black dialect is the prime example, characters on many other shows also spoke in dialect. *The Goldbergs* (1929–1945) was the first major Jewish radio comedy. The show was created by Gertrude Berg, who did not rely on pronunciation as much as on intonation and on the proverbs and the sentence patterns she had learned from her Yiddish-speaking grandmother, as in this ad-libbed line, "Better a crust of bread and enjoy it than a cake that gives you indigestion."

On *The Jack Pearl Show* (1931–1936), Pearl took a character out of German history, Baron von Munchausen, and used him as the central figure in a running skit. Using his own voice, Pearl spoke the straight man's lines under the name of Sharlie, and then shifted to a German dialect for the Baron:

> *Baron*: Und dere in frundt off me wuz a green elephant.
>
> *Sharlie*: Now wait a minute, Baron; do you mean to tell me you actually saw a green elephant?
>
> *Baron*: (with great indignation) Vas you dere, Sharlie?

In the mid-1930s, "Vas you dere, Sharlie?" was the country's most famous catch phrase.

In the 1940s, *Allen's Alley*, a part of the Fred Allen show, was inhabited by a number of dialect speakers. Minerva Pious played the role of Mrs. Pansy Nussbaum, a muddle-headed Jewish housewife who uttered such malapropisms as *Talooraloora Bankhead;* the *Meyer Brothers Clinic; lemons, oranges, and tambourines;* and *spinach, turnips, and rutabagels.* There was also a loudmouth Irishman named Ajax Cassidy, a farmer named Titus Moody, and a pompous Southerner named Senator Beauregard Claghorn, whose signature line was "that's a joke, son!" Kenny Delmar modeled the Claghorn character after a Texas rancher who during the depression had given Delmar a ride in his Model-T Ford. In 1946, Claghorn was a national sensation, and even today his name and his signature line are invoked by a Foghorn Leghorn, one of Warner Brothers' cartoon characters.

Duffy's Tavern (1940–1951) was created as a comic rendition of Irish Americans, while in *Meet Me at Parky's* (1945–1947), Nick Parkyakarkus was the proprietor of a Greek diner. *Life with Luigi* (1948–1953) was about Italian immigrants. Each week Luigi would write home to Mama Basko in Italy, "Dear-a-Mamma-Mia! It's a now summertime in-a-Chicago, and everybody's-a-feelin' very very hot-a!"

Of all the radio performers, Mel Blanc was the most impressive. He started learning dialects as a child in Portland, Oregon. His first was Yiddish, picked up from an elderly couple who ran a neighborhood grocery story; then he started on the Asian dialects that he heard in Portland's Chinatown. While still in high school, he had become a semi-professional entertainer, and by the time he moved to Hollywood in 1935 he was labeled the "Heinz 57-Variety" man because of the many dialects and voices he had mastered. For Warner Brothers he provided the voices of Bugs Bunny, Daffy Duck, Tweety Pie, and the stuttering Porky Pig. On *The Jack Benny Program*, he was the huffing, puffing Maxwell car, as well as Professor LeBlanc, the violin teacher, and the announcer at the train station who shouted out, "Anaheim, Azusa and Cuc—amonga!" On *The Judy Canova Show* (1943–1953), Blanc was Pedro, the Mexican handyman who each week got laughs with "pardon me for talking in your face, senorita; 30 days hacienda, April, June and sombrero—I theenk!" His Mexican accent had to compete for attention with Canova's own lines spoken in a hillbilly dialect.

In 1944, Marlin Hurt, a white man who had developed a female impersonation of the Black nursemaid who had cared for him when he was growing up in Illinois, was written into the script of *Fibber McGee and Molly* as their maid, Beulah. Hurt was such a sensation with his "love dat man!" and "somebody bawl fo' Beulah?" that within 18 months he was given his own *The Marlin Hurt and Beulah Show*. On the new show, he switched out of his falsetto voice to also play Beulah's irresponsible boyfriend. After Hurt's unexpected death, the part was played by another white man, Bob Corley, but eventually went to Hattie McDaniel, the African American actress famous for her role as Mammy in *Gone with the Wind*.

Social attitudes about the portrayal of minorities began to change in the 1950s, gathering momentum in the 1960s and 1970s, and people began to look at how minority group members were characterized by their speech. Few people were bothered by the portrayal of white speakers' differences; for example, the Brooklyn accents of Ralph Kramden (Jackie Gleason) in *The Honeymooners* (1955–1956) and of Sergeant Bilko on *The Phil Silvers Show* (1955–1959) were viewed as simply amusing, much like the accents of the German officers on *Hogan's Heroes*, a show that in the 1966–1967 season was ranked in the top 20 of all television programs. Part of the charm of *The Andy Griffith Show* (1960–1968) was the southern accents of the characters and the contrasts between the speech of Sheriff Taylor and Barney Fife (Don Knotts), Gomer Pyle (Jim Nabors), Opie (Ron Howard), and Aunt Bee (Frances Bavier). Television's *Beverly Hillbillies* (1962–1971) spoke with a heavy Appalachian accent, but because they were white millionaires, viewers felt free to laugh. In contrast, the earlier *Ma and Pa Kettle* movies starring characters with similar hillbilly accents began to make newly sensitized viewers feel uncomfortable in laughing at the downtrodden.

These relatively benign uses of dialect contrasted with the heavy use of dialect for African Americans, Hispanics, and other immigrant groups. With such groups, heavy accents provided only part of the humor; the rest came from a multitude of language errors that implied that the speakers were less than bright. So many people were offended by this kind of humor that toward the end of his career Groucho Marx began to worry that some of the most talented comedians he knew were going to be out of work because dialect humor was falling out of fashion.

Marx had, indeed, seen the writing on the wall. The inscrutable Charlie Chan's pidgin English disappeared from the airwaves and so did Tonto's manly grunting. Children no longer read *El Gordo* comic strips, and both *Beulah* and *Amos 'n' Andy* disappeared. In 1970, Bill Dana gave up telling jokes through the voice of his popular Jose Jimenez character, and Frito-Lay discontinued its *Frito Bandito* commercials.

While dialect humor did not totally disappear from public entertainment, its nature changed. The new medium of television played a part by demanding more honesty. Because television characters could be seen as well as heard, white men, for example, could no longer play the roles of Black women. On radio, no one had worried that the role of the "Greek" Nick Parkyakarkus on *Meet Me at Parky's* was the creation of Harry Einstein, who mimicked the Greeks working at his father's warehouse, nor that the "Italian" *Life with Luigi* set in Chicago starred an Irishman and was created by a Jew from New York. In contrast, it was authentic for Desi Arnaz to mix Spanish and English on television's *I Love Lucy* (1951–1957). Arnaz's authentic dialectal speech made it to television only because of Lucille Ball's insistence that her husband play the part. However, the success of the show set an example for others to follow, as when Eva Gabor was cast to speak in her own Hungarian accent while playing Lisa on television's *Green Acres* (1965–1971). Having respected characters, who were obviously bright and appealing, speak with an accent broke away from the old vaudeville idea that speaking with an accent correlated with stupidity.

In the early days of dialect humor, script writers would make all the members of a particular group, and only the members of that group, speak in a particular way, but with the greater realism that came to television, more variety was displayed. For example, on television's *Sanford and Son* (1972–1977), Redd Foxx, who played Sanford, spoke with a stronger dialect than did the younger Demond Wilson, who played the role of his son Lamont. Yet viewers were left with the idea that Sanford was sophisticated in both his language and his logic. Also, it wasn't so offensive to have some African American characters speaking Black dialect as long as there were other African Americans using standard English as on *The Jeffersons* (1975–1985) and *The Cosby Show* (1984–1992).

Probably the biggest single difference between early dialect humor and contemporary dialect humor is that in the early years it was created by people outside of the groups. Today, it is mostly people inside particular groups who use dialect humor. A whole generation of comedians, actors, talk show hosts, singers, and rapsters are now using Black dialect for shock and amusement, while Hispanics are doing something similar with Spanglish where they drop Spanish words and phrases into everyday English, not because they don't know the English words, but because they want to be different and to show pride in their culture. They are following the example of the Jewish comedians of a generation ago who made a lasting impact on American English and American humor by the way they incorporated Yiddish patterns and proverbs into their performances. *See also* BLACKFACE COMEDY, JEWISH HUMOR, RADIO, REGIONAL HUMOR

Disabilities and Humor

Humor about disabilities comes in two types; that which is created and shared by people with disabilities and that which the mainstream culture creates and shares about disabilities. This latter kind of humor includes Helen Keller and Little Moron jokes, as well as such stories as the one about a blind man entering a department store, picking up his guide dog by its tail, and swinging it high in the air. When a clerk rushes over and says, "Can I help you, sir?" the man replies "No thanks, I'm just looking around."

Some people are appalled by the dark humor in jokes like the one about a little boy who is showing off his homemade motor scooter:

Where'd you get the motor?
From my dad's iron lung.

What'd your dad say about that?
AARRGGHHH!

and:

What do you do when an epileptic has a fit in your swimming pool?
Throw in a box of Tide and your laundry!

An alternate point of view is that such jokes are beneficial because they help take away the uncomfortable sense of pity that many people hold toward the disabled. According to this theory, it is a positive sign that such jokes have increased since 1992 when the Americans with Disabilities Act went into effect. Because this act forbids bias in hiring and requires businesses, schools, and public offices to accommodate the disabled, people in the mainstream culture have been forced to associate with, and think about, people with various kinds of disabilities. The jokes are evidence that people are trying to adjust.

Joking by and among disabled individuals may have similar effects as shown by such articles as "Sign Language in the Production and Appreciation of Humor by Deaf Children" written by Danielle Sanders (*Sign Language Studies* 50 [1986]) and "Defusing Awkward Situations: Comic Relief as an Interactive Strategy for People with Disabilities" by Robert A. Stebbins (*Journal of Leisurability* 23.4 [1996]).

Cartoonist John Callahan, who is himself paralyzed from an automobile accident shortly after his 21st birthday, says that "I'm sick and tired of people who presume to speak for the disabled. The question of what is off-limits should not be defined by some special-interest group. The audience—the readers—should decide." Callahan asks only, "Is it funny?"

An article by Timothy Egan published in *The New York Times* (Jun. 7, 1992) told about some of Callahan's most controversial cartoons, including one showing a dark-skinned beggar in the street wearing a sign that read: "Please help me. I am blind and black, but not musical." In the midst of the controversy, a Black man approached Callahan in a restaurant and asked him if he drew "that Black and blind strip." When Callahan said "Yes," the man shook his hand and thanked him. Something similar happened when a man who had lost his hands in Vietnam approached Callahan at a concert and thanked him profusely for his cartoon showing a bartender refusing to pour another drink for a man who had two prosthetic hooks in place of hands. "Sorry Sam," says the bartender, "you can't hold your liquor."

Cartoonist John Callahan plays with stereotypes as in the message on this man's placard: "Please help me. I am blind and black but not musical." ©*John Callahan/ Levin Represents*

In 1991 the American Civil Liberties Union of Oregon gave Callahan its Free Expression Award, citing him for a "history of facing challenges to artistic and intellectual freedom." He has also been honored by the Media Access Office in Los Angeles, while Royce Hamrick, a paraplegic who is president of the San Diego chapter of the National Spinal Cord Injury Association, has praised him saying, "In the disabled community, we make a lot of jokes that stay within that community. What John is doing is bringing those out to everyone else."

However, not everyone is so pleased. When Callahan drew a cartoon called "The Alzheimer Hoedown," showing confused couples at a square dance scratching their heads because they were unable to follow the instructions, "Return to the girl that you just left," he got an angry letter from the St. Louis chapter of the Alzheimer's Association.

Callahan complains that there is a double standard. Right after any major disaster, creative people recycle old disaster jokes into new formats and tell them on the street and on the Internet as well as through e-mail, fax, and long distance telephones. But when Callahan puts a similar kind of black humor into his "disabled-humor" cartoons, he is criticized.

Callahan's defenders use his disability as a way of defusing criticism, but Callahan says he does not want special treatment because he is in a wheelchair. Most readers don't know that he is paralyzed, and that's fine with him. Veteran cartoonist Sam Gross says that being in a wheelchair "has nothing to do with" why Callahan can get away with doing the things he does. "He is in the vein of sick humor—but sick humor that's funny. He's intelligent and witty—that is why he gets away with it."

An increasing number of disabled comedians are doing something similar to what Callahan does by using their "differentness" as a way to stand out from the crowd and to be remembered. Comedian Gene Mitchener, who has to be lifted on stage in his wheelchair, explained:

> The things I want to say concerning the disabled, I couldn't say without using comedy. Society wouldn't accept it; they'd be too hard, too cold. Before I get on stage, the audience is talking, drinking, making noise. As soon as I come on, there's dead silence, like someone dropped a bomb. Quiet! I must break the silence immediately and I do it with a joke. Comedy removes tension; then people are ready to listen and more willing to learn and to treat me just like any person.

In the mid-1980s, Mitchener told John Shaughnessy, a writer for *The Indianapolis Star*, that "laughter heals. It knocks down defenses. Everyone is handicapped in one way or another. At least mine shows up on the outside where we have to deal with it." One of Mitchener's monologues is about the beautiful woman he is dating. She could have any man she wants, and when I ask, "Why me?"

she says, "It's because you're so easy to push around." Once when they had a quarrel, he was so depressed he went all the way to Lovers' Leap, but it didn't have a wheelchair ramp.

One of the pleasures that audiences get from listening to comedians from outside the mainstream is that they get to see a different point of view and to become privy to inside jokes. For example, the deaf protagonist in the 1986 movie *Children of a Lesser God* reveals her cynical attitude by signing "bullshit." In American Sign Language, the word for "bull" is signed with two fingers representing a bull's horns placed against the forehead. However, Marlee Matlin laid her right arm over her left and signed the bull's horns lifting up from the inside of her elbow while the fingers of her left hand wagged back and forth as if the bull were relieving itself.

When *The New York Times* television critic John J. O'Connor reviewed an upcoming PBS special *Look Who's Laughing* (Nov. 28, 1994), he said he winced at the prospect of "watching people with physical disabilities tell jokes." However, he was pleasantly surprised at how artfully the producers tweaked "preconceptions with profiles of six professional comics whose physical disabilities are, to varying degrees, worked into routines that aim, as one puts it, to break down barriers and build bridges." Performers included Brett Leake, who has muscular dystrophy; Chris Fonseca and Geri Jewell, who both have cerebral palsy; Kathy Buckley, who is hearing-impaired; Alex Valdez, who is blind; and J. D. England, who is paraplegic.

Geri Jewell works her involuntary muscle movements into her act with such lines as "I used to have a job as a waitress, but they didn't like the way I tossed salads," and in reference to having sex, "I just tell him it's one long orgasm." The blind Alex Valdez says that he stopped drinking when he started hearing double, while Chris Fonseca says, "I'm handicapped and I'm Mexican, but if I was also a woman, I could get any government job I want."

The PBS show alternated between showing performance clips and interviewing the comedians, who talked about such things as the fear of getting "sympathy laughs," the democracy of comedy clubs in that "owners only care about one thing: are you funny?" and the belief that a gimmick is good in performance "for about two minutes. Then it's a matter of substance and quality." *See also* AGING AND HUMOR, COMIC ZEITGEISTS, SELF-DISPARAGEMENT

Further reading: John Callahan, *Don't Worry, He Won't Get Far on Foot* (1989).

Drama

Since the 1500s, *drama*, from the Greek *dran* meaning "to do," has meant the telling of stories through action and dialogue performed onstage as a play in a theater. Because plays are filled with conflicts and emotions, the word *drama* is also used to describe situations that in real life involve interesting events or intense conflicts.

In a general sense, **comedy** is a type of drama meant more to interest and amuse audiences than to make them think seriously about issues. Dramatic comedy is usually less boisterous than farce or burlesque, and it usually has a sustained plot, characters, and actions that might be found in real life as well as dialogue that is weighted with meaning.

While in formal literary studies, tragedy is often considered to be more significant than comedy, throughout history people have expressed a preference for comedies. Shakespeare wrote almost twice as many comedies as tragedies, and in both his tragedies and his histories he included light moments. And many of the longest-running plays on Broadway have been comedies; for example, Mary Chase's *Harvey*, which opened in 1944 for 1,775 performances; Joseph Kesselring's *Arsenic and Old Lace*, which opened in 1941 for 1,444 performances; and Bernard Slade's *Same Time Next Year*, which opened in 1976 for 1,453 performances.

In formal literary criticism, "comedy" is given a more specific meaning than "humor." Northrop Frye (1912–1991) has explained that comedy is based on an unjust law or tradition that in the course of the play is somehow broken. While there are always complications, the comedy ends in the reestablishment of the natural order of things; for example, with young lovers paired off and ready to go forth and live happily ever after. Much of the tension in a comedy is provided by the steps that must be taken to overcome the unjust law. A good example is the French playwright Beaumarchais's 1784 *The Marriage of Figaro*, which was later made into an opera by Mozart. The unjust law at the core of the play is that the lord of the manor had the right to take the virginity of any woman marrying one of the lord's serfs. The plot of the play revolves around how Figaro and his bride repeatedly outwit the lord of the manor until after the couple is married and the lord is no longer entitled to the privilege.

In Shakespeare's *The Merchant of Venice*, the unjust law relates to the pound of flesh that Shylock is authorized to receive. Portia, the lawyer, overturns the unjust law by arguing that while Shylock may be allowed to take his pound of flesh, he cannot shed one drop of blood in obtaining it.

In contemporary drama, the "unjust law" is not as likely to be an actual law as it is to be a social expectation. Humorous conflicts come from clashes between the expectations of characters, often from different ethnic groups, different genders, or different ages. Lorraine Hansberry's *A Raisin in the Sun* (1959) made audiences weep as well as laugh with pleasure as she explored the struggles of a Black family making its way in middle-class culture. The tension in George Axelrod's *The Seven Year Itch* (1956) was caused by conflicting ideas about marital fidelity. Differences between the expectations of gay and straight communities provided the basis for the humor in Mart Crowley's *The Boys in the Band* (1968) and Harvey Fierstein's *Torch Song Trilogy* (1982), while in Caryl Churchill's *Top Girls* (1982) some of the humor is based on the differences among the dinner guests who have been gathered from such different places as Chaucer's "The Clerk's Tale" and Brueghel's painting *Dulle Griet*.

Comedies of Humors go back to the belief from medieval physiology that the human body contains four basic fluids (phlegm, blood, black bile, and yellow bile) and that their relative proportions determine a person's health and temperament so that a particular individual might be either phlegmatic, sanguine, melancholic, or bilious.

Although dramatists no longer believe in an actual relationship between the fluids of the body and someone's temperament, they do believe in creating characters whose dispositions are exaggerated. Neil Simon's *The Odd Couple* (1965) would not be nearly as funny without the exaggerated sloppiness of Oscar Madison, which is placed in opposition to the meticulousness of Felix Unger. In *Life with Father* (1939), based on Clarence Day's book, the humor centers around the stubbornness of the father in refusing to be "properly baptized." In Garson Kanin's *Born Yesterday* (1946), the humor comes from the way that ex-chorus girl Billie loses her exaggerated innocence as she realizes how she is being used by Harry Brock, the vulgar and egotistical millionaire junkman.

Comedies of Manners are realistic plays that treat, often satirically, the manners and conventions of high society. The term was first used with the Restoration comedies of late 17th-century England, which feature witty dialogue and repartee, often targeting jealous husbands; fops; would-be wits; and awkward, stiff, or pretentious social misfits.

Social class in the United States has never been as clear-cut as in England, and so in American Comedies of Manners the class distinctions are created by specific circumstances. For example, in Thomas Heggen and Joshua Logan's *Mister Roberts* (1948), the hierarchical structure of the military creates a class difference that traps Lieutenant Roberts between the enlisted men and the captain on a U.S. Navy ship. In John Patrick's *The Teahouse of the August Moon* (1953), the comic confrontation occurs between American occupation forces on Okinawa and the local residents who have no intention of being "Americanized." In Herb Gardner's *I'm Not Rappaport* (1986), the comic confrontation is between two elderly New York men who meet in Central Park. One is a middle-class Jew and the other an African American janitor.

The most respected playwrights of the last half of the 20th century are skilled at creating humor, but as shown by this alphabetical sampling of authors who are either American or have had a major influence on American drama, they are less inclined to write plays for simple amusement and more inclined to write plays that will stimulate audiences to serious thought. The humor they create is new and different and like a chef skilled in food presentation, they frame their humor and place it between heavy courses so that it serves purposes ranging from tasty appetizer to satisfying dessert or from spicy accompaniment to main course.

Edward Albee (1928–): Albee's *The American Dream* (1960) is a bitterly funny attack on how families treat the young and the old, while the title of his first full-length play, *Who's Afraid of Virginia Woolf?* (1962) is adapted from *Who's Afraid of the Big Bad Wolf?* In this stunning example of black comedy, there is just as much huffing and puffing as in the old folktale, only in the play no one escapes. George and Martha, whose names are generally perceived as an allusion to the first U.S. president and his wife, are a middle-aged faculty couple at a small college. They invite a younger couple in for a get-acquainted evening, which turns savage. The witty viciousness shocked as well as mesmerized audiences, and the play won virtually every award available, except for the Pulitzer, whose trustees stated that the subject matter and the language made the play an inappropriate choice.

Samuel Beckett (1906–1989): Beckett was Irish, but moved to Paris in 1937 where he worked for the French resistance movement. Shortly after World War II, he wrote his first play, *Waiting for Godot*, which, when it was produced in 1953, became an international sensation. Beckett was doing for theater what the Absurdists were doing for painting. Audiences were shocked and fascinated by the way he could hold their attention even after stripping away such stage conventions as movement, dance, music, costumes, action plots, and stage settings. Four characters

make up the *Waiting for Godot* cast: two tramps, Vladimir and Estragon, and a master and his slave, Pozzo and Lucky, who are roped together. They are all on stage "waiting for Godot," who never comes, but yet they wait on and in the midst of telling stories, eating carrots, and contemplating suicide, they solemnly go through vaudeville scenes drawn from the Marx Brothers, Charlie Chaplin, and Buster Keaton. In the first act of *Happy Days* (1961), Winnie is buried up to her waist in a mound of sand, but still she has a gift for comic irrelevance as she rummages through her large shopping bag discovering bits and pieces of her life.

Christopher Durang (1949–): Best known for his parodies, Durang came to public attention in 1974 when he played a role in the Yale Repertory Theatre production of *The Idiots Karamazov*, a satire of Dostoyevsky's *The Brothers Karamazov*, which Durang wrote with Albert Innaurato. In 1978 Durang's *A History of the American Film*, which parodies some 200 motion pictures as a chronicle of American life, was nominated for a Tony Award. The actors, who sit on stage in movie theater seats facing forward, alternate between playing roles as moviegoers and as actors in such films as *The Grapes of Wrath*, *Citizen Kane*, and *Casablanca*. Durang's later satires of American suburban life include *The Vietnamization of New Jersey*, *The Nature and Purpose of the Universe*, and *Sister Mary Ignatius Explains It All for You*, a parody about the Roman Catholic church. Critic Frank Rich said about the Obie-winning *Sister Mary* that "anyone can write an angry play—all it takes is an active spleen, but only a writer of real talent can write an angry play that remains funny and controlled even in its most savage moments." Durang plays first produced in the 1990s include *Naomi in the Living Room*, *Media Amok*, *Putting It Together*, *For Whom the Southern Belle Tolls*, and *Sex and Longing*.

A. R. Gurney (1930–): While he doesn't like to be described as a "WASP writer," Gurney told London *Times* reporter Sheridan Morley that instead of writing about rebels and dissenters, he writes "about my own people, the Americans you see haunting Harrods in midsummer." This means that Gurney's humor is more low-key, the kind found in John Cheever and John Updike novels and short stories. In *Children*, Gurney explores the tensions of a middle-class family over a Fourth-of-July weekend, while in *The Dining Room* he takes a satiric and rueful look at upper-middle-class customs by showing different families gathered around their dining room tables. In *The Perfect Party*, a middle-aged professor puts on a grand party for all the notable people he can gather together. *Another Antigone* and *The Cocktail Hour* are deeply critical of upper-class attitudes. After seeing *The Cocktail Hour* in 1988, *New York Times* reviewer Frank Rich wrote that Gurney "still has new and witty observations to make about a nearly extinct patrician class that regards psychiatry as an affront to good manners, underpaid hired help as a brithright, and the selling of blue-chip stocks as a first step toward Marxism." Gurney plays newly produced in the 1990s include *The Snow Ball, The Old Boy, The Fourth Wall, Later Life, A Cheever Evening: A New Play Based on the Stories of John Cheever, Sylvia, Overtime, Let's Do It* (a musical), and *Labor Day*.

Charles Ludlam (1943–1987): Ludlam co-founded New York's Ridiculous Theatrical Company, but because of internal disagreements left in 1967 to co-found the Off-Broadway Ridiculous Theatrical Company. He wrote, directed, and acted in all of the troupe's plays, winning four Obie Awards, a Drama Desk Award, and a Rosamond Gilder Award. His best-known plays include *The Mystery of Irma Vep: A Penny Dreadful, Conquest of the Universe, Camille: A Tearjerker*, and *The Artificial Jungle*. In most of his campy and satirical productions, he left room for the actors to improvise and interact with the audiences. His sense of the ridiculous became apparent in his 1970 *Bluebeard*, about a mad scientist trying to create a third genital, while in his 1972 *Eunuchs of the Forbidden City* the empress kills her son thereby triggering the Boxer Rebellion, while the eunuchs explain, "We

have no power to love. . . . We must love power." Ludlum held adjunct teaching or writing positions with Yale, Carnegie Mellon, and New York universities, as well as with Connecticut College for Women. After his 1987 death from AIDS, Steven Samuels edited *Ridiculous Theatre: Scourge of Human Folly: The Essays and Opinions of Charles Ludlam,* published by the Theatre Communications Group in 1992.

Terrence McNally (1939–) writes not only plays, but also screen and television plays. Movie scripts that he has adapted from his stage plays include the 1977 *The Ritz*, 1991 *Frankie and Johnny*, and the 1994 *Love! Valour! Compassion!* which on stage won the 1995 Tony Award for best play. McNally set a record by also winning the 1996 Tony Award for best play with *Master Class*, a biographical play about the legendary opera diva Maria Callas. One of his most acclaimed plays is his 1991 *Lips Together, Teeth Apart* in which two affluent couples spend a Fourth-of-July weekend at a Fire Island beach house. One of the women inherited the house from her brother who died of AIDS. The situation triggers some heavy thinking, ricocheting off McNally's usual wit. *A Perfect Ganesh* is the story of two middle-aged Connecticut women touring India, while *Love! Valour! Compassion* is an account of the lives of eight gay men holidaying at an upstate New York country home. McNally was only 24 years old when he wrote his first play produced on Broadway, *The Lady of the Camellias*. He has worked consistently ever since and is commended for continuing to develop his skills. In 1993, he helped found a play-writing department at the Juilliard School.

Ntozake Shange (1948–): Shange is an African American who writes in nonstandard English, believing that "in murdering the King's English we free ourselves." However, she stresses that nonstandard writing must come from a position of complete control, from knowing "your enemy so well that you're able to do something with his weapon." Her first play, *for colored girls who have considered suicide/when the rainbow is enuf*

(1975), is about both sexual and racial stereotyping, which she treats with pain and anger but also with humor. The subtitle to her *spell #7* is "geechee jibara quik magic trance manual for technologically stressed third-world people." The play is especially interesting from the standpoint of humor because the stage setting and the style are taken from old minstrel shows. Incorporated are all the periods of "afro-american entertainment: from acrobats, comedians, tap-dancers, calindy dancers, cotton club choruses, and apollo theatre du-wop groups." Although Shange does not think that stereotypes disappear, she argues that they can be transformed, which is what she tries to do by evoking the energetic creativity of such contemporary performers as Tina Turner, Chuck Berry, Butch Morris, Bob Marley, and Stevie Wonder.

Sam Shepard (1943–): Some critics rank Sam Shepard, with his over 40 plays and his numerous awards, as the preeminent playwright of his generation. Many of his plays pay homage to a mythical West of our imaginations. *Operation Sidewinder* (1970) features a six-foot rattlesnake that is also an Air Force computer. *The Tooth of Crime* (1972) re-enacts an old West shootout between Hoss, an established rock star, and Crow, a "gypsy" challenger. As a bonus, it includes a referee and cheerleaders. Shepard's people live on the edge, both literally and figuratively, whether in the junkyard of Azusa as in *The Unseen Hand* (1969) or in a barren motel room on the edge of the Mojave Desert in *Fool for Love* (1983). Audiences laugh nervously at his characters' dysfunctional behavior as when in *Suicide in B-flat* (1979) everyone ends up quarreling in Laurel and Hardy style because they can't get a dead friend's body to fit into the outline chalked on the floor.

Neil Simon (1927–): Neil Simon began his career working with his brother, Danny, as a comedy writer for Goodman Ace on radio. The two went on to write for Phil Silvers, Tallulah Bankhead, Sid Caesar, Garry Moore, and Jackie Gleason. After 10 years of "prac-ticing," the brothers launched themselves as successful playwrights with *Come Blow Your Horn* (1960). Danny then moved to Hollywood to become a producer, and Neil stayed in New York writing plays including *Little Me* and *Barefoot in the Park* (1962), *The Odd Couple* (1965), *Plaza Suite* (1968), and *Last of the Red Hot Lovers* (1969). Critics were never as kind to Simon as were theatergoers, but they did praise him for giving priority to honest emotion and to the story lines in his autobiographical trio of plays *Brighton Beach Memoirs* (1982), *Biloxi Blues* (1984), and *Broadway Bound* (1986). Simon has said that while he used to look for funny things to write about, now he looks for sad things and tries to figure out how to tell them in a funny way.

Tom Stoppard (1937–): Although Stoppard is British, his plays are well known to Americans. His *Rosencrantz and Guildenstern Are Dead* (1966) parodies not only Shakespeare's *Hamlet* but also Beckett's *Waiting for Godot*. Stoppard's humor comes from intrinsically funny plots as well as from puns, sight gags, poses, jokes, games, aphorisms, double takes, double talk, cross-conversations, and asides to the audience. *Albert's Bridge* (1967) begins with four men working in their continuous job of painting a bridge, but ends with the bridge collapsing when "management" decides to have it painted in one day and so sends out 1,800 men equipped with brushes and full buckets of paint. *The Real Inspector Hound* (1968) burlesques an Agatha Christie mystery in which the detective proves to be the murderer, while *Artist Descending a Staircase* is a play on Marcel Duchamp's famous *Nude Descending a Staircase*. When one of the artists in the play makes an edible statue out of cubes of sugar, he is told "it will give cubism a new lease on life." Critic Susan Rusinko places Tom Stoppard in the ranks of such dramatists as Oscar Wilde and George Bernard Shaw because of his dazzling wit and vivid imagery, his daringly plagiaristic usages of other writers' plots and characters, and the incongruous situations that he creates by placing characters outside of their times.

Individual plays old enough to have proven their staying power as delightfully funny include Ben Hecht and Charles MacArthur's *The Front Page* (1928), Eugene O'Neill's *Ah, Wilderness* (1933), George S. Kaufman and Moss Hart's *You Can't Take It With You* (1936), Kaufman and Hart's *The Man Who Came to Dinner* (1939), Howard Lindsay and Russel Crouse's *Life with Father* (1939), William Saroyan's *The Time of Your Life* (1939), Barry Philip's *The Philadelphia Story* (1939), James Thurber and Elliott Nugent's *The Male Animal* (1940), John Van Druten's *I Remember Mama* (1944), Herb Gardner's *A Thousand Clowns* (1962), Harvey Fierstein's *Torch Song Trilogy* (1983), and Alfred Uhry's *Driving Miss Daisy* (1988). Many of these have also been made into movies. *See also* MOVIES, MUSIC

Further reading: Lee A. Jacobus, *The Bedford Introduction to Drama,* 3rd ed. (1997). Carl H. Klaus, Miriam Gilbert, and Bradford S. Field Jr., *Stages of Drama: Classical to Contemporary Theater,* 3rd ed. (1995).

E

Erotic Humor

Erotic humor is devoted to arousing sexual love or desire. A fine line separates erotic humor from scatological humor. An oversimplified definition is that erotic humor relates to sex while scatological humor relates to excrement, but what to one person may seem erotic and perhaps romantic, to someone else may seem scatological and vulgar.

Erotic drawings, showing exaggerated sex organs and sexual play, have a long history. They were placed as "teasers" in the waiting rooms of ancient brothels, and before photography made nude photos commonplace, "girlie" cards were appreciated both for their humor and their salaciousness. In some ways these drawings are the ancestors of the sexy cartoons that today appear in print and animated forms as well as online.

Erotic wordplay ranges from the stage names of striptease dancers to an impromptu advertisement to share a bumper crop of lemons: "Take me! Hold me! Squeeze me!" Multivolume books are filled with sex-related riddles, funny definitions, puns, one-liners, and jokes. In the late 1800s creating suggestive limericks was a popular form of adult party entertainment, while during the late 1960s and 1970s grafitti writers included almost as many sexual as political messages.

Because in social situations risque jokes are so often floated as trial balloons to measure listeners' attitudes about sexual matters, they are specifically mentioned in sexual harassment policies. People who engage in sexual joking in the workplace may simply be relieving boredom and trying to have fun. However, if the joking is viewed by recipients of the humor as a campaign of flirtation, seduction, or harassment, and the recipients let it be known that they are offended, then the person doing the joking must stop or run the risk of being formally charged with sexual harassment.

Since the 1970s, the most popular medium for erotic humor has been late-night talk shows. Because these are assumed to be broadcast to basically adult audiences, television censors have always been more lenient, but during the 1998 White House sex scandal, the number of sex-related jokes on late-night television rose sharply. According to the *Los Angeles Times* news service (Jan. 30, 1999), in 1998 late-night comedians David Letterman, Jay Leno, Conan O'Brien, and Bill Maher told 1,712 jokes about President Clinton and an additional 749 about others associated with the scandal. This more than doubled the number of jokes (810) that were told about Clinton in 1997. The figures were compiled by the nonpartisan, nonprofit Center for Media and Public Affairs in Washington. The organization's president Robert Lichter explained the numbers by saying that the scandal was revealed early in 1998 and the story "unfolded slowly and, with every twist and turn," there was new "fodder for the late-night joke mill."

In *Time* magazine (Feb. 22, 1999), linguist Deborah Tannen, in an article entitled "Freedom to Talk Dirty," wrote that the "Lewinsky matter is only the latest in a series of episodes that have made graphic sex talk more common." Earlier contributors to changing attitudes included the AIDS epidemic, the Clarence Thomas hearings, the rape trials of William Kennedy Smith and Mike Tyson, and the development of Viagra with its advertising campaign featuring Bob Dole. Tannen wrote that the enduring legacy of the Clinton scandal "may simply be the adding of the term *oral sex* and its vernacular synonym to the list of once avoided phrases that are now used openly. . . ."

As various networks and newspaper columnists and cartoonists competed for bigger shares of the audience, they grew more bold with the result that sex-related humor was not restricted to late-night television. For example, in Mark Russell's February 1999 special for PBS, he quoted Monica Lewinsky's statement that had been played the day before on national television. During the taking of depositions, she had avoided a direct answer to one of the prosecutor's questions by saying that she looked at Clinton "more as a man than as president." In an allusion to oral sex, Russell quipped, "From that angle, I should think so!"

Even without the impetus of sex-related scandals, the producers and creators of television talk shows have consistently looked for ways to focus on sex-related topics. While daytime talk shows take a pseudo-serious approach to sex, billing themselves as helping people with sex-related problems (what some critics have labeled "pious pornography"), the late-night shows have taken a light-hearted approach. Topics for conversation between male hosts and their beautiful women guests are chosen for their potential to elicit sexual references and joking. The same process was used in the popular *Dating Game* show in the 1960s and 1970s and its various spinoffs. While sophisticated audiences are turned off by "canned" sexual jokes, they like joking that appears spontaneous and original.

Skilled authors of novels, plays, movies, and short stories have more room to develop sexual allusions that are well integrated into a story. John Updike in *Couples*, as well as in several of his short stories, is skilled at creating moments that are both sexy and funny; so is Saul Bellow in *Adventures of Augie March* and Philip Roth in *Goodbye Colum-*

"I've contacted your husband. He's at http://hottalk.com and wants to know what I look like naked."

This cartoon succeeds because Robert Mankoff uses a new twist on an old topic. ©*1999 Robert Mankoff from Cartoonbank.com. All rights reserved.*

bus and *The Breast*. Vladimir Nabokov's *Lolita* is filled with both sexuality and humor, albeit a dark humor.

The title of Lisa Alther's *Kinflicks* is close enough to *skinflicks* to make readers expect something sexual; she did not disappoint them. However, as critic John Leonard wrote in the *New York Times*, when he compared protagonist Ginny Babcock to J. D. Salinger's Holden Caulfield, Saul Bellow's Augie March, and even Mark Twain's Huckleberry Finn, *Kinflicks* is a very funny book about very serious matters.

Woody Allen is the most successful screenwriter and producer of films that are both funny and sexy as in his 1977 *Annie Hall* and his 1986 *Hannah and Her Sisters*. His 1972 *Everything You Always Wanted to Know about Sex but Were Afraid to Ask* was less successful, but was still an interesting experiment in getting audiences to look on sex as comedy material.

Nora Ephron's 1989 romantic comedy *When Harry Met Sally* is about a couple of New Yorkers whose 12-year friendship evolves, against their wishes, into a courtship. Meg Ryan and Billy Crystal play the lead roles, and the scene in which Ryan fakes an orgasm while the two are eating lunch at a restaurant is considered one of the funniest movie scenes of the 1980s.

Neil Simon draws people into his plays with the promise of sex-related humor in such titles as *Barefoot in the Park*, *Plaza Suite*, and *Last of the Red Hot Lovers*. Bernard Slade wrote the screenplay for the 1978 movie *Same Time Next Year*, which starred Alan Alda and Ellen Burstyn meeting for an annual affair over a 25-year period. Marilyn Monroe is still remembered for her 1955 role in *The Seven Year Itch*. Visually, people remember the scene where she stands over a sidewalk air vent to catch the breezes blowing up her skirt, but orally they remember her explaining to co-star Tom Ewell how when it's so hot she keeps her underwear in the refrigerator.

Erotic humor is a matter of teasing and sexual play. If and when it crosses the line into passion, then it is no longer funny. Popular culture critic Hamlin Hill has explained

that in their desire to ridicule hypocrisy, black humorists moved a step beyond the socio-pornographic level. They found sexual behavior inherently funny, and in the process lost some of the audience. "Sex in the bedroom was one thing; laughter there was something else."

The opposite situation occurs in comedy clubs where people want laughter and titillation, but not real sex. For example, comedian Judy Carter says that just as laughter interferes with orgasm, sexual stimulation also gets in the way of the mental focus necessary for comedy. She is quoted in Susan Horowitz's *Queens of Comedy*:

> Breasts aren't funny. If I have something tight on, they don't hear me. They look at me. It hits a different region. Comedy hits the mind — they laugh — it's an idea. But if you're hitting the groin . . . (She tilts her head to the side in an idiot version of the RCA Victor dog.) Ever watch men in a strip club?

Horowitz goes further to conjecture that if comedians are in a kind of conflict with their audiences in which the audience is saying, "I dare you to make me laugh," then it stands to reason that they aren't going to feel sexually aroused by a woman who has just won the competition by making them laugh. Another gender-related difference between male and female comedians is that a woman onstage is in a vulnerable position and must remain in control. While both Sandra Bernhard and Judy Tenuta play up their sexuality, they also have techniques to put the brakes on and to squelch overly zealous fans. As Horowitz says, a man can threaten a heckler by saying something like, "I could pee on from you from here!" but if a woman made such a statement, the audience would most likely cheer and clap and shout encouragement.

Older women have been much freer to make erotic jokes without fear of losing control. Touchstone examples are Sophie Tucker (1884–1966), "The Last of the Red Hot Mamas," and Mae West (1893–1980). Although West always wore clothes that were more elegant than revealing, she made a lasting contribution to legitimate theater by challenging the censors with her indirect speech. When in the 1920s, she was arrested for "corrupting the morals of youth," her jail sentence of 10 days provided a publicity bonanza because she demanded that she be allowed to wear her own silk underwear rather than the coarse prison garb. Eight days later, there were new headlines when she got off two days early "for good behavior," a situation similar to when an admiring woman complimented West with, "Goodness, what lovely diamonds," and West responded, "Goodness had nothing to do with it!"

Belle Barth (1911–1971) took Mae West's and Sophie Tucker's kind of titillation a step closer to shock comedy. She sang ribald songs and told bawdy jokes and "blue" stories. Besides working in Las Vegas and Miami hotels, she performed in the Borscht Belt hotels of the Catskills, where she attempted to evade censors (not always successfully) by translating obscenities into Yiddish.

Another example is Rusty Warren (1930–), the "knockers-up girl" most famous for her party albums and for including women in her observational and sex-related humor. For example, she would argue that women enjoy sex more than men do: "Put your little finger in your ear. Wiggle it around. Now which feels better, your finger or your ear?"

More recently Zsa Zsa Gabor has played the role of the sexy wit as when she was asked how many husbands she'd had, and she replied, "You mean apart from my own?" *See also* GENDER AND HUMOR, SCATOLOGY AND OBSCENITY

Further reading: Susan Horowitz, *Queens of Comedy* (1997). Richard Lederer, *Nothing Risque, Nothing Gained: Ribald Riddles, Lascivious Limericks, Carnal Corn, and Other Good, Clean Dirty Fun* (1995).

Ethnic Humor

The word *ethnic* is related to the words *ethnicos* and *nation*; its meaning is that of a group of people classed according to common religious, national, tribal, racial, linguistic, or cultural origins or backgrounds. Ethnic humor relates to the unique characteristics of such groups and appears across a wide spectrum of genres, for example

- The play and movie *I Remember Mama* from Kathryn Forbes's novel, *Mama's Bank Account*, is the tender and humorous story of a family of Norwegian immigrants living in San Francisco in 1910.

- Comedian Andrew Dice Clay is known almost exclusively for telling hostile, sexist, and racist jokes.

- In the late 1970s, comedian Don Novello spoke with an Italian dialect and dressed in clerical garb when doing comedy skits about Father Guido Sarducci. He was a hit on *Saturday Night Live* and on *The Smothers Brothers Comedy Hour*, but when he went to the Vatican to pose for publicity photos he was arrested for impersonating a priest.

- Richard Rodgers and Oscar Hammerstein's 1958 Broadway musical, *Flower Drum Song*, is filled with cross-generational humor about an American family that had emigrated from China.

- The now defunct *El Gordo* comic strip was filled with humor about Hispanics.

- Web pages prepared by hate groups often contain ethnic-related jokes, most often about recent groups of immigrants.

- Funny Irish-Americans on radio included Ed Gardner playing the role of Archie on *Duffy's Tavern* and Jackie Gleason playing the role of Chester Riley on *The Life of Riley*.

- Russian immigrant Yakov Smirnoff entertained Americans through the cold war and beyond with such jokes as "I have a Russian Express Card. It says, 'Don't Leave Home!'" and "One of the biggest differences between America and Russia is that in American you can always find a party, but in Russia, the party always finds you."

As these examples show, ethnic humor ranges from good-natured teasing to hostile hate speech. The discomfort that accompanies the latter has caused people to make such statements as "ethnic humor has no place in the work environment." At the other extreme are people who say that ethnic humor is simply a reflection, or a bubbling up, of the discomfort that speakers feel about changing social situations. Christie Davies, who has published several books about ethnic humor, says that "to become angry about such jokes and to seek to censor them because they impinge on sensitive issues is about as sensible as smashing a thermometer because it reveals how hot it is."

Many of the people who agree with the idea of forbidding ethnic joking fail to realize how prevalent it is and that it can serve positive as well as negative purposes. Skilled speakers often use ethnic humor to challenge an audience's assumptions and to surprise listeners by making them bump up against some of their own prejudices. They say that audiences are more receptive to lessons that come with a smile than with a scolding.

Folklorist Elliott Oring says that for listeners to appreciate an ethnic joke they must know enough about the group to catch on quickly and easily, but at the same time they have to have a "measure of emotional distance from the subject matter of the humor." When the aspect of a culture that is being disparaged in a joke is "the focus of intense emotion . . . the communication may be regarded as slander rather than as humor," but on the other hand, a mild sense of discomfort may make the surprise and relief of the joke that much funnier.

Joke collector Larry Wilde claims that ethnic settings fill a literary need. They foreshadow the surprise but without giving it away. For example, Garrison Keillor's stories of his Minnesota Lutherans are more fun because readers have a context for understanding Keillor's statement that when the residents of Lake Wobegon come down with the "Swedish flu," "it's the usual flu with chills, fever, diarrhea, vomiting, achiness, and personal guilt, but it's accompanied by an overpowering urge to put things in order.

Before you collapse into bed, you iron the sheets. Before you vomit, you plan your family's meals for the upcoming week" ("The Speeding Ticket" from *Leaving Home*, 1987).

Ethnic references provide unlimited opportunities for inserting clever details that keep jokes from all sounding the same. They also provide keys to the stereotypes that enable jokesters to tell relatively complicated stories in only a few sentences.

Anthropologist Alan Dundes theorizes that Americans have more ethnic than political jokes because America has a free press where politicians and politics are lambasted on a daily basis. Americans therefore have little need for oral political jokes. But because people are often uncomfortable discussing such subjects as sexuality or racism, these tend to become the hidden subjects of joke cycles.

University of Maryland professor of American Studies Larry Mintz has described four developmental stages in ethnic humor. During the first stage, ethnic humorists tend to be critical of the outgroup. During the second stage they are critical of their own group in a kind of self-deprecation. In the third stage, the ethnic humorists become "realistic" in seeing laughable aspects of both their own group and the outgroup, while in the fourth stage the oppressed minority gains revenge by making fun of the majority.

The most amusing jokes are usually found in the middle ranges because this is where the hostility does not overpower the humor. But even in the same performance, a skilled entertainer may use all four levels. Dick Gregory, one of the first African Americans to perform in front of predominantly white audiences, found that people were too nervous to laugh if he started right off by drawing attention to his race. He would therefore start with neutral topics, but once the audience had laughed with him he would move on to tease them about their prejudices.

Often when people use self-deprecating humor in their own groups, they are chiding friends about the frailties to which human beings are prone. For example, a cartoon that appeared in the Brigham Young University newspaper in Utah showed a bloodied and battered student rising from a pile of stones that had apparently been thrown at him. As a campus police officer comes up, the student explains, "All I said was 'Let he who is without sin, cast the first stone.'"

Because BYU is a Mormon school, the joke was not anti-Mormon as much as it was a gentle reminder about smugness and self-righteousness. It was teaching the same lesson as the story about St. Peter taking visitors around Heaven and telling them to tiptoe past the room where the Mormons are "because they think they're the only ones here."

When a group member tells this kind of ethnic joke, it opens the door for inner-group communication and invites group members to examine their attitudes and behavior. But if outsiders tell the same joke, the effect is quite the opposite because the outsider focuses on the group's most obvious characteristics and implies that these characteristics belong to everyone in the group. Because outsiders have little power to bring internal change, the effect is to stereotype the group, which actually lessens the chances for change.

One of the complications of living in today's multicultural world is that group boundaries are unclear, especially in relation to immigrants. For example, noted Chinese writer Frank Chin has criticized Maxine Hong Kingston for *Woman Warrior* (1976), Amy Tan for *The Joy Luck Club* (1989), and David Henry Hwang for his plays *F.O.B.* and *M. Butterfly*. He accuses these writers of "boldly faking" Chinese fairy tales and childhood literature. Kingston, in a personal statement made for the Modern Language Association's *Approaches to Teaching Kingston's* The Woman Warrior (1991) explained her point of view:

> Sinologists have criticized me for not knowing myths and for distorting them; pirates [those who illegally translate her books for publication in Taiwan and China] correct my myths, revising them to make them conform to some traditional Chinese version. They don't understand that myths have to change, be useful or be forgotten. Like the people who carry them across oceans, the myths become American. The myths I write are new, American. That's

why they often appear as cartoons and Kung Fu movies. I take the power I need from whatever myth.

The difficulties of sorting out these kinds of subtleties were illustrated in 1996 when *The New Yorker* generated controversy with a "Black in America" issue, which was advertised as "keeping up with, even staying ahead of, a changing world." Richard Goldstein, writing in *The Village Voice* (May 7, 1996) said that

> In many respects, the black issue met that claim. There was bold writing by black authors, including a provocative (if arguable) profile of Farrakhan by Henry Louis Gates Jr. and some striking illustrations by black artists. But the cartoons clashed with the rest of the issue. Unlike the articles, they were inordinately concerned with the anxieties of white people around African Americans.

Goldstein conjectured that this was because only one of the 13 cartoonists featured in the issue was Black. In fact, the editors had contacted nine Black cartoonists and purchased eight of their cartoons, but when it came to making final decisions they were "nervous." Hendrik Hertzberg, *The New Yorker*'s editorial director explained, "We were worried about perpetuating stereotypes that people—especially Black readers—might see instead of the humor. It's something that wouldn't have been a problem in a context that wasn't so fraught with firstness as this issue."

One of the cartoonists, whose cartoon was paid for but not used, Barbara Brandon, wrote in a follow-up letter to the *Village Voice*, "What could be better for a cartoonist than being published in *The New Yorker*? I'm here to say being a black cartoonist whose work made them too 'nervous' to print. . . ." In the top panel of her two-part cartoon, a white woman was saying to a Black woman, "Why don't you get off your butt and get a job." The picture in the lower panel was identical except that the Black woman was now sitting at a desk and dressed for business. The white woman was saying, "Hey, wait a minute, I wanted that job!"

In conclusion, the following principles are ones that most humor scholars agree on in relation to ethnicity:

- Someone else's ethnic identification does not seem as important as does one's own.

- The appreciation of ethnic humor correlates with how much one knows about, and identifies with, the joke target.

- Humor is a tool that can be used either for building up or tearing down relationships.

- A joke told by a member of the targeted ethnic group is quite different from the same joke when it is told by an outsider.

See also AFRICAN AMERICAN HUMOR, AMERICAN INDIAN HUMOR, COMIC ZEITGEISTS, DIALECT HUMOR, HISPANIC HUMOR, JEWISH HUMOR, POLITICAL CORRECTNESS, REGIONAL HUMOR

Further reading: Joseph Boskin (ed.), *The Humor Prism in Twentieth-Century America* (1997). Michael Rogin, *Blackface, White Noise: Jewish Immigrants in the Hollywood Melting Pot* (1996). Mark Winokur, *American Laughter: Immigrants, Ethnicity, and 1930s Hollywood Film Comedy* (1996).

Exaggeration

Exaggeration is the enlarging of stories or things so that they are beyond belief or beyond normal expectations. Exaggeration, also referred to as *overstatement* and *hyperbole*, is a basic component of humor. Pantomimists, clowns, and comic dancers exaggerate gestures and facial expressions, while storytellers rely on such overstated contrasts as Clark Kent changing into Superman, frogs and beasts changing into princes, and old crones changing into beautiful maidens. The success of comedy teams often depends on exaggerated differences between the members as in the physical differences between the comic strip characters Mutt and Jeff and the emotional differences between Felix Unger and Oscar Madison in Neil Simon's *The Odd Couple*. Viewers expected comedy as soon as they saw short and chunky Danny DeVito co-starring with tall and muscular Arnold Schwarzenegger in the 1988 movie *Twins*. The same idea was the basis for the less successful 1998 movie *My Giant*, which starred short and slight Billy Crystal and the towering basketball star Gheorghe Muresan.

The secret of caricature is the artist's ability to select and exaggerate such prototypical features as Jimmy Carter's front teeth, Richard Nixon's nose, Gerald Ford's awkwardness, Ronald Reagan's forelock, George Bush's ordinariness, and Bill Clinton's sexual proclivities. Exaggeration inspires funny images as when Bill Dana tells the same hyperbolic joke disguised three ways.

First telling: A large group is assembled in an auditorium when from the loudspeaker comes the message, "Will the person with New York license plate BL 74468459030 623145098725, kindly remove it? Your license plate is blocking traffic."

Second telling: Two cowboys are talking, and the first one explains that the name of his ranch is the *Bar Nine, Circle Z, Rocking O, Flying W, Lazy R, Happy Two, Flying Nun Ranch*. When the second cowboy asks if he has many cattle, the first cowboy wistfully responds, "Not many survive the branding."

Third telling: Two football players are talking and one of them begins describing an especially heroic run that he made during the final football game of the season. When the opposing team could not stop him, "They brought the cannon out on the field, and they shot me with the cannon, and then the airplanes came down with machine guns, and still they couldn't stop me, and finally I made the touchdown." The other player indignantly interrupts with, "Anybody who was in the stadium that day could prove that's a lie!" to which the first player responds, "There were no survivors."

With literary humor, some authors prefer to sneak up on readers. Joseph Heller has explained that when he wrote *Catch-22* he exaggerated almost every incident, but in each case he developed his exaggerations so gradually that readers were unaware of just when the story reached a point beyond reality. In contrast, Marshall Dodge and Robert Bryan in their *Bert and I* records and books use such hyperbole that readers don't even look for credibility as shown by this account of a discouraged hunter named Kenneth, who had walked all day without seeing a single animal.

> He was all set to quit about sundown when he spied a fox about 20 yards distance. Takin' careful aim, he almost squeezed the trigger when he saw another fox about five feet from the first. He aimed somewhere in between and pulled the trigger. The shot hit a rock, split in two, and killed both foxes. The kick from the gun knocked Kenneth into the stream behind, and when he come to, his right hand was on a beaver's tail, his left hand was on an otter's head, and his trouser pockets were so full of trout that a button popped off his fly and killed a partridge.

This story sounds like the exaggerated wish-fulfillment that is part of frontier folklore. It is in opposition to the other kind of frontier humor that exaggerated the hardships that pioneers underwent. In relation to theories of relief and release, hyperbolic statements about hardships are comforting because people's real-life frustrations pale when compared to humorous exaggerations, as in the story of a Kansas farmer who had a hole in the roof of his sod house. When a traveler asked him what it was for, he explained that it was a crowbar hole: "Every morning I stick a crowbar through it, and if it doesn't bend, then I know it's not too windy to go out."

Advertisers who use hyperbolic humor have a good chance of putting across their desired point while not bearing the burden of proof that goes along with serious claims. Benjamin Franklin used this persuasive technique in a 1765 letter that he wrote to counteract British claims that American farmers did not raise enough sheep to provide wool for even one pair of stockings for each inhabitant. In his letter, Franklin said that "the very Tails of the American Sheep are so laden with Wooll, that each has a little Car or Waggon on four little wheels, to support and keep it from trailing on the ground."

When people conduct roasts or use other kinds of put-downs, hyperbole is the clue that humor is intended. An insult doesn't sound cruel when it is so exaggerated that it surprises listeners into laughing as with this 1990s anti-lawyer joke.

> A lawyer gets in a wreck and lies by the side of the road lamenting that his $60,000 Lexus has been destroyed. The disgusted policeman who is trying in vain to document the accident finally says, "You lawyers are all alike, so selfish and materialist. Just look at yourself. Your left arm has been torn off, and all you care about is your car." The shocked lawyer looks down at what used to be his left arm and gasps, "Oh, my God! Where's my $3,000 Rolex?"

See also COMEDY TEAMS, DIALECT HUMOR, FRONTIER HUMOR, LANGUAGE PLAY

F

Fiction

Novels and short stories are the two kinds of writing generally counted as fiction, but today some critics say that there is no more fiction or nonfiction—only narrative. As soon as any event is recorded on paper, it ceases to be the actual event but is instead a fictional event as seen by the writer and interpreted by the reader. Even though it is difficult if not impossible to clearly separate fiction from nonfiction according to this theory, the writers listed below are generally considered to have provided 20th-century Americans with healthy doses of humor through what is generally considered to be fiction.

Lisa Alther's (1944–) flawed characters irritate and annoy readers, but they also make them laugh. *Kinflicks* (1975) is her best-known book; others are *Bedrock* (1990), *Other Women* (1984), *Original Sins* (1981), and *Five Minutes in Heaven* (1995).

Thomas Berger (1924–) is famous for his dark humor and his ability to stretch readers' emotions through telling stories that are both real and fantastic. His *Crazy in Berlin* (1958) ushered in the era of dark humor, while he is best known to the general public through his *Little Big Man* (1964), which was made into a 1970 film starring Dustin Hoffman. Other titles include *Regiment of Women* (1973), *Sneaky People* (1975), *The Feud* (1983), *Nowhere* (1985), *Being Invisible* (1987), *The Houseguest* (1988), *Orrie's Story* (1990), *Meeting Evil* (1992), and *Suspects* (1996).

Richard Brautigan's (1935–1984) most famous book, *Trout Fishing in America* (1967), is a novel of the absurd that uses food to illustrate American's mixed-up values as trout becomes waste and fruits and seeds become sour and infertile. Other Brautigan titles include *A Confederate General from Big Sur* (1964), *The Pill Versus the Springhill Mine Disaster* (1968), *Abortion: An Historical Romance 1966* (1971), *Dreaming of Babylon: A Private Eye Novel, 1942* (1977), and *June 30th, June 30th* (1978).

Rita Mae Brown (1944–) says she tries to do what Flip Wilson did in helping white people understand Blacks through humor. Her first novel, *Rubyfruit Jungle* (1973), tells the "exuberant, picaresque, and semi-auto-biographical" story of Molly Bolt, who is "a kind of Lesbian Huck Finn." Brown's most obviously funny books are the mysteries that she's written, citing her cat, Sneaky Pie Brown, as co-author: *Wish You Were Here* (1990), *Rest in Pieces* (1992), *Murder at Monticello, or, Old Sins* (1994), *Pay Dirt, or, Adventures at Ash Lawn* (1995), and *Murder She Meowed* (1997).

Peter De Vries (1910–) has written nearly 25 novels filled with puns, parodies, paradoxes, epigrams, repartees, and wordplay. Word lovers call him a genius, while others complain that his cleverness interrupts his stories. Among his best-known novels are *But Who Wakes the Bugler?* (1940), *The Blood of the Lamb* (1961), *Let Me Count the Ways* (1965), *Madder Music* (1977), *Slouching toward Kalamazoo* (1983), and *The Mackerel Plaza* (1984).

Clyde Edgerton (1944–) delighted readers of *Raney: A Novel* (1985) with the sustained tone and the sound of Raney Bell's voice as she tells the deliciously funny story of her marriage. She is a Southern Free Baptist and her husband is an Episcopalian. The *Washington Post Book World* described Edgerton's writing as what James Thurber "might have written had he lived in North Carolina rather than Connecticut." Other humorous Edgerton books are *The Floatplane Notebooks: A Novel* (1988), *Killer Diller: A Novel* (1991), *Redeye: A Western* (1995), and *Where Trouble Sleeps: A Novel* (1997).

Stanley Elkin (1930–1995) mixes triumph and catastrophe in his dark comedies. A pervasive irony runs through most of his books, including *The Bad Man* (1967), *The Franchiser* (1976), *The Living End* (1979), *The Rabbi of Lud: A Novel* (1987), *The Six-Year-Old Man* (1987), *The Magic Kingdom* (1991), and *Pieces of Soap: Essays* (1992).

William Faulkner (1897–1962) was heavily influenced by the old Southwest humorists and borrowed many of their techniques. The humor in his novels and short stories ranges from crackerbox philosophy to black humor and from broad satire to sophisticated intellectual humor. In *The Hamlet* (1940), *The Sound and the Fury* (1956), *As I Lay Dying* (1957), *The Town* (1957), *The Mansion* (1959), and *The Reivers* (1962), he uses frame narratives around mock oral tales. His male and female con-artists are intriguing, as are his allusions and his names for characters and places. *The Faulkner Reader* (1954) and *The Portable Faulkner* edited by Malcolm Cowley (1966) are good sources for his short stories.

Joseph Heller (1923–) served in the U.S. Air Force from 1950–1952 and used his experience as the basis for writing what is ac-

knowledged as a masterpiece of black humor, *Catch-22: A Novel* (1961). He wrote a play *We Bombed in New Haven* (1968) and since has written several novels, including *Something Happened* (1974), *Good as Gold* (1979), *God Knows* (1984), *No Laughing Matter* (1986), *Picture This* (1988), *Closing Time* (1994), and *Now and Then: From Coney Island to Here* (1998).

John Irving (1942–) was fortunate in that the movie production of his 1978 novel *The World According to Garp* was almost as good as the book, which is filled with comic scenes that act as a counterbalance to what is basically a melancholic and sad story. Other Irving novels include *The Water Method Man* (1972), *The Hotel New Hampshire* (1981), *The Cider House Rules: A Novel* (1985), *Prayer for Owen Meany* (1989), *Trying to Save Piggy Sneed* (1996), and *A Widow for One Year: A Novel* (1998).

Erica Jong (1942–) startled the literary world in 1973 with *Fear of Flying: A Novel*, which talked openly and wittily about Isadora Wing, the protagonist, and her fantasies of "the zipless fuck." Isadora's story is continued in *How to Save Your Own Life: A Novel* (1977) and *Parachutes and Kisses* (1984). Other Jong novels include *Any Woman's Blues: A Novel of Obsession* (1990), *Fanny: Being the True History of the Adventures of Fanny Hackabout Jones: A Novel* (1980) and *Fear of Fifty: A Midlife Memoir* (1994).

Ken Kesey's (1935–) *One Flew Over the Cuckoo's Nest* (1963) is the story of Randal Patrick McMurphy's confinement to a mental hospital because he refuses to knuckle under to authority. The book is studied in literature classes and was made into a popular film and an off-Broadway play; however, its critics argue over whether it is a macho and sexist romance, or a black comedy in which readers are expected to see that the hero's actions are absurdist and farcical. Other Kesey satires include *Sometimes A Great Notion: A Novel* (1977), *Demon Box* (1986), *The Further Inquiry* (1990), and *Sailor Song* (1992).

W. P. Kinsella (1935–) is a Canadian author most famous for his hundred stories about a Cree Indian named Silas Ermineskin and for his baseball stories including *Shoeless Joe Jackson Comes to Iowa* (1980), which was adapted and produced as the 1989 movie *Field of Dreams*. Other baseball collections are *The Iowa Baseball Confederacy* (1986) and *The Dixon Cornbelt League and Other Baseball Stories* (1993).

Ring Lardner (1885–1933) is admired for his novel *You Know Me, Al: A Busher's Letters* (1925), but is even more revered for his biting glances at American culture in such short stories as "Haircut," and "The Golden Honeymoon." For straight humor, it is hard to beat "Alibi Ike" and "My Roomy." In 1995, Scribner's republished three of his books: *You Know Me Al*, *Gullible's Travels, etc.*, and *The Big Town: How I and the Mrs. Go to New York to See Life and Get Katie a Husband*.

Bernard Malamud (1914–1986) retells Yiddish prankster tales, writes about schlemiel-schlimazel twins (mostly father/son pairs), and mixes the natural and the supernatural. His 1961 *A New Life* is a satire dedicated, in effect, to the college where he taught undergraduates from 1949 to 1961 while writing his first three novels and several short stories. As Philip Roth observed about Malamud's *The Natural* (1952), this is "not baseball as it is played in Yankee Stadium, but a wild, wacky game." Several Malamud books are in print, including *The Stories of Bernard Malamud* (1984) and *Talk Horse: Bernard Malamud on Life and Work* (1996).

Flannery O'Connor (1925–1964) is considered by some critics to be the greatest American writer of short stories. Many of her stories, such as "A Good Man Is Hard to Find," "Everything That Rises Must Converge," and "Good Country People" are "grotesques" in which she blends humor and horror as she writes about clashes between males and females, the Old South as compared to the New South, and people's multiple approaches to religious faith. Unlike most writers of black humor, O'Connor was deeply religious and said she used her extreme

techniques to get the attention of people who were both blind and deaf to spirituality. O'Connor's short stories can be found in the collection, *The Complete Stories* (1990).

Philip Roth's (1933–) most famous book is *Portnoy's Complaint* (1969). While some critics describe the protagonist as a whining, stand-up comedian delivering a self-deprecating comic monologue, others say that beneath the cheap actions is a subtle and poignant human cry. Roth's other books include *Goodbye Columbus* (1959), considered to be one of his funniest works, *Our Gang: Starring Tricky and His Friends* (1971), *The Breast* (1972), *Zuckerman Unbound* (1981), *Zuckerman Bound* (1985), *Operation Shylock, A Confession* (1993), and *American Pastoral* (1997).

Damon Runyon (1880–1946), during the first half of the century, was one of the most popular writers of humorous short stories. Collections republished fairly recently include *Romance in the Roaring Forties and Other Stories* (1986), *The Bloodhounds of Broadway and Other Stories* (1981), and *Guys and Dolls: The Stories* (1992).

Jean Shepherd (1929–1999) often wrote short stories about the lost innocence of youth as in his funniest book *Wanda Hickey's Night of Golden Memories and Other Disasters* (1976). Additional short-story collections include *The Ferrari in the Bedroom* (1973) and *A Fistful of Fig Newtons* (1981). Novels include *In God We Trust, All Others Pay Cash* (1967) and *Phantom of the Open Hearth* (1977). Between 1960 and 1967, he wrote a column for *The Village Voice* while between 1968 and 1977 he wrote a column for *Car and Driver*. Indiana University has honored him for the originality of his fiction, while in four different years *Playboy*, where he has been a frequent contributor, gave him its humor and satire award. The 1983 movie *A Christmas Story*, is based on part of *In God We Trust, All Others Pay Cash*. This movie narrated by Shepherd himself, hilariously tells the story of a young boy in the 1940s and his scheming quest to get a Red Ryder BB gun for Christmas. Often shown on television at

Christmas time, it has become something of a cult classic.

Max Shulman (1919–1988) said he became a humorous writer because life was bitter, but he was not. He wrote novels, short stories, plays, screenplays, television scripts, and a syndicated column for college newspapers. His first book was *Barefoot Boy with Cheek* (1943), followed by *Max Shulman's Guided Tour of Campus Humor* (1955), *Rally Round the Flag, Boys* (1957), and *Potatoes Are Cheaper* (1971). His *The Many Loves of Dobie Gillis* (1956, reprinted in 1993) became a popular TV series running from 1959 to 1963.

Isaac Bashevis Singer (1904–1991) immigrated to the United States from Poland in 1935. Using Jewish folktales as a base, Singer first wrote his stories in Yiddish and later translated them into English. His stories are filled with irony often brought about through the way he treats realism side by side with fantasy and the supernatural. *The Collected Stories of Isaac Bashevis Singer* was published in 1982. The best known of his novels are *The Family Moskat* (1950), *The Manor* (1967), *The Estate* (1969), and *Enemies: A Love Story* (1972). He won the Nobel Prize for literature in 1978.

Jane Smiley (1949–) published her first novel *Barn Blind* in 1980, but it is her 1995 *Moo*, set in an agricultural college affectionately called Moo U, that gained her a reputation for the humorous writing that she continues in her 1998 *The All-True Travel and Adventures of Lidie Newton, A Novel*. She has published stories in many anthologies and in *Redbook*, *Atlantic*, *Mademoiselle*, *Fiction*, *TriQuarterly*, and *Playgirl*.

John Steinbeck (1902–1968) with his *The Grapes of Wrath* (1939) wrote the most widely read protest novel to come out of the Depression, but he also wrote lighter stories. His 1945 *Cannery Row* about the canning industry in Salinas Valley, California, is a biting and often funny satire of American values. Among his books where humor is mixed with seriousness are *Cup of Gold: A Life of Sir Henry Morgan, Buccaneer* (1936), *In Dubious Battle* (1936), and *Travels with Charley: In Search of America* (1962).

Mark Twain (1835–1910) is not a contemporary writer, but certainly his influence has been felt by 20th-century readers. In his *Green Hills of Africa* (1935), Ernest Hemingway credited Mark Twain's *Huckleberry Finn* (1885) with being the foundation of all American literature: "There was nothing before. There has been nothing as good since." Many of the writers in this list have relied on the techniques that Twain developed:

- A well-developed main character with whom readers can identify. Huck Finn was an outsider and an innocent, which made his observations and his thoughts fresh and insightful.

- A limited number of other interesting characters who provide the humor as they interact with the protagonist; for example, the dark humor connected to Pa and to Huck's staged death to get away from Pa, the slave hunters who are taken in by Huck's fib about his family's illness, and the Trickster characters of the Duke and the Dauphin.

- A picaresque plot in which the protagonist is on a journey (either figurative or literal) so that the plot moves basically in one direction as with Huck and Jim's trip down the Mississippi River.

- Spacing out the humor as comic relief for the treatment of thought-provoking and significant issues such as questions related to slavery, racism, religion, and morality.

- Interesting dialogue from a variety of voices and attitudes. Scholars are still studying the authenticity and the differences among the various dialects that Twain had his characters use.

Anne Tyler (1941–) creates original characters, who are believable even though she puts them in unusual occupations and settings. She writes with affection and humor

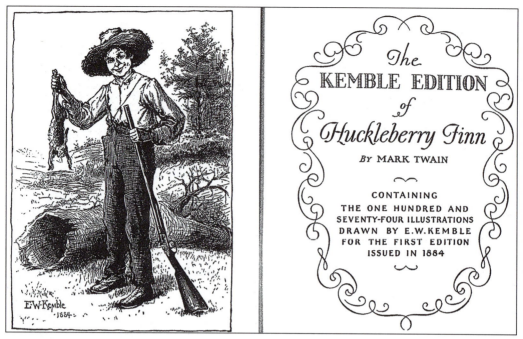

Ernest Hemingway credited Mark Twain's 1884 *Huckleberry Finn* with being the foundation of all American literature. While this may be an exaggeration, there is little doubt that it is a benchmark against which other fiction is measured.

about the communication challenges that people face in their most intimate relationships. *The Accidental Tourist* (1985) and *Breathing Lessons* (1988) have been made into well-received movies. Among her other popular novels are *A Slipping Down Life* (1970), *The Clock Winder* (1972), *Earthly Possessions* (1977), *Dinner at the Homesick Restaurant* (1982), *Saint Maybe* (1991), *Ladder of Years* (1995), and *A Patchwork Planet* (1998).

John Updike (1932–) is one of the keenest observers of contemporary life and one of the most prolific writers of the century. Short story collections include *Pigeon Feathers, and Other Stories* (1962), *The Music School, Short Stories* (1966), and *The Afterlife and Other Stories* (1994). He has written plays, poetry, and essays, as well as novels. The general public probably knows him best for *The Witches of Eastwick* (1984), which was made into a 1987 movie starring Jack Nicholson, Cher, Susan Sarandon, and Michelle Pfeiffer; however, his readers are partial to the witty observations in his books recounting the life of a high school basketball player: *Rabbit Run* (1960), *Rabbit Redux*

(1971), *Rabbit Is Rich* (1981), and *Rabbit at Rest* (1990).

Kurt Vonnegut Jr. (1922–) is described as a writer of science fiction, a satirist, and a black humorist, but running through all of his stories are clever jibes and observations about human behavior. His best known novels are *Player Piano* (1952), *Cat's Cradle* (1963), *God Bless You, Mr. Rosewater, or Pearls Before Swine* (1965), *Slaughterhouse-Five, or the Children's Crusade* (1969), *Breakfast of Champions: Or, Goodbye Blue Monday* (1973), and *Timequake* (1997). Short stories are collected in *Canary in a Cathouse* (1961) and *Welcome to the Monkey House* (1968).

Eudora Welty (1909–) is considered by some critics to be second only to Faulkner in the original and insightful ways that she portrays her fellow Southerners. She writes succinct and funny dialogue and is clever in the way she incorporates mythical allusions to reveal character. In 1984, Welty published her autobiographical *One Writer's Beginnings*. In *The Ponder Heart* (1954), a girl is literally tickled to death, while in *Losing Battles* (1970) Welty develops humorous interplay through the characters' dialogue. The family relationships in *The Optimist's Daughter* (1972) and in "Why I Live at the Post Office," published in *The Collected Stories of Eudora Welty* (1980), are so uniquely mean-spirited that readers end up laughing.

P. G. Wodehouse (1881–1975) was born in England, but died in America while working at age 93 to complete a 22-chapter novel (he got to chapter 16). During his long life, he wrote more than 93 full-length books, published 23 omnibus volumes of stories, wrote 12 plays, and created the lyrics for 300 songs in some 45 musicals. He also worked on the scripts of 48 films and wrote over 500 articles, short stories, essays, and verses for *Punch* and other magazines. His funny stories about Jeeves (a butler) and Bertie Wooster (Jeeves's intimidated boss) are the most famous. Sample titles include *Carry on Jeeves!* (1927), *The Code of the Woosters* (1938), and *Jeeves and the Tie That Binds* (1973). Chances are good that any humorous television show or film that includes a British butler has been influenced by P.G. Wodehouse's funny imaginings. *See also* BLACK HUMOR, HUMOROUS ESSAYISTS

Further reading: *American Authors on the Web,* http://www.lang.nagoya-u.ac.jp/~matsuoka/ AmeLit.html (August 1999). Don L. F. Nilsen, *Humor in American Literature: A Selected Annotated Bibliography* (1992).

Frontier Humor

Frontier humor is a unique blend of exaggeration, optimism, creativity, propaganda, and tomfoolery. America has had basically two frontiers, first the frontier of the Old Southwest (Arkansas, Kentucky, Missouri, Oklahoma, Tennessee, and Texas), and then the frontier of the far West. Writers from the Old Southwest included Joseph Glover Baldwin, George Washington Harris, Johnson Jones Hooper, Henry Clay Lewis, Augustus Baldwin Longstreet, Thomas Bangs Thorp, and Mark Twain. Many of their stories are framed tales in which an Eastern narrator starts the story in standard English and then introduces the comic characters who present the vernacular humor. Except for

Mark Twain, these writers used such heavy dialect that few contemporary readers find their humor worth the effort demanded in their reading. Critic Pascal Covici says in his *Humor and Revelation in American Literature* that "brutality and coarseness were blown up out of all proportion in order to solidify the position of the detached witness." Most of the events could not have been enacted by mere human beings. "In fact, a whole menagerie of frontier titans were used to accommodate the Gentleman's need for low behavior from which to disassociate himself."

Humor of the far West served different purposes. It was a kind of test, an elaborate initiation ceremony for newcomers. Mountain men, scouts, cowboys, and Texas Rangers wanted to know the temperament of their companions. Folklore collector Mody Boatright in *Folk Laughter on the American Frontier* explains that when each man's survival depended upon the other men in the group, these frontiersmen would not admit to their fraternity anyone who could not "take a joke." Being able to tell good lies was also part of the fun. Davy Crockett bragged, "I can outspeak any man," while the epitaph on Pecos Bill's tombstone is said to read, "Here lies Pecos Bill. He always lied, and always will. He once lied loud. He now lies still."

Another reason for the popularity of humor is that frontiersmen faced bigger-than-life challenges and conditions of nature that had never been seen or even dreamed of. In the mid-1800s, scout Jim Bridger sent reports back east on his explorations of the Yellowstone region. Boatright says that Bridger's "accurate reports of geysers, petrified trees, and obsidian mountains gained for him the reputation of being the most fertile liar in the West." No one believed other people's reports of rivers teeming with so many fish that they could be coaxed to jump into boats or of upside down rivers where the sand was on top and the water running underground—"to keep from getting sunburned," joked Arizona's Dick Wick Hall.

True stories this fantastic inspired many exaggerations based on at least a kernel of truth. These exaggerated stories, which provided all-around amusement as well as emotional release, explore a relatively small set of archetypal situations and characters.

Frontier Justice: Stories about frontier justice illustrate the belief that people joke about what makes them nervous. What justice there was was unpredictable and happenstance. Boatright tells about the discovery of a man's body dangling from the limb of a tree. Pinned to his clothing was a note reading, "In some respects this is a very bad man. In other respects he is a damn sight worse." Another Boatright story is about Jack Smith, whose body was taken to the town coroner for a decision on how he died. The coroner attributed his death to heart disease: "We found two bullet holes and a dirk knife in the organ, and we recommended that Bill Younger be lynched to prevent spreading of the disease."

The Greenhorn: Frontiersmen loved making fun of greenhorns, especially if they were visitors from England. In one story, a visitor is found along a stream in Texas near death from thirst. His tongue is swollen and bulging from between his blistered lips. When his rescuers find him, they ask why he didn't drink from the stream. His explanation: "I didn't have a cup!" Another greenhorn story is about a newcomer who bought a herd of mules and then gave them away because they wouldn't reproduce. Yet another is about a visitor calling a country boy an ignorant fool because the boy can't give the city man directions to the next town. After his berating, the boy responds, "I knows I don't know nothing. I knows I's a fool. But I *ain't* lost."

Even a man as astute as Charles Dickens could not comprehend the American West. When he came on his grand tour of America, the farthest west he got was St. Louis. Upon his return to England, he declared "the American West" was a fraud.

The Inarticulate Cowboy: In a kind of self-deprecating humor, cowboys joked about their lack of the finer social graces. A man was hanged, and when no one wanted to report the bad news to his wife, lots were drawn and the losing cowboy reluctantly went to the wife's cabin and knocked on the door. When she answered, he asked, "Does the widow Smith live here?" The woman responded, "I'm Mrs. Smith, but I am not a widow," to which the man replied, "I'll bet you 10 dollars you are!"

In another story about poor communication skills, a cowboy walks up to a friend and asks, "Didn't you say that Bill Jones said that I was a hot-headed, overbearing sort of man?" "Naw, you mistook me. I didn't say that he said that." "Well now, that's too bad. I've killed an innocent man."

The Judge: Frontier judges earned a kind of grudging respect as in the story about a trial in which one attorney called the opposing attorney a "lying son of a bitch." The rival attorney promptly replied, "You're a lying son of a bitch yourself." After this exchange, the judge calmly declared, "Now that you gentlemen have got acquainted with each other, we will proceed with the argument."

The story of Colorado Judge M. B. Gerry, who in 1883 sentenced Alferd E. Packer to death for cannibalism during a Colorado snowstorm, illustrates one of the ways that exaggeration worked. Judge Gerry pronounced the sentence in standard legalese, but the situation was so bizarre that it inspired a reporter to run from the courtroom to the local bar and announce that the Judge had said, "There were only seven Democrats in all of Hinsdale County and you, you son of a bitch, ate five of them." This quote was printed in Eastern newspapers and made both Judge Gerry and Alferd Packer folklore heroes. For example, at the University of Colorado in Boulder, the student cafeteria is named the Alferd Packer Grill and souvenir sweatshirts bear the messages "Serving All of Mankind" and "Keep Your Eyes on Your Thighs!"

Pour Quoi Stories: Many folk legends are "Pour Quoi" stories giving explanations for natural phenomena. Pecos Bill dug the Rio Grande because he was tired of packin' water from the Gulf of Mexico. One year when he was bored, he put thorns on trees and horns on toads and as a joke invented the centipede and the tarantula. Icebergs and tidal waves are leftovers from the days when Paul Bunyan threw chunks of ice out into the Great Lakes for Babe the Blue Ox to retrieve. The San Francisco earthquake was caused by Stackalee's getting mad at a bartender who refused to sell him a drink. He "laid a-holt of the bar with both hands and give one powerful jerk and down come the ceiling and whole building" followed by the entire city of San Francisco. "It was the watah pipes," he said. "They was fastened together all over town."

The Preacher: Like the judge, frontier preachers earned grudging respect. In the early days of the Republic of Texas, a Baptist preacher preparing for a trip was carefully cleaning and loading his long rifle. A friend, who knew the preacher believed in predestination, challenged him on why he needed a rifle to defend himself. If he were predestined to die he should just be ready to meet his maker. "Yes, I know all about that," replied the preacher, "But it might not be my time to die; it might be the other feller's."

Boatright quotes a popular preacher's prayer filled with the same kind of irony that Mark Twain used in his "War Prayer." The preacher is asking that a cowboy might recover from the bite of a snake that the Lord had sent, and become the Lord's faithful servant:

> And we pray thee, O Lord, to send also a rattlesnake to bite his brother Tom that he may likewise repent for his wickedness and be saved from hell. And we supplicate thee, O Lord, most earnestly to send another and a larger rattlesnake to bite their father, who has led these fine young men into a life of wickedness, that he may likewise repent of his crimes and turn to thee before it is too late. These things we ask in Jesus' name. Amen.

Unusual Animals: Horses were often the heroes of animal tall tales. On signal, Wild Bill Hickok's Black Nell was said to drop to the ground "as if a cannonball had knocked the life out of her." This often saved Wild Bill because when they came upon enemies she would drop out of sight in the tall grass before anyone saw them. Other "realistic" animals included bears that would sit down

and talk to men and dogs that knew exactly when to bark and who to bite. Cracker-barrel philosopher Josh Billings adopted an understated tone when he observed that the principle food of the fly was "anything," that the ant "has no holidays, no eight-hour system, nor never strikes for higher wages," and that "it is impossible to do anything well with a flea on you except swear."

An opposite approach was taken by humorists writing about Paul Bunyan's Babe the Blue Ox and the mosquitoes at Big Mantisque Lake, which made droning noises like airplanes and were big enough to carry off cows. Purely imagined animals include the *hoop snake,* which moves by rolling along, the *splinter cat,* which dives headfirst into trunks of trees looking for honey bees, and the *hugag,* which because it has no knees sleeps propped against houses or fences or barns, which is why there are so many leaning structures in the West.

Weather Conditions: Changing weather conditions are spoofed in a story about a cowboy deciding to take a swim. He takes off his clothes and dives from a high bluff, but just as he jumps, a drought comes along and dries up the pool. He is sure he is going to dash his brains out on the rock bottom, but then a cloudburst opens up just in time to save him. However, he suffers some slight injury because in the meantime a "norther" has blown in from Canada and when he hits bottom the ice is thick enough to cause a considerable knot on his head.

In another weather-related story, a cowboy is riding along and sees a pretty good hat lying in the mud. He dismounts to pick it up when a voice underneath shouts, "Hey, what you doing there?" When the cowboy realizes that the hat is still on a man's head, he asks if he can help. "No, thank you," comes the reply. "I'm riding a mighty good horse and I guess I'll make it through."

Western Women: Men far outnumbered women on the frontier and frontiersmen made exaggerated jokes about their size, their power, and their looks. One stanza of the song "Old Dan Tucker" goes:

The purtiest gal I ever saw
Was Old Dan Tucker's daughter-in-law.
Her eyes bugged out and her nose bugged in,
And her lip hung down over her chin.

One night when Mike Fink crawled into an alligator's hide to frighten Davy Crockett's wife, "She threw a blast of eye-lightnin' upon him that made it daylight for half an hour." Boatright says that Sal Fungus could "scalp an Indian, laugh the bark off a pine tree, swim stark up a cataract, gouge out an alligator's eyes, dance a rock to pieces, sink a steamboat, blow out the moonlight, tar and feather a puke, ride a panther bare-back, sing a wolf to sleep, and scratch his hide off." Luke Logroller's bride was "six feet high in her stocking feet; that is she would have been only she'd got no stockings." A girl who once rescued Davy Crockett from eagles was "as tall as a sapling and had an arm like a keel-boat's tiller." On their wedding day, Pecos Bill's Slue-Foot Sue insisted on riding his horse Widow-Maker. When Widow-Maker bucked her off she bounced so high on her spring bustle that she orbited the moon and they had to throw jerky to her to keep her from starving to death. In one version, Bill gets her back by lassoing her, while in another he has to shoot her.

Wish-Fulfilling Work Heroes: The most archetypal of all the characters were the wish-fulling work heroes who gave hope that help was on its way. Of course people didn't really believe the stories about work heroes, but they enjoyed dreaming of men who could accomplish impossible tasks with one hand tied behind their backs, as shown by these brags quoted by B. A. Botkin:

- Joe Barnes was "sired by a yoke of cattle, suckled by a she-bear . . . , and had three sets of teeth and gums for another set."

- Mike Fink was "a Salt River roarer . . . a ring-tailed squealer . . . half wild horse and half cock-eyed alligator and the rest crooked snags and red-hot snappin' turtle."

- Nimrod Wildfire was "a touch of the airthquake"; he had the "prettiest sis-

ter, fattest horse, and ugliest dog in the district."

- Wirt Staples has "a shadow that can wilt grass, breath that can poison mosquitoes, and a yell that can break windows."

While "the folk" undoubtedly contributed to the creation of frontier humor and to stories about work heroes, professional writers were more responsible than is generally acknowledged. Almanac makers, newspaper writers, and advertisers eager to get Western copy of interest to Eastern readers began adapting anecdotes and old jokes into "westerns." They used suffixes to create such new words as *poundiferous* for "heavy," *circledicular* for "round," *golumgumtiated* for "confused," and *bodacious* for "awesome." To give a frontier flavor to their stories, eggs were referred to as *hen apples*, coffee as *belly wash*, an upset stomach as *collywobbles*, and something on a slant as *antigodlin* or *catawampus*. All around modifiers include *all-fired* as in "She's all-fired sweet," and "He's all-fired rambunctious," *seldom* as in "There's something seldom about that dog [person, tree, horse, etc.]," and *rip snorter* or *rip roarer* as in "That was a rip snorter of a trip," or "He's a regular rip roarer." *So . . . that* was used as a productive pattern for creating exaggerations as in

- He is so stingy that he sits in the shade of the hackberry tree to save the shade of the porch.

- His feet are so big that he has to put his pants on over his head.

- Her teeth stick out so far that she can eat a pumpkin through a rail fence.

Individuals with name recognition (Sam Bass, Davy Crockett, Mike Fink, John Henry, Jesse James, Billy the Kid, etc.) were connected to whatever anecdotes or stories seemed appropriate. Paul Bunyan stories were written during the 1920s as part of a publicity campaign for the Red River Lumber Company. James Stevens wrote many of the stories, while another writer, W. B. Laughead, was largely responsible for the names. He chose *Babe* as an ironic name for a huge animal. *Johnny Inkslinger* was a natural because camp clerks were called inkslingers. *Shot Gunderson* and *Chris Crosshaul* were in the lingo of lumberjacks as nicknames for any Scandinavian, and *Sourdough Sam*'s name was taken from the name of a cook who lost an arm and a leg when his sourdough barrel blew up.

Other writers who collected, polished, and published frontier folklore include W. H. Auden, John Lee Brooks, Max Gartenberg, Herbert Halpert, Luc Lacourciere, James MacGillivray, James Kirk Paulding, Albert Peterson, William Trotter Porter, Vance Randolph, John S. Robb, Matt Surrell, Louis Untermeyer, Dale Warren, and Homer A. Watt. The effect of journalists putting their professional stamp on frontier folklore was twofold. It brought about a kind of centralization in that the stories of hundreds of local heroes were attached to a couple of dozen nationally known figures. This means that many of the true locations and sources were lost, but on the other hand, professional writers made the stories accessible to many people far removed in time and space from any American frontier. Because of this, frontier humor has enhanced the following characteristics of American humor:

- An uninhibited and playful kind of boasting and exaggeration.

- The professional creation of humor disguised as folk humor through the use of nonstandard speech.

- An irreverence for authority as shown through making fun of religious, judicial, and political leaders.

- Glorification of the common person at the expense of the intellectual.

- The enjoyment of bizarre events and the making light of such gruesome topics as starvation, accidents, and even death.

See also DIALECT HUMOR, HOAXES AND PRACTICAL JOKES, REGIONAL HUMOR

Further reading: C. L. Sonnichsen, *The Laughing West: Humorous Western Fiction, Past and Present. An Anthology* (1988).

G

Gay and Lesbian Humor

Because homosexuality is such a sensitive issue in American life, the subject is often treated indirectly through jokes created both by and about gays and lesbians. Such joking appears in genres as different as comedy skits, sitcoms, hate speech, cartoons, and witty rejoinders, such as when Noel Coward approached Edna Ferber, who was wearing a mannish looking suit, and commented, "You look almost like a man." Her response was, "So do you."

For as long as drama has been in existence, playwrights have been able to get laughs by having men dress in women's clothing. Even today this is the main technique of the Ballet Trocadero de Monte Carlo dance troupe where male dancers perform such traditionally feminine ballets as "Swan Lake." Much of the humor in the screwball comedies of the 1930s and early 1940s came from incidents of cross-dressing and from such stock comedians as Edward Everett Horton and Franklin Pangborn playing the roles of dandified fops. Even Stan Laurel and Oliver Hardy had a kind of sissy-buddy relationship, and in Hal Roach's 1932 *Their First Mistake* they lived as husband and wife and were shown in bed together with a baby between them. These kinds of "soft" male friendships disappeared in the 1940s as people began to view such characters as coded homosexuals instead of eccentrics. For the next two decades, gays were either excluded from the movies or were cast as psychopaths or suicides. Not until after the social and sexual revolution of the 1960s would cross-dressing again appear in comic movies, for example in the 1978 *La Cage aux Folles*, the 1982 *Tootsie* starring Dustin Hoffman, the 1982 *Victor/Victoria* starring Julie Andrews, and the 1993 *Mrs. Doubtfire* starring Robin Williams. While not all of these are overtly about homosexuality, there is a kind of titillation underlying males dressing as females, even when it is something as innocent as a male principal of an elementary school promising to wear a dress if every student reads 15 books.

Homosexuals are a unique kind of minority in that they are not born into homosexual families so they lack the built-in support system from family that racial or religious minorities have. Also, many gays and lesbians do not recognize their sexual orientation until they are in their teens or beyond. Some religions teach that homosexuality is a sin, and in spite of the fact that the American Psychological Association no longer identifies homosexuality as "deviant," many people still view it as such and make fun of homosexuals as a way of turning young people against the idea. Such persuasion tactics range from overt hate jokes to exchanged glances, raised eyebrows, smirks, and the lifting of a limp wrist. People anxious to dissuade young people from homosexuality also condone, or at least do not discourage, the use of humor targeting gays and lesbians by children and teenagers.

However, not all critics agree on the effects of such humor. Some feel that, as with humor about ethnicity and disabilities, the joking may serve to relieve tensions by satisfying curiosity and showing that the subject is open for discussion. As gay and lesbian activists have become more assertive, they turned anti-gay humor on its head. By bringing homosexuality out into the open, comedians encourage the general public, including young people, to examine and perhaps argue about the underlying assumptions about homosexuality.

M. E. Kerr, a witty and popular writer for teenagers, has been including references to homosexuality in her books for nearly 25 years. In her 1977 *I'll Love You When You're More Like Me*, protagonist Wally has a best friend, Charlie Gilhooley, who is gay. Wally's dad, who runs a mortuary, "has an assortment of names for Charlie: *limp wrist, weak sister, flying saucer, fruitstand, thweetheart, fairy tale, cupcake*, on and on," but he never uses those names to Charlie's face because "after all, everybody's going to die someday, including the Gilhooleys; why make their only son uncomfortable and throw business to Annan Funeral Home?"

In Kerr's later books, she made homosexuality a main theme. In her 1986 *Night Kites* about a young man with AIDS coming home to die, she includes several old jokes about gays, partly as a counterbalance to the sadness of the story and partly to demonstrate how hard the younger brother has to work to overcome his own prejudices and fears. The title of her 1994 award-winning *Deliver Us from Evie*, which is told by the brother of a teenage lesbian, comes from the way one of Evie's "friends" teases her in church by loudly misstating a line from "The Lord's Prayer."

People who believe homosexuality is a sin are on the lookout for "normalization." In February of 1999, Reverand Jerry Falwell was given credit for "outing" Tinky Winky, one of the four Teletubbies in the British-made television show for infants. As the controversy gathered momentum, Falwell denied being responsible for the article in his *National Liberty Journal* whose headline read "Parents Alert: Tinky Winky Comes Out of the Closet." Evidence given in the article to support the assertion that Tinky Winky is gay included his being purple (the gay pride color), his antenna being triangle-shaped (a gay pride symbol), and his carrying a magic bag resembling a purse.

The story resulted in abundant free publicity for the Teletubbies and a surge in Tinky Winky sales. In newspaper columns and on television, commentators ridiculed the charge by noting that Barney is also purple, joking about finally understanding the meaning of those triangle-shaped road signs saying "Yield," and repeating old accusations about the friendships of Fred Flintstone and Barney Rubble, Bert and Ernie on Sesame Street, and Batman and Robin. In relation to the latter, Leonard Pitts of the Tribune Media Services (Feb. 14, 1999) asked, "How obvious can it be? Two single guys, living together, carrying on a double life. Worse, they tooled around in the Batmobile, a powerful machine they kept driving into the dark, mysterious recesses of the Batcave."

In spite of this kind of apparent support for gays, being a gay comedian is still not easy according to Tom Kunz, writing in *The New York Times* (Sep. 28, 1997). He acknowledged Ellen DeGeneres's coming out as a lesbian after "she hit the bigtime in television," as a good thing, but still, he said, networks "aren't exactly stampeding to gay comics with offers of sitcoms, fame, and fortune." Nevertheless over the past few decades, many openly gay comedians have become steady performers in comedy clubs. Kunz presented a sampling "minus the raunch and bad taste" from a compendium of the works of some 30 gay comedians collected by Ed Karvoski Jr. For example, Robin Tyler, who has been openly lesbian since the 1970s, advises, "If homosexuality is a disease, let's all call in queer to work. 'Hello, can't work today. Still queer.'"

Three gay comedians in New York, Bob Smith, Danny McWilliams, and Jaffe Cohen, work under the name *Funny Gay Males*. They told a *New York Times* reporter (Apr. 11, 1993) that they like working as a team because there's safety in numbers. While Cohen is the "Jewish New Yorker," Danny represents "blue-collar Queens," and Bob is the "all-American guy from Buffalo," no one has to be the "official gay comic."

Across the continent in San Francisco, a street theater group calling themselves the *Sisters of Perpetual Indulgence* also finds it more comfortable to act as a group. The Sisters include some 30 gay, lesbian, bisexual, and transgender members who dress as far-out nuns and use such names as Sister Dimanda Tension, Sister Ann R. Key, Sister Phyllis Stein, and Sister Reyna Terror. They hold parties and perform in gay pride parades and at charitable events. They were in the news (*New York Times*, Mar. 26, 1999) because of protests from Catholics about the San Francisco Board of Supervisors approving the closing of one block of Castro Street for their Easter Sunday 20th-anniversary celebration.

Karen Ripley from Berkeley, California, gets laughs by telling how when she came out to a straight friend and told her she was lesbian, the first thing the friend said was, "Really? Do you know Jill McGee? She's a lesbian in Philadelphia!" "Pardon me for laughing," says Ripley, "but straight people are so funny! They think we all know each other! Actually, I do know her. But, hey, it's just a coincidence!"

One of the best known gay comedians is Tom Ammiano, who defines homophobia as "the irrational fear that three gays will break into your house and redecorate it against your will." In the early 1990s, Ammiano was the San Francisco School Board president in his day job and a gay comedian in his night job. The two roles often crossed over as he would bring his sense of humor into public meetings and his meetings into his comedy act. As a former teacher, he did a school routine in which he talked about California Governor Pete Wilson wanting to put God back in the classroom. "But thanks to Pete, instead of 25 kids, I've got 35. If God can find a desk, She's more than welcome." And when

a school board member once told him there was no such thing as a gay Boy Scout, he responded, "I beg your pardon, I was a gay Boy Scout. I was the Avon representative for my troop."

During the early 1990s, Tom Ammiano was both president of the San Francisco School Board and a gay comedian. *Photo by Rink Foto*

In their book, *The Story of English* (1992), published in conjunction with the PBS television series, Robert McCrum, William Cran, and Robert MacNeil write that the general population is now adopting gay usages into everyday language; for example, referring to office clothes as *business drag*, making known one's personal views as *coming out of the closet*, and watching and observing something as *cruising*. While such playful usages are not the kind of humor that makes one laugh out loud, the fact that they are neutral or even positive in tone shows that the general public is becoming less uncomfortable about homosexuality.

Theater critic Laurie Stone in her 1997 *Laughing in the Dark* traces the evolution of this change by describing the role of such activists as Jack Smith with his 1963 *Flaming Creatures* and a whole group of celebrities dedicated to turning "depravity into chic." Andy Warhol was one of these as were Jackie Curtis, Holly Woodlawn, and Candy Darling. In 1967, Charles Ludlam, Black Eyed Susan, and Lola Pashalinski founded the *Ridiculous Theatrical Company*. Two years later in 1969 when police raided the Stonewall bar on Christopher Street under the New York City law forbidding a man from wearing more than three articles of women's clothing in public, drag queens including Marsha P. Johnson and Sylvia (Ray) Rivera fought back. In 1971, the *Cockettes*, a San Francisco glitter queen troupe, performed in New York. Although it was not a polished show, it gave confidence to New York gay theater pioneers. Jimmy Camicia's dancing troupe *Hot Peaches* was formed and so was the *Ballet Trocadero de Monte Carlo*. In 1983, Ira Siff began singing soprano roles in public and founded *La Gran Scena Opera*.

At first these theatrical groups performed only for other gays and lesbians, but gradually they began appearing on talk shows and in movies. It was a matter of pride that they not be manipulated by mainstream media. In 1986 Holly Woodlawn outfoxed Geraldo Rivera when he was trying to "out" her in an interview. In 1993, k.d. lang did the same thing in a Connie Chung interview. Their point was that they wanted to be in control when they talked about their own sexuality.

Throughout the 1970s, what Stone calls "Warholian sass" began seeping into the movies; for example, in the 1976 *Rocky Horror Picture Show*, Tim Curry performs "Sweet Transvestite" in a manner that Vito Russo described in his 1981 *The Celluloid Closet* as "the essence of what every parent in America fears will happen if our sexual standards are relaxed. It becomes the living horror of making deviant sexuality visible and tangible."

Music videos and documentaries have also played a part in bringing drag and queer theater from the margins to the mainstream, especially Madonna's "*Vogue*" and Jennie Livingston's *Paris Is Burning*, a documentary about the drag balls of Harlem. Since stand-up comedy is more business venture than art form, it took longer for gay and lesbian com-

ics to be hired in mainstream clubs. Among the earliest New York clubs to book gay comedians were the Duplex and Caroline's. In the spring of 1996, Club Casanova in Alphabet City began a weekly drag king night. While drag queens have long been considered hilarious, drag kings seem to make the public more nervous because the idea that women can get along without men is a newer and therefore more threatening social idea. But proponents of either drag group say that they are not so much interested in becoming members of the opposite sex as they are in freeing themselves from assigned gender roles, no matter what they are.

News of such revolutionary ideas and the increasing appearance of gay comedians on cable TV and in mainstream movies has elicited protests from the Christian right and from government conservatives who object to funds being expended by the National Endowment for the Arts to support gay theater, gay writing, or art such as that created by Robert Mapplethorpe. However, the ensuing publicity may have helped as much as it harmed gay causes. In the mid-1990s, mainstream jokesters ranged from such "acceptable" lesbians as Sandra Bernhard's character on *Roseanne*, Lisa Edelstein's role on *Relativity*, and Ellen DeGeneres's role on her own show to such far-out comedians as Lea DeLaria who stole Arsenio Hall's show in March of 1993. One of her jokes is not that she doesn't like penises, she "just doesn't like them on men." In 1994, Bob Smith did an HBO show "queering the mainstream" by unclosseting gayness behind a calm demeanor, shamefacedly admitting to having experimented with heterosexuality in college where, he said, "I slept with a straight guy." Then he apologized, "I was really drunk."

Such group names as Split Britches, Bloolips, Pomo Afro Homos, and Five Lesbian Brothers reflect the playful sense of rebellion that is inherent in making jokes against the majority culture. And while such groups are hoping to change the majority culture, critics worry that becoming mainstream also changes the rebels. For example, Laurie Stone accuses drag queen RuPaul of having created "a vanilla-friendly version" of himself. She

Androgyny, as demonstrated here by Lea DeLaria, has a long comic history. ©*Mark Allan/Alpha London/ Globe Photos Inc.*

describes his raw humor while "doing drag downtown," but "on *Oprah* his message is: 'Go after your dreams.'" *See also* GENDER AND HUMOR, STAND-UP COMEDY

Further reading: Julian Fleisher, *The Drag Queens of New York: An Illustrated Guide* (1996). Ed Karvoski, *A Funny Time to Be Gay* (1997). Laurie Stone, *Laughing in the Dark: A Decade of Subversive Comedy* (1997).

Gender and Humor

Gender is related to humor in at least three ways. *Gender*, as used here, includes not just the physical differences between males and females, but also the cultural beliefs and expectations that have developed around these basic differences. That so many jokes involve issues of gender illustrates the theory that jokes will flourish on whatever topics make people nervous. The most obvious kind of gender-related humor is that used by one gender to put down the other. A second type of gender-related humor is a step removed and is more sophisticated in that it is humor about conflicts between the sexes. The third related area is the differences between males and females in the creation, performance, and appreciation of humor.

Sexist humor, which makes fun of the real or imagined characteristics of males and females, is seen in the oldest myths, fairy tales, folk tales, nursery rhymes, and sacred writings. Because jokes are a kind of shorthand, creators do not start with a whole new cast of characters for each joke; instead they rely on familiar scripts that include exaggerations and stereotypes. This enables listeners to fill in the details from the material that their minds have already absorbed from the popular culture.

Common foils for sexist jokes include virgins, older women (especially mothers-in-law), cuckolded males, talkative women, unattractive women, and both males and females who act stupid in gender-related ways, for example, John Belushi crushing a beer can against his forehead in *Animal House* and Goldie Hawn giggling when she muffed her lines on *Laugh-In*.

Early radio, in its search for natural-sounding ways to hold audiences with different voices, paired males and females in such popular shows as *The Easy Aces*, *Vic and Sade*, *Burns and Allen*, *The Bickersons*, *The Honeymooners*, *Fibber McGee and Molly*, *Amos 'n' Andy*, and *The Jack Benny Program*. These shows were the foundation of what today is domestic comedy, where a large portion of the humor is based on male/female differences and quarrels. Women have complained that they are the ones always given the stupid roles, but actually in the domestic realm there has been enough stupidity to go around. In the 1990s, William R. Mattox Jr. the director of Research and Policy Analysis for the Family Research Council in Washington, DC, studied Father's Day vs. Mother's Day cards and found that one in four Father's Day cards (as compared to one in seven Mother's Day cards) was intended to be funny. The humor came from poking good-natured fun at the Man of the House, as in "Happy Father's Day to the smartest, kindest, most generous and loving dad in the whole world—Hey! Look at me when I'm praising you," and "You're such a great dad. You deserve a 21-gun salute—Would you settle for 10 belches, 7 knuckles cracking, and 4 armpit sounds?" The humor in the Mother's Day cards was more likely to be self-deprecating or insulting to someone else, as in "Mom, I can't find the words to tell you how much I love you—I know, I know, 'Look it up,'" and "It's Mother's Day, Mom, and I just wanted to say—Thanks for stomping that imaginary brake that way when Dad drives. Probably saved our lives dozens of times."

In spite of this kind of evidence, the general perception has been that because men have been the ones in power, sexist jokes have traditionally targeted women. However, in the early 1990s women launched their own joke wars with such riddles as

- Why are all the dumb-blonde jokes one-liners? (So men can understand them.)

- What do you call a man with his hands handcuffed behind his back? (Trustworthy)

- How do you force a man to do sit-ups? (Put the TV remote between his toes.)

- What did God say when he created man? (Hey, I can do better than this.)

For a *Los Angeles Times* article (Oct. 6, 1992), Nancy Wride interviewed several authorities about this wave of male-bashing jokes. Historian Joseph Boskin explained that for the first time in American history, minority groups were able to openly retaliate against their oppressors through the use of humor. Some observers believed that this "year of the woman" (1992) and the round of male-bashing jokes were triggered by outrage over the Clarence Thomas confirmation hearings. Others weren't so sure. Feminist Susan Brownmiller, author of *Against Our Will* (1975), said that while she's laughed at a few of the jokes, she doesn't feel like dignifying the joke war by giving it great significance. "It's just a blip on the screen." "Lighten up," said comedian Diane Ford, who thinks that even if the white-men-as-slime era goes on for 30 years, "we still wouldn't even the score." Anthropologist Alan Dundes said he noticed a fresh wave of men-as-nincompoops

jokes in the early 1990s. He predicted they will be around for a couple of years or until the war between the sexes balances out. Greg Howard, the creator of the nationally syndicated *Sally Forth*, a feminist-inspired comic strip, used the jokes for material when he had Sally's husband, Ted, complain, "Stand-up comics, sitcoms, comic strips . . . more and more it's men who are the butt of the jokes. . . . Pretty soon we'll be hearing jokes about how many husbands it takes to fix a faucet." "Two," says Sally. "One to get out the Yellow Pages, and one to dial the phone."

A second type of humor is closely related to male/female insult humor, but is more sophisticated because the amusement comes not so much from putting down one gender or the other as from the larger issue of the differences between the way males and females view the attitudes and perceptions of the opposite sex. An illustration is the following one about whether people should refer to their computers with masculine or feminine pronouns. Those who think computers are basically masculine give the following reasons:

1. In order to get their attention you have to turn them on.
2. They have a lot of data but are still clueless.
3. They are supposed to help you solve problems, but half the time they are the problem.
4. As soon as you commit to one, you realize that if you had waited a little longer, you could have had a better model.

Those who claim that computers are basically feminine give these reasons:

1. No one but the Creator understands their internal logic.
2. The native language they use to communicate with other computers is incomprehensible to everyone else.
3. Even your smallest mistakes are stored in long-term memory for later retrieval.
4. As soon as you make a commitment to one, you find yourself spending

half your paycheck on accessories for it.

A riddle that made the rounds in the mid-1970s illustrates how listeners can be tricked by their own expectations.

> A boy and his father are in an automobile wreck. The father is killed and the boy is rushed to the closest hospital. The surgeon enters the emergency room, looks at the patient, gasps, and says, "I can't operate on this boy. He's my son."

When the teller would stop and ask, "How could this be?" it took most listeners a long time to figure out that the surgeon was the boy's mother.

It isn't always possible to know whether a piece of humor is promoting or making fun of gender-related roles in life, and, in fact, the same piece of humor may affect different receivers in opposite ways. With light-bulb jokes and other simple riddles, it is easy to identify the targets and therefore who is most likely to enjoy the joke, but with more sophisticated humor motivations and identifications aren't always so clear. For example, some feminist critics have complained that such humorous writers as Erma Bombeck, Jean Kerr, and Judith Viorst have done a disservice to feminist causes by focusing on their domestic experiences. However, other critics argue that these women are not supporting domestic expectations but are instead questioning and making fun of them.

In the early 1970s when Senator Margaret Chase Smith was being discussed as a possible candidate for president, she garnered headlines when a reporter asked her what she would do if she should wake up one morning and find herself in the White House. Without batting an eye, this elegant and accomplished woman responded, "I would go to the President's wife, apologize, and then leave at once."

Some people interpret this as the same kind of self-deprecating humor that so many women comedians used in the 1960s and 1970s, but others think that it is instead a humorous reversal because everything about Margaret Chase Smith's life contradicted the stereotype that a woman would be valued in the White House only for a one-night stand.

While most people agree that males and females differ in the ways they create and appreciate humor, there is little consensus on the extent or the causes of these differences. In his book *Gender, Fantasy, and Realism in American Literature* (1982), Alfred Habegger quotes a commonly held 18th-century opinion:

> Women have sprightliness, cleverness, smartness, though but little wit. There is a body and substance in true wit, with a reflectiveness rarely found apart from a masculine intellect. . . . We know of no one writer of the other sex, that has a high character for humor. . . . The female character does not admit of it.

He also quotes Kate Sanborn's argument from a century later:

> There is a reason for our apparent lack of humor. . . . Women do not find it politic to cultivate or express their wit. No man likes to have his story capped by a better and fresher [story] from a lady's lips. What woman does not risk being called sarcastic and hateful if she throws back the merry dart, or indulges in a little sharp-shooting. No, no, it's dangerous if not fatal. . . . Though you're bright, and though you're pretty, they'll not love you if you're witty.

In the 1990s, Regina Barreca has argued that women have always had jokes of their own, but that "men, who decide what is universally applicable and empirically true, have declared that women do not have a sense of humor because we do not necessarily laugh at what they find funny." Among the things that men find funny but women do not, she lists the Three Stooges, fat men dressed up in women's clothing, the bad luck of underlings and foolish people, misogynist jokes, and jokes at the expense of ideas that women value.

Comedy clubs are one of the places where differences between male and female humor is apparent. In 1988, Budd Friedman, owner of the Improv, said that women made up 15 percent of stand-up comedians as compared to ½ of 1 percent when he went into business in the early 1960s. A 1990 article

"Sauce, Satire and Shtick" in a special issue of *Time* magazine, which focused on the changing roles of women, said that by 1990 the figure was 20 percent and still rising, as compared to 2 percent in 1970. Ronald L. Smith in his 1992 book, *Who's Who in Comedy*, wrote entries on 400 male comedians as compared to 90 female comedians.

Although these figures differ, they all reflect the fact that while increasing numbers of women are entering the tough field of stand-up comedy, this aspect of show business is still a long way from the 50–50 percentages in the overall field of entertainment. Reasons that have been given for the lopsidedness include

- Making people laugh is taking power, and in spite of the feminist movement, many people aren't ready for women to take this kind of power.

- Stand-up comedy is extremely competitive, and men, who have not wanted the competition, have sought to maintain separate camps. Elayne Boosler, like many other women comics, has instructed her publicist never to refer to her as a *comedienne* because the word, like *aviatrix* and *authoress*, classifies women as second class.

- Women on stage are more likely to be heckled and insulted; even one or two misogynist patrons can have a devastating effect on a comedian's mood and on the show as a whole.

- Even today when many three-person shows feature two males and one female, club owners tend to say that a woman isn't "loud enough" or "strong enough" to close the show (the closing act gets a bigger percentage of the profits).

- Women comedians report that it is a lonely business. After a show, both men and women will join male performers to talk and joke at the bar, but patrons seem shy or hesitant to approach female performers.

- Some people believe that women do not have the same option of falling back on sex-related shock jokes. Tony Camacho, a talent consultant to several New York comedy clubs, has said that "society just isn't ready for raunchy women comics. Instead of laughing, people would be looking at each other and saying, 'Who is that slut?'"

In the 1960s and 1970s, the first women comedians to succeed on a grand scale were Phyllis Diller and Joan Rivers. They used self-deprecating humor to entice their audiences to laugh even if it was *at* them instead of *with* them. Feminists in the 1970s and 1980s were highly critical of this technique. Their criticism was similar to that expressed by African Americans in the 1960s against the offensive stereotypes in the *Amos 'n' Andy* and the *Beulah* television shows. However, as time passed and there were many more images of Blacks in the media, such comedians as Flip Wilson and Dick Gregory began to successfully manipulate the old stereotypes for laughs. Something similar has been happening in women's comedy so that there's now room for playing with both old and new stereotypes. For example, on *Saturday Night Live*, when Jane Curtin would play the straight woman to the giddy characters created by Gilda Radner, the audience was well aware of the fact that Curtin was doing comic interpretations, not real imitations, of uptight, overly efficient newscasters, sneering housewives, sour hostesses, and irritated sophisticates. And because the late Gilda Radner created so many different characters, no one thought she was the obnoxious Roseanne Rosanadanna or the "Never mind!" Emily Litella, who offered confused editorial commentary on such subjects as "Soviet Jewelry," and "Violins on Television."

While there is a downside to the fact that so few women in the past were professional comedians and that they were so limited in the roles they played, Rita Rudner points to a benefit for today's comics. She says there is more variety among female than male comedians because male comedians grew up watching other males perform and so a lot of men adopted the same "cynical approach to life, but we're all unique." Judy Tenuta says that in the new generation most women's comedy comes from living, from the relationships that women have with family, friends, and lovers. Rudner and Tenuta were talking to Charles Leerhsen in relation to a July 1988 article he wrote for *Savvy* magazine, where he said that "indeed, for every Rudner who speaks too softly to suit some cigar-chomping club owners, there is a booming Roseanne. . . . For every clean-talking Carol Leifer there is a Susie Essman telling a loud table at Catch a Rising Star to 'Shut the f— up, already.'"

Rita Rudner thinks that women exhibit more originality than do men in their comedy acts because women had few role models and so were forced to develop their own techniques. *Lisa Ross/Globe Photos Inc.*

A *Psychology Today* "News and Trends" column (Sep./Oct. 1993), under the title of "Last Laugh: Battle of the Sexes," made the point that today's women are changing the rules for comedy and that many male comedians are following along. According to the editors, women are using humor that is cooperative instead of competitive; relies on caring concern rather than distrust, hostility, envy, or jealousy; brings people together rather than singles out victims; lets everyone feel good instead of making some people feel good at the expense of others; uses kidding instead of sarcasm; focuses on what any of us might do instead of what one of us did; spotlights issues rather than relies on rhetorical one-upmanship; and targets the powerful rather than the weak. *See also* COMEDY TEAMS, RADIO, SELF-DISPARAGEMENT, SITCOMS

Further reading: Jane Curry, *Marietta Holley* (1996). Susan Horowitz, *Queens of Comedy: Lucille Ball, Phyllis Diller, Carol Burnett, Joan Rivers, and the New Generation of Funny Women*, 1997. Marilyn Jurich, *Scheherazade's Sisters: Trickster Heroines and Their Stories in World Literature* (1998).

Gothic Humor

The term *Gothic* was first used to refer to a Germanic tribe of medieval times, but was expanded to refer to anything Teutonic or Germanic and later to anything medieval and then to anything associated with medieval ideas or customs. Gothic humor is powerful because of the freedom that its creators have to explore both this and the supernatural world. It also treats such powerful human emotions as religious faith, sexuality, and fear. Humor became part of Gothic traditions partly because humans attempt to assuage their fears by laughing at what makes them uncomfortable.

For example, Gothic cathedrals often included grotesque gargoyles and frightening figures worked into tapestries, stained glass windows, and paintings. While their initial purpose was to inspire fear of the supernatural, the figures gradually evolved into objects of amusement rather than awe-inspiring reminders of supernatural powers. Stone masons working on scaffolding high above the main floor began creating their own little jokes by carving mischievous looking imps instead of angels or devils. They were confident that clergymen would never climb high enough for a close inspection.

In a similar way, as soon as Gothic novels became popular with their mysterious sights and sounds, supernatural elements, dark and stormy nights, villainous relatives and neighbors, and old houses or castles with underground passages and trap doors, authors began writing parodies and spoofs. The most notable is Jane Austen's *Northanger Abbey*

(1818), which was a gleeful parody of Ann Radcliffe's 1797 *The Mysteries of Udolpho* and other Gothic novels of the day including Horace Walpole's 1764 *Castle of Otronto* and Matthew Gregory Lewis's 1796 *The Monk*. Austen's heroine is Catherine Morland, an imaginative reader of Gothic romances, who has her chance to become part of the Gothic tradition when she goes to Bath for a vacation and is invited by Captain Tilney and his daughter Eleanor to visit their old country home, Northanger Abbey. Catherine suspects that Tilney had long ago murdered his wife and so she begins looking for clues. She assigns stereotypical Gothic roles to everyone she meets and believes she discovers a cryptic record of secret crimes, which turns out to be a laundry list.

The same year that Austen published *Northanger Abbey*, Mary Shelley published *Frankenstein* about a brilliant student at the University of Ingolstadt who learns the secret of creating life. From butcher shops and dissecting rooms, he obtains the materials he needs to create an eight-foot monster, which he endows with life. The original *Frankenstein*, in contrast to hundreds of imitations and parodies, is rich in Gothic details presented through a complex plot and fully developed characters.

In 1897 Bram Stoker published *Dracula*, which established the conventions about vampires that have become standard in Western culture. Stoker's story is based on the 15th-century Prince Vlad Tepes, the ruler of Transylvania and Walachis (now Romania). The Prince was nicknamed "The Impaler" because he would spear his victims on wooden poles and leave their bodies displayed in front of his castle as a deterrent to both domestic criminals and foreign invaders. His people could not believe that such blood lust was possible in a human being, so they considered him to be a vampire and gave him the nickname of Dracula, which can be translated as either "son of the devil" or "son of a dragon."

Ion Barbu and Mihai Barbu, two Romanian cartoonists and journalists, reported to the 1998 International Society of Humor Studies conference in Bergen, Norway, that during most of the 24-year reign of Romanian dictator Nicolae Ceausescu, who in 1989 was executed for crimes against the people (including causing an alleged 60,000 deaths), Bram Stoker's story was not allowed to be printed in Romania, nor were any of the American movies allowed to be imported. This was because popular media had begun to portray Ceausescu as Dracula, and Ceausescu, understandably, did not want to help publicize such an image. But after the revolution, popular singers and cartoonists revived the story, and a cartoon on the subject was first-place winner in an International Black Humor Festival, "Humorror," held in Bucharest in 1997, the centennial year of the publication of Stoker's book. If Romanians decide they want to make up for lost time by importing all the *Dracula* movies, they missed, they can choose from a wide selection, ranging from the 1931 classic starring Bela Lugosi and Helen Chandler to the 1992 *Bram Stoker's Dracula* starring Gary Oldman, Winona Ryder, Anthony Hopkins, and Keanu Reeves. In between are some 20 other Dracula movies, ranging from scary to funny ones.

Gothic novels, as well as their sequels and parodies, have provided playful icons that are a part of Halloween celebrations: spider webs, skeletons, black cats, bats, ghosts, coffins, tombstones, monsters, and haunted houses. Halloween is itself an illustration of how the sacred and the feared can evolve into amusement and fun. The festival began as All Hallowed Even, a prelude to All Saints' Day, which falls on 1 November. The holiday is now second only to Christmas in the amount of money expended for costumes (many of them scary), parties, and candy to be given to trick-or-treaters.

Parents, teachers, and the public at large worry about children's fascination with Gothic humor especially after the perpetrators of the 1999 high school massacre in Littleton, Colorado, were identified as "Goths," kids who dressed all in black, held themselves aloof from other students, and communicated on the Internet with like-minded kids. In the first few days after the event, newspapers were filled with stories about kids' fascination with Gothic icons, but the focus of concern soon moved away from Gothic elements to gun control and to the entertainment media in general with its portrayals of modern rather than Gothic violence.

Nevertheless, parental and goverment concerns are reminiscent of the early 1950s when the popularity of American horror comics inspired an alliance so unlikely that it is still talked about in Great Britain. The Church of England, the Communist party, and the National Union of Teachers successfully worked together to convince Parliament to outlaw the importing of American comic books into Britain. Shortly after this, the American Congress launched its own investigation into horror comics. In fear of being censored from outside, the publishing industry drew up a comic book code that limited the kinds and the amount of horror that could be portrayed. But this did not stop children from telling scary stories at slumber parties or from gathering their friends to watch the horror films shown on *Tales from the Crypt*, hosted in the late 1950s by John Zacherle on WABC-TV in New York. He was a creepy creature who ate spider soup, told about his collection of human heads, shared recipes for fried bat wings, gave lessons on the wrapping of mummies, and presented the latest news from Transylvania. A woman host on a rival station performed similar antics under the name of Vampira.

Bud Abbott and Lou Costello were among the earliest comedians to take advantage of the possibilities of film for stretching viewers' emotions between the frightening and the ridiculous. Their 1948 *Abbott and Costello Meet Frankenstein* still appears on all-time best comedy lists, with such other films as *Abbott and Costello Meet the Killer, Boris Karloff* (1948); *Abbott and Costello Meet Dr. Jekyll and Mr. Hyde* (1953); and *Abbott and Costello Meet the Mummy* (1955) also getting starred reviews.

In the mid-1960s two successful television shows, *The Munsters* and *The Addams Family*, satirized the kind of family life shown on most sitcoms. *The Addams Family* was adapted from Charles Addams's ghoulish cartoons that had been published in *The New Yorker*. A generation later, children who had enjoyed watching the televised *Addams Family* took their own children to see the feature films *The Addams Family* (1991) and *Addams Family Values* (1993) starring Angelica Huston, Raul Julia, and Christopher Lloyd. Laughs came mostly from the surprise of seeing ordinary family life conducted by a spooky-looking group with such names as Uncle Fester, Morticia, Gomez, Wednesday, and Pugsley. They lived in a medieval-style house with its own cemetery, ghosts, hidden treasures, wandering body parts, and questionable relatives.

In the 1990s, virtually every American was made aware of Gothic humor through the Warner Brothers' films: *Batman* (1989), *Batman Returns* (1992), *Batman Forever* (1995), and *Batman and Robin* (1997). The extensive advertising and marketing campaign put a black bat silhouetted against a golden moon on everything from toy batmobiles to T-shirts and from keychains to lunch boxes. The original comic book characters of Batman and Robin were created in the early 20th century as a parody—a reversal—on the all-American image of the humble but capable Superman. But by the time the movies were made, Batman and his apprentice Robin were folk heroes in their own right. In the movies, New York City is renamed Gotham City, and the city's underground tunnels and sewer systems serve as modern substitutes for the secret passageways, hidden entries, and basement crypts of the castles and mansions in the Gothic novels. The maidens in distress, who proved themselves to be every bit as resourceful as those in the Gothic novels, were played by Kim Basinger, Michelle Pfeiffer, and Nicole Kidman. Michael Keaton, Val Kilmer, and George Clooney played Batman with the roles of creepy, but funny, bad guys being filled by Jim Carrey, Jack Nicholson, Danny DeVito, and Arnold Schwarzenegger.

Book publishers have capitalized on children's interest in Gothic humor. Even easy-to-read books have such riddles as:

What do ghosts like to eat?
BOO berries.

What are vampires' favorite fruits?
NECtarines.

Why didn't the skeleton cross the street?
He didn't have the guts.

HarperCollins produces The Black Cat Book Club, which publishes scary stories for second and third graders. Alvin Schwartz, a folklore collector, was happily surprised when his *Scary Stories to Tell in the Dark* (1981), *More Scary Stories to Tell in the Dark* (1984), and *Scary Stories 3: More Tales to Chill Your Bones* (1991) began winning state contests where children voted on their favorite books. The stories he collected were kids' versions of some of the urban legends published in such adult books as Jan Harold Brunvand's *The Vanishing Hitchhiker: American Urban Legends and Their Meanings* (1989) and Paul Dickson and Joseph C. Goulden's *There Are Alligators in Our Sewers and Other American Credos* (1983).

Noting children's interest in scary stories and the popularity with teenagers of books by V. C. Andrews and Stephen King, the Scholastic book company in the mid-1980s asked one of its writers to create a series of scary stories for kids. They went to Robert Lawrence Stine, who had written joke books, as well as a *How to Be Funny* manual under the pen name of "Jovial Bob Stine." Under the name of R. L. Stine, he created the Goosebumps series for eight-, nine-, and 10-year-olds, and the Fear Street series for older children. Stine has become a publishing phenomenon. As of 1996 the books and related merchandise (T-shirts, CD-ROMS, TV shows, and games) had grossed $450 million. While children say they read the Goosebumps books because they "like to be scared" or because the books "are funny," parents worry that their children are either "wasting their time" or are being negatively influenced to believe in ghosts, voodoo, and other supernatural horrors. Almost every issue of the American Library Association's *Newsletter on Intellectual Freedom* cites one or more cases where parents have asked school libraries not to stock the Goosebumps or the Fear Street books.

The Fear Street series best illustrates the influence of the Gothic novels in that the events take place on Fear Street, which is named after a mansion built by the Fear family in the 1800s. Fear Cemetery rests behind the mansion, and nearby are the Fear Woods and Fear Lake. Stine's Fear Street is a junior version of Elm Street, which was the setting of the evil action in the 1984 *A Nightmare on Elm Street* film and the four sequels that followed. Many of the people who went to see these movies were teenagers, just as it is mostly teenagers and young adults who communicate on the Internet about vampires and witches and who still dress in costumes and make a ritual out of going to midnight showings of *The Rocky Horror Picture Show*.

In the 1990s when Warner Brothers began its WB network and decided to focus on teenagers as its niche audience, it gave Joss Whedon a chance at adapting his moderately successful 1992 movie *Buffy the Vampire Slayer* into a series about an ex-cheerleader who discovers her true profession to be killing vampires. The series, which went on the air in 1997 starring Sarah Michelle Gellar, has been surprisingly successful in helping WB gain its desired teenage audience. While the show has been praised for its campy dialogue, its action, its humor, and its realistic portrayal of contemporary teenage life (what *USA Today* described as "90210 with a 666 suffix"), even its producers were made wary by the Littleton massacre and postponed a show they had prepared about violence at a high school graduation.

Among the better Gothic films that have attracted both critical acclaim and wide audiences are the 1984 *Ghostbusters* and *The Witches of Eastwick* (1987), the latter based on John Updike's novel, and the 1986 *Little Shop of Horrors,* which includes a plant that eats people. *See also* BLACK HUMOR, PARODY, URBAN LEGENDS

Further reading: Carol J. Clover, *Men, Women and Chain Saws* (1992). Katherine A. Fowkes, *Giving Up the Ghost: Spirits, Ghosts, and Angels in Mainstream Comedy Films* (1998). Paul William, *Laughing Screaming: Modern Hollywood Horror and Comedy* (1994).

H

Health and Healing

The idea that humor is good for one's health is as old as this biblical verse from Proverbs, "A merry heart doeth good like a medicine; but a broken spirit drieth the bones," and as new as the 1998 *Patch Adams* film starring Robin Williams. In this movie, which is based on a true story, Williams plays the part of an unconventional medical student who upsets the hierarchy in his school's hospital by breaking into patients' rooms and playing the role of a clown against the orders of the administration, but with the tacit approval of the hospital's nursing staff. While the controversial film probably offended more doctors than it converted to the power of humor, the general public warmed to its wish-fulfilling message that laughing and acting silly can work as a tool for healing.

Although the film is exaggerated, it nevertheless illustrates a controversy among nurses, doctors, and the general public. In a review of the movie by Bob Fenster (*Arizona Republic*, Dec. 24, 1998), Fenster objected to what he called a "two-hour lecture from a guy who has mixed up the Hippocratic oath with the song lyrics, 'Be a clown, be a clown, be a clown.'" He went on to say that if he were the real Patch Adams, he would sue for malpractice because "no doctor could be this smarmy and self-righteous and still heal anybody." While agreeing that humor can make you feel better, Fenster thought the movie didn't acknowledge the occasional need for "medicine and surgery," and concluded with, "Some people will buy into *Patch Adams*. But you have to be able to stomach a heaping platter full of hokum to do it."

The idea that humor has curative powers was brought to the general public's attention in 1979 when Norman Cousins, a talented writer and former editor of *The Saturday Review*, published his book *Anatomy of an Illness as Perceived by the Patient: Reflections on Healing and Regeneration*. In the 1960s, Cousins had returned exhausted from a trip to the Soviet Union. His immune system was down and he fell ill with a serious collagen disease that affected the connective tissue of his spine and joints. The disease was life-threatening, his pain was intense, and doctors gave him little hope of a full recovery. During the course of his treatment, Cousins grew so frustrated with hospital routines and the slow progress he was making that he checked himself out of the hospital and into a nearby hotel. He was close enough that his doctors could still see and care for him, but he was free enough to put into practice his own ideas for getting better. He developed what he called a humor-intervention therapy in which he read books by his favorite humorous authors and watched funny movies and tapes of *Candid Camera* and other television shows that he enjoyed. He found that the more he had laughed at something, the longer his body was without pain.

While Cousins may have been the most effective writer, he was not the first person to explore connections between humor and health. In 1971, Dr. William F. Fry, a faculty member at the Stanford School of Medicine, was already doing empirical studies about the effects of laughter on the body as shown by the publication of "Laughter: Is It the Best Medicine?" in Vol. 10 of *Stanford M.D.* and "Mirth and Oxygen Saturation of Peripheral Blood" in Vol. 19 of *Psychotherapy and Psychosomatics*. Dr. Fry continued his interest in, and research on, the topic over the next three decades. In 1977, nurse educator Vera M. Robinson published the first edition of her *Humor & The Health Professions*. She too has stayed interested in the idea and has continued to speak and write about the benefits of humor in health care settings.

Nurse Patty Wooten, who has been president of the American Association for Therapeutic Humor and an executive board member of the International Society for Humor Studies, sometimes entertains other health care workers dressed as clown Nancy Nurse. In a *USA Today* article (Oct. 31, 1996), she talked about 25 specific hospital humor programs but said there are hundreds more. Morton Plant Hospital in Clearwater, Florida, has a clown school on site. Graduates patrol the halls and give out smiley faces, joke books, and little clown babies. The Fox Chase Cancer Center in Philadelphia has a humor cart with a six-foot-high clown on the front. On the inside are comedy tapes, squirt guns, yo-yos, whoopee cushions, Slinkys, and such other toys as kaleidoscopes and Mr. Potato Head. The Oasis Room at Baptist East Hospital in Louisville, Kentucky, has a player piano, humorous books, cartoon albums, and Nintendo game sets for patients and family members to use together. In New York City, a not-for-profit group, The Clown Care Unit of the Big Apple Circus, sends clowns to the pediatric units of several hospitals.

The Carolina Health and Humor Association (Carolina Ha Ha) was founded in 1986 in Durham, North Carolina, by Ruth Hamilton as a nonprofit educational service organization dedicated to promoting a healthy lifestyle through humor and entertainment. One of its best-known contributions is the founding of the Duke University Medical Center Humor Project and its donation of the Laugh Mobile for use by cancer patients. The organization sponsors classes in humor therapy and trains volunteers to manage the Laugh Mobile.

Items frequently passed around the Internet include "Funny Comments found in Medical Records," "Medical Terminology for the Layman," "O.R. Humor—Top Ten Signs That This Case Has Been Going WAY Too Long," and "You might be an ER Nurse if . . . " Some sites also print cartoons, while others offer a collection of humor-related articles designed for nurses and other health care professionals.

Just as in the *Patch Adams* movie, nurses are more enthusiastic about humor both for themselves and their patients than are doctors. One reason is that they work more closely with patients; another reason is that they have a greater need for humor to relieve their own stress. Scott Adams, the creator of the *Dilbert* comic strip, says that the more hierarchical is a working environment the more likely are people in the middle to be frustrated. Nurses are often caught between patients' wishes, doctors' orders, hospital rules, supervisors' admonitions, and their own judgment about a situation. One of the ways they relieve their stress is to joke with their patients, often at the expense of those higher in the chain of command—usually doctors and hospital administrators.

The real goal is for patients to feel empowered to make their own jokes. One of the happiest scenes in the *Patch Adams* movie occurred when a group of inmates at a mental hospital took over a therapy session, each contributing to a group joke. In this case the unenlightened doctor stormed out, but in most support groups leaders recognize the importance of group members making jokes. Even those who are skeptical about the role of humor cannot disagree with the critic who compared humor to changing a baby's diaper. "It doesn't permanently solve any problems, but it makes things more acceptable for a while."

At the 1998 International Society for Humor Studies conference, Melvin Pollner and Jill Stein from the UCLA Department of Sociology presented a paper, "Doubled-Over in Laughter: The Humor of Self-Deprecation and Self-Transcendence in Alcoholics Anonymous," in which they said that "despite a public image of dire seriousness, the social world of Alcoholics Anonymous is replete with humor and laughter." They used several examples transcribed from meetings to show how, in the words of one member, "through the laughter . . . I could clear out the wreckage of my past." In one example, a woman told her laughing audience how she was always drunk or hung over, but because she was "trying to be what society says you're supposed to be," she was always volunteering to do things. One afternoon at Cub Scouts they were making moccasins, "and I remember sewing it, honest to God I can still feel it, onto my finger."

Pollner and Stein concluded that sharing humor with the group about past misbehaviors, disorientations, and lapses in judgment, and about members' newly found sense of being in tune with, and attracted to, the group was crucial in helping people construct an image of their alcoholic selves as "tricksters within" separate from their real selves. They concluded with an example of a man explaining his attraction to the group:

> The thing I did like about the meeting, though I didn't let any of you know it, was that I liked that fact that you guys would laugh at inappropriate things. (*laughter*) I liked that. (*laughter*) There was a guy who was sharing that while drunk, backing out of his driveway, he accidentally ran over his wife. (*laughter*) And everybody laughed. (*laughter*) Even his wife was there, sitting in the front row, and she was laughing. (*laughter*) She limped a little bit, but she was laughing. (*laughter*) What a crazy place.

Critics of the humor movement do not object to these kinds of observations. What they worry about are the few humor consultants, writers, and inspirational speakers who promise, or at least imply, that humor can do more for people than has been proven. A gullible public is eager to grab onto the wish-fulfilling idea that humor can cure illness because everyone is frustrated about the rising costs for medical care and the lessening of personal contact between caregivers and patients. These trends are especially frustrating at a time when media stories and advertisements from drug companies lead people to expect long and happy lives without pain and suffering.

Humor researchers worry that the good research will be thrown out with the bad if people become disappointed because after having provided a loved one with funny videos and joke books, "she died anyway." These more cautious scholars are asking the following questions:

- Knowing that people have individualized senses of humor and that what makes one person laugh might annoy or insult someone else, how can we expect mass-produced humor programs to work for individuals?

- Even if we had well-documented evidence that people with a good sense of humor live longer, how would we know that their sense of humor is the cause? Perhaps these individuals are happy because they are healthy and things are going well in their lives.

- And when people are sick, could it be that those patients who are pleasant and find things to laugh about have broader support groups and also get better care from doctors and nurses?

- While it is true that a hearty laugh pumps adrenalin and other "good" chemicals into people's blood streams, don't other positive emotions do the same thing? For example, in some children's hospitals volunteers bring pets in to visit with patients, and throughout the United States more people are visited by members of the clergy than by clowns (note how many more hospitals have chapels than humor rooms). Should researchers be comparing the results of these visits with those from a clown?

- If laughing actually produces enough chemicals to strengthen one's immune system, should we keep people who have implants from laughing lest their strong immune systems make them reject their implants?

Internet sites likely to provide useful information related to health and humor include

American Association for Therapeutic Humor
   http://aath.org/

Carolina Health and Humor Association
   http://rtpnet.org/~cahaha/

Humor and Health Home Page
   http://www.intop.net/~jrdunn/

Jest for the Health of It!
   http://www.jesthealth.com/FAVS.HTML

See also ACADEMIC STUDY OF HUMOR, AGING AND HUMOR, ANTIAUTHORITY HUMOR

Further reading: William Fry and Waleed Salameh (eds.), *Advances in Humor and Psychotherapy* (1993). Allen Klein, *The Courage to Laugh: Humor, Hope, and Healing in the Face of Death and Dying* (1998). Patty Wooten, *Compassionate Laughter: Jest for Your Health* (1996).

Hispanic Humor

In the late 1990s, 26 million Hispanics lived in the United States. Their backgrounds varied tremendously with some families having lived in areas of Texas, New Mexico, Arizona, and California before the land became part of the United States, while others immigrated more recently from Mexico, Central or South America, Europe, or such islands as Puerto Rico, Haiti, and Cuba. The group used to be tied together by their use of Spanish, but that is only partially true today because many second- and third-generation Hispanics have grown up speaking English. It is an oversimplification to expect such a large and diverse group (known variously as *Hispanics, Chicanos/Chicanas, Latinos/Latinas, Mexican Americans* and *Americans*) to agree on what constitutes Hispanic humor. Nevertheless, there are some commonalities.

Magical realism, which consists of a blending of exaggeration, fables, and cultural lore is distinctively Hispanic as seen in Rudolfo Anaya's *Bless Me, Ultima* (1972) and in Laura Esquivel's novel and award-winning movie *Like Water for Chocolate* (1992). The title of Esquivel's novel comes from a Spanish colloquialism alluding to water that is agitated or "ready to boil." It is the story of Tita, the youngest of three daughters in a Mexican ranching family. She was born in the kitchen, which is why she has an affinity for cooking and for food. An example of the magical realism is the solemn way that Esquivel writes that so many tears were shed at Tita's birth that when the flood dried there was enough salt to last the family for many years. And again, when Tita is forced to bake the wedding cake to celebrate her sister's marriage to the man that Tita loves, Tita cries so many tears that her sorrow is baked into the wedding cake and the guests become ill.

In 1984, Jose R. Reyna, a professor in the foreign language department at the University of New Mexico, made a presentation at an Arizona State University humor conference where he said that "unlike other ethnic groups in the U.S., Chicanos have not joined in the American tradition of professional stand-up comedy as a major medium for comic relief. Instead, humor is expressed in folk genres such as jokes, jests, and anecdotes." Mexican proverbs are used around the world: "En boca cerrada, no entran moscas" (If you keep your mouth shut, flies won't enter), while many of the *corridos*, the songs that Sandra Cisneros describes in *The House on Mango Street* as "the Mexican records my father plays on Sunday mornings when he is shaving, songs like sobbing," include humorous allusions to both American and Mexican folk culture heroes. They are like the warning that Horsethief Shorty gives a forest ranger in John Nichols' novel *The Milagro Beanfield War* (1974), "These people wouldn't confide in you, in that uniform, Carl, if you was Cesar Chavez, Pedro Infante, Cantinflas, and Lee Trevino all rolled into one."

Professor Reyna went on to say that most jokes were either sex related or were about conflicts between Hispanics and other ethnic groups. The other major category of joking is language play between Spanish and English. This latter kind of "inside" Hispanic humor appears in settings as different as gang graffiti and tagging, the names of businesses, and mainstream movies and television. Even young children—those who describe bilingual education as "when the teacher says everything twice, but you only understand once"—create such jokes as

> Knock knock.
> *Who's there?*
>
> Kelly.
> *Kelly who?*
>
> Que le importa? (Spanish for "What's it to you?")

At a more sophisticated level, bilingual tennis players might say their score is "without elbows." In Spanish this would be "sin codos," which with a little respacing, becomes "Cinco dos" or "five-two."

Laurence Peter and Bill Dana ended their 1982 book *The Laughter Prescription* with a truly bilingual story:

> There was un ratoncito, a little mouse, and he was hiding in his little hole in the living room. He was very frustrated, because he knew where there was some queso, some cheese. But, he heard the "miao" of el gato, the cat.
>
> This was no ratoncito estupido, because he knew that gatos eat ratoncitos. So he waited until he heard "Woof, woof," and he knew it was el perro, the dog. He knew that perros scare away los gatos, and also that perros don't eat ratoncitos. So he walked out and saw, no perro, pero el gato!
>
> And el gato gulped him up and said: "¡Que bueno ser bilingue!"

Bill Dana is the Caucasian comedian who grew famous telling jokes through the voice of Jose Jimenez. Because of protests from Chicano groups who viewed the jokes as negative stereotyping, Dana stopped telling them in 1970, but some of the anecdotes were so funny and the accent so easy to imitate that the stories are still circulating. Also, children much too young to have heard Bill Dana

routines use the rhyming "No way, Jose!" as an all-purpose denial.

Hispanics are sensitive about stereotyping because as the fastest growing minority group having sizable numbers in every geographical area, they have long been the targets of negative jokes:

> Why do Hispanics wear shoes with pointed toes?
> *So they can step on the bugs in the corner!*
>
> Why is Mexican beer named XX?
> *Because the owner of the company had to have a co-signer.*

While such jokes are still around, there are also many counterbalancing forces. Mexican restaurants, which have become increasingly popular over the last two decades, provide a pleasant and light-hearted meeting ground between Hispanic and mainstream culture, but even here some people worry about negative stereotyping because although it's done with good humor, many restaurants are made to look "tacky" and run down with chandeliers made from beer bottles, ceiling fans from the legs of old levis, and booths and tables from worn wagons or old car seats. In the late 1990s, Taco Bell, the largest chain restaurant for Mexican food, launched an advertising campaign featuring a Mexican chihuahua announcing "Yo quiero Taco Bell" (I crave Taco Bell) to startled human bystanders. Some Hispanics found it funny, while for others it was reminiscent of the same kind of negative stereotyping that led to the cancellation of a "Frito Bandito" advertising campaign in the early 1970s.

As with other ethnic groups, a major factor in the acceptance of humor is whether Hispanics are telling the joke among themselves as a way of bonding or whether the joke is being perpetuated by the majority culture as a way of making themselves feel superior. However, being Hispanic does not necessarily guarantee acceptance of jokes. In 1991, *Time* magazine (Oct. 28) devoted a page to the controversial Colombian-born comedian John Leguizamo. The article, "Mocking the Ethnic Beast," gave an account of Leguizamo's negative portrayals of "Latin lowlifes, louts, and losers." His defense was that "Latin culture is very subliminal. There's still a lot of self-hate. It's underneath this mat and rug hidden in the basement, and it's the beast that wants to come out and chop our heads off. I'm letting out a lot of monsters."

One of the monsters he let out was as likely to offend Japanese as Hispanics. In a "Crossover King" sketch, he transformed himself into a Japanese businessman encouraging and cajoling all those named *Tito* to work hard enough to transform themselves into *Toshino*, "the quiet, well-dressed, manicured, well-groomed, somewhat anal-retentive over-achiever who is ready to enter the job market at the drop of a dollar." At this point in the skit, Leguizamo would regress to himself and begin dancing and shouting Spanish phrases.

By the late 1990s, Professor Reyna's 1984 statement that Hispanics had not adopted the American custom of stand-up comedy was no longer true. According to an article in the 1997 July-August issue of *Hispanic* magazine entitled "Tickled Brown: Latino Comics Take Center Stage," Hollywood writer-producer Jon Mercedes III actively encourages young Hispanic talent. At the Improv in Los Angeles he sponsors a year-round competition called The Latino Comedy Olympics. There are preliminary, semifinal, and final rounds in several categories: sketch, improvisation, stand-up, group, clowns, impressionists, and ventriloquists. Mercedes has compiled a list of 300 performers and every three months, in conjunction with Entertainment Consulting Services, releases a ranking of the top 100 Latino comics. Among the comedians whose names appeared near the top of the mid-1997 list were Paul Rodriguez, Jeff Valdez, George Lopez, Vic Dunlop, Pablo Francisco, Willie Barcena, Greg Giraldo, Luke Torres, Carlos Alazraqui, Johnny Sanchez, Gilbert Esquivel, and Rudy Moreno.

Efforts to get Hispanic comics into mainstream media are of two kinds. At one level, producers are being encouraged to include Hispanic actors in situations when, for example, a script calls for three friends: "Why," activists ask, "Couldn't one of those friends be a Hispanic?" At another level, Hispanic comedians are getting into straight stand-up comedy with new repertoires extending be-

yond the old favorites of sex and ethnic conflict. For example, consider this Jeff Valdez joke:

> My brothers' names are Alfonso, Lorenzo, Ramon . . . [and me] Jeff. I guess that was right about the time my parents assimilated . . . right there!

A George Lopez joke is more typical of insider ethnic joking in the way it extols the virtues of the minority group at the expense of the majority:

> I liked the original Batman because the Joker was Latino—Cesar Romero—but I thought Batman should have been Mexican because that car was way too nice for a white man to be driving.

In Los Angeles, the three main comedy clubs, the Comedy Store, the Improv, and the Laugh Factory, sponsor Latino nights that often have sell-out crowds. As has happened with other ethnic groups, non-group members of the audience find the humor new and refreshing, while Hispanic members gradually become more relaxed about one of their own revealing cultural "secrets."

In 1994, a group of women, Sully Diaz, Marilyn Martinez, Lydia Nicole, Dyana Ortelli, and Ludo Vika, formed the Hot and Spicy Mamitas because "the guys had taken over." The women each take a topic and use it as the basis for real or fictional "sharing." For example, Martinez satirizes telephone sex, Diaz talks about being a single mom, Nicole shares memories from a childhood in which her mother was a prostitute and her father a pimp, and Ortelli tells about the difficulties of being a Hispanic actress in Hollywood.

Vika says the group's success comes not just from their new sense of confidence but also from the increase in the confidence of their audience: "Latinos used to just laugh about sex—now we laugh about ourselves." Early in her career she remembers telling a joke about Puerto Rico and her mother getting calls from people saying, "How dare she say that about our country?"

Jackie Guerra got her start as a comedian after spending years as a labor organizer for the Hotel Employees and Restaurant Employees Union. When in 1993 her friends dared her to go onstage at an open-mike competition in a West Hollywood comedy club, she wowed the audience with the originality of her monologue, which was pretty much a factual account of her day as a labor organizer.

Jackie Guerra's first comedy performance was an only slightly exaggerated recounting of her day as a labor organizer. *Fitzroy Barrett/Globe Photos Inc.*

In New York, Mike Robles began his career with a cable-access show, *Comedy Rhumba*, where he would do man-in-the-street interviews with Hispanics. A typical technique was to share a far-fetched version of an actual news story and then record his "victims'" unpredictable reactions. He has now gone on to host a Sunday night show, *Comedy Picante*, on Galavision.

Other unusual comedy groups include the CIA (*Chicano Inteligencia Agency*) founded by Roen Salinas, director of a ballet folklorico group, and Rodney Garza, director of a theater company in Austin, Texas. The group puts on full-length shows, bringing in performers from local communities to augment their own comedy sketches and such headliners as Esteban Zul, talk show host Crustino, and Juan El Sancho del Rancho.

The impetus for the 1997 article in *Hispanic* magazine was the American Airlines Latino Laugh Festival, which was being held in San Antonio August 14 through 17. The first year of the festival resulted in 13 30-minute television segments that played on Showtime in the fall of 1996. Cheech Marin, along with Paul Rodriguez and Daisy Fuentes, hosted the show, which consisted of four kinds of performances. "Latinologues" were comedy sketches written by producer Jeff Valdez and performed by such celebrities as Maria Conchita Alonso and Geraldo Rivera, while stand-up acts from novice performers were billed as "Diamonds in the Rough." The third part consisted of film clips and novelty acts, including Elvis imitator El Vez, while the fourth part was made up of performances from such established comedians as John Mendoza and Paul Rodriguez. Marin described the comedy as running "the gamut from suburban to urban voices, from family humor to political satire."

Jeff Valdez, whose first show, *Comedy Compadres*, aired in the early 1990s on cable, describes the Hispanic sense of humor as "Dramedy," a combination of drama and comedy. Valdez's comedy show introduced some 60 comedians during its one-year run in 1993–1994 on Superstation KTLA. At about the same time, a troupe called *Culture Clash* also had a ground-breaking show. Carlos Mencia, one of the comedians who got his start on Valdez's show, said that there used to be so few Hispanic stand-up comics performing in clubs that he started by emulating Sam Kinison and Richard Pryor. He was unaware of the pioneering television work of Desi Arnaz and Freddie Prinze, and so concluded that Paul Rodriguez "was our entire army."

Thanks to the work of such people as Jon Mercedes, Mike Robles, and Jeff Valdez, today's aspiring Hispanic comedians have no shortage of models to follow, whether they choose to specialize in what some of them call "beaner" humor or whether they want to go beyond their ethnic identification and be appreciated simply as someone funny. *See also* ETHNIC HUMOR, POLITICAL CORRECTNESS, REGIONAL HUMOR

Further reading: Clara E. Rodriguez (ed.), *Latin Looks: Images of Latinas and Latinos in the U.S. Media* (1997). Jonathan Tittler, *Narrative Irony in the Contemporary Spanish-American Novel* (1984).

Hoaxes and Practical Jokes

The term *hoax* is thought to be a contraction of the word *hocus* as in "hocus pocus." The first use of the word was recorded in the late 1700s and currently is used as both a verb and a noun to identify tricking or duping others into thinking that something false or preposterous is true. *Hoax* differs in connotation from such words as *fraud*, *scheme*, and *conspiracy* in that hoaxes are usually conducted for amusement and fun rather than for financial gain. While many hoaxes are, in effect, practical jokes, there are practical jokes that are not hoaxes; for example, putting a balloon over a car's exhaust pipe, covering a toilet with plastic wrap, short-sheeting a bed, dismantling a car and reassembling it in some "impossible" location, and tricking friends with props from fun shops such as bars of soap that make hands dirty, ice cubes containing fake bugs, pizzas covered with cockroaches, remote-controlled fart machines, and basic tools that squirt users with water or surprise them with recorded messages such as "Get your dirty hands off me."

Max Eastman says that practical jokes exemplify not only the sense of mischief involved in the search for a national American character, but also the art of laughing at oneself. In frontier America, cowboys played practical jokes on the cook, on each other, and especially on newcomers partly for comic relief and partly to initiate or test the mettle of greenhorns. Newcomers were sent off on "snipe" hunts or on "gopher" trips to mountains that looked close but were actually miles away, and they were set up for scares from animals—both dead and alive.

A modern hoax with frontier roots is the 1,500 jackalopes that Jim Herrick, a taxidermist in Douglas, Wyoming, creates each year and sells to tourists. He attaches the antlers of young deer to the bodies of jackrabbits. His uncle got the idea in 1939 when he and a friend were hunting rabbits running through the grass and thought how much easier they would be to follow if they had horns. The town of Douglas promotes itself on its Web site and through the Chamber of Commerce as the "Home of the Jackalope" and sponsors a jackalope hunt every June 31st.

Jim Herrick, a Wyoming taxidermist, creates Jackalopes by attaching young deer antlers to jackrabbits. His company is a major industry in the town of Douglas, which advertises itself as "Home of the Jackalope" and sponsors a jackalope hunt every June 31st. *Photo by A.P. Nilsen*

Actually, as shown by the fact that April Fools' Day is celebrated in many countries, practical joking is not limited to America. Various theories offered to explain April Fools' Day include the observation that it simply fits the season. As winter ends and spring begins, people want to get out and to have fun, typified by Mardi Gras celebrations. More specific explanations are that it developed from a Roman festival honoring Hilaria, the goddess of nature, or from a commemoration of Ceres's search for her kidnapped daughter. As Ceres followed the echo of Proserpine's cries, she was on the archetypal fool's errand, which may be the inspiration for sending people on fruitless errands.

In India, the Hindus have a five-day festival ending on 31 March when people are sent on silly errands. In France the custom dates from the late 1500s when the Gregorian calendar was adopted in place of the Julian calendar. The Gregorian calendar started the new year in January instead of April. Either for fun or because of being resistant to change or simply uninformed, many people continued to celebrate 1 April with visits, gifts, and parties. These people came to be known as April fools and the celebrations as "fooling the April fish." The fish connection may have come about because fish are an archetypal symbol of Christianity or of life, or because on the Julian calendar the sun was identified as leaving the house of Pisces on 1 April, or simply because fish are easily caught at the beginning of spring. Still in France on 1 April, confectioners make chocolate fish and people send their friends unsigned "fish" cards, in addition to playing tricks on each other.

A story in the *New York Times Business Day* (Jul. 13, 1998) asked, "What's the difference between New York and Boston?" and then answered, "In the Boston area, an April Fool's Day broadcast hoax on WAAF-FM about the Mayor's death costs two afternoon disk jockeys their jobs." "In New York it earns the pair, known as Opie and Anthony, a shot at the big time on WNEW-FM, a rock station. No joke."

Some jokes are presented in the format of a hoax, but virtually everyone knows from the beginning that the event isn't real. Lila Green of Ann Arbor, Michigan, bears a striking resemblance to Queen Elizabeth II and so began making "royal appearances" carrying clunky purses and wearing garden party hats, long white gloves, and sensible low-heeled shoes. Green says the real queen is "more bosomy, but I wear a better bra." When Ms. Green went to London in 1996, she felt she had the necessary qualifications to be given an audience with the Queen because she has crowns on her teeth, sleeps in a queen-sized bed, and uses a Royal typewriter and a Prince tennis racket. She sends homemade cards to the royal family on their birthdays and gives them homespun advice as the occasion demands. When the Queen's staff sent her a photo of the royal grandson and future King William, Green returned the favor with a picture of her own grandson. According to an article in *The Wall Street Journal* (May 30, 1996), Ms. Green frequently drives her own Toyota Camry with its "QEII" li-

cense plate to meetings of health professionals where she lectures about relationships between humor and health. "Unlike the stony-faced Defender of the Faith, Ms. Green always looks as though she's just heard—or told—a good joke." The only time she gets angry is when someone mentions abdication. "Never," she says, pounding on her dining-room table. "I took this job for LIFE."

The Boring Institute, founded by Alan Caruba from Maplewood, New Jersey, is another hoax where for the fun of it people suspend their disbelief. Caruba's Institute sponsors National Anti-Boredom Month during which he distributes lists of the year's most boring celebrities and movies, while explaining that boredom is the country's most ignored, and yet its most prevalent, malady. High on his list of boring events is Macy's annual Thanksgiving Day parade, which he claims is the most carefully orchestrated charade in history. The parade actually took place only once, he claims, and every year afterwards has been merely a rerun of a videotape.

Part of the fun of hoaxes is the way that victims gradually realize they have been had. This means the hoaxer must provide clues, as when professional hoaxer Joey Skaggs uses trick names. When he launched his "Campaign to Rename the Gypsy Moth," he used the alias of Jo Jo the Gypsy. When he was promoting a healing serum extracted from cockroaches, his alias was Dr. Joseph Gregor, reminiscent of Kafka's Gregor Samsa. As Joe Bones, he advertised the Fat Squad, a gang of commandos who for $300 a day would move into your home and keep you from eating. One of his more complex hoaxes was the founding of "Hair Today Ltd.," advertised as the "first medically safe scalp-transplant process to cure baldness." Hair Today would pay potential full-hair scalp donors $1,000 for agreeing that when they die their scalp could be removed and attached to the shiny bald pates of live recipients. Skaggs was especially interested in getting donor commitments from people working in such dangerous fields as deep-sea diving and inner-city police work. The charge to recipients would be $3,500. Skaggs explained to a reporter from *The Boston Globe* (Dec. 10, 1990) that with their new hair pieces recipients could probably find jobs as television news anchors or as real-estate executives, not only because they would be looking their best, but because if they could afford the fee they were probably already in line for such high-visibility jobs.

Alan Abel, the creator of "Media Hoaxes," has been in business for 30 years. He began his career with the now-classic story about G. Clifford Prout, a wealthy prude who was willing to dedicate his fortune and his life to covering up the indecency of animals by having them wear clothing. He cheerfully brags that he can pull off a good hoax for only $1,200, which means that it takes only eight fun-loving people to kick in $150 each.

Stand-up comedian Harry Friedman hires himself out to speak before large groups of corporate employees under the guise of a medical doctor, a safety expert, a stock broker, an authority on health-care reform, or whatever else the company wants. He begins his speeches with slightly off-base propositions, which grow increasingly ridiculous until the majority of people in the audience figure out they have been bamboozled. As a health-insurance expert, he touts the advantage of his company's policy, which covers people only for those illnesses that worry them: tuberculosis for $50 per year and for just another $5 each he will add salmonella or bubonic plague. While posed as a regulator from the Federal Deposit Insurance Corporation, in the 1980s he addressed 400 chief executives at the Independent Bankers Association of New York and theorized that the savings and loan crisis was not actually caused by greedy bankers, but by careless tellers. "Some tellers don't check these coin rolls very carefully, and it turns out later there were only 98 cents inside. You add up a few pennies here, a few pennies there, and the next thing you know, you're down $500 billion."

It takes nerve to pull hoaxes, but this is something many performers have in abundance. Baseball player Mickey Mantle loved to trick teammates. When he raffled off a nonexistent ham at a dollar a chance, he calmly explained to the winning teammate, "This is one of the hazards of entering a game of chance." W. C. Fields used to practice his acting ability while at the same time studying audience reactions by going to the beach, wading out until the water was neck high, and then crying for help. Someone would save him and carry him to Fortescue's Pier and place his limp body over a sideways barrel to dry out while barkers sold beer and sandwiches to the excited onlookers. According to biographer Wes Gehring, Fields would sometimes "drown" three or four times in a single day.

Hoaxes sometimes take on lives of their own with unfortunate results. In 1991 when the United States Treasury Department printed new $100 bills embedding a polyester thread in the paper to foil counterfeiters, Russian television's *Tele-Courier* announced as a joke that Russian citizens had three days to exchange their old $100 bills. The newspaper *Izvestia* picked up the story, which resulted in a panic at banks all over Russia. Vladislav Nechayev, director of *Tele-Courier*, apologized while lamenting, "It's very sad that our citizens have lost any sense of humor."

The Internet with its potential for anonymous postings and quick and easy forwarding of messages provides a wealth of new opportunities for hoaxes, including advertisements for such agencies as "Adopt a Runaway" and "Guaranteed Mensa Sperm Bank." In late March of 1989, someone forged a message from Eugene Spafford, a computer science professor at Purdue University, warning that with April 1 approaching, users should beware of fake missives. Professor Spafford has no idea how the message got posted, but each year when it mysteriously appears again he gets about 50 messages from people thanking him for the warning.

Time magazine (Aug. 4, 1997) recounted a more elaborate hoax under the title, "Is Denny Really Dead?" Through several different messages, the prank got viewers involved in an imagined story of embezzlement and suicide. *Time* writer Michael Krantz wasn't sure whether to call the created story "art" or "an edgy e-mail prank." But either way, he said that the incident "retold the Internet's oldest cautionary tale: online exchanges may be virtual, but the emotions they provoke are quite real." *See also* FRONTIER HUMOR, INTERNET INFLUENCES, PARODY

Humorous Essayists

In this entry, we are defining "essayists" very broadly. In the days of E. B. White and James Thurber, *The New Yorker* printed what it called "casuals." If the term were better known today, it is the one we would have used because of its breadth. Many of *The New Yorker* casuals were fairly traditional essays, but others were news accounts (some true, some fanciful), personal observations, opinion pieces, exaggerations, light verse, reminiscences, short stories, parts of longer books, and pure whimsy. The only requirement was that they be short and enjoyable.

The authors listed below are among those who, over the past century, have provided short and enjoyable pieces to millions of Americans. While many of them have also written full-length books, screenplays, novels, and collections of short stories, they are included here because of their inventive nonfiction.

Woody Allen (1935–) is best known as a screenwriter, actor, and director, but some critics say that his books are far wittier and have better one-liners than do his films. Beginning in the 1960s, Allen contributed comic essays and short stories to such national magazines as *Life*, *Esquire*, *The New Yorker*, and *Playboy*. These pieces have been collected into three books: *Getting Even* (1971), *Without Feathers* (1975), and *Side Effects* (1989).

Richard Armour (1906–) has written some 6,000 humorous essays or poems published in over 200 magazines. He published one of his first books in 1953 when he was dean of the faculty at Scripps College: *It All Started with Columbus, Being an Unexpurgated, Unabridged, and Unlikely History of the United States*. Among his books in print are *Armoury*

of Light Verse (1962), *Our Presidents* (1983), and *Golf Is a Four-Letter Word* (1993).

Russell Baker (1925–) retired on Christmas Day of 1998 after 36 years of writing his nationally syndicated "Observer" column for *The New York Times*. In his farewell column, he thanked his readers "for listening for the past 3 million words." Baker won the Pulitzer Prize in 1979 for commentary and again in 1983 for his autobiography, *Growing Up*. In 1993, he succeeded Alistair Cooke as host of public television's *Masterpiece Theatre* and published *Russell Baker's Book of American Humor*.

Dave Barry (1947–) won the 1988 Pulitzer Prize for commentary, the same year that some of his best newspaper columns were reprinted in *Dave Barry's Greatest Hits* (1988). Both *Dave Barry Slept Here: A Sort of History of the United States* (1989) and *Dave Barry Turns 40* (1990) reached *The New York Times* bestseller lists. *Dave Barry's Guide to Marriage and/or Sex* (1987) weighs in on the battle of the sexes as does *Dave Barry's Complete Guide to Guys: A Fairly Short Book* (1996).

Henry Beard (1946–) began his career as a humorist working on the *Harvard Lampoon*. In 1969, he and a couple of fellow students founded *National Lampoon*. After three years, Beard sold his interest for $3 million and went sailing. In 1981, he and Roy McKie wrote *Sailing*, a book of yachting "daffynitions." It became a bestseller and made him a millionaire for the second time. He has since written similar daffynitions for other sports including fishing, golfing, and skiing. His books for Random House include *The Official Exceptions to the Rules of Golf* (1992), *Poetry for Cats: The Definitive Anthology of Distinguished Feline Verse* (1994), and *What's Worrying Gus? The True Story of a Big City Bear* (1995).

Robert Benchley (1889–1945) began his career while in college working on the *Harvard Lampoon*. There he met Gluyas Williams, an illustrator who did a wonderful job of drawing Benchley's "little man" character. Benchley was known for writing superb comic essays, for parodying and mocking the excesses of other writers, "luxuriating in the absurd," and for being an amiable and comic figure. He acted in more than 40 of the approximately 50 short movies that he wrote. Among Benchley's books are *My Ten Years in a Quandary* (1936), *Of All Things* (1947), and *Chips Off the Old Benchley* (1949).

Roy Blount Jr. (1941–) wrote in a *New York Times Book Review* article (Dec. 11, 1994), on the occasion of the publication of his edited anthology, *Roy Blount's Book of Southern Humor*, "In the South, humor (like argumentativeness in New York) is not so much a specialization as a requisite element in discourse, and Southern humor tends to work best when it isn't trying to be any funnier than life and death are." Blount's own books include *One Fell Soup, Or, I'm Just a Bug on the Windshield of Life* (1982), *About Three Bricks Shy of a Load* (1989), *First Hubby* (1990), and *Be Sweet: A Conditional Love Story* (1998).

Erma Bombeck (1927–1996) was an Ohio homemaker with three children when she decided to write a humor column—sort of a grown-up version of the one she had done for her high school newspaper. She began in a small weekly newspaper, and within two years was being published in the *Dayton Journal Herald* on her way to national syndication. At the time of her death from kidney failure, she was still writing her column and had 12 books in print including *The Grass Is Always Greener over the Septic Tank* (1971), *I Lost Everything in the Post Natal Depression* (1973), *If Life Is a Bowl of Cherries, What Am I Doing in the Pits?* (1978), and *I Want to Grow Hair, I Want to Grow Up, I Want to Go to Boise: Children Surviving Cancer* (1989).

Peg Bracken (1920–), like Jean Kerr and Erma Bombeck, undermined the seriousness with which homemakers were expected to play their roles in post–World War II America. Her *Complete I Hate to Cook Book* from the 1960s was reprinted both in 1988 and 1992. She describes a humorist as a person who is able to find the snail beneath the prettiest leaf, a philosophy she demonstrated in her 1969 book *I Didn't Come Here to Argue, but I Wouldn't Have Missed It for the World*.

Art Buchwald (1925–) chortles at the irony of earning his living by criticizing the powers that be. He has been called "a political cartoonist in words" based on the way he uses symbolism, exaggeration, and reinforcement. Buchwald began his career writing from Paris just after World War II, an experience he recounts in his 1996 *I'll Always Have Paris: A Memoir*. In the late 1980s, he was the most widely syndicated political satirist in America, appearing in 550 newspapers. Among his 30 books are *Son of the Great Society* (1966), *I Think I Don't Remember* (1987), and *Whose Rose Garden Is It Anyway?* (1989).

Christopher Buckley (1952–) began his writing career as an editor at *Esquire*, then went on to be a speech writer for vice president George Bush, and to edit *FYI*, a *Forbes* magazine insert. He also contributes to such periodicals as *Commonweal* and *The New York Times*. After college, he took a couple of years off to go sailing, an experience he recounts in the witty and incisive *Steaming to Bamboola: The World of a Tramp Freighter* (1982). He has since gone on to do satirical novels including *The White House Mess* (1986) and *Wet Work* (1991).

People still argue over whether Erma Bombeck's humor perpetuated or fought against the stereotyping of women as homemakers. *Reuters/Michael Mertz/Archive Photos*

Nora Ephron (1941–) is best known to the general public for writing the screenplays for *When Harry Met Sally, Sleepless in Seattle,* and *You've Got Mail,* romantic comedies starring Meg Ryan, and the autobiographical novel *Heartburn* (1983 book, 1986 film). Before these successes, Ephron was a reporter, a freelancer, a columnist, and a contributing editor to *New York Magazine* and *Esquire.* Her essays are reprinted in *Crazy Salad: Some Things about Women* (1975), *Scribble Scribble: Notes on the Media* (1978), and *Selections* (1991). In *Crazy Salad* she wrote that "all I wanted in this world was to come to New York and be Dorothy Parker. The funny lady . . . The woman who made her living by her wit . . . Who always got off the perfect line at the perfect moment."

Ian Frazier (1951–) was chosen in 1997 by the James Thurber House Foundation in Columbus, Ohio, to receive the first biennial Thurber Prize for American Humor. The prize of $5,000 was given for Frazier's 1996 collection *Coyote v. Acme.* Michael J. Rosen, the literary director of Thurber House says that they are hoping to make the $5,000 prize "the National Book Award in humor writing." Frazier's comic and ironic essays about such topics as food, family, and travel have mostly been printed in *The New Yorker* and collected in such books as *Dating Your Mom* (1986), *Nobody Better, Better Than Nobody* (1987), *Great Plains* (1989), and *Family* (1994).

James Finn Garner (c. 1960–) identifies himself as a descendant of dead white European males. He is a writer and performer in Chicago, where he appears on Chicago Public Radio and writes for the *Chicago Tribune Magazine.* In 1994, he irritated a few people but amused millions more with his *Politically Correct Bedtime Stories: Modern Tales for Our Life & Times,* followed in 1995 by *Once Upon a More Enlightened Time,* and in 1997 by *Apocalypse Wow: A Memoir for the End of Time.*

Lewis Grizzard (1941–1994) was still a popular columnist when he died after heart surgery in 1994. His column written for *The Atlanta Journal-Constitution* was syndicated in over 400 newspapers. He was known for parading his southern roots and good ol' boys style. Books include *They Tore Out My Heart and Stomped that Sucker Flat* (1982), *My Daddy Was a Pistol and I'm a Son of a Gun* (1986), and *When My Love Returns from the Ladies Room, Will I Be Too Old to Care?* (1987).

James Herriot (1916–1995) was a British veterinarian, but it was American readers who first loved his homey stories about what the *Atlantic Monthly* described as "recalcitrant cows, sinister pigs, neurotic dogs, Yorkshire weather, and pleasantly demented colleagues." His first book was *All Creatures Great and Small* (1972), followed by *All Things Bright and Beautiful* (1974), *All Things Wise and Wonderful* (1977), and *The Lord God Made Them All* (1981).

Molly Ivins (c. 1944–), a Texas newspaper columnist, has been described as "H. L. Mencken without the cruelty," "Will Rogers with an agenda," and "fresh in every sense of the word." The essays reprinted in her bestselling *Molly Ivins Can't Say That, Can She?* (1991) and *Nothin' but Good Times Ahead* (1993) were originally printed in such diverse publications as *The Dallas Times-Herald, Wigwag, Savvy, Mother Jones,* and *Washington Journalism Review.*

Shirley Jackson (1919–1965) is best known for her Gothic short stories, especially her chilling "The Lottery," but her autobiographical accounts of motherhood, *Life Among the Savages* (1953) and *Raising Demons* (1957), are the books that place Jackson on humor lists. Humor scholar Barbara Levy has noted that Jackson's two kinds of writing are not so different; in both she consistently relies on humorous descriptions and quirky characters.

Garrison Keillor (1942–) came to the general public's attention through his PBS radio show *Prairie Home Companion,* but as early as 1970 he was contributing pieces to *The New Yorker,* mostly satires on fads, movements, passing fancies, and the oh-so-serious causes championed by various groups of Americans. Keillor was listening to the Grand

Garrison Keillor's distinctive voice seems perfectly matched to his hometown humor from the upper midwest. *UPI/Corbis Bettmann*

Ol' Opry in Nashville, when he began thinking of a Minnesota version of a "gospel show." He wrote a script including his opening monologue. Keillor books growing out of the radio show include *Happy to Be Here* (1983), *Lake Wobegon Days* (1985), *Leaving Home* (1987), and *Wobegon Boy* (1997).

Jean Kerr (1923–) wrote comic plays including *Mary, Mary* (1963), *Poor Richard* (1965), *Finishing Touches* (1972), and *Lunch Hour* (1981), but she also wrote humorous sketches about such mundane matters as composing letters of complaint, buying a house, traveling, dieting, juggling household expenses, and caring for children. The title of her most famous book, *Please Don't Eat the Daisies* (1957), came from her experience of bringing guests home for a beautifully prepared luncheon and finding that her children had devoured the centerpiece, the one action she forgot to warn against. Other essay collections include *The Snake Has All the Lines* (1960) and *Penny Candy* (1970).

Paul Krassner (1932–) founded *The Realist* in the summer of 1958. He billed it as "an angry young magazine" and stayed on as its editor and chief writer for the next 40 years. For a "small" satirical magazine with no advertisements, it became surprisingly big time,

at its peak having a subscription list of 40,000. Today, the best place to get acquainted with Krassner's humor is his 1993 book *Confessions of a Raving, Unconfined Nut: Misadventures in the Counter-Culture.*

Fran Lebowitz (1950–) published a monthly satirical column during the 1970s in *Interview*, and between 1977 and 1979 in *Mademoiselle*. Her first book of essays, *Metropolitan Life*, came out in 1978, followed by *Social Studies* in 1981. They were both bestsellers, which did not surprise Lebowitz; however, she was surprised at how many reviewers treated her as a "new" author. She thought her columns had already made her famous. The two books were republished as a single volume in *The Fran Lebowitz Reader* (1994).

Betty MacDonald (1908–1958), in the 1940s, brought a fresh voice to domestic humor because she was tired of "all those good sports." In *The Egg and I* (1945), she wrote "a bad sport's account" of the four years she spent living "in the wilderness without lights, water or friends and with chickens, Indians, and moonshine." In *The Plague and I* (1948), she focused on the frustrating aspects of living for a year in a tuberculosis sanatorium. Two other books from the 1950s about more typical suburban life were recently republished: *Onions in the Stew* (1984) and *Anybody Can Do Anything* (1993).

P. J. O'Rourke (1947–) began his humor career writing for underground newspapers in the late 1960s. After a break in by a militant group determined to "free" the staff, O'Rourke decided he liked some establishment people better than some revolutionaries, so he cut his hair and got a job. He went to work for the *National Lampoon* and between 1978 and 1981 was editor-in-chief. In the mid-1970s, National Lampoon published two of his bestselling spoofs: *The 1964 High School Yearbook* (co-edited with Douglas C. Kenney) and *Sunday Newspaper Parody*. Since then, he has gone on to become head of the international affairs desk at *Rolling Stone*, while writing such bestselling satires as *All the Trouble in the World: The Lighter*

Side of Overpopulation, Famine, Ecological Disaster, Ethnic Hatred, Plague, and Poverty (1994); *Everybody Had His Own Gringo: The CIA and the Contras* (1992); *Give War a Chance: Eyewitness Accounts of Mankind's Struggle against Tyranny, Injustice, and Alcohol-Free Beer* (1992); *Parliament of Whores: A Lone Humorist Attempts to Explain the Entire U.S. Government* (1991); *The Bachelor's Home Companion: A Practical Guide to Keeping House like a Pig* (1987); and *Modern Manners: An Etiquette Book for Rude People* (1983). A good retrospective of his work is contained in the 1995 *Age and Guile Beat Youth, Innocence, and a Bad Haircut: Twenty-Five Years of P. J. O'Rourke.*

Dorothy Parker's (1893–1967) reputation for put-downs and rejoinders was so great that almost any witty repartee that happened to be going around New York City would be ascribed either to her or to Fanny Brice. She resented the fact that her wit overshadowed her serious commentary and social criticism. Her works have been collected into seven books, including three of verse and one of short fiction. *Laments for the Living* (1930) is short stories and sketches, while *Constant Reader* (1970) is a compilation of her *New Yorker* articles. *The Portable Dorothy Parker,* with an introduction by W. Somerset Maugham, was originally published in 1944, but enlarged and republished in 1973. Her *Complete Stories* was also released in 1995.

S. J. Perelman (1904–1980) was a writer for the Marx Brothers and several of the sketches in *The Most of S. J. Perelman* (1958) and *The Last Laugh* (1981) suggest the wackiness of Marx Brothers comedies. Other books include *Crazy Like a Fox* (1944) and *Monkey Business* (1972). During the years he wrote for *The New Yorker,* Perelman contributed 178 comic sketches (a little more than half of his lifetime total). They were inspired by travel, domestic woes, financial problems, show business, and the daily annoyances of life. He began his 50-year career in humorous writing when he was a student at Brown University and edited its humor magazine.

Andy Rooney (1919–) makes the most of playing the role of a friendly curmudgeon who takes the side of ordinary citizens against big business, fat-cat politicians, and modern gadgetry. Since 1978, his "A Few Minutes with Andy Rooney," has closed out CBS's *Sixty Minutes* news program. He polishes these three-minute commentaries into short essays before publishing them in such books as *A Few Minutes with Andy Rooney* (1981), *More by Andy Rooney* (1982), *Pieces of My Mind* (1984), and *My War* (1995).

Mike Royko (1932–1997) wrote columns for *The Chicago Daily News* in the 1960s and early 1970s, *The Chicago Sun Times* in the late 1970s and early 1980s, and *The Chicago Tribune* in the mid-1980s until his death in 1997. He won the 1972 Pulitzer Prize for commentary, and while he was considered the spokesperson for Chicago, his columns were syndicated and appreciated nationally. His wit and ability to reveal the ironies of modern life are the most appreciated aspects of the books reprinted from his columns, which include *Up against It* (1967) and *Like I Was Sayin'* (1984). He was also the author of the critically acclaimed book *Boss: Richard J. Daley of Chicago.*

James Thurber (1894–1961) helped set the tone and style of *The New Yorker.* He also published some 25 books of humor, with contents ranging from such famous stories as "The Secret Life of Walter Mitty" and "The Catbird Seat," to his cartoons of dogs, people, and seals lounging on the head of the bed. Recently released books include *The Thirteen Clocks* (1950, reprinted in 1990), *The Thurber Carnival* (1945, 30th printing in 1998), and *People Have More Fun Than Anybody: A Centennial Celebration of Drawings and Writings by James Thurber* (1994).

Calvin Trillin (1935–), who is known for understated tongue-in-cheek humor, began his writing career as a reporter for *Time* magazine. In 1963, he became a staff writer for *The New Yorker,* and in 1978 a columnist for *Nation.* Since 1986, his "Uncivil Liberties" column has been nationally syndicated and collected in *Uncivil Liberties* (1982),

With All Disrespect: More Uncivil Liberties (1985), *If You Can't Say Something Nice* (1987), and *Enough's Enough (And Other Rules of Life)* (1990). Three of his books about searching for the perfect American meal were reprinted in *The Tummy Trilogy* (1994).

Judith Viorst (1936–) went to a good college and received a liberal education, but she was caught between the attitudes of her parents' generation (they did not think nice girls from nice families should prepare for a profession) and the new attitudes of her own generation. Her solution was to become a homemaker *and* a writer. Besides writing clever poetry and popular books for children, she writes pieces for today's women, printed in such books as *It's Hard to Be Hip over Thirty, and Other Tragedies of Married Life* (1968), *People & Other Aggravations* (1972), *Necessary Losses* (1986), and *Forever Fifty and Other Negotiations* (1989).

E. B. White (1899–1985) will long be remembered for introducing generation after generation of children to sophisticated humor through his children's books, *Charlotte's Web* (1952), *Stuart Little* (1964), and *Trumpet of the Swan* (1972). Along with James Thurber, with whom he co-authored a spoof of 1920s sex manuals, *Is Sex Necessary, Or Why You Feel the Way You Do* (1929, reprinted in 1977), White was a key player in the early *The New Yorker. Every Day Is Saturday* (1934), *Quo Vadimus: Or, the Case for the Bicycle* (1939), and *Writings from the New Yorker: 1927–1976* (1989) are collections of his *New Yorker* columns. His *The Second Tree from the Corner* (1954) is considered one of the great works of American literature. *One Man's Meat* (1944) was republished with a new introduction in 1982. White was hired at *The New Yorker* by Katharine Sergeant Angell, who later became his wife. Together they edited *A Subtreasury of American Humor* (1962).

See also COMEDIAN AUTHORS, FICTION, MAGAZINES

Further reading: Steven H. Gale (ed.), *Encyclopedia of American Humorists* (1988). George Plimpton et al. (eds.), "Whither Mirth?" special issue of *The Paris Review* 136 (Fall 1995). Barry Sanders, *Sudden Glory: Laughter as Subversive History* (1995).

Humorous Icons

Humorous icons are cartoon figures, mylar balloons, decorations at a Mexican restaurant, clever T-shirts, conversation starters, funny earrings, and all the other visual paraphernalia that people display to communicate a cheerful or "fun" attitude. In traditional usage, an *icon* was a pictorial representation of a religious figure, but partly because of being used to name the small pictures on computer screens the term is moving away from purely religious denotations and is being used to refer to any symbolic representation. People now come in contact with more humorous than sacred icons, and as shown by these examples, icons appear in a wide variety of settings.

- In honor of the 100th anniversary of the comic strip, the U.S. Postal Service distributed sheets of commemorative stamps. Each of the 30 stamps in the set pictured a classic comic strip character with miniature histories printed on the sticky side. This project was so successful that two years later, in 1997, postal officials sold not only stamps, but also ties and caps decorated with Warner Brothers' *Bugs Bunny* characters. Marketing Evaluation Inc., a Manhasset, New York, firm that studies fame, noted a jump in popularity for Warner's Bugs Bunny, Road Runner, and Tasmanian Devil, with Bugs Bunny ranking as 1997s number-one money-making cartoon character.

- After the 1991 death of children's author Dr. Seuss, his widow Audrey Geisel took the advice of lawyers and began Dr. Seuss Enterprises to license his characters. Seuss had always resisted such licensing, but Geisel found it necessary to keep Seuss's storybook characters out of the public domain and to guard against counterfeiting. In 1995 when Macy's began offering

In offices and daily life, humorous icons establish a friendly tone, often serving as conversation starters. *Photo by A.P. Nilsen*

Cat in the Hat toys (including the famous hat) for $13.95, over 200,000 items were sold in the first season.

- In 1995, the Walt Disney Company was portrayed in national news stories as a Scrooge because it made the owner of a nursery school paint over the Disney characters she had painted on the walls of her classrooms without seeking permission and paying a fee. Such vigilance is part of an aggressive marketing campaign that between 1991 and 1995 caused Disney's revenue for licensed goods to triple to $2.2 billion (*Wall Street Journal*, Oct. 15, 1995).

- At the start of the travel season in 1996, the *Wall Street Journal* uncovered some vacation destinations where the lines were shorter and the costs less than at Disneyland, Six Flags, and Knott's Berry Farm. They found two Flintstones Bedrock Cities, one near the Grand Canyon in Arizona and another in Custer, South Dakota, where restaurant customers can eat Brontoburgers, Dino Dogs, and Gravelberry Pie. There's an Alley Oop park in Iraan, Texas, while Yogi Bear's Jellystone Park Camp/Resorts are scattered throughout Michigan, Ohio,

Pennsylvania, and Wisconsin where an actor costumed as Yogi Bear wanders around greeting visitors.

- In a 1996 issue of the *Journal of Nursing Jocularity*, an emergency-room nurse told about a precocious four-year-old brought in with a bad cough. While the nurse was trying to diagnose the girl's lung sounds by listening through a stethoscope, the child kept up a non-stop conversation. Finally the nurse said, "Shhh, I have to see if Barney is in there." The child gave her a withering look and said, "I have Jesus in my heart. Barney is on my underwear."

Much of the underwear and bedroom furnishings sold for babies and children comes decorated with pictures of either cartoon or storybook characters, while T-shirts for teenagers come emblazoned with messages, most of which are intended to be funny. At Halloween and Christmas, merchandisers are happy to sell clothing with seasonal icons guaranteeing that it will be worn only for a month, while throughout the year businessmen and other professionals are now donning humorous ties that a decade earlier only such people as pediatricians and kindergarten teachers wore. Humorous ties feature such icons as The Three Stooges, W.C. Fields, the Marx Brothers, and characters from comic strips, picture books, animated cartoons, and *Sesame Street*.

The first comic-strip character to catch the public's fancy was Richard F. Outcault's *Yellow Kid* published in 1895 in Joseph Pulitzer's *The World*. In his relatively short life, the Yellow Kid served as a salesman for merchandise ranging from crackers to cigars and cigarettes. In 1902, Outcault began drawing another comic strip, *Buster Brown*, which he marketed as a logo to manufacturers visiting the 1904 World's Fair in St. Louis. One result is that long after the comic strip has disappeared, American kids are still wearing Buster Brown shoes.

Mickey Mouse, whose distinctive ears were inspired by the silhouette of a movie camera, got his start as a salesman at the beginning of the Depression when an enterprising stationer recognized Walt Disney in the lobby of a New York hotel. He introduced himself and asked Disney if for $300 he could put a picture of Mickey Mouse on his stationery. Disney, who at the moment was short of cash, said "Yes," and the deal was finalized on the spot.

Such casual dealing is unheard of today when franchise decisions require not only lawyers, but artistic advisors, business and sales representatives, and perhaps even psychologists to estimate the appeal of a particular icon. When Gary Larson retired in January of 1995 from drawing his *Far Side* cartoons, Thomas N. Thornton, chief executive officer of the publishing company that controlled most of the $500 million merchandising empire based on *Far Side* cards, calendars, T-shirts, and mugs, admitted in a *New York Times* interview (Oct. 17, 1994) that he was nervous because no one knew whether without the continuing exposure in the newspaper demand would drop or if it would increase because *Far Side* fans would have nowhere else to turn.

Lee Salem of Universal Press Syndicate, which carries *Doonesbury*, *Cathy*, and *Garfield*, along with such columnists as William F. Buckley Jr. and Abigail Van Buren, explained to a *New York Times* reporter (Oct. 28, 1996) that it is the comic strips that pay the bills for syndication companies because characters from the comic strips can be developed into other properties. "One best-selling calendar will make more money than all of the papers pay for the comic in a year." Then he added, "Nobody ever bought a lunch box with a Bill Buckley column on it."

Bill Watterson, creator of *Calvin and Hobbes*, which by the time he retired in 1995 was among the five most popular comic strips in the country, waged a war against the licensing of his characters. In *The Calvin and Hobbes Tenth Anniversary Book* (1995), he explained that licensing causes over saturation and that commercial products rarely respect how a comic strip works: "Cartoonists who think they can be taken seriously as artists while using the strip's protagonists to sell boxer shorts are deluding themselves."

Ironically, on the same day that Watterson announced he was retiring "from the constraints of daily deadlines and small panels," the *Chronicle of Higher Education* (Nov. 10, 1995) carried a photo of students on Bucknell University's fraternity row moving into a new house named CALVIN & HOBBES. The name is an acronym for "Creating A Lively, Valuable, Ingenious New Habit of Being at Bucknell and Enjoying Sobriety." Two hundred members of the group (only 23 live in the house) have promised to abstain from drugs and alcohol. The *Chronicle* did not say whether Watterson had been consulted.

As with most other kinds of humor, playful icons garner their share of criticism as when in 1997 an NFL player was given an inappropriate-celebration-of-a-touchdown fine for lifting his jersey and showing the crowd that he was wearing a *Superman* undershirt.

According to the *Los Angeles Times* (Dec. 15, 1997) a study conducted under the auspices of Dartmouth Medical School found that 32 percent of teenagers in grades six through 12 owned at least one piece of promotional merchandise bearing the logo of a brand of cigarettes. The most popular of all such logos was the cartoon-style Joe Camel, which in 1997 was forced into retirement by widespread concern that it was unfairly tempting children and teenagers to smoke.

Many people are bored or even offended at the overuse of cheerful icons. For example, the smiley face symbol is so easy to draw that some people routinely attach it to their messages or signatures. One such individual, Texas Judge Charles J. Hearn, was nationally criticized in 1993 for signing his name and drawing a smiley face on the bottom of an execution order. But in spite of such occasional problems as this, humorous icons are well entrenched in popular culture. *See also* ANIMATION, CLOWNS, COMIC STRIPS

Further reading: Cynthia Erb, *Tracking King Kong: A Hollywood Icon in World Culture* (1998). Robert C. Harvey, *The Art of the Funnies: An Aesthetic History*, 1994.

I

Impersonation

Impersonation is a comedy technique in which a performer, pretends to be a celebrity, a politician, another performer, or other such well-known personality. It differs from skit comedy and dialect humor in that the audience must be able to recognize the real person whose words and actions are being parodied or caricatured.

Some critics prefer the term *impressionist* over *impersonator* because of negative connotations associated with the word *impersonator*. For example, it is not funny when a soldier impersonates an officer or when a lab technician in a hospital impersonates a doctor, but in an elementary school classroom nearly everyone laughs when an unpopular teacher leaves the room and a clever student stands up and gives an impromptu performance imitating the teacher's voice and mannerisms.

Impressionists are like cartoonists in finding key characteristics to exaggerate and lampoon. During the 1950s and early 1960s, Will Jordan was a well-known impressionist who made "R-r-really big shew!" a signature line for Ed Sullivan, even though Sullivan never said it. Jordan also invented Ed Sullivan's knuckle cracks, his upwardly rolled eyes, and his crazy body spins. When impersonating, Bing Crosby, Jordan arched his eyebrows; when doing Alfred Hitchcock, he bulged out his cheeks; and when doing Groucho Marx, he leered at the audience.

The better known is the individual being impersonated, the more audiences can appreciate the subtleties of the impersonation. Because of the way the mass media has created a culture that knows, and in some ways worships, celebrities, impersonation is more popular today than it was before television gave the public access to the appearance, voices, mannerisms, and attitudes of hundreds of public figures. Nevertheless, in the first half of the century, Belle Barth successfully impersonated Al Jolson, Sophie Tucker, George Jessel, and strippers Gypsy Rose Lee and Lili St. Cyr.

Because U.S. presidents are so often in the public eye, they make a perfect target for impressionists. Vaughn Meader's *The First Family* comedy album about the Kennedys set records by selling five million copies. Meader physically resembled President Kennedy, and his satire was basically friendly. For example, in a fake interview, he asks President Kennedy if he thinks the United States will ever have a Jewish president. Kennedy responds, "Well, let me say this, I ah, don't see why a member of the Jewish faith should not have a chance for the office. I know that I as a Catholic could never vote for him, but other than that. . . ." When Kennedy was assassinated in November of 1963, the horror outweighed the humor and Meader's career was stunted. Nevertheless his initial success served as a model for later U.S. presidential impersonations.

David Frye impersonated Lyndon Johnson with a benign smile and a harsh Southern accent, "Mah fellow Americans. . . ." but he really came into his own with his Richard Nixon impersonations because he could mimic not only Nixon's voice and mannerisms, but also his face and body. He would furrow his brow, shrug his slumping shoulders, puff out his jowls, and shift his eyes back and forth, while declaring, "I *am* the president." Nixon never said this, but Frye made the public think he had. Frye made the most of the Watergate scandal with such lines as

- They call me Tricky Dickie. But I can't imagine why. I've got two good arms, two good legs, and two good faces.

- My administration has taken crime out of the streets and put it in the White House, where I can keep an eye on it.

- As the man in charge, I, of course, accept the full responsibility. But not the blame.

Dan Akyroyd used a clipped and hesitant speech style when doing Jimmy Carter. Rich Little says that he values the joke more than politics and so he did "nice guy" impersonations of Jimmy Carter, Gerald Ford, and Ronald Reagan. Dana Carvey was especially good with his George Bush act, while the count is not yet in on whether a single individual will become known as the best impressionist of Bill Clinton.

Chevy Chase became so famous doing his imitation of President Gerald Ford stumbling down the steps of Air Force One that he was invited to a humor conference celebrating the opening of the Ford Presidential Library in Grand Rapids, Michigan. The most-published photo from the event was of Ford sticking out his foot to trip Chevy Chase.

Other performers who have become famous doing impressions include Joe Piscopo, who on *Saturday Night Live* impersonated Frank Sinatra, Jerry Lewis, and David Letterman; Martin Short, who moved from Canada's SCTV to *Saturday Night Live* where he impersonated Bette Davis, Katharine Hepburn, Jerry Lewis, and fellow Canadian David Steinberg; and Billy Crystal, who impersonated Sammy Davis Jr. singing "We Are

Former President Gerald Ford got the last laugh at a "Humor and the Presidency Symposium" at the Gerald R. Ford Museum in Grand Rapids, Michigan. Here he trips Chevy Chase, who made a career out of impersonating Ford as he stumbled and fell while disembarking from Air Force One. ©*David Hume Kennerly/Corbis Sygma/Time-Life Photos Laboratories*

the World." Besides impersonating presidents, Rich Little does the voices of more than 150 celebrities including John Wayne, Groucho Marx, James Stewart, Frank Sinatra, Humphrey Bogart, and Boris Karloff. In 1975, Frank Gorshin joined Rich Little, George Kirby, and other impressionists in a wild television series called *The Kopykats*. Gorshin said that he secretly craved to be like some of the people he impersonated including Richard Burton, James Cagney, Kirk Douglas, Jackie Gleason, Alfred Hitchcock, Burt Lancaster, George C. Scott, Ed Sullivan, and Richard Widmark. David Frye is especially good with strong and antagonistic people. He did a viciously giddy George C. Scott playing the role of General Patton, a lizard-tongued William F. Buckley Jr., a nasally snide Howard Cosell, and a wheedling and obnoxious Truman Capote. His best joke for George Wallace was "Ah'm heah to say Ah'm sick and tard of the lootin' and riotin.' Last week they burned mah library down in Alabama—both books! And one of them Ah ain't even colored yet."

Phil Hartman, before he left *Saturday Night Live* in 1994 to star on the *NewsRadio* sitcom, did more than 50 impressions. After he was murdered in 1998, a *Time* magazine obituary (Jun. 8, 1998) included photos of him impersonating Ronald Reagan, Burt Reynolds, and Frank Sinatra. Editors praised his "elastic voice" impressions that were "dead-on yet laced with hilariously cartoonish anger as well as amiable vulgarity." Hartman jokingly complained about being the perfect model for Sears and Roebuck because his size and appearance were so "ordinary." This was both an advantage and a disadvantage. The advantage was that with the help of wigs and makeup, he could be made to physically resemble his targets. The disadvantage was that he blended so seamlessly into the impersonations that audiences had difficulty remembering him as an individual. *See also* DIALECT HUMOR, PARODY, STAND-UP COMEDY

Implication

An implication is a veiled hint about something, usually with negative connotations. Related terms are *innuendo* and *insinuation*. While implication, innuendo, and insinuation are not new communication devices, they have become increasingly sophisticated and subtle. They are effective tools for humor because they force the listener or reader to become involved in solving a puzzle. Success brings intellectual pleasure.

Most readers can easily get the implied message in a note that President Woodrow Wilson sent to an outspoken and foulmouthed political opponent: "Sir, being a gentleman, I cannot write what I think of you. My stenographer, being a lady, cannot type it. You, being neither, will understand what I mean." However, it takes more background knowledge to understand why humor consultant Mark Katz had the Bill Clinton White House say about Pete Wilson's and Arlen Specter's early withdrawals from the presidential primaries that "they terminated in their first trimester." This specific wording, which is usually used to describe abortions, implies a connection between the men's failed campaigns and their opposition to pro-choice.

In another grim example, listeners need to know the facts of the story to catch onto the implications of the joke that went around after the young Mary Jo Kopechne drowned on 18 July 1969, when Ted Kennedy's car in which she was riding home from a party went off a bridge in Massachusetts:

Kopechne: But Ted, what if I should get pregnant?

Kennedy: Don't worry; we'll cross that bridge when we come to it.

Two decades later, the same implications were being made when a cartoonist suggested that U.S. Justice Rehnquist should respond to questioning by Senator Kennedy with such statements as, "Let's not dredge up the past . . . You're sinking to new depths . . . That's water under the bridge . . . You're all wet."

Stereotypes work mainly through implication in that their truth is not put on the table for concrete appraisal. Stereotypes don't appear in statements as new information, but instead are used where there is a presumption of shared knowledge and agreement, as in this old joke about Heaven and Hell:

Heaven is the place where the cooks are French, the police are English, the mechanics are German, the lovers are Italian, and everything is organized by the Swiss. Hell is where the cooks are English, the police are German, the mechanics are French, the lovers are Swiss, and everything is organized by the Italians.

In another old story that shows the dangers of implication, at least for serious communication, a college wrote to complain about the letter of recommendation it had received from the college where its new professor had previously taught. The recommendation had said that the departing professor could be compared to Solomon, Socrates, Demosthenes, and Einstein. In defending his letter, the man's previous chair explained, "We told you the truth. This professor can be compared to Solomon because, like him, he knows no English; like Socrates, he knows no French; like Demosthenes, he speaks as if he has pebbles in his mouth; and like Einstein, hardly anyone knows what he is talking about." *See also* ALLUSIONS, LANGUAGE PLAY

Incongruity and Surprise

Incongruity and surprise are among the few characteristics that humor scholars agree are necessary attributes of humor. E. B. White illustrated the point with a story about sitting in a restaurant when a waitress walked by and spilled a pitcher of buttermilk over his shoulder and down the front of his dark blue suit. White and the people at his table burst out laughing because of the sudden way their expectations of an orderly world had been upset.

There may occasionally be a surprise without incongruity, and more frequently incongruity without surprise, but in general the two concepts go together. However, this doesn't mean that the result is automatically humorous. The humorous moment comes when the mind draws together and resolves the jarred reality with what was expected. If the incongruity is so great that one doesn't recognize a relationship to what is normal, then there is no humor. Humor scholars use the example that it is funny when a two-year-old picks up a spoon and places it on his cheek between his ear and his mouth and says "Hello!" The child's parents can share the joke because the shape of a spoon resembles the shape of a telephone, but if the child says "Hello!" to a cup or a plate it would be more of a mistake than a joke. The same thing could be said for the difference between a child looking at a dog and mischievously saying "Nice kitty!" as opposed to saying "Nice kitty!" while looking at a chair or at the kitchen sink.

Nor is incongruity humorous when it elicits fear, pain, or embarrassment. William Hazlitt in the early 1800s explained that while we laugh at what disappoints our expectations in trifles, "We weep at what thwarts or exceeds our desires in serious matters." If we laugh at surprising or incongruous aspects of serious matters, it will be in retrospect after the negative emotions have dissipated, or it will come from those who are far enough away from the event not to feel personally threatened. For example, while readers smile when they see a news story about a robber whose attempt to hold up a grocery store clerk was foiled when the clerk noticed water dripping from the man's pistol, it is quite likely that at the time neither the robber nor the clerk were laughing. Similarly, the people working in the New York bank where this sign is posted, probably don't find it nearly as funny as did the reporter who noticed it and put it in a news story:

> Notice to Would-Be Robbers!
> This is a Spanish-speaking bank.
> If you wish to rob us, please be patient
> while we arrange for an interpreter.

The theory of incongruity was first proposed in the 1600s by Blaise Pascal, French scientist and philosopher, who said, "Nothing produces laughter more than a surprising disproportion between that which one expects and that which one sees." Toward the end of his life, Scottish philospher Frances Hutcheson turned his attention to humor and his book *Reflections upon Laughter* was published after his death in 1750. In the book, Hutcheson argued against Thomas Hobbes's century-old superiority theory. He pointed out that people don't go to asylums to laugh at the "inferior" beings, nor do we laugh at animals unless they resemble human beings. We laugh at someone who slips on a banana peel not because we feel superior but because of the incongruity between our expectations and the sudden insight.

In the late 1700s, German philosopher Immanuel Kant added to the incongruity theory through focusing on physical rather than mental reactions. He said that when people's expectations are upset, they suffer an intellectual disappointment, but are compensated for this disappointment by a physical sensation. The surprise gives a wholesome shock to the body. He illustrated the irony in an incongruous situation by telling about the heir of a wealthy man who wanted to arrange an imposing funeral. The heir was frustrated because the more money he paid the mourners to look sad, the happier they became.

Arthur Schopenhaur, who died in 1860, but whose work was not translated into English until 1907, made similar observations when he wrote on what he called "the true theory of the ludicrous." He believed that all laughter is occasioned by a paradox or an unexpected happening either in words or actions. The reason that the words *ludicrous* and *absurd* are insulting is that they are usually said with scorn as a speaker points out to an adversary the difference between the adversary's cherished expectations and the reality that is now being revealed. Schopenhaur's interpretation shows a closer alliance than do other theories between incongruity and feelings of superiority.

Surprise and incongruity are such essential features that they are a subtext to practically all humor. For example, an Associated Press story (Apr. 19, 1999) about the most popular movies of the previous weekend illustrates how hard movie producers work to create situations where audiences will not expect to find humor. The result is that when the humor appears, viewers are surprised and doubly amused. The top-grossing film on that date ($20.7 million) was *Life,* starring Eddie Murphy and Martin Lawrence, who as strangers in 1932 were sent south from Harlem to pick up bootleg whiskey. They were arrested on false murder charges and sentenced to life terms on a notorious black prison farm in Mississippi. The humor that helped the two keep hope until their escape some 60 years later was all the funnier because the circumstances were so grim.

Coming in third that week ($8.7 million) was the teen movie *Never Been Kissed,* starring Drew Barrymore playing a young newspaper reporter who is sent back to high school as an underground reporter. She finds that she is just as much a social misfit in high school the second time around as she was the first. The movie coming in fourth was *Analyze This* ($4 million), starring Billy Crystal playing the role of a psychological family counselor and Robert DeNiro as a mafia don who demands help for his panic attacks. The incongruities from both sides of the fence are genuinely funny.

In conclusion, while incongruity and surprise can come from something as obvious as John Cleese playing the part of a dancing transvestite in the 1999 film *The Out-of-Towners,* it can also be much more subtle as when good authors manage to entice readers into a willing suspension of disbelief so that they can sit back and enjoy characters and situations too zany to be real. *See also* ACCIDENTAL HUMOR, FICTION, HUMOROUS ESSAYISTS, SUPERIORITY AND HOSTILITY

Further reading: Robert L. Latta, *The Basic Humor Process: A Cognitive Shift Theory and the Case against Incongruity* (1998). John Morreall, *The Philosophy of Laughter and Humor* (1987).

International Wordplay

International wordplay is a direct result of the increased business and communication that is now occurring on a worldwide basis. Both intentional and unintentional humor results as businesses export and import trademarks as well as products. Few of the American children who play with *Lego* building blocks know that the name comes from Danish *leg godt,* which means "play well." Nor do people connect the name of *Rambo,* the violent hero in David Morrell's *First Blood,* with the French Rambeaux apples that Morrell's wife happened to bring home on the day that the author was looking for a memorable character name.

Most players of the *Pac Man* video game do not know that its name comes from a Japanese slang word *paku-paku,* which describes a person's mouth opening and closing while one eats, nor have they heard the story about the almost-as-popular *Donkey Kong,* which features an aggressive gorilla. According to the story, the Japanese manufacturer intended to name the game *Monkey Kong* in honor of *King Kong,* but confused a *d* for an *m.*

Bill Bryson begins a chapter in his book, *The Mother Tongue: English & How It Got That Way,* with this account of how English is faring on its way to becoming the world's business language:

In Hong Kong you can find a place called the *Plastic Bacon Factory.* In Naples, according to the London *Observer,* there is a sports shop called *Snoopy's Dribbling,* while in Brussels there is a men's clothing store called *Big Nuts,* where on my last visit to the city it had a sign saying: *SWEAT — 690 FRANCS.* (Closer inspection revealed this to be a sweatshirt.) In Japan you can drink *Homo Milk* or *Poccari Sweat* (a popular soft drink), eat some chocolates called *Hand-Maid Queer-Aid,* or go out and buy some *Arm Free Grand Slam Munsingwear*.

John Murphy, a names consultant in London, has a collection of products whose English names are "unusual." From Morocco he has a hair straightener named *Stiff* and from Japan a moisturized tissue named *Pocket Wetties*. In the book *Japanese Jive: Wacky and Wonderful Products from Japan*, Caroline McKeldin cites *Crunky Kids* as the name for a crunchy chocolate bar, *Dew Dew* dried apples, *NFL Grease* hair dressing for men, and *Brown Gross Foam* hair mousse.

Today's Americans do not need to travel to come up against cultural differences and translation problems because many of the differences come to them. A Knight-Ridder story (May, 10, 1997) told about a cultural clash occurring when the Nike company put a logo on the back of athletic shoes that resembled the world *Allah* in Arabic script. "Nike said the logo was meant to look like flames for a line of shoes to be sold . . . with the names *Air Bakin'*, *Air Melt*, *Air Grill* and *Air B-Que*." A company representative said it had caught the problem before the shoes went into production, and altered the logo; however, Nihad Awad, president of the Council on American-Islamic Relations, displayed a pair of the controversial shoes and said they were still seen in retail stores. Hakeem Olajuwon, a Muslim who endorses another brand of athletic shoe, wrote a public letter to Nike president Tom Clarke, "It is offensive to us when a major corporation such as Nike publicly shows disrespect for Allah's name." The conflict was more strongly felt because two years earlier, Nike had put up a billboard near the University of Southern California that showed a basketball player with the heading, "They called him Allah."

Because of the money involved in designing, naming, and promoting particular makes of cars and related products, the choice of names is crucial. Only after General Motors was well into production and advertising for its popular Nova model, did it learn that in Spanish "no va" means "it won't go." The Standard Oil Company was going to use *Enco* as its trademark until learning that in Japan the name would be translated as "car trouble."

They chose to go instead with *Exxon*, but then had trouble registering the new trademark in France. An American living in Paris read about the choice of the new trademark and registered *Exxon* and various combinations including *Exxon Provence*, a play on the French *Aix-en-Provence*. Standard Oil could not use *Exxon* in France until it purchased the rights from the forward-thinking entrepreneur.

Hyundai, as a car name, has been criticized because its pronunciation is unclear, and in one version sounds like "high and dry," as in the nautical term for "stranded." Also, some Japanese speakers resent this Korean name because they think it was purposely designed to borrow the positive connotations of *Honda*. In 1989, Ford dropped its luxury German-made *Mercury Merkur* because of poor sales, which they blamed partly on name difficulties. *Merkur* is German for Mercury (pronounced "Mare-cure") and English speakers never felt comfortable with it. Neither do English speakers feel comfortable with the Swedish *Saab*, as shown by the joke: "What you do when it's time to make the payments." The *Toyota MR2* is no longer marketed in France because with a French pronunciation the last part of the name sounds like a word for excrement. The *Yugo* looks and sounds too much like *yucko*, while the best-selling car in Russia, the *Zchiguli*, had to be given a new name for export because Europeans pronounced the name as *gigolo*. *See also* ACCIDENTAL HUMOR, LANGUAGE PLAY, METAPHORS

Further reading: Bill Bryson, *The Mother Tongue: English & How It Got That Way* (1990). Caroline McKeldin, *Japanese Jive: Wacky and Wonderful Products from Japan* (1993).

Internet Influences

Internet influences can be seen on both the creation and the distribution of humor. Many of the early users of the Internet (of which the World Wide Web is a part) came from the 1960s counterculture, and their feelings about big business and the evils of conformity still provide the Internet "with attitude." In her end-of-the-year column (Dec. 30, 1996), Denise Caruso, technology writer for

The New York Times, complained about "what the mega-mondo corporations" are doing to the World Wide Web "with their multimillion-dollar attempts at mass appeal." She judges many of today's corporate sites as "the polar opposite of the homegrown, wildly original sites that drove the Web's early popularity." In a spirit of nostalgia, she recommended a dozen sites that still epitomize the quirkiness of the early days; for example, the *Center for the Easily Amused* <http://www.amused.com>, which specializes in "Random Silliness" such as a page devoted to Peeps (candy chicks popular at Easter), and another to "Bathrooms of Madison County." *Anagram Insanity* <http://anagram.avatartech.com>, allows people to type in their names or other words and within seconds get hundreds of words spelled from the letters; for example, *dirty room* is an anagram of *dormitory*, while *Alas! No more Z's* is an anagram of *snooze alarm*. She concluded that "turning the Internet into a mass medium is fine, but it is far more thrilling to contemplate what might happen in a world where more people have the means to express their creativity to each other—without the censors, filters, and gatekeepers that the mass media employ."

While many people agree with Caruso's attitude, others worry about the potential of the Internet to influence young minds because much of what used to be underground is now easily available to anyone online. Second only to worries about pornography, parents fear that teenagers will be seduced into hate groups or cults, many of which use jokes and cartoons both for getting attention and for persuading viewers to a particular way of thinking. Some humor scholars who are more worried about hate speech giving humor a bad name than they are about the underlying political messages say there's nothing funny about translating hate speech into simplistic riddles and jokes. Other scholars argue that some hate jokes are indeed funny, especially to their creators, who are relieving frustrations caused by a changing social order. At the 1997 meeting of the International Society for Humor Studies in Edmond, Oklahoma, Elliott Oring, a professor of anthropology at the University of California,

Los Angeles, showed hate jokes from the Web pages of a white supremacist group. Even though the audience was generally resistant to this kind of humor, when Oring put on an overhead of a cartoon showing a down-and-out member of a minority group holding up a sign: "Will make excuses for food!" there were smiles and chuckles. Oring did not argue about whether the cartoon was good or bad. Instead, he talked about the joke in relation to Sigmund Freud's theory that humor lets people reveal repressed or suppressed impulses. Since the writings from this particular group show undisguised hostility, Oring asked why, then, do these overtly hostile people still use jokes to communicate?

Another interesting question that the Internet is encouraging scholars to pursue is the source and the cause of the disaster jokes that pop up following such events as the Challenger explosion, the Jeffery Dahmer murder trial, the fire at the Branch Davidians' Waco complex, and the O. J. Simpson trial. Collecting such jokes used to be a time-consuming task, but now within a few hours after such news events they begin appearing on the Internet almost as if by magic.

A kind of humor unique to the Net revolves around the names that people create for their sites. On the "Web Winners of 1997" page in the December issue of *Time Digital*, *Pookie* was chosen as the best one-word-name site, while lamentations were offered for the demise of such "former must-click destinations" as *Now What?* (a site for insomniacs), *WebBraille* (an experiment in onscreen finger reading for the blind), and *BathTime* (an interactive "soap").

People have fun creating enigmatic and puzzling names for their sites and incorporating such names into their addresses. One user by the name of *Eddie*, follows his signature with "Ceci n'est pas une signature," a parody of the title Rene Magritte gave to his famous painting, "Ceci n'est pas une pipe."

Most Web sites have a Web master. Maddi Sojourner, a 34-year-old technical writer for Centigram Communications Corp. in San Jose, was interviewed by the *Wall Street Journal* (May 2, 1994), in relation to the couple of hours a week she spent weeding out about 95 percent of the 20 or so witticisms that were submitted daily to the *Rec.Humor.Funny* page <http://www.netfunny.com/rhf>, which is apparently now managed by Brad Templeton. Sojourner said that she graded submissions on a seven-point scale from "doubt it" to "sidesplit." A major criterion is whether the jokes make "a profound comment on the human condition," or just "put someone down." Her favorite from the Gulf conflict was "What if Kuwait's main product had been broccoli?" During the 1993 U.S. presidential campaign, she also liked the riddle, "What's the difference between Bill Clinton, Dan Quayle, and Jane Fonda?" "Jane Fonda went to Vietnam."

Chat networks allow group members to communicate in real time (simultaneously), but other than that they work much like e-mail list serves, bulletin boards, and news groups in that members' comments go out unedited. Susan Herring, a member of the Linguistics Program at the University of Texas, Arlington, found that even if a chat group was not designated as a place for humor, there could be lots of humor. On one group that she studied, 54 percent of the information involved joking, 22 percent was marked as laughter/smiling, 17 percent was presented as bona fide information, with another 6 percent being bona fide but humorous. She classified the humor techniques as

imaginary situations = 20 percent
a mock persona = 14 percent
teasing = 13 percent
irony = 6 percent
name play = 5 percent
silliness = 4 percent
real situations = 3 percent
riddles = 2 percent
pretended misunderstandings = 2 percent
puns = 1 percent

According to *The New York Times* (Oct. 28, 1996), 12,000 locations on the Internet feature the word "comic strip." While a few are academic forums on the subject and others are commercial sites selling comic books, the majority appear to be individual Web sites put up by cartoon-venturers hoping to be noticed by newspapers and/or by advertisers who will buy space. Chris Butz, the product and online marketing manager at Electric Classifieds, Inc., in San Francisco, explained

to a *New York Times* reporter (Jan. 8, 1995) that underground artists of the 1960s had a terrible time getting their work known, but today "the Internet . . . takes publishing out of the hands of the big corporations and places it into the hands of individuals, like what the printing press did in making literature available to the masses."

In the same article, Dan Perkins, who draws *This Modern World,* which is syndicated in 80 papers and also put on the Internet, said, "The truly great thing about publishing electronically is e-mail," because it allows readers to respond directly with criticism and ideas.

Another way that the Internet is changing the nature of the humor that people share is in providing a forum for longer pieces. Because of the limitations of human memory and attention spans, people in the past mostly shared relatively brief jokes. Now with the Internet, where it isn't necessary to retype or even read something fully, when people receive something funny they forward it to their friends or they recommend such sites as the *Atheist Humor Links,* <http://www.infidels.org/misc/humor> which contains such pages as "God's Total Quality Management Questionnaire," "21 Actual Announcements Taken from Church Bulletins," and "Easter Cancelled This Year."

A British site, *The Joke Factory* <http://www.webscope.co.uk/jokefactory/jokes.htm>, carries a warning at the top, "All the jokes on this page have been submitted by our visitors . . . Please do not scroll down the page if you are easily offended by rude or obscene jokes!" *Joke Email* <http://www.jokeemail.freeservers.com/royal.htm> lets people subscribe so that every Monday morning they will be sent "some seriously funny jokes." Those under 12 can sign up for *Kid's Joke Email.* Categories to click on include "Bloke in a bar," "Cracker," Little Johnnie," "Putdowns," "Quasimodo," "Tasteless," and "Viagra." The *Funnymail* site <http://www.funnymail.com/lawjcrim.html> is set up for lawyers and people in criminal justice. The pages to click on are ranked for suitability (G, PG, and R) and for funniness. "Bank Robbery?" had a funniness rating of 3.49, "Keeping Yourself

Busy in Prison" ranked 2.99, while "Good and Bad News on Death Row" was ranked 1.36. The date of submission is given and "submitted by": (either first name or "unknown").

This kind of anonymity, and the general lack of documentation and giving of credit, is a troublesome by-product of the ease with which things can be put on the Web. In August of 1997, a piece that Kurt Vonnegut identified as "funny and wise and charming," but also as something he never wrote, made the rounds of the Internet identified as a graduation speech that he had given at M.I.T. When Vonnegut's wife, photographer Jill Krementz, received a copy, she was so pleased at her clever husband that she forwarded copies to his children. Actually, the "speech" was a newspaper column written by Mary Schmich and published under her own name in the *Chicago Tribune* on 1 June of that year. Her column, in the form of a graduation speech, began with "Ladies and gentlemen of the class of 1997: Wear sunscreen." It ended with:

> Be careful whose advice you buy, but be patient with those who supply it. Advice is a form of nostalgia. Dispensing it is a way of fishing the past from the disposal, wiping it off, painting over the ugly parts and recycling it for more than it's worth.
>
> But trust me on the sunscreen.

Mary Schmich is as baffled as anyone about how her column, which she said she wrote while on "a coffee and M&M's high," got on the Net and who decided to identify it as Vonnegut's. Ian Fisher, writing about the incident in *The New York Times* (Aug. 6, 1997), explained that as long as readers thought the piece was Vonnegut's, they viewed the Internet as a wonderful tool for keeping "people in touch instantaneously, free and around the world." But as soon as the essay was identified as having been clipped from a newspaper column, "the other perception of the Internet—as unreliable hotbed of hoaxes and wild-eyed-conspiracies—took the fore." Among the readers was one doubter who refused to believe the words weren't Vonnegut's. He predicted that the whole thing was "part of a promotion for an upcoming Vonnegut book" that will have a newspaper columnist character named Mary Schmich. *See also* COMPUTER HUMOR, JOKE PATTERNS, LANGUAGE PLAY, LEGAL ISSUES

Further reading: Katharine English (ed.), *Most Popular Web Sites: The Best of the Net from A2Z* (1996). Preston Gralla, *How the Internet Works* (1997). David Siegel, *Creating Killer Web Sites* (1996).

Irony

The word *irony* is related to the Greek *eiron* meaning "dissembler in speech." In modern usage it commonly refers to speech incidents in which the intended meaning of the words is contrary to their literal interpretation or to the expected meaning. Irony is often a part of such humor-related techniques as satire, sarcasm, and wit, where its indirectness sometimes softens people's messages. In conversations, people are often unaware that they are being ironic when, for example, they want to change the subject and they begin with, "Not to change the subject, but . . . ". Similarly, a speaker who wants to emphasize a point he is making starts with fake humility: "Far be it from me to say, but . . . ", while someone with an unproven argument might begin with, "Clearly . . . ", or "As is well known . . . "

Approximately 2,000 years ago, the philosopher Quintilian suggested three ways that irony could be achieved: First is *pronuntiato* or tone of voice; second is *persona* or the character of the speaker; and third is *rei natura* where the irony is provided by accident or nature. Irony can occur when any one of these situations is inconsistent with what is being said.

Many modern critics make only the two-way distinction between **linguistic** and **situational irony**. Linguistic irony requires a sender and a receiver, while situational irony requires only an observer with a clever mind as when Lily Tomlin tells about buying a waste basket. The clerk puts it into a paper sack so she can take it home, and the first thing Tomlin does when she gets home is to put the paper sack into the waste basket. Derek Evans and Dave Fulwiler's *Who's Nobody in America* (1981) is filled with such ironic complaints as the one from James M. Gatwood of San Ramon, California. In seven visits to his dentist he spent $2,800 and the dentist still calls him Sidney. Gatwood asks in frustration, "Who the hell is Sidney?"

The ability to catch on to and appreciate linguistic irony comes fairly late in language acquisition. Unless the speaker gives such clues as twinkling eyes and a smile, children and unsophisticated adults may interpret ironic statements as either mistakes or lies. In contrast, sophisticated adults know that irony is a form of "lying" that gives itself away through elements of playfulness. And even those ironic statements that are delivered deadpan style are all the funnier when listeners catch on.

Literary critic Wayne Booth uses the term **stable irony** to refer to that which humans create to be heard or read and understood with some precision. He says that stable ironies allow readers glimpses into authors' most private thoughts. What Quintilian called *rei natura*, Booth calls **observable irony**, such as when a premature monsoon ruins an army's invasion plans or lightning strikes just as a preacher raises his arms to make a dramatic point about God. In such situations, all that is needed is an aware observer. Writers and dramatists often work such observable ironies into their plots.

In George Bernard Shaw's *Major Barbara*, Unterschaft asks Bilton, the foreman, if anything is wrong, and Bilton responds that a "gentleman walked into the shed and lit a cigarette, sir; that's all." The stage directions are that Bilton is to say this "with ironic calm." The irony is obvious only when the audience learns that the shed is filled with high explosives.

Irony is a popular technique for humorists because it provides for multiple vision, and in many ways that is what humor is about. A good example is Jerzy Kosinski's novel and the 1979 movie *Being There*. The movie starred Peter Sellers as a mentally disabled gardener named Chance. Those around him treat him as though he is a sage and a great visionary. They supply grandiose metaphorical meanings for what are the simple and sometimes inane observations of an ordinary gardener.

Dramatic irony occurs when the audience knows things that the characters do not know. **Tragic irony** is used for situations where there are terrible consequences, as in the Greek drama *Oedipus Rex*. **Socratic irony** occurs when a person pretends to be ignorant and willing to learn from another, but then asks adroit questions that expose the weaknesses in the other person's argument.

There is double irony in O. Henry's story "The Gift of the Magi" in which a husband sells his watch to buy combs for his wife's hair and she sells her hair to buy a gold chain for his watch. This is similar to the joke about the two friends, one a Catholic and one a Protestant, who try to convert each other. They present such convincing arguments that the Protestant becomes a Catholic and the Catholic becomes a Protestant.

The period in literary history in which irony was most developed was the Age of the Enlightenment, the time of Voltaire, Hume, Pope, Dryden, Swift, Addison, Steele, and Diderot, but irony has been included in literature throughout history. In Chaucer's 14th-century *Canterbury Tales*, an unhappily married merchant grandly praises marriage. In William Shakespeare's 16th-century *Julius Caesar*, Marc Antony's extravagant praise of Caesar is ironic, while Jonathan Swift's 18th-century "Modest Proposal" that the English begin eating Irish babies was in no sense modest. An additional irony is that some of Swift's opponents read his ironic proposal as legitimate rather than ironic and attempted to have Swift committed as mentally ill.

Critic Northrop Frye makes a distinction between satire and irony. He says that satire is a criticism of society with a clear understanding in the author's mind of what society should be like, but is not. The author of a satire hopes to persuade readers to work for the author's vision as does C. S. Lewis in his *Screwtape Letters* (1943). Those who create black humor and irony do not intend to point their readers in a particular direction, but instead to leave them shaking their heads in wonderment. As Frye says, "Whenever a reader is not sure what the author's attitude is or what his own is supposed to be, we have irony with relatively little satire." *See also* BLACK HUMOR, SATIRE

J

Jewish Humor

Jewish humor is defined here as humor that contains familiar references to customs, names, language patterns, locations, individuals, and stereotypes commonly perceived as Jewish.

Some critics argue that a more accurate definition would be humor that is understandable and enjoyable only to Jews. However, this definition is complicated by whether being Jewish is considered to be a religious or an ethnic characteristic and by the different languages and national origins of Jews. Still another opinion is that in America there is no such thing as Jewish humor because the Jewish influence on U.S. humor has been so strong that American and Jewish humor are one and the same. People who make this claim point to the 1978 study by psychologist Samuel Janus, who found that although Jews constituted only 3 percent of the U.S. population, 80 percent of the nation's professional comedians were Jewish. The percentage of comedians is less today, not because there are fewer Jewish comedians, but because in response to ethnic and gender identity movements, many new comedians have come from groups that were previously under-represented.

Impressive support for how great has been the influence of Jewish humorists comes from Darryl Lyman's 1989 *The Jewish Comedy Catalog,* which presents biographical information on nearly 150 stars; for example, vaudeville and early radio performers Jack Benny and Mary Livingstone, Milton Berle, George Burns, Eddie Cantor, the Marx Brothers, Sophie Tucker, and Ed Wynn; comic actors Beatrice Arthur, Red Buttons, Billy Crystal, Gertrude Berg, Willie Howard, Bert Lahr, Molly Picone, Zero Mostel, and Phil Silvers; television stars Sid Caesar, Imogene Coca, Goldie Hawn, Estelle Getty, Gabe Kaplan, Jerry Lewis, Andy Kaufman, Mike Nichols and Elaine May, Gilda Radner, Roseanne, and Soupy Sales; comic musicians Victor Borge, Fanny Brice; Danny Kaye, Mickey Katz, and Bette Midler, and movie stars and directors Woody Allen, Mel Brooks, Joey Bishop, Marty Feldman, Buddy Hackett, Judy Holliday, Madeleine Kahn, Peter Sellers, The Three Stooges (Larry Fine, Moe Howard, Curly Howard), and Gene Wilder; and stand-up comedians Joey Adams, Sandra Bernhard, Shelley Berman, Elayne Boosler, Lenny Bruce, Myron Cohen, Bill Dana, Rodney Dangerfield, Totie Fields, Shecky Greene, George Jessel, Alan King, Robert Klein, Sam Levinson, Joe E. Lewis, Jackie Mason, Don Rickles, Joan Rivers, Mort Sahl, Adam Sandler, Jerry Seinfeld, and Steven Wright. In addition to these performers, humorous Jewish writers for young readers include Judy Blume, Paula Danziger, Norma Klein, E.L. Konigsburg, Robert Lipsyte, Mary Rodgers, and Shel Silverstein. Humorous Jewish writers for general adult audiences

Elayne Boosler gives a new twist to an old Jewish stereotype when she jokes: "My brother's gay. My parents don't mind as long as he marries a doctor." *Bob Scott/Archive Photos*

include Edward Albee, Saul Bellow, Art Buchwald, Nora Ephron, Erica Jong, Dorothy Parker, Philip Roth, Neil Simon, Isaac Bashevis Singer, and Judith Viorst.

The fact that Jews have a history of marginalization has had at least two effects on the development of humor. One is that by viewing life from "the edge," Jews come up with fresh and funny observations as, for example, when in the 1950s Mel Brooks and Carl Reiner invented the 2,000-year-old man. Reiner explained to a writer for *New York Magazine* (Oct. 6, 1997) that after seeing a bizarre interview on a television program, he turned to Brooks and said, "I understand you were actually at the scene of the Crucifixion." Brooks responded, "Ooooooh, boy!" and then continued in character saying that yes, he had known Christ. "He was a thin lad, always wore sandals. Came into the store but never bought anything."

Brooks and Reiner performed their "2,000-Year-Old Man" act many times for friends at parties. When Steve Allen suggested they should broaden their audience, the two hesitated fearing that the material would be offensive, their Jewish accents would be con-

sidered anti-Semitic, and the Yiddish cliches would be understandable only to people who grew up in the Bronx or Brooklyn. Nevertheless, they went ahead and made a record that became an all-time bestseller.

More recently, Gilbert Gottfried has made jokes about the Old Testament—if you flip the pages one direction he says, you get Jesus riding a horse and in the other direction a fat lady with a hula hoop. "Back then, everyone thought *she* would be the famous one."

A second result of being marginalized was that Jews were attracted to careers in the theater, popular music, and vaudeville because the world of entertainment was also marginalized. Earlier immigrant groups such as the Irish worked in burlesque and early radio and films, but Jews were more successful and made room for each other. In many cases, show business became a family affair.

Comedian Albert Brooks grew up in Hollywood as the son of the famous radio comedian Harry Einstein (better known as Parkyarkarkus) and was a successful stand-up comedian by the time he was 21. Actor and producer Rob Reiner is the son of writer and producer Carl Reiner. Danny Thomas, who although he was not Jewish, told Yiddish stories and was the first producer to give writer Larry Gelbart a job. Gelbart, who went on to be one of the most successful writers of comedy (*A Funny Thing Happened on the Way to the Forum*, *M*A*S*H*, *Oh, God*, and *Tootsie*), was only 16 years old when his father, who was Danny Thomas's barber, convinced Thomas to give Larry a chance at writing jokes for him.

In the Winter 1997 issue of *Culturefront* focusing on "Jews in America," Joseph Boskin observed that one of the ways Jewish humorists have shaped the course of urban comedy is by arranging collisions between 20th-century urban experiences and the Jewish stockpile of ethnic folk humor as shaped over a measureless past. "Jews have wrought a distinctively hard-driving, spontaneous humor of concrete immediacy, one that bursts with retaliation." Its sarcastic rejoinders, rapid-fire jokes, and happy quips reflect the rhythms and pace of the city itself. As Stephen Leacock noted in the 1930s, urban humor "must be as short as possible and then a little shorter still."

Henny Youngman's rat-a-tat style quickly outpaced the droll and folksy rural humor that had worked for Mark Twain and Will Rogers. Such jokes as "Fellow walks up to me and says, 'You see a cop around here?' I say, 'No,' and he says 'Stick 'em up!'" reflected the frustrations of urban existence while laying a foundation for the absurdist humor of today. Steven Wright's jokes exemplify this absurdist humor as he solemnly brags that he has the world's largest collection of sea shells, which he stores on the beaches of the world, and when he says he has a microwave fireplace that he lies in front of every evening for eight minutes.

Ridicule is a big part of Jewish humor. Marvin Koller in *Humor and Society: Explorations in the Sociology of Humor* (1988) points out, for example, that in the annual celebration of Purim, there is rejoicing among Jewish people over the hanging of the wicked Haman on the gallows he had prepared for the execution of Persian Jews. And "to this day, Jewish children are given hand-held *greggars* or noise makers to drown out the name of Haman when the story of Esther is recited." Haman is the ancient counterpart of Adolf Hitler, who was the target of heavy ridicule in Mel Brooks's 1968 movie *The Producers*, which has "Springtime for Hitler" as the title for a hit musical. Brooks explained that if he had gotten on a soapbox, his words would have been blown away in the wind. But people have a long memory for the chaotic scene in which dozens of dancers, singers, actors, and pantomimists of every race and shape audition for the role of Hitler. The show's opening production number culminates in the formation of a slowly turning swastika and in the pillars at the back of the set being lowered to a horizontal position and transformed into cannons.

Israeli humor scholar Avner Ziv credits the Jewish education system, which has existed for nearly 2,000 years, with influencing the style and rhetoric of Jewish humor. Boys started school at age four and were taught to examine issues from all angles: to speculate, to find contradictions, to shift back and forth

between abstract and concrete thought, to ask all possible questions, to clarify various points, and to find subtle and simple answers to highly complex problems. "This way of thinking, in which endless argumentation, sometimes for its own sake, could lead anywhere" is called *pilpul* and is highly valued. Besides being good practice for Talmudic scholars, pilpul correlates with the intellectual processes of creating successful humor, including the practice of answering a question with a question or piling one question on top of another:

What do I look like?
A dictionary?

Wordplay is a big part of Jewish humor because for generations Jews have been multilingual, speaking Yiddish at home, Hebrew at the synagogue, and the language of the surrounding community at work. In the early 1900s, many Jewish immigrants came to America speaking Yiddish, and while their children and grandchildren learned English as their first language, they nevertheless were like Richard J. Fein, who wrote in *The Dance of Leah: Discovering Yiddish in America* (1986):

Yiddish was in my bones, but hidden from my tongue. I did not know Yiddish as a language, but I felt reared in its resonance, pitch, and tone. I recognized a few words uttered in isolation, grasped nothing of its structure, but felt washed in its rhythms. Although I could not speak Yiddish, it was not a foreign language. I never possessed it, but sensed it possessing me.

Belle Barth substituted Yiddish for English when she wanted to fool English-speaking censors with risque jokes. Other comedians in the Catskill Mountains "Borscht Belt" used Yiddish as insider jokes with Jewish patrons and then as fresh ways to create humorous images for general audiences; for example, saying *schmooz* for a heartfelt visit, *nebish* for a loser or sad sack, *schmaltz* (literally "chicken fat") for sentimentality, *schmear* for bribing or "greasing the palm," *nosh* for a snack, *shlep* for carrying things (including oneself) in an undignified manner, *mishmash* for flagrant disorder or confusion, *ki-*

bitz for kidding around, *ganeff* for a thief or a mischievous prankster, *chutzpah* for gall or incredible nerve, *bobehla* as a term of endearment (literally "little grandmother"), *shlimazl* for a fall guy or a luckless oaf, *schlemiel* for someone clumsy and inept, and *shnorrer* for a beggar.

Patterns taken from Yiddish include making up rhyming words as in *virus/schmirus* and *Charley/smarley* or adding the Slavic participle *nik* as in "a no-goodnik" or "a real no-goodnik." Author Leo Rosten says that these irreverent and jocular expressions are direct translations from Yiddish:

- Get lost!
- You should live so long!
- Who needs it?
- He should excuse the expression.
- It shouldn't happen to a dog.
- On him it looks good.

Comedian Danny Hoch's mother was a speech pathologist, and he inherited her good ear and learned to do impersonations from the four distinct sections of the New York neighborhood where he grew up. There was Forest Hills (middle class, white, and Jewish), Corona (Italian, Dominican, Puerto Rican, and Cuban), Rego Park (mixed from Sierra Leonese to Madagascans to West Indians), and Lefrak City (predominantly Black). By the time he was in junior high, Hoch was entertaining at parties and bar mitzvahs where he impersonated Indira Gandhi, Billy Graham, and Mae West. In 1993, he was doing a one-man show *Some People* featuring 11 characters with completely different voices.

Dolf Zillman, in Paul McGhee and J. H. Goldstein's *Handbook of Humor Research* (1983), refers to Jewish humor as "dispositional." He says it consists of two antithetical types: disparagement and superiority. A joke that illustrates such conflicted feelings is the story about Mendelson's dying. "Call the Priest," he says to his wife. "I want to convert." "But Max, you've been an Orthodox Jew all your life. What are you talking about you want to convert?" Mendelson's response was: "Better one of them should die than one of us."

A second joke illustrating the wavering between humility and pride is about the Israeli Knesset lamenting all of the challenges that Israel faced. One member proposed going to war against the United States. "What?" said his startled companions. "Such a war wouldn't last 10 minutes." "I know, I know," said the man with the idea. "Then we would be a conquered country and the Americans would send aid. They would build roads and hospitals and send food and agricultural experts to help!" "But," said another worried member, "what if we win?"

Discussing the dual nature of Jewish humor, author Henry Spalding says that much of it comes in the form of "honey-coated barbs at the people and things" Jews love most. "They verbally attack their loved ones and their religion—all done with the grandest sense of affection—a kiss with salt on the lips, but a kiss nevertheless."

Many of these "salty kisses" are planted on such comic stereotypes as the shrewd businessman, the overbearing mother, the Jewish American Princess, and the persecuted Jew. Arthur Naiman illustrates the stereotype of the overbearing Jewish mother with a story about a psychiatrist who tells a Jewish mother that her son has an Oedipus complex. The mother responds, "Oedipus, schmoedipus, just so long as he loves his mother." In the late 1980s, so many Jewish American Princess jokes about spoiled young women were circulating on college campuses that serious objections were voiced. Many people suspected that the jokes were not so much anti-Semitic as they were anti-feminist. The jokes were attached to Jewish American Princesses because that stereotype was already in the public consciousness, but they were actually a reaction against the feminist movement in general.

Christie Davies in Avner Ziv's *Jewish Humor* illustrated the Jewish sense of persecution combined with pride in survival with a joke about a Jewish rabbi who was brought before a Court of Inquisition and told that his fate would depend on the power of his own God. The judge put two slips of paper into a box, saying that the word "guilty" was on one of the slips and the word "innocent" was on the other. In fact, however, the judge, who was seeking the slaughter of all Jews, had written "guilty" on both slips of paper. The rabbi pulled out a slip, and without looking at it popped it into his mouth and swallowed it. "What are you doing?" cried the judge, "How will the Court know?" "That's simple," replied the rabbi. "Examine the slip that's in the box. If it reads "innocent" then the paper I swallowed obviously must have read "guilty." But if the paper in the box reads "guilty" then the one I swallowed must have read "innocent.""

Many Jewish comedians, for example, Jack Benny, Milton Berle, Jerry Lewis, and Roseanne, seldom rely on their ethnic background as a subject for jokes, while others, including Woody Allen, Rita Rudner, and Don Rickles, frequently remind viewers of their Jewishness by joking about it. Richard Lewis explains that his family had a tree every December: "It wasn't Christmas, and it wasn't Chanukah. It was Chronica." When a Christmas tree was placed on the set of Jon

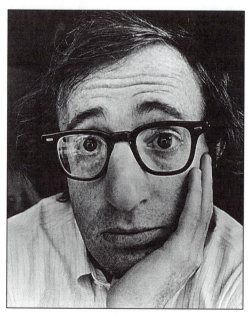

Woody Allen, known for personifying the classic schlemiel, gets much of his humor from juxtaposing the commonplace with the profound, as when he describes his parents' values as "God and carpeting." *Corbis/Hulton-Deutsch Collection*

Stewart's late-night TV show, he jumped back saying, "Not too close! It's like Kryptonite for Jews, it sucks the energy out of you." Richard Belzer, in reference to Israeli attacks on Palestinians, told an audience, "I used to be a Jew until I saw some guy break a girl's arm with a rock."

Some Jews worry that because much of this joking is self-deprecating it contributes to anti-Semitism. Sarah Blacher Cohen has said that it is as if the message of Jewish humor is to tell oppressors, "You don't have to injure us. We'll take charge of our own persecution. And we'll do it more thoroughly than you ever could."

Beloved Jewish comedians are nevertheless careful to walk the fine line between self-deprecation and insult. Fanny Brice, for example, said that she never did a Jewish routine that would offend Jews, "because I depended on my race for the laughs. . . . I wasn't standing apart making fun. I was the race, and what happened to me onstage is what could happen to my people. They identified with me, which made it all right to get a laugh because they were laughing at me as much as at themselves." *See also* DIALECT HUMOR, RELIGIOUS HUMOR

Further reading: Shirley Kumove, *More Words More Arrows: A Further Collection of Yiddish Folk Sayings* (1999). Darryl Lyman, *The Jewish Comedy Catalog* (1989). Richard Raskin, *Life Is Like a Glass of Tea: Studies of Classic Jewish Jokes* (1992).

Joke Patterns

Joke patterns that become widely popular are based on simple and clear-cut formulas that inspire listeners to create their own variations. These patterns or formulas come in and out of fashion just as do fads in clothing, slang terms, music, and other icons of popular culture. As explained in the entry "Comic Zeitgeists," historians, sociologists, and anthropologists seek to explain the popularity of joke cycles based on how the content of jokes ties into current social concerns. Here, the focus is on how the forms of certain jokes contribute to their popularity because of the ease with which they can be remembered and passed from one joke teller to another.

Anyone who has tried to create humor knows how much easier it is when a pattern has been established. Just as people can get a feeling of success by painting with numbers, people can have fun writing parodies of maxims and proverbs, as in "laugh alone and the world thinks you're an idiot," "Where there's a will, I want to be in it," and "He who laughs last, thinks slowest."

An easy kind of pattern humor is the creating of new names for established eponyms as when USC students say their school's initials stand for *Ubiquitous Service Charge*, and students at many colleges identify the degrees they are working for as

B.S. = Bull shit
M.S. = More of the same
Ph.D. = Piled higher and deeper

One reason acronym humor is popular is that people resent the overwhelming number of acronyms they are expected to interpret on a daily basis. But a more important reason is that creating negative-sounding names is an easy way to vent frustrations as when IBM employees, who are subject to frequent transfers, say the company's initials stand for *I've Been Moved*. Patients who are frustrated by voice mail or busy signals when they call their CIGNA health care center say the initials stand for *Called In, Got No Answer*. Fiat owners say the name stands for *Fix It Again Tony*, while GMC owners say the initials stand for *Garage Man's Companion, General Mess of Crap* or *Gotta Mechanic Coming*. Because BMW's are frequently vandalized, owners interpret the initials as *Break My Windows*.

The humor on vanity license plates differs from acronym humor in that words are often given in clipped forms or letters and numbers are put together so as to sound like words, for example:

10SNE1 = Tennis, Anyone?
RM4U = Room for you
XQUSME = Excuse me
IMNLUV = I am in love
4RGRAN = For our gran(dmother)

There's more room on a bumper sticker than a license plate, but the messages still need to be short and easy to read so people can "get them" at 60 miles an hour. In the 1980s, messages alluding to sexual intercourse were popular:

Nurses do it with care.
Electricians do it shockingly.
Cowboys do it in the dust.
Engineers do it with precision.
Pilots do it at 40,000 feet.
Teachers do it with class.
Librarians do it by the book.

Their popularity can be partly explained by the subject—perhaps the last big hurrah for sexual freedom before fear of AIDS set in. But equally important was their simplicity and the way labor unions, professional organizations, and individuals rose to the challenge of seeing that their professions were included.

A popular joke pattern in the 1950s and 1960s was based on the idea of wind-up dolls, as in these examples:

The Elizabeth Taylor doll: Wind it up and it wrecks two marriages.

The Frank Sinatra doll: Wind it up and it chases another doll.

The Eisenhower doll: Wind it up and it doesn't do anything.

The Nixon doll: Wind it up and it goes through a crisis.

The Helen Keller doll: Wind it up and it bumps into walls.

The Lenny Bruce doll: Wind it up and it laughs at the Helen Keller doll.

This is such an easy pattern to follow that it could have gone on indefinitely since there are always celebrities engaging in behavior that not everyone approves of. But as with most patterns, the public sooner or later grows bored and moves onto something more challenging.

A characteristic of pattern humor is that the jokes are funnier when seen as variations on a theme than when they are looked at individually. Alan Dundes in an essay "Many Hands Make Light Work," published in Joseph Boskin's *The Humor Prism in 20th-Century America,* showed that light-bulb jokes do not pass on new information. Instead they rely on stereotypes already in the popular culture; hence, the surprise and the fun comes from the creativity shown by those who make up the different answers:

How many New Yorkers does it take to screw in a light bulb?

Three — One to do it and two to criticize.

How many graduate students . . . ?

Two and a professor to take credit.

How many Jewish mothers . . . ?

None — I'll just sit in the dark!

How many mice . . . ?

Only two but they have to be really small.

How many Los Angeles police . . . ?

Six — One to do it and five to smash the old bulb to smithereens.

How many Dolly clones . . . ?

As many as you'd like. As many as you'd like. As many as you'd like . . .

And in an adapted form:

What's the difference between a pregnant woman and a light bulb?

You can unscrew the light bulb.

Obviously the mass media plays a role in spreading joke patterns; however, such promotion isn't always necessary to the process as shown by the fact that long before children had access to print media or television, they used word-of-mouth techniques to pass on patterns of insults, riddles, knock-knock jokes, jump-rope rhymes, and chants. *Tom Swifties* are based on this pseudo quote from a popular series of kids' books: "'My name is Tom,' he said *Swiftly*." Since the 1940s, punsters have enjoyed this gentle kind of word play as in

"Get to the back of the boat!" he said *sternly*.
"Would you like another pancake?" she asked *flippantly*.
"She works in the mines," he roared *ironically*.
"I'd like my egg boiled," she whispered *softly*.

In a literary adaptation, listeners are to guess the title of a book that is being referred to; for example, "'I don't care how earnest you are,' he said wildly," "'But Rochester, you already have a wife!' she said airily," and "'Where's my wife?' Gatsby asked lackadaisically." Another variation relating to geography is played frequently on the Internet by former staff members of Radio Free Europe. Examples include: "'Check!' she warned in Slovak," "'Have you seen my falcon?' he asked in Maltese," "'Well, I'm glad that's over!' she exclaimed in Finnish," and "'It's awfully crowded in here,' he protested in Sardinian."

These puns are more sophisticated than ordinary *Tom Swifties* because with electronic mail people have more time to think than if they are engaged in face-to-face conversations. Also, with chat groups and with friends who have something in common, the jokes can be focused and therefore more challenging.

E-mail and the Internet have given a tremendous boost to pattern jokes. For example, people in a conversation usually cannot automatically come up with the kind of "Top 10" list that David Letterman and his joke writers have made famous. But e-mail allows the time to devise such lists or re-create and adapt a Letterman list that they found amusing. When in 1993 Letterman bade farewell to NBC before moving to a better time slot at CBS, his "Top 10 Things I Have To Do Before I Leave NBC" was so funny that several of the items found their way into various print formats:

• Drop off hairpiece at security desk.

• Vacuum out Wendell (his announcer) and write down his mileage.

• Steal my weight in office supplies.

• Let my plastic surgeon step out and take a bow—this has been his show as much as mine.

• Get one more cheap laugh by saying the word *Buttafuoco*.

When sets of jokes are sent out to a group, receivers read and enjoy them, and then in pyramid style forward the jokes on to the people they regularly communicate with. Along the way, there are likely to be clever individuals who will think of new versions or adaptations that they add to the set. A set that kept growing and growing were names of fictional viruses including

- AT&T Virus: Every three minutes it tells you what great service you are getting.
- MCI Virus: Every three minutes it reminds you that you're paying too much for the AT&T virus.
- Paul Revere Virus: This revolutionary virus does not horse around. It warns you of impending hard disk attack— once if by LAN, twice if by C:>.
- New World Order Virus: Probably harmless, but it makes a lot of people really mad just thinking about it.

Lexicon humor is another pattern that works better in print than orally. One example of this is new definitions given to ordinary words; for example, a university is defined as "Something held together by a central heating plant and a parking problem." Someone hearing that definition is inspired to add his own, "A circus that never leaves town," while someone else contributes, "A conglomerate that, from the outside, looks like General Motors, but is really 162 Mom and Pop shops."

A lighthearted medical dictionary begins with "*Artery*: The study of painting, *Bacteria*: The back door of a cafeteria, and *Barium*: What doctors do when patients die." A mock college catalog offers such continuing education courses as "Self Improvement 107: Whine Your Way to Alienation," "Home Economics 634: 27 Ways to Wok Your Dog," and "Business 471: Money Can Make You Rich."

A second kind of lexicon humor is the creation of what in the 1980s author Rich Hall labeled *sniglets*; these are new words that the language doesn't have but should have. For example, included in a list of 10 recently being circulated on the Internet under the title "Humor for the language lover . . . " were these examples:

- Elbonics (el bon' iks) n. The actions of two people maneuvering for one armrest in a movie theater.
- Pupkus (pup'kus) n. The moist residue left on a window after a dog presses its nose to it.
- Phonesia (fo nee' zhuh) n. The affliction of dialing a phone number and forgetting whom you were calling just as they answer.

Since the headers had been "snipped," it was impossible to know who created these and whether it was the work of a group or an individual. However, it is easy to see how someone receiving these new words and their "daffynitions" might be inspired to think of other "needed" words.

This sampling of joke patterns is far from comprehensive, a goal that would be impossible to achieve because humor, by its definition, incorporates the unexpected. There are so many variables that no one knows whether the next great joke pattern has already been conceived and is waiting in the wings for a push to stardom or whether it will arise from a current event or a sound-bite as did the *Mother of all . . .* quips that were popular in the early 1990s based on Saddam Hussein's Gulf War statement that he was preparing for *the Mother of all battles. See also* ADAPTATION, COMIC ZEITGEISTS, LANGUAGE PLAY, PUNS

Further reading: Joseph Boskin (ed.), *The Humor Prism in 20th Century America* (1997). Gilda Feldman and Phil Feldman, *Acronym Soup: A Stirring Guide to Our Newest Word Form* (1994).

L

Language Play

Language play includes any use of language that is creative and unusual and has a purpose beyond the communication of basic information. Cultures throughout the world and throughout time have had language play. When ancient ruins are uncovered, graffiti is found written on the walls, while some of the oldest tales in the world are fables about talking animals. Such basic English words as *janitor, cereal, volcano, atlas, narcissism, psychology, nymphomania, erotic*, and *venereal* come from language play connected with the Greek and Roman myths, while in the Judeo-Christian tradition, the Bible is full of creative and metaphoric uses of language, which often cause people to argue over whether a particular story should be interpreted literally or symbolically. Exaggerations, and even lies, are forms of language play; and so are poems and songs and riddles and jokes.

Even though humans have always enjoyed playing with language, today's entertainment and media industries, both supported by advertising, have contributed to an increase in the amount and the variety of language play that people meet on a daily basis. A couple of generations ago, it would have been possible for someone who lived in a rural society to speak to others only occasionally on matters of business and to go through the daily routines of life meeting very little creative or playful language. In fact, certain religious sects encouraged this kind of life because a frivolous tongue was thought to be sinful. Today, few people believe in such proscriptions as illustrated not only by the specific techniques and examples given here, but also by the many techniques treated more fully in separate entries and illustrated throughout this encyclopedia.

Antithesis occurs when opposite concepts are connected so as to make a surprising kind of sense as in a Master Card advertisement showing a picture of a tall man looking at a shirt. The caption reads, "You found a 50 long. But you're $17.00 short." The *World Book Encyclopedia* ran a summertime advertising campaign under the slogan, "Schools are closed. . . . Minds are open," while the Hoover Company advertised its irons with "The iron with the bottom that makes it tops." Shortly after Gerald Ford assumed the U.S. presidency, he amused an audience at Ohio State University by making a reference that is antithetical in tone. He said:

> So much has happened in the few months since you were kind enough to invite me to speak here today. I was then America's first instant Vice-President and then I became America's first instant President. The Marine Corps Band is so confused they don't know whether to play "Hail to the Chief" or "You've Come a Long Way, Baby."

In a related joke, he told other audiences that "I only know two tunes; one of them is 'Hail to the Chief'—and the other one isn't."

Chiasmus is the literary device in which words from the first part of a sentence are repeated in an inverted order in the second part of the sentence as in Mae West's famous line: "It's not the men in my life that count; it's the life in my men." A senior-citizen bumper sticker reads, "Aging is a matter of mind: If you don't mind, it doesn't matter." One from the 1960s reads, "Marijuana is not a question of 'Hi, how are you?' but of 'How high are you?'" A one-liner that is popular around tax time reads, "The IRS: We've got what it takes to take what you've got."

Coordinate Conjoining occurs when two sentences are put together in such a way as to force the reader to see an incident or an issue in a new light. Sometimes a coordinate conjunction like *and*, *but*, or *for* is used as in "You were never lovelier, and I think it's a shame," "One swallow does not a summer make, but Humpty Dumpty makes a great fall," and "Eat, drink, and be merry, for tomorrow you may be radioactive." In other examples, just a semicolon is used:

- There's no fool like an old fool; you just can't beat experience.
- An apple a day keeps the doctor away; an onion a day keeps everyone away.
- Rome wasn't built in a day; the pizza parlors alone took several weeks.

Eponyms are created when the name of a real or mythical person is used in reference to something other than the individual. While most eponyms are like dead metaphors in that speakers use them without thinking about their sources, newly coined eponyms require the same kind of energy that goes into creating or understanding other forms of humor as with the 1992 coinage of *Frankenfood* for genetically altered tomatoes or other foods.

During the Gulf War, American soldiers said they were taking *Johnny Weissmuller showers* because the cold water made them scream like Tarzan. When Ross Perot was running for president, John Chancellor described Perot as holding "the *Daddy Warbucks* theory of presidential qualifications," and when a report stated that over 500 out of the 700 shooting incidents in which Los Angeles police were involved between 1987 and 1994 were potentially life-threatening mistakes, a union leader observed that officers had succumbed to the *John Wayne syndrome*.

A different kind of eponym nearly always used in a jocular fashion is taken from common first names rather than last names as in the noun *Lazy Susan*, the verb *to peter out*, or the expressions *Great Scott!* and *By George!* Many of the terms developed because of sound patterns as with the rhyming of *even Steven*, *flap jack*, and *ready for Freddie*; the alliteration of *gloomy Gus*, *dumb Dora*, and *nervous Nellie*, and the assonance of *alibi Ike*, *fancy Dan*, *sneaky Pete*, *long johns*, and *screaming Meemie*.

Outside of these types of inventions, only a handful of fairly short and easy-to-pronounce names are used. *Joe* is a favorite as in *Joe Six-Pack*, which is a refinement of the *Good Old Joe* concept, seen earlier in *Joe Blow* and *Joe Schmo*, and in the more specific *G. I. Joe* (from "General Issue") for a soldier, *Joe* (or *J.*) *Random Hacker* for a computer whiz, *Holy Joe* for an army chaplain, *Joe College* for a student, and even *Joe Camel* for the controversial cartoon character that sold Camel cigarettes.

Faulty Parallelism brings smiles as in this signature ditty of Chuckles the Clown on the *Mary Tyler More* show:

> A little song . . .
> A little dance . . .
> A little Seltzer down your pants!

Naturalist Joseph Wood Krutch wrote that "the most serious charge that can be brought against New England is not Puritanism, but February," while Henry Clay declared that he "would rather be right than President."

The pleasure comes in breaking from an established pattern as when William F. Buckley Jr. was campaigning for mayor of New York City in 1965 and railed against the restrictions being put on New York City police. He complained that they couldn't use clubs or gas or dogs and then concluded with, "I suppose they will have to use poison ivy." In a Mexican skit, Sid Caesar established his pattern by talking about tequila being "our national drink" because "it kindles the spirits of our hearts." Then he added, "And it keeps our cigarette lighters working." A *Wall Street Journal* cartoon by D. Cresci pictured a bank robber informing the teller, "You won't get hurt if you hand over all the money, keep quiet, and validate this parking ticket."

Metonymy occurs when something is named for a quality that is in some way associated with the item. In the days of CB radios, people often chose "handles" that were descriptive of their physical characteristics or their hobbies, just as today with e-mail and the Internet some people choose nicknames that are metonymous. Jeff Gordon, a professor of geography at Bowling Green State University in Ohio, collects interesting names of antique shops. He has over 300, including these maxims: *Another Fine Mess*, *As You Were*, and *The Collected Works*; adapted maxims: *Fourscore and More*, *A Touch of Glass*, and *Den of Antiquity*; and names that incorporate the owners' names as in *Suzantiques*, *Shair's Wares*, *Young's Oldies*, and *Fine's Finds*.

In a world-famous example of metonymy, the *Watergate* scandal was named after the hotel where the break-in of the national Democratic headquarters occurred. Language observers smilingly observe that history, and the English language, would have been different if the first news reports had referred instead to the general area in Washington, DC, (*Foggy Bottom*) or to the group Richard Nixon had assigned to stop the leaks (code-named *The Plumbers*). Today's dictionaries give more room to the metonymous meaning of Watergate than to the literal meaning of "a gate controlling the flow of water." *Gate* has now become a suffix meaning "scandal" as in *Irangate*, *Contragate*, *Iraqgate*, *Pearlygate*, *Rubbergate*, *Murphygate*, *Gennifergate*, *Nannygate*, *Monicagate*, ad infinitum.

Diseases are sometimes given metonymous names. For example, the *Pickwickian Syndrome* gets it name from Charles Dickens's *The Pickwick Papers* in which Joe the Fat Boy constantly falls asleep. The disease is a condition in which blood veins going to the brain are squeezed so that people fall asleep in the midst of activities. *Ondine's Curse* describes a condition in which sleeping people cease breathing and die without awakening. It is named for a mythological water nymph who cursed her mortal lover when he betrayed her. *Legionnaires disease* is named for 29 victims who died after attending a 1976 American Legion convention in a hotel with a contaminated air-conditioning system.

Nonsense in relation to humor does not have the literal meaning of "without sense." There is no humor in something that is truly nonsensical because it is unintelligible as in the ravings of an insane person or in random words or sounds spewed out by a computer. To be humorous, the communication has to be in a recognizable pattern and has to seem to make sense, but then to surprise listeners or readers with something unexpected. Nonsense verse, for example, is carefully put together so that it has a strong rhythmic quality that serves to highlight logical infelicities and *nonce* words. *Nonce* (cognate with *once*) words are coined for a particular use as in Lewis Carroll's "Jabberwocky" poem where he created *frabjous* and *galumphing*, new words which caught on so that most people at least recognize them today. Nonsense can also be found in the logic of some seemingly serious piece as in Charles Dickens's story for children "The Magic Fishbone," in which he makes fun of large Victorian families by describing Princess Alicia's family, "They had nineteen children and were always having more. Seventeen of these children took care of the baby, and Alicia, the eldest, took care of them all. Their ages varied from seven years to seven months."

Oxymoron comes from two Greek words *oxys* meaning "sharp," and *moros* meaning "foolish or dull," hence the meaning of "con-

180

tradictory terms" as when a product for arthritis relief is named *Icy-Hot*, a line of shoes is named *Cool Fire*, and a floor covering is named *Soft Brick*. In the mid-1980s, Warren S. Blumenfeld, a professor at Georgia State University, brought oxymorons to the attention of the general public. *People* magazine (Mar. 3, 1986) began an article about him with this paragraph, which contains 14 oxymorons:

It was a new tradition—the First Annual Florida Snowmobilers' Ball. As he gazed across the crowded room, he saw her sitting on the real vinyl banquette. She was a relative stranger, but he was attracted by her seductive innocence. Sophisticated good ole boy that he was, he adopted an air of studied indifference as he mused upon the planned serendipity of their meeting. "What if she is a closet exhibitionist?" he wondered. "What if she thinks my minor surgery is old news?" Still she was his only choice.

While some people have this kind of playful fun with the contradictory terms, others take a more pessimistic view, saying that oxymorons are purposefully misleading. They don't think it's funny that in 1955 the Supreme Court ordered schools to desegregate with all *deliberate speed*, nor do they think that wars are ever *civil*, or that there's such a thing as *friendly fire*, or that what the United States launched in Vietnam was a *peace offensive*. But even the most cynical can smile at an *Anarchists Unite* button or at the *May we live long and die out* motto of the Voluntary Human Extinction Movement, a group devoted largely to producing humorous mailings.

Personification is an unusually common process. Even before infants have mastered language, they respond to toys as if they were human, and in the earliest nursery rhymes and stories, animals, dolls, "choo-choo" trains, and teapots come to life. This kind of personification is a kind of fun that we never outgrow as shown by this paragraph from an often reprinted lament to old age:

As soon as I wake, Will Power helps me get out of bed. Then I go see John. Then

Charley Horse comes along, and as soon as he leaves, Arthur Ritis shows up and for the rest of the day we go from joint to joint. After such a busy day, I'm tired and glad to go to bed—with Ben Gay. What a life!

More sophisticated examples of personification are these various definitions of puns. Richard Lederer in the introduction to his *Get Thee to a Punnery* said that puns are "a three-ring circus of words: words clowning, words teetering on tightropes, words swinging from tent-tops, words thrusting their heads into the mouths of lions." Tony Tanner said that a pun was like an adulterous bed in which two meanings that should be separated are coupled together, while Debra Fried defined them as "the weird accidents, amazing flukes and lucky hits that the one-armed bandit of language dishes up. . . ." This last example is a case of once-removed personification, since a "one-armed bandit" is itself a personified reference to a gambling machine.

Synecdoche is a specific kind of metonymy in which a part of something is used to represent the whole thing, as when referring to the movies as *the big screen* or to television as *the tube*. In a popular joke about the *Lone Ranger* show, Tonto uses synecdoche when he responds to the Lone Ranger's announcement that "We are being followed by Indians," with "What you mean *we*, Paleface?" Football kicker Lou Grosa was called *The Toe*, while the outspoken baseball player and coach Leo Durocher was called *The Lip*. Actress Betty Grable was called *The Million Dollar Legs*, while actor Jimmy Durante was called *The Schnoz*. In a Brant Parker *Wizard of Id* cartoon, a girl brings a boy home and introduces him with, "Father . . . This is Marvin! He's asked for my hand." The father replies, "Marv . . . It's the whole package or nothing." *See also* ACCIDENTAL HUMOR, ALLUSIONS, AMBIGUITY, EXAGGERATION, JOKE PATTERNS, METAPHORS, PUNS, SLANG, UNDERSTATEMENT

Late-Night Talk Shows

Late-night talk shows were originally devised as a way to squeeze advertising dollars out of what was basically television's dead time. As the concept proved viable, a fairly standard format evolved. A genial host provides continuity and makes sure there is at least some humor and excitement as different guests perform or visit with the host and other guests. The shows start after 10 or 11 P.M. when children are assumed to be asleep, which means that censors are less likely to object to "adult" topics and risque language. Other assumptions are that people will be coming and going so it is best to organize the shows in small segments, and because people use the shows as a way to relax before going to sleep, they do not want to be troubled with the problems of the world. If serious problems are discussed, they are joked about.

In 1986 when NBC commemorated its 60th anniversary, it brought together Jerry Lester, Steve Allen, Jack Paar, and Johnny Carson to celebrate the founding of the late-night talk show. This was an appropriate gathering because each of these men made contributions to the genre that is now imitated and admired around the world, not only as a source of entertainment but also as an influence on public opinion.

In 1950, the first late-night host, Jerry Lester (1911–1995) of *Broadway Open House*, established the humorous tone, which is the key difference between late-night and daytime talk shows. He took on his pioneering role almost by accident when he was invited to appear on a talk show with Tex McCrary and Jinx Falkenburg. His "shameless mugging, corny jokes and irrepressible energy" lit up the NBC telephone switchboard so that on the spot Pat Weaver, president of NBC, offered Lester the job of hosting the newly planned show.

Besides Lester's comic style and his humorous quips ("What do you give a man who has everything? Penicillin."), Lester brought in the light-hearted sexual teasing that is still a staple on late-night talk shows. His most popular guest was the blonde Dagmar (Virginia Ruth Egnor). She dressed in a long, strapless gown, which accentuated her full figure, as she played the role of the dumb blonde, reciting ridiculous poetry filled with malapropisms and sexual innuendos. The

show ran for approximately a year before Lester went on to other activities and Dagmar went on to her own show, *Dagmar's Canteen*.

The time slot under the name of *The Tonight Show* was given to 30-year-old Steve Allen, who had inherited a talent for comedy from his mother Belle Montrose, a performer described by Milton Berle as "the funniest woman in vaudeville." Allen adapted some of the techniques and the humorously teasing tone that Groucho Marx used in his popular *You Bet Your Life*. Through his "Man in the Street Interviews" and "The Answer Man" (people would give him an answer to which he made up a funny question) Allen instituted the repeating gimmick, similar to what Dave Letterman does with his "Top 10" lists and Jay Leno does with his funny newspaper headlines. More important, Allen brought intellectual content to the program, similar to what Dick Cavett would do nearly two decades later. Allen has wide-ranging interests that over his lifetime made him a scholar of comedy, a dramatic actor, a director, a musician, a writer, and a political activist. In *The Tonight Show*, he put these interests to good use through interviewing a variety of guests. His knowledge also gave him the confidence to tease the high and the mighty as when he was asked, "Do they get your program in Boston?" and he responded, "Well, they see it, but they don't get it."

In 1957 Jack Paar (1918–) was chosen as Steve Allen's replacement. He had already hosted *Up to Paar, Bank on the Stars*, and *The Jack Paar Program*. On *The Tonight Show*, he arranged for types of guests who had never before been seen on talk shows including Robert Kennedy, John F. Kennedy, Fidel Castro, and Richard Nixon. He also had performance guests, one of the most famous being Cliff Arquette playing the character of Charlie Weaver reading "letters from Mama." Television critic John J. O'Connor devoted his "Television View" column (*New York Times,* Feb. 2, 1997) to a retrospective on the contributions of Paar. He wrote that "Before Paar, . . . the formats tended to be straightforward comedy or variety. Paar introduced the panel set that to this day remains the late night altar before which an endless parade of guests eagerly genuflect." Part of Paar's success was that he built up a repertory of regulars and "as he never tires of pointing out," he was the one who introduced the Beatles to America. He was also the first to put Bill Cosby and Liza Minnelli on television. Paar told O'Connor, "I like to think of myself not as a comic but as a humorist. To me, a comic says funny things. A humorist thinks funny things." Paar, whose signature line was, "I kid you not," observed that "I've been doomed all my life to the small chuckle," which inspired O'Connor to conclude, "When it comes to being doomed, other comics and talk-show hosts should be so lucky."

The next host of *The Tonight Show* was Johnny Carson, who came in 1962 and was so successful that he stayed for 30 years. As a boy growing up in Nebraska, Johnny Carson got into performance through teaching himself magic tricks and ventriloquism. The magic gave him practice in performing before an audience, while the ventriloquism gave him a head start in making snide asides and speaking to both sides of an issue. When after World War II he moved from Nebraska to California, one of his first show-business jobs was as a script writer for Red Skelton, who just before a performance accidentally knocked himself out on a prop door. Carson went on in his place and earned good reviews. He also had fairly good reviews when he hosted a daytime show *Who Do You Trust?* which was similar to Groucho Marx's defunct *You Bet Your Life*. In contrast to Paar, Carson was cool, in control, and self-assured. Rather than inviting controversial guests, he invited entertaining guests. As a talented mimic, he played such costumed roles as aging Aunt Blabby, redneck Floyd Turbo, magician El Moldo, television pitchman Art Fern, and psychic Karnak the Magnificent. He encouraged audience involvement ("It was really hot today . . ." "How hot was it?") and he took his audiences into his confidence by telling them when he was going "for the biggie," or when he thought his monologue was "heading for the dumper."

As competition increased in the world of television and as people began anticipating Carson's retirement, various contenders—both individuals and networks—began vying for the late-night audience. The earliest serious contender was Dick Cavett, who had such a successful daytime show that in 1969 ABC moved the *Dick Cavett Show* to late night to compete with Carson. Cavett was praised for combining wit and cerebral humor with urban sophistication and down-to-earth boyishness. Cavett invited as regular guests such luminaries as Norman Mailer, Groucho Marx, and Mort Sahl. Ronald L. Smith wrote that "not since Paar's heyday did newspapers breathlessly quote the outrageous opinions and witty rejoinders." Cavett worked first with ABC, but later also worked with PBS, USA cable, and NBC cable.

In the late 1980s, Joan Rivers, who had frequently substituted for Carson, had a short-lived show with the Fox network. In 1993, Chevy Chase had a show that was abruptly canceled, to which he responded: "My hat is off to those guys who do this kind of work." In the early 1990s, Arsenio Hall, described as having "more personality than jokes," also did a successful show for Fox, while Keenan Ivory Wayans did one in the late 1990s. Other comedians who took a turn at late-night hosting included Paula Poundstone, Dennis Miller, and Jon Stewart.

David Letterman, who in the 1980s and on into the 1990s had been Carson's biggest competitor, stayed in the business to go head-to-head against Jay Leno, who in 1992 became Carson's replacement. Letterman, who is described as an over-six-foot "loveable scamp," sends a camera out to roam the streets, participates in stunt comedy, needles his guests, and pretends that his unruly hair is a toupee.

When Leno became Carson's replacement, he had a rocky beginning partly because the audience was so accustomed to Carson, and Leno's "anvil-shaped" face and moody voice were so different. But like Carson, Leno smiles and chuckles lightheartedly when he manages to squelch a heckler, and although he avoids four-letter words, he is not afraid to be nasty. In its 9 February 1998 issue, *Time* magazine pictured him in its "Winners" column for his Clintongate monologues, which "are cruel, unfair—and riotously funny."

As with other aspects of television, at the end of the century there was more competition, which provides viewers with more choice. Besides the *Late Show with David Letterman* on CBS and *The Tonight Show with Jay Leno* on NBC, viewers could watch *Politically Incorrect with Bill Maher* on ABC or *The Charlie Rose Show* on PBS. Insomniacs and people whose jobs kept them awake even later at night could also watch *Later* on NBC, the *Late Late Show with Tom Snyder* on CBS, and *Late Night with Conan O'Brien* on NBC. Also, cable TV channels were increasingly offering shows with formats that resemble the late-night talk shows; for example, *The Chris Rock Show* Friday nights on HBO.

The fact that late-night television is a popular genre does not mean that it goes without criticism. A two-page feature in *The New York Times* (Aug. 22, 1993) tried to answer the question of "Why Late-Night TV Is a Man's World." Psychologist Midge Wilson from De Paul University said that all the

By the time Conan O'Brien came to late-night television, the genre had moved a long way from being a gimmick designed to squeeze advertising dollars from "dead time." ©*NBC/Globe Photos Inc.*

late-night hosts and virtually all of their writers are male because late-night humor leans toward put-down humor, which "has a male bent."

According to Nielsen ratings, on an average night in the summer of 1993, 20 percent more women than men were watching *The Tonight Show*, 40 percent more women than men were watching Arsenio Hall, while about the same number of men and women were watching David Letterman. Elizabeth Kolbert, the author of the article, wrote that "Freud never got a chance to tune in to late-night television, but if he had he would almost certainly have found his theories confirmed. After 11:00 p.m., the aggression is everywhere. . . . The laughs belong to the winners." Some of the male writers that Kolbert interviewed denied that the humor was as aggressive as it was "self-protective—learned in school by little boys trying to get by." Robert J. Thompson, a communications professor at Syracuse University who specializes in television, said that the training ground for teaching "sly, knowing, ironic humor isn't available" to girls. Follow-up letters to the editor (Sep. 5, 1993) pointed out that the article was in itself perpetuating a myth: "If you haven't found as many funny women as men, you haven't looked hard enough." Another writer said it was because young men don't often watch television, except for sports, and so advertisers were behind the male appeal because they want the commercial time to sell beer and cars. *See also* GENDER AND HUMOR, RADIO, TELEVISION

Laughter and Smiles

One dictionary defines *laughter* as "showing mirth, joy, or scorn with a smile and chuckle or explosive sound." However, some humor scholars do not agree that smiling and laughing are the same. They feel that the difference between the two actions is not so much a matter of intensity or degree as of kind. While smiles sometimes evolve into laughs and laughs usually taper off into smiles, smiles are more likely to express feelings of satisfaction or good will while laughter comes from surprise or a recognition of incongruity.

"Getting the giggles," a phenomenon that most people have experienced, seldom happens when one is all alone. In contrast, people frequently smile when they are reading or even when having private thoughts. The idea that laughter is contagious is so well established that the first line of Ella Wilcox's folksy poem "Laugh and the world laughs with you . . ." has become a cliche. The idea it expresses underlies the radio and television practice of "sweetening" the responses of live audiences by adding a laugh track so that listeners and viewers at home will feel more like laughing.

Over the centuries, scholars have offered various definitions of laughter including the following:

> The sudden glory arising from the sudden conception of some eminency in ourselves, by comparison with the infirmity of others. (Thomas Hobbes, *Leviathan*, 1651)

> Laughter is an affection arising from a strained expectation being suddenly reduced to nothing. (Immanuel Kant, *The Critique of Judgment*, 1790)

> The essence of the laughable is the incongruous, the disconnecting one idea from another, or the jostling of one feeling against another. (William Hazlitt, *Lecturers on the Comic Writers, Etc. of Great Britain*, 1819)

> The phenomenon of laughter always signifies the sudden apprehension of an incongruity between a conception and the real object. (Arthur Schopenhauer, *The World as Will and Idea*, 1844)

> Something mechanical encrusted on the living causes laughter. (Henri Bergson, *Laughter*, 1900)

> [Laughter arises from] the release of previously existing static energy. We should say that laughter arises if a quota of psychical energy which has earlier been used for the cathexis of particular psychical paths has become unusable, so that it can find free discharge. (Sigmund Freud, *Jokes and Their Relation to the Unconscious*, 1905)

These definitions are each influenced by the particular scholar's philosophy and beliefs about the nature of humor, but they all reflect an assumption that for most people laughter is tied to humor and that it is a quick response of the body to something that the mind has perceived. Three out of the six use the word *sudden*, while the others use such terms as *jostling*, *arise*, *release*, and *free discharge*, none of which would be appropriate terms for defining *smiling*.

Laughing and *smiling* are hard to define because they occur in so many situations and for so many reasons. Perpetrators of violent acts have been known to exhibit menacing smiles or to laugh demonically. As Jacob Levine has pointed out in *Motivation in Humor* (1969), "No pattern of human behavior is so full of paradoxes. . . We may laugh in sympathy, from anxiety or relief, from anger or affection, and from joy or frustration." Conditions that can evoke laughter include shyness, triumph, surprise, tickling, a funny story, an incongruous situation, a sense of well-being associated with good health, and a desire to conceal one's inner thoughts. Anthropologist Gary Alan Fine has explained that a smile in one society may portray friendliness, in another embarrassment, while in still another it may be a warning of hostilities and attack if tension is not reduced.

Laughter varies by intensity as well as by situation. At the 1998 meeting of the International Society for Humor Studies, D. G. Kehl, a scholar in 20th-century American literature, cited James Thurber's essay "The State of Humor in the States" in which Thurber says "there are a dozen different kinds [of laughter], from the inner and inaudible to the guffaw, taking in such variants as the laughter of shock, embarrassment and . . . she-laughed-so-I-laughed-too, and even he-laughed-so-I-didn't." A decade earlier, author James Agee had classified the laughter of screen comedians into four categories: the titter, the yowl, the belly laugh, and the boffo.

Kehl went further in finding literary examples to illustrate nearly 20 kinds of laughter in ascending order of intensity: the simper or smirk (what Thurber identified as "inner and inaudible"), the snicker or snigger, the titter, the giggle, the chuckle, the simple laugh, the cackle, the cachinnation, the chortle, the belly laugh, the horse laugh, the Olympian or Homeric laugh, the guffaw, the boff or boffo, the crack up, the roar, the yowl or howl, the bellow, the hoot, and the shriek.

While both smiling and laughing are motivated internally, they are also influenced by social situations. Psychologists are currently working to measure how smiles differ in intensity and duration and how different kinds of smiles have different effects. For example, while the "polite" smile is often forced, "sardonic" or "threatening" smiles may be sincere but there is the question of whether or how such smiles relate to humor.

Researchers have recently studied relationships between laughing and tickling. Among their findings are that people who laugh from being tickled are not necessarily put in a more receptive mood for enjoying the humor in jokes. Apparently, laughing from being tickled occurs in a part of the brain different from where laughter that is intellectually stimulated occurs. Another study reported in the November 1998 issue of *Nature Neuroscience* found that people cannot tickle themselves because the cerebellum in the lower back of the brain somehow sends an interfering message to the part of the brain that controls laughter.

Laughter is in many ways similar to talk in that it serves as a means of social interaction. British psychologist Antony Chapman, writing in the *Handbook of Humor Research*, reported on a study in which he compared the actions of a group of children who knew they were being observed with a group who did not know they were being observed. The children who knew they were being watched laughed four times as often as did those in the other group; however, they smiled only half as much. Chapman also compared the reactions of three sets of seven-year-old children listening to humorous material through headphones. One set of children listened individually, while the other two sets were paired. With one of the paired sets, one child listened to humorous material while the other listened to non-humorous material. In the other paired set, both children listened simultaneously to the humorous material. As might

be expected, the children listening by themselves laughed the least; those who had a listening partner laughed more even though the partner was not laughing, while those whose partners were listening to the same humorous material laughed significantly more. The participants who laughed the most also rated the material as funnier. Chapman concluded that humor was both the result and the cause of laughter. In a follow-up study, he found that a lack of laughter or inappropriate laughter served as an inhibitor of laughter quite as effectively as "good" laughter served as a stimulant.

Further reading: Salvatore Attardo, *Linguistic Theories of Humor* (1994). *Researching Humor and Laughter*, http://www.uni-duesseldorf.de/WWW/MathNat/Ruch/research%26people.html (June 1999). Barry Sanders, *Sudden Glory: Laughter as Subversive History* (1995). Daniel Wickberg, *The Sense of Humor: Self and Laughter in Modern America* (1998).

Legal Humor

Legal humor consists of jokes targeting lawyers as well as jokes that lawyers tell about themselves, their clients, and frustrations connected with their profession. It might also include anecdotes, reminiscences, humorous laws and events, and discussions about the place of humor in law schools and courtrooms. One of the reasons that jokes targeting lawyers are a popular form of legal humor is that lawyers are high enough on the social scale that people can translate old hostile jokes into lawyer jokes without feeling guilty for picking on the disadvantaged. Anti-lawyer jokes range from the riddle

> What do you have when you've got a lawyer buried up to his neck in sand?
>
> *Not enough sand!*

to Woody Allen's observation that

> Some men are heterosexual, some are bisexual, and some men don't think about sex at all . . . they become lawyers.

Both William Shakespeare and Charles Dickens used lawyers as comic foils and so did the French artist Honore Daumier (1808–1879). In his set of lithographs *Les*

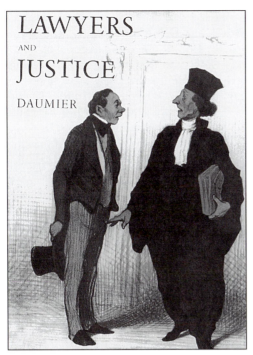

The great French caricaturist Honore Daumier drew dozens of cartoons satirizing lawyers and the legal profession.

Gens de Justice, Daumier shows pretentious and haughty lawyers speaking such lines to their disadvantaged clients as "It's true you lost your case . . . but at least you had the pleasure of hearing me make my plea," and "My dear Sir, it is quite impossible for me to take on your case . . . You lack the most important piece of evidence . . . [aside] Evidence that you can pay my fee!" Law students are encouraged to study such anti-lawyer jokes to get an idea of the public perceptions they will have to deal with.

Another explanation for the popularity of anti-lawyer jokes is that people relieve moderate levels of tension through joking, and tension is an integral part of the law profession. Most people hire a lawyer only when they are having a disagreement or when they are hoping to forestall disagreements by drawing up such documents as contracts, wills, and prenuptial agreements. The tensions people feel about these situations, and about how quickly billable hours add up, often get transferred to their attorneys, sometimes with disastrous results. In the summer of 1992 after a disgruntled client opened fire in a San Francisco law office killing eight people and wounding six others before turning the gun on himself, Harvey I. Saferstein, president of the California Bar Association, called a news conference to ask people "to stop the lawyer-bashing . . . that sometimes can incite violence and aggression toward lawyers." It was his opinion that lawyer jokes can push "a fringe person" over the edge. The man, Gian Luigi Ferri, who did the shooting was disappointed in the help he had received from the law firm regarding a 10-year-old real estate venture. Although it is impossible to know what was going on in Mr. Ferri's mind, people who believe in the theory of humor as release and relief could argue that had Mr. Ferri been telling jokes and making fun of his lawyers over the past 10 years his hostility might have drained away instead of festering into the tragedy.

Lawyers are not immune from the stress that is part of their jobs and so they too have jokes about their profession as when students in law school compare it to a besieged city; everybody outside wants in, and everybody inside wants out. Humor from the perspective of lawyers appears in such books as Arnold B. Kanter's *The Ins & Outs of Law Firm Mismanagement: A Behind-the-Scenes Look at Fairweather, Winters & Sommers* (1994) and Daniel R. White's *Still the Official Lawyer's Handbook* (1991) and *Trials & Tribulations: An Anthology of Appealing Legal Humor* (1991). White, who dropped out of practice to become a comedy writer and editor, told a *New York Times* reporter (Aug. 8, 1993) that "Law like wine and opera," lends itself to pretension and that people hate lawyers because they don't understand their language or the judicial system. "What lawyers see as a legitimate part of the adversarial process (casting facts in the light most favorable to one's client) a lay person sees as telling a half-truth, or even a lie. They see lawyers' opinions as purchasable."

Law professors liven up boring lectures with humorous analogies, anecdotes from trials, true stories about bumbling criminals, and discussions on obsolete or strange laws. Henry Ward Beecher observed that "it usually takes a hundred years to make a law; and then, after it has done its work, it usually takes a hundred years to get rid of it." In the 1880s, the good citizens of South Foster, Rhode Island, passed a law saying that any dentist who accidentally pulls a patient's wrong tooth must willingly have his own identical tooth pulled by the town's blacksmith. The citizens of Chicago's 7th Ward presumptuously declared it against the law for pigeons to fly overhead, while a town in California passed a law banning animals from publicly mating within 1,500 feet of any tavern, school, or place of worship. An entrepreneurial druggist, William C. Garwood, in Evanston, Illinois, invented ice cream sundaes when the town passed a law forbidding the selling of ice cream sodas on the Sabbath. He first called his invention *Sundays*, but was forced by the town's clergy to change the spelling.

James Gordon, a professor of law at Brigham Young University, sometimes tells students that the day's topic is so boring that it fits Mark Twain's description of "chloroform in print," and he is ashamed to be teaching it. Then he turns away for a minute and reappears in a simple disguise. When he submitted a satirical article on "How Not to Succeed in Law School," the *University of Chicago Review* returned it with its own brand of satire, "We have worked long and hard to establish a grim and humorless reputation, and we are not about to let you threaten it." The article was later published in the spring 1991 *Yale Law Journal*. In defending his use of humor as a teaching technique, Professor Gordon says that "when students are having fun, the class time virtually flies by, and the 50 minutes of class seem like a mere 48."

Even though humor may be welcome in law school classes and in firms where it is found to be beneficial in staff relations and in negotiations with clients, attorneys who joke in actual trials are taking a risk. Humor has a leveling influence, which is contrary to the hierarchical nature of courtrooms. Humor also involves ambiguity and implication so that the same joke or allusion might be interpreted differently by different judges or members of a jury.

In a 1992 case, comedy writers E. J. Novak and Debra Studer sued NBC for allegedly pirating and using material on *Saturday Night Live* that Novak and Studer had written for *Video Vault*, a comedy show that ran on WOR-TV in the mid-1980s. The two writers not only lost their case but were fined $3,500 because trial judge Robert W. Sweet of Federal District Court in Manhattan wanted to teach them that "Federal litigation is no playground for comics." Novak claims that he and his wife, who represented themselves, lost their case because they spoke in "plain, barbed English rather than in the acceptable huffing and puffing and pompous circumlocutions of traditional legal discourse." According to *The New York Times* (Jan. 24, 1992), throughout the trial, Novak referred to the NBC lawyers as Laurel and Hardy, "a reference not to the defense lawyers' comedic skills but to their respective physiques." When the lawyers, James Sandnes and Thomas Jones, objected, Novak wrote a letter addressing them simply as "Stan" and "Ollie." Early on, even the judge joined in by asking Mr. Sandnes, "Which one are you?" "I'm Stanley, your Honor," Mr. Sandnes replied. But from there the situation degenerated into "the rudeness zone," and after the fine was levied, Novak protested that he would rather be called "Laurel and Hardy" than "dilatory and deceitful." He then went on to say that the only people defamed were the real Laurel and Hardy "because they were compared to these lawyers." *See also* LEGAL ISSUES, SCHOOL HUMOR

Further reading: Michael Gilbert (ed.), *The Oxford Book of Legal Anecdotes* (1986). Sidney Harris, *So Sue Me! Cartoons on the Law* (1993). Charles M. Sevilla, *Disorder in the Court: Great Fractured Moments in Courtroom History* (1992).

Legal Issues

Most legal issues related to humor center around people's claims of having been harmed by someone's use of humor. Defamation claims can be straightforward as when in the spring of 1992, the father of a sixth-grade boy in Tucson, Arizona, sued his child's school because following the school's ceremony where it distributed end-of-the-year awards, the teacher returned to her classroom and passed out joke awards to her 15 students. The boy, who since kindergarten had spent part of his time in special education classes, received a Pigsty Award, a Procrastinator's Award, and a World's Worst Athlete Award. The school agreed to pay the father's attorney fees of $15,600 and to set up a college annuity fund to pay the boy $8,900 annually for his four years after high school. It also agreed to buy the boy a mountain bike for immediate use.

In a more complicated 1991 defamation claim, the Milford Place Hotel in New York City unsuccessfully sued the syndicated *Atlanta Journal-Constitution* columnist, Lewis Grizzard, for engaging in the kind of New York bashing that his Southern readers loved. The Milford Place Hotel came to his attention when its commercials repeatedly interrupted his watching of an Atlanta P.G.A. golf tournament. Grizzard took umbrage at the dancing show advertising the "Lullabuy of Broadway," which included breakfast and cocktails and a night's stay in midtown Manhattan, all for $50 a person. In his column, Grizzard urged hotel visitors to check their beds "for things that crawl" because "any hotel in Manhattan, that would offer you a room at that meager cost might also offer you the risk of catching Lyme disease."

The hotel's lawyers argued that " . . . just because something is said with humor does not make it any less damaging," while the newspaper's lawyers argued, first, that a humorous essay containing both opinion and parody could not be considered libelous, and second, the hotel could not prove that the column had caused it any damage.

Since 1980 when the Equal Employment Opportunity Commission (EEOC) issued guidelines defining certain kinds of behavior in the workplace as unacceptable because they contributed to a hostile working environment, joking and teasing based on sex or ethnic differences have been grounds for filing EEOC complaints and follow-up lawsuits. In one of the first such cases (*Kyriazi vs. Western Electric*, 1981), a woman industrial engineer won a class-action suit for sexual harassment against male coworkers whose "tasteless behavior, joking, and innuendos" made working intolerable for her. Under EEOC guidelines, management is responsible for maintaining a work climate that is reasonably free from harassment, but in this particular case the judge specified that the company could not absorb the costs; the woman's coworkers were required to pay their own $1,500 fines.

Over the years as government agencies and private companies have worked to clarify EEOC guidelines, several distinctions have been developed. The Department of the Army Training Program on the Prevention of Sexual Harassment, for example, makes a distinction between "sexual static" and "sexual harassment." "Static" is everyday customary joking, which is not *intended* to make any one person uncomfortable. However, if this kind of joking makes someone uncomfortable, and the uncomfortable individual lets either the joker or the supervisor know of the discomfort, and there is no resultant change, then the situation becomes one of "harassment." Joking and kidding around are particularly inadvisable where there is a power difference by rank or position and/or where there is a numerical imbalance between groups by age, gender, race, and so forth. If a person complains and is counseled with something like "Where's your sense of humor?" or "You should be able to take a joke," the situation will likely be judged as harassing because the targeted individual is being told that his or her "rights and feelings don't count."

In a training manual or a workshop this sounds fairly straightforward, but real-life situations are seldom so clear-cut. In 1995, Mohamoud M. Ismail, a Trenton State College sociology professor from Somalia, sued two colleagues for collecting and distributing cartoons to sociology students, 10 of which were displayed in court. One depicted two African Americans—one picking cotton in 1790 and one picking up trash in 1990. Another showed an African American man drinking beer in a seedy-looking room. From a group of rats on the floor comes the comment, "And—get this—we're not rats anymore. We're *Rodent-Americans*." Murray S. Davis, a sociologist and humor scholar from Berkeley, California, was called as an expert witness. He testified that cartoons are "used to illustrate various social processes. One sociologist should expect another sociologist to find them interesting because the cartoons are part of the subject matter that both of them are presumably studying." Davis went on to explain about the portrayals of African Americans in 1790 and 1990, saying that he interpreted the cartoon "as saying that the plight of blacks in America has not changed as much as people might want to believe." However, the same cartoon could offend an African American who interprets the message as saying, "It's their fault that they haven't improved their lot in the past 200 years. But there's nothing in the cartoon itself that shows who's responsible for this." The jury sided with Davis's interpretation of the cartoons as being professionally relevant to the study of sociology rather than as harassing to a fellow faculty member.

Problems of trademark infringement are more numerous and more varied than they were a generation ago because in the buying and selling of abstractions, the dealings are complex and involve many people. Those who initiate an agreement are not necessarily the ones to carry it out. In 1997, the student-run *Harvard Lampoon* hired attorneys to try to collect $226,000 in royalties from J2, the Los Angeles owners of the *National Lampoon*. When *National Lampoon* was founded in 1969, it agreed to pay the Harvard magazine 2 percent of the revenues from any publication using the *Lampoon* name. All went well until 1990 when J2 purchased *National Lampoon* and began attaching the *Lampoon* name to Chevy Chase films, videos, TV shows, CD-ROMs, and some proposed comedy-themed restaurants.

When business names are parodied, the owner of the original name can institute legal action based on trademark infringement. Although companies sometimes sue for damages, the usual result is simply a cease-and-

desist order as when MGM succeeded in keeping a gay rights group from calling itself the *Pink Panther Patrol*, and when Johnny Carson kept a portable toilet company from using *Here's Johnny* as a trademark. The judge decided in favor of Carson, not because of an invasion of privacy or a demeaning of the plaintiff's reputation, but because the *Here's Johnny* toilet company might be confused with Carson's *Here's Johnny* restaurants and *Here's Johnny* line of clothing. The portable toilet company had added insult to injury with the slogan, "The World's Foremost Commodian."

In 1994, Jacques Cousteau and the Cousteau Society received an undisclosed amount of money after taking the Clover-Stornetta Farms to court for a billboard advertisement that parodied Jacques Cousteau. It showed the dairy's *Clo the Cow* dressed in a wet suit and snorkeling gear, sporting the name *Jacques Cowsteau*.

In other cases, judges have come down on the side of humor as when the *Jordache* company was unsuccessful in its suit against *Lardashe Jeans*, a company in Albuquerque, New Mexico, that manufactures oversize jeans for women. The 10 U.S. Circuit Court of Appeals rejected the *Jordache* argument that *Lardashe* was an attempt to confuse the public. Other names considered by the New Mexico company included *Vidal Sowsoon*, *Calvin Swine*, and *Seambusters*.

Two graduates of Iona College in New Rochelle, New York, started a pizza shop that they named *A No. 1 (Iona* spelled backwards) and adopted a slogan that resembled the college's. The college sued on the grounds of "a misuse of the Iona identity." In siding with the graduates, the judge said, "At best, the similarities that do exist can be interpreted as a satirical play on familiar symbolism."

Most colleges and universities now market the use of their logos and their team mascots, as when the University of Georgia's bulldog played a substantial role in the movie made from John Berendt's 1994 novel *Midnight in the Garden of Good and Evil*. Town/gown conflicts often arise in communities where there has been a long-time tradition of showing local support for the team by painting its mascot on the sides of trucks, decorating restaurants with it, and imprinting it on checkbooks. Such "friends of the school" are offended when a new policy is put in place and they are asked to pay a permission fee or, even worse, to cease using the logo because it is not in keeping with the school's desired image.

Humorous parodies are often created under the philosophy that it is easier to ask for forgiveness than for permission. The matter becomes more complicated when music is involved, as was shown in 1994 when the Supreme Court unanimously overturned a lower court's judgment that when the rap group 2 Live Crew recorded its parody version of "Pretty Woman" it was infringing on Roy Orbison's copyright of the rock classic. The Capitol Steps, a satiric Washington singing group, along with political comedian Mark Russell, lent support to 2 Live Crew because, as they pointed out, the success of their own work depends on its timeliness, which means they cannot wait for permission to use parodies of well-known works. In the original decision against 2 Live Crew, the judge wrote that "a parody in the sense of a critical commentary on the original work could be fair use but that a parody that sought only to make a profit could not be." 2 Live Crew argued that all song parodies have commercial value, and that if the Supreme Court accepted the district court's rationale, "the effect would be to prohibit all forms of parody."

The New York Times described the Supreme Court decision as deftly splitting the difference between the argument over whether a parody was a "commercial ripoff" or "the sincerest form of flattery." The Court declared that parody can indeed qualify as fair use and called on lower courts to decide, case by case, whether a particular work qualifies—or infringes on copyright. In a follow-up letter to the editor (Mar. 15, 1994), lawyer Steven M. Berkey protested the Court's failure to consider that "song parodies strike at more than the funny bone. They are music, too, and appeal to the consumer on a primal,

nonintellectual level. . . . A song parody without melody is just a long joke with a short life."

In 1996, broadcaster David Brinkley had an experience illustrating how commercialized humor has become. Shortly after publication of his autobiography, *Everyone Is Entitled to My Opinion*, he received a letter from former history professor, Ashleigh Brilliant, who explained that creating and copyrighting pithy mottoes has been his livelihood since 1967. So far he has copyrighted 7,540 aphorisms, which he licenses for postcards, T-shirts, and other products. In 1974 he copyrighted No. 461, "Everybody Is Entitled to My Opinion." In what the *Wall Street Journal* (Jan. 27, 1997) labeled "Mr. Brilliant's racket," he has now settled 134 infringement cases. Brinkley had already paid $1,000 to a friend of his daughter who thought up the title over dinner, but Mr. Brilliant claimed that the friend had probably seen the saying on one of Brilliant's products. Brinkley and Random House paid the former professor $1,000 without agreeing to or contesting his claim of ownership.

With the reprinting of ordinary jokes there have been two schools of thought. One is that jokes are ever-changing and that they are folk-humor creations and so cannot be copyrighted. A second theory, which has been upheld in some court cases, is that jokes are like poetry in being so condensed and so specifically worded that they deserve copyright protection. Court cases are usually complex, not only because of the vagueness of these two interpretations, but because of questions about the "borrowed" material; for example:

- Was it a whole sketch or only one or two isolated jokes?
- What is the proof that the person bringing the suit originated the joke?
- What is the proof that the person being sued didn't happen to think of the same joke?
- What damages did the creator of the joke suffer?
- Was there intent to defraud?

- Did the "borrower" use the material for commercial purposes?

California attorney Roger Richman's career, which is unusual even by Hollywood standards, illustrates still more complications brought about by the commercialization of humor. According to the *Los Angeles Times* (Oct. 12, 1997), he is "Guardian of the Image" for 45 dead celebrities including Albert Einstein, Sigmund Freud, W. C. Fields, Jimmy Durante, Mae West, and the Wright Brothers. Among the images he has fought against are pictures of Albert Einstein with his head half-shaved advertising a product for hair loss, John Wayne lending his name to a brand of toilet paper, Judy Garland and Clark Gable in pornographic and sadomasochistic poses, and a nearly nude W. C. Fields look-alike. Richman works under the California Celebrity Rights Act passed in 1984 (a dozen states have since passed similar laws), which for 50 years after a person's death forbids the unauthorized use of a celebrity image, including a name, voice, signature, photograph, or likeness, without the family's permission. Richman is the one who forced the U.S. Postal Service to pay for using W. C. Fields's image on a postage stamp. Richman got his start in 1974 when an 80-page court decision about the use of the image of film legend Bela Lugosi ruled that while the family could not control a celebrity's image, "no one else could appropriate it either—as long as one could show proof that the artists had merchandised themselves while alive." Gathering this proof of prior merchandising is a big part of Richman's job and one of the reasons that he has agents in 19 countries who frequent flea markets, clip newspapers, and monitor television and radio in search of both new, unauthorized references and authorized commercial usages made during the celebrities' lifetimes.

As many comedians have learned, in this day of reruns, videotapes, computer-altered photos, and the clipping and inserting from one medium to another, it is not just deceased performers who need protection for their images. In 1993, comedians Robert Schimmel and Carol Siskind sued the Improv when Schimmel happened to pick up a comedy video at a gas station convenience store and discovered that he was one of the featured performers. Schimmel and Siskind said that in 1992 when they performed at the Improv on Melrose Avenue in Los Angeles, they were taped without their knowledge or consent. The tape, along with others, was sold by the Improv to a production company in Atlanta, which packaged the material in two series of six tapes labeled "Live from the Improv" and "Comedy after Hours." The production company said it had been assured that the performers had given permission. Other performers on the tape, who also said that they had not given permission, were hesitant to join in the lawsuit for fear of not being invited back to any of the 15 Improv clubs.

Computers and the World Wide Web have introduced several new areas of legal skirmishes, including quarrels about the names that people use as Internet addresses. For example, the *Princeton Review* and the Kaplan Educational Centers compete with each other in the lucrative business of preparing college students for admissions exams to graduate school. In 1994, the *Princeton Review* signed itself onto the Internet under the name of *Kaplan.Com* and then used the bulletin board to post complaints about the Kaplan company. Kaplan executives were not amused: "How would you feel if you called up your BMW dealer and were automatically connected to Hyundai?" asked president Jonathan Grayer. An Internet arbitration panel put a stop to the "prank," and predicted that regulating names on the Internet will probably be necessary in the not-too-distant future.

Other kinds of regulation are also likely to be developed for the Internet. Because by moving a mouse around and clicking a few buttons it is possible to copy the look of someone else's Web page or to lift a logo and then alter it slightly, many computer users create online parodies and mock other people's Web pages. And except for sites with Web masters, there are no "gatekeepers" on the Internet, which means that virtually anyone can post anything, including rumors, spoofs, hate jokes, and even lies, which, if questioned, are likely to be defended as "jokes." Also, the speed and the anonymity with which things can be put on the Internet complicate questions of authorship. Much of the "anonymous" humor that is posted on the Internet and passed from friend to friend has actually been taken from copyrighted material. And as written about in the entry "Internet Humor," material is sometimes posted and credited to the wrong person.

In summary, the major legal issues connected with humor include

- Charges of defamation and harassment where one side receives as offensive what the other side offers (or claims to have offered) as humorous.

- Intellectual property questions about who owns jokes and one-liners and about "being inspired by" vs. "pirating" someone's ideas.

- Protection of the images and the names of both institutions and individuals, including deceased celebrities.

- Deciding on fair pay when materials are adapted from one medium to another.

- Copyright and trademark infringement in relation to business names and parodies.

- Complications related to the Internet where virtually anyone can post material without being responsible for it.

See also CENSORSHIP, INTERNET INFLUENCES, LEGAL HUMOR, POLITICAL CORRECTNESS

Further reading: Sheryl L. Andrew (ed.), *Brigham Young University Law Review: Symposium on Humor and the Law* (1992:2). J. T. Knight, "Humor and the Law," *Wisconsin Law Review* (1993: 897–919). Robert Riggs, Patricia Murrell, and Joanne Cutting, *Sexual Harassment in Higher Education: From Conflict to Community* (1993).

M

Magazines

The original meaning of *magazine*, a word that English borrowed from French and that French speakers borrowed from Arabic, was "a warehouse or storage place." The common meaning today is a periodical containing miscellaneous pieces such as articles, short stories, advertisements, poems, photos, cartoons, and illustrations. Recently, this meaning has been extended to include television news and feature shows made up of various short segments, and even more recently to include online "magazines," which have various segments so that they are more comprehensive than Web sites.

In 1987, David E. E. Sloane edited a 600-page book *American Humor Magazines and Comic Periodicals* filled with brief descriptions of humor-related magazines between 1757 and 1985. In the foreword, Stanley Trachtenburg noted how the subjects treated in the publications provide a running commentary on American history:

> The politics and social life of the Federal era are mirrored in Washington Irving's *Salmagundi* and in the Washington *Champagne Club* and similar periodicals; the Civil War intruded into the pages even of *Vanity Fair*; *The Knickerbocker* magazine and the *Spirit of the Times* dominated the comic assessment of our growth in the years between 1830 and 1860. The colorful New York *Bee* reflected the feeling about the Spanish-American War, while Thomas

Nast and Joel Chandler Harris along with *Life*, *Puck*, and *Judge* brought an often satiric irreverence to current events and the corruption they concealed.

From more recent periods, he cited *Ballyhoo*, *The Realist*, *MAD Magazine*, *Spy*, and *National Lampoon* as "the gadflies of our national institutions." Perhaps the most influential of all has been *MAD Magazine*, which was founded in 1952, when cartoonist Harvey Kurtzman approached publisher William Gaines with an idea for a satirical comic book *Tales Calculated to Drive You MAD: Humor in a Jugular Vein*. Kurtzman, who was making fun of the popularity of horror comics, chose young adolescent males as his target audience. In 1955, Gaines agreed to let Kurtzman turn the comic book into *MAD Magazine*, both to make it more distinctive and to keep it free from the self-censorship code developed by the comic book industry.

Some observers give *MAD Magazine* credit for ushering in the hippie movement and shaping the generation that protested Vietnam. Grant Geissman, who put together *Collectibly Mad: The Mad and E.C. Collectibles Guide*, said that in its early years *MAD* was an oasis in a cultural wasteland. At a time when there was no other satire, here was an anti-establishment magazine for kids attacking with machine-gun force the man in the gray flannel suit. Rock singer Patti Smith quipped that "after *MAD*, drugs were nothing."

Abe Peck, director of the magazine program at Northwestern University's Medill School of Journalism, says that by the end of the 1960s, *MAD* had achieved the status of an institution. It was printed in seven languages, and, because it could rely for funding on its nearly three million subscribers, did not have to sell advertising and so could carry a joke in every panel. Peck thinks that as a political publication, *MAD* may have "influenced more readers than Tom Paine and maybe even Karl Marx."

MAD's main tool was parody. In the first issue, Kurtzman parodied only other E.C. comics, but he soon turned to parodying the full range of American popular culture and entertainment. A back page "fold-in" provided visual and lexical ironies cleverly illustrating the fact that things may be different from what they first appear. In these parodies television's *Bonanza* was renamed *Bananas*; Irving Berlin's "A Pretty Girl Is Like a Melody" became "Louella Schwartz Describes Her Malady"; Hollywood's *Top Gun* became *Top Gunk*, and *King Kong* became *Ping Pong* connected with the native tribe of *Ookabolaponga*. The *MAD* lexicon included a generous supply of exclamation marks following such words as *blecch*, *yecch*, *va-va voom*, *aargh*, *potrzebie*, *veeblefeztering*, *farshimmelt*, and *furshlugginer*.

In addition to influencing readers, *MAD* has influenced the media and the entertainment world. Mark Cohen, a collector whose traveling exhibit of *MAD* original art has been displayed in 24 cities, says that if it weren't for *MAD*, we wouldn't have had *Laugh-in*, *Beavis and Butt-head*, and *Saturday Night Live*. *MAD* introduced generations of suburban kids to the themes of existential angst, hypocrisy, snobbery, and the new kinds of crime and sexual misadventures they would later meet in the novels of John Cheever, Joseph Heller, Philip Roth, Terry Southern, and John Updike.

MAD also served as a training ground for a new generation of cartoonists, including Mort Drucker, Jack Davis, Will Elder, Wallace Wood, Don Martin, Dave Berg, and Antonio Prohias, who sketched the well-loved *Spy vs. Spy* series making fun of the Cold War.

Paul Krassner, who in the 1960s and 1970s edited *The Realist*, worked first for *MAD*. Throughout his career, *MAD* founder Harvey Kurtzman, who soon moved away to work for Hugh Hefner and *Playboy*, provided various kinds of apprenticeships for some of today's leading cartoonists and taught classes at the School of Visual Arts in New York City. Adam Gopnik, in a 1993 *New Yorker* obituary article about Kurtzman, wrote that "there has been scarcely a single cartoonist or animator of note in the last forty years—from R. Crumb and Art Spiegelman to Monty Python's Terry Gilliam and the French cartoonist Goscinny, co-inventor of 'Asterix'—who did not come under his direct influence and encouragement."

By the mid-1990s, *MAD*'s subscriptions had fallen to something like 400,000, and the magazine was redesigned to include more women and minorities and to compete with Nintendo games by having its own Web page. Co-editors Nick Meglin and John Ficarra philosophically explained in a *New York Times* article (Jun. 30, 1997) that in some ways they were victims of their own success. Across the board, today's humor is more in-your-face and coarse, and to stay on the edge, *MAD* editors are pushing the boundaries still further so that some staff members no longer feel comfortable bringing the magazine home to their kids.

At the other end of the social spectrum is *The New Yorker* magazine, founded in 1925 and described by its editor Harold Ross as "a reflection in word and picture of metropolitan life." *The New Yorker* made such writers as James Thurber, E. B. White, and Dorothy Parker into household names, while also doing more than any other medium to influence the development of cartoon art and the respect that it enjoys in the United States. What the trade refers to as "gag cartoons," the general public often calls *New Yorker* cartoons, regardless of where they are published. This is especially true of cartoons that feature characters from the upper levels of society who rely on urbane wit to make observations that are more social than political.

When *The New Yorker* was founded, most cartoon art, even that which appeared in England's renowned *Punch*, consisted of illustrated dialogues. The dialogues, which carried the joke, were printed like a script, with the characters identified either by name, gender, or the role they were playing. Ross worked with his first art director, Rea Irvin, to change such stilted and wordy dialogues into short and pithy captions. For this new approach to succeed, artists had to move the action into their drawings, and they had to develop techniques (an open mouth, a tilt of the head, a face direction, a hand gesture, etc.) to clarify who was speaking. Ross was happiest when a cartoon needed no caption, as with the famous 1940 Charles Addams drawing of two skiers. One is looking back in wonderment at his fellow skier's tracks each of which mysteriously appears on the opposite side of a large pine tree.

The caption to Peter Arno's 1941 drawing of a group of military personnel looking on as an airplane crashes into the tarmac caught the public fancy so that it became a popular rejoinder in a variety of contexts. A civilian engineer with a roll of plans under his arm is walking away from the disaster and saying, "Well, back to the old drawing board."

In the early days of *The New Yorker*, choosing the cartoons, as well as choosing gags to be assigned to the magazine's regular cartoonists, was often a group effort accomplished in staff meetings, which may be one of the reasons that the magazine developed such a consistent and recognizable style.

Helen Hokinson, a fashion illustrator, was among the earliest cartoonists that Ross hired. She drew "the Hokinson Girls," amiable but basically empty-headed society matrons. Arno drew the kinds of lecherous men and sexy young women that soon became commonplace in *Esquire* and *Playboy*, while George Price specialized in the eccentricities of mean-tempered old men and working-class couples. When Price died at age 93, a three-column obituary article in *The New York Times* (Jan. 14, 1995) identified him as "Cartoonist of Oddities," and the last surviving member of the generation of artists who shaped the look of *The New Yorker* in its early years.

Other early contributors included Gluyas Williams, Alan Dunn, Gardner Rea, Al Frueh, and Mary Petty. In the 1930s came Charles Addams, Perry Barlow, Whitney Darrow Jr., Robert Day, Richard Decker, Syd Hoff, C. E. Martin, Garrett Price, Barbara Shermund, William Steig, and Richard Taylor, while in the 1940s Sam Cobbean, Joseph Farris, Dana Fradon, Frank Modell, Mischa Richter, Saul Steinberg, and Barney Tobey joined the cartoonists under contract. Rea Irvin served as art director from 1925 to 1939, with James Geraghty succeeding him until 1973, when Lee Lorenz took over and stayed in the position for the next 23 years. In 1997, cartoonist Robert Mankoff was chosen as his replacement.

More recently founded humor magazines include *Bonkers: A Magazine for Our Times* (1992), which tries for a balance between light-heartedness and realism. It is heavy on cartoons and illustrations, and about half of the advertisers try for the same light-hearted approach. *The New Humor Magazine*, a quarterly founded in 1994, is printed as an oversized tabloid and contains numerous cartoons, anecdotes, short witticisms, and stories from readers and freelance writers. In

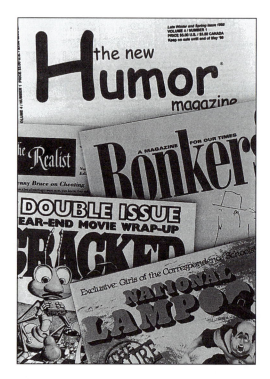

1988, *The Onion* was started (and is headquartered) in Madison, Wisconsin, as a college-town alternative newspaper. Another official version is published in Chicago and a separate version in the Boulder/Denver area under license. By November of 1998, when *The Onion* had a circulation of 160,000 from newstands in Milwaukee, Madison, Chicago, and Denver, national bookstores began carrying it, "as a trial run toward eventually distributing a truly national magazine." But according to *The Onion* PR department, the magazine actually considers its online version to be its major publication: http://www.theonion.com.

Jamie Malanowski wrote in *Time* magazine (Nov. 16, 1998), "You say the real headlines are too wacky to parody these days? Then you haven't seen *The Onion*." Dikkers's moment of epiphany came in 1995 when he realized, "I'm not particularly interested in humor. Nothing really makes me laugh. I thought if we could do a straight news parody, that could be really funny. That's when we found our voice."

"And a funny little voice it is too," concluded Malanowski, who quoted such headlines as, "U. S. Students Lead World in TV Jingle Recall," "Grecian Formula Falls into Non-Grecian Hands," and "Health Insurance: Are You Paying Enough?"

Malanowski, who used to write for *Spy*, said that of course people are comparing *The Onion* to *National Lampoon* and *Spy*, both magazines that are editorially more ambitious and cover a wider range of interests and use more varied approaches. Her conclusion was that *National Lampoon* and *Spy* feature better writers but "right now readers of *The Onion* should just be grateful for the laughs."

Malanowski's use of *right now* hints at what a challenge it is for humor magazines to stay in business. Once readers have gotten over their initial surprise at the kind of humor a magazine offers, then it is hard to surprise and amuse them. Readers grow out of, or beyond, particular kinds of humor, so that such humor magazines as *Cracked* have to continually recruit new subscribers. *Cracked* is read by kids of the age that used to read *MAD*, which has tried to hold onto its readers by moving toward an adult content. Even a magazine as famous as *National Lampoon* has trouble keeping readers. It suspended publication after the April 1992 issue, but resumed as a quarterly in February 1993 to tie in with release of the movie *National Lampoon's Loaded Weapon 1*, the first company movie to be released since the 1989 *National Lampoon's Christmas Vacation*. According to an article in *Advertising Age* (Feb. 22, 1993), during the 1980s, *National Lampoon* steadily lost subscribers and advertisers, partly due to a boycott by antipornography groups. An article in *Folio* (Apr. 1, 1994) had as its headline "National Lampoon: A Magazine or a Theme Park?" Even the British *Punch*, the famous granddaddy of humor magazines, ceased publication with its 8 April, 1992, edition, but was revived four years later thanks to $5 million invested by Mohamed al-Fayed, an Egyptian-born businessman who specializes in acquiring British emblems. According to articles in *The New York Times* (Sep. 18, 1996) and London's *The Sunday Times* (Sep. 1, 1996), new editor Peter McKay laughed in a jolly fashion at the dire predictions and the "fusillade of dead cats coming over the wall." He wondered about a world in which if he had announced that he was producing and selling chemical weapons to third-world nations, "the press would have shown no interest. But say you are reviving a humorous magazine, and the entire press is at your door." He quoted Malcolm Muggeridge, a former *Punch* editor, who once observed, "England is the only place where trying to be funny is considered an insult."

Starting a new magazine is even more challenging than keeping an old one going. Because so many magazines are now published, there is tremendous competition for the rack space in stores, not to mention advertising dollars and money from subscribers and newsstand customers. Magazines have to offer more than jokes because jokes are plentiful on the Internet and the Comedy Channel, and consequently many editors have turned to specialized audiences.

The advent of desktop publishing has enabled hundreds of people to launch small humor magazines or newsletters aimed at specific groups. Ministers subscribe to magazines providing "jokes you can tell on Sunday," literature teachers look for analyses of the humor written by their favorite authors (at least five scholarly journals are devoted to Mark Twain's writings), nurses look for hospital humor, psychologists for humor they can use with their patients, public speakers for timely or witty references, and teachers for school-related humor. Sample specialty magazines include *Political Pix*, a six-page weekly consisting entirely of political cartoons chosen from newspapers; *Sons of the Desert* for fans of Laurel and Hardy; *Hysteria*, a quarterly focusing on women, feminism, and humor; *The Journal of Polymorphous Perversity* satirizing psychological research and writing; *CARtoons* and *Cartoon Cavalcade* specializing in cars and sexy humor; the *American Comedy Network*, which supplies humor pieces to radio stations; and *The Comedy Channel Comic Book*, which is part entertainment and part mail-order catalog for the offerings of the Comedy Channel.

The Annals of Improbable Research (AIR), is an academic spoof run by the staff that from 1955 to 1994 produced *The Journal of Irreproducible Results*. The new journal appears in print six times a year supplemented by a free electronic version each month. It is published by the MIT Museum, the group that gives out the "Ig Nobel" awards each spring to people or organizations whose research achievements "cannot or should not be reproduced."

College humor magazines feel particularly challenged in these times of political correctness. In an article, "No Laughing Matter: Humor Magazines Face a Campus Climate of Indignation and Apathy" (*The Chronicle of Higher Education*, Nov. 30, 1994), writer Christopher Shea said that college humor magazines have become more marginal in recent years: "Once thick, glossy, and packed with national advertising, the magazines now—with a few exceptions—are lucky to get ads for pizza joints." A number have folded for lack of interest. He cited contro-

versies over articles in *Howl* at Bryn Mawr College, *Jabberwocky* at Duke University, *Below the Belt* at Oberlin College, and the *Gargoyle Magazine* at the University of Michigan. Audrey Kennan, editor at Bryn Mawr, was quoted as saying, "Humor is a social tool and it is important that women learn how to use it." Sibi Lawson, co-chair of Abusua, the black-student group at Oberlin College, was quoted as saying, "People of color cannot laugh at some things." The controversy at Oberlin occurred when the college's humor magazine made fun of the minority-student newspaper *The Collective* and changed its slogan from "a safe space for students of color" to "a safe space for bad writing." Lawson agreed that the parody was "very effective" and "very witty," but it was nevertheless "as detrimental as a hate crime."

Stephen Levinson, editor at the University of Michigan, was also accused of racism for parodying what he called some "bad jokes." He said that as a result of being accused of racism, he looks more carefully at what is published, but the protest was actually an anomaly. "The main feeling is apathy." Editor of *The Harvard Lampoon*, John Aboud, said that when he includes racist humor it is to make fun of intolerant people. "Racism is not funny, but racists are."

The Harvard Lampoon is more fortunate than most college magazines because it is housed on the Harvard campus in a mock castle financed by newspaper magnate William Randolph Hearst. "Poon" alumni who have gone on to distinguish themselves as humorous writers include John Updike, Robert Benchley, James Thurber, and Conan O'Brien. More recent graduates have found jobs writing for David Letterman, *Saturday Night Live*, *The Simpsons*, *The Larry Sanders Show*, Comedy Central, and various networks. Alumni Kurt Andersen co-founded *Spy*, while Doug Kenney, who wrote the screenplays for *Animal House* and *Caddyshack*, co-founded *National Lampoon*, which resulted in a "licensing windfall" for the Harvard magazine. The *Harvard Lampoon* selects a variety of major magazines to parody. The all-time best seller was a *Cosmopolitan* parody in the 1970s when 1.2

million buyers were enticed with such tantalizing sell-lines as "10 Ways to Decorate Your Uterine Wall" and "Myth of the Male Orgasm." Johnny Carson boosted sales by holding up a nude centerfold of Henry Kissinger. In the 1990s, comic actor and talk-show host Chris Rock financed a humor magazine at Howard University to try to provide the same kind of launching pad for writers that the *Harvard Lampoon* has. *See also* CARTOONS, HUMOROUS ESSAYISTS, PARODY

Further reading: Glenn C. Ellenbogen, *The Directory of Humor Magazines and Humor Organizations in America (and Canada),* 3rd ed. (1992). Lee Lorenz, *The Art of The New Yorker, 1925–1995* (1995). *Ulrich's International Periodicals Directory.*

Metaphors

Metaphors are analogies that connect two objects in the minds of communicators by ascribing to the second object one or more qualities of the first object. Metaphors give people a way to talk about the unknown through references to the known. Many of the "cute" things that children say are original metaphors created because the speakers do not know the standard way of expressing an idea. Adults create metaphors for the same reason, but they are more aware of what they are doing. Editors said that of the 100,000 new words added to the 1961 edition of Webster's unabridged dictionary, nearly half came into the language through metaphorical processes (most of the others were the result of blending).

Adults create metaphors for both serious and humorous purposes, but for either kind, listeners' minds have to go through a process similar to unraveling a joke. They must see the item being referred to (the goal) in relation to the basis of the comparison (the source) and then they must figure out the nature of the grounding, which is what the source and the goal have in common. Powerful metaphors result in a sudden insight that resembles "catching onto" a joke. In writing about this "thrill," Ralph Waldo Emerson used six comparisons:

When some familiar truth or fact appears in a new dress, mounted as on a fine horse, equipped with a grand pair of ballooning wings, we cannot enough testify our surprise and pleasure. It is like a new virtue in some unprized old property, as when a boy finds that his pocketknife will attract steel filings and take up a needle.

While some critics would call all of these comparisons metaphors, others would say that technically speaking the instances from this quote where Emerson used *like* ("like the new virtue") or *as* ("as on a fine horse") are similes because *like* and *as* give notice to readers that a comparison is being made. The "pure" or true metaphors, as when Emerson wrote that a fact "appears in a new dress," and that a fine horse is "equipped with a grand pair of ballooning wings," force readers to expend more intellectual energy. Because listeners or readers have to discover on their own that a comparison is being made, they are more relieved and pleased when they come to a sudden insight about the intended comparison.

With metaphors created for comic effect, listeners have to engage in an extra level of mental gymnastics or they will miss the point, as with Gabriel Kaplan's statement on television's *Welcome Back, Kotter*, "When you walk through the cow pasture of facts, you are bound to step in some truth." The following newly coined metaphors from the field of business provide vivid mental images, but only if listeners think about the information provided in parentheses.

Jell-O Principle: The ability of an organization to survive meddling and intervention. (When an object is placed into and removed from moderately set Jell-O, the Jell-O will flow back to its original shape.)

Kangaroo Strategy: A company trying to increase its inadequate holdings. (Sometimes the companies with the emptiest pockets are the ones that take the greatest leaps.)

Mouse-milking: A venture that has reached the point of diminishing returns. (Because of a mouse's size, milking it would be an intricately challenging operation producing very little milk.)

Queen Bee Syndrome: When a powerful woman strictly limits the development of her female subordinates. (In a swarm of bees, only one superior bee is allowed to lay the eggs.)

One's whole life experience goes into creating and understanding metaphors. As Cynthia Ozick wrote in a May 1986 *Harper's,* "Metaphor is what inspiration is not. Inspiration is ad hoc and has no history. Metaphor relies on what has been experienced before; it transforms the strange into the familiar."

Dead metaphors are ones that have been in the language so long that speakers take them for granted; they hardly think about the source, as with such body metaphors as a *head* of cabbage, a bottle*neck* in traffic, the *shoulder* of a road, an *arm* of the government, and so forth. However, body metaphors can be funny if there is something to attract readers' or listeners' attention to contradictory images in a metaphor's source and goal, as when a "virgin forest" is defined as one "in which the hand of man has never set foot," or when "virgin territory" is described as being "pregnant with possibilities." S. J. Perelman startled his readers with this mixed metaphor, "The color drained slowly from my face, entered the auricle, shot up the escalator, and issued from the ladies' and misses' section into the housewares department."

Winning entries in the annual Bulwer-Lytton Fiction Contest, which honors the "best of the worst" from some 10,000 "bad" book beginnings, often include overdone or confused metaphors as in this 1990 winning sentence written by Linda Vernon:

Dolores breezed along the surface of her life like a flat stone forever skipping along smooth water, rippling reality sporadically but oblivious to it consistently, until she finally lost momentum, sank and, due to an overdose of fluoride as a child which caused her to suffer from chronic apathy, doomed herself to lie forever on the floor of her life as useless as an appendix and as lonely as a 500-pound barbell in a steroid-free fitness center.

See also ACCIDENTAL HUMOR, ADAPTATION, COMPUTER HUMOR, LANGUAGE PLAY

Further reading: Roland Bartel, *Metaphors and Symbols: Forays into Language* (1983). George Lakoff and Mark Johnson, *Metaphors We Live By* (1982).

Mimes

Mimes take their name from the word *pantomime.* Its general meaning is communication through gestures, as when performers use their bodies, faces, and hands instead of their voices, and in formal mime, imaginary, rather than real, props.

Evidence exists of prehistoric cultures using pantomime dances relating to animals and weather conditions, while later societies incorporated mime dances into religious ceremonies and into the presentations of legends and myths. Modern Western customs are mostly taken from classical Greek and Roman practices, where during dramatic performances a chorus would mime the action that characters were speaking about. Comic miming developed during the 15th and 16th centuries in the Italian commedia dell'arte, which was soon imitated in France where the Italian Pedrolino clown was changed into the French Pierrot clown, the first mime to wear white makeup.

In the early 1800s in Paris, Jean-Baptiste Gaspard Deburau established a popular mime theater. His story was told in the 1944 French film *Les Enfants du Paradis* (*Children of Paradise*). Playing the role of Deburau's father was Etienne Decroux, who throughout his life promoted the art of mime and formalized its movements. Decroux was the teacher of Jean-Louis Barrault, who played Deburau in the film, as well as of Marcel Marceau, who for 50 years entertained audiences with his clown-tramp character named Bip. Marceau's Bip, with his tight-fitting and high-waisted pants and his dark jersey designed to set off his whitened face and serve as a backdrop to his expressive hand movements, was a modern interpretation of the French Pierrot. In some of his most memorable acts, Marceau's Bip would try to walk against the wind or to find his way out of an imaginary box. His facial expressions ranged from toothy glee to frowning outrage. Mel Brooks set up the ultimate irony when he hired Marceau to say the only spoken line in his 1976 *Silent Movie*.

Decroux is known as the "father of modern mime" partly because he was the first one to document and formalize a system of specific movements representing universal meanings. He identified the stylized movements that he taught as *mime*, while classifying other performing practices as *pantomime*. Although not everyone agrees with Decroux's classification system, most people do associate mime with stylized techniques and with more dramatic and serious matters, while they think of pantomime as more spontaneous and less structured, hence more likely to include surprise and humor.

According to this interpretation, Marcel Marceau did mime while Charlie Chaplin did pantomime. Even though as a youngster Marceau admired Chaplin and because of him decided to become a professional performer, their styles differed considerably. Unlike most mimists, the great pantomimists of American silent film, including Chaplin, Buster Keaton, and Harold Lloyd, relied heavily on real props and on spontaneous reactions to whatever situations developed.

An obvious advantage of mime and pantomime is that the artforms transcend language barriers. Charlie Chaplin was the first movie star recognized and appreciated around the world—one reason was that his movies could be understood with only minimal translation. Another advantage of mime is that it works in arenas too large or too noisy for people to hear well. This is why circus clowns and the mascots for athletic teams rely for their humor on exaggerated body movements. Emmett Kelly, the famous Ringling Brothers clown who died in 1979, was so skilled in pantomiming the role of Weary Willie that he was allowed to remain in the circus arena throughout entire performances. He was at liberty to do any of his pantomime bits or to enter into the act and interfere with the performers. His most famous act was to

sweep the circle of light thrown by a spotlight into a smaller and smaller circle, and then to chase it under a rug or into a dustbin. As he would straighten up and bow with an air of satisfaction, another circle of light would appear on the floor in front of him.

In one of the Marx Brothers first films, Al Shean accidentally wrote only a few lines for Harpo. He compensated for his mistake by asking Harpo to use pantomime, and this is how the world got one of its most beloved pantomimists. Harpo's most successful disguise was that of a mute with unruly hair who could communicate with others only by means of honks, whistles, and pantomime. He wore a fright wig and an overcoat with enormous inside pockets from which he pulled such objects as an ice-cream cone, a cup of coffee, and various pieces of hardware including a blowtorch. Somewhere in every movie, he pulled a face called a "Gookie," in which he puffed out his cheeks and crossed his widened eyes. Harpo remembered the look from when he was a youngster working in a cigar store and his boss would contort his face as he concentrated on rolling a cigar. Harpo's best known pantomime scene is in the 1933 movie *Duck Soup*. Groucho chases Harpo, who accidentally breaks a floor-length mirror. When Groucho looks in the empty frame, Harpo is standing on the other side and deftly reflects back every one of Groucho's intricate moves.

Miming is a talent that can be worked into almost any skit. Fanny Brice included mime in her imitations of Madame Pompadour and Theda Bara, while Jack Gilford was known for his pantomime of split-pea soup coming to a boil. Shecky Greene, Tim Conway, and Carol Burnett are so good at impromptu pantomiming that they have been known to break up their co-stars with their silent interruptions. *See also* BODY HUMOR, CLOWNS, SILENT FILMS

Further reading: Tony Montanaro with Karen Hurl Montanaro, *Mime Spoken Here: The Performer's Portable Workshop* (1995).

Movies

In the first decade of the 20th century, producers and inventors used such terms as *stereoscopy*, *kinetoscopes*, *motion photography*, and *motion pictures*, but the American public embraced the less technical term of *movies*. This diverse genre developed in the modern sense between 1930 and the present to include color, sound, and both realistic and enhanced photography. While today we have made-for-TV movies, home videos, documentaries, educational films, and artistic short films, in the early years "the movies" were simply whatever films were shown in theaters to which people paid admission fees. Going to the movies most often meant seeing a cartoon, a newsreel, previews of forthcoming attractions, and a feature film lasting somewhere between 80 and 180 minutes. The feature film was usually the acting out of a fictional story or the re-creation of an event from history.

In relation to humor, today's films illustrate the variation in what makes people laugh. In hopes of being amused, people buy tickets to movies as different as the 1988 film *Who Framed Roger Rabbit?* a whodunnit spoof made through combining live action and animation, and 1998's *Wag the Dog*, an uncannily realistic foretelling of the Monica Lewinsky/President Clinton scandal. Moviegoers also pay money to see annual collections of the world's best television commercials, most of which are humorous, and the life stories of comedians as in *Lenny* (1974), starring Dustin Hoffman as Lenny Bruce; *Buster Keaton: A Hard Act to Follow* (1987), narrated by Lindsay Anderson; and *Chaplin* (1992), starring Robert Downey Jr. *Richard Pryor: Live in Concert* was a box office success in 1978 and was followed by such other comedy performance films as *Bill Cosby, Himself* (1982), *George Carlin at Carnegie Hall* (1983), *An Evening with Robin Williams* (1988), and *Live from Washington It's Dennis Miller* (1988).

While such miscellaneous offerings find audiences, the majority of humorous films are created from fictional stories, with many following similar themes. One such theme is the "quest" or journey in which a protagonist sets out to find something or to get someplace. Quest stories provide opportunities for humor in that individuals are away from home and therefore meet different kinds of people and are subject to new expectations and challenges. Some of the greatest comedies of all time are quest stories including Charlie Chaplin's *The Gold Rush* (1925); Frank Capra's *Mr. Smith Goes to Washington* (1939), starring Jimmy Stewart; the French comedy *Monsieur Hulot's Holiday* (1953); Michael Todd's *Around the World in Eighty Days* (1956), whose cast was a virtual who's who of Hollywood; and *It's a Mad Mad Mad Mad World* (1963), in which another all-star cast competed in a frenzied search for buried treasure. In 1940, Bing Crosby, Bob Hope, and Dorothy Lamour began a series of light romantic comedies that started with *Road to Singapore* and got zanier as the cast went on to *Zanzibar* (1941), *Morocco* (1942), *Utopia* (1945), *Rio* (1947), *Bali* (1952), and *Hong Kong* (1962).

Humorous quest stories can be as realistic as *Biloxi Blues* (1988), the autobiographical story of Neil Simon's 1945 conscription into the army, or as ridiculous as *Pee-wee's Big Adventure* (1985), in which Pee-wee Herman goes searching for his lost bicycle. *ET: The Extraterrestrial* (1982) was on an intergalactic quest, while Albert Brooks and Julie Hagerty played two harried L.A. yuppies on an interstate quest in *Lost in America* (1985). Woody Allen's *Bananas* (1971) is a spoof on America's quest for influence in third-world countries, while *Planes, Trains, and Automobiles* (1987) gets its humor from exaggeration, as a frustrated advertising executive played by Steve Martin tries desperately to get home for Thanksgiving while saddled with an obnoxious traveling companion played by John Candy.

Because in quest and travel films, people come in contact with strangers, the exploration of cultural differences is a natural development. *The Russians Are Coming, The Russians Are Coming* (1966) is an amiable exploration of the cold war panic when a Russian submarine lands on a Connecticut island. Part of the fun in *A Fish Called Wanda* (1988), starring John Cleese, Jamie Lee

Curtis, and Kevin Kline, is the difference between British and American sensibilities. In *"Crocodile" Dundee* (1986), Paul Hogan, an Australian outback hero, startles New Yorkers with his way-out approach to life. In *Beverly Hills Cop* (1984), Eddie Murphy plays a Detroit policeman who tracks the killer of his best friend to Beverly Hills and shocks the Los Angeles police with his street-wise approach. In the 1989 *Splash,* Tom Hanks and Daryl Hannah have a cross-species romance; he's a regular guy while she's a mermaid who grows legs for love. In the 1983 *Local Hero,* a Texas oil executive played by Peter Riegert moves to a sleepy Scottish village whose people are almost as much fun as the Irish villagers in the 1998 *Waking Ned Devine* or the Welsh villagers in the 1995 *The Englishman Who Went Up a Hill but Came Down a Mountain.*

Writers and producers look for ideas and gimmicks that will allow comedy stars to shine in new ways. The stage play *Harvey* was a perfect movie vehicle (1950) for tall and lanky Jimmy Stewart, who looked up to an even taller, imaginary white rabbit. In *Sister Act* (1992), Whoopi Goldberg is a singer on the run from the Mafia. She hides in a convent where she transforms the nuns into singing performers. In *Twins* (1988), the large, muscular, and blond Arnold Schwarzenegger discovers that he was born as part of a genetic experiment and that he has a short, plump, and dark-haired twin played by Danny DeVito. One of the most popular movies that bodybuilder Schwarzenegger has made is *Kindergarten Cop* (1990), where his size and strength contrast with the kindergarteners he teaches while on assignment as an undercover cop.

Even in the early days of silent film, viewers showed a preference for scenes they would be unlikely to see in everyday life. The same is true today, but because of technological advances in filmmaking, expectations are higher. Viewers hardly batted an eye when President Kennedy shook hands with Tom Hanks in *Forrest Gump* (1994), nor were they astounded when in *Memoirs of an Invisible Man* (1992), Chevy Chase was most often seen as a walking and talking set of clothes

Exaggeration and incongruity are only part of the fun in *Twins,* where Arnold Schwarzenegger and Danny DeVito play the roles of twins born as part of an experiment in genetics. *Archive Photos*

with no person inside. In *Multiplicity* (1996), Michael Keaton plays the roles of a construction worker plus his less-than-perfect clones, similar to the way that in the 1998 production of *The Parent Trap,* Lindsay Lohan plays the parts of both twins. In *The Nutty Professor* (1996), Eddie Murphy is an overweight and shy chemistry professor who discovers a formula that changes him into a slim and dashing man-about-town. He plays both parts with vigor and comic effect. In *Look Who's Talking* (1989), starring Kirstie Alley and John Travolta, adult words and attitudes are funnier because they come from the mouth of a baby.

Special effects in science fiction movies started with *King Kong* in 1933 and today are seen in such humorous characters as *The Coneheads* (1993) played by Dan Aykroyd and Jane Curtin, the robot R2D2 (its name comes from Reel 2, Dialogue 2) in *Star Wars* (1977), the leading characters in *Planet of the Apes* (1968), and other aliens such as those in *Gremlins* (1984).

One particular kind of special effect comedy revolves around size changes as in *Attack of the 50-Foot Woman* (1993), starring

Darryl Hannah as a sexy giant, and in *Honey, I Shrunk the Kids* (1989) in which an inventor accidentally changes his children into creatures approximately the size of rats. A 1992 sequel *Honey, I Blew Up the Kid,* in which the same inventor, played by Rick Moranis, turns his two-year-old into a 50-foot giant was more predictable and less popular, proving that there needs to be something more than an overused gimmick. Tom Hanks starred in the more originally concepted *Big* (1988), in which a 13-year-old boy's wish to grow "big" is granted by a carnival wishing machine. Part of the humor in Woody Allen's *Everything You Always Wanted to Know about Sex* (1972) comes from the giant breast that chases people and the miniaturized figures that travel through a human body.

Film makes it possible to treat the supernatural in a variety of ways. There is sophisticated charm in the 1958 *Bell, Book, and Candle,* starring Jimmy Stewart, Kim Novak, and Jack Lemmon and in the 1987 *The Witches of Eastwick,* starring Jack Nicholson, Cher, Susan Sarandon, and Michelle Pfeiffer. The humor in the 1977 *Oh, God!* was touted as "an almighty laugh." Pauline Kael described star George Burns as "God in a baseball cap." Bill Murray, in *Groundhog Day* (1993), is a cynical TV weatherman sent to cover an annual festival. He finds that he is being forced to relive the day over and over until he gets it right. The theme is similar to that of such stories as *Heaven Can Wait* (1943 and 1978) in which the main character dies by mistake and is put back into other people's bodies. In the 1984 *All of Me,* serious lawyer Steve Martin is invaded by the spirit of the rich, crabby, and deceased Lily Tomlin.

Exaggerated plot lines that audiences don't see in real life become scenes of wish-fulfilling excess: candy for children in *Willy Wonka and the Chocolate Factory* (1971), beer for young adults in *National Lampoon's Animal House* (1978), and post-divorce hostility for adults in *War of the Roses* (1989). Chase scenes and utter madness fill such movies as *Smokey and the Bandit* (1977), starring Burt Reynolds, Jackie Gleason, and

Sally Field; *Every Which Way but Loose* (1978), starring Clint Eastwood, Sondra Locke, and Ruth Gordon; and *The Blues Brothers* (1980), starring John Belushi and Dan Aykroyd.

Chaos reigns in *Home Alone* (1990) when a couple of inept burglars try to rob the home where a young boy (Macaulay Culkin) has accidentally been left by his vacationing family. A bonus to the chaos is that the audience has the satisfaction of witnessing a David-and-Goliath ending in which the boy outwits the burglars. In *The Mask* (1994), audience emotions are similar, but speeded up because of the digital special effects. Here a wimpish, young bank clerk played by Jim Carrey finds a mask that transforms him into a comic book hero capable of humiliating his former enemies.

Because today's audiences have already seen hundreds of movies, producers can build on their viewing backgrounds. Director Mel Brooks made his career out of spoofing stories that people already knew. His 1974 audiences had seen so many westerns, especially on television, that when they went to see *Blazing Saddles*, they laughed not only at the antics of Brooks and the townspeople (who all bore the last name "Johnson"), but at earlier westerns they were reminded of. Brooks worked with Gene Wilder to write the script for *Young Frankenstein* (1974), in which the grandson of the infamous scientist tries to live down the family scandal by pronouncing his name "Frahnkensteen" and by teaching the monster he creates to dance in top hat and tails. Brooks's *High Anxiety* (1977) spoofs Alfred Hitchcock–type thrillers, his *Spaceballs* (1987) spoofs such space epics as *Star Wars*, while in his *History of the World, Part I* (1981), Brooks plays the roles of Moses, Louis XVI, and Comicus, a "stand-up philosopher" who can't get a job and so has to work as a waiter, asking at the Last Supper, "Are you all together, or is it separate checks?"

In the 1990 *The Freshman,* Marlon Brando parodies his own performance in the 1972 *Godfather* gangster movie, and in the 1991 *Hot Shots* (1991), Charlie Sheen parodies the 1986 *Top Gun* and other glorified fighter pilot movies. *Monty Python's Life of Brian* (1979) is an irreverent parody of the story of Christ, *Roxanne* (1987) is an inspired imitation of *Cyrano de Bergerac*, while *Men in Black* (1997) parodies the whole genre of movies about secret government agencies and aliens from outer space. The 1980 *Airplane*, which is described as having more laughs per minute than any other movie in history, parodies all the disaster movies that were produced in the 1970s. While audiences are not amused at old gags, they are amused at the creativity that goes into setting them up, as when Leslie Nielsen asks Robert Hays if he can fly the plane and Hays responds, "Surely you can't be serious!" Back comes the old line: "Don't call me Shirley."

Most professions have customs, practices, and inside jokes that when exaggerated and incorporated in a movie for general audiences lend an aura of originality and authenticity. For example, *Caddyshack* (1980), starring Chevy Chase, Rodney Dangerfield, Ted Knight, and Bill Murray, has extra meaning for golfers, while *Stir Crazy* (1980), starring

Gene Wilder and Richard Pryor, lets general audiences in on prison humor. *Bull Durham* (1988), starring Kevin Costner and Susan Sarandon, focuses on baseball, while *Analyze This* (1999), starring Robert DeNiro and Billy Crystal, focuses on psychiatric counseling. Mel Brooks's *The Producers* (1968) and *Silent Movie* (1976), along with Woody Allen's *Bullets over Broadway* (1994) and Neil Simon's *The Sunshine Boys* (1975), have numerous inside jokes about show business. *Nine to Five* (1980), starring Jane Fonda, Dolly Parton, Lily Tomlin, and Dabney Coleman, makes fun of clerical work and inter-office competition. The *Pink Panther* (1963) and *The Naked Gun* (1988) are detective spoofs, while the *Police Academy* films beginning in 1984 are police spoofs.

The best comedies are those that appeal to large general audiences, while providing something extra for special interests. For example, lawyers in the audience were probably the most appreciative of the quip in *Cookie's Fortune* (1999) about the complications of a "one-lawyer town," while

Tony Curtis and Jack Lemmon in *Some Like It Hot*. Film critic Pauline Kael described the film's "transvestism, impotence, role confusion, and borderline inversion" as "hilariously innocent, though always on the brink of really disastrous double-entendre." *Archive Photos*

Shakespeare scholars undoubtedly caught on to more of the allusions in *Shakespeare in Love* (1999) than did the general audience.

Light romantic comedies are fun to watch because of the beautiful people involved, especially if they are young and vulnerable as was Matthew Broderick in *Ferris Bueller's Day Off* (1986) and Michael J. Fox in *Back to the Future* (1985). Adult romantic comedies are likely to include more sexual allusions, if not sexual acts, as in *Some Like It Hot* (1959), starring Jack Lemmon, Tony Curtis, and Marilyn Monroe; the British *Carry On Camping* (1969); Woody Allen's *Annie Hall* (1977); and *10* (1979), starring Dudley Moore and Bo Derek. Meg Ryan successfully combines sexuality and humor in *When Harry Met Sally* (1989), where she co-stars with Billy Crystal, and in *Sleepless in Seattle* (1993), and *You've Got Mail* (1998), both of which co-star Tom Hanks.

There are far too many humorous movies for this entry to be more than a sampling, and because film is such an important part of the American entertainment scene many movies are discussed in other entries. But listed below as a partial summary are techniques showing how producers and advertisers rely on humor as a tool for both creating and marketing their films:

1. Producers and theater managers are putting humor in the peripherals that surround moviegoers. For example, a comic Charlie Chaplin or Harold Lloyd scene comes on the screen accompanied by this message: "Watch movies in the old fashioned way—in Silence!" The advertisement for the theater's THX sound system is done as a sophisticated cartoon. Many producers entice viewers to stay and watch the credits by including funny outtakes or original messages, as when at the end of *Spice World*, the five Spice Girls stare out at the audience and Sporty says, "Why do people sit there at the end of the film and watch the credits go up?" Ginger answers, "It's probably the sad anticlimax. It's all over, back to reality."

2. Most producers have given up trying for "mass appeal." Instead, they create humor to appeal to teenagers, particular ethnic groups, fans of various kinds of music, intellectuals, and other niche audiences.

3. Name recognition is increasingly important in helping potential moviegoers recognize that humor is intended. This is why a comedian whose name is known to the public will have a better chance of being cast in a starring role than will a newcomer, even if the newcomer is a better fit. *National Lampoon* pays millions to the *Harvard Lampoon* for the privilege of using the *Lampoon* name, and even though many sequels could be better described with new titles, the producers stick to such easily recognized names as *Ghostbusters II* and *Back to the Future II* and *III*. A slightly more creative approach was used with *Grumpy Old Men* and *Grumpier Old Men*.

4. Remaking popular films is similar to doing sequels in that the producers are hoping to attract audience members who either remember the pleasant experience they had with the original movie or have heard about the original's success. Critics often prefer the original to the remake, and in most instances the general public won't feel motivated to pay money to see a new release of a movie they have already seen. However, a combination of nostalgia and curiosity entices people into theaters to see new versions. For example the 1999 *Out of Towners,* starring Steve Martin and Goldie Hawn, was seen by many people who remembered the 1970 version starring Jack Lemmon and Sandy Dennis.

5. As shown in the entry on black humor, writers and producers are increasingly relying on tragicomedy. Serious themes are being treated in combination with humor. This kind

of experimentalism attracts media attention while also creating powerfully emotional viewing experiences. For example in the fall of 1998, before the general U.S. release of the Italian film *Life Is Beautiful*, which is set in a Nazi death camp, both individuals and media critics were questioning the appropriateness of turning the Holocaust into "a joke." But as people saw the film and experienced its power, which won the Best Actor Oscar for Roberto Benigni, most such criticism disappeared. By serving as a foil, the humor made the horror all the more terrible. Its success is likely to encourage more experimentation with dark humor in exotic and unexpected settings.

See also ANIMATION, BLACK HUMOR, GOTHIC HUMOR, SCREWBALL COMEDIES, SILENT FILMS

Further reading: Kristine Brunovska Karnick and Henry Jenkins, *Classical Hollywood Comedy* (1995). Robert Sklar, *Movie-Made America: A Cultural History of American Movies*, 2nd ed. (1994). Mark Winokur, *American Laughter: Immigrants, Ethnicity, and 1930s Hollywood Film Comedy* (1996).

Museums

The word *museum* is related to the concept of the Greek *muses*. A museum is an institution devoted to the procurement, care, study, and display of objects of lasting interest and value. Art museums occasionally put together shows of humorous art; concert halls may prepare displays of unusual or comical instruments for patrons to look at during intermissions.

In addition to formal "museums," many other institutions devote energy and space to preserving and displaying humor-related items. For example, one of the secrets to the success of the Planet Hollywood restaurants, a chain whose primary investors are movie stars Sylvester Stallone, Arnold Schwarzenegger, Bruce Willis, Demi Moore, and Whoopi Goldberg, is that each restaurant features unique displays of Hollywood memorabilia connected to popular movies.

Unfortunately, Planet Hollywood is now having financial problems and many of the restaurants are being closed.

University libraries collect and display both memorabilia and papers related to entertainment. Howard Gottlieb, director of Boston University's special collections, has been working since 1963 to collect memorabilia from 20th-century performers, artists, journalists, authors, screenwriters, producers, and directors. Over 1,700 celebrities including Robert Benchley, Al Capp, and Douglas Fairbanks Jr. have donated their working papers to the library, which also has the original artwork for Harold Gray's *Little Orphan Annie* and Hank Ketcham's *Dennis the Menace* comic strips.

In 1998, Kent State University in Ohio was thrilled to be given a $200,000 collection of memorabilia about the storybook character King Babar, the elephant who has taught children about life and language for almost 70 years. The 3,600-piece collection includes first-edition Babar books, toys, and collectibles ranging from tiny chocolates to a six-foot model of the French pachyderm wearing his customary green suit and sparkling yellow crown.

In 1997, the Popular Culture Library at Bowling Green State University, where Tim Conway went to school, accepted a collection of some 200 hours of video with other treasures to come later, including the moustache and toupee that Conway wore as he played the character of Mr. Tudball on *The Carol Burnett Show*, the white fright wig he wore as "the Old Man," and the shoes he wore on his knees when he played Dorf, the stubby-legged schmo. The library was grateful for the timing because it was preparing to host a conference "Celebrating 50 Years of American Television Situation Comedy, 1947–1997."

The Ohio State University Library, in cooperation with Bowling Green, Kent State, and Michigan State belongs to the Consortium of Popular Culture Libraries in the Midwest (CCPCL). It specializes in cartoons and owns more than 200,000 original drawings and related manuscript materials, 14,000 books, and more than 600 periodicals. Because the material is so fragile, researchers need to make prior arrangement to study materials in the reading room. They can find out what is available through the Online Library Computer Catalog.

Museums large enough to have revolving displays, along with those affiliated with multi-purpose institutions, are advantaged over single-purpose museums because once the people in a particular area have seen the display of a small museum, then proprietors must rely on attracting tourists to generate needed revenue. This is a challenge in today's entertainment-rich society. When we tried telephoning humor-related museums listed in Bill Truesdell's 1985 *Directory of Unique Museums*, many of the listed telephone numbers were no longer working. Among those that have apparently gone out of business are Lum 'N Abner Museum in Pine Ridge, Arkansas; the Nut Museum in Old Lyme, Connecticut; the Toy Museum of Atlanta; the Uncle Remus Museum in Eatonton, Georgia; the Circus City Festival Museum in Peru, Indiana; the Perelman Antique Toy Museum in Philadelphia; the Enchanted World Doll Museum in Mitchell, South Dakota; and the Bing Crosby Historical Society Museum in Tacoma, Washington.

However, it isn't just small museums that have financial problems. Montreal's Museum of Humor, which had been built with $13.5 million in start-up assistance from Ottawa, the Quebec government, and the city of Montreal, closed in 1994. The museum opened in 1993 with great fanfare, and although it attracted 3,000 visitors the first year, twice that many were needed to meet expenses and debt obligations.

The same year that the Montreal museum closed, groundbreaking took place in Boca Raton, Florida, for a $15 million International Museum of Cartoon Art. "It's the start of a dream," said Mort Walker, museum founder and creator of the comic strip *Beetle Bailey*. "All we can hope for now is that it doesn't turn into a nightmare. After all, we still have $10 million to raise." *Peanuts* creator, Charles Schulz donated $1 million, while *Garfield* creator Jim Davis agreed to head the fund-raising committee. Eight Pulitzer Prize–winning editorial cartoonists helped design the exhibits. The museum opened to visitors in March of 1996. Fund-raising and building have continued so that more exhibits are being opened on a regular basis. The feature exhibit in the summer of 1999 was "Tarzan from Burroughs to Disney." It included the original manuscripts from Burroughs's 80-year-old book, along with comic strip stills and animated versions leading up to the 1999 Disney movie. Plans are to eventually include an accredited school of cartooning and to have a resident cartoonist who will draw for visitors and answer questions. The museum's address is 201 Plaza Real, Boca Raton, Florida, telephone (561) 391-2200.

The ease with which people can create Web pages on the Internet has inspired many people to create "virtual reality" comedy museums. Examples include The Mad Martian Museum of Modern Madness <http://www.madmartian.com>, Kooks Museum <http://www.teleport.com/~dkossy>, The Whole World Toilet Paper Museum and Society <http://www.tagyerit.com/tp.htm>, and The Mozilla Museum <http://www.snafu.de/~tilman/mozilla>.

The brief descriptions given below provide a sampling of actual museums. Even though not all-inclusive, the list illustrates the variety of humor-related items and activities in American life.

- American Museum of Magic, 107 East Michigan Avenue, Marshall, Michigan, (616) 781-7666.

  Housed in a 130-year-old historic building, this museum contains 250,000 magic-related items, including the six massive padlocks and the oversized milk can that Houdini escaped from under water. Such magicians as Blackstone, Fu Manchu, Kellar, Levante, Okita, Sorcar, and Thurston are honored with posters, photographs, books, programs, films, sculptures, paintings, and equipment.

- The Exotic World Burlesque Hall of Fame, 29053 Wild Road, Helendale/

The newest and most ambitious of humor-related museums in the United States is the $15 million International Museum of Cartoon Art, which opened to visitors in 1996 in Boca Raton, Florida. *Courtesy International Museum of Cartoon Art*

Silverlakes, California (between Victorville and Barstow), (760) 243-5261.

National Public Radio, *Smithsonian Magazine*, and MTV have featured this museum in documentaries about burlesque and strip-tease dancing and how they went the way of vaudeville and silent film when "talkies" and television arrived. On display are pasties, tassels, breakaway gowns, rhinestone G-strings, sequined and blinking-light bras, and the trunk used by Gypsy Rose Lee. Manager Dixie Evans, who in her stripper days imitated Marilyn Monroe, founded the museum in 1991. She says that the shows that featured such strippers as Sally Rand, Blaze Starr, Tempest Storm, and Lili St. Cyr, and such comedians as Red Skelton, Phil Silvers, and Jackie Gleason brought working-class glamour to Depression-weary Americans who, for 25 cents, could escape the boredom and drudgery of everyday life.

- The Lewis Grizzard Museum, 2769 Highway 29 (P. O. Box 67), Moreland, Georgia 30259, (770) 304-1490.

The late Lewis Grizzard grew up and developed his humor skills in the warmth of this small southern town, which now honors his writing career with a community museum.

- The Liberace Museum, 1775 East Tropicana, Las Vegas, Nevada, (702) 798-5595.
Liberace's million-dollar wardrobe is on display, along with what is considered to be the world's best collection of rare pianos.

- The Lucy-Desi Museum, 212 Pine Street, Jamestown, New York, (716) 484-7070.
Jamestown, New York, was Lucille Ball's hometown. A 90-minute presentation, interactive exhibits, larger-than-life wall panels, audio and video segments, and trivia contests summarize the career of Lucille Ball and Desi Arnaz.

- McCurdy Historical Doll Museum, 246 North, 100 East, Provo, Utah, (801) 377-9935.
Three thousand dolls dressed in folk costumes from around the world are displayed. Also featured is a Parade of Fashion and Famous Women of History.

- Mummers Museum, Two Street at Washington Avenue, Philadelphia, Pennsylvania, (215) 336-3050.
  As visitors enter, they encounter a mirrored display of New Year's costumes and then move on to a self-guided tour. One room creates the illusion of actually marching in a mummer's parade. These parades go back to pre-colonial European, British, and black American heritages, with some of the customs being traced to the 1600s. In 1901, the parade became a city-sponsored event.

- Museum of Norman Rockwell Art, 227 S. Park Street, Reedsburg, Wisconsin, (608) 524-2123.
  On display are more than 3,000 covers, ads, illustrations, prints, and other paper memorabilia of painter Norman Rockwell. Also included are some specialty items.

- Museum of Television and Radio, (East Coast) 25 West 52nd Street, New York, (212) 621-6600; (West Coast) 465 North Beverly Drive, Beverly Hills, California, (310) 786-1000.
  Many of the daily screenings, radio presentations, and seminars by performers, critics, writers, directors, producers, and journalists relate to humor. For example, from March 19 to September 19, 1996, the New York museum presented a special program on stand-up comedians on television. Nearly 70 individuals were pictured on the oversized exhibit program, which listed daily events related to various types of comedians.

- National Toy Train Museum, Paradise Lane, Strasburg, Pennsylvania, (717) 687-8976.
  Hundreds of toy trains manufactured from the 1880s to the present are displayed along with movies about trains, three huge operating layouts of trains, and some rare and unusual specialty trains.

- Ripley's Believe It or Not! 7850 Beach Blvd., Bueno Park, California, (714) 522-7045; 6780 Hollywood Blvd., Hollywood, California, (213) 466-6335; 175 Jefferson Street, San Francisco, California, (415) 771-6188; 301 Alamo Plaza, San Antonio, Texas, (210) 224-9299.
  Located near other tourist attractions; for example, a wax museum and the Alamo in Texas, and the Guinness World Book of Records Museum and Mann's Chinese Theater in Hollywood, these museums of oddities are based on the concept started by explorer and newspaper writer Robert Ripley. For over 40 years, he visited out-of-the-way places and collected both strange and unusual facts and artifacts.

- Vent Haven Museum, 33 West Maple, Fort Mitchell, Kentucky, (606) 341-0461.
  Five hundred ventriloquist figures, hundreds of volumes on ventriloquism, scripts, pamphlets, playbills, records, tape recordings, films, and ventriloquism courses make this the largest known collection of ventriloquist material in the world. Eight different languages are represented and some of the manuscripts date back to the 18th century.

- Will Rogers Memorial, Will Rogers Blvd., Claremore, Oklahoma, (918) 341-0719
  This museum houses the largest collection of Will Rogers memorabilia in the world, and includes his papers, personal effects, photographs, films, and memorabilia. Free films are shown daily.

See also HUMOROUS ICONS, INTERNET INFLUENCES

Further reading: American Association of Museums, *The Official Museum Directory.* Victor J. Danilov, *University and College Museums, Galleries, and Related Facilities: A Descriptive Directory* (1996). Christopher D. Geist (ed.), *Directory of Popular Culture Collections* (1989).

Music

Humor can be a part of virtually any kind of music. Mothers amuse their babies by singing funny nursery rhymes and playing musical games. Kindergarteners, who can't say their ABCs, can sing them, along with songs from *Sesame Street* and humorous advertising jingles. Middle-grade children sing funny songs when they go off to summer camp; teenagers revel in the dark humor of rock music and videos; and the general population enjoys the regional humor country-western music, the character development in musical comedies, and the wit that finds its way into operas and classical music.

Musicians have an advantage in creating humor because music has the power to increase the intensity of people's emotions. Music establishes mood and tone; for example, in Sergei Prokofiev's *Peter and the Wolf* when the narrator is talking about Peter the music is light and playful, but when he starts talking about the wolf the tone becomes dark and threatening.

Even in the most serious operas, composers include light moments for comic relief. For example, Richard Wagner in his *Ring Cycle* has the young Siegfried turn the brown bear loose on Mime so that he and the audience can relish the dwarf's fright. And one of the funniest lines in all of opera is the bit of dramatic irony when Siegfried slices open Brunnhilde's breastplate with his armor-piercing sword, and exclaims, "Das ist kein Mann!" ("This is not a man!").

Humor in classical music has a long tradition as shown by such playful vocabulary items as the French *gavotte*, which like the Irish and English *gigue* or *jig* is music for a fast-moving dance. A *scherzo* is a musical joke; a *cappricio* is a composition that is irregular in form and usually lively and whimsical in spirit; a *divertimento* is a light and entertaining instrumental composition in several movements; and a *rondo* is a composition whose principal theme is repeated three or more times in the same key, interspersed with subordinate themes.

In the 1700s, Franz Joseph Haydn was distressed by the number of people who fell asleep while listening to his chamber pieces.

Taking matters into his own hands, he wrote *Symphony Number 94* (*The Surprise Symphony*) in the key of C using a slow tempo and soft and repetitive sequences. At the end of each stanza, he modulated the music to the key of G and ended with a resounding fortissimo chord guaranteed to wake up anyone who was dozing.

The Farewell Symphony is another example of Haydn's humor, but to catch on audiences need to know the story behind the music. As the symphony draws to its end, various musicians put out the lights on their music stands and depart from the stage. While audiences are amused at the gradual diminishing of the performing force, Haydn's original intention was sending a message to sponsors that the musicians were lonely for their wives and wanted to go home for the summer. This same technique of a diminishing number of performers was later used in *The Sound of Music* as the von Trapps left the stage and were individually smuggled out of the theater past Nazi guards.

Wolfgang Amadeus Mozart was a contemporary of Haydn and in his *The Village Musicians*, also known as *A Musical Joke*, burlesqued the nonprofessional playing that was often done by amateur community bands. Ludwig van Beethoven also satirized local musicians in his *Pastoral Symphony* where he portrayed a sleepy village in which the musicians doze off, wake up, play a few notes, and then doze off again.

In a Pulitzer Prize–winning book, *Godel, Escher, Bach: An Eternal Golden Braid*, Douglas Hofstadter compares artist M. C. Escher's fascination with visual loops in which a waterfall, for example, appears to become its own source, to Johann Sebastian Bach's fascination with acoustic loops. In his *Endlessly Rising Canon*, Bach seems to be drawing to a conclusion but instead slips out of the key of C-minor and into D-minor. This false "ending" ties smoothly into a new beginning where Bach repeats the process and returns in the key of E, only to start over again. Hofstadter says that "these successive modulations lead the ear to increasingly remote provinces on tonality, so that after several of them, one would expect to be hopelessly far away from the starting key. And yet, magically, after exactly six such modulations, the original key of C-minor has been restored!"

The humor in operas and musical comedies can be extensive and sophisticated because of the interplay between words, dance, and music, and also because the pieces are long enough that the composers have time to develop and solve humorous complications. Because of the repetition that is part of musical comedy, audiences have time to get to know characters and to savor their idiosyncrasies and the situations they get into. In Mozart's *The Abduction from the Seraglio*, Giovanni Rossini's *The Barber of Seville*, and Jacques Offenbach's *Orpheus in the Underworld*, dramatic irony comes into play as characters become victims of Tricksters and suffer from misidentifications and misunderstood events. An extra irony in relation to Offenbach's *Orpheus* is that one of its musical sequences was so lively that it became famous (or infamous) throughout Paris and the world as "The Can Can."

Examples of composers making their music match the plot are the popping staccato of Mozart's "Popagano-Popagana" duet in *The Magic Flute*, the flourishes and strikes in Giocchino Antonio Rossini's *The Thieving Magpie*, the "bump de bump de bump dedadadada . . ." of the donkeys on the trail in Ferde Grofe's *Grand Canyon Suite*, and the expressively cross-sensory sounds of "The Painted Desert" in Anton Dvorak's *New World Symphony*.

At the same time that music increases people's emotional reactions, it decreases the intensity of their intellectual reactions by inspiring a willing suspension of disbelief. For example, with both musical comedies and videos made for MTV, audiences don't think to question the coincidence of a band or an orchestra, waiting just off-stage or off-screen ready to accompany whoever suddenly feels inspired to break into a heartfelt song expressing their emotions. Nor are audiences as critical of messages that if delivered in straight speech would be controversial. This is true not only for contemporary hip-hop and rap, but also for such counter-culture rock musi-

cals as Jerome Ragni and James Rado's *Hair*, *Beatlemania*, based on the music of John Lennon and Paul McCartney, and Jim Jacobs and Warren Casey's *Grease*. An air of the forbidden also circles around such musicals as *Cabaret, Hellzapoppin'*, and *Oh, Calcutta!*

Two-thirds of the 60 Broadway shows that have had runs of over 1,200 performances have been musicals. They include such comedies of manners as *Cats*, based on T. S. Eliot's witty personifications of humans in cat fur; *Oklahoma* where the big city dudes in Kansas City have "gone about as far as they can go"; *La Cage Aux Folles* with its confusion of cross-dressed characters and sexual innuendo; and *Funny Girl*, the true story of comedian Fanny Brice and her gambler husband Nick Arnstein.

Musical comedies are mostly exaggerations with people and events bigger than life, and regular rules of time, space, and expectations of normality violated. Few theatergoers know people as dynamic as Auntie Mame in Jerry Herman's *Mame*, Dolly in Herman's *Hello Dolly*, and Annie Oakley in Irving Berlin's *Annie Get Your Gun*. When characters are this exaggerated and charismatic, trivial events and random activities have rich comic possibilities. Many comic heroes are outcasts who do not play by the rules. Audiences nevertheless identify with these high-spirited "underdogs," as they engage in guerrilla warfare against society. Musicals of this type usually end in compromise; roguish characters are brought a bit closer to society's ways of thinking but society is also brought a bit closer to the rogue. For example, in Meredith Willson's *The Music Man*, Professor Hill is a charlatan who can't read a note of music, yet he convinces the townspeople of River City, Iowa, that they need a brass band. As he transforms a dull town into a singing and dancing community, he too is transformed into a good citizen with the help of "Marian, the librarian." In Abe Burrows and Frank Loesser's *Guys and Dolls*, Nathan Detroit, an inveterate gambler, is involved in all kinds of shady dealings, including making bets about Sarah Brown, the woman who runs the street-corner mission, yet audiences cheer for the "good man" hidden inside the gambler. In Carol Hall's *Best Little Whorehouse in Texas*, the madam has to close down her lively, "almost wholesome," establishment, but as a consolation prize she gets to elope with the sheriff.

Musical theater goes back at least to the 13th century where there are records of a musical telling of the story of Robin Hood and Maid Marion. By the 1500s, such theater had been influenced by the commedia dell'arte and by farcical Punch and Judy puppet shows so that it leaned heavily toward slapstick comedy. In the 1600s, the Italians developed their *Opera Buffa,* leading the way to comic opera, which in France became the *Comedie Francais* and in Germany the *Komische Oper*. Musicologist Karl Haas says that in England it led to John Gay and John Christopher Pepusch's 1728 *The Beggar's Opera*, in the 1850s and 1860s to Offenbach's satirical masterpieces, and in the 1870s through the 1890s to the work of Britishers W. S. Gilbert and Arthur Sullivan, whose still popular comedies include *The Gondoliers, H.M.S. Pinafore, Iolanthe, The Mikado, Patience, The Pirates of Penzance, Princess Ida, Ruddigore, The Sorcerer, Trial by Jury*, and *The Yeoman of the Guard*.

In *Better Foot Forward: The History of American Musical Theatre*, Ethan C. Mordden says that in the 1920s, Jerome Kern and Oscar Hammerstein "led the revolution from empty-headed musical comedy to adult musical theater." Before they started working together, musical comedy was "a haphazard melding of stars, tunes, and jokes made for fun but not form." Kern and Hammerstein turned the corner with *Show Boat* (1927), based on Edna Ferber's novel about life among Mississippi River entertainers. Telling the stories of musicians, dancers, actors, and writers is popular because it provides a natural vehicle for singing, dancing, and other theatricals. When in the 1940s, Hammerstein teamed up with Richard Rodgers, Americans were ready for a new level of sophistication in music, staging, subject matter, and humor—this is what Rodgers and Hammerstein provided. In a 1998 tribute piece to their partnership in *Time* magazine (Jun. 8, 1998), Andrew Lloyd Webber said that Rodgers and Hammerstein were the first to truly blend music, action, and words. Nearly 40 years after Hammerstein died from cancer in 1960, their partnership "has not yet been equalled. It probably never will be."

The contemporary musician who comes closest to matching Rodgers and Hammerstein's talents is probably Stephen Sondheim. Among his many credits are being lyricist for *Gypsy* (1959) and composer and lyricist for *A Funny Thing Happened on the Way to the Forum* (1962) and *Sweeney Todd: The Demon Barber of Fleet Street* (1979).

The editors of *The Entertainment Guide to the Greatest Movies* (1994) offer one of the reasons that current discussions about musicals sound somewhat historical: "Once, they made musicals. Now they make music videos. The difference? Musicals made a show of optimism, music videos make a show of cynicism." Because of this cynicism, people don't generally think of music videos as being humorous; but, as rock musicians strive to outdo each other and to be memorable, they make heavy use of such comic techniques as incongruity and shock. Movies that served as a transition between musicals and music videos include the Beatles' animated fantasy *Yellow Submarine* (1968); *Grease* (1978), starring Olivia Newton-John and John Travolta; *Rock 'n Roll High School* (1979); *Fame* (1980), which inspired the long-running TV show set in a fine arts high school; *Michael Nesmith in Elephant Parts* (1981) which is a collection of comedy bits and minimovies made by the man who some critics credit with founding MTV; and *Little Shop of Horrors* (1986), in which Steve Martin impersonates Elvis Presley as a sadistic dentist while Levi Stubbs of the Four Tops provides the voice of the man-eating plant.

The way that rock musicians take a name or a phrase from one context and use it in another illustrates the humor technique of pointing listeners' minds in one direction and then forcing them to make a sharp turn in a different direction. For example, singer *Marilyn Manson* surprises people by being a male with a female-sounding name. He wanted to make people think of both Marilyn

Monroe and Charles Manson. Although people may have a hard time remembering the exact spelling, the name of singer *Snoop Doggy Dogg* attracts attention because of Charles Schulz's Snoopy, while singer Engelbert Humperdinck's name is memorable, first, because of its cacophonous sounds, and second, because it was the name of a famous German composer who lived from 1854 to 1921.

Other naming techniques change the order of the words as with *T-Model Ford*, or alter the spelling, as with *T-Rex* from the tyrannosaurus rex dinosaur and *Deflator Mouse* from the famous *Die Fledermaus* opera. Still another humor technique is to simply steal someone else's famous name as with *Magoo* (Mr. Magoo, the cartoon character), *Toto* (Dorothy's dog in *The Wizard of Oz*), *Uriah Heap* (a Charles Dickens character), and *Blondie* (a comic strip character). Album names chosen to relate semantically to a groups' name include "The Pick, the Sickle, and the Shovel" put out by the *Gravediggaz*, and "Disassembly Required" by *Beta Minus Mechanic*.

In 1977 the revolutionary *Sex Pistols* shocked the world by picturing Queen Elizabeth with a safety pin through her nose on the cover of their single "God Save the Queen." Their rebelliousness contributed to an atmosphere in which groups relied on black humor for names that would be both shocking and memorable as in the *Dead Kennedys*, *Agent Orange*, *The 13th Floor Elevators*, and *Urge Overkill*.

In summary, because music provides an extra level of emotional involvement, musicians are in a good position to stretch audiences' reactions from pathos to amusement. Musicians work to surprise audiences by experimenting with new rhythms and sounds produced either by the human body or by musical instruments; for example, rap and hip-hop are new kinds of singing, while computers and such inner-city street items as garbage can lids, sticks, and brooms are new musical instruments. In addition, musicians have the same opportunities that poets and storytellers have to create humor with words,

plus they can use the staging techniques of dramatists and dancers. *See also* MUSICAL COMEDIANS

Further reading: Classical Net, http://www.classical.net (September 1999). Karl Haas, *Inside Music* (1984). Meryle Secrest, *Stephen Sondheim: A Life* (1988).

Musical Comedians

Comedians and music are related in two major ways. First, comedians use music as raw material to be manipulated in ways that will make audiences laugh. They do this by coaxing funny sounds from musical (and nonmusical) instruments, creating novelty songs, changing and parodying the words of standard songs, and making fun of the sacred customs of serious musicians and those who appreciate serious music. A second, less obvious connection has not been proven but is strongly suspected: musically oriented comedians, even when not performing music, often are better comedians because their musical talent and their training have helped them develop a stage presence and a sense of timing, which in performance often makes the crucial difference between laughs and groans.

Comedians with musical talents include clarinet players Phil Silvers and Woody Allen, drummers Johnny Carson and Charlie Callus, and conductors Danny Kaye and Jerry Lewis. Sid Caesar used to make his living as a concert saxophonist, while Morey Amsterdam, whose father was first violinist for the San Francisco symphony, played the cello. Henny Youngman played the violin and "Bob Hope sang like an angel." When Bobcat Goldthwait was 16 years old he was the lead singer of the Dead Ducks in Syracuse, New York. Chevy Chase was a drummer and keyboardist in 1968 for the Chamaeleon Church, which made one recording.

Phyllis Diller, in an interview with Susan Horowitz for Horowitz's *Queens of Comedy*, talked about her training at the Sherwood Music School in Chicago. She played concert piano and harpsichord, and early in her career as a comedian played and sang parodies; and in *Wonderful Town*, the musical version of her book *My Sister Eileen*, she played herself. Under the name of Dame Illya Dillya she appeared as a piano soloist with 100 symphony orchestras, playing serious music including Bach and Beethoven. As her success in stand-up comedy increased, she gave up performing music because of the challenge of arranging for daily practice time and grand pianos while traveling as a performer. Nevertheless, she says, "Comedy is listening—the ear, rhythm, and timing." With her kind of humor, "Every word is timed and choreographed . . . and the joke word is the last word in the payoff. That last word preferably should end in an explosive consonant. For example, 'He bought a zebra and named it *Spot!*'"

Diller chose her signature prop of a cigarette in a long holder merely to portray a certain type of woman, but found that she felt comfortable and natural in using it, much like the conductor of an orchestra uses a baton, signaling for attention, punctuating the end of a joke, pointing at someone, expressing hostility, and in general, controlling the audience.

Goldie Hawn did not have formal music training, but she had dance training, where she learned the importance of timing in building a comic effect. She told Horowitz about working with an actor "who couldn't get the scene, couldn't get the timing. So I beat it out with my hands. It was like percussion, so he could understand the arch of the scene and the power it had to have. It's as if I hear the beats in my head."

When Jack Benny's success as a comedian is analyzed, his sense of timing is always mentioned. He knew exactly when to speed up a joke and when to drag it out. Even though he used his violin mostly as a comedy prop, he was in reality an accomplished player and appeared as a soloist with almost every major symphony orchestra. (They slowed their tempo so that he could keep up.)

Hillbilly comedian Judy Canova came from a wealthy family who gave her extensive training as a classical singer. During the Depression, her mother suggested that her three children put together a hillbilly act. They did, but Judy was the only one to continue in

show business. She had a three-octave range and sang spoofs of country-western songs, with a bit of yodeling thrown in. She wore long pigtails, a straw hat, and checkered "country" clothes. She carried a battered suitcase and played the role of a man-chasing hillbilly. Because she was "country," she could express a kind of crass sexuality forbidden to more "ladylike" performers.

Jerry Colonna started in the orchestra on Bing Crosby's 1937 radio show, but soon was moved up front to work as a supporting comedian to Crosby. His abrupt nonsequiturs brought laughs as did his singing, where he would land on a note and hold it for an insanely long period. Before suffering a stroke in 1966, he was compared to Henny Youngman and the Marx Brothers.

Without their music, the Marx Brothers would not have been nearly as funny. Chico made his piano-playing comic by "shooting the keys." In an arpeggio, he would play all of the notes but one, and then would point to that key with his index finger and using his thumb as a "trigger" would shoot the key. Harpo played both the piano and the harp. He was famous for his glissandos (sliding music), for shooting the keys like Chico did, and for getting his finger stuck between the keys.

From the mid-1940s through the mid-1960s, Spike Jones and his City Slickers played classical music, opera, and Tin Pan Alley hits using cowbells, horns, pistols, pans, pots, saws, tire pumps, washboards, and whistles. Their fame came in 1942 with "Der Fuehrer's Face," which was filled with Bronx cheers, also called raspberries. The group also had zany renditions of "Cocktails for Two," and "Chlo-e." As leader, Jones wore loud plaid suits, laconically chewed gum, and used a gun in place of a baton. He occasionally pulled the trigger to add to the musical chaos. Clarinetist Mickey Katz provided vocal "glugs" and other funny throat sounds. In 1994, Thomas Pynchon, a long-time fan, wrote a 3,000-word booklet to accompany a newly compiled CD of the band's hits.

Other humorous bands of the period included the *Firehouse Five Plus Two* specializing in Dixieland music and the *Hoosier Hot*

Shots, which got its start doing cornball humor on the *National Barn Dance* radio show in 1935. Their clown, Hezzie, played on washboards, auto horns, slide whistles, and other noisemakers. Ernie Kovacs invented *The Nairobi Trio*: three people in gorilla outfits wearing bowler hats. They moved like clock figures to a tune played on a tin whistle. Suddenly the drummer, with no change of expression, would use his drumsticks to pummel the head of the gorilla in front of him, and then they would all go back into the clock-work routine.

Easygoing band leader Phil Harris played specialty tunes like "That's What I Like about the South." On the *Jack Benny Program*, he developed a boozy comic character who displayed his hip ego and annoyed Benny with the greeting "Hiya, Jackson!"

Redd Foxx started his career as a street musician playing on the corner for tips. He then joined a group called "The Four Hep Cats," which changed their name to "The Five Bon-Bons" when they took on an extra player. Stan Freberg's group of "Tuned Sheep" was unusual even for the world of comedy. Each sheep wore a bell that played a particular musical note. He would direct the sheep to shake their heads in the appropriate sequence for playing "Lullaby of Birdland."

Comedians who moved from vaudeville to radio had an advantage if they could sing, because on radio, where listeners were deprived of seeing performers, it was important to have different voices making different sounds. As a radio and stand-up performer, George Burns would sing his old vaudeville songs with the words crunched together. This is similar to the gimmick that Ish Kabibble (Merwyn Bogue) used in his 1940's hit "Mairzy Doats." The lines to this intriguing song were "Mares eat oats, and does eat oats, and little lambs eat ivy. A kid will eat ivy too, wouldn't you?" Ish Kabibble's most popular novelty song was "Three Little Fishes," which sold five million copies, with his "Hold Tight, Boorri-yaki-taki" selling almost as many. He got into show business in the 1930s as a trumpet player in Kay Kyser's radio band.

Jimmy Durante, who began his career as a nightclub pianist, also sang novelty numbers, but admitted that he never had "much of a verce." He nevertheless became famous for singing "Inka Dinka Do," a piece he composed himself: "Say it with flowers, say it with drink/But always be careful not to say it with ink. . . ."

Carol Burnett liked to include a "singing spot" on her network television shows where she featured such musically accomplished co-stars as Julie Andrews, Beverly Sills, Dolly Parton, and Placido Domingo. Burnett explains that her love of music goes back to her childhood, when her mother would sit in the kitchen and play her ukelele while Carol sang. She had a wonderful ear for music and taught her daughter all kinds of old songs. While Carol sang, her mother did the harmony.

Brooks Atkinson, critic for the *New York Times* declared Victor Borge "the funniest man who ever lived" after he attended the opening night of Borge's *Comedy in Music*. The show set a Broadway record for a one-man show, running for 849 performances over three years. Borge, a concert pianist, got into the comedy business when he found himself on stage with a conductor who had lost his place. Borge stood up, walked over to the conductor's stand, pointed to the right place in the score, and then returned to his piano bench and finished the concerto. As a serious musician, Borge had never experienced the kind of laughter and applause that came from the crowd. He decided to change his approach and become a piano comedian. One of his gags is to look befuddled as he examines a score of music and tries to play it. After false starts and pondering, he realizes it is upside down, turns it over and plays it beautifully. Other tricks are to shift slyly from a piece of classical music into a piece of pop music, to demonstrate how such pop culture pieces as "Happy Birthday to You" would sound if composed by Bach or Brahms, and to engage in wordplay, as when he solemnly announces that the piece he is playing by Rachmaninoff was written in four flats because the composer had to keep moving while he was working on it, and that another piece he is playing is by Bach, but he can't remember whether it is by Johann Sebastian or Jacques Offen.

"The Cynic Who Never Soured" was the headline on a *New York Times Magazine* (Nov. 2, 1997) article about Tom Lehrer and the nearly 1,000 Web sites devoted to his music. Even though he hasn't recorded a new song in more than 30 years, he has been nominated for Entertainment Weekly's Humor Hall of Fame as one of the 50 funniest people of all time. Lehrer is a Harvard professor who, between 1953 and 1965, took time off from teaching to make recordings of some 40 songs of musical parody and political satire. While some of his current students occasionally bring him albums to autograph, he says they are divided in their enthusiasm between the old albums and his contributions of about a dozen songs to *Sesame Street*. He can't envision returning to live performing because he is a songwriter, not a performer, and he doesn't need "anonymous affection." The only reason he originally went on tour was to perfect his songs. He is still fascinated by the genre and ponders why putting verbal wit and music together is so effective. "Clearly," Lehrer said in 1991, "it has something to do with expectancy. A well-known tune sets up a challenge. There's a template. Now, can he do it? The trick is to avoid what the listener has provisionally guessed. You have to satisfy the task but avoid predictability. That's what is creative, the surprise." Among Lehrer's surprises were songs about poisoning pigeons in the park, hometown perverts, and charred bodies in a nuclear holocaust. "The Vatican Rag" with its "bow your head with great respect and—genuflect! genuflect! genuflect!" was one of his most shocking. Today, he says, it's harder to be shocking, and besides, it isn't very interesting, because the typical topics of flatulence, menstruation, and genitalia are things that people can relate to even without reading a book.

Political satirist Mark Russell began doing song parodies in the early 1960s at the Shoreham-Americana Hotel in Washington, DC where politicians, patrons, and columnists started dropping by for drinks and the lively piano player's take on the latest news. Russell's formula, which he still follows on PBS television specials as well as in individual performances, is to take a popular tune and give it new words. For example, during Reagan's presidency he took the tune of "My Bonnie Lies over the Ocean" and sang, "My ship of state's practically grounded, for want of a policy plan. I deny all the charges—unfounded—since the state of my ship hit the fan . . . . Bring back, bring back, oh bring back my Teflon to me, to me . . . ."

P.D.Q. Bach is proported to be the last of Johann Sebastian Bach's 20-odd children. He was "discovered" by Peter Schickele, the first person to occupy the General Electric Chair at the University of Southern North Dakota at Huppel. Schickele publishes a newsletter named *The Schickele Rag*, which gives information about the activities of Peter Schickele and P.D.Q. Bach, along with music (usually rondos), crossword puzzles, miscellaneous articles, atrocious puns, and assorted hype. P.D.Q. Bach wrote such music as "Sonata for Viola Four Hands and Harpsichord," which is considered to be the only extant piece of music written to be played by two musicians on the same viola. Schickele keeps unearthing various P.D.Q. Bach "schleptetas" and "pervertimentos." Schickele reasons that P.D.Q. has a wider appeal than other classical musicians because whenever someone hears the music of Mozart or Beethoven it is so perfect that it gives everyone an inferiority complex, whereas when a person hears something by P.D.Q. Bach, that person feels capable of writing something as good. The "Schickele Mix" on National Public Radio is a combination vaudeville show and concert, made up of strange music and strange instruments as well as parodies of real music.

Among the younger parodists is Weird Al Yankovic with his wild, curly hair, loud Hawaiian shirts, and what *TV Guide* described as "the worst mustache in show business. Yankovich turned Michael Jackson's "Beat It" into "Eat It," and The Knacks's "My Sharona" into "My Bologna." His "I Lost on

Jeopardy" makes fun of both the television quiz show and Greg Kihn's "Our Love's in Jeopardy." *See also* STAND-UP COMEDY, VAUDE-VILLE AND BURLESQUE

Further reading: Susan Horowitz, *Queens of Comedy* (1997).

P

Paradoxes

Paradoxes are statements that seem contradictory, unbelievable, or absurd, but in some sense are nevertheless true. Because paradoxes highlight breakdowns in our expectations of a logical universe, they are sources of both delight and consternation as the human mind works to figure out how people can in good faith talk about a "large mouse" running between the legs of a "small elephant" or can make sense out of the Yiddish curse, "He should drop dead, God forbid!"

Speakers found the *Catch-22* that Joseph Heller outlined in his 1961 antiwar book so intriguing that the book's title is now in dictionaries as the name for any tricky problem, especially one for which the only solution is denied by a circumstance inherent in the problem. In Heller's book, the character Yossarian would be excused from flying bombing missions if he were declared insane. However, the fact that he is trying to get out of flying bombing missions proves his sanity; he therefore has to keep flying. People who can't get a job until they have experience and who can't get experience until they have a job are in a Catch-22, and so are authors who can't get their manuscripts published until they have an agent but can't get an agent until they have been published. A newspaper story under the headline "Texas in Catch-22" told about a Texas state law forbidding the execution of anyone insane and a prisoner on death row who refused to take the medication that would keep him sane. This is the kind of irony illustrated by many urban legends and contemporary novels, films, and plays.

People are especially fascinated by paradoxes at times of great change and intellectual growth. Greek philosophers wrestled with paradoxes, the most famous being the one credited to the Cretan philosopher Epimenides: "All Cretans are liars." The puzzler is whether Epimenides, who is a Cretan, is lying. If he is lying, then the statement must be true. But if the statement is true, he must be lying.

The Industrial Revolution and the Victorian period leading up to World War I inspired a widespread interest in paradox. Jacques Offenbach relied on paradox for humor in his *Tales of Hoffman* and so did Gilbert and Sullivan in their operas—for *The Pirates of Penzance* they composed a song about paradoxes:

> How quaint the ways of paradox!
> At common sense she gaily mocks!
> A paradox, a paradox,
> A most ingenious paradox!
> Ha! ha! ha! ha!

The most often cited or parodied quotes from Lewis Carroll's *Alice in Wonderland* and *Through the Looking Glass* are paradoxes:

- Why, sometimes I've believed as many as six impossible things before breakfast.

- The rule is, jam to-morrow and jam yesterday—but never jam *to-day*.

- Now, *here*, you see, it takes all the running *you* can do, to keep in the same place. If you want to get somewhere else, you must run at least twice as fast as that.

That people relate *Alice in Wonderland* quotes to current events illustrates the fact that paradoxes are more than wordplay. They are explorations of philosophy, logic, and social criticism; that is, a verbal means of acknowledging real world conditions and frustrations. When put into "other" worlds (science fiction or fantasy), paradoxes can be even more intriguing. For example, the "grandfather paradox" in science fiction is a variation on the plot technique in which a time-traveler goes back and murders his own grandfather before the time-traveler's parent was born. This is a brain teaser because if the grandfather were prematurely killed then the grandchild couldn't have been born and wouldn't have been able to go back and commit the murder.

This sampling of paradoxical quotes illustrates the kinds of topics treated as paradoxes. They are arranged in chronological order according to the birth of the speaker:

- Sits he on ever so high a throne, a man still sits on his bottom. (Michel Elyquem de Montaigne, 1533–1592)

- We have just enough religion to make us hate, but not enough to make us love one another. (Jonathan Swift, 1667–1745)

- I laugh, so that I may not cry. (Pierre Augustin Caron de Beaumarchais, 1732–1799)

- When a feller says, "It hain't th' money, but th' principle o' th' thing," it's the money. (Josh Billings [pseudonym for Henry Wheeler Shaw], 1818–1885)

- Nowadays people know the price of everything and the value of nothing. (Oscar Wilde, 1854–1900)

- There ain't any answer. There ain't going to be any answer. There never has been an answer. That's the answer. (Gertrude Stein, 1874–1946)

- The vital question today is not whether there will be life after death, but whether there was life before death. (Marshall McLuhan, 1911–1990)

- When I grow up I want to be a little boy. (Joseph Heller, 1923–)

- [in reference to cartoonist Garry Trudeau] As with all anti-Establishment figures, Mr. Trudeau will soon be an honored member of the Establishment. (Art Buchwald, 1925–)

See also BLACK HUMOR, IRONY, LANGUAGE PLAY, SATIRE, URBAN LEGENDS

Parody

A parody is a conscious imitation of someone else's creative work, usually literary but sometimes musical or artistic. What caricature is to art, parody is to literature. Through exaggeration, it makes fun of the style of the original and calls its content into question. In the 1930s, *The New Yorker*'s Wolcott Gibbs said that parody is the hardest form of creative writing because the style of the subject must be reproduced in slightly enlarged form, while at the same time holding the interest of people who haven't read the original. Further complications are posed since it must entertain at the same time that it criticizes and must be written in a style that is not the writer's own. He went on to say, "The only thing that would make it more difficult would be to write it in Cantonese."

Parodies are created for fun and amusement as well as for persuasion. Even those people who create parodies for fun usually have a desire to undermine the message of the original. For example, Lewis Carroll in his *Alice in Wonderland* books had fun changing "Twinkle, twinkle, Little Star, How I wonder where you are," into "Twinkle, twinkle, Little Bat, How I wonder where you're at." But with most of his parodies, he was protesting the didacticism and the sentimentality imposed on Victorian children and their parents. This well-known poem by G. W. Langford not only preached at parents but threatened them with a reminder of the high mortality rate for young children:

> Speak gently to the little child!
> Its love be sure to gain;
> Teach it in accents soft and mild;
> It may not long remain.

Carroll thumbed his nose at the grim message by turning it into a song for the Duchess to sing to a piglet wrapped in baby clothes:

> Speak roughly to your little boy,
> And beat him when he sneezes.
> He only does it to annoy
> Because he knows it teases.

When Alice "tries" to recite Isaac Watts's "Against Idleness and Mischief":

> How doth the little busy bee
> Improve each shining hour
> And gather honey all the day
> From every opening flower!

it comes out:

> How doth the little crocodile
> Improve his shining tail
> And pour the waters of the Nile
> On every golden scale?

The original goes on to extol the glories of an industrious individual who never has time for mischief, but Carroll's version depicts a crocodile grooming itself while waiting with a many-toothed grin for whatever might float by.

When the characteristics of a genre are standardized and well known, then the whole genre might be parodied, as in Quentin Tarantino's 1994 film *Pulp Fiction*, which parodies the kinds of flamboyant characters, mystery, and personal greed found in thriller fiction. In the 1970s, the manufacturers of Virginia Slims cigarettes designed an advertising campaign to win the hearts of women through parodying fairy tales. Full-page magazine advertisements showed the silhouette of a castle foregrounded by a "Once-upon-a-time . . ." story in old-fashioned typeface. The condensed story was about a prince who was looking for a good wife to keep him company, to cook his meals, to clean the many rooms of his castle, and to bear him many sons who would carry on his noble name. It ended with, "And the prince lived happily ever after."

Mark Twain's "War Prayer" is another example of a genre being parodied:

> Oh Lord our God, help us to tear their soldiers to bloody shreds with our shells; help us to cover their smiling fields with their patriot dead; help us to lay waste their humble homes with a hurricane of fire; help us to wring the hearts of their unoffending widows with unavailing grief; help us to turn them out roofless with their little children to wander unfriended the wastes of their desolated land in rags and hunger and thirst. Lord, blast their hopes, blight their lives, protract their bitter pilgrimage, make heavy their steps, water their way with their tears. We ask it in the spirit of love, of Him Who is the Source of Love, and Who is the ever-faithful refuge and friend of all that are sore beset and seek his aid.

Among today's political parodists is Mark Russell, who, because of his piano playing and singing, calls himself "a political cartoonist for the blind." Pat Paulsen, who died in 1997, was identified in his *New York Times* obituary as "A Parodist of Presidential Doubletalk." His name became a household word in 1968 when he announced on *The Smothers Brothers Comedy Hour* that he was running for president on the ticket of the Straight Talking American Government or S.T.A.G. party. The joke took on a life of its own, and he campaigned in five presidential elections under such slogans as "We Cannot Stand Pat," "We Can Be Decisive, Probably," and "United We Sit." His promise at the 1996 Democratic National Convention in Chicago was "If elected, I will win."

In today's world of commercialized graffiti, people undermine slogans and maxims with parodies so succinct they can go on bumper stickers and T-shirts. The army's slogan of "Be All That You Can Be. Join the Army." is changed into "Be All You Can Be. Work for Peace." "Envision World Peace" becomes "Envision Using Your Turn Signal" or "Envision Whirled Peas." "A Woman's Place is in the Home" is altered to "A

Woman's Place is in the House—and the Senate Too," while a horseback riding club created its own version, "A Woman's Place is on a Hunter."

E-mail and the Internet encourage people to create parodies because they can act on

impulse and send them out to a wide audience with little cost or effort. Also, they can lift a logo or graphic and alter it according to their whims. Parody sites that have been created using Netscape as a subject include *Ninscape, Nutscape, Netape*, and *Veggiescape*. Microsoft is parodied as *Microsnot, Mike Rasoff*, and *Micrososo*, while America Online is parodied as *America Outaline* and *America On Hold*. One of the most visited sites is *Stale*, a parody of Microsoft's *Slate* magazine. Daniel Radosh and Michael Tritter, creators of *Stale*, conveniently provide links to the real *Slate* so readers can see how cleverly they have parodied the original. When the *Wall Street Journal* (Mar. 13, 1997) interviewed Eugene Volokh of the U.C.L.A. law school about these parodies, he said that "in order for there to be trademark infringement, there has to be a likelihood that consumers would be fooled into believing the parody site is authorized by the company or organization."

Periodicals that rely mainly on parody are as mainstream as *MAD Magazine* and *National Lampoon*, and as specialized as *Adbusters*, a Canadian quarterly founded in 1990, and *Stay Free!* a small desktop-published 'zine produced in New York City. *Adbusters*, which has some 30,000 U.S. sub-

scribers, and the smaller *Stay Free!*, devote themselves to "culture-jam." Kalle Lasn, *Adbusters'* editor and founder, says that "economic progress is killing the planet," and so the magazine is doing what it can to fight the advertising industry and its ubiquitous sales messages. It employs mockery as with a photo of a man whose mouth is stuffed with big denomination, green dollar bills over the tagline, "The True Colors of Benetton." A recent back cover of *Stay Free!* was a glossy replica of the Dewars campaign featuring attractive, sophisticated young drinkers over the tagline, "Remember how liquor used to make you vomit?"

In an "If-you-can't-beat-them-join-them" attitude, some corporations have begun to use parody in their own advertising. In 1996 Dana Carvey debuted on a weekly ABC show that deliberately spoofed advertisements of the show's sponsors: Taco Bell, Pepsi-Cola, and Pizza Hut. In 1997, Boston Chicken Inc., had an ad campaign that mocked the anorexic models used by Calvin Klein. When a Nissan ad featured Barbie and Ken look-alikes, the Mattel toy company immediately protested. Nike also wrote a cease-and-desist letter to Candie's Inc. whose ad featured actress Jenny McCarthy wearing colorful new sneakers under the tagline, "Just Screw it."

While parodies are legally protected as fair use, there are difficulties in determining the difference between parody and plagiarism. For example, a photograph taken by Annie Leibovitz of nude and pregnant Demi Moore was on the cover of a 1991 issue of *Vanity Fair*. In 1994, Paramount's ad campaign for the movie *Naked Gun 33 1/3: The Final Insult* was a parody of Leibovitz's cover. A pregnant model was photographed in the same seductive pose as Moore, but the model's head was replaced by that of Leslie Nielsen, the film's star.

According to the *Wall Street Journal* (Dec. 20, 1996), photographer Leibovitz sued Paramount, saying that the ad copied too much of her original photo and that it was done solely for commercial purposes. U.S. District Judge Loretta Preska in Manhattan denied Leibovitz's claim on the grounds that using a portion of someone's work for criticism or commentary is fair use. She said that the ad clearly took "a satiric aim" and that it "intended to make a mockery of an image that had become a 'cultural icon.' . . . In fact, without reference to the Moore photograph, the Nielsen ad is simply not very funny."

The judge rejected the relevance of the argument about the parody being created for commercial purposes based on a 1994 Supreme Court decision in relation to a 2 Live Crew parody of the song "Pretty Woman." In that decision, the justices unanimously agreed that even though parodies are created for commercial benefits, they can nevertheless be legitimate artistic commentary on the original work. The justices left it to lower courts to decide case by case when artistic thievery was being disguised as satire. Earlier courts had already given fair-use protection to a parody of "When Sunny Gets Blue" called "When Sonny Sniffs Glue" and to a *MAD Magazine* parody of Irving Berlin's "A Pretty Girl Is Like a Melody," entitled "Louella Schwartz Describes Her Malady." However, in 1995, *Snicker*, a St. Louis-based humor magazine, lost in court when Anheuser-Busch charged the editors with trademark infringement for a "Michelob Oily" ad. Manhattan attorney Lawrence Savell said about the case in *Folio* (Mar. 15, 1995), "The bottom line is that your ad parody must make it clear to readers that it is a parody or editorial, and that it is not what it seeks to make fun of or comment on." Attorney David Korzenik added that the court's action "continues a pattern in which judges have ruled in favor of trademark owners when they deem the parody pornographic, obscene or possessing some other displeasing characteristic."

While "straight" magazines occasionally run parodies, they do so reluctantly, for fear of being misunderstood by today's speed-readers. In 1995, when the American Society of Business Press Editors sponsored a TRAMP (TRAde Magazine Parody) contest, only five submissions came in from the 80 members. Top honors went to an April Fools' Day four-page insert created by *National Jew-eler* and called *National Fooler*. It was a piece about the extramarital jewelry market. Second prize went to Helmers Publications's *Sensor* for a May 1993 parody entitled *Non-Sensors* with a probing article on "Vacuum Sensors: Do They ALL Suck?" Third prize went to Cahners Publishing Company's *EDN* (*Electronic Design News*) for its April Fools' edition, which included an etiquette column for socially backward electronics engineers and a probing article about how savvy engineers take credit for other people's work.

When the *California Lawyer* magazine ran a three-page "LL.B. Catalog" (a simultaneous reference to a law degree and to the L. L. Bean catalog), it used staff members to model items "every lawyer needs." Dozens of readers had their secretaries telephone to inquire about ordering the products, which included a "java-derm" attachment to inject caffeine directly into the arm "for all-nighters and mornings-after" with no "messy rings on the conference table"; a "bottomless briefcase" that flipped open to release a cargo net with wheels for lugging around extra case files, a change of underwear, and golf clubs; and a $99 "pocket pay-point," a calculator-sized machine topped with a handkerchief so it can be worn discreetly in a breast pocket and pulled out as needed to take a client's automatic-teller card and deposit the money directly into the lawyer's account.

Parodies are fun to create. In literature classes, high school instructors encourage students to write parodies of Sherlock Holmes mysteries and of such classics as J. D. Salinger's *Catcher in the Rye* and Edgar Allan Poe's "Annabel Lee." The University of Mississippi has contests for would-be Faulkners, while California English professor Scott Rice sponsors the Bulwer-Lytton Fiction Contest in which writers imitate the overblown style of the Victorian author who was second to Charles Dickens in 19th-century popularity. Snoopy, in the *Peanuts* comic strip, is only one of the many aspiring to write the "Great American Novel" beginning with Bulwer-Lytton's "It was a dark and stormy night. . . ." *See also* ADAPTATION, HUMOROUS ESSAYISTS, IMPERSONATION, JOKE PATTERNS, MAGAZINES, POSTMODERNISM, SATIRE

Further reading: Linda Hutcheon, *A Theory of Parody* (1986). Gao Yan, *The Art of Parody: Maxine Hong Kingston's Use of Chinese Sources* (1996).

Poetry

The word *poetry* comes from the Greek *poiein*, "to make," hence its meaning of using words to create an intense or emotionally concentrated experience. From the beginning, humor has been one of these emotional experiences provided by a creative person putting exactly the right words in the right places.

Poetry can be divided into three major types. Narrative poetry relates a story; lyric poetry is more subjective and emotional as in sonnets and elegies; and dramatic poetry is written like a play, in which the poet presents an idea or a sentiment through showing, rather than telling, using such techniques as dramatic monologues and striking metaphors and symbols. Humor can be incorporated into any of these kinds of poetry, with even "serious" poets relying on humor for a change of pace and for contrast.

In the first half of the 20th century, Gertrude Stein provided such surprises when she began using words for their sounds more than for their meanings. In 1956, when Allen Ginsburg ushered in the age of "Beat" poetry with "Howl," people were amazed that a poem about depression and suffering could also be exuberant and exciting and filled with such fresh and humorous images as "angel-headed hipsters," from "Zen New Jersey," eating "the lamb stew of the imagination," and being "run down by the drunken taxicabs of Absolute Reality."

While these are examples of playful moments found in serious poetry, the more common place to find humor is in light verse, which comes in many forms. It is characterized by a bantering tone, a sportive mood, a worldly attitude, and oftentimes a witty, humorous, ingenious, or satirical approach. Frederick Locker-Lampson, who in 1867 published an anthology of *vers de societe* (a French term often used to refer to light verse), said that light verse has somewhat the same relation to the poetry of lofty imagination and deep feeling that the Dresden china shepherds and shepherdesses of the last century bore to the sculpture of Donatello and Michelangelo. W. H. Auden, in the introduction to his *Oxford Book of Light Verse* (1973), wrote that the source of the difference is not so much in the poetry as in the relation between the author and society. "When the things in which the poet is interested, the things which he sees about him, are much the same as those of his audience . . . his language will be straightforward and close to ordinary speech." Auden divided light poetry into three categories: that created to be spoken or sung before an audience, that which will be read by people interested in everyday social dealings, and that which is primarily humorous or nonsense—what some people call "light, light poetry."

Light verse shares many of the characteristics of other humorous literature, but it is usually more succinct and therefore has an advantage over essays, short stories, and novels. The appeal of Ogden Nash's humorous verse is shown by the fact that 25 years after his 1971 death, 16 of his books were still in print including *The Adventures of Isabel, Bed Riddance: A Posy for the Indisposed, The Cruise of the Aardvark, Everyone but Thee and Me, A Penny Saved Is Impossible,* and *The Pocket Book of Ogden Nash.* For today's generation, the most famous writers of light verse have been Dr. Seuss and Shel Silverstein. Silverstein's collection of poems and drawings, *Where the Sidewalk Ends* (1974), is number 11 on *Publisher's Weekly* list of all-time best selling hardcover books. His 1981 *The Light in the Attic* and his 1996 *Falling Up* have also been popular with both adults and children. When a few years before his death in 1991, Dr. Seuss was awarded an honorary doctorate at a college graduation, the audience stood and recited *Green Eggs and Ham.* That students and their parents could remember this story demonstrates how poetry works as an aid to memory.

Other successful poets who have written light verse as part of their life's work include Roy Blount Jr., John Ciardi, William Cole,

Donald Hall, Randall Jarrell, Maxine Kumin, David McCord, Phyllis McGinley, Marianne Moore, Marge Piercy, Jack Prelutsky, Gary Snyder, William Stafford, Wallace Stevens, May Swenson, and Judith Viorst.

Good poets are like skilled joke writers in making every word count and in getting maximum benefit from connotations and metaphorical and symbolic meanings. While not all poetry rhymes or follows a set rhythm, all poets are cognizant of sounds. They work with alliteration, assonance, repetition, cadence, and rhyme so that when words are said aloud the rhythm and the flow will contribute to the idea being communicated. These techniques are used to greater or lesser degrees in each of the following kinds of light verse.

Clerihews were invented in the early 1900s by Edmund Clerihew Bentley. The witty genre is a satirical verse form designed to target historical, political, and literary figures as in

> When their lordships asked Bacon
> How many bribes he had taken
> He had at least the grace
> To get very red in the face.

The rules of the game are that the person's name must form one of the rhymes and that the idea is expressed in two couplets of irregular meter.

Dialect poetry relies for its humor on the poet's use of dialect or the inclusion of characters who speak a dialect. Dialectal speech is the mark of an outsider, of someone who is different and therefore a likely target for humor. With cowboy and regional poetry, writers exaggerate local speech patterns and look for words and phrases unique to an area. In the mid-1800s, James Russell Lowell, a respected professor at Harvard University, was opposed to the Mexican War and used a character he named Birdofredum Sawin as a satiric spokesperson for his anti-war sentiments. Birdofredum had lost an arm, a leg, and an eye in the war, so he planned to go into politics as a way of cashing in on his "disfigurements."

> If, while you're lectioneerin round, some
>   curious chap should beg
> To know my views o' state affairs, just an-
>   swer WOODEN LEG!
> If they ain't satisfied with that, and kinda
>   pry and doubt,
> And ax for somethin' definite, just say ONE
>   EYE PUT OUT!

In talking about his "platform," Birdofredum continues:

> Then you can call me "Timbertoes"—that's
>   what the people likes! . . . .
> "Old Timbertoes," you see, 's a creed it's
>   safe to be quite bold on,
> There's nothin in't the other side can any
>   ways get hold on.

Lowell was using a comic technique already popular in fiction and in vaudeville where listeners enjoyed feeling superior to a character speaking what they considered to be an inferior form of English.

In contrast, contemporary poets use small bits of dialect humor for quite a different purpose. Those who belong to minority groups include words, phrases, or pronunciations that are characteristic of their group as a matter of cultural pride. Writers Sandra Cisneros, Pat Mora, and Gary Soto, for example, mix English and Spanish as they make observations—some funny, some not so funny—about the ironies of living in two cultures. Imamu Amiri Baraka (LeRoi Jones), Maya Angelou, Nikki Giovanni, and Alice Walker do much the same with African American speech.

Epigrams are pithy, pointed concise sayings, many of which rhyme, as in "Man proposes but God disposes," and Dorothy Parker's "Men seldom make passes at girls who wear glasses." While most epigrams are couplets or quatrains, the distinguishing characteristic is not so much the shape as the tone and the wit, as illustrated in this 17th-century example written in defense of poets by Matthew Prior:

> Sir, I admit your general rule,
> That every poet is a fool:
> But you yourself may serve to show it,
> That every fool is not a poet.

Epitaphs in modern American usage are the brief messages engraved on tombstones. Because the overwhelming majority of epitaphs are serious, humorous ones are all the more surprising. Among the examples of folk literature that Fritz Spiegel collected for his *A Small Book of Grave Humor* (1973) are several that rhyme including this one:

Here Lies
Lester Moore
Four Slugs
From a 44
No Les
No More.

Experimentation is important to poets who try to follow Ezra Pound's admonition of "make it new." Poets commonly play word games. Ogden Nash frequently switched into phonetic spellings to better catch a rhyme, while Leigh Hunt wrote a series of triplets in which he achieved rhymes by dropping the initial letter from the word ending the previous line. Alaric A. Watts wrote a poem in which he devoted one line to each letter of the alphabet beginning with:

An Austrian army awfully arrayed
Boldly by battery besieged Belgrade.

Other ways that poets surprise readers and listeners into smiling is by not following standard conventions of English as with e e cummings' refusal to use capital letters and his putting words together in unexpected order as in "spring is like a perhaps hand." Don Marquis, in his book *Archyology: The Long Lost Tales of Archy and Mehitabel*, gave an amusing explanation for the lack of capitals in his poems. Archy is a cockroach who lives in a warehouse and at night writes his poetry by jumping down onto the keys of a typewriter. Because he can hit only one key at a time, he has no underlining or capital letters. Such an explanation puts readers in the mood to appreciate Archy's fantasies about Mehitabel, the cat.

Limericks were almost called *Learics* after Edward Lear. He is the Victorian poet and artist who made the form popular with his illustrated 1848 *Book of Nonsense* that included such offerings as

There is a young lady whose nose,
Continually prospers and grows;
When it grew out of sight,
She exclaimed in a fright,
"Oh! Farewell to the end of my nose!"

The form is easy to imitate and thousands of limericks, both published and unpublished, have been devised. Because limericks are a kind of nonsense verse, the creators operate in a framework of play and games, which gives them poetic license to treat in a nonserious manner such serious topics as illness, physical violence, sexuality, death, and madness. This is why many of the limericks created by adults have suggestive overtones or playfully recount the chopping off of heads and other appendages. In 1896, the poems were given the name of *limerick*, after a popular song about Limerick, Ireland.

Nonsense verse, as a term, has been in English since 1799, but the concept has been around much longer. Rather than referring to poems that make no sense, it refers to poems that make just enough sense to be intriguing and amusing, as in Lewis Carroll's famous lines from his 1871 *Through the Looking Glass*:

'Twas brillig, and the slithy toves
Did gyre and gimble in the wabe:
All mimsy were the borogoves,
And the mome raths outgrabe.

Nonsense rhymes have been found in ancient Greek literature, including this one from around A.D. 200:

I boiled the hot water in an urn
Till it was cold as ice;
I blew the fire to make it burn,
Which froze it in a trice.

The technique of relying on opposites and contradictions makes the following piece of children's folklore so funny that generations have memorized it:

Ladles and jelly spoons:
I come before you
To stand behind you
And tell you something
I know nothing about.
Next Thursday,
Which is Good Friday,

There'll be a mothers' meeting
For fathers only.
Admission is free;
So pay at the door.

Occasional Verse can be as serious as the poem Robert Frost wrote for John F. Kennedy's inauguration or as flip as those recited by Henry Gibson, who during the late 1960s did quavering recitations of mini-poems on television's *Laugh-In*.

Amateur poets often write occasional verse "to honor" friends at parties, retirements, and roasts. The humor in these latter poems can be either intentional or unintentional. Unintentional humor results when the poems are overly sentimental and have flawed scansion and rhyme so that they come across as loosely styled or trivial "doggerel" rather than poetry.

Funeral poems, created in dead seriousness during the late 1800s, are today considered wonderfully funny examples of doggerel verse. One of the writers was Howard Heber Clark, who wrote about "Little Willie," who "had a purple monkey climbing on a yellow stick, And when he sucked the paint all off it made him deathly sick . . . ." Julia Moore, "the Sweet Singer of Michigan," is the most famous writer of funeral poems, perhaps because she did tours where she recited such poems as

One morning in April, a short time ago.
Libbie was alive and gay;
Her Savior called her, she had to go,
Ere the close of that pleasant day.
While eating dinner, this dear little child
Was choked on a piece of beef.
Doctors came, tried their skill awhile,
But none could give relief.

Mark Twain confessed to studying Julia Moore's poetry to learn the art of writing funny poems, and apparently used Moore as the model for Emmaline Grangerford and her "Ode to Stephen Dowling Bots, Dec'd," in *The Adventures of Huckleberry Finn*.

Parodies are usually intended to be funny in that they exaggerate the features of the original. In 1902, Harry Graham, an English soldier, produced a book of "Little Willie" or "Little Billie" poems parodying funeral po-

ems. He used the pen name Col. D. Streamer (he was in the Coldstream Guard) and published his book under the title of *Ruthless Rhymes for Heartless Homes*. It included

Billy, in one of his nice, new sashes,
Fell in the fire and was burned to ashes.
Now, although the room grows chilly,
I haven't the heart to poke poor Billy.

and

Father heard his children scream,
So he threw them in the stream,
Saying, as he drowned the third,
"Children should be seen, not heard."

The book was such a success that it inspired a kind of parlor game where people sat around making up ruthless rhymes, many of which found their way into print in local and national newspapers and magazines.

Gelett Burgess was made famous by his 1901 playful parody of Emily Dickenson's "I Never Saw a Moor":

I never saw a Purple Cow,
I never Hope to See one
But I can Tell you Anyhow,
I'd rather see than Be one!

He was forced to recite the ditty so often that in desperation he wrote:

Oh Yes, I wrote "The Purple Cow."
I'm Sorry now I Wrote it.
But I can Tell you Anyhow,
I'll Kill you if you Quote it.

There is no end to the parodies of Mother Goose rhymes and of such famous poems as Edgar Allan Poe's "Bells," "Annabel Lee," and "The Raven."

In conclusion, the catagories of clerihews, dialect poetry, epigrams, epitaphs, experimentation, limericks, nonsense verse, occasional verse, and parodies are a sampling, rather than a complete list, because as with other examples of humor, creative minds are always thinking of something new. Perhaps not too far in the future, computers will be successfully programmed to write interesting light verse. *See also* CHILDREN'S LITERATURE, DIALECT HUMOR, HUMEROUS ESSAYISTS, MUSIC, PARODY

Further reading: The Academy of American Poets, http://www.poets.org/ (August 1999). Ronald Wallace, *God Be with the Clown: Humor in American Poetry* (1984).

Political Correctness

Political correctness is the practice of operating under the belief that language and practices that could offend political sensibilities (as in matters of sex or race) should be eliminated. The lively debate now occurring in the United States, as well as in other parts of the world, about political correctness is evidence of an interested citizenry undergoing social change.

Political correctness relates in at least two ways to humor. First is the inhibiting effect on joking and humor caused by the belief that people should refrain from making references that "could offend political sensibilities." As Richard Zoglin wrote in *Time* magazine (Oct. 25, 1993), "Telling jokes has always been somewhat at odds with the p.c. ethos. To be politically correct, one must be constantly sensitive to the feelings of others. To be a comedian, one frequently has to ignore them." Zoglin then went on to describe the second relationship between humor and political correctness when he wrote, "Political correctness, once the province of a small band of liberal reformers, has been around long enough to become establishment orthodoxy—which means it is fair game for satire. It is now p.c. to make fun of p.c."

Dennis Baron, a professor of English at the University of Illinois, did a computer-assisted search of how the term *political correctness* was used in news stories and found that between 1980 and 1995 it was increasingly used with negative connotations, while the reverse concept, *politically incorrect* was used with increasingly positive connotations. In 1992, comedian Jackie Mason proudly argued in the Federal District Court in Manhattan that he had been "associated with the phrase politically incorrect for 10 years. . . . My whole attitude was always politically incorrect; it's my expression of independence." He was arguing for the right to call a new show *Jackie Mason, Politically Incorrect*.

Comedy Central cable television channel had filed an injunction against the new name because of their program *Politically Incorrect,* hosted by Bill Maher.

A complicating factor with humor and political correctness is the mass media, which demands instant stories in jokes, commercials, cartoons, advertisements, and television programming. Cartoonists, for example, who have only one frame in which to tell a story, and comedians, who are expected to make an audience laugh within 30 seconds, are forced to rely on the stereotypes that are already in people's minds. To make their stories obvious, creators exaggerate the aspects on which the jokes hinge and downplay all other characteristics. The result is a set of exaggerated stereotypes (the dumb blonde, the drunk Irishman, the Jewish American princess, the irritating mother-in-law, the inscrutable Asian, the Italian mafioso, the stoic American Indian, etc.) that for many years were used as the hooks on which to hang jokes.

It used to be that when people told offensive jokes, they selected audiences that did not include members of the stereotyped group. But modern media makes it harder to limit or assess one's audience. "The world is a rough room to work," Billy Crystal said after two Italian American organizations protested one of the jokes he made while hosting a Hollywood Oscars ceremony. He had speculated that the proposed purchase of MGM by an Italian businessman "could mean the famed MGM lion would stop roaring and take the Fifth instead." Fifty-two members of Congress wrote to say that Crystal "soiled the reputations of the 38 members of Congress who are descended from Italian parents and grandparents as well as 26 million citizens of Italian heritage who live throughout this free and loving land." *Newsday* columnist Linda Winder defended Crystal by pointing out that he wasn't questioning the integrity of 26 million Italian Americans; instead he was making fun of "one Italian businessman, one Giancarlo Parretti—a flashy, mysterious new Beverly Hills resident whose controversial Pathe Communications offered to buy MGM-UA for $1.3 billion." According to *Variety*, Parretti had been arrested in Sicily and Rome and, in 1986, had stopped doing business in Italy because he did not want to disclose the identity of his stockholders when he was being investigated for fraud.

Other examples of people being surprised to have the world as an audience include President Reagan who made a joke about bombing Russia to an insider group of American reporters and then had his statement broadcast internationally; Vice President George Bush who forgot that he was in a public situation when he bragged about his performance in a debate with Geraldine Ferraro, "We tried to kick a little ass last night"; night-duty police officers who forget that outsiders with short-wave radios are listening in when they tell jokes to each other; and people who use e-mail, forgetting that their friends might forward the jokes they have told.

People protest against what they see as politically incorrect humor in hopes of educating the public about their particular special-interest groups, as, for example, when the Concerned Relatives Alliance for the Mentally Ill and the Mental Health Association of Broward County, Florida, protested the 1990 Paramount Films' *Crazy People,* starring Dudley Moore and Daryl Hannah, and when the St. Louis chapter of the Alzheimer's Association protested a John Callahan cartoon called "The Alzheimer Hoedown," in which confused couples at a square dance are scratching their heads, unable to follow the instructions, "Return to the girl that you just left." As more and more protests get in the news, people feel almost duty-bound to speak out or to take some action if they see something that they interpret as maligning of a member of their family or a group to which they belong. Some people also protest if they think undeserving individuals or groups are being "glorified." This was at the root of complaints that Callahan received for his cartoon showing two Ku Klux Klansmen in sheets leaving a house in the middle of the night. One of them is saying, "Don't you just love it when they're still warm

from the dryer?" It could be argued that Callahan was trivializing rather than glorifying the Klan, but what often happens with cartoons and jokes is that people, who are accustomed to devoting less than ten seconds to a joke, jump to conclusions based simply on the subject matter rather than stopping to think about the situation, the tone, and the point of view.

In 1997, a California history professor wrote to the newsletter of the International Society for Humor Studies that "alas, these days the squinty-eyed, pursed-lipped, sour-faced, humorless vigilantes of the p.c. thought police are busy 'round the clock, rooting out laughter in any nook or cranny where humor is displayed. I know university professors who manage to get themselves upset over three things every day before breakfast. Four years ago, a male colleague . . . mindlessly destroyed all the clippings, cartoons, sayings, and news blurbs that I'd posted on my bulletin board outside my university office door because, he said, 'they were inappropriate.'" The letter writer filed unprofessional conduct charges against the self-appointed "enforcer," who was reprimanded by the president of the university.

When John O'Sullivan, editor of the *National Review*, was asked to apologize for a cover cartoon making fun of the 1996 Democratic National Party's acceptance of campaign contributions from Chinese businessmen, he responded with an op-ed piece in the *Wall Street Journal* (Apr. 17, 1997). The *Review* had used a cartoon by Roman Genn on its cover showing Bill Clinton "wooing Chinese interests and so acquiring some stereotypical Chinese features," Al Gore "wearing the robes of a Buddhist monk and holding a begging bowl full of dollars," and a toothy Hillary Clinton "exaggerated in the style of all caricature." O'Sullivan had been invited to speak on the Yale University campus. The speech went fine, but afterwards he was surrounded by what he described as a mini-mob of honor students who "pulled at my clothes, struck a few glancing blows, waved placards denouncing a recent *National Review* cartoon cover as 'racist' and 'anti-Asian' and shouted loudly a few inches from my face."

Among the points that O'Sullivan made in his op-ed piece were that "not all stereotypes are objectionable." Cartoons without stereotypes—the Brit in his bowler, the Frenchman with his beret, the Russian in his fur hat—would require written explanations. What is objectionable is the stereotype that holds up an entire group to ridicule and contempt. But that was not what Roman Genn—a fine caricaturist—created. He was lampooning the "2½ most important WASP politicians in America." O'Sullivan compared the demands for a *National Review* apology to the way victims of the Red Guards during China's Cultural Revolution were forced to confess and then were sentenced to political re-education, which he correlated with "sensitivity training" for Americans.

Other people take a more lighthearted approach when protesting political correctness, as when Stan Freberg amused people by singing "Old Man River" filled with such substitutions as *elderly* for *old* and *perspire* for *sweat*. Several people have used the same idea to write parodies of such folk tales as "Little Red Riding Hood" and "The Three Little Pigs." In 1996, California Attorney General Dan Lungren asked California newspapers to add a note identifying a Garry Trudeau cartoon treatment of a raid on the San Francisco Cannabis Buyers' Club as "false and misleading." Lungren's request was met mostly with ridicule, as when Bob Wieder suggested in the February 1997 *Playboy Forum* that several other comic strips should also have warning notes; for example:

- *Hagar the Horrible:* "Vikings were not suburban family men with horned helmets but savage marauders who spent their lives enduring bitter cold and recovering from battle wounds. Their mortality rate was appalling. There is no actual record of an amusing Scandinavian prior to Victor Borge."
- *The Family Circus:* "The characters in this strip are impossibly wholesome, pleasant, even-tempered, devout, optimistic and content. There haven't been any actual families such as this since 1962."
- *Alley Oop, Prince Valiant, Blondie, Mary Worth*: "These characters do not age in a normal or realistic manner. If these were actual people, they would have died of natural causes or lapsed into advanced stages of senility by now. The strip's implication that life goes on forever is a cruel deceit."

See also ANTIAUTHORITY HUMOR, CENSORSHIP, LEGAL ISSUES, POLITICS AND HUMOR

Further reading: Joseph Boskin (ed.), *The Humor Prism in 20th-Century America* (1997). Murray S. Davis, *What's So Funny: The Comic Conception of Culture and Society* (1993). Elliott Oring, *Jokes and Their Relations* (1992). Robert W. Terry, *Authentic Leadership: Courage in Action* (1993).

Politics and Humor

Humor used in politics includes that which politicians create and use, as well as that which is produced by professional comedians, essayists, authors, scriptwriters, cartoonists, and the general public about politicians and political situations. Whether such humor is distributed on the Internet, worn on a T-shirt, shared by a comedian, or printed in the daily newspaper, its overall aim is to entertain, but it may also attract attention to individuals and to issues, influence public opinion, disarm political foes and critics, communicate information in ways that straight language does not, relieve stress, and build a sense of community among like-minded individuals.

Political humor ranges from the historical observations of Mark Twain and Artemus Ward to the contemporary points made by editorial cartoonists Herb Block and Pat Oliphant or by Garry Trudeau in his *Doonesbury* comic strip. It appears in the sophisticated language of author Robert Penn Warren and journalist William F. Buckley Jr., as well as in the vernacular of Finley Peter Dunne's Mr. Dooley character and in the journalistic prose of Molly Ivins, Russell Baker, Calvin Trillin, and Art Buchwald.

Political comedian Mark Russell gives television the credit for extending the popularity of political humor as entertainment. When he first started doing his satirical political songs, he performed mainly in Washington, DC, but during the 1990s his television specials were among the most popular on the Public Broadcasting System, and he performed outside of the Washington area 200 times a year. Other groups doing political humor, most notably The Capitol Steps and Gross National Product, have similar success stories.

Achieving name recognition is a prerequisite to getting elected to public office, and making people laugh is one way to become famous. Bud Clark, known locally as "The Budster," was mayor of Portland, Oregon, between 1984 and 1992. Clark's election stunned his opponent, incumbent Frank Ivancie, who had derided Mr. Clark as nothing more than "a man whose claim to fame is exposing himself to a downtown statue." Clark owned a Portland bar and had been active in civic affairs, but was known mainly

Mark Russell started his career of playing the piano and making fun of national politics at a bar in Georgetown. *Courtesy of WNED, Buffalo/Photo by Diana Walker*

for being the man in a 1979 "expose yourself to art" poster, which sold over 500,000 copies to benefit a local arts group. The photo on the poster was shot from behind and showed a bare-legged Clark wearing an open raincoat and standing in front of a nude statue.

In 1995, Ray Wardingly, a part-time clown in Chicago, won the Republican nomination for mayor after spending only $200. As expected, he lost in the final election to the firmly established Democrat, Richard Daley. However, Japanese voters in both Tokyo and Osaka elected comedy performers as governors (equivalent to American mayors). Both performers ran as independents and surprised the established party candidates, much as professional wrestler Jesse Ventura did when, in 1998, he won the race for governor of Minnesota. Also in 1998, New York voters gave over 50,000 votes to Al Lewis, known for his television role as Grandpa Munster. The Green party recruited Lewis to run, hoping that his fame would outweigh the disadvantages of being a third-party candidate.

The most publicity that President Ford received after leaving office was in the fall of 1986 when the Gerald R. Ford Museum hosted a Humor and the Presidency Symposium in Grand Rapids, Michigan. The late comedian Pat Paulsen, himself a frequent candidate for president, likened the event to an "Ayatollah Khomeini Symposium on the Sexual Revolution." Speakers and discussants at the three-day event included Art Buchwald, Chevy Chase, Robert Klein, Mark Russell, Mort Sahl, and cartoonists Jeff MacNelly and Berkeley Breathed.

Presidential speech writer Robert Orben expressed a consensus opinion when he said that self-deprecating humor is a president's best friend and weapon because it helps a politician to be seen as warm and relaxed. "Humor reaches out, puts a warm, affectionate arm around an audience and says, 'I am one of you. I understand you.' If we can laugh together, we can vote together." When Ford gave speeches written by Orben, he muffed the lines so often that Orben attached a 3x5 card on the inside cover of Ford's speech binder. It read, "I told my wife I knew this speech backwards and that's how I'm delivering it." Ironically, this became one of Ford's most successful lines, and he began bungling speeches just so he could use it.

Besides building a sense of community, self-deprecating humor can be effective in disarming political foes if a candidate is able to beat his critics to the punch by making voters laugh about something that worries them. As the country's oldest president, Ronald Reagan was well aware of the potential for concern about his age so he looked for opportunities to make jokes that would relieve people's worries. At a Gridiron Club dinner in Washington, DC, he noted that the club had been founded in 1885, and lamented that he was not invited to their *first* dinner. In front of the Washington Press Club, he mentioned its having been founded in 1919 and wistfully added, "It seems like only yesterday." One of his best quips came during a televised debate with opponent Walter Mondale when, with a twinkle in his eye, he declared, "I will not exploit, for political purposes, the youth and inexperience of my opponent."

Jokes about a politician's age can also come from the other side of the coin, as when in 1956, U.S. Senator William Langer spoke against the second-term nomination of President Eisenhower. Eisenhower was in his late 60s and during his first term had undergone intestinal surgery and suffered a heart attack. Langer solemnly declared, "I deserve the nomination more than Eisenhower does. I'm older. I'm sicker. And I need the rest more than he does!"

John F. Kennedy countered those critics who charged that he had an unfair campaign advantage because of his family's wealth by pulling an envelope from his pocket and reading a fake telegram from his father: "Don't buy one vote more than necessary. I'll be damned if I'll pay for a landslide."

When Arizona's Representative Morris (Mo) Udall was campaigning against Jimmy Carter, who had shocked his public by granting an interview to *Playboy* in which he confessed to having "lusted in his heart," Udall

got laughs by saying, "You think Plains, Georgia, is small; my hometown of St. Johns, Arizona, was so small you couldn't even lust in your heart." When Udall died in December of 1998, one of the headlines on an obituary article in the *Arizona Republic* (Dec. 14, 1998) read, "Udall never met a joke he didn't write down." The reference was to a collection of stories, anecdotes, jokes, and one-liners that Udall kept in three loose-leaf notebooks. On a regular basis he would browse through his notebooks so that he could nearly always pull from memory some appropriate rejoinder or anecdote. Some of Udall's jokes had been used by his grandfather in frontier Arizona in the late 1800s, while others came from a collection kept by his father, an Arizona judge and church leader. In his book *Too Funny to Be President*, Udall apologized for not having indexed all the jokes he included. He noted that his father's collection included one set for "Funerals (stock)" and another for "Funerals (special)," which Udall said showed something about both his father's organizational abilities and his dry sense of humor.

On the occasion of Udall's death, fellow Arizonan, Secretary of the Interior Bruce Babbitt, said about him, "Sure, he was funny, but he was not antagonistic. He would have been out of place in this Congress. There was always time to tell a story, to philosophize a little bit, and to laugh at ourselves. He would have been very uncomfortable in a Congress like we have now."

Humor allows politicians to be both less specific and more specific than they could be with ordinary language. For example, when Abraham Lincoln wanted to urge Civil War General George McClellan to move a little faster with his attack on Richmond, Virginia, he wrote in a letter, "Dear General, if you do not want to use the Army, I would like to borrow it for a few days."

When in 1994 in Trevose, Pennsylvania, The Three Stooges were remembered on the occasion of the 60th anniversary of their first short film, one of the topics discussed was the historical significance of the group's propagandistic war efforts. Donald B. Morian, comedy film historian from the University of

Dayton in Ohio, pointed out that The Stooges virtually got "away with murder" at a time when even hints of anti-Nazi sentiment in feature films drew the wrath of isolationists. But isolationist critics ignored slapstick, and so were unaware of how influential The Three Stooges were in influencing public opinion with their movie *You Nazi Spy*. It was released in theaters on 19 January 1940, nearly two years prior to the bombing of Pearl Harbor and nine months before Charlie Chaplin's *The Great Dictator*.

Invective given without the counterbalance of a smile comes across as hostile and is likely to be dismissed as offensive, but when listeners or readers are made to chuckle, or at least smile, they become intellectually involved. This means that they at least think about the criticism that underlies the quip, as when in the 1980 presidential election, comedian Mort Sahl remarked that people did not vote *for* Ronald Reagan so much as they voted *against* Jimmy Carter. "If Reagan had been unopposed, he would have lost." From the same era, Mike Peters gained national attention with a cartoon showing George Washington saying, "I cannot tell a lie," Richard Nixon saying, "I cannot tell the truth," and Jimmy Carter saying, "I cannot tell the difference."

In an earlier election, Adlai Stevenson managed to save face while playfully insulting the American electorate. A man complimented Stevenson on his astuteness and knowledge and concluded, "Every thinking American will vote for you," to which Stevenson replied, "That won't be enough!"

Political experts and scholars undoubtedly have grounds to quibble with humorous over-simplifications of political concepts. Nevertheless, the public finds them so clear and memorable that they adopt them as popular culture icons. For example, in *The Humorous Dictionary of Economics* (1983), Jere Moorman expanded on an old joke about the meaning of communism by devising a more extensive set of "cow-definitions":

- **Capitalism**: If you have two cows, you sell one and buy a bull.

- **Communism**: If you have two cows, you give them to the government and the government gives you some milk.

- **Fascism**: If you have two cows, you keep the cows and give the milk to the government and the government then sells you some of the milk.

- **New-Dealism**: If you have two cows, you shoot one and milk the other and then pour the milk down the drain.

- **Socialism**: If you have two cows, you give your neighbor one.

- **Totalitarianism**: If you have two cows, the government shoots you and keeps the cows.

On 1 October 1974, Craig Hosmer, Republican from California, published in the *Congressional Record* an often-quoted statement on how to tell Republicans from Democrats, which reads in part as follows:

Democrats buy most of the books that have been banned somewhere.

Republicans form censorship committees and read them as a group.

Republicans employ exterminators.

Democrats step on the bugs.

Democrats name their children after popular sports figures, politicians, and entertainers.

Republican children are named after their parents or grandparents, according to where the money is.

Republicans tend to keep their shades drawn, although there is seldom any reason why they should.

Democrats ought to, but don't.

Republican boys date Democratic girls. They plan to marry Republican girls, but feel they're entitled to a little fun first.

Republicans sleep in twin beds—some even in separate rooms. That is why there are more Democrats.

Citizens who are frustrated by their government often seek relief from their frustrations by making jokes at politicians. As the "Cowboy Philosopher," Will Rogers with his folksy, country drawl brought smiles to Depression-weary Americans when he said such things as "Politics is the best show in town," and "This country has gotten where it is in spite of politics, not by the aid of it." Rogers's political statements have been the basis for such shows as James Whitmore's *Will Rogers U.S.A.*, Robert Hays's made-for-television biography of Rogers, and Keith Carradine's 1991 Broadway show *The Will Rogers Follies*. Through these forums, more people have seen reconstructed views of Rogers than ever saw him in real life, where many of his jokes about nonpolitical matters would not be considered funny today.

A "real-time" example of how humor can bring relief in political situations came in 1992, when at a formal state dinner in Tokyo, President George Bush suddenly became ill and vomited on Japanese Prime Minister Kiichi Miyazawa and then fainted for a moment. Immediately after the president was helped from the room, Barbara Bush stood and made an accusation. She said that the incident was the fault of Emperor Akihito and Crown Prince Naruhito because they had beaten George in tennis that afternoon, "and we Bushes aren't used to losing." The incident was recorded by television security cameras, and when Mrs. Bush first made the accusation the audience notably stiffened. However, as they realized she was making a joke, relief washed over the room and both Japanese and Americans burst out laughing. They knew she would not be joking if she thought her husband had been poisoned or was having a heart attack. This was comparable to the sigh of relief that echoed around the world in 1981 after President Reagan was shot by John Hinckley and proved that he was still in his right mind when, as he was being wheeled into the operating room, he quipped to the doctors, "Please assure me that you are all Republicans." *See also* ANTIAUTHORITY HUMOR, CARTOONS, COMIC RELIEF, POLITICAL CORRECTNESS, SATIRE

Further reading: Gerald Gardner, *Campaign Comedy: Political Humor from Clinton to Kennedy* (1994). ———. *The Mocking of the President: A History of Campaign Humor from Ike to Ronnie*

(1988). Charles Henning, *The Wit and Wisdom of Politics* (1989).

Pop-Up Books

Pop-up books have movable parts, so that one picture can evolve into another and three-dimensional items can suddenly appear from between flat pages. The first pop-up or movable book was an astronomy text published in 1540, and was designed to show readers how stars and planets revolve. While today there are still some educational pop-up books, and even whole kits or packs designed to teach about nature, parts of the body, architectural styles, and other three-dimensional concepts, the majority of pop-up books are designed for children's or adults' amusement. There is something incongruous and pleasantly surprising about books that contain more than printed words.

Readers of early pop-up books were delighted by such creative printing techniques as lift-up flaps, holes drilled through books so as to create different effects on each page or each fold-out, fancy paper dolls and other figures inserted into slots, and the appearance in fold-outs of three-dimensional scenes or clothing. The golden age of movable books is generally considered to be the period between 1878, when German artist Lothar Meggendorfer began developing his famous moving characters, and 1910, when World War I halted production. In the 1890s, Ernest Nister, another German artist, created numerous kinds of movable pictures, including circular dissolves, which were soon being produced and distributed by Dutton in New York. Both Meggendorfer's and Nister's pictures are available in modern reproductions.

Other turn-of-the-century "fun" books included Raphael Tuck's fold-out panoramas and complex peep shows, as well as books that could be turned inside out to create doll houses. A forerunner to modern holograms were moire patterns that came covered with a finely striped piece of acetate. When laid over a drawing and moved or jiggled, the acetate caused an illusion of movement. When placed over a picture of a train, for example, the wheels appeared to revolve while smoke billowed from the engine.

According to book collector Gene Valentine, proprietor of the Almond Tree Press in Tempe, Arizona, throughout most of the 20th century, movable books were consigned to historical collections and viewed with nostalgia. In 1975 Waldo Hunt founded Intervisual Communications, Inc., a Los Angeles firm that launched a second era of movable books. Other companies now producing movable books to be distributed by mainline publishers include Compass Productions, Sadie Fields, and White Heat. Jan Pienkowski, who works with paper engineers and other book illustrators, is the best known of the pop-up designers. His Intervisual *Toilet Book: Don't Forget to Flush,* distributed for young readers in 1994 by Price/Stern/Sloan, is part of a series (*Phone Book, Doorbell,* and *Road Hog*) with three-dimensional pictures and buttons to push for appropriate noises. *The Naughty Nineties: A Saucy Pop-Up Book for Adults Only,* also produced by Intervisual and distributed by Price/Stern/Sloan in 1982, proves that pop-up books are not just for children. Another book appreciated by adults is Jan Pienkowski's *Botticelli's Bed & Breakfast,* which folds out like an ornate, three-story doll house filled with classical art. In addition to M. C. Escher–like stairways, there are paintings on every wall and famous figures peopling the rooms. For example, da Vinci's "Mona Lisa" is bringing a bottle of wine from the cellar where Rodin's "Thinker" sits amongst packing crates. In the living room, "Whistler's Mother" stares at a television portrayal of Michelangelo's outstretched man, while in the bathroom Botticelli's "Venus" stands shyly in the shower. Rodger Smith and Helen Balmer, with help from Hilary Saunders, were the paper engineers. Intervisual produced the book for a 1996 Simon & Schuster distribution.

Valentine, who collects not only pop-up books but also cartoons about them, has one showing a professor counseling a student, "Well, a pop-up doctoral dissertation is certainly an original idea." In Dan Piraro's "Bizarro," a husband shows his wife the new IRS 1040 booklet with "a pop-up federal penitentiary," while in Bob Thaves's "Frank and Ernest," Frank is trying to convince a book publisher to produce his "perfect" pop-up book on "The History of Toasters."

Comedian Ernie Kovacs built a television routine around his own specially designed pop-up books. While silently browsing through his library, he would pick up a thick book. When he opened it at the beginning, a miniature cannon shot out a puff of smoke; when he opened it near the end, out flew a dove. Only when he put it back on the shelf, did viewers see the title, *War and Peace.* Another book started with a little cough, which grew worse and worse as he turned the pages. The book was Alexandre Dumas's *Camille,* the ironic story of a beautiful socialite dying from tuberculosis. *See also* ANIMATION, CARTOONS, CHILDREN'S LITERATURE

Further reading: Ann R. Montanaro, *Pop-Up and Movable Books: A Bibliography* (1993). Albert Tillman, *Pop-Up! Pop-Up!: Pop-Up Books: Their History, How to Collect Them, and How Much They're Worth* (1997).

Postmodernism

Postmodernism is a term created almost playfully in 1949 to describe the wave of artistic creativity that followed what in art and architecture had been labeled *modern.* The postmodern movement was in many ways a reaction against the theory and practice of modern art or literature. The term spread from its use in the arts and literature to the popular culture so that in the 1980s and 1990s it became a buzzword, sometimes shortened to *pomo.* An *Arizona Republic* feature story on the topic (Apr. 18, 1999) distinguished between modern and postmodern with such examples as Captain Kangaroo vs. Pee-Wee Herman; James Joyce vs. Donald Barthelme; JFK vs. WJC (William Jefferson Clinton); Madonna vs. Jewel; the peace symbol vs. the happy face; B. Dalton vs. Amazon.com; the movie *Halloween* vs. the movie *Scream 2*; Kukla, Fran, and Ollie vs. the Teletubbies; reading vs. channel surfing; having your own bike vs. having your own

Web site; writing essays vs. making lists; and the real Jay Leno vs. the fictional Larry Sanders.

Related to postmodernism are the noun *deconstruction* and the verb *deconstructing*. Just as the term *postmodernism* developed as a playful rejection of the concept of *modernism*, the term *deconstruction* developed as a rejection of the idea that everything is orderly or structured. At mid-century, it was common for philosophers, linguists, and literary scholars to claim that human behavior and the products of human brains were regularly patterned and that these patterns or structures could be revealed through careful study based on authors' intentions. A new generation claimed instead that careful study from different points of view could reveal entirely different patterns. This means there can be multiple conflicting interpretations of a text based on the philosophical, political, or social implications of the use of language in a text rather than on the author's intention.

Woody Allen's 1997 movie, *Deconstructing Harry*, was a comedy about a successful writer with more than his share of family and personal problems. While the movie was criticized for being too confessional and too autobiographical, it nevertheless introduced a mass audience to the concept of deconstruction as the process of going beneath the surface to explore matters from different viewpoints.

Postmodernism and deconstruction relate to humor in that they provide insights from unexpected points of view. Also, both postmodernism and deconstruction are intertwined with the mass media so there is often a crossover to popular culture humor. The lack of privacy in a postmodern world provides new arenas for humor as illustrated through the Bill Clinton/Monica Lewinsky affair and through the jokes created in reaction to media coverage (some critics say overcoverage) of disasters and crimes.

Like seeing reflections of oneself in facing mirrors, it is sometimes hard to tell what are real and what are fantasy reflections. We live our lives according to media images. For example, instead of grieving, we go through "the seven-step grieving process," and instead

of coming to the end of something, we "bring about closure." Leslie Savan, in *Time* magazine (Dec. 16, 1996) under the title "Yadda, Yadda, Yadda," wrote "Oh, pulleeze, save us from choking on media-marinated catchphrases." Among the ones she listed were *No-brainer*; *Clueless*; *I hate when that happens*; *Same old, same old*; *Blah blah blah*; *Been there, done that*; *He's history*; *Not even close*; and *Hel-lo-oh!* She thinks these phrases are popular because they make speakers feel clever and in control: "It's as if they come with a built-in laugh track."

When 13 journalists played fictional roles as reporters in the 1997 Robert Zemeckis movie *Contact*, which starred Jodie Foster as a scientist decoding messages from outer space, there was an outpouring of criticism. In reaction, CNN instituted a new policy forbidding its reporters from appearing in movies. Marvin Kolb, who directs a center on the press and public policy at Harvard University, wrote in *Newsday* (Jul. 21, 1997): "If a reporter is to retain his credibility as a truth-teller, he has to stick to his craft and not confuse the viewer by playing an actor who plays a reporter telling fictional truths about space flight." Kalb also criticized Zemeckis for taking tapes of President Clinton speaking in totally different contexts and splicing them into the movie without White House permission. He warned that, in less playful hands, "the use of the presidential image and voice, deliberately misused for malicious purpose, could kick off a political or diplomatic crisis that no one needs."

When Jane Pauley was interviewed about the controversy by the *Philadelphia Inquirer*, she said that she was a real journalist and would never portray a fictional one on TV or in the movies. "It blurs the line. Viewers are confused enough about the hair and the makeup and the glamour. We already confuse them so much without crossing the line and suddenly becoming make-believe." Pauley had earlier declined to appear on the *Murphy Brown* television sitcom where real women journalists were invited to a fictional baby shower being given for the famous character played by Candice Bergen.

Connie Chung was featured as one of the journalists who went to the sitcom shower. Richard Nilsen posed the question in his *Arizona Republic* article on postmodernism: What's more real: Murphy Brown (Candice Bergen) doing *60-Minutes* segments on her television sitcom or Connie Chung, along with other "real" newswomen, making a guest appearance on *Murphy Brown* when they attended a shower for Murphy's fictional baby?

Because Dan Quayle chose to use the example of Murphy Brown having a baby "without a father" in one of his vice-presidential campaign speeches, Brown's fictional baby became very real on the political scene. *Murphy Brownism* entered the language, at least temporarily, to name the influence of the entertainment media on politics, as shown, for example, in the way life seemed to imitate art and the way public opinion was influenced in relation to the movies *Primary Colors* (1997) and *Wag the Dog* (1998).

Robert Klein in a *New York Times* article, "This Funny Business about Comedy and Politics" (Nov. 3, 1996), wrote that "somewhere along the line, the separation between theater and state broke down, and show biz and politics came crashing together with a blurry, amorphous thud." He added that in this "era of the unsubtle, of a hundred television channels, of music videos where no image dare linger on the screen for more than a nanosecond, the audience is assumed to have the attention span of an Egg McMuffin, and pyrotechnics are required to keep its attention."

Humor is part of the pyrotechnics. For example, in August of 1996, Comedy Central sent the team of Arianna Huffington, Chris Rock, Al Franken, and Bill Maher to cover the Democratic and Republican conventions under the title of "Indecision '96." Also, during that summer, polls found that one-fourth of the voting-age population got some of their information about presidential candidates from listening to the opening monologues of such TV comedians as David Letterman, Jay Leno, and Conan O'Brien. *New York Times* reporter James Bennett observed that "late-night comedians have an uncanny ability to peg which candidates'

qualities and what public miscues will stick in people's minds."

Another example of postmodernism is the way that the media makes fun of itself. Woody Allen's 1994 screenplay *Bullets over Broadway* relied for much of its humor on the fact that it was a play about a play. The 1987 comic movie *Hollywood Shuffle*, with Ludie Washington, Robert Townsend, and Keenen Ivory Wayans, provided starring roles for African Americans in Hollywood while making clever jokes about the lack of such jobs. Both the 1998 *The Truman Show* and the 1999 *ED TV* are about people being constantly on television.

The producers of the 1998 animated movie *A Bug's Life* went to painstaking efforts to create extra scenes to show during the closing credits. They were modeled after the outtakes (accidental goofs made during filming) that in the last decade have become popular jokes. Audiences were all the more amused because they realized that with animation there are no such things as quickie mistakes. As an added joke, after the first four weeks these "outtakes" were changed to a new set for the benefit of repeat viewers.

Stories and icons based on ideas related to artificial intelligence, morphing, and mutating have become increasingly popular, adding further to the confusion over what's real and what isn't. Children's toys based on such concepts started in the 1980s with the Teenage Mutant Ninja Turtles and progressed to the Mighty Morphin Power Rangers. At the turn of the century, some of the most popular children's books are about *animorphs*, while with adults the concepts are explored through science fiction and fantasy.

Because of this image overload many people long for the good old days when they didn't have so many facts and images to keep track of. "Yesterday's News May Be Antidote to '90s Overload" read a headline on a Marc Fisher story in the *Washington Post* (Feb. 4, 1997). Fisher told about both MSNBC and the Fox News Channel devoting hours each evening to showing old newscasts, while for 24 hours a day, the Classic Sports Network "recycles old Muhammad Ali fights, Michael Jordan's college games, Nolan Ryan no-hitters and the like." In a similar way, "Nick at Nite" shows reruns of old comedy shows. Fisher proposed that "the phenomenon has tapped into a popular desire to slow down the march of events just enough to comprehend something. There's so much new news that no story, no character has time to jell in the public mind." *See also* COMIC ZEITGEISTS, PARODY

Puns

The English meaning of *pun*, which comes from the Italian word *puntiglio* meaning "fine point," is the humorous use of a word in such a way as to suggest two or more of its meanings or the meaning of another word similar in sound. Even though puns are as often met with groans as with smiles, they still bring pleasure and surprise because the mind is forced to travel along at least two different routes when interpreting the same word or phrase. For example, when Victor Borge and his wife were introduced to figure skater Sonja Henie, Mrs. Borge complimented Henie by saying how young she looked. "Why not?" quipped Victor, "She's been on ice all her life."

Headline writers often use puns because in just a few words they can make a joke or an interesting allusion. Forward-thinking people also choose product names that have a potential for punning. This is what Henry Luce and Briton Hadden did in 1923 when they founded *Time* magazine. Here are just some of the puns that have been worked into marketing messages:

- *Time* flies (1924)
- *Time* marches on! (1932)
- *Time* to get the facts (1932)
- *Time*; it's brief (1938)
- It's *Time* (1944)
- *Time*—to get it straight (1951)
- A man hardly ever has *Time* all for himself (1954)
- This is the time to start reading *Time* (1960)
- Make time for *Time* (1989)

- Understanding comes with *Time* (1994).

Johnny Carson, in his *Tonight Show* routine as Karnak the Magnificent, was given the answers to which he would provide the questions, which often relied on puns. For example, for *Catch-22*, he came up with the question, "What would the Los Angeles Dodgers do if they were hit 100 pop flies?"

The majority of the winners in a *Boating* magazine contest for funny names on registered boats were puns: *Nauti By Nature, Ahoy-Vey, Pier Pressure, Berth Control,* and *Harvey Wharfbanger*. On Chinese New Years in Albuquerque, the New Mexico Race Walkers sponsor an annual *New Year Wok*, while in Big Sur, California, sponsors of a marathon solicited these names related to classical music to honor the orchestras and pianists who provide music along the route: *The Unfinished Hill, Crescendo at De Endo, Go-for-Baroque Hill,* and *Trouble Cliff*.

Not everyone is enchanted with such puns. Author Dennis Baron likens such names as *Mustard's Last Stand* (a hot dog restaurant), *The Wizard of Ooze* (a septic tank cleaner), *Currier and Chives* (a catering service), *Wreck-Amended* (an auto body shop), and *Curl Up and Dye* (a beauty shop) to "overripe camembert." He calls them "public cutespeak" and conjectures that enjoying these names has to be "an acquired taste." While he may be right, there are undoubtedly many people who have acquired the taste. Business consultants say that such names are memorable and that they help a business stand out from competitors in a shopping mall or in the yellow pages of a phone directory. However, they also caution against playful names for companies wanting to go national or worldwide because cute names sound too frivolous to inspire investors. *Arby*'s (from the initials of *Roast Beef*) is one of the few national companies whose name is a pun. Like other "good" puns, it succeeds because of its subtlety. But speakers don't actually want to be so subtle that their joke is missed. When it looks like there's some danger of that happening, they offer the pseudo-apology, "no pun intended," which, contrary to the meaning of the spoken words, has the effect of focusing attention on the pun.

Groaning at puns usually occurs after long, shaggy-dog stories contrived to accommodate a pun or when a conversation is interrupted by someone plucking out a word and creating a pun that doesn't relate to what's being said. More than 200 years ago, lexicographer/writer Samuel Johnson said, "People that make puns are like wanton boys that put coppers on the railroad tracks. They amuse themselves and other children, but their little trick may upset a freight train of conversation for the sake of a battered witticism." In spite of this criticism, Johnson's poetry contains many puns, just as Shakespeare's does. The best puns are those that fit so well into a conversation that they increase the level of understanding for those who catch on without interrupting the conversation's flow for those who miss the point. For example in *Romeo and Juliet*, when Mercutio is bleeding to death and says, "Ask for me tomorrow and you shall find me a grave man," listeners are not inspired to stop and laugh; in fact, it may be only on a subconscious level that the pun helps them understand the "graveness" of the situation.

In 1979, John Crosbie, a Canadian writer and publisher, founded the International Save the Pun Foundation, which publishes a monthly newsletter, *The Pundit*, and produces a list of the "Ten Best Stressed Puns of the Year." After Crosbie's death in 1994, Norman Gilbert, a financial planner in Toronto became "Chairman of the Bored." More than 1,500 members from around the world belong to the organization, which also honors a POTY (Punster of the Year). The year that author and collector Richard Lederer won, he said as part of his acceptance speech at the annual April First dinner in Chicago, "A good pun is like a good steak—a rare medium well done." *See also* JOKE PATTERNS, LANGUAGE PLAY

Further reading: Dennis Baron, *Declining Grammar and Other Essays on the English Vocabulary* (1989). Jonathan Culler (ed.), *On Puns: The Foundation of Letters* (1988). Don Hauptman, *Cruel and Unusual Puns* (1991).

Puppets and Puppeteers

Puppets are similar to dolls except that they are used for theatrical purposes and are moved mechanically by a puppeteer, who tries to make it look like the puppet is in control. Puppet-like figures have been found in 4,000-year-old tombs and ruins of ancient Egypt, Greece, and Rome. These early figures were apparently used for entertainment as well as for links to the underworld or afterlife. Ancient stories are told about devious leaders manipulating superstitious followers by secretly moving the eyes or arms of icons or religious puppets.

In the Middle Ages, court jesters used mock scepters topped with blown-up pigs' bladders. When the jester wanted to say something critical or scathing, he would "hide" behind the scepter and use it as his alter ego to express social satire and dissatisfaction. Since the criticism was in the form of comedy and coming from an inanimate object, kings were free to either accept or ignore the information, much as today's politicians do when they are criticized by comedians.

At the same time, puppet shows were being used to educate the masses about important stories, concepts, and morals found in the Bible. The term *marionette* ("little Mary") is thought to be an eponym based on the Mother of Christ, who was one of the most popular figures in such religious performances.

As puppeteers became increasingly humorous and used puppets to tease the clergy, priests began to worry that such burlesques were inappropriate in sacred meetings. Their discomfort was exacerbated by the fact that performances outside the church, in fairs and parks, were becoming racier and more entertaining. As a result, puppets were excluded from church and installed only as street entertainment.

Lifelike puppets engaged in buffoonery, and slapstick, situational, and verbal humor. Even though these early puppets had rigid features and body parts, and their physical characteristics were exaggerated, they exerted an enigmatic appeal; the unseen puppeteer manipulated miniature people just as an unseen God seemed to manipulate the lives of those watching the shows. An extra bonus for audiences was that the street puppets would often "rebel," and express themselves in sexual or vulgar ways not allowed to real people.

There are basically four kinds of puppets: hand, shadow, string (or marionettes), and the dummies used by ventriloquists. The most common and the simplest to operate are hand puppets, sometimes augmented by hidden rods that help to bring extra movement. Throughout Asia, shadow puppetry, using a bright light shining from behind a cotton or silk screen, is a serious and respected form of theater. The audience sits on the opposite side of the screen and sees only the moving shadows of the puppets, whose sizes can be increased or decreased depending on how far from the light they are held. The most common shadow puppets are cut from flat pieces of leather and are operated by rods made of bamboo or animal bone.

In the 18th century, permanent puppet theaters were established throughout Europe and in Mexico City, New York, and Quebec. Sophisticated audiences enjoyed parodies of the fashionable operas and dramas of the time, performed mostly by marionettes or string puppets. They also enjoyed satire and witty commentary on social and political events of the day. In the 1870s, several U.S. puppet companies made round-the-world tours performing musical fantasies, pantomimes, minstrel shows, and variety programs.

During the early 1900s, as vaudeville became fashionable in the United States, large puppet companies shrank and puppet shows were shortened to fit into the 10-minute slots allotted to vaudeville acts. As puppets lost some of their popular appeal, they returned to being viewed as an artistic or educational medium. Between 1920 and 1940, several colleges offered courses in puppet making, and puppets again became teaching tools. During World War II, many puppeteers were called into service; even so, puppetry gained status as an inexpensive and portable form of entertainment for the troops and for people in war-torn countries. And at home, people

who lacked the money necessary to produce most kinds of shows found that they could make puppets and produce shows, as depicted in Anne Tyler's 1980 novel, *Morgan's Passing*.

Today, the art of puppetry is a respected medium in both education and entertainment. The Puppeteers of America is an international organization with members from the United States, Canada, and 20 other countries. The Union Internationale des Marionettes (UNIMA), with headquarters in Warsaw, Poland, has national chapters in the United States, Canada, and 15 other countries. Puppet centers have also been established in Atlanta; Boston; Toronto; London; and New York.

In September 1998 the Jim Henson Foundation in New York City, assisted by several other sponsors, presented an 18-day International Festival of Puppet Theater. Shows were performed in 13 theaters throughout the city with puppet troupes coming from 16 different countries. Productions ranged from an adaptation of the opera *Sweeney Todd*, featuring masks, life-sized puppets, and special effects, to an unusual example of shadow theater by Balinese master I Wayan Wija and San Francisco theater artist Larry Reed. Of the 28 shows, 17 were specifically identified as "for adults." This major undertaking is planned for every other year, with some of the shows touring nationally after the event.

Given below in chronological order are brief descriptions of some of the world's most famous puppets and puppeteers. The listing illustrates the changes that have taken place, while also revealing some of the features that make puppets both emotionally and intellectually appealing.

Punch and Judy: Around 1600, an Italian actor from Naples invented a puppet named *Polcinella* ("little chicken"). Polcinella became so popular that many imitations were made, and by 1660 the beak-nosed little man was appearing in London under the name of *Punchinello*, shortened to *Punch*. By 1742, "Punch and Joan his Wife" were playing in Philadelphia. Punch's humor was outrageous and physical. His ribald and hilarious escapades inevitably ended in a fight either with his wife (who came to be called *Judy*), the law, or death itself. Audience members expressed their pleasure or displeasure by the hitting of wooden "slapsticks," similar to those later used in vaudeville. The sheer lunacy of Punch's anti-social behavior combined with audience participation made these shows popular. In the 1870s, many "Punch men" came to the United States from England. They used portable booths and worked alone, operating Punch on their right hand and all other characters on their left. By the turn of the 20th century, practically every American was familiar with Punch and Judy.

Pinocchio: Although there have been thousands of pictures and hundreds of reproductions made, Pinocchio's beginning was not as an actual puppet but as a puppet character in a children's book published in 1883. Its author, C. Collodi (Carlo Lorenzini), lived in Florence, Italy, where he was a government official and a journalist. In this most successful of his children's stories, Collodi captured such universal archetypes as the creator (Gepetto), the wise and good mother (the Blue Fairy), the temptations of life (Pinocchio's waywardness), the journey of discovery and reuniting in a new relationship (Gepetto and Pinocchio meeting in the belly of the Dogfish), the young person passing a significant test and being rewarded (Pinnochio managing their escape and soon afterwards becoming a real boy).

Edgar Bergen and Charlie McCarthy: The first radio performers were forced to be creative in devising ways to represent different voices on the air. Edgar Bergen's technique was to use dummies. He had several, but Charlie McCarthy is the one that found his way into the hearts of Americans. It was fortunate for Bergen that he and Charlie could grow famous on radio because, while Bergen was a genius at creating both sides of a conversation, his skill at ventriloquism was limited; he moved his lips. Nevertheless, Charlie McCarthy became such a part of American life that even Candice Bergen (Edgar's daughter) said she was jealous—Charlie had his own room and more clothes than she did.

Charlie was the only one in all of show business who could get away with insulting W. C. Fields.

Kukla, Fran, and Ollie: Wesley Hyatt wrote in *The Encyclopedia of Daytime Television* that "if any children's series designed for television can be termed a 'classic,' *Kukla, Fran, and Ollie* deserves that distinction" for the seamless way the show was put together with ad-libbed lines, songs, and advertisements for RCA Victor. The show was first seen in 1939 in Chicago and became a series in 1947. In 1948 it was made a Midwest network show, and in 1952 became an NBC national daytime show. *Kukla, Fran, and Ollie* ran first as a half-hour Sunday show, and then daily from 5:00 P.M. to 5:05 P.M. The Sunday show had a studio audience, pianist Jack Fascinato and his 12-piece orchestra, and announcer Hugh Downs, who at the time was a Chicago TV personality. Puppeteer Burr Tillstrom worked the hand puppets from beneath the stage, while actress Fran Allison appeared in front and interacted with the puppets. Kukla was a bald-headed and round-nosed, somewhat whiny little man, while Ollie (Oliver J. Dragon) was a lovable creature with one large tooth coming out from his upper lip. Miscellaneous characters (known as Kuklapolitans) included Buelah the Witch, Madam Ooglepuss, Colonel Crackie, Cecil Bill, Doloras Dragon, Mercedes Rabbit, and Fletcher Rabbit.

The Howdy Doody Show: The first children's television show to become a hit was hosted by radio star Buffalo Bob Smith. It premiered on 27 December 1947, and stayed on the air through 24 September 1960, for 2,343 episodes. Its original name, *The Puppet Playhouse*, was soon changed to honor its star, Howdy Doody, a marionette who missed the grand opening because creator Frank Paris was still working on him. The puppet who was destined to become a pop culture hero got his name from the "Howdy Doody" greeting of a stock cowboy character on Smith's NBC radio show, *The Triple B Ranch*. Howdy Doody was designed to fit in with the Western theme of the show and was given 48 freckles, one for each state. He interacted not only with the show's host Buffalo Bob, but also with such other marionettes as Phineas T. Bluster and Dilly Dally. He became the star both because of his appearance (the cowboy doll in Disney's 1995 *Toy Story* looks a lot like him) and his euphonious name. In his daily greeting to the studio audience, Smith would shout, "What time is it?" and the kids would shout back, "It's Howdy Doody time!"

Beany and Cecil: During the 1950s, *Time for Beany*, a 15-minute puppet adventure for children, was an Emmy-winning show syndicated from Los Angeles. The main characters were Beany, a cheerful boy who always wore a propellor-topped beanie; Beany's uncle, Captain Huffenpuff, owner of the Leakin' Lena boat; and Beany's pet, a seasick serpent named Cecil. Director Bob Clampett also created such miscellaneous characters as Moon Mad Tiger, Jack Webfoot, Marilyn Mongrel, Louis the Lone Shark, Dizzy Lou and Hey You, and the Double Feature Creature with the Stereophonic Sound. Each show included four adventures, puns galore, and great spoofs. Voices were provided by Stan Freberg, Daws Butler, and Jerry Colonna. The close relationship between puppetry and animation was illustrated in 1961 when the live puppet show was changed into a *Beany and Cecil* cartoon, which ABC showed as a weekend feature from 1963 until 1988.

Shari Lewis and Lamb Chop: Next to Lamb Chop, Shari Lewis's most famous hand puppets were Hush Puppy and Charlie Horse. Lewis began her career in 1952, when at age 19 she was winner of an Arthur Godfrey talent show and was hired as a regular performer on the *Captain Kangaroo Show*. This led to her own *Shari Lewis Show*, which for many years was a Saturday morning offering on NBC. She later moved to PBS where her show was *The Charlie Horse Music Pizza*. She was awarded a dozen Emmys, a Peabody Award, seven Parents' Choice Awards, and a ROMMIE for her 1995 CD-ROM *Lamb Chop Loves Music*. Much of her humor was based on wordplay and tricks, as in the non-

sense of her "Never-Ending Song." Besides performing for children, Lewis did nightclub shows in Las Vegas and Southern California, where she worked with puppets named Zsa Zsa and Phyllis. They compared measurements and went on unending searches for men, while a tipsy Lamb Chop, in his adult mode, went searching for martinis. Lewis's latest show was still being syndicated when she was diagnosed with uterine cancer in June of 1998. She died two months later at age 65.

Jim Henson and the Muppets: When in June of 1998, *Time* magazine chose its 100 most influential people of the 20th century, it honored Jim Henson for having "had the most profound influence on children of any entertainer of his time; he adapted the ancient art of puppetry to the most modern of mediums, television, transforming both." Henson had just graduated from high school when he made his first puppet and applied for a job on a children's television show. While he studied art and theater design at the University of Maryland, he did a twice-daily five-minute

Not only did Jim Henson's Muppets help make *Sesame Street* the most popular children's show of all time, they also proved that puppets still held a charm for adults. *NBC/Globe Photos Inc.*

Sam and Friends puppet show on a Maryland television channel. Kermit, his famous frog, was one of the "Friends," and through the 1960s, Henson and Kermit made appearances on the *Today* show and other variety programs. His big break came in 1969 when Joan Ganz Cooney, the director of the Children's Television Workshop hired him for *Sesame Street*. While Henson, who died unexpectedly in 1990, was careful not to take credit for the success of *Sesame Street*, everyone agreed that Henson's muppets: Bert, Ernie, Big Bird, Grover, the Cookie Monster, and others, were a big part of the show's appeal. Cooney is happy to give him credit, saying that the group had a collective genius, but that Henson was the only individual genius. "He was our era's Charlie Chaplin, Mae West, W. C. Fields, and Marx Brothers." With *The Muppet Show*, which was syndicated from 1976 to 1981, Henson proved that adults could be as charmed by his muppets as were children. The show was the most widely viewed series in the world. Some 235 million viewers watched the antics of Miss Piggy, Fozzie Bear, Gonzo, The Swedish Chef, and Dr. Strangepork. Guest stars, pleased at the chance to interact with the world's most famous puppets, included George Burns, Zero Mostel, Steve Martin, and Peter Sellers. Rudolf Nureyev danced a *pas de deux* from "Swine Lake" with Miss Piggy, and Elton John sang "Crocodile Rock" backed by a chorus of Muppet crocodiles. *See also* ANIMATION, CHILDREN'S TELEVISION

Further reading: Wesley Hyatt, *The Encyclopedia of Daytime Television* (1997); Harold B. Segel, *Pinocchio's Progeny: Puppets, Marionettes, Automatons, and Robots in Modernist and Avantgarde Drama* (1995). Dina Sherzer and Joel Sherzer, *Humor and Comedy in Puppetry: Celebration in Popular Culture* (1987).

Put-Downs and Rejoinders

Put-downs and rejoinders are the witty insults and the come-backs that clever people devise, especially when they think they have been insulted. Put-down humor is best appreciated when it occurs between people of equal status who respect each other and so can enjoy the teasing as a display of wit rather than meanness. Celebrity roasts succeed because the person being roasted is clearly respected, but when put-down humor crosses levels of power as when parents or teachers use it against children, bosses use it against employees, or popular kids use it against unpopular kids, then the discomfort may outweigh the humor. Snappy rejoinders are also funnier when the person on the receiving end has somehow "asked for it."

A classic example is the exchange between George Bernard Shaw and Winston Churchill in which Shaw sent Churchill two tickets to a new play with an accompanying note, "Dear Sir Winston. Here are two tickets to the opening night of my latest play, for you and a friend, if you have one." Churchill returned the tickets with, "Dear Mr. Shaw. Unfortunately, I am unable to attend the opening night; however, I would appreciate two tickets to the second night performance, if there is one."

Shaw was a notorious curmudgeon, especially with aspiring authors who had the nerve to send him their manuscripts in hopes of getting some hints on their writing or a recommendation to a publisher. Shaw wrote back to one, "The covers of your book are too far apart," and to another who had glued two pages together as a test to see whether the whole manuscript was read, "You don't have to eat a whole egg to know it's rotten." A country parson, after hearing that Shaw was an expert at brewing coffee, wrote and asked for his secrets. When Shaw forwarded the recipe, he added the note, "I hope this is an honest request and not a surreptitious mode of securing my autograph." The parson wrote back, enclosing Shaw's signature cut from his letter, "Accept my thanks for the recipe. I wrote in good faith so allow me to return what is obviously to you infinitely prized, but which is of no value to me, your autograph."

When William Gladstone attacked fellow statesman Benjamin Disraeli in front of the British Parliament by saying that Disraeli would die "either on the gallows or of a horrible disease," Disraeli responded, "That depends on whether I embrace your principles or your mistress." On another occasion, Disraeli said that if a traveler should come to England and be informed that such a man as Lord John Russell was leader of the House of Commons, the stranger would begin to comprehend how the Egyptians once worshipped an insect.

When the sexy, blonde actress Jean Harlow was introduced to Lady Margot Asquith, widow of the former British prime minister, Harlow kept mispronouncing Lady Asquith's first name, calling her *Mar-gott*. In exasperation, Lady Asquith explained, "My dear, the *t* is silent, as in *Harlow*." A "friend" who met actress Ilka Chase shortly after Chase had published a book said, "I enjoyed it immensely; who wrote it for you?" Chase responded, "I'm so glad you liked it; who read it to you?"

A particularly nasty kind of put-down is the one that on a first hearing sounds like a compliment, but which on examination turns out to be an insult, as when Dorothy Parker remarked on Katharine Hepburn's performance in a Broadway play: "She runs the gamut of emotions from A to B." Within professions and groups, comments that sound fine to outsiders are really insults to the insider. When a comic fails, for example, the next comic bounding to the stage offers the pseudo-sympathetic, "Gee man, tough crowd!" When architects say something like, "Obviously, there were very difficult aspects to the project and the site that had to be dealt with," they are usually saying that the building is a failure. Teachers frustrated by a student's lack of progress may say, "While there's no such thing as an error, if there were one, this would be it," and "You've really

worked hard here, and I know you will do even better next time." In academia, to say that a professor is a "good committee member" is to say he or she isn't a scholar; in legal circles, it is damning with faint praise to say that an attorney "is a member of all the regular organizations."

Put-down humor became popular on television in the late 1960s and 1970s when it provided running gags for the Smothers Brothers, Sonny and Cher, and Donny and Marie Osmond. A currently popular pattern of insult humor is the "Full Deckism," named from the cliche, "He's not playing with a full deck." Other examples of this pattern are ". . . a few bricks shy of a load," and ". . . a few sandwiches short of a picnic." Other formulaic insults include, "He was fired from McDonald's for having a short attention span," "His family tree doesn't fork," and "She has a room-temperature IQ." The influence from modern technology is seen in such put-downs as

- She's not running on full thrusters.
- He fired his retro rockets a little late.
- She dropped her second stage too soon.
- His solar panels are aimed at the moon.
- She's running at 300 baud.
- His reset line is glitching.

See also EXAGGERATION, POLITICS AND HUMOR, WIT

Further reading: Reinhold Aman, *Maledicta Monitor* (1992). James C. Humes, *The Wit and Wisdom of Benjamin Franklin* (1995). ———, *The Wit and Wisdom of Winston Churchill* (1994). Maria Leach (ed.), *The Ultimate Insult* (1996).

R

Radio

Radio humor developed through music, vaudeville acts, variety shows, skits, sitcoms, talk shows, quiz shows, and the work of commentators whose acts ranged from reading the Sunday "funnies" to discussing the news of the day. In the history of comedy, radio fills a surprisingly brief time slot. It began in the late 1920s and was, for the most part, gone by the early 1960s when the American public turned to television for its laughs. However, the influence of radio humor is still felt on virtually all performance humor that has followed.

Radio audiences were not satisfied with the constant repetition of the gags that had worked in vaudeville: thus comedians were forced to create characters and to place them in contexts. Because radio left so much for listeners to fill in, audiences were grateful when they had some knowledge to fall back on, as when the programs or the jokes centered around characters who were familiar. Audiences appreciated long-running gags as well as recognizable stereotypes and locations. They looked forward to their weekly visit to *Duffy's Tavern* and their weekly chance on *Vic and Sade* to catch up with news from the Gook family's hometown of Crooner, Illinois.

Radio was the first medium to make it possible for the entire country to know and relate simultaneously to the same comedians, characters, and stories. Suddenly radio listeners had many new names to remember; it helped considerably when producers thought up names that not only identified their characters but also gave hints about their roles or their personalities as with *Fibber* McGee, *Baby* Snooks, the *Great* Gildersleeve, and the *Bicker*sons. Scriptwriter Paul Rhymer used a different kind of name humor for *Vic and Sade* where he wrote about a man named *Rishigan Fishigan of Sishigan, Michigan,* who married *Jane Bane of Pane, Maine.* One of Uncle Fletcher's friends was an armed guard at the *Ohio State Home for the Tall*, and another one died after moving to *Dismal Seepage, Ohio,* by way of *Sweet Esther, Wisconsin.*

Many of today's jokes are built on the comic foils that were developed in the early days of radio, such as the high school English teacher played by Eve Arden on *Our Miss Brooks* (1948–1957) and the "dumb blonde" created by Jane Ace on *The Easy Aces* (1930–1949), as well as Gracie on *Burns and Allen* (1932–1950), Marie Wilson on *My Friend Irma* (1947–1954), and Lucille Ball on *My Favorite Husband* (1948–1951). The generation gap is still illustrated by portray-

Note: Program names are the ones that proved most lasting, but specific names were frequently altered to accommodate new sponsors or network changes. Dates are also approximate because, when shows were between sponsors or when cast members were drafted into World War II military service, the shows would be off the air for a few months or in some cases a year or more.

als of befuddled parents and raging teenagers much like those shown on *A Date with Judy* (1941–1950), *Meet Corliss Archer* (1943–1955), *The Adventures of Ozzie and Harriet* (1944–1954), and *My Little Margie* (1952–1955). The most popular of all the family shows, *The Aldrich Family*, premiered in July of 1939 and was a hit for the next 14 years. It always opened with Alice Aldrich calling "Hen-Reee! Henry Aldrich!" which was answered by a cracking adolescent voice, "Coming, Mother!"

This opening line demonstrates the importance of voice humor on radio. Audiences appreciated such unique voices as the gravelly voice of Eddie Anderson, who played Rochester on *The Jack Benny Program*; the down-to-earth alto of Shirley Booth, who, long before she played *Hazel* on television, was a star on *Duffy's Tavern*; and the Brooklynese "Ink-a-dink" style of Jimmy Durante, who on his show (1943–1950) mangled "da big woids just ta hear 'em scream." To make characters sound different from each other, performers stuttered, used nasal twangs, and spoke in falsetto and in various dialects. Marian Jordan's voice on *Fibber McGee and Molly* aroused an image of a strong and long-suffering wife, but when she played Teeny, she used a totally different baby voice, "Whatcha doin', huh, mister, whatcha doin'?" Three other "children" who played prominent roles in early radio were Fanny Brice's Baby Snooks, Edgar Bergen's Charlie McCarthy, and Red Skelton's Junior, more commonly known as the "mean widdle kid." Baby Snooks was the darling of the three, while Charlie McCarthy and Junior were the bad boys.

The need for different-sounding voices encouraged the creation of comedy teams in which one person would serve as a stooge. The different ranges of male and female voices provided a natural advantage for such teams as George Burns and Gracie Allen, Fred Allen and Portland Hoffa, and Jack Benny and Mary Livingston. When a comedy team was made up of two men, the men would exaggerate their differences, as did Bud Abbott, the level-headed straight man, and Lou Costello, his screaming and hair-brained partner. One of Eddie Cantor's stooges was The Mad Russian, played in a thick Slavic accent by Bert Gordon, while Phil Baker did skits with his butler, Bottle, a "veddy-veddy English chap" played by Harry McNaughton.

Because radio humor had to be communicated only through sound, language play was a big part of it. Danny Kaye was a master at tongue-twisters, doubletalk, and dialects. The malapropisms spoken by Jane Ace on *The Easy Aces* became the witticisms of her day as when she complained about "the fly in the oatmeal," and said that "time wounds all heels," "Congress is still in season," and "I've been working my head to the bone." On *Duffy's Tavern* the writer of the show, Ed Gardner, played the role of Archie and offered such malapropisms as "I tink you've give me da mucous of an idea," and "Listen, Eddie, wit good management, dis place could show a nice overhead."

Some radio performers moved directly from vaudeville to radio and then directly to television, but the transitions were not always successful because radio had its unique demands, one of which was speed. Except for being a foil for Edgar Bergen's Charlie McCarthy, W. C. Fields failed on radio because he took too long to develop his jokes. Milton Berle also failed on radio, but was a huge success on television where audiences could see his facial and body humor and his bizarre costumes. Art Linkletter's *People Are Funny* (1942–1959) was equally successful on radio and television, as was Bob Hope, who began his first radio show in 1935. Hope used a rapid-fire approach that barely gave audiences time to catch their breaths between punch lines. Although Hope's humor was topical, it was the forerunner of the comedy monologues now seen on late-night TV.

The dozen shows listed here in roughly chronological order are not necessarily the "best" of radio humor, but they are a representative sampling chosen to illustrate the evolution of radio humor.

The Amos and Andy Show (1929–1954): Two white actors, Freeman F. Gosden and Charles J. Correll, created the leading characters for this sitcom, which is generally acknowledged as the first great radio show. The characters were Black, and part of the humor was in the way Gosden and Correll performed more than 100 distinct voices, ranging from that of the conniving Kingfish to the shuffling Lightnin' who in a high pitched drawl would say "Yazzah. Ah'll jus' whiz right on ovah deah!" The show was such a favorite that in the 1930s, movie theaters had a nightly intermission at seven o'clock when they would pipe in the 15-minute radio program so that moviegoers could keep up with the story. After his visit to America, George Bernard Shaw said, "There are three things I'll never forget about America: The Rocky Mountains, Niagara Falls, and *Amos and Andy*.

Stoopnagle and Budd (1931–1938): The Frederick Taylor and Budd Hulick partnership was formed in an emergency when the Buffalo, New York, station where they had minor jobs failed to receive a network show. To fill in, Taylor played the organ while Hulick made chatter and kept referring to Taylor as *Colonel Stoopnagle*. They were a local sensation and were soon brought to New York City where they did a *Gloom Chasers* show. Their humor was a forerunner to that of Bob and Ray. On *Stoopnocracy* they read fake letters from listeners giving advice on such things as how to "eliminate the backward swing of hammocks" or making such suggestions as cutting out the insides of soap bars so they would be all gone when the good part was used up.

The Eddie Cantor Show (1931–1949): Eddie Cantor was the first of the headliners from vaudeville to make it big in radio. He preceded by a year or more Al Jolson, Ed Wynn, Fred Allen, and Jack Benny, and by several years Bing Crosby and Bob Hope. One of his lasting contributions is that he arranged to have a studio audience as participants, in fact, two of them—one for dress rehearsal and another six hours later for the performance. In the experimental days of the 1920s, audiences were either banned or were warned by "On the Air" signs to be absolutely quiet. Cantor changed all that by encouraging laughing, clapping, and cheering. He made his family life a part of his routines, and in their own way the five Cantor daughters were almost as famous as the Dionne quintuplets. Cantor took credit for having introduced such performers as George Burns and Gracie Allen, Bobby Breen, Deanna Durbin, Billie Burke, and Margaret Whiting.

The Jack Benny Program (1931–1955): Jack Benny was a master at timing and delivery. With his wife, whose stage name was Mary Livingston, Benny became one of the all-time great radio performers. While he was not known for writing his jokes (Fred Allen quipped that Benny couldn't ad-lib a belch after a Hungarian dinner), he was a master at judging what audiences would find funny. He became his own longest-running joke by doing variations on the theme of his stinginess: putting only one precious gallon of gas in his Maxwell car, installing multiple locks on his safe, and having both a human and a polar-bear guard. In a 1948 episode, Benny went to Ronald Colman's house to borrow the Oscar that Colman had won for his role in *A Double Life*. A hold-up man shoved a gun in Benny's ribs and demanded, "Your money or your life." The audience's tittering grew as the silence extended. Then came the robber's questioning, "Well?" followed by an even longer pause. While the audience waited, nervously giggling, the pause grew and grew, followed by another "Well?" After an excruciating silence, Benny responded with an irked, "I'm thinking! I'm thinking!" What followed was the longest laugh in radio history.

Vic and Sade (1932–1944): Paul Rhymer was the creator of this story of "radio's homefolks" who lived "in the little house halfway up in the next block." Vic Gook was played by Art Van Harvey, whose unique manner of speaking was a mixture of Hoosier accent and second-generation German. Sade Gook was played by Bernardine Flynn, a talented actress who spoke her lines with a nasal twang. Vic and Sade lived in Crooper, Illinois, with Rush, a "son" they had inherited from a poor relative. Although Crooper townspeople never appeared on the show, listeners learned all about them from letters, one-sided phone calls, and the Gooks's conversations. In 1940 Van Harvey had a heart attack, and rather than trying to bring in a new Vic, Rhymer brought in Clarence Hartzell to play the part of a visiting Uncle Fletcher. When Van Harvey recovered and returned to the show, Uncle Fletcher stayed on.

Burns and Allen (1932–1950): George Burns and Gracie Allen moved to radio from vaudeville and then went on to succeed a third time when they moved to television. Probably because of their long apprenticeship in vaudeville, Gracie had difficulty adjusting to radio. To get away from her "mike fright," Burns and Allen insisted on having live audiences. They brought continuity to their show through running gags, one of which was about Gracie looking for her lost brother, while another one was about Gracie running for president on the Surprise party ticket. Her campaign booklet was published by the Gracie Allen Self-Delusion Institute. Even though Burns and Allen were married in 1926, they first performed as singles. By the early 1940s they began appearing as husband and wife and they moved away from the style they had used in vaudeville and closer to that of situation comedy.

The Fred Allen Show (1934–1949): In 1934, Fred Allen began his *Town Hall Tonight* weekly show, often remembered for the feud that Allen started with Jack Benny. Allen's show was on Wednesday nights and he began by wisecracking about Benny's violin. On Sunday, Benny bristled back and on it went, until on 14 March 1937, the "battle of the century" was staged in which Allen and Benny went off-mike for a fight. Audiences were never told exactly who won, but it didn't matter because the feud kept going through the next decade, culminating in a "King for a Day" spoof where Benny posed as a contestant on Allen's show and won the grand prize. It included a pressing job on his baggy suit. Benny was stripped to his shorts and awarded his prize right there in front of the studio

audience. In 1940, *Town Hall Tonight* was renamed *The Fred Allen Show*. The format included the Mighty Allen Art Players, a gimmick borrowed three decades later by Johnny Carson, who openly acknowledged his admiration for Fred Allen as the wittiest man he ever knew.

Fibber McGee and Molly (1935–1957): Jim and Marian Jordan were Midwestern childhood sweethearts, whose first radio job was playing the O'Henry twins for $10 a week on a station in Peoria, Illinois. It was a lucky day for all concerned when, in 1931, they met Don Quinn, a cartoonist who wanted to write for radio. They had a lifelong collaboration, which began with Quinn writing a show called *Smackout* about a neighborhood grocer who was always "smackout" of whatever the customers wanted. The show ran for four years in Chicago, but when it went national in 1935 it was changed to *Fibber McGee and Molly*. The McGees lived at 79 Wistful Vista and early on did mostly vaudeville tricks, including the famous opening of Fibber McGee's closet. Over the years, Marian insisted that the show become more realistic, a move that apparently pleased listeners. In 1941, the show won the ratings wars by topping Jack Benny and Bob Hope.

The Henry Morgan Show (1940–1950): Henry Morgan was "the bad boy of radio," who livened up the reading of commercials by throwing in barbs about the product, while he livened up the reading of weather reports with such statements as "snow tomorrow, followed by small boys with sleds and dignified old men getting conked . . . ." The U.S. Navy put a stop to Morgan's frivolous weather forecasts, while more than one sponsor put a stop to his comments by canceling their support. He lost his sponsorship from the makers of Life Savers after he offered to sell *Morgan's Mint Middles* made from the centers drilled out by the conniving manufacturers.

The Red Skelton Show (1941–1953): When Red Skelton received his first radio job offer, he was best known as a pantomimist, something virtually useless on radio. He solved the problem by creating a cast of characters and giving them unique names and unique voices. The best known was Junior, "the mean widdle kid," whose signature line was "I dood it again!" Skelton also created Clem Kadiddlehopper, the singing cab driver, and Deadeye, the fastest gun in the West. Ozzie Nelson was the bandleader on Skelton's show, and it was here that Harriet Nelson developed her own comic talent. Ozzie and Harriet became regulars interacting with Skelton, but when Skelton was drafted into the army in 1944, Ozzie and Harriet went off to their own radio show. When Skelton came back in December of 1945, he regrouped and went on to a new success, followed by even greater success when, in 1953, he moved to television where he could put his talent at miming to use.

The Bob and Ray Show (1946–1953): Bob Elliott and Ray Goulding brought spontaneity to radio comedy. They were the forerunners of skit-comedy and improv, and continued working as a team long after their own show ended. They worked without a script and had great fun spoofing sportscasters, other performers, and especially advertisers. While ribbing the commercial premium offers that were popular, they offered their own "Little Jim Dandy Burglar Kit" and "The Bob and Ray Home Surgery Kit." Their closing lines were "This is Ray Goulding, reminding you to write if you get work . . ." "And Bob Elliott, reminding you to hang by your thumbs."

Groucho Marx's **You Bet Your Life** (1947–1959): People thought it was a comedown for comedian Groucho Marx to take the job of hosting a radio quiz show, but he soon made the job into something worthy of his reputation. Contestants went through a series of interviews and tryouts, but for the sake of preserving spontaneity Marx did not meet them or see them until the show. By the third year of Marx's reign, the show was among the top 10 radio shows, and by 1951 *You Bet Your Life* was also broadcast on television. If the contestants were funny, Marx would let them shine, but if they were sobersides, he would shine. Once, when he had a woman

going on and on about how much she loved her husband, he stopped her with, "I love my cigar, but I take it out of my mouth once in a while."

While today's radio humor reaches smaller audiences, it still has loyal followers. Many disc jockeys and talk show hosts have a community of listeners that they entertain with a running patter of jokes and witty observations between records and phone calls. Shock-jock Howard Stern is one of the most famous for his satire and his insult humor.

National Public Radio (NPR) has been unusually supportive of humorous programs and several shows have developed niche audiences. NPR brought fame to both Garrison Keillor and his comedy/musical show and to Peter Schickele and his musical spoofs. The Peabody Award–winning *Car Talk* features brothers Tom and Ray Magliozzi, who on Saturday mornings answer questions about car repair and maintenance. They have been compared to the Smothers Brothers, Monty Python, A. J. Foyt, and the Marx Brothers. Their show has become so well known that the producers of *This American Life*, which is a blend of poignancy, observations, and humor, began describing their nebulous show, which each week has a different theme treated by various writers and performers, as *Car Talk* "except just one guy hosting. And no cars."

Wait Wait . . . Don't Tell Me is a weekly news quiz asking such questions as this one in July of 1999: "When Senator Daniel Patrick Moynihan said the following, 'I hope she goes all the way. I mean to go all the way with her,' about whom was he speaking?" (Hint: This was the week before he hosted Hillary Clinton's exploratory campaign meeting for the New York senatorial race.)

Michael Feldman's NPR show *Whad'Ya Know?* is also done in the style of a quiz show, but a four-page article in the July 1999 Delta *Sky* magazine teased that it was no more a quiz show than was Groucho Marx's *You Bet Your Life*. Since 1984, Feldman has broadcast from Madison, Wisconsin, where he specializes in Midwestern humor and laughingly admits that the live audiences are "there mainly for my benefit . . . I sort of prey on them." Unlike serious television talk show hosts, Feldman convinces his guests to share such secrets as did the truck driver who confessed to parking at truck stops but eating at other restaurants and the two women who went on a self-described *Thelma and Louise* weekend and "picked up two guys on campus last night—but it was dark and they couldn't tell how old we were." *See also* COMEDY TEAMS, DIALECT HUMOR, GENDER AND HUMOR, SITCOMS, TELELVISION

Regional Humor

Regional humor overlaps with country humor because the characteristics and the speaking patterns unique to a region of the country are more likely to show up in rural than in urban areas. Humor focusing on the values and traits of rural people appears across many genres, ranging from ancient fables (Aesop's *The Country Mouse and the City Mouse*) to comic strips (Al Capp's *L'il Abner*), from old-time radio (*Lum and Abner*) to movies (*Ma and Pa Kettle*), from personal memoirs (Betty MacDonald's *The Egg and I*) to variety shows (television's *Hee Haw*), from cowboy poetry and country-western songs to television sitcoms (*The Beverly Hillbillies* and *Northern Exposure*), from Texas "Aggie" jokes to Internet humor ("You Know You're in Maine if . . ."), and from such real-life events as greased pig contests at county fairs to tin cans tied on vehicles of newlyweds.

Country humor, whether created by outsiders or by rural people, serves both to amuse and to relieve frustrations. Its relationship to the term *corny* for something old-fashioned, sentimental, and unsubtle, hints at the lack of sophistication in most country humor. The term *corn belt* was used by comedians as a contrasting term to the upstate New York *Borsht Belt* where audiences were mostly Jewish vacationers from New York City. Robert Hendrickson in *The Henry Holt Encyclopedia of Word and Phrase Origins* (1987) says that "corn came to be known as 'what farmers feed pigs and comedians feed farmers.' Soon *corn-fed humor* became simply *corney jokes*, the phrase possibly helped along by the Italian word *carne* 'cheap meat,' being applied to the 'cheap jokes' the comedians told."

Between 1910 and 1920, one-third of all Americans lived on farms, but by the late 1990s fewer than 2 percent did. It is to be expected that such a change in demographics would be reflected in American humor. Cynthia Crossen writing in the *Wall Street Journal* (Jan. 31, 1997) said that 100 years ago typical American jokes were burlesques about naive immigrants, but today they are grotesques about yuppies. This change of subject matter, as well as a change in tone from beaming to whining, "mirrors the changes in America's soul . . . . The record shows the evolution of a people from innocent, hopeful, rural and God-fearing to plugged-in, ironic, inward-looking and dripping with ennui." Crossen quoted Mark O'Donnell, who recently adapted Moliere's *Les Fourberies de Scapin* for Broadway, "You can live out on the farm and still be jaded. It used to be the circus had to come to town. Now you have the circus 24 hours a day."

The appeal of country humor lies in its exaggerated and uninhibited tone inherited from frontier days when America was a country on the move. Those early settlers who painted "California or Bust!" on their wagons were the inventors of today's bumper stickers. Those who "signed" their names by carving them in sandstone walls along the trails were the precursors of today's taggers and graffiti artists, while frontiersmen with their tall tales and their ridiculing of greenhorns are the models for today's urban legends.

Jim Garry of Big Horn, Wyoming, who earns a living collecting and performing western stories, says that farmers and ranchers are subject to three uncontrollable forces: the weather, the bank, and the government. Thus, their humor is consistently fatalistic, even though in one region you'll hear stories about blizzards, in another floods, and in another droughts. The only rancher Garry ever saw smiling as he walked away from meeting with a loan officer at a bank explained, "I've won! There's no way I'll live long enough to have to pay this note off!"

Down East (Yankee) humor is stereo-typed as taciturn and reluctant, as in this story about Calvin Coolidge. He was seated next to a woman at an official White House function. When she leaned toward him and confided that someone had bet her that she couldn't make him say three words, he responded: "You lose."

While southern, and to a lesser extent western, dialects are filled with what are generally viewed as grammatical errors, New England dialects are instead shown through the use of archaic or old-fashioned verbs such as *clumb*, *tonk*, or *holp*. They make the characters sound quaint rather than ignorant. Tim Sample's "Postcards from Maine" are regularly shown on *CBS Sunday Morning*. He is an illustrator, writer, and performer in the style of Marshall Dodge, who in 1958 began recording *Bert & I* stories with Robert Bryan. Robert Skoglund, aka "The Humble Farmer," has a weekly radio show originating on Maine Public Radio. Joe Perham, Gary Crocker, Mark Easton, and Kendall Morse are other Maine humorists.

Francis Colburn specialized in Vermont humor when, in the early 1960s, he recorded "The Commencement Address." The New England Press published his *Letters from Home and Further Indiscretions* in 1979. Frank Bryan and Bill Mares have published *Real Vermonters Don't Milk Goats* and *Out! The Vermont Secession Book*. Since 1985, Jack Maxson has written a "Fenwick Snade" column for the Keene, New Hampshire, *Sentinel*. Snade lives in the fictional town of Piddlington and, according to the newsletter of the American Humor Studies Association, makes observations worthy of a latter-day Seba Smith, the frontier author who created Jack Downing of Downingville, the prototype for such later literary figures as Hosea Bigelow and Josh Billings.

The humor in Garrison Keillor's stories from the fictional Minnesota town of Lake Wobegon, "Where all the women are strong, all the men are good-looking and all the children are above average," comes as much from Keillor's revelations about small-town America as from his illustrations of characteristics unique to midwestern Lutherans.

Tourists in the upper Midwest can search out the Paul Bunyan Logging Camp near Eau Claire, Wisconsin, or while driving near Brainerd, Minnesota, they can stop at the legendary logger's mailbox and climb the ladder to drop in their letters. Other roadside attractions in Minnesota include a huge ear of corn mounted on a water tower near Rochester, a Jolly Green Giant near Blue Earth, an oversized snowman near North St. Paul, a huge Uncle Sam near Virginia, and the "World's Biggest Revolver" near Mankato. Each state has its own pieces of roadside architecture, whose creators have wanted to make a town or a business memorable through making viewers smile.

People in rural areas make jokes about their neighbors, especially if the neighbors are even more rural. Ohio residents have "Briar" jokes about newcomers from the "briar patches" of the South, people in New England have "Newfie" jokes about their neighbors from Newfoundland, Californians have "Zonie" jokes about visitors from Arizona, and people in Montana have jokes about those from the Dakotas.

Author Marvin Koller has described rural humor as "down-to-earth," as in the small Oklahoma town that each summer sponsors a "cow chip" throwing contest and the rural Ohio town that has a "chicken-flying" contest that measure how far a hen will fly when released from her coop. Vermillion, Ohio, stages a "wooly bear" festival to celebrate the amount of "fur" or "fuzz" on black and brown caterpillars. Other than having fun, the purpose of this festival is to predict whether the coming winter will be severe or mild, based on the kind of "wisdom" that has traditionally been offered in farmers' almanacs. *The Old Farmer's Almanac*, which has been published continuously since 1793, was founded by R. B. Thomas, who hit upon the idea of putting advice to rural readers in the form of salty comic speeches supposedly from a fellow farmer. Today, the *Old Almanac* resembles a cross between a magazine and a trivia book slanted toward rural interests. The editors do not include jokes as such but are still looking for ways to be entertaining as well as informative. For example, the 1999 edition had the expected weather predictions and humorous write-ups on various climatic conditions, plus such feature articles as "A Brief History of Briefs, and Boxers, Drawers, and Breeches," "Alcatraz Was Never No Good for Nobody," and "Why Elvis Carried His Own Utensils."

Ever since early Americans thumbed their noses at the British by turning the British-created *Yankee Doodle* song into a robust celebration of American independence, music has been one of the ways to celebrate being both American and "country." Singers in vaudeville and minstrel shows made jokes to the accompaniment of banjos and guitars, while country bands made music with washboards, buckets, gourds, and wooden whistles. In the 1940s, country singer and comedian Judy Canova was Republic Studio's top female star. She had her own radio show, considered the *Hee Haw* of its day, and earned over $8,000 a week. She wore clodhopper shoes, carried a cardboard suitcase, and braided her hair in pigtails. Republic Studios gave her a movie contract after she co-starred on Broadway with Buddy Ebsen in the 1939 *Yokel Boy*, where her most memorable scene was scrubbing the floor with brushes tied to roller skates.

During the 1950s, Homer and Jethro (Henry D. Haynes and Kenneth Burns) were popular musicians on radio's *National Barn Dance*, where Homer played a guitar and Jethro a mandolin. They gradually began to work more and more humor into the show. Their catch phrase of "Oooh, that's corny!" came out of an advertising campaign for cornflakes. During the 1960s, they were frequent performers on *Hee Haw* and later on Garrison Keillor's *Prairie Home Companion* public radio program.

Minnie Pearl was a singing teacher in the early 1940s when she performed her comical man-starved spinster act at a banker's convention near her home in Centerville, Tennessee. She was invited to appear on Tennessee's WSM radio and *The Grand Ole Opry*. Through the late 1960s and on into the 1970s, she was a favorite on CBS's *Hee Haw* variety show. In 1988 when she ap-

peared on *Comic Relief III*, she told the same corny jokes, wore her straw hat with its hanging price tag, and greeted the audience with "How-deeee! I'm just so proud to be here!"

The roots of today's country music industry, centered around *The Grand Ole Opry* in Nashville, Tennessee, go back to the Scottish and Irish immigrants who came through the Cumberland Pass and settled in the Ozarks. Part of the "fun" in country western singing and in the CB radio talk that was popular during the 1970s is the nasal twang and the southern drawl. However, there is also an abundance of "moonshine" humor, as illustrated by these excerpted lines, at least one of which was used for book titles by the late Lewis Grizzard:

- The shoes I bought and paid for are walking out on me.
- My daddy was a pistol, and I'm a son of a gun.
- If you want to keep the beer real cold, put it next to my ex-wife's heart.
- Drop-kick me, Jesus, through the goal posts of life.
- Don't cry down my back, baby, you might rust my spurs.
- My wife ran off with my best friend, and I miss him.
- She stepped on my heart and stomped the sucker flat.

In the 1950s, Andy Griffith was a stand-up comedian doing country humor. He became nationally known when Capitol Records released a five-minute recording of his hillbilly view of football. From there, he was given a part in *No Time for Sergeants*, and then, from 1960 to 1968 he played Sheriff Andy Taylor on *The Andy Griffith Show* (renamed *Mayberry R.F.D.* after Griffith quit the show). In the 1980s, Griffith returned to television to star in a serious role as a lawyer on *Matlock*. In each of these roles, he became more mainstream and his southern accent was less noticeable. Many American families have gone through similar transformations; however, the changes took place over two or three generations. Nevertheless, many such families still identify with their country roots, and may recognize personalities of friends and relatives in some of the exaggerated character portrayals in such popular 1960s sitcoms as *Mayberry R.F.D.*, *Gomer Pyle*, *Green Acres*, *The Beverly Hillbillies*, and *Petticoat Junction*. These shows were canceled in the early 1970s, not because they were no longer popular, but because their high ratings came from rural areas and from older viewers who had lower incomes. Advertisers wanted to sponsor shows that would attract young, affluent city dwellers because such viewers would be more likely to purchase the sponsors' products.

Since in all these shows the characters spoke "Southern," the image of the South as a generic representative of country humor was furthered. In 1997, Rick Bragg wrote in *The New York Times* (Jun. 6, 1997) that people from Alabama felt particularly picked on because the state had become the butt of jokes made by talk show hosts, disc jockeys, newspaper cartoonists, and columnists, and such national figures as Conan O'Brien, Bill Maher, and Jon Stewart. A car repair expert on National Public Radio suggested that the state's license plates should read, "Alabama: Illiteracy Ain't That Bad," and a joke that popped up on the Internet stated that "there are people in Alabama who are their own fathers."

Wayne Flynt, professor of history at Alabama's Auburn University, explained that the situation was a result of Alabama trying to "invent a world consistent with our ideals, and it's a world that doesn't exist anymore. We're trying to squeeze rural values into an urban world." The incidents that led him to this conclusion included the display of a homemade plaque of the Ten Commandments in a Gadsden courtroom, Governor Fob James threatening to call in the National Guard to defend the judge's right to display the plaque, the same judge being removed by the State Supreme Court from a case in which he had barred a lesbian from contact with her own child, a Birmingham television station refusing to broadcast the coming-out episode of the television show *Ellen*, and an elemen-

tary school principal in Mobile publicly warning a group of animal rights advocates that she could not be responsible for their safety if they came to school and presented a program aimed at convincing students that fishing was wrong.

Thanks to modern mass media and improvements in public education and transportation, the geographical location of one's home is not the determining factor that it used to be in shaping a person's worldview and speaking style. Socioeconomic levels, including one's job and one's education, play a bigger role; however, these matters are harder to joke about, and so humorists nostalgically search for regional differences and for eccentric characters whose dialects they can exaggerate and laugh about while exploring challenges in human interactions. *See also* DIALECT HUMOR, FRONTIER HUMOR

Further reading: Marvin R. Koller, *Humor and Society: Explorations in the Sociology of Humor* (1988). James P. Leary (comp. and ed.), *Midwestern Folk Humor* (1991). *Roy Blount's Book of Southern Humor* (1994).

Religious Humor

Religious humor is tied in some way to the service and worship of God or the supernatural. Religion is a common topic for humor because it is full of mystery and ambiguity. It allows people to transcend their everyday concerns and tempts them into such philosophical meanderings as trying to discover "How many angels can stand on the head of a pin?" and whether, "If the earth is held up by a turtle, what is holding the turtle up?" Philosopher Joseph Campbell noted that the chief difference between what in Western culture is viewed as religion and what is viewed as mythology is that with myths people feel free to create and enjoy humor, while with religion most people have ambivalent feelings and aren't quite sure what territory is permissible for joking.

One of comedian Judy Tenuta's lines is "So I went out with this guy, and he kissed like, you know, *a Pez dispenser*. I mean, his head fell back 180 degrees and his tongue popped out like he wanted me to give him *communion.*" People laughed, not only because of the incongruous images, but also because they were surprised at Tenuta bringing this kind of a religious reference into a comedy act.

In 1994, *New York Newsday* cartoonist Doug Marlette pictured the Pope wearing a "No Women Priests" button. Marlette drew an arrow pointing to the Pope's head and quoted the scripture from Matthew 16:18, "Upon this rock I will build My Church." The newspaper received so many protests that the editors devoted their 16 June 1994 "Viewpoints" page to the matter, letting Marlette have his say, along with Francis J. Maniscalco, director of the Office for Media Relations of the United States Catholic Conference. Maniscalco's view was that, of course, editorial cartoons are not expected to give both sides of an argument: "a well-balanced cartoon is probably by definition a boring and forgettable one." But on the other hand, people have limits on what can be treated irreverently: "For religious people, especially off limits is all we have been taught to hold sacred. The sacred is really another realm. It is not the realm of health-care reform, or China policy, or defensive cigarette manufacturers, or any other mundane matter, as important as it may be in its own right."

Marlette's argument was that "the Catholic Church I know is big enough and secure enough to laugh at this cartoon. . . . I have drawn cartoons of this Pope for years. I have drawn positive cartoons when he was standing courageously toe to toe against communism's Evil Empire, and I have drawn cartoons critical of him for his positions on population control and women priests. It is not disrespectful to satirize and criticize. On the contrary, satire shows true respect because it takes seriously public figures and the stands they take."

One of the classes taught by University of Michigan history professor Thomas Tentler in a 1992 Comedy Semester program was entitled, "Comedy in Catholic Contexts," and it came under Board of Regents scrutiny because of the course description. The brochure explained that Catholic traditions have produced a variety of comic responses because such features as a celibate clergy, an hierarchical structure, and elaborate rituals and traditionalist values "invite opposition: heresy, rebellion, reform, protest and satire." The structure and traditions "give comic writers a firm place from which to satirize the outside world as well as the visible society of the church." Professor Tentler denied that the course would ridicule Catholicism; instead, he explained, it would simply illustrate how "shared values and assumptions define a community that will get the joke." The writings being studied ranged from Boccaccio's 14th-century *Decameron* to works by 20th-century authors including Flannery O'Connor, Walker Percy, and Frank O'Connor.

Such basic disagreements as these are likely to continue, especially as the United States becomes more culturally diverse, so that people need an expanding level of knowledge to know what different religions consider sacred and off-limits for humor. A running controversy throughout the 1990s at the University of Illinois has focused on the team mascot, Chief Illiniwek. Protests have centered around charges that sacred beliefs and symbols have been manipulated to create a character who lacks authenticity and whose roles as a crowd pleaser and a cheerleading clown are insulting to the religious beliefs of Native American tribes.

In the spring of 1997 the Islamic Council publicly protested a logo on athletic shoes that resembled the word *Allah* in Arabic script. Nike said the logo was meant to look like flames for a line of shoes to be sold with the names *Air Bakin'*, *Air Melt*, *Air Grill,* and *Air B-Que.* A spokesperson also said the company had caught the problem and altered the logo before the shoes went into production; however, Nihad Awad, president of the Council on American-Islamic Relations, displayed a pair of the controversial shoes and said they were still seen in retail stores. Hakeem Olajuwon, a Muslim who endorses another brand of athletic shoe, wrote in a public letter to Nike President Tom Clarke, "It is offensive to us when a major corporation such as Nike publicly shows disrespect for Allah's name." Two years earlier, Nike advertisers had offended Muslims with a billboard picture of a high-jumping basketball player accompanied by the slogan "They called him Allah."

In spite of these complications, many people are working within organized religion to make humor a part of pastoral work, church management, counseling, storytelling, eulogizing, and preaching. They quote Proverbs 17:22, "A merry heart is a good medicine, but a downcast spirit dries up the bones." Rabbi Albert Lewis, from Temple Beth Sholom in Cherry Hill, Pennsylvania, has explained that "for a message to be understood, it has to have wheels," and humorous stories are "the best wheels of all." Rev. Edward V. Avery, who is a priest and chaplain at Nazareth Hospital in Pennsylvania, says that in today's world, where busy families are accustomed to getting information in sound bites, they want sermons to be memorable and to the point. He thinks that the "people who need to be lambasted" are the ones who don't come to church; those who come should be cheered and affirmed with stories that relate to their real lives.

The Rev. Henry H. Mitchell, a professor at the Interdenominational Theological Center in Atlanta, says that "Black preaching is much less formal and self-consciously dignified" than the preaching in most white churches, and so it sets the stage for the use of humor. Besides, Black culture, out of necessity, has learned to use laughter as a buffer against hardship and oppression.

An interdenominational newsletter, *The Joyful Noise*, distributed by the Fellowship of Merry Christians, includes news stories about the use of humor in religious circumstances, letters from subscribers, cartoons donated by nationally known artists (including *Family Circus's* Bill Keane and *B. C.'s* Johnny Hart) for reprinting in church newsletters, and humorous quotes that could liven up church bulletins. Amusing anecdotes are also reprinted, as in the story about Milton Berle visiting actor Jim Backus in the hospital a few months before Backus died. Berle told jokes

for two hours. As he got up to leave, Berle said, "I hope you get better." Backus replied "You, too."

The Door is a bimonthly magazine that bills itself as "the world's pretty much only religious satire magazine." The cover of its "Special 25th Anniversary Issue" (Nov./Dec. 1996) was an elegant painting of "Madonna with Child." The child was Chicago Bulls star Dennis Rodman, complete with green hair and basketball shoes. A 1997 cover showed Billy Graham with a gun being held to his head over the cutline, "Buy this magazine or Billy gets it." Billy Graham declined to be interviewed, but the editors went ahead and prepared an "interview" by devising questions that they answered with excerpts from Graham's autobiography.

The Rev. Doug Adams, author of *Humor in the American Pulpit*, says that scholarship about humor in the Bible has helped legitimize the growth of clerical humor. Examples he cites include Samson testing his new in-laws with a riddle, while Isaac was given a name meaning "laughter" because both his elderly mother and father laughed with joy when God told them they would have a son. Rebekah's twins, Esau and Jacob, fought while they were still in her womb, and when Esau was born first, Jacob's hand came out grasping Esau's heel as if to keep him from being the first born. In the New Testament, Jesus' listeners were probably amused by several of his parables, including the one about it being as hard for a rich man to get into heaven as for a camel to go through the eye of a needle. The story of perverse Jonah and how God had to follow him even into the hold of a ship, into the belly of a whale, and onto a barren beach before Jonah would listen to Him is the forerunner of today's picaresque novel, while the way Abraham haggled with God over how many good people it would take to save Sodom is the forerunner of hundreds of conversation-with-God jokes, including one in which a man goes hiking in the mountains and falls over a cliff. At the last second, he grabs onto a small branch growing out of a crack so that he is dangling helplessly hundreds of feet above the rocks.

No one answers his frantic calls for help, and so in desperation he lifts his eyes to heaven and calls,

"Is there anyone up there?"
A great booming voice answers, *"I'm here."*
"Who are you?"
"It's me, God. I am who I am. I'll help you. Just let go of the branch."
"If I let go of the branch I'll fall and die."
"Trust me," God says. *"Let go of the branch and I'll save you."*
The man raises his eyes to heaven again and cries out: "Is there anybody else up there?"

See also CENSORSHIP, POLITICAL CORRECTNESS, SATIRE

Further reading: Doug Adams, *Humor in the American Pulpit from George Whitefield through Henry Ward Beecher* (1992). Peter L. Berger, *Redeeming Laughter: The Comic Dimension of Human Experience* (1997). A. Roy Eckardt, *On the Way to Death: Essays toward a Comic Vision* (1996). Conrad M. Hyers, *The Spirituality of Comedy: Comic Heroism in a Tragic World* (1996).

Riddles

The word *riddle* is from the same root as *read*, and since the 12th century has meant a mystifying, misleading, or puzzling question—something that needs interpreting. Author Northrop Frye says that "read a riddle" was once a common verb phrase similar to "tell a tale" and "sing a song." "And just as the connections of charm are close to music, so the riddle has pictorial affinities related to ciphers, acrostics, rebuses, concrete and shape poetry and everything that emphasizes the visual aspects of literature."

In *Crosbie's Dictionary of Riddles*, John Crosbie, editor of *The Pundit*, describes three types of riddles: those that have logical answers; those whose answers are pure nonsense; and those which are conundrums, or plays on words, so that their answers cannot be guessed on the basis of logic alone. As an example of a conundrum, he asks, "What does a person confronted with conundrums and a person facing a firing squad have in common?". . . "They are both about to get riddled!"

Riddles range from the childish to the philosophical. Perhaps the most famous of all is the "Riddle of the Sphinx," which appears in the story of Oedipus. The Sphinx in this story is not the Egyptian Sphinx, but a female form with the wings of a bird, the body of an animal, and the breast, neck, and face of a woman. She represents the destiny of life and has sent a plague on the land. To rid the land of the plague, the hero has to answer her riddle, "What is it that walks on four legs, then on two legs, and then on three?" The answer is "Man." As an infant he crawls on hands and feet, as an adult he walks on two legs, but when aged he walks with the help of a "third leg" or a cane. Philosopher Joseph Campbell suggests that the Sphinx is presenting the image of life through time: childhood, maturity, old age, and death. When people have accepted life and death with understanding and without fear, they have faced and accepted the Riddle of the Sphinx. At this point, death has no further hold, and the curse of the Sphinx disappears.

Alvin Schwartz, in his 1983 children's book *Unriddling*, presents such patterns as the "No Way Out Riddle." A girl is locked in a room that is empty except for a piano, a wooden table, a saw, and a baseball bat. The door is locked and there are no windows, no keys, and no other openings. "How does she get out?" In addition to such trite answers as, "She broke out with the chicken pox," more creative answers include:

- She used the saw to cut the table in half. Since two halves make a whole, she crawled out through the hole.

- She played the piano until she found the right key. Then she unlocked the door and let herself out.

- She ran around the room until she wore herself out.

- She swung the baseball bat three times. It was three strikes, and she was out.

In a category called "Riddle Jokes," Schwartz asks, "What has 18 legs and red spots and catches flies?" . . . "A baseball team with measles." In a "Tricky Question" category, he asks "What word with five letters becomes shorter when you add two letters?" ... "The word *short*." In an "Elephant Jokes" category, he asks "How do you make a statue of an elephant?" ... "Get a piece of stone and cut away everything that does not look like an elephant."

In a 1977 article in volume 13, number 2 of *Developmental Psychology*, J. Kenneth Whitt and Norman M. Prentice illustrated the stages of riddle appreciation that children experience:

1. Pre-riddle: "What did the big firecracker say to the little firecracker?"
   You're too little to pop!

2. Homonymic Neutral Riddle: "Why is a packed baseball field always cool?"
   It has a fan in every seat!

3. Homonymic Superiority Riddle: "Why did the little girl eat bullets?"
   She wanted her hair to grow out in bangs!

4. Improbable Relationship Riddle: "Where can you find roads without cars?"
   On a map!

5. Riddle Parody: "What do squirrels have that no other animal has?"
   Baby squirrels!

A sophisticated type of riddle told by Ennis Rees in his 1964 *Pick-a-Riddle* (collected from oral traditions and folk literature) involves not only punning, but also visual trickery:

> There were 710
> Women and men
> At sea in a boat
> That ceased to float.
> When it spun around
> And turned upside down,
> What was left then
> Of the 710?

To get the answer of "OIL," a listener has to visualize the number 710 and turn it upside down to change it into a word.

Leo Rosten, in his 1968 *The Joys of Yiddish,* tells a joke about a riddle that involves even more trickery. A father asks his son, "What is it that hangs on the wall, is green, wet, and whistles?"

When the boy cannot guess, the father responds, "It's a herring." "But," the son says, "a herring doesn't hang on the wall," and the father responds, "So hang it there." "But," the son continues, "a herring isn't green," and the father responds, "So paint it green." "But," the son continues, "a herring isn't wet," to which the father responds, "It is if it's painted." Finally, in exasperation, the boy says, "But a herring doesn't whistle." "Right," smiles the father, "I just put that in to make it hard." *See also* LANGUAGE PLAY, METAPHORS, PUNS

S

Satire

Satires are humorous literary works, artistic pieces, performances, or informal speech in which such human frailties as greed, self-indulgence, stupidity, and various kinds of abuses are held up to ridicule and contempt for the purpose of inspiring reform. The word *satire* comes from the Latin *satura* meaning a dish filled with mixed fruits. This was the usual dessert tray after a banquet, and an early meaning for the word was "to be well fed" as seen in such cognates as *sated*, *saturated*, and *satisfied*. The contemporary meaning is metaphorically related in that the creators of satire present a full plate for readers, listeners, and viewers whose immediate satisfaction comes from the inherent humor. Satire also provides food for thought because satirists use their humor to inspire reform and change. If creators do not have a reform or a solution in mind but are simply holding up an aspect of the world as ridiculous, then they are creating irony or black humor rather than satire.

Satirists do not usually aim their criticism at a particular person, but instead at groups of people or at institutions. They follow the example of Joseph Addison, who, in the 1700s, chose to "pass over a single foe to charge whole armies." The armies he charged were not knights on noble steeds, but common fools, knaves, tricksters, pedants, and hucksters. Satire has a long history and occurs across genres ranging from Aesop's fables and Shel Silverstein's poetry to Art Buchwald's newspaper columns and Paul Krassner's newsletter *The Realist*. It also includes political and social cartoons, such television programs as late-night talk shows and Bill Maher's *Politically Incorrect*, such movies as *Wag the Dog* (1997) and *The Truman Show* (1998), and such novels as C.S. Lewis's *Screwtape Letters* (1967) and Aldous Huxley's *Brave New World* (1965).

Satire can be divided into two basic types: informal or indirect, as in stories, poems, plays, or novels; and explicit or formal, in which the satirist speaks directly to readers or listeners. Because explicit satire is more efficient, it is the kind most likely to be presented by comedians. For example, in 1996, when the Museum of Television and Radio in New York City put on a six-month exhibit, "Stand-Up Comedians on Television," one of the major sections was "Social Satire." It was divided into three categories: The Instigator, The Politico, and The Sage. Exhibit notes explained that social satirists follow in the tradition of Mark Twain and Will Rogers. "The sacrosanct tenets of the Establishment are rings on a dartboard to the socially conscious comedian, whose sole mission is to make you think before you laugh."

Identified as Instigator satirists were Lenny Bruce, Mort Sahl, Nipsey Russell, Godfrey Cambridge, Dick Gregory, and Richard Pryor. Bruce, Sahl, and Gregory were the pioneers working in edgy San Francisco and New York clubs where they challenged the facade of Eisenhower America. First branded as "sickniks," they were often censored, and, in the case of Bruce, arrested for indecency. Sahl was the least controversial, not because his satire was less biting, but because he dressed and looked "collegiate" and focused on politics, while Bruce was challenging sexual and religious conventions and Gregory was giving voice to the civil rights movement. The museum's brochure stated that Gregory's work "made it possible for African American entertainers to openly rib Jim Crow" while paving "the way for Richard Pryor's brazen commentaries on discrimination."

Politico satirists that the museum chose to feature included Bob Hope, Johnny Carson, Jack Paar, David Frye, Jackie Mason, Arsenio Hall, Tom and Dick Smothers, Jay Leno, Pat Paulsen, David Letterman, David Steinberg, Dennis Miller, Dan Rowan and Dick Martin, and Mark Russell. Hope was praised for his longtime rattling of "Washington like a Gatling gun, skewering the sanctimony of politics and securing a soapbox for topically minded comedians," while Rowan and Martin's *Laugh-In* and *The Smothers Brothers Comedy Hour* were praised for blending "critical views with a counterculture sensibility." Johnny Carson had such a hold on the American public that he "was one of the few personalities who could safely fire one-liners at Capitol Hill." His cynicism came from the daily news "inspired by the politicians who spoke with at least one foot in their mouths."

Sages were described as those who warn us of the pitfalls of everyday life. The exhibit included performance clips from Bob Newhart, Mike Nichols and Elaine May, George Carlin, Alan King, Mark Russell, Bill Maher, Dennis Miller, Paul Mooney, Chris Rock, Robin Williams, Billy Crystal, and Whoopi Goldberg. Carlin, Newhart, and Nichols and May were praised for exploring the frustrations of bureaucracy and the dehumanizing effects of technology, while King, Maher, and Russell were cited for lampooning society's lack of ethics and its focus on pop culture, and Rock for challenging class disparities. One of Rock's funniest skits is about the absurdity of giving surplus cheese to welfare families. Robin Williams played with this same idea in a *Comic Relief* skit where he impersonated a farmer whose land has been taken over by the mortgage company so that he is left pondering how to turn wedges of surplus cheese into all the things needed for daily living.

Edgar Johnson in his *The Anatomy of Satire* (1962) praises satire as a corrective for bad behavior. "If we ever become civilized," he writes, "it will probably be satire almost as much as poetry that will have accomplished it." Arthur Pollard in *Satire* (1970) says that satirists move readers to criticize and condemn through "various emotions ranging from laughter through ridicule, contempt and anger to hate." The feelings that are evoked will depend on the seriousness of the faults being attacked as well as the author's view of "the gap between the ideal and reality."

Writers or performers who feel so strongly about their subject that they cannot view it with detachment and humor will probably not be able to create satire. As writer Henry Rule has confessed, "In truth I don't ever seem to be in a good enough humor with anything to satirize it; no, I want to stand up before it and curse it, and foam at the mouth—or take a club and pound it to rags and pulp."

Some critics divide satire into gentle satire called "Horatian" after the writing style of the Roman poet Horace, who lived at the time of Christ, and heavy or biting satire called "Juvenalian" after the Roman poet Juvenal, who lived in the first century after Christ. One of the characteristics of gentle satire is that it includes a higher percentage of humor. For example, Jonathan Swift's 1726 *Gulliver's Travels* comes closer to being gentle satire than does his 1729 "A Modest Proposal for Preventing the Children of poor People in Ireland, from being a Burden to their Parents or Country; and for making them beneficial to the Publick." In this latter piece, his intention was to move his readers to understand the plight of the Irish and to do something about it. He suggested that at the age of one year, poor Irish children should be sold as food to be eaten by landlords and other members of the upper class. Irish mothers should be encouraged to let their children "suck plentifully in the last Month, so as to render them plump, and fat for a good table. A Child will make two Dishes at an Entertainment for Friends; and when the Family dines alone, the fore or hind quarter will make a reasonable Dish; and seasoned with a little Pepper and Salt, will be very good Boiled on the fourth Day, especially in *Winter*." Few people who read Swift's "Modest Proposal" ever forget it. Because it touches such deep psychic nerves, it illustrates the satirist's major tool, which is playing with the emotions of readers or listeners.

Swift's *Gulliver's Travels* stands in contrast to this grim essay; the accounts of Gulliver's voyages to Lilliput, Brobdingnag, Laputa, and the Country of the Houyhnhnms can be read and enjoyed as adventure stories, even by children. Funny images from the stories remain in readers' minds, such as the picture of Gulliver awakening to find himself pinned down by hundreds of threads placed on him by the tiny people in Lilliput and the image of him putting out the fire that was burning the Queen's Palace by urinating on it.

Because of the extensive accumulation of details in *Gulliver's Travels* and because Swift is trying to influence mental attitudes as much as actual change, some critics identify the work as an example of *Menippean satire*, named after the Greek cynic Menippus.

A technique often used in satirical novels is the contrast between utopian and dystopian societies. The author usually introduces what at first appears to be a utopian society, but which the reader soon realizes is actually grotesque or dystopian. Lois Lowry's prize-winning children's book *The Giver* (1993) is of this type, as is George Orwell's *Animal Farm* (1954). These books both have antitotalitarian messages just as does Orwell's much heavier and grimmer *1984* (1949). But because *Animal Farm* comes closer to being Horatian satire with its nostalgic barnyard and its "lovable" set of farm animals, when it was first submitted to American publishers they missed the point and turned it down saying the prospective market for "animal stories" was too small.

The grimmer a story, the less likely it is that readers will miss the intended satire, but also, with such grim satires as Anthony Burgess's dystopian *A Clockwork Orange* (1963), William Golding's anarchic *Lord of the Flies* (1955), and Ray Bradbury's anti-censorship *Fahrenheit 451* (1967), if there is humor, it is black humor or irony, which does not stretch readers' emotions as tightly from laughter to crying as is done in satires, where the humor is mixed in with the lessons. Readers shudder at these books if they think they are predicting the future, but Ray Bradbury has made it clear that he is trying to prevent, not predict, the future. It is this call to action that distinguishes satire from black or gallows humor.

Aristophanes's antiwar fourth-century B.C. *Lysistrata* is a classic example of the lighter kind of satire that blends humor with a serious story. The story has an antiwar message, with the humor coming from the wives' refusal to have sex with their husbands until they quit fighting. A contemporary example of a satire that includes humor along with serious elements is John Nichols's *The Milagro Beanfield War* (1974), in which village farmers in New Mexico are pitted against developers who are coming in to take what water is available for building a golf course and resort.

Matthew Hodgart in *Satire* (1969) wrote that in ancient Eskimo cultures, satirical prose and rhyme were used to shame individuals who had violated community standards. The punishment was worse than a physical punishment because the criminal would be made to look foolish while the other villagers watched. Hodgart also wrote that when going to war, the ancient Arabs would send a satirist from both sides into battle to see which satirist could be the most clever. The morale of the two armies would be determined by the skill of their satirists, and occasionally a humiliated army would simply give up and retreat.

Both of these situations have modern counterparts. During international conflicts, each country cranks up its propaganda machines to convince its citizens of the rightness of its own cause and the wrongness of the enemy's. More clearly related to satire are the shaming penalties meted out by cartoonists, comedians, and writers who use the mass media to make fun of individuals who have gone against behavioral codes, whether in business, sex, or politics. Although most such jokes have as their immediate target one or two individuals who are involved in current scandals, the goal of the satirist is to capitalize on the public's interest in a current event to shape society's long-term attitudes and behaviors. *See also* ANTIAUTHORITY HUMOR, BLACK HUMOR, POLITICS AND HUMOR, WIT

Further reading: Arthur Asa Berger, *Li'l Abner: A Study in American Satire* (1994). Steven Weisenberger, *Fables of Subversion/Satire and the American Novel: 1930–1980* (1995).

Scatology and Obscenity

Scatology came into English from the Greek *scato* meaning "feces" or "excrement" and *logy* meaning "the study of." *Obscene* came into English from Middle French to refer to anything repulsive, abhorrent, or taboo in polite society. *Obscenity* and *scatology* are often used as synonyms, although *obscenity* has a broader meaning and is often used in relation to sexual matters or to refer to any crass disregard for morals or ethical principles.

In reference to humor, scatology refers to jokes about bodily functions, excrement, and the parts of the body not usually talked about in "polite" company. In science, scatology refers either to the study of fossil excrement or to judging the health of individuals through examining their body excrement. When watching historical movies, audience members smile when the king's or the emperor's chamber pot is solemnly taken out for examination by the wise men of the court. Yet, these same people comply with their doctors' requests for stool specimens, urine samples, and semen deposits.

Scatology relies for its effectiveness on shocking the audience with verboten references to body parts or excrement, as when a six-year-old chants, "Red, Red, wet the bed.

Sop it up with gingerbread!" or a 10-year-old boy teases the girls by sneaking a sign onto the door of their bathroom "4 U 2 P." The following joke, collected from a Los Angeles junior high school, illustrates that while children have a continuing interest in toilet humor, as they grow older they expect more cleverness than a simple reference to a verboten subject as in the earlier jokes.

> What does a man do standing up, a woman sitting down, and a dog on three legs?
> *Shake hands.*

Scatological humor has beeen said to serve as an antidote to modern preoccupations with cleanliness and to accomplish what Sigmund Freud referred to as an "unmasking" in reminding us of humanity's animal nature. Political analyst Charles E. Schutz says that when scatological or "phallic humor is employed against personages who have attained social eminence, it not only has the pleasure in it of permissibly expressing sex and flaunting its taboo, but it also levels the superiors to a common equality. They too are vulnerable, and thus inferior. Ergo, we are delightfully superior to our superiors."

Stand-up comedians use obscenity to shock their audiences into paying attention. However, one of the reasons given for the mid-1990s slump in the popularity of comedy clubs was that audiences were turned off by comedians' heavy reliance on vulgarity. Jokes about such subjects as incest, bestiality, pedophilia, and genital mutilation surprised audiences into laughing, but it was more often a nervous than a full-hearted laugh.

Paul Krassner, editor of *The Realist*, has noted the irony of Lenny Bruce being arrested in 1962 for using certain words on stage in San Francisco, while a couple of decades later Meryl Streep used the same words in the movie *Sophie's Choice* and won an Academy Award.

George Carlin, who in his early days as a "straight" comedian had admired Lenny Bruce and after Bruce's 1966 death became in some ways Bruce's successor, uses dirty words as his signature performance. For three decades, he has gotten laughs from audiences by shouting out "the seven words not allowed on television." He jokes about the absurdity of word taboos as when he laughs about getting fired from the Frontier Hotel in Las Vegas for saying *shit*—"in a town where the big game is called *crap!*" And about people who say *shoot*, he confided, "They can't fool me, man. *Shoot* is *shit* with two *o*'s."

A thousand years ago, in German, Old English, and Middle English, *bitch* simply meant a female dog. By the 1400s, it had acquired the additional meaning of an insulting name for a woman, while by the mid-1700s it was used to refer to any troublesome person in the phrase *son of a bitch*. By the mid-1900s, speakers had added a verb form, meaning "to complain."

Gilda Radner on *Saturday Night Live* shocked and amused her television audience when as Emily Litella, she called Jane Curtin, who was playing the "Weekend Update" anchor, a *bitch*. Although the word had already been broadcast in such popular music as Miles Davis's 1969 *Bitches Brew*, the Rolling Stones's 1971 *Bitch*, and Elton John's 1974 *The Bitch Is Back*, listeners were surprised that the word wasn't bleeped, because standards for speech are usually more strict than they are for music. In 1984, Barbara Bush lost points with feminists when she said that Geraldine Ferraro could be described by a word that "rhymes with rich," and in 1995 both Kathleen Gingrich and Connie Chung were criticized when Chung aired part of an interview in which the mother of Newt Gingrich said her son thought of Hillary Rodham Clinton as "a bitch." Obviously the word is still considered an insult, but as with all obscenities, the more it is used the less sting it has.

Twice a year since the early 1980s, Reinhold Aman has published—"fate willing"—*Maledicta: The International Journal of Verbal Aggression*. Scholars from such academic areas as psychology, sociology, communications, literature, linguistics, popular culture, humanities, and drama contribute articles about verbal abuse and insults; scatology; euphemisms; the jargon of subcultures; libel and slander; stereotypes; names of groups, places, and things; and language

play related to sex, body parts, and physical aggression. Aman also publishes occasional books developed from materials in the journal.

In 1997 the British Broadcasting Standards Commission conducted a study to see what words were most offensive to television viewers. On their top-30 list, religious swear words (*Jesus Christ, Bloody, God,* and *Damn*) were in the bottom five, while during the 1700s, they would probably have led the list. The top five were considered so obscene that when the *Independent* (Feb. 22, 1998) printed an article by Boyd Tonkin they were excised (*C——, Motherf——, F——, W——er,* and *Bastard*). When shown this list, many Americans couldn't figure out the fourth word, which is in itself an illustration of cultural differences. Tonkin noted that *queer*, which a few years ago was a highly insulting term, wasn't even on the new list. Today, we've seen it on academic letterheads: "Only the crustiest don would now bat an eyelid at the professor of queer studies," Tonkin writes.

Tonkin's article was written in reaction to the public outcry when political leader Gerry Adams told the world—and BBC News—that he was *pissed off* by the announcement that Sinn Fein might be excluded from the Northern Irish peace talks. *Pissed off* was mid-way down the top-30 list. For those who were offended by it, Tonkin reminded readers of the occasional appropriateness of taboo language by quoting former U.S. president Lyndon Johnson, who in the 1960s explained his reluctance to fire J. Edgar Hoover from his position as director of the FBI by saying it was "better to have him inside the tent pissing out, than outside the tent pissing in."

In *Comic Visions, Female Voices: Contemporary Women Novelists and Southern Humor*, Barbara Bennett shows how, since the 1970s, such authors as Kaye Gibbons, Gail Godwin, Bobbie Ann Mason, Anne Tyler, and Alice Walker have begun to include scatological humor in their writing. She concludes that

> Because of its reputation as a low form of humor, some people might see the emergence of scatological humor in fiction by

women as a devolution, but the recognition and incorporation of scatological humor is a kind of liberation. Like the use of black humor, the use of scatological humor is one more barrier broken, one more limitation challenged, and one less secret kept, allowing women to explore areas once considered taboo.

See also ACQUISITION OF A SENSE OF HUMOR, FICTION, PUT-DOWNS AND REJOINDERS

Further reading: Reinhold Aman (ed.), *Talking Dirty: A Bawdy Compendium of Colorful Language, Humorous Insults and Wicked Jokes* (1994). Lars Andersson and Peter Trudgill, *Bad Language* (1990). Barbara Bennett, *Comic Visions, Female Voices: Contemporary Women Novelists and Southern Humor* (1998).

School Humor

School humor can be divided into two categories: that which is used in relation to intellectual development and that which is used for the emotional purposes of having fun and relieving tensions and frustrations. Teachers and students use both types. Teachers use humor as a technique for getting children's attention, communicating information in understandable and memorable ways, and helping students develop higher-order thinking skills, as well as for making light of stressful situations, whether their own or children's. In a similar way, children challenge themselves and each other intellectually as they struggle to catch on to jokes and to create such wordplay as riddles and puns. They also use humor as a way to relax and to try out social roles through pretense, teasing, name calling, and joking.

Performance Learning Systems devoted its August 1991 newsletter to the subject of humor in the classroom. In the newsletter, educational consultant Bill Haggart encouraged teachers to list common situations that made them uncomfortable or concepts that they had trouble communicating to students and then to search through joke books and collections of school-related anecdotes, as well as their personal experiences, with the goal of finding applicable jokes. "There needs to be a connection," he stressed, between the joke or anecdote and what the teacher wants to communicate. "When there's a connec-

tion, a lot of learning goes on and a lot of tension is relieved."

One of the examples he gave from his own teaching was the strategy he developed to deal with the issue of cheating on tests. Instead of giving a threatening speech, he would tell the class he was looking for nominees for the Rubber Neck Award. If he saw any candidates, he would list their names on the board, and consider them for the grand prize to be given at the end of the year. And, "because it's such a prestigious award, your parents will of course be notified." This approach not only provided comic relief for students nervous about taking an exam, but also provided a socially acceptable way for students to "nominate" classmates for the award. One student was so amused by the idea that he donated an old basketball trophy, from which he had severed the top and then reattached it with a rubber band.

Haggart came up with another humorous solution to a difficult problem when he grew tired of hearing student excuses for not getting homework done. He put a three-way chart on the wall identified as "Helpless," "Hopeless," and "Not in Control of the Body." Whenever he got an excuse he hadn't heard before, he would ask the class to help him decide the category. As the year went on, students grew less interested in making excuses and more interested in making a joke out of the situation while taking whatever punishment was involved. He concluded, "Teachers are way ahead of the game if they can change anxious situations into humorous ones that evolve into shared experiences."

First-grade teacher Steve Kissell gave several such examples in "Laughing and Learning: Humor in the Classroom" (*Virginia Journal of Education*, Feb. 1991) where he told how a little girl was terribly upset when she opened her lunch box and found it full of ants. After he helped her dispose of her lunch and get a charge slip for the cafeteria, he began jumping around and scratching his back, legs, and stomach. As the girl and her classmates stared at his exaggerated movements, he exclaimed, "I've got ants in my pants!" The first graders were highly amused by their teacher's antics, and they learned "a valuable lesson not found in any textbook — the lesson of humor. We need to teach children that it's all right to laugh at our daily problems — in fact it's healthy! Laughter is the great communicator and stress reliever." At Kissell's school, one table in the faculty lounge is labeled "No Griping Table" and on a bulletin board with enlarged cartoons, teachers are invited to create their own captions.

Humorous class activities that have worked well for elementary school teachers include helping students rewrite proverbs or maxims; doing new versions of old stories, as in the style of Jon Scieszka's *The True Story of the Three Little Pigs* (1989) and *The Stinky Cheese Man: And Other Fairly Stupid Tales* (1992); rewriting nursery rhymes with local references and names; composing a dictionary of made-up words and definitions; keeping diaries of funny jokes and anecdotes; using the public address system one morning a week to present a riddle with many possible answers and to read the best answers the same afternoon; including jokes as fillers in written tests; providing classroom "Humor Centers" where students can sit and read funny stories or draw their own cartoons; and, on a designated day, replacing "Show and Tell" with "Show and Smell" (students bring funny, smelly items in zip-lock bags).

Although teachers are advised to make sure their humor is related to the lesson, some teachers follow the example of teachers on educational TV and use props that go beyond rubber noses and Groucho Marx glasses. They may start a lesson with a magic trick or by blowing bubbles or juggling balls. Texas educator Mike Currier has a foam-rubber cinder block with which he hits himself on the head when he makes a mistake or does something for which he's sorry. He also has traveling trophies: silk flowers for the desk of a student who says something nice about another student and an inflatable light bulb for someone who has "enlightened" the whole class.

Max Coderre, author of "Humor in My Class? Never!" in *Teaching Today* (Mar./Apr. 1991), recommended silliness, surprise, exaggeration, understatement, and even puns, as long as the teacher is comfortable and can make kids laugh. He estimated that students learn and remember up to five times more when they are involved and smiling than when they are frowning, afraid, or bored. But he also warned teachers against using hostile wit or irony. It is both unfair and unwise for adults in positions of power over students, especially children, to use sarcastic, harsh, or cutting humor.

At the 1998 International Society for Humor Studies conference in Bergen, Norway, Kay Caskey and Laurie Young from Western Michigan University in Kalamazoo talked about the multiple uses of humor that they observed when teaching in a women's prison, where many of the prisoners were Black and most of the guards were white males. While a few of the guards used humor to reduce tensions and gain cooperation, most used humor for purposes of establishing control and belittling prisoners. With these guards, the women prisoners upset the hierarchy, reacting with "get even" tactics by using humor related to such vulnerable areas of male sensitivity as baldness and body build. Teachers who humiliate students with sarcasm are justifiably afraid of losing control when students turn such humor back onto them.

Also at the ISHS conference in Bergen, Stefan Bucher, who teaches in the Chinese University of Hong Kong, made a distinction between the effects of humor used in lecture-type classes and the humor used in foreign-language classes, where the teacher is not transmitting knowledge but instead is interacting with students. He said that a light-hearted and humorous approach is especially important in skills-oriented classes where students need to feel secure enough to take chances. This includes not only the learning of new languages, but learning in any class where performance is involved, such as in athletics, dancing, studio art, public speaking, and acting.

With high school and adult students, many argue for the incorporation of humor as part of the curriculum. The March 1999 issue of *English Journal*, which goes to high school teachers belonging to the National Council of Teachers of English, focused on humor.

Arguments made for bringing the study of humor into high schools included the following:

- Through studying humor, teachers can help students enlarge their understanding and appreciation of different kinds of humor in both print and film.

- Analyzing humor is a good way to entice students into other kinds of literary analysis. Humor is an obvious emotion, and students are genuinely interested in figuring out what causes them to laugh.

- Because humor is such a part of everyday life, it is a good way to help students see the relevance of literary studies to real life.

- While young people may have a slim chance of growing up to become comedy performers or professional writers, it would be hard to name a career where being able to use and appreciate humor would not contribute to success.

- Humor gives people practice in creative problem solving because much humor incorporates hidden angles.

One article concluded with the observation that in the production of humor some students will probably be more skilled than their teachers. However, this is a healthy balance because teachers have the advantage in virtually every other activity. Teachers who shudder at the thought of having a future comedian in their class can take hope from the story that comedian Jim Carrey has told: as long as he didn't interrupt the class all week, his junior high teacher allowed him to do a 10-minute stand-up routine on Friday afternoons.

Topics for research and writing recommended by the *English Journal* for high school students included the following:

- Humor on the Internet

- Analysis of the humor techniques used by a favorite children's author, such as Dr. Seuss, Roald Dahl, A. A. Milne, Lewis Carroll, or William Steig

- Relationships between popular jokes and current events or concerns

- Humor in politics

- Humor in television commercials

- Humor in the names of popular music groups and musicians

- Accidental humor, as in bloopers and blunders

- The humor of a special group, such as a student's ethnic group or employment group

- The biography of a comic performer or humor writer

- The stories behind a humorous television show or movie

- An analysis of the humor about school or teachers

Because stories about teenagers naturally appeal to youth, they often are featured in sitcoms and movies. Teens spend a significant part of their time going to school; thus, high school teachers and classrooms often are portrayed in books, such as Max Shulman's 1955 *Guided Tour of Campus Humor* and his 1953 *Many Loves of Dobie Gillis;* in movies, such as *The Breakfast Club* (1985), starring Molly Ringwald and Emilio Estevez, and *Dead Poets' Society* (1989), starring Robin Williams and Peter Weir; and in such television sitcoms as *Welcome Back Kotter,* which, from 1975 to 1979, starred Gabe Kaplan as a wild street kid who after going to college returned to Brooklyn to teach kids with backgrounds similar to his own.

Sam Levenson's first career was teaching school, and in his comedy routines he often talked about school experiences. Bill Cosby earned a doctorate in education and created the characters of Fat Albert, Old Weird Harold, and their buddies in an inner-city grammar school. They were the inspiration for the CBS cartoon show *Fat Albert and the Cosby Kids.*

For nearly 50 years, Irwin Corey entertained audiences by playing the role of a befuddled double-talking professor. He wore an overlarge frock coat, a bedraggled string tie, tennis shoes, and a mop of flying hair. He would jab his finger in the air to make dramatic but nonsensical points, such as "We must first sublimate the imponderable eventualities, but only if we finalize the extemporaneous intricacies of the universal consciousness." One of his best-loved lectures stressed that before Sir Isaac Newton discovered the law of gravity apples fell up, not down. Leo Rosten's *The Education of Hyman Kaplan* (1937) is a humorous book about the teaching of English-as-a-second language to adults. George Bernard Shaw's *Pygmalion* (1942), Lerner and Lowe's *My Fair Lady* (1958), and the 1983 movie *Educating Rita* all rely for their humor on the involved relationships that develop between adult students and teachers. *See also* ACADEMIC STUDY OF HUMOR, ACQUISITION OF A SENSE OF HUMOR, CHILDREN'S LITERATURE, JOKE PATTERNS

Further reading: Marilyn Droz and Lori Ellis, *Laughing while Learning: Using Humor in the Classroom* (1996). Deborah J. Hill, *School Days, Fun Days: Creative Ways to Teach Humor Skills in the Classroom* (1993). Fred Stopsky, *Humor in the Classroom: A New Approach to Critical Thinking* (1992).

Screwball Comedies

Screwball comedies are full-length, zany, but romantic, movies produced in Hollywood during the Depression and on into the early 1940s. The movies are 1930s American versions of such early comedies of manners as Moliere's *The Doctor in Spite of Himself* and Sheridan's *The Rivals*. Directors and performers relied for humor on the kinds of sight gags, slapstick, extended violence, and disguises and masquerades that previously had been used only in the two-reel films produced by Hal Roach and Mack Sennett, with such actors as Charlie Chaplin and Harold Lloyd.

Virtually all of the screwball comedies included a male/female conflict, with either the man or the woman, sometimes both, being wealthy. Setting the stories among the elegant surroundings of the idle rich, with occasional visits to the poorer sides of life, provided glamour and excitement for Depression-weary viewers, as shown by such wish-fulfilling titles as *The Richest Girl in the World* (1934), *We're Rich Again* (1934), and *You Can't Take It with You* (1938). When the stories ended with the characters choosing true love over wealth, viewers were comforted by the idea that they too, could do the same. And viewers were amused along the way by the intrigue and the often funny results of millionaires masquerading as bums, ghosts as people, adults as children, men as women, and women as men.

Also contributing to the success of screwball comedy was that, in 1933, Hollywood moviemakers passed a self-censorship "Production Code," which severely restricted the sexual content of movies. As a substitute for sexuality, these new comedies were filled with slapstick and playful violence. Beneath the conflicts lay considerable sexual tension; movie titles often were designed to encourage fantasies. The pleasures of pursuit, of "the chase," were hinted at in such titles as *Woman Chases Man* (1937), *Boy Meets Girl* (1938), *Third Finger Left Hand* (1940), *The Lady Eve* (1941), and *The Lady Has Plans* (1941). *Bachelor* was a popular word, as shown by *Bachelor Apartment* (1931), *Bachelor's Affairs* (1931), *Bachelor Mother* (1939), *Bachelor Daddy* (1941), and *The Bachelor and the Bobby Soxer* (1947). Producers also hinted at marriage irregularities in such titles as *The Ex-Mrs. Bradford* (1936), *Four's a Crowd* (1938), *Wife, Husband, and Friend* (1939), *Hired Wife* (1940), *My Favorite Wife* (1940), *Too Many Husbands* (1940), *Too Many Blondes* (1941), *Weekend for Three* (1941), and *Fired Wife* (1943).

The screwball comedies were full of rebelliousness, not just against the Production Code, but also against the stilted dialogue that early scriptwriters had created because they thought of "talkies" as stage plays. The scripts also reflected the rebelliousness of women, who now had the vote, and whose roles had changed considerably during the "roaring 20s." The assertiveness of the women in these movies was probably as far removed from real-life conditions as were the grand mansions and the luxurious estates of the characters, but they gave women viewers something to dream about. As a balance to appeal to male viewers, women were beautiful but often dumb or ditzy. While the male characters, many of whom were the forerunners of the literary anti-hero or the little man, were challenged both by the women in their lives and by the frustrations of a changing world order, the female leads were portrayed as so ditzy that male viewers did not feel intimidated by them.

Wes Gehring, in his book on screwball comedy, has identified eight performers as having been the most influential in shaping the genre: actors Cary Grant, Fred MacMurray, Melvyn Douglas, Carole Lombard, Irene Dunne, Katharine Hepburn, Claudette Colbert, and Jean Arthur. A discussion of their roles serves as a general illustration of the genre.

Cary Grant was the ideal male lead for screwball comedy because he could exude sexuality, even when playing the role of a comic anti-hero. He was tall, dark, and handsome, with a pleasant sounding voice. And because he began his career as a teenage acrobatic comic in the music halls and variety theaters of England, he was comfortable doing slapstick and physical comedy. In *Gunga Din* (1939), he teetered on a rope bridge and yelled in a manner reminiscent of stooge Curly Howard, while in *Arsenic and Old Lace* (1944), he suffered from pop-eyed jitters. In *Bringing up Baby* (1938), he took several pratfalls while playing a professor/scientist whose interests oscillated between assembling a giant skeleton of a brontosaurus and socializing with rich patrons of the arts to solicit contributions for his museum.

In *Topper* (1937) and *Topper Takes a Trip* (1939), Cary Grant and Constance Bennett are husband-and-wife ghosts who are prevented from entering the afterlife and must therefore return to earth. Although the sequel does not include Grant, except in a flashback, it is smoother and has sophisticated trick photography, as when Bennett confuses a bartender by levitating Topper's hat.

Arsenic and Old Lace (1944) is only one of several screwball comedies that make fun

In the classic *Bringing Up Baby* Cary Grant and Katharine Hepburn take care of a pet leopard. *Archive Photos*

of death. Cary Grant, plays the only normal Brewster, in the role of the hapless nephew of Josephine Hull and Jean Adair, two charming and beloved elderly sisters who, as a work of charity, serve elderberry wine laced with arsenic to lonely old gentlemen. Their equally mad nephew believes he is Teddy Roosevelt, and buries the bodies in the cellar thinking they are yellow-fever victims and the cellar is the Panama Canal. Another member of the family is a sadistic serial killer (Raymond Massey) who comes in disguise to hide out at the Brewster home. Cary Grant worries that he can never marry because "insanity runs in our family; it practically gallops!" But there is a happy ending when Grant discovers that he isn't a Brewster after all; rather he was the son of the cook and raised by the "kindly" sisters. In the stage play, the character joyfully exclaims, "I'm not a Brewster; I'm a bastard!" However, the movie censors changed Grant's line to "I'm not a Brewster; I'm a son of a sea cook!"

Other screwball comedies starring Grant include *The Awful Truth* (1937), *Holiday* (1938), *His Girl Friday* (1940), *My Favorite Wife* (1940), *The Philadelphia Story* (1940), and *Once Upon a Honeymoon* (1942).

Fred MacMurray played the less dramatic role of a steady and unspectacular regular American guy, similar to what he later played as the father on television's *My Three Sons* (1960–1972). His appearance and his manner of acting made him a good foil for the comedy talents of the women who co-starred with him in *The Gilded Lily* (1935), *Hands across the Table* (1935), *True Confessions* (1937), *Too Many Husbands* (1940), and *Take a Letter Darling* (1942).

Melvyn Douglas played the leading man to just about every leading lady in Hollywood. Greta Garbo was his co-star in *Ninotchka*, a picture advertised under the slogan "Garbo Laughs" because it went against Garbo's typecasting in serious roles. Douglas starred in *She Married Her Boss* (1935), *Theodora Goes Wild* (1936), *I Met Him in Paris* (1937), *Good Girls Go to Paris* (1939), and *Too Many Husbands* (1940).

Other males who took roles as romantic leads in various screwball comedies include Brian Aherne, John Barrymore, Lionel Barrymore, Ralph Bellamy, Charles Coburn, Gary Cooper, Bing Crosby, Douglas Fairbanks Jr., Errol Flynn, Clark Gable, Rex Harrison, John Hubbard, David Niven, William Powell, Charles Ruggles, Jimmy Stewart, and Rudy Vallee. Supporting characters, friends, and father figures include Edward Arnold, Robert Benchley, Herman Bing, Charles Butterworth, Walter Connolly, Harry Davenport, Frank Jenks, Edward Everett Horton, Lionel Stander, Robert Warwick, Charles Winninger, and S. Z. Sakall.

Carole Lombard was a beautiful and eccentric heroine. As a child she was a tomboy and even took boxing lessons, so she was willing to engage in actual combat in her movie roles. Her most famous screwball comedy scene occurred in *Nothing Sacred* (1937), when she and newspaper reporter Fredric March knock each other out. She knocks him out in revenge for him knocking her out as a ploy to help in her masquerading as terminally ill. Another deception in *Nothing Sacred* occurs when reporter March has Troy Brown, a janitor, pose as the Sultan of Marzipan for a "news" story that March is writing.

In *Hands across the Table* (1935), Lombard plays a manicurist who is out to snare millionaire Ralph Bellamy even though she is in love with Fred MacMurray, an impoverished playboy. In *True Confession* (1937), every time Lombard would start to tell a lie to Fred MacMurray, she would put her tongue in her cheek. Lombard played the role of an idle young woman on a party scavenger hunt in *My Man Godfrey* (1936), which explored differences between the extremely rich and the extremely poor. She is looking for "a forgotten man" (a cliche of the Depression), when she finds William Powell in a junkyard. He is not really a "forgotten man" but a millionaire in disguise. He is so taken with Lombard that he lets her hire him as her butler. In one part of the movie, Lombard pretends to be drunk and is dunked in a cold shower, while in another scene, Mischa Auer does his ambling ape impression. His facial contortions and his hopping over the furniture create one of the funniest scenes in all screwball comedy. Lombard also starred in *Twentieth Century* (1934) and *Mr. and Mrs. Smith* (1941).

Irene Dunne co-stars with Melvyn Douglas in *Theodora Goes Wild* (1936). She plays a small-town, ultra-respectable church organist who in her spare time writes a risque novel. When it is published she goes to New York, where she has a fling with the artist who designed the cover. Dunne's formal and businesslike aura made her stand out from the more flighty and giddy actresses who usually played in screwball comedies. During the course of a movie, Dunne would become as "goofy" as others, but it was always precipitated by situations that developed out of the plot. Because of the contrast, audiences found her giddiness funnier.

The Awful Truth (1937), starring Dunne and Cary Grant, illustrated the kind of happy ending that left viewers with amused satisfaction. A married couple seeking a divorce because each has chosen new mate find themselves reunited in a deserted mountain cabin just minutes before their marriage is to legally end. Other movies starring Irene Dunne include *Joy of Living* (1938), *My Favorite Wife* (1940), *Unfinished Business* (1941), and *Lady in a Jam* (1942).

Katharine Hepburn starred with Cary Grant in *Bringing Up Baby* (1938), which is now considered a classic of the screwball comedy genre. Baby is a young pet leopard, who in typical screwball fashion is mistaken for a vicious circus leopard; the mistake leads to havoc throughout the film. Hepburn played the part of a madcap heiress determined to "capture" the scientist/professor character played by Cary Grant. While he is in the shower at her aunt's house, she sends his clothes to the cleaners as a ploy to keep him from leaving. When he gets out of the shower, he has to dress in her frilly negligee. Such cross-dressing was a guaranteed laugh-getter in screwball comedy.

Off-screen, Hepburn had the nickname of "Katharine of Arrogance," and so her zaniness in this role was especially appreciated. As critic Molly Haskell observed, Hepburn acted her parts with "a kind of ruthless, upper-class eccentricity, that was more a revenge on, than an expression of, her personality." Hepburn also starred in the comedies *Holiday* (1938), *The Philadelphia Story* (1940), and many others.

Claudette Colbert played the lead opposite Clark Gable in *It Happened One Night* (1934). In this prototypical plot, Colbert is a rich heiress who, to spite her father, jumps off his yacht and runs away to marry a basically worthless man whom she barely knows. En route to the clandestine wedding, she encounters Clark Gable, a newspaper reporter assigned to cover the story of her disappearance. He accompanies Colbert on her quest and helps her learn some valuable lessons about the value of money, humility, and loyalty. A running gag is that the two have to sleep in the same room, so each night Gable hangs a wire between their beds and throws a sheet over it. They refer to this separating sheet as "the walls of Jericho," which as might be expected, fall by the end of the film.

Bluebeard's Eighth Wife (1938) is a romantic farce in which a recently impoverished father pushes his daughter, played by Colbert, into a romance with multimillionaire Gary Cooper. Colbert meets Cooper in a French haberdashery where he asks to buy only half a pair of pajamas—the bottom half. Coincidentally, Colbert also wants to buy half a pair of pajamas; however, she wants the top half. When Cooper takes the shopkeeper aside to ask him the reason for her odd request, the shopkeeper responds, "Love has its little secrets, m'sieur." At first, Colbert resists Cooper's advances, but they eventually marry. She then discovers that Cooper is a romantic philanderer and that she is actually wife number eight. She launches into a campaign to keep from consummating the marriage. Her ploys include having fake affairs in hopes of driving Cooper to jealousy and frustration so that he will divorce her and give her a handsome settlement. She is so successful with her schemes that Cooper winds up straitjacketed in an insane asylum. Colbert gets her settlement, and once she is independently wealthy, decides to approach Cooper on her own terms.

Jean Arthur is a young salesgirl who gets involved with her older boss while he is masquerading as a shoe salesman in *The Devil and Miss Jones* (1941). Charles Coburn plays a millionaire store owner whose workers hate him so much that they burn him in effigy and constantly attack him at their labor meetings. In an attempt to gather evidence for his revenge, which would involve a wholesale purge of recalcitrant employees, Coburn becomes a shoe salesman in his own store. Of course he is inept, but he is guided and helped by Arthur's character, and the two strike up a warm friendship. The ironic twist is that Arthur's boyfriend, played by Robert Cummings, is the leader of the labor agitators. Coburn gets to savor the joys of Coney Island with Arthur, but ends up being matched with another woman.

In the opening scene of *Easy Living* (1937), Arthur is riding a bus to work when a mink coat falls from a penthouse window and lands in her lap. Later in the movie when she wears the coat to a Horn and Hardart automat cafeteria, an employee behind the rows of little square food-dispensing boxes sees her, assumes that she is a mistress of a millionaire, and so reaches through the glass door to personally hand out her piece of pie. Other movies starring Jean Arthur include *The Whole Town's Talking* (1935), *The Ex-Mrs. Bradford* (1936), *Easy Living* (1937, *You Can't Take It With You* (1938), *Too Many Husbands* (1940), and *The More the Merrier* (1943).

Other females who took leads in screwball comedies include Bette Davis, Jean Harlow, Myrna Loy, Ginger Rogers, Rosalind Russell, Barbara Stanwyck, and Loretta Young. Billie Burke and Edna May Oliver are two of screwball comedy's grande dames, who played the roles of mothers or aunts.

After World War II, tastes changed and so did fashions in moviemaking. However even today many people enjoy old screwball comedies. They also watch more recent comedies made in the same madcap style and in-

corporating many of the motifs that were first developed in the screwball comedies. One of these traditional screwball comedy motifs involves playing with death and questions about reincarnation, as in the 1964 *Goodbye Charlie,* in which Walter Matthau is murdered and then reincarnated as a libidinous Debbie Reynolds. Masquerading, usually as someone of the opposite sex, is the basis for slapstick humor in the 1959 *Some Like It Hot,* starring Jack Lemmon and Tony Curtis, the 1982 *Tootsie,* starring Dustin Hoffman and Jessica Lange, and the 1993 *Mrs. Doubtfire,* starring Robin Williams and Sally Field. The 1989 *War of the Roses,* in which a divorcing couple (Michael Douglas and Kathleen Turner) fight to utter destruction, is a modern exaggeration of the kinds of fights Carole Lombard had with her leading men, while the 1981 *Arthur,* starring Dudley Moore and John Gielgud, and the 1983 *Trading Places,* starring Dan Aykroyd and Eddie Murphy, play on the differences in lifestyles between the very rich and the very poor that had amused viewers in the 1930s. *See also* GENDER AND HUMOR, MOVIES, SITCOMS

Further reading: William K. Everson, *Hollywood Bedlam: Classic Screwball Comedies* (1994). Wes D. Gehring, *Screwball Comedy: A Genre of Madcap Romance* (1986). Mark Winokur, *American Laughter: Immigrants, Ethnicity and 1930s Hollywood Film Comedy* (1996).

Scriptwriters

In the business of comedy scriptwriting, most professionals either work in groups, preparing television scripts for sustained monologues, skits, sitcoms, and variety shows, or they work for producers, writing and rewriting movie scripts. However, there are still a few writers who primarily write jokes marketed through specialized publications to public speakers, comedians, politicians, and radio commentators. Sheldon Keller and Howard Albrecht, who, in the early 1990s, prepared and distributed *Funny Stuff from the Gag Gang* and *Daily Almanac,* said that disc jockeys were their prime subscribers because they need more jokes in a month than stand-up comedians need during their whole careers. Disc jockeys are on the air for long hours and can't get away with repeating their jokes, because night after night the same people are likely to be listening.

The group writing of scripts for television sitcoms and for the skits and monologues that distinguish today's variety shows is a fairly recent development. Bob Hope was one of the first comedians to publicly praise—or even to admit he had—joke writers. He continued his generosity in May of 1998, when at age 95, he was honored at the British Embassy in Washington, DC, and quipped, "If only my writers were here, I'd have a good ad lib."

The image of comedy writing that most nonprofessionals hold in their minds resembles that portrayed in television's *The Dick Van Dyke Show* (1961–1966), where Van Dyke played the role of television writer Rob Petrie, with Mary Tyler Moore playing the role of his wife Laura. Co-stars Morey Amsterdam and Rose Marie Mazetta played the roles of fellow writers, all trying to please producer Mel Cooley, played by Richard Deacon. The show was a success partly because of the talent of the actors, but also because of its format. Rob and Laura's marriage allowed for domestic humor, while the work situation allowed for group conflicts and experimentation with other kinds of humor, under the guise of preparing it for the fictional show.

Today, many of the children who grew up watching *The Dick Van Dyke Show* in its original form or in reruns have the kind of job that Rob Petrie made look so appealing. A *New York Times* article (Jul. 17, 1995) said that in the summer of 1995, 59 television comedies went into production compared to 45 during the 1994 season. That meant that 500 to 600 writers were needed, and there weren't that many with experience. The result was a bidding war and raids from one studio to another. Jamie McDermott, senior vice president in charge of prime-time series programming for NBC, complained that "as more comedies get onto the air, more and more talent and less and less experience is getting raided."

In another *New York Times* article (Aug. 26, 1997) entitled "Looking for Laughs? Call a Harvard Grad," James Sterngold said that dozens of Harvard graduates, as well as many other Ivy League scholars, are writing for television comedies. Some of them who got their start on the *Harvard Lampoon* are attracted by the excellent salaries, the chance to associate with other writers, and the fact that they can dress casually. In 1997, four of 13 writers for *The Simpsons* were Harvard graduates, as were five of the 14 writers for *King of the Hill*, and three of the eight writers for *Party of Five*. There were also Harvard alumni writing for *Saturday Night Live, Late Show with David Letterman, Cracker, News Radio, Third Rock from the Sun, Seinfeld, Veronica's Closet, The Larry Sanders Show, Suddenly Susan, Murphy Brown*, and *The Naked Truth*. Sterngold said that bright young Ivy Leaguers prefer writing for television to movies because of the higher prestige and the greater chance for media coverage. Also, in comparison to movies, which seem to be run by deal makers, television writers feel more in touch with their craft because the loop between writing and production is shorter and therefore less likely to be tampered with by outsiders.

Neil Simon tried to capture the challenge and the excitement of comedy-team writing in his 1993 Broadway play *Laughter on the 23rd Floor*. It was about his days working on what some people judge to be the first truly successful team of comedy writers. Neil Simon and his brother Danny worked along with such legends as Mel Brooks, Carl Reiner, Larry Gelbart, Mel Tolkin, Sheldon Keller, Aaron Ruben, and Gary Belkin as writers for Sid Caesar's *Your Show of Shows* and *Caesar's Hour*, both at the top of the charts in the 1950s. Nine of Caesar's writers met with him in a 1996 reunion, which resulted in a 90-minute PBS television special and numerous articles about the event. Journalist William Grimes said that the group was "the most brilliant collection of talent since the 1927 Yankees took the field," while Ron Simon, curator at the Museum of Television and Radio in Manhattan explained that the team was "sometimes stumblingly but more often brilliantly, working out a comic language for a new medium." They "came to television without any extensive background in radio or vaudeville. They did something unique, creating skits with a visual quality that would play well on television."

The relationship between a performer and his or her writers is a crucial element. Gene Perret, who has been a head writer for Bob Hope, Phyllis Diller, Bill Cosby, Carol Burnett, John Travolta, and Gabe Kaplan, smiles when he tells about how Gabe Kaplan put so many demands on his writers that the staff threatened to walk. Instead, they began writing scripts that left Kaplan delivering only a few lines at the beginning and the end of each episode. Historically, for the groups that have been most successful, writers and performers have worked side by side or have been one and the same, as with the Monty Python group, the Sid Caesar group, and Mike Nichols and Elaine May. Many well known performers have worked as members of writing teams for other comedians. In the early 1950s, for example, Johnny Carson wrote for Red Skelton, while in the 1970s both Jay Leno and David Letterman subsidized their stand-up earnings by writing for other comedians.

Writers are hired for teams sometimes on the basis of having submitted a "spec," that is, a script for speculation, sometimes on the basis of having published humorous pieces in magazines or newspapers, and sometimes on the basis of a performance. Alan Zwiebel, who, from 1975 to 1980, was a writer for *Saturday Night Live* and who created *It's Garry Shandling's Show*, said that when he first started out, he performed his own jokes. In 1972, *SNL's* Lorne Michaels was in his audience one night and came up afterwards to say, "You know, you are the absolute worst comic I have ever seen in my life," but he nevertheless liked the material and asked Zwiebel for a sample. Zwiebel went to his mother's house, sat at her kitchen table, and typed up 1,100 of his best jokes. They were good enough to get him his first regular job working for NBC.

Teams work especially well for sitcom writing because the members inspire each other and bring in different points of view. Matt Williams and John Markus of the Museum of Television and Radio have explained that jokes are less important than believability and character development. A team needs someone who can write funny dialogue, someone who can create interesting plots, someone who can coordinate the male voices with the female voices, and someone who can create unique but believable characters. And most importantly, the team has to be able to blend all these differences into a coherent and significant show with a poignant point of view.

Larry Gelbart, who helped create *A Funny Thing Happened on the Way to the Forum*, *M*A*S*H*, *Oh God*, *Tootsie*, and *City of Angels*, told a *Writer's Digest* (Apr. 1995) reporter that authors should not crush their work with the weight of their cleverness. Part of writing is editing. In short, "Say it once. Say it well. Say it quickly." When asked about the future of the entertainment industry, Gelbart responded, "The future of the entertainment industry has already been written in its past. The only thing that changes is the medium. We're moving into "superhighways—that's just another way of saying we've figured out a new way to bring you *The Three Stooges*. Whatever the hardware, the software is always going to be the human condition— how we relate to one another, how we love, how we hate."

According to Michiko Kakutani, writing in the *New York Times Magazine* (Feb. 1, 1998), Gelbart is disappointed with what he calls "table writing" in which "a draft will be prepared by one or two writers, and the staff will sit around a table and try to get in as many new lines as possible. It is not an art being practiced here. It's a product being manufactured to as rigid a set of standards as getting all the right ingredients inside a bottle of Coca-Cola."

Chuck Tatham, television critic for *The New York Times,* has also criticized the tried-and-true techniques that writers overuse. One technique, the rule of three, places two regular items in front of the "blow" or the "joke" item, as in "The anti-fur activists are at it again in Beverly Hills. They're protesting fur coats, mink stoles, and that thing on William Shatner's head." *Implication by omission* is at work when a character quips, "People say I'm involved with the Mafia and that I'm gay.

I am not gay." *Literalization* is the technique of having a character ask, "What kind of an idiot do you think I am?" and another one respond, "A cute one." There is no end to the jokes based on *misunderstandings*, as when a dad says, "Well, kids, the doctor says Grandma has a cataract," and little brother responds "A cataract! I thought she had a Lincoln Continental."

Cartoonist and writer Garry Trudeau, in a *New York Times* spoof (Aug. 1, 1993) titled "Anatomy of a Joke," protested how a profession that started with a few friends sharing laughs has evolved into big business. He solemnly explained that the *Tonight Show* has a staff of 12 "clippers" who peruse some 300 newspapers every day, focusing on headlines since that is as far as anyone reads. Their mountains of clippings are sent to the "comedy engineers," who decide how many parts the jokes should be broken into, how many red herrings or false clues to include, and the velocity of the buildup. The jokes then go to the "stylists," who are the prima donnas of the team, often the best paid and the worst dressed. They fashion the raw jokes, which then go to the "polish man" and then to the timing coach. Finally the joke is e-mailed to "the talent" (Jay Leno). "Once Leno approves the joke, it is transferred to a hard disk and laser-printed on cue cards with a special font to make it look hand-lettered. Finally, at exactly 5:30 P.M., California taping time, Leno walks out on stage and reads it to 15 million people." *See also*: COMEDY TEAMS, MOVIES, RADIO, SITCOMS

Further reading: Arthur Asa Berger, *The Art of Comedy Writing* (1997). Larry Gelbart, *Laughing Matters* (1998). Gene Perret, *Become a Richer Writer: Shift Your Writing Career into High Gear* (1997).

Self-Disparagement

Self-disparagement or self-deprecating jokes often surprise and amuse listeners or readers and leave them feeling superior to the comedian or writer. The form has become so common that advertisers can parody it with slogans that at first appear to be self-deprecating, but are really clever plays on words, as in these examples:

When you think of pests, think of us. (Terminix Pest Control)

Eight million people walked all over us. And they don't even know our name. (Champion International Trend Carpet)

Our new menthol is a lemon. (Twist lemon-menthol cigarettes)

Quaker Oats: Breakfast of losers. (Quaker Oats as a diet food)

Simmons beds are a lot of bunk. (Simmons bunk beds)

Comedians often use self-deprecating jokes as a way of breaking the ice with an audience, as when Jackie Mason solemnly confides to a new audience, "The way you look at me, I think you're waiting for the comedian to show up." Red Buttons used to joke about having taken the economy flight to whatever city he was in: "The airline couldn't afford to show movies, but the pilot flew low over drive-in theaters." Dick Cavett has quipped that, although he doesn't mind being short, he was insulted when *Playgirl* magazine offered him a half-centerfold. Billy Crystal, who also is short, says he collects miniature furniture because it gives him a feeling of great height.

In the mid-1970s, newly appointed President Gerald Ford opened a speech at Ohio State University by telling the audience, "So much has happened in the few months since you were kind enough to invite me to speak here today. I was then America's first instant Vice-President, and then I became America's first instant President. The Marine Corps Band is so confused they don't know whether to play, 'Hail to the Chief' or 'You've Come a Long Way, Baby.'"

Rodney Dangerfield has based his career on a claim of getting no respect. He says that when he was a kid he was so ugly they tried to make him a poster boy for birth control, and in games of "Hide and Seek" nobody would come looking for him. Dangerfield claims his pet rock died, and the last sweepstakes letter he got began with "You may already be a loser." He notes that he tried to forget his troubles by going to the horse races, but that when they shot off the starting pistol they killed the horse Dangerfield had bet on.

He says he sought help from a psychologist, but when he confided that he had suicidal tendencies the psychologist asked for payment in advance.

In the 1960s, Phyllis Diller, with her blonde fright wig, her garish clothes, and her cackling laugh, became the first female stand-up comedian to be offered top billing in big clubs and on television. Most of her jokes were self-deprecating, even those that she made about her husband, Fang, her sister-in-law, Captain Bligh, and her mother-in-law, Moby Dick. She said she combed her hair with an electric toothbrush and was chosen for inclusion in *What's That?* instead of in *Who's Who?* Audiences loved it when she said her Playtex Living Bra died from starvation and that she was unable to get Lloyds of London to insure her face: "What the hell more could happen to it?" Overweight Totie Fields made similar jokes about being fat, while Joan Rivers, claiming she was the ugliest child ever born in Larchmont, New York, said, "Oh, please! The doctor looked at me and slapped my mother."

During the 1970s, feminist critics took umbrage at the way women entertainers put themselves down and also made fun of other women. As more women have become comedians, such criticism has softened, because self-disparagement is only one of many techniques female comedians now use. Also, critics have become more understanding. In an article about women comedians, "Stand and Deliver" in the July 1988 *Savvy* magazine, Charles Leehsen quoted author Betsy Borns as explaining that early women comedians had to use self-disparagement "because to be in a position of power and be beautiful would have been terrifying for the audiences of the day. You know, if Eleanor Roosevelt looked like Jayne Mansfield, people wouldn't have been able to handle it." *See also* DISABILITIES AND HUMOR, GENDER AND HUMOR

Further reading: Susan Horowitz, *Queens of Comedy: Lucille Ball, Phyllis Diller, Carol Burnett, Joan Rivers, and the New Generation of Funny Women* (1997). Ronald L. Smith, *Who's Who in Comedy* (1992).

Silent Films

In 1890, inventors in France, Germany, Great Britain, and the United States competed to develop a machine that could project a series of pictures resembling movement in real life. Thomas Edison was one of these inventors, and although he was unable to meet his pre-release promises, he put together a kind of projector that showed a 90-second "movie"—basically a peep show—at the 1893 Chicago World's Fair. Edison's major contribution was the idea of perforating the edges of the film at equal distances so that it would move smoothly in front of the projector lens.

The first projectors were installed in penny arcades, but within a few years, the machinery was refined enough that pictures could be shown on large screens. The most obvious place to find audiences for these short movies was at vaudeville shows; thus, up-and-coming owners of vaudeville theaters began showing short, silent films, usually as concluding numbers. Many of the films produced by Edison's company had sexually titillating titles, which were tricks or jokes, as when *The Pouting Model* (1902) turned out to be a nude little girl with her back to the camera, and *What Happened on 23rd St., NYC* (1901) showed a strong wind that blew up women's skirts. Edison hired Edwin S. Porter, who, in 1903, made the first highly acclaimed American movie, *The Great Train Robbery*, which was 12 minutes long. Prior to creating this dramatic action thriller, Porter directed some of the earliest satire. His *Terrible Teddy, the Grizzly King* (1901) made fun of Vice President-elect Theodore Roosevelt, while *Uncle Josh at the Moving Picture Show* (1902) made fun of a country bumpkin who is so excited by a kissing scene in a movie that he tears down the screen.

When in 1900, New York vaudeville performers went on strike over a salary dispute, some managers filled their entire programs with short films. Audiences kept coming, and the strike was broken. By 1906, silent films had moved permanently out of penny arcades, nickelodeons, and vaudeville houses and into hundreds of storefront, neighborhood theaters. In 1908, the more than 600 nickel theaters in greater New York were collecting between 300,000 and 400,000 admission fees each day. The price climbed from a nickel to a quarter, but working-class people (laborers, homemakers, and teenagers, many of them immigrants) still found the money and the time to go to the movies. The programs lasted only 20 to 30 minutes, so that workers and children could stop to view them on their way home and women could use them as a shopping break, often bringing their babies with them. Because of such support from the working class, movies became well established as entertainment for the masses before the middle classes sat up and took notice. It was 1913 before a theater was built especially for movies, and it was 1914 before S. L. "Roxy" Rothapfel entered the scene. He was the first great showman to see a potential audience of middle-class customers. In keeping with his philosophy, "Don't 'give the people what they want'—give 'em something better," he provided special lighting, uniformed ushers, splendid restrooms, and orchestral music.

Much of the film from the pre-1912 movies has faded or crumbled away, but fortunately for historians, producers wanting to protect their work from being plagiarized sent paper copies to the Library of Congress. Nearly one-third of these pre-1912 films were comic in nature. Some were simply photographed acts from vaudeville; audiences were not as impressed with these as with pictures of exotic places and grandly moving waterfalls, running horses, crashing stagecoaches, and roaring locomotives. Scripts were sometimes read by a narrator in the theater, usually in English, but occasionally translated to the language of the neighborhood. Some theaters had small orchestras or a piano player, while most films included cards for the audience to read.

The fewer cards needed, the faster paced the movie could be, so there was a premium on performers who could pantomime and use gestures or facial expressions to move the plot along or to get a laugh. Cross-eyed Ben Turpin is a prime example. His eyes were injured in a childhood accident, but the rumor was that they had slipped permanently off-center because of the way he held them when playing his signature character of Happy Hooligan. Besides having eyes that were askew, Turpin had a short and agile body well suited for slapstick and pratfalls, a comically high forehead, and an Adam's Apple that jutted out as punctuation for his emotional outbursts. In 1914, he co-starred with Charlie Chaplin in *The Champion* and *A Night Out*, and later made his own short films. One of the best was a parody of Rudolph Valentino in *The Shriek of Araby* (1923).

Humor had to be obvious in the early pictures to make up for the poor quality of the film and the flickering of the hand-cranked projectors. Favorite comic techniques included running film backwards so that a diver moved out of instead of into the water, speeding up, and then slowing down, a train or a horse, racing cars backward through city streets, and setting a table or washing dishes at breakneck speed. Fights, chases, accidents, and pratfalls could all be funnier with changes in directions and speeds. Kurt Vonnegut in his 1966 antiwar novel *Slaughterhouse-5* refers wistfully to this old comic film technique when he watches a war movie backwards and happily sees the bombs float up and tuck themselves inside the airplanes and the shattered buildings put themselves back together.

Between 1912 and 1929, over 10,000 silent films were made, many of which are now enjoying a second life because of college film courses, videotapes, and television. Charlie Chaplin, Buster Keaton, Harold Lloyd, and to a lesser extent, Harry Langdon, are considered the all-time great comedians of silent film. In the late 1920s American studios were producing around 700 feature films a year; the closest any other country came was Germany with nearly 250; Britain with fewer than 50; and a half dozen other countries with fewer than 25. In a 1972 worldwide poll of the best-ever films, Buster Keaton's *The General* (1926) was ranked in the top 10, while Charlie Chaplin's *The Gold Rush* (1925) was in the top 20.

One of the first producers of silent films was D. W. Griffith. Although he was not particularly interested in humor, one of his actors and directors, Mack Sennett, was. In 1912 Sennett left Griffith to form his own Keystone Studio where his first four films foreshadowed all that followed. *Cohen Collects a Debt* ridiculed the mistakes of ordinary people. *The Water Nymph* challenged standards of modesty and flirted with sexuality by showing a girl in a bathing suit. *The New Neighbor* went further by introducing sexual competition, while *Riley and Schultz* introduced incompetent police officers—forerunners to the Keystone Kops.

Sennett had learned from Griffith to cut his scenes and to move from one locale to another, but in his own work he far outdid anything that Griffith had done. Violent energy and a fast pace were his trademarks as he produced pictures of a society in total disorder. Such disarray was to be put aright by the arrival of proper authority, but when the Keystone Kops came, the chaos was made worse rather than better.

Although relatively little footage was devoted to them, it is the Keystone Kops that the Sennett studios are remembered for. In his autobiography, Sennett modestly gave credit for the development of filmed slapstick to the French Pathe studios and their star, Max Linder, but in reality Sennett's Keystone Kops have their own uniqueness. Their helmets looked like inverted spittoons, and they lurched past the camera so fast that it was a challenge to figure out who was doing what. For the chases, such scenery as trees, telephone poles, city buildings, and street signs was painted onto a moving panorama. Collisions were filmed by backing two cars away from each other and then reversing the film so that it looked like a crash. Audiences cheered as they watched authority figures topple out of their patrol cars and slip and fall as they ran down the streets in pursuit of justice. Critics worried that the movies would inspire a general lack of respect for authority.

Sennett recruited Charlie Chaplin to work for him after Chaplin had already developed his style while growing up in the poorer parts of London and working as a pantomimist in British vaudeville. Chaplin worked for Sennett for only one year, but in that time acted in 35 movies, half as many as he made in his lifetime. Sennett wanted to be more obvious and more vulgar than did Chaplin, and they continually argued over style and details. Once Chaplin had broken with Sennett and began making his own movies, he slowed his pace and achieved his greatest comic effects when he gave audiences time to observe and appreciate the subtleties of his actions.

It was Sennett's idea that Chaplin adopt a persona that he could use regularly. Chaplin's choice of the tramp was both inspired and practical. British, French, and Italian film comedies had already featured character clowns dressed as tramps, but Chaplin saw more in the character than did anyone else. Fatty Arbuckle, another Sennett star, provided Chaplin with his own oversized shoes and pants. Chaplin, who added the tight-fitting coat, the bowler hat, the moustache, and the cane, explained to Sennett that his character was many-sided, "a tramp, a gentleman, a poet, a dreamer, a lonely fellow, always hopeful of romance and adventure." The "Little Tramp" became a world figure, easily recognized, but able to play many roles. He brought pathos to the screen by solving problems, not through anarchy and rebellion, but through imaginative magic. Rather than changing conditions or events, he changed the way people looked at them.

Buster Keaton grew up in vaudeville and in 1917 began making short movies with Fatty Arbuckle. In 1920, he set out on his own and between 1923 and 1928 made 10 features, three of which are considered classics, along with his earlier *Cops* (1922). Keaton personified the "Little Man" as he was shown in long shots running away from giant boulders, battling a windstorm, eluding cops, or gazing into the face of some other disaster. He capitalized on America's increasing fascination with mechanical things. In one of the funniest scenes in *The General* (1926), Keaton is so busy chopping wood to stoke a train engine that he doesn't notice the whole Union Army passing behind him. Keaton was one of the first directors to insist on authenticity,

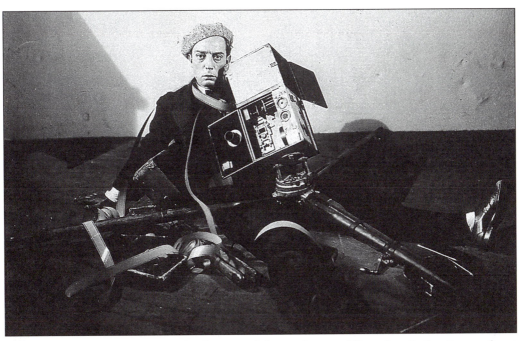

Buster Keaton's calm demeanor charmed audiences partly because it was so different from the frenetic pace of most silent films. *Archive Photos*

and he shocked the world of moviemaking by burning a real bridge and plunging a real train into the water below. In *Steamboat Bill Jr.* (1928) he fights a cyclone, while in a later scene a two-ton wall falls on him. As "the Great Stone Face," Keaton is unscathed because he happens to be standing in the spot of an open window frame. As the protagonist in *The Navigator* (1924), he christens a ship and then exhibits no emotion as he watches it sink. In *Sherlock Jr.* (1924), Keaton is a movie projectionist who is wrongly accused of theft and therefore fired by the woman he loves. He falls asleep in the projection booth, and in a dream, leaves his body and walks down the aisle of the theater and into the movie screen where he remains in the same position, while all around him dramatic and scary events happen. In *The Cameraman* (1928), Keaton plays a street photographer who poses as a newsreel cameraman in hopes of wooing a young star.

Harold Lloyd also experimented with sight gags and breathtaking danger as his protagonists came face to face with the menaces of modern living. His 1923 *Safety Last* is the story of an innocent young man who, in a literalization of the upward-mobility meta-phor, moves to the city and climbs a sky-scraper to impress his girlfriend. Before he reaches the top and falls into her arms, he must overcome pigeons, a tennis net, a painter's scaffolding, a weather gauge, and a giant clock whose minute hand temporarily gives him something to hang on to.

Harry Langdon was hired by Mack Sennett in 1923 after a 20-year career in vaudeville. His style was the opposite of Sennett's, who was frenetic while Langdon was slow and lugubrious. Laughs came when he did nothing but stare wide-eyed and try to make sense out of a puzzling world. According to *New York Times* writer David Everitt (Mar. 30, 1997), in the 1920s, Harry Langdon's "pudding-faced man-child was considered as endearing and uproarious as Chaplin's Little Tramp, Keaton's stoic dare-devil, and Lloyd's indefatigable go-getter." Everitt said that while contemporary viewers aren't as comfortable with Langdon's sheet-white face, his dark eyes, and his curlicue mouth accented by theatrical lipstick, they may nevertheless enjoy the newly released and digitally enhanced videos of his three best movies made in 1926 and 1927: *Tramp, Tramp, Tramp, The Strong Man,* and *Long Pants.*

Stan Laurel and Oliver Hardy teamed up in 1927 to make silent films, and unlike most silent film stars, were able to move on, in 1929, to be equally successful in talkies. They looked funny, they talked funny, and they moved funny. Their comedy was uncompromising slapstick as illustrated by the "pie fight of all time," which occurs in *Battle of the Century* (1927).

The development of recording sound equipment in the late 1920s was not altogether an advantage. One problem was that the placement of microphones and the machinery necessary for recording sound forced camera operators to stay in one place. New techniques and equipment had to be developed to get back to the free movement that audiences had gotten used to. Also, according to Robert Sklar, in his 1994 book *Movie-Made America*, when moviemakers tried to translate the chance-taking of Buster Keaton, the romanticism of Charlie Chaplin, and the sexual innuendo and antiauthoritarian attitudes of Mack Sennett into words, censorship was an unexpected side effect. Silent films had not been censored because it was hard to pin down exactly what someone's facial expression was communicating or what social message viewers were taking away along with their chuckles. But once characters started speaking, social critics moved in to question and to protest. "Comedy, of course, survived," Sklar says, "but the rich comic traditions, with its roots in social conflict, ridicule, exaggeration and license, largely vanished from the commercial screen." *See also* ANIMATION, MOVIES, SCREWBALL COMEDIES

Further reading: David Robinson, *From Peep Show to Palace: The Birth of American Film* (1996). Robert Sklar, *Movie-Made America: A Cultural History of American Movies* (1994). John Walker, *Halliwell's Film and Video Guide: 1998.*

Sitcoms

Television sitcoms (situation comedies) are continuing stories about casts of characters who find themselves in jams and mild predicaments mostly of their own making. The characters try to solve the problem of the day, but their efforts usually make things worse.

Just before the closing commercial, someone or something usually comes in from the outside and sets things right so that the show ends with the characters, the music, and the closing scene much as it was at the beginning.

The sitcom was originally developed for radio because listeners grew tired of hearing performers retell the kinds of random jokes that had been the fashion in vaudeville—radio listeners wanted contexts and familiar characters. When television came along, the visual element was an added bonus. Among the early radio sitcoms that moved to television (sometimes with a different cast) were *The Goldbergs* (1949–1955); *The Life of Riley,* starring William Bendix and later Jackie Gleason (1949–1958); *The George Burns and Gracie Allen Show* (1950–1958); *The Jack Benny Program* (1950–1965); *Ozzie and Harriet,* starring the Nelson family (1952–1966); *Father Knows Best,* starring Jane Wyatt and Robert Young (1954–1962); and *The Honeymooners,* starring Jackie Gleason, Audrey Meadows, and Art Carney (1955–1956).

In general, sitcoms are either about family life or are connected to a work environment or a job. Shows in either category often center on an intriguing individual and will be named after the star, as with *The Patty Duke Show* (1963–1966); *The Dick Van Dyke Show* (1961–1966); *The Mary Tyler Moore Show* (1970–1977); and *The Bob Newhart Show* (1972–1978), which was followed by *Newhart* (1982–1990), and *Bob* (1992–1993). With shows named for a character rather than a performer, viewers tend to remember the star as the character: Dwayne Hickman as *Dobie Gillis* (1959–1963); Shirley Booth as *Hazel* (1961–1966); and Marlo Thomas as *That Girl* (1966–1971). To lend variety to this type of show, characters were sometimes given supernatural or out-of-this-world powers as was Ray Walston in *My Favorite Martian* (1963–1966), Elizabeth Montgomery in *Bewitched* (1964–1972), Barbara Eden in *I Dream of Jeannie* (1965–1970), and Robin Williams in *Mork & Mindy* (1978–1982). In *Mr. Ed* (1960–

1966) the title role was given to a horse whose voice was provided by Rocky Lane.

Occupation-related settings provide variety and open possibilities for a wider range of humor. Early examples include the school-teacher settings for *Mr. Peepers* (1952–1955) and *Our Miss Brooks* (1952–1956), and the police or spy settings for *Car 54: Where Are You* (1961–1963) and *Get Smart* (1965–1970). Other workplace sitcoms include *WKRP in Cincinnati,* starring Loni Anderson (1978–1982); *Taxi,* starring Judd Hirsch, Marilu Henner, and others (1978–1983); *Night Court,* starring Harry Anderson and Marsha Warfield (1984–1992); *Murphy Brown,* starring Candice Bergen (1988–1998); and *Coach,* starring Craig T. Nelson and Jerry Van Dyke (1989–1997). Unusual sitcom locations adding interest and further possibilities for humorous situations are represented by *The Phil Silvers Show* (1955–1959), *McHale's Navy* (1962–1966), *Gilligan's Island* (1964–1967), *F-Troop* (1964–1967), *Gomer Pyle, USMC* (1964–1969), *Hogan's Heroes* (1965–1971), *M*A*S*H* (1972–1983), and *Private Benjamin* (1981–1983).

The earliest and still the most popular sitcoms are family oriented; they are set in people's homes, and the humor comes from the daily frustrations and pleasures associated with sharing one's living space and one's life. *Leave it to Beaver* (1957–1963), a prototypical example, was soon followed by *Dennis the Menace* (1959–1963). Larger families allowed for more humorous possibilities, as in *The Brady Bunch* (1969–1974) and in the fatherless *Partridge Family* (1970–1974). Atypical families included those without mothers: *My Three Sons,* starring Fred MacMurray (1960–1972); *The Courtship of Eddie's Father* (1969–1972); and *My Two Dads* (1987–1990). *The Jeffersons* (1975–1985), an upwardly mobile African American family, provided a contrast to *Sanford & Son,* a show about a streetwise father and his adult son. Non-related adults living together provided new grist for old jokes in *The Odd Couple* (1970–1975), *Three's Company* (1977–1984), and *The Golden Girls* (1985–

1992). *The Munsters* (1964–1966) and *The Addams Family* (1964–1966) stood out because of their horror-movie appearances and spooky lifestyles.

During the past 50 years, only 10 sitcoms have been ranked as the most popular of all television shows during a season. Because of the luck involved regarding competition, these 10 may not be the all-time "best." Nevertheless, brief descriptions illustrate the changing characteristics of sitcoms.

I Love Lucy (1951–1957): Critic Gerard Jones says that Lucille Ball and Desi Arnaz's comedy about a young married couple living in a Manhattan apartment was "a complete synthesis of TV comedy up to that time: It had the music and burlesque of Berle, the plot strength and slickness of *Amos 'n' Andy*, the behind-the-scenes charm of *Burns and Allen*, and the naturalism of *The Goldbergs*." As the first sitcom to be filmed before an audience, it had the quickness and the intensity of live television combined with the sleekness and the shifts of camera angles associated with Hollywood filmmaking.

In 1999, the Comoros Islands beat the United States Postal Service by several months in issuing postage stamps bearing pictures of Lucille Ball.

But more important than any of this was Lucille Ball's comedic talent and the story line. The show had an honesty and a strength of feeling that reached many viewers in post-war America. Domesticity was being held up as the ideal role for women because their men had come home from the war and needed to "take over." Lucy agreed in principle, but she was too bright and too ambitious to settle into the kitchen without a struggle. Millions of women identified with her ambitions even though the shows always ended with the lesson that Lucy would have been better off not to have dreamed so forcefully.

The Andy Griffith Show (1960–1968):

Andy Griffith, a folksy singer and comedian from North Carolina, came to national attention when Danny Thomas hired him for one episode on *The Danny Thomas Show* (also known as *Make Room for Daddy*). He played the part of a country sheriff nailing an arrogant big-city driver. Audience response was so positive that the mythical town of Mayberry, North Carolina, was created with Andy Griffith playing the role of Sheriff Andy Taylor. The show was first called *The Andy Griffith Show,* then changed to *Mayberry R.F.D.* when Griffith left the show. Griffith played the part of a widower sheriff raising his son Opie (Ron Howard) with the help of Aunt Bea, played by Francis Bavier. Comedy came mainly from Don Knotts playing the role of Deputy Sheriff Barney Fife; from Jim Nabors and George Lindsey, who played the roles of Gomer and Goober Pyle, attendants at Wally's gas station; and from an assortment of town folks. Sheriff Taylor cajoled, persuaded, tricked, and occasionally forced characters to do what was for everyone's best interest. This left viewers with a comforting sense that all would be well if only people would communicate with each other. However, as critics have pointed out, the show totally skirted the issue of race relations. Unlike any other town in the South, Mayberry had not a single black citizen. The show appealed to midwestern and southern viewers; in the East, both Jackie Gleason and the Smothers Brothers were more popular.

The Beverly Hillbillies (1962–1971):

The cast included an Ozark widower Jed Clampett, his mother-in-law Granny, his daughter Elly Mae, and his son Jethro. The characters were played by Buddy Ebsen, Irene Ryan, Donna Douglas, and Max Baer Jr., respectively. When oil is discovered and the O. K. Oil Company pays the Clampetts $25 million for their swamp, they move to Beverly Hills to live the life of millionaires. The cast was rounded out by the Drysdales, with Mr. Drysdale as president of the Beverly Hills bank, and Miss Jane Hathaway, the bank's secretary. Producer Paul Henning, who had worked on *The Real McCoys,* modeled the Clampetts after Al Capp's *Li'l Abner* characters and brought in country-hick gags from vaudeville and from *The Grand Ole Opry.* While critics were appalled at the stereotypes, the unsophisticated jokes, and the country-style "Ballad of Jed Clampett," the public loved the show as a 1960s version of the screwball comedies that had kept America laughing through the Depression. The show was aimed at an audience of working-class viewers and was shown early in the evenings to attract both old and young. Elly Mae and her "critters" appealed to kid viewers while teen girls idolized her sexiness and teen boys lusted after her. Boys were comforted to realize that no matter what social mistakes they made they would never appear as unsophisticated as Jethro. Adults fantasized about sudden wealth and about how much better they would be than the Clampetts at adjusting to a new life. Producer Henning took some of the same themes and motifs and reworked them to create the popular *Petticoat Junction* (1963–1970) and *Green Acres* (1965–1971).

All in the Family (1971–1979):

When he created *All in the Family,* Norman Lear purposely set out to shatter the blandness that was on television and to prove to sponsors that their fear of controversy was unjustified. He was inspired to make an American version of the cynical and hard-nosed British sitcom *Till Death Do Us Part.* Lear first thought of Mickey Rooney for the part of Archie Bunker, but Rooney declined saying, "If you go on the air with that, they're going to kill you dead in the streets." Carroll O'Connor, an actor without the baggage carried by the more famous Rooney, took the role and made himself both lovable and ridiculous as the world-weary, racist, and xenophobic blue-collar worker from Queens. Jean Stapleton played Archie's "dingbat" wife, Edith, while Rob Reiner and Sally Struthers played newly wed son-in-law Mike Stivik and daughter Gloria. The success of the show was based as much on the chemistry among these four characters as on Norman Lear's scripts, which dared to demonstrate bigotry and to mention such topics as abortion, birth control, mate-swapping, menopause, and homosexuality. *All in the Family* proved that serious issues could be treated in comic fashion.

Happy Days (1974–1984): The Cunningham family lived in Milwaukee, Wisconsin, during the 1950s and early 1960s. The viewing audience was filled with children and teenagers who related to the Cunningham's son Richie (played by Ron Howard, the grown-up Opie from *The Andy Griffith Show*) and his friends (played by Donny Most, Henry Winkler, and Anson Williams). During the first two years, the show received 15,000 fan letters; 10,000 of them were regarding Winkler's role of Fonzie. "The Fonz" was a little older than the other boys; he wore his dark hair in a ducktail, dressed in a black leather jacket, and rode a motorcycle. The scriptwriters moved Fonzie into a room over the Cunninghams' garage so he could be almost, but not quite, family. Critic Gerard Jones says the show placed itself squarely in popular culture ideas of what a sitcom should be. Soda fountain scenes came right out of *Dobie Gillis*, while characters compared themselves to *Ozzie and Harriet* and other television characters. Jones said that the show jumped up and screamed, "'I'm a sitcom! Not modern, not daring, not sophisticated! I'm a sitcom, just like *Beaver!*' (which was, of course, a pretty modern, daring, sophisticated position to take . . . .)." Part of the appeal of the 1950s setting was that the boys could think, talk, and dream about the pursuit of girls without the complications of 1970s sensitivities brought about by the feminist movement.

Laverne and Shirley (1976–1983): When ABC hired Fred Silverman away from CBS in 1975, Silverman set about pouring even more resources into whatever successes ABC had. Silverman proposed a spin-off from *Happy Days* based on two of the guest characters, Laverne and Shirley, played by Penny Marshall and Cindy Williams. ABC producer Garry Marshall said about viewers, "You have to do something silly to get their attention. Then I like to knock them off their chairs with laughter. I go for the gut. I want them to laugh *hard*. I don't want them quietly staring at a bright, witty show." Laverne and Shirley lived in Milwaukee during the 1960s and worked in the bottle-capping division of Shotz Brewery. The remaining characters included relatives and drivers of the brewery's trucks. After the newness wore off, popularity plummeted, and in 1981, the locale was changed. Laverne and Shirley moved to Los Angeles and became co-owners of the Squignoski Talent Agency of Burbank.

Cheers (1982–1993): Just as the title of the theme song says, people long for a place, "Where Everybody Knows Your Name." This place for the characters, and vicariously for millions of viewers, was the *Cheers* bar located at 112 1/2 Beacon Street in Boston. Main characters included former Boston Red Sox relief pitcher Sam Malone (played by Ted Danson), who started out as the bar's owner; his main love interest Diane Chambers, a prim and proper barmaid with intellectual ambitions (played by Shelley Long); Rebecca Howe, a gorgeous Boston immigrant from San Diego (played by Kirstie Alley), who was first the manager and then the owner; and Carla, an outspoken waitress (played by Rhea Perlman) who had eight children fathered by assorted men. The group was rounded out by several regulars including naïve bartender Woody, mailman Cliff, psychiatrist Frasier, accountant/housepainter Norm, and occasional walk-ins. The characters operated through a protective covering of insults and practical jokes, especially Sam and Diane, whose love-hate relationship failed to evolve into a happy-ever-after love story. The bar was a refuge for troubled individuals who seemed to feel better after blowing off steam. Fall-down drunks have a long history as comic foils, but on *Cheers* the part that alcohol played in making people feel better was sanitized. The show was aimed at an upper echelon of viewers, at people who were turned off by slapstick and the corniness of *The Beverly Hillbillies*. The industry was surprised to find how many such viewers there were.

The Cosby Show (1984–1992): An obvious purpose of *The Cosby Show* was to counterbalance old entertainment stereotypes about poor, shuffling Black folks. The educated, kid-loving, and enormously appealing Bill Cosby played Dr. Heathcliff Huxtable, an obstetrician, who with his lawyer wife, played by Phylicia Rashad, lived in a New York town house and conscientiously raised an ideal family. Black heritage was shown through stories about a grandfather who worked as a Pullman porter, Dr. Huxtable's knowledge of Harlem Renaissance painting and modern jazz, and the fact that the children were expected to go to traditional Black colleges. However, the scriptwriters did send Sondra, the oldest daughter, to Princeton, so the Huxtables could complain about the $79,648.72 that it cost them. Children quarreled and made up, earned bad grades, applied for jobs, argued with their parents, and got married and gave birth to the Huxtable grandchildren. Much of the humor was straight out of 1950s sitcoms, but the setting and the characters made it fresh. What criticism the show received came mostly from a segment of the Black community that said the show was "too white," and from critics who remarked that there was never a problem too severe to be resolved with a clever speech from Cosby.

Roseanne (1988–1995): Roseanne Barr (later Roseanne Arnold and then just Roseanne) transferred her stage persona, as an outspoken comedian representing the frustrated homemakers and mothers of America, into a successful television sitcom about the Conner family. As a mother, Roseanne is as different from June Cleaver and Harriet Nelson as, in the words of Mark Twain,

"lightning is from the lightning bug." But while June Cleaver and Harriet Nelson made viewers feel guilty, Roseanne made them feel superior, by declaring that if the kids were still alive when her husband got home at night, she had done her job. Yet, viewers never doubted that Roseanne loved her kids and was willing to take tough stands with them. In a reversal from the old days when kids had all the "smart" lines, Roseanne said things to her kids that millions of mothers wish they had the cleverness and the nerve to say to their owns kids. Viewers loved Roseanne for her spunkiness; since she brought home the bacon and cooked it too, they were willing to forgive her for being outspoken and a little overweight.

Seinfeld (1990–1998): *Seinfeld*, along with *Frasier*, starring Kelsey Grammer; *Ellen*, starring Ellen DeGeneres; *The Larry Sanders Show*, starring Garry Shandling; and *Friends*, starring Courteney Cox, Matthew Perry, and others, was one of the "smart" comedies of the 1990s, written for college-educated audiences. It ended its nine-year run in 1998, while it was still on top. The sitcom's four New Yorkers, played by Jerry Seinfeld, Julia Louise Dreyfus, Jason Alexander, and Michael Richards, were such fully developed characters that much of the audience's pleasure came from being able to predict the different reactions of each to various incidents. For a cover story on the final episode of Seinfeld, *People* magazine polled celebrities about their favorite episode from the shows nine-year run. Liz Carpenter liked the "spongeworthy" episode in which Elaine wonders if a potential suitor is worthy of using up her supply of scarce contraceptive sponges, while Paula Abdul liked the episode in which Jerry drops his girlfriend's toothbrush in the toilet, doesn't tell her, and then doesn't want to kiss her.

Because of increased diversification, modern TV marketing makes it easier for a show to get a number-one ranking in the polls, but harder for it to become part of the mass consciousness. As far as the rankings go, to be number-one a show does not have to appeal to "everyone," or even to the 40 percent of the viewing audience that watched *I Love Lucy*. With all the competition from new networks, cable channels, and reruns, a show can be the number-one show while being seen by only 20.2 percent of viewers, which was *Seinfeld*'s ranking. *See also* DIALECT HUMOR, RADIO, SCREWBALL COMEDIES, TELEVISION

Further reading: Marc David, *Comic Visions: Television Comedy and American Culture*, 2nd ed. (1997). Rob Owen, *Gen X TV: The Brady Bunch to Melrose Place* (1997). Vincent Terrace, *Television Character and Story Facts* (1993).

Slang

Slang is language at play; it is the metaphors, abbreviations, nicknames, euphemisms, and coinages that people use for purposes of relieving boredom, communicating efficiently, being creative and original, protesting conformity and pomposity, identifying with occupational or social groups, sending insider messages, treating abstractions concretely, camouflaging scary and unpleasant matters, and, in the words of H. L. Mencken, making language "more pungent and picturesque" by increasing our "store of terse and striking words." Teenagers are especially clever about creating slang because they use their own way of talking as a sign of their growing independence from parents and teachers.

"Spanglish" is a new kind of slang finding its way not only into conversations but also into short stories, novels, popular music, comedy acts, and television sitcoms. Sprinkled throughout English sentences are such insertions as *Que no?*, *tambien*, *Yo se*, and *Oye, oye*, as well as combined words as when *barber shop* and *peluqueria* become *barberia*, *chilling out* and *relajar* become *chileando*, and *to park* and *estacionar* become *parkear*. Users explain that Spanglish has moved far away from the clumsy slang of newcomers striving to learn English; it's now used for humor and for giving a comforting sense of identity to people who want to acknowledge that they live in two coexisting worlds.

In 1979, James Baldwin published a celebrated essay in *The New York Times*, "If Black English Isn't a Language, Then Tell Me, What Is?" One of his points was how white American speech has adopted African American slang, and in the process changed the meanings:

> *Jazz*, for example, is a very specific sexual term, as in *Jazz me, baby*, but white people purified it into the *Jazz Age*. *Sock it to me*, which means, roughly, the same thing, has been adopted by Nathaniel Hawthorne's descendants with no qualms or hesitations at all, along with *let it all hang out* and *right on*! *Beat to his socks*, which was once the black's most total and despairing image of poverty, was transformed into a thing called the *Beat Generation*, which phenomenon was, largely, composed of *uptight*, middle-class white people, imitating poverty, trying to *get down*, to *get with it*, doing their *thing*, doing their despairing best to be *funky*, which we, the blacks, never dreamed of doing — we were funky, baby, like *funk* was going out of style.

Occupational slang serves as insider language for everyone from short-order cooks to drug dealers to astrophysicists. In 1967, Princeton physicist John Wheeler coined *black hole* for something, which by definition, no one will ever see. Thirty years later, astronomers, with the help of the Hubble telescope, obtained evidence of real black holes, and the word entered mainstream English. In the process the term became parent to a new generation of slang, as when used to refer to the Chicago branch of the U.S. Post Office, the Russian economy, and the United States national debt.

Code names are a kind of formalized slang. In the mid-1990s, *Newsweek* magazine reported that college admissions officers refer to applicants with such terms as *Woofer*, *Swims*, and *Q & D*. A *Woofer* is a "loser"; a *Swims* gets thrown back in the pool for a second chance; while a *Q & D* is "quiet and diligent but lacks imagination and energy." "Country kids" are called *Rural Reps* or *GRTS* (pronounced "grits") while an *SPI* is a "special interest admit"—most likely the child of parents who donated money to the school.

Long before the days of mass media, slang was effectively spread by word of mouth, but with today's media it can be spread instantaneously and around the world. *Yada, yada, yada, master of my domain,* and *it's in the vault* all made their way into popular culture through television's *Seinfeld* sitcom, while *D'oh!* was adopted from cartoon character Homer Simpson's expression of disappointment or self-disgust.

Earlier generations picked up such signature lines as Will Rogers's "All I know is what I read in the papers," W. C. Fields's "Tain't a fit night out for man nor beast!" Jimmy Durante's "Everybody wants ta get inna the act!" and Jackie Gleason's "How sweet it is!" Later catch phrases adopted from entertainers include Jack Paar's "I kid you not!" Arte Johnson's "Verrrry interesting!" Flip Wilson's "The Devil made me do it!" Gilda Radner's "It's always something!" Joan Rivers's "Can we talk?" Don Adams's "Would you believe . . .?" Rowan and Martin's "Look that up in your Funk & Wagnall's!" and Dennis Miller's "I'm outta here!" *See also* EXAGGERATION, LANGUAGE PLAY, METAPHOR

Further reading: Eric Partridge and Paul Beale, *Shorter Slang Dictionary* (1993).

Sports Language

Sports language often has a humorous side, whether in the chatter of broadcasters filling in time between plays, both real and satirical names for teams, sports-based metaphors, player nicknames, and the names chosen for racehorses. It is to be expected that humorous language would develop around sports because sports engender many of the same intellectual processes and emotional reactions that are part of humor: surprise, incongruity, the venting of hostility, feelings of superiority, and competition between winners and losers. Even though games have predetermined rules and expectations of behavior, players and spectators still want surprise. This is why footballs are designed to bounce in unexpected directions and why, in lopsided competitions, fans often cheer for the underdog. Because games involve skill as well as luck, fans experience feelings of superiority

when they can identify with the winners. They also enjoy relieving hostile feelings by jeering opponents and officials. Only at sports events, is it socially acceptable for sophisticated adults to give raspberry cheers and to yell insults at public officials.

Because sports provide legitimate avenues for playing out conflicts and expressing hostilities, college teams aren't often named after *Bunnies* or *Robins*; but instead have more aggressive names such as *Eagles, Tigers, Cougars, Bulldogs, Panthers, Wildcats,* and *Bears.* Even religious names from church-sponsored schools are adapted to sound aggressive as in the *Fighting Saints,* the *Crusaders,* and the *Battling Bishops.* Over a dozen college team names include *Devil* or *Demon;* for example, the Duke *Blue Devils,* the DePaul *Blue Demons,* and the Wake Forest *Demon Deacons.*

Sportscaster Lindsey Nelson on CBS extended this kind of playful negativity when he suggested we needed a few more bowl games: "the *Probation Bowl*—only schools currently on NCAA probation for rule violations can be considered, the *Punch Bowl*—featuring the teams that led the nation in number of players ejected for fighting, the *Caraway Bowl*—limited to colleges with seedy-looking campuses, and the *Ty-Dee Bowl*—a posh affair. Winners each receive a free dinghy."

When a sports team isn't doing well, the fans take out their frustrations with such temporary name changes as *Cincinnati Beagles* (Bengals), *Denver Buncos* (Broncos), *Houston Castros* (Astros), *Indianapolis Count On a Loss This Sunday* (Colts), *L.A. Lambs* (Rams), *New Orleans Aints* (Saints), and *New York Mutts* (Mets).

Omni magazine sometimes sponsors renaming contests, one of which was won by a Canadian when he suggested that the Norris Division of the National Hockey League was so terrible that it should be called the *Porous Division,* with the five teams being the *Chicago Slackhawks,* the *Detroit Deadwings,* the *Minnesota No Stars,* the *St. Loseit Blues,* and the *Toronto Makebelieves.* Editor Scot Morris in the "Games" column of *Omni* magazine chose this entry as the winner because the team names were phonologically clever while contributing to the semantic idea that the league was full of holes.

While journalists are quick to criticize the choice of team names, they are happy to take advantage of every potential for a pun and every nuance in meaning. In dead moments between plays, broadcasters comment on players' names, and on days when no games are played reporters often look to names for a story. As Roy Blount Jr. once remarked, "To suggest to a sportswriter that he write about names is like suggesting to a fat man that he eat pie."

There are two kinds of nicknames in sports; one is the short, easy-to-shout name that develops naturally among teams working outdoors and needing to communicate quickly and efficiently. The other type includes literary names concocted by publicists and journalists. One of these is *The Real McCoy*, now a common phrase meaning "the real thing." While its origin is disputed, many lexicographers think that it comes from *Kid McCoy*, the professional name of Norman Selby, welterweight boxing champion from 1898–1900. Selby was billed as *The Real McCoy* and would prove he was aptly named by boxing with doubters until they conceded.

Obviously the Chicago Bears' William Perry with the nickname *The Refrigerator* had to be more successful at tackling than running. Lanky basketball star Wilt Chamberlain wanted to be called *The Big Dipper*, but fans preferred the rhyme in *Wilt the Stilt*. New York Yankee's catcher Lawrence Peter Berra became so famous as *Yogi Berra* that he inspired the cartoon character, *Yogi Bear*, and a generation grew up more familiar with his namesake than with him. In the summer of 1997, it was the cartoon character, not the man, whose name was given to one of the rocks found on Mars.

As in other areas of tremendous growth, it's harder than it used to be for schools to come up with team names that will stand out. This has caused many schools to look for a humorous touch that will communicate something about the school's history or location: Columbia College in California has the name of *Claim Jumpers*; the Vassar *Brewers* are named for the occupation that earned

Matthew Vassar, the school's benefactor, his millions; and the *Moles* of Nazareth College in Kalamazoo, Michigan are named in honor of the tunnels that connect campus buildings. ESPN sports broadcaster Chris Fowler nominated these high school teams for a "Scholastic Sports America" nickname hall of fame: *Awesome Blossoms* from Blooming Prairie, Minnesota; *Bats* from Belfry, Montana; *Bubblers* from Boiling Springs, Pennsylvania; *Cavegirls* and *Cavemen* from Carlsbad, New Mexico; *Ghosts* and *Spooks* from Chillicothe, Illinois; *Headless Horsemen* from Sleepy Hollow High in Tarrytown, New York; *Hi-Tides* from Miami Beach, Florida; and *Sparkplugs* from Speedway, Indiana.

Amateur athletes in a playful mood often do mental gymnastics to figure out clever names. Over the last several years, teams running in the Nike Capital Challenge, a footrace held in Washington, DC, have included *The Peacock Strutters* from NBC; *See Span Run* from C-Span; *Writ Runners* from the Supreme Court; *Appellate Briefs* from the Circuit Court of Appeals; *Running Concurrently* from the U.S. Sentencing Commission; *Elliott Fit Ness's Runtouchables* from the Bureau of Alcohol, Tobacco, and Firearms; and *The Boxer Shorts* captained by U.S. Representative Barbara Boxer.

The names for racehorses must meet several stringent requirements and be approved by The Jockey Club located in Lexington, Kentucky. Nevertheless, owners still have fun with them. *Tentiltwo*'s front legs resembled the hands of a clock, while *Rose's Record* was purchased minutes after Pete Rose broke Ty Cobb's record for career hits. The cleverest names are those that reflect a horse's pedigree as in these examples:

Racehorse Names		
DAM	+ SIRE	= FOAL
Joanne Behave	Hatchet Man	Ax Me Nicely
Fur Scarf	Stop the Music	Muffler
Masked Moment	Dixieland Band	Dixieland Bandit
Top o' the Morning	The Axe II	Splitting Headache
Bridal Party	Blue Ensign	Naval Engagement
Safely Home	Double Zeus	Safe on Second

Creative naming sometimes brings more than smiles. After the 1993 earthquake did severe damage to the campus of California

State University at Northridge, the athletic department staff began a campaign to name their sports arena *The Epi Center* and to change their logo from *The Matadors* to *The Quakes*. As memories of the earthquake faded, so did enthusiasm for the change, but as university spokesman Barry Smith explained, for a while it made a difficult situation easier to bear. *See also* ADAPTATION, METAPHORS, SUPERIORITY AND HOSTILITY, TELEVISION

Further reading: Marvin Terban, *Dictionary of Idioms, Phrases, and Expressions* (1996).

Stage Names

Stage names are the pseudonyms that entertainers give themselves for purposes of professional identification. Of "The *People* 400" list of performers chosen as the "fastest-rising and indisputably established stars and starmakers" by *People* magazine for its 1996 *Entertainment Almanac*, almost one-fourth (98 out of 400) were listed under both "real" and professional or stage names.

Names authority Leslie Dunkling has given an explanation of why performers so often create new names for themselves. He says that for a name "to be widely used and remembered, other people must be able to say it and spell it easily, and it must not suggest anything undesirable or silly. At the same time, a slight dash of the unusual is welcome to provide the necessary individuality."

Humor often enters the picture in relation to this last criterion. When Caryn Johnson changed her name to *Whoopi Goldberg*, she both acknowledged her conversion to Judaism and identified herself as a comedian. Other comedians who have chosen names with humorous connotations include *Woody Allen* (formerly Alan Stewart Konigsberg), who, at age 16, contributed a joke to a newspaper under a name partially borrowed from *Woody* Woodpecker. Comedian *Spike Milligan* is a name with more "punch" than Terence Alan Milligan, while *Phyllis Diller* sounds more like "a dilly" than does Phyllis Driver. *Flip Wilson* was more likely to "flip out" an audience than was someone named Clerow; likewise *Gene*

Wilder sounds more like a "wild and crazy" guy than does Gerald Silberman. *Soupy Sales* sounds more like a pie-in-the-face kind of guy than does Milton Supman, while *Minnie Pearl* sounds like a gem compared to Sarah Ophelia Colley. *Rip Taylor* sounds more exciting than Charles Elmer *Taylor*, *Buster Keaton* sounds more likely to "bust up" an audience than Joseph Frances Keaton, and *Red Buttons* more likely to "pop your buttons" than Aaron Chwatt.

When the late Cecil Martin adopted the stage name of *Boxcar Willie*, he provided himself with that "slight dash of the unusual," which Dunkling said is necessary. The early African American performer Dewey Markham did the same thing when he chose the name *Pigmeat Markham*, as did Sheldon Greenfield when he chose *Shecky Greene*. *Sigourney Weaver* is more distinctive than the original Susan, as is *Barbra Streisand* compared with the original Barbara, *Garrison Keillor* compared with the original Gary, and *Spike Lee* compared with the original Shelton Lee.

Comedians Werner Groebli and Hans Mauch performed under the names *Frick* and *Frack*, respectively, a name now parodied by two brothers who as mechanics do the lighthearted *Click and Clack* PBS radio show and also write a newspaper column on car repairs.

Even when a newly chosen name is not overtly humorous, the creator may be looking for a lighter tone, as when Frances Gumm changed her name to *Judy Garland* and Melvin Kaminsky changed to *Mel Brooks*. It is surprising how many male comedians have chosen first names with the diminutive -y or –ie ending, often thought to be more appropriate for women and children: Joseph Levitch changed to *Jerry Lewis*, David Daniel Kaminsky changed to *Danny Kaye*, Leonard Hackett to *Buddy Hackett*, Herbert John Gleason to *Jackie Gleason*, Jacob Cohen to *Rodney Dangerfield*, Frederick Pruetzel to *Freddie Prinze*, Joseph Abramowitz to *Joey Adams*, Anthony Dominick Bennedeto to *Tony Bennett*, and Joseph Gottlieb to *Joey Bishop*. The effect seems to be one of making audiences feel closer and more intimately connected.

To make his name manageable and to get away from sounding so "foreign," *Liberace* dropped his first two names of Wladziu Valentino. For similar reasons, Alphonso D'Abruzzo changed to *Alan Alda*, Benjamin Kubelsky to *Jack Benny*, and Doris von Kappelhoff to *Doris Day*. On the other hand, some comedians chose names to emphasize the ethnic role they play. Russian stand-up comedian Yakov Pokhis changed to *Yakov Smirnoff*, a name associated with Russian vodka; Wenceslao Moreno changed to *Senor Wences*; and Mario Moreno Reyes changed to *Cantinflas*, from Spanish *cantinflear* meaning to talk gibberish and nonsense. Merwyn Bogue took the name *Ish Kabibble* because its meaning in Yiddish is "I should worry?"

When Herbert Khaury changed his name to *Tiny Tim*, he took advantage of the fame that Charles Dickens had already given the name, plus he made an ironic allusion to himself because he was anything but "tiny." This is the opposite of what Paul Rubenfeld (aka *Reubens*) did when he chose the name of *Pee-Wee Herman*, because he really is small in stature. Giving fans help in connecting names and faces, or names and bodies, was the motivation behind comedian David Akeman's choice of *Stringbean*, roly-poly Samuel Joel Mostel's choice of *Zero Mostel*, Dallas Burrows's choice of *Orson Bean*, Roscoe Conkling Arbuckle's choice of *Fatty Arbuckle*, and Loretta Mary Aiken's choice of comedian *Moms Mabley*.

In 1921, Fatty Arbuckle was involved in a scandal when a girl died at a party he was hosting. He was legally exonerated of responsibility, but was virtually banned from filmmaking. Finally, William Randolph Hearst allowed Arbuckle to direct *The Red Mill*, starring Hearst's protegee Marion Davies, but only on the condition that Arbuckle use another name. Buster Keaton suggested *Will B. Good*, but Arbuckle thought this was too transparent and chose instead *William Goodrich*.

The Marx Brothers have an inspired set of names created by stand-up comedian, Art Fisher, who the brothers sometimes talked with back stage. Fisher's inspiration came from the *Sherlocko, The Monk* comic strip

by Gus Mager. It featured a monkey-faced detective and his assistant Watso. Ronald L. Smith quotes Groucho recalling, "I was the moody one, so he called me *Groucho*. The harp player Adolph—who, after Hitler's rise to power changed his name to Arthur—would be known as *Harpo*. The fellow who wore the gumshoes (Milton, who had a habit of sneaking around backstage) would be known as *Gummo*. And the one constantly chasing the pretty chicks would be called *Chicko*." The brothers weren't as enthused about their new names as were audiences. When a typesetter accidentally left the *k* out of Chicko's name, he became *Chico*. As Milton became successful in the garment industry, his place was taken by Herbert, who was nine years younger than any of the others. He was something of an acrobat, so the brothers named him *Zippo*, after a famous trained chimpanzee. Insisting that he wasn't going to share his name with a monkey, Herbert changed the spelling to *Zeppo*. *See also* ADAPTATION, ALLUSION, LANGUAGE PLAY

Further reading: Leslie Dunkling, *The Guinness Book of Names,* 6th ed. (1993). Michael Cader, *1996 People Entertainment Almanac* (1995). Ronald L. Smith, *Who's Who in Comedy* (1992).

Stand-Up Comedy

Stand-up comedy developed as its own genre during the last half of the 20th century. It grew out of the traditions of burlesque and vaudeville, but differs in that it is limited to only the spoken or comedy part of such shows; it omits the music, the skits, and the variety acts. In comedy clubs, a typical format features three performers: someone who opens the show, warms up the audience, and serves as emcee; a middle performer; and then the "headliner" who closes the show. The headliner is paid the most, especially if he or she has a recognizable name that will draw people into the club.

Starting in the early 1960s, comedy clubs became an increasingly important part of the entertainment industry, with their popularity peaking in the late 1980s and early 1990s. One reason that comedy clubs took hold is that they are fairly simple to operate. Without the variety and the music, only a few performers are involved and there is no need for elaborate staging. A prototypical example of a small, independent comedy club is Pips, in Brooklyn. It was started by George Schultz, a 1950s comedian who dropped out of doing stand-up so he could spend more time at home with his family. Wanting to stay involved with comedy, he found a coffeehouse that he could turn into a club. He chose Sheepshead Bay for its waterside charm, even though he knew it was too far outside of the city for the club to be a big money maker. For his fairly modest business, he booked only comedians, and did not bother with the musical numbers that nightclubs had. Other owners noticed his success and were soon imitating the format.

Rosie O'Donnell was only 18 when she played Pips. David Brenner, Joan Rivers, Richard Lewis, Robert Klein, Rodney Dangerfield, and Billy Crystal also played the landmark comedy club when they were beginning their careers. Brenner remembers one rainy night when only about four people were in the audience and he didn't want to go on. Schultz insisted, and encouraged Brenner to ask the audience what they wanted him to talk about. They first said "subways," and then went from topic to topic. At the end of the evening, an exhausted Brenner said to Schultz, "Thanks for nothing." Schultz told him he would be surprised when he listened to the tape recording and found that he had written a whole new act. Brenner was skeptical, but the next day when he listened he was delighted to discover 20 new jokes. Ever since this experience, Brenner has taken time to talk to his audiences.

The big-city comedy club with the strongest track record is Chicago's Second City, which has been in business since December 16, 1959. Among the comedians who started there are Dan Aykroyd, Alan Alda, Alan Arkin, Ed Asner, the Belushi brothers (John and Jim), the Murray Brothers (Bill, Joel, and Brian Doyle), John Candy, Shelley Long, Elaine May, Mike Nichols, Joan Rivers, Martin Short, Jerry Stiller, and Gilda Radner. Multi-city clubs in business during the 1990s included the Funny Bone, Punch Line, Laff Shop, Comedy Store, Comedy Connection, Yuk-Yuks, and Catch a Rising Star. The Improv Comedy Clubs are one of the largest franchises, which gives them advantages in name recognition and in booking stars. The walls in each Improv, displaying the faces of visiting performers, have been compared to the "Vice-President's Hall of Fame" because some of the performers have gone on to become known around the world, while others remain unrecognizable to general audiences.

In December of 1996, Clifford D. May, the associate editor of the *Rocky Mountain News* in Denver, Colorado, wrote that "Throughout American history, there have been mythologized characters who hold sway over the culture and over the public imagination. Examples of these archetypes might include the rugged cowboy, the eccentric inventor, the rags-to-riches entrepreneur, the hell-bent soldier, the suffering artist and the daring astronaut. So who is the ascendant icon of the current era? It's the stand-up comic. I kid you not."

Two years later in November of 1998, May's observation was given unusual support when Jay Leno, comedian host of the *Tonight Show*, was chosen as the one "earthling" to be connected to the orbiting *Discovery* shuttle to talk with John Glenn and the other astronauts. "This is the most amazing thing that has ever happened to me," said an excited Leno as the National Aeronautics and Space Administration Mission Control linked him to the shuttle from Burbank, California. On the *Tonight Show*, one of Leno's jokes had been that the other astronauts should let Glenn, age 77, pre-board the *Discovery*. Leno kept up the theme by asking the other astronauts, "Does Senator Glenn keep telling you how tough it was in the old days, how cramped it was, how small it was, how lucky you young punks are?" "Well, Jay, actually no," replied commander, Curtis Brown Jr., "He doesn't *always* do that, only when he is awake."

For its 7 September 1998 issue, *Time* magazine polled eight comedians for their best joke about the political crisis in Russia. Yakov Smirnoff's answer was that "the reason Yeltsin fired the whole government was that he wants to replace everyone with interns."

Television, with its extensive broadcasting of stand-up comedy, is responsible for bringing comedians into virtually every American home, but the overall effects on the genre have been mixed. On the positive side, broadcasting has provided working opportunities for many more comedians while introducing the genre to a broad audience. This encouraged people from previously underrepresented groups to try doing stand-up. In the fall of 1998 Mike Robles began hosting *Comedy Picante*, a bilingual stand-up show, broadcast on Sunday nights by Galavision, the nation's largest Spanish-language cable channel. He also dreamed up *Comedy Rhumba*, a public-access cable show. *The Chris Rock Show* and *Def Comedy Jam* are successful comedy shows aimed at African American audiences, while Margaret Cho makes jokes based on being a second-generation Asian American.

On the negative side, television has raised the public's expectations for smooth and quick-moving shows because the slow moments in these taped "live" comedy shows are edited out. The new owner of the venerable club Pips, Michael Palmiero, reluctantly announced in September of 1997 that he would cease booking new comedians because his audiences no longer have the patience to sit through lags or stumbles.

For better or worse, cable television has opened the door to less restrictive comedy. "Screamers" such as Sam Kinison and Bobcat Goldthwait could never have performed their type of humor on network television. But once such humor was allowed on cable, network television became less restrictive because it did not want to be "that" different from cable.

The popularity of stand-up comedians on television built a comedy market and encouraged crossovers with other kinds of television shows. Shows have been created, with varying degrees of success, for such comedians as Tim Allen, George Carlin, Dana Carvey, Chevy Chase, Ellen DeGeneres, Dennis Miller, Kevin Nealon, Paula Poundstone, Rosie O'Donnell, Ray Romano, Roseanne,

Chris Rock has been unusually successful in getting laughs from both Blacks and whites by teasing them about their prejudices. *Globe Photos*

Martin Short, Jerry Seinfeld, Jon Stewart, and Sinbad. Dozens of stand-up comedians have written humor books, also with varying degrees of success.

On the negative side, critics complain that what used to bring success to a comedian was having a point of view, an original style, and a unique take on life. But today when someone's whole career depends on a few minutes of performance at something like the United States Comedy Arts Festival in Aspen, Colorado, or the annual festival in Montreal, where invitations are extended and deals are made, what it often comes down to is having a gimmick or some memorable characteristic. Jimmy Shubert, one of the "Outlaws of Comedy," uses the gimmick of painting half his face like a clown and teasing one side of his hair, while Dennis Miller keeps audiences off-balance with such lines as "There's nothing wrong with being shallow as long as you're insightful about it."

Many performers turn to alternative comedy, sometimes called "the thinking person's comedy," because it is so free-flowing that it can include anything. Alternative performances from the 1997 festival in Aspen included a duo under the name of Tenacious

Jerry Seinfeld believes that a comedian's skills are best honed in stand-up. *Corbis/David Turnley*

D parodying the cliches of classic rock on acoustic guitars, and Rich Hall telling stories from the viewpoint of small-town Midwesterners. Because each performer of alternative comedy is truly "different," the genre does not translate well to television, where audiences have their expectations already in place and find it hard to adjust their thinking for each short snippet. In the mid-1990s, small New York clubs sponsored alternative comedy including Surf Reality, Luna Lounge, Upright Citizens Brigade, El Flamingo, Rebar, and Collective Unconscious. Luna Park in Los Angeles, the Velveeta Room in Austin, Texas, and the Subterranean Cabaret in Chicago also had special nights for alternative comedy.

Improvisation is another alternative to traditional stand-up, but nearly all comedians do some improvising and interacting with their audiences. Jonathan Winters, who was awarded the 1999 Mark Twain Prize for humor by the Kennedy Center (Richard Pryor was the first awardee in 1998), was praised for influencing the entire field of improv, especially Robin Williams and Jim Carrey. With true improv the audience is in control, calling out the subjects or even the situations they want the comedian, or group of comedians,

to relate to. The fun comes in seeing how creative the performers and the audience can be in adjusting to each other's wishes. However, the resulting skits aren't as novel as they might appear to the audience, because most audience requests are so similar that the group has had previous experience with the topics.

Clubs also stage special interest evenings such as contests and celebrity hosts. Refinements on the idea of an open mike include offering performance opportunities for amateurs from specific professions such as accounting, dentistry, and teaching. Clubs provide new performers with free admission in hopes they will bring their own audiences (the two-drink minimum is still enforced). Some clubs have featured children as performers, while others have special evenings playing toward the interests of immigrant populations.

New York Magazine (Jun. 19, 1995) devoted its cover and a nine page feature written by Larry Doyle to pointing out that the popularity of comedy clubs had already peaked and was on the way down. In 1992, there were 475 full-time comedy clubs in the United States, and perhaps 2,500 other places that offered comedy nights. In 1995, of the 350 comedy clubs still operating, only 76 were doing comedy seven nights a week. While some people were staying at home to get their laughs more conveniently from cable television, others were bored with comedy and had turned to Karaoke bars or to sports and music for relaxation.

Critics suggested that comedy was simply suffering from overexposure and that like the stock market was suffering a "downward adjustment." David Brenner told Doyle that in the 1970s he talked to some guys who were trying to interview every working comic in America for a book they were writing. Their list included only 145, as compared to the 1995 *Comedy USA* directory listing nearly 5,000 comics, a statistic that fits with George Carlin's observation that "America can be counted on to take any good idea, or any bad idea, and absolutely run it into the ground."

Doyle's article inspired some thoughtful letters to the *New York Magazine* editor (Jul.

17, 1995). One writter blamed the trend on the quality of the material. "Why," he asked, "were the Bennys, the Aces, the Allens (Steve and Fred, both), Berles, Benchleys, Parkers, Woollcotts intuitively brilliant and where are their kind now?" In answering his own question, he said these individuals "were the products of a literate society, widely read or with extensive cultural experience, which gave them backgrounds upon which to draw. . . . They knew how to think and were well edited, either by erudite editors or by perceptive audiences." Another writer commented, "I've seen many articles examining the current state of comedy but almost none that use the word *humor*. Looking for humor in comedy clubs is like looking for true love in a strip joint. There is plenty of delightful wit being produced in this country, but it is in written form, in comic novels and essays.*"

William Grimes, writing in *The New York Times* (Jun. 6, 1995), explained that "many of the top names have fled the field and gone on to make careers in television and film. Cable television, quick to pick up on a hot trend and desperate for cheaply produced entertainment, overfished the talent pool that remained." Another reason given for the downturn was comedians' heavy reliance on obscenity and the nervous laughter guaranteed to come from shocked audiences. Brinton Banta in *Manhattan Spirit* (Jun. 8, 1995) quoted comic Sam Brown explaining that "open mikes can be tough because it's just a bunch of other comics sitting around waiting to hate you." Performer Jeremy Rabb added that "everyone is thinking in the back of their mind, 'It's going to be me who gets a sitcom, it's me versus this other guy.' By virtue of the fact that it's a solo effort, that competition is inevitable."

Banta concluded his two-page article by comparing stand-up comedy to bullfighting and the way audiences look for two kinds of pleasure: the enjoyment from watching a fresh and truly talented performer, as well as the sadistic enjoyment of seeing someone "crash soundlessly into a sea of vacuous stares." Banta described comedy clubs as "an evening's entertainment where people go to cheer the hero, but understand that the true sport lies in the certainty that, every once in a while, the bull is gonna win." *See also* CO-MEDIAN AUTHORS, COMEDY TEAMS, GENDER AND HUMOR

Further reading: Ronald L. Smith, *Who's Who in Comedy: Comedians, Comics and Clowns, from Vaudeville to Today's Stand-Ups* (1992). Robert A. Stebbins, *The Laugh-Makers: Stand-Up Comedy as Art, Business, and Life-Style* (1990). Laurie Stone, *Laughing in the Dark: A Decade of Subversive Comedy* (1997).

Stereotyping

The word *stereotype* in the world of printing refers either to the technical process by which an image is created over and over again or to the plate from which prints are made. In literary contexts, *stereotyping* consists of the use of such stock characters as the bumbling clown, the pedantic teacher, the arrogant politician, the bad boy, and the dumb blonde. All writers and storytellers rely on stereotyping for background characters because stories would fall from their own weight if each character had to be fully developed as a unique individual.

Because joke tellers have even less time and space for character development, they rely more heavily on stereotyping than do other writers. In the late 1960s and 1970s, as people's social consciousness grew, so did their dislike for stereotyping. Minority groups complained that their members were stereotyped in menial roles, feminists complained that women and girls always took a back seat to men and boys, while men pointed out that robbers, rapists, and criminals in general were stereotyped as males. This concern about negative stereotyping has added to a general distrust of humor.

Humor scholars, however, point out that a society's cultural stereotypes are not exactly the same thing as are its humor scripts. A stereotype is an idea that many seriously believe in and act upon, while joke or comic scripts are more literary than sociological or political. They are amusing ideas that serve as the nucleus for folklore. The difference is illustrated by this joke:

I'm going to tell you a funny story.
I must warn you, I'm Polish.
That's okay. I'll tell it very slowly.

Only people who recognize that there is a difference between a joke script and a stereotype will be amused by this joke. The humor comes because listeners have a joke script in their head that they don't expect anyone to take seriously. They are surprised when the person proposing to tell the funny story confuses the joke script with a stereotype.

Joke scripts are sometimes based on seriously held stereotypes, but there is a wide variation in how closely the scripts match the stereotypes. For example, Americans don't really believe that Poles are stupid, nor do New Englanders believe that French-speaking Canadians are stupid, nor do the British believe that the Irish are stupid. Nevertheless there are extensive joke scripts circling around these and many other groups.

Sometimes the joke script develops from a skewed interpretation of facts or of a stereotype believed of one group, but applied to another group in the joke script. For example, beliefs about the citizens of a particular country are applied to Americans whose ancestors came from that country. Another mismatch is when a group displays a certain characteristic and people's minds transfer that generalization to individuals. Sociologist Christie Davies gives this example of a comic script about Italians surrendering in battle:

How would you recognize an Italian tank?
It has five gears: four reverse and one forward—in case the enemy attacks from the rear.
From where do you view the Italian Navy?
From a glass-bottomed boat.
What is the flagship of the Italian navy?
Chicken of the Sea.

These jokes are part of an 800-year-old humor script that Rabelais, Montaigne, and Erasmus all played with. For centuries Greeks have told such jokes about Italians, but as shown by their proverb, "One face; one race," they considered the matter to be political rather than racial. It is true that the Italian army has repeatedly run away from battles, but throughout history, the decisions to surrender have been political as much as individual. They say more about the sense of patriotism and coalescence of Italians than about the lack of individual bravery.

Humor scripts ignore such fine distinctions, but in real life it would be foolish to conclude that all Italians are cowardly. In the United States, for example, the stereotype of the strong Mafia hitman directly contradicts the joke script of Italians as cowards.

The concept that joke scripts develop rather haphazardly out of the history of particular countries helps to explain why people from different cultures have a hard time catching onto each other's jokes. One has to be privy to the joke scripts of a culture before one can be amused by new variations on old themes or by the surprise of one's expectations being suddenly violated, as in the stereotypical situation of a man eating dinner in a fine restaurant.

The man, who has been a customer for twenty years, sits down to his regular dinner and immediately calls the waiter to his table and demands that he "Taste the soup!" The waiter is most apologetic and says, "I'm sorry sir. What's wrong? Here let me get you another bowl."

"Taste the soup!" demands the irritated customer.

Again, the waiter apologizes and leans forward to whisk away the offending bowl. "No!" demands the customer, who by now is irate: "Taste the soup!"

The humbled waiter leans over to obey and asks in surprise, "Where's the spoon?"

"Ah, ha!" says the man. "Now you've got it!"

See also ETHNIC HUMOR, JOKE PATTERNS

Further reading: Joseph Boskin (ed.), *The Humor Prism in 20th-Century America* (1997). Christie Davies, *Ethnic Humor around the World: A Comparative Analysis* (1990).

Superiority and Hostility

Some humor scholars believe that for any joke or incident to be funny it must contain the tension that goes along with feelings of superiority and/or hostility. Terms used in connection with theories of superiority and hostility include *superior adaptation*, *self-asserting tendencies*, *aggressive-defensive* humor, *derision*, and *playful aggression*.

Humor-related terms that reflect a general belief that humor contains at least moderate levels of hostility include a *punch line*, *biting satire*, *sharp-tongued wit*, a *pointed remark*, a *barbed joke*, to *crack* (or *break*) someone up, to *knock 'em dead*, to *slay 'em*, to tell a *killer* or a *side-splitting* joke, and to *bomb*. In England the most famous humor magazine is named *Punch*, while in the United States some readers think of *National Lampoon* as more of a National "Harpoon." Humor magazines in other countries have names that translate to "lemon," "crocodile," and "porcupine," all terms that hint at the possibility of some level of discomfort. However, these words appear within a "play frame"; they are part of joking and so refer to a kind of aggression that is as different from real flesh-and-blood aggression as is a chess game from an actual battle.

Robert Priest, a psychologist at West Point Military Academy, has proposed what he calls the *MICH Theory* for Moderate Intergroup Conflict Humor. He says that people will not use humor with each other unless there is some kind of tension or strong feeling. For example, tricksters play practical jokes only on their good friends. Few people would bother to send a singing telegram or have 100 pink plastic flamingos delivered to someone they don't know well; nor would they send such "gifts" to someone they hate, for fear of being sued or arrested. There must be enough conflict between individuals to inspire the energy it takes to create humor, but when feelings go beyond a moderate level then humor exacerbates, rather than helps, a negative situation.

Proponents of superiority and hostility theories trace their beliefs back to Plato (428–348 B.C.) and Aristotle (384–322 B.C.). Plato said that people laugh at what is ridiculous in their friends, which is why he campaigned *against* humor and laughter, while Aristotle defined comedy as "an imitation of people who are worse than the average." Philosopher Rene Descartes (1596–1650) outlined six human emotions: wonder, love, hatred,

desire, joy, and sadness. He said that laughter accompanies half of these emotions: wonder, (mild) hatred, and joy. As explained by contemporary philosopher and humor scholar John Morreall, Descartes felt that derision or scorn was "a sort of joy mingled with hatred." The joy comes from observing "some small evil in a person whom we consider to be deserving of it." We feel hatred for the evil, but joy that it is in someone else rather than in ourselves. When we come upon it unexpectedly, the surprise or wonder causes us to burst into laughter.

Philosopher Thomas Hobbes (1588–1679), a contemporary of Descartes, placed humor within his generally pessimistic view of humankind. He wrote that people laugh at the infirmities of others to set off and illustrate their own abilities. We laugh at jests when we discover some absurdity in another person or when we look at ourselves and suddenly recognize that we, too, have had our ridiculous moments. Our new self recognizes and feels superior to our old self.

Arthur Koestler, in his book *The Act of Creation*, explained that while sophisticated forms of humor evoke mixed and sometimes contradictory feelings, the one ingredient that is indispensable is "an impulse, however faint, of aggression or apprehension. It may be manifested in the guise of malice, derision, the veiled cruelty of condescension, or merely as an absence of sympathy with the victim of the joke—a 'momentary anesthesia of the heart, as [Henri] Bergson put it.'" Koestler says that in subtle humor, the tendency may be so "discreet that only careful analysis will detect it, like the presence of salt in a well-prepared dish—which however, would be tasteless without it."

Charles Gruner, a communications professor at the University of Georgia, is a strong advocate of superiority and hostility theories, and in his book *The Game of Humor*, issues a challenge to readers to send him examples of humor that do not contain superiority or hostility. He makes the case that laughter equals winning, and that even with puns, riddles, and conundrums there is a winner and a loser. The winner is the person who knows the answer, while the loser is the one who feels foolish and tricked, and in the case of puns, gets even by groaning at the teller.

While virtually all humor scholars agree that most humor contains some elements of superiority and hostility, they disagree on the amount and on whether it is always present. For example, researchers in the child development laboratory at Purdue University have videotaped mothers and babies playing together and have found that mothers are constantly laughing at their babies' mistakes, such as when a sitting baby reaches for a rolling ball and tumbles over or when a baby tries to clap hands and misses. According to the superiority theory, the mothers laugh because they feel so much smarter than their babies, but someone else could interpret the mothers' laughter as merely amusement or as a loving way to encourage their babies to try harder.

Critics of the hostility theory ask how it is possible to describe what is in each joke teller's or listener's mind. In an example taken from a meeting of a tenure and promotion committee at a large university, the group was trying to decide whether several articles written by an engineer on the subject of prestressed concrete were original contributions or "borrowed" from existing information. One committee member offered the comment, "Well, at least he's steady." From across the table came, "Definitely one of the hard sciences," followed by comments from other committee members: "Yes, very solid," "A weighty topic!" and "Lots of concrete data." Observers with a strong belief in the theory of superiority and hostility might say that these group-created jokes revealed the committee's hostility toward the man asking for tenure and promotion, and that the committee members were competing to see who could be the most clever. An alternate viewpoint is that, by playing with language in this spontaneous fashion, the committee members were not competing with each other, but instead were bonding together as they created the extended joke (which, in fact, led to the man's promotion).

This incident illustrates some of the difficulties in studying real-life humor. Each situation is different, and it is impossible to get inside the heads of participants, who in such a fast-moving scenario probably could not honestly assess whether their contribution to the joke gave them a stronger sense of bonding or of competing with each other.

It is much easier to judge humor created for entertainment because it has been designed for a particular effect, with many of the real-life complications stripped away. When watching a *Roadrunner* or a *Beavis and Butthead* cartoon, such sitcoms as *Roseanne* and *Married with Children*, and such performers as Andrew Dice Clay and Don Rickles, viewers can hardly doubt that hostility and superiority play a major role. *See also* ANTIAUTHORITY HUMOR, LEGAL ISSUES

Further reading: Charles R. Gruner, *The Game of Humor: A Comprehensive Theory of Why We Laugh* (1997). John Morreall (ed.), *The Philosophy of Laughter and Humor* (1987).

T

Television

In addition to the humor found in televised situation comedies, late-night talk shows, and children's programming, humor appears in news broadcasts, through human interest stories and in the kinds of editorial commentary that Andy Rooney provides for the closing of *Sixty Minutes*. Because of cable television, viewers can tune in at almost any hour to see videos of comedy performances or reruns of favorite situation comedies or variety shows. Many of the advertisements that are awarded prizes and featured in the annual film of *The World's Best Commercials* include humor through mini-dramas, parodies, clever wordplay, trick photography, or animation. Advertisers cash in on sports events by paying broadcasters to use their names in key places, as when in baseball a vacuum cleaner company sponsors "the Hoover pick-up" and when in basketball a paint company sponsors "Dutch boy in-the-paint" points.

Sports broadcasters also use language play to make their announcing more interesting. For example, announcer Al McGuire calls a tall basketball player an "aircraft carrier," a player standing alone under his team's basket "a cherry picker," and a score that's over 100, "a dollar plus change." Between periods, he entertains his listeners with stories, such as one explaining the difference between recruiting for basketball and football. For either sport, he says, you take all the kids to the edge of a forest and tell them to run as fast as they can to the other side. Those who smash into the trees are assigned to football and those who run around the trees are assigned to basketball.

In the early days of television, Bishop Fulton J. Sheen offered anecdotes and light-hearted lessons on his weekly *Life Is Worth Living* program. He spoke from what looked like a cleric's study and illustrated his points by drawing on a chalkboard. A running gag was how one of his "angels" (really the TV crew) would erase the board when he moved away from it. From 1952 to 1955, his show was in the same time slot as *The Milton Berle Show*, and TV critics were amused at how many viewers chose the beneficent and kindly humor of Bishop Sheen over the loud and raucous clowning of Berle.

Berle's show, which grew out of his work on *The Texaco Star Theater*, featured "Uncle Miltie," who was surrounded by outrageously costumed stooges screaming out one-liners. Berle was an aggressive put-down artist who never used cue cards. When he muffed his lines, he made them funnier by using ad-libs drawn from his years of working in vaudeville and nightclubs.

Comic variety shows were a mainstay in the early days of television. In most cases, the host or master of ceremonies provided much of the humor, supplemented by skits and novelty acts that included music and dance numbers, trained animals, magic tricks, and whatever else enterprising performers could think of. According to the Nielsen ratings, the variety shows listed below were among the 20 most-viewed programs in the years identified in parentheses. Most were on the air for several additional years.

The Texaco Star Theater and *The Milton Berle Show*, NBC (1950–1955)

Your Show of Shows (Sid Caesar), NBC (1950–1953)

The Colgate Comedy Hour, NBC (1950–1954)

Arthur Godfrey's Talent Scouts, CBS (1950–1957)

The Red Skelton Show, NBC (later moved to CBS) (1951–1970)

The Red Buttons Show, CBS (1952–1954)

The Bob Hope Show, NBC (1953–1955)

The George Gobel Show, NBC (1954–1956)

The Ed Sullivan Show, CBS (1955–1968)

The Garry Moore Show, CBS (1962–1963)

The Dean Martin Show, CBS (1966–1971)

The Smothers Brothers Comedy Hour, CBS (1966–1968)

Rowan and Martin's Laugh-In, NBC (1968–1971)

The Carol Burnett Show, CBS (1969–1971)

The Flip Wilson Show, NBC (1970–1973)

Hee Haw, CBS (1970–1971)

The Sonny and Cher Comedy Hour, CBS (1973–1974)

Not since *The Sonny and Cher Comedy Hour* did in the 1973–1974 season has a variety show ranked in the top 20. This is not because viewers became less interested in humor, but because offerings became more diverse and viewers wanted characters and situations they could relate to over an extended period of time. Puppets were popular because they gave comedians dependable partners with whom they could interact. Edgar Bergen's Charlie McCarthy was treated as if he were a human actor. Mario Prego's tiny Topo Gigio made 50 appearances (the all time record) on the Ed Sullivan Show, while Senor Wences and his hand puppets appeared 23 times.

Audiences also wanted to see real people whose spontaneous actions were funny. Groucho Marx's *You Bet Your Life*, consistently among the top 20 shows throughout the 1950s, was in the format of a quiz program, but actually was more of a showcase for the witty Groucho, whose risque comments often had to be edited out. The success of Alan Funt's *Candid Camera*, in the top 20 from 1960 to 1964, illustrates the superiority theory of humor; the viewers, who were "in the know," got pleasure from laughing at the victims, who were being surprised or fooled by the trick situations that the producers set up and filmed. *America's Funniest Home Videos*, in the top 20 during the 1991–1992 season, succeeds for similar reasons, except that in most cases, the surprising event happens without anyone preparing and setting it up, much like the incidents shown in *TV's Bloopers and Practical Jokes*, a top-20 program in 1983 and 1984.

As the years went on, the variety shows that succeeded were those that had continuity as well as spontaneity and interaction. In each of their shows, Tom and Dick Smothers produced dozens of predictable jokes about sibling rivalry, but they also provided something new by tackling political issues, through inviting such controversial guests as Mort Sahl, Joan Baez, and Pete Seeger, and by showing film clips, such as one of the Democratic Convention with Harry Belafonte singing, "Lord, Lord, Don't Stop the Carnival."

Dan Rowan and Dick Martin held *Laugh-In* together with their skits, which included a spy routine in which Rowan would pass instructions to Martin, who would parrot them back, all wrong. In other sketches, Rowan would stand with a cigarette in hand and tolerantly watch Martin's nudges, winks, and snickering as he made sexual allusions. Catch phrases that caught on with the general public included "You bet your bippy!" "Look that up in your *Funk and Wagnall's*!" and "Here come da judge!" The latter came from a skit by Sammy Davis Jr., who had borrowed the line from vaudeville comedian Pigmeat Markham. Cast members who regularly appeared in *Laugh-In* skits included Ruth Buzzi, Goldie Hawn, Arte Johnson, Lily Tomlin, and Judy Carne.

Carol Burnett's hour-long weekly show was popular for over a decade. The show opened with a dialogue between Carol and the audience. She then performed skits with Harvey Korman, Vicki Lawrence, Tim Conway, and various guest stars. Some of the skits were quite memorable, as when Burnett coughed her way through Ali McGraw's death scene in *Love Story* and when she played Scarlett O'Hara from *Gone with the Wind,* neglecting to remove the heavy iron rod from the velvet drapes before turning them into a ball gown. Other skits centered around favorite characters she had created, including a serio-comic charwoman, a psychotic silent film actress, and an obnoxious little girl who used subtle blackmail to sell her Girl Scout cookies.

Part of the fun of *The Flip Wilson Show* was to see his various impersonations, especially when he cross-dressed and played the assertive Geraldine. *Hee Haw* was a mixture of country music and country humor at its best—or worst—depending on one's viewpoint. *Sonny and Cher* also combined music and humor, with much of their humor coming from domestic bickering.

In October of 1975, NBC launched *Saturday Night Live*. Although it never reached the top 20, it was so successful as a comedy show that more than 20 years later other pro-

ducers, including its own changing staff, are left trying to recreate the show's magic. Regular segments included the satiric news program, "Weekend Update," and continuing sketches with the Conehead aliens, a Japanese Samurai Warrior, and the Blues Brothers. Guest hosts have included Ralph Nader, Julian Bond, George Carlin, Candice Bergen, Lily Tomlin, Steve Martin, Michael Jordan, football player Fran Tarkenton, and New York Mayors Ed Koch and Rudolph Giuliani. Performers in *SNL's* often outrageous comic sketches included Chevy Chase, John Belushi, Dan Aykroyd, Gilda Radner, Jane Curtin, Bill Murray, Joe Piscopo, Eddie Murphy, Lorraine Newman, Jim Belushi, Billy Crystal, Chris Rock, David Spade, Chris Farley, Julia Sweeney, Julia Louis-Dreyfus, Adam Sandler, and Rich Hall.

When comedy is truly original it is more likely to reach a specialized rather than a broad audience. This was true for *Saturday Night Live* and even more so for the British imports of *The Benny Hill Show* and *Monty Python's Flying Circus*.

Each year since the mid-1980s, the Academy of Television Arts and Sciences has inducted individuals (usually six or seven) into

Among the most memorable of *Saturday Night Live* skits were the running arguments between the rattle-brained Gilda Radner and the uptight Jane Curtin. *Corbis/Lynn Goldsmith*

the Television Hall of Fame. The following individuals have been honored because of their contributions to humor:

1986

Lucille Ball (1911–1989) not only starred in various *Lucy* shows, but, as the co-owner of Desilu Productions, pioneered in using Hollywood filming techniques for television.

Milton Berle (1908–) was known as "Mr. Television." Historians say that his Tuesday night show caused more people to buy television sets than did any advertising campaign.

Norman Lear (1922–) created Archie Bunker and produced the revolutionary *All in the Family* sitcom. He is still an important figure in the media as he crusades against censorship.

1987

Carol Burnett (1933–) after starring in a 1959 off-Broadway production of *Once Upon a Mattress* and being a regular on *The Garry Moore Show* hosted her own show between 1966–1977, where she was a master at relating to her audience and at creating skits.

Sid Caesar (1922–) produced and starred in *Your Show of Shows,* which is credited with being the first program to demonstrate the difference between television and radio comedy. Mel Brooks, Neil Simon, Larry Gelbart,

The remarkable chemistry between Sid Caesar and his writers made his *Your Show of Shows* the first really successful television comedy. *NBC/Archive Photos*

and Woody Allen were among the brilliant writers working with Caesar between 1949 and 1954.

Ed Sullivan (1901–1974) was not a humorist, but he was a master at getting guests of all kinds to appear on his Sunday night variety show and then standing back and letting them shine. His show contributed to the demise of variety shows by discouraging competition; other shows were reluctant to go up against such a successful show.

1988

Steve Allen (1921–) helped to shape late-night television when he was given the *Broadway Open House* time slot when host Jerry Lester left in 1951. Allen began *The Tonight Show* and has since appeared in some 15 other television shows and has written approximately 40 books, mostly on aspects of humor.

Jackie Gleason (1916–1987) played Ralph Kramden in *The Honeymooners*, a sitcom second in memorability only to Lucille Ball's *I Love Lucy*. For variety shows, he did skits involving such characters as "The Poor Soul," "Joe the Bartender," and "Reginald Van Gleason III."

Mary Tyler Moore (1936–) played the role of sitcom wife Laura Petrie on *The Dick Van Dyke Show* from 1961 to 1966 and the role of an independent single woman on *The Mary Tyler Moore Show* from 1970 to 1977. The show won 27 Emmy Awards and was parent to three spin-offs: *Rhoda*, *Phyllis*, and *Lou Grant*.

1989

Johnny Carson (1925–) had a 30-year run as host of *The Tonight Show*. He wrote his college thesis on Jack Benny, Bob Hope, and Fred Allen, men whose comic styles he admired and blended into his own. Among the alter egos he repeatedly used in sketches were elderly Aunt Blabby, redneck Floyd Turbo, magician El Moldo, television pitchman Art Fern, and psychic Karnak the Magnificent.

Jim Henson (1936–1990) was the creator of the Muppets including the famous *Sesame Street* characters: Big Bird, Elmo, Bert, Cookie Monster, and Oscar the Grouch. In

1975, he produced *The Muppet Show,* which was aimed at adult viewers and included such unforgettable characters as Kermit the Frog, Miss Piggy, Fozzie Bear, Gonzo the Great, Scooter, and Rizzo the Rat.

Bob Hope (1903–) was a boxer in his first career, which he says gave him the nerve to be a comedian. He starred on *The Colgate Comedy Hour* (1952–1953), and had his own top-ranked show from 1953 to 1955. *Bob Hope Presents* from 1963 to 1967 was popular but not in the top 20. Many later television appearances were undoubtedly helped by the success of his movies and by the indefatigable spirit he showed in traveling and performing for American troops.

1990

Jack Benny (1894–1974) was one of the few radio stars who moved successfully to television, where his show, under various names, ran between 1950 and 1965. Up until his death, he continued to perform in television specials and as a guest on other people's shows.

George Burns (1896–1996) and Gracie Allen (1902–1964) were one of the most beloved husband-and-wife acts in television history. They met each other in vaudeville and became a team in 1923. By the time they moved to television in 1950, they had dropped the flirty boy-chases-girl gags that had worked in vaudeville and were doing domestic skits about married life.

Red Skelton (1913–1997), with his sketches of hayseed Clem Kaddiddlehopper; inebriated Willie Lump-Lump; bumptious San Fernando Red; hobo Freddie the Freeloader; and the Mean Widdle Kid, with his "I dood it!" confession, set records for having the longest-running comedy show in the top 20 (1951–1970).

1991

Carroll O'Connor (1924–) starred as Archie Bunker on *All in the Family,* which premiered in 1971 and shocked audiences by being a "serious" sitcom that dealt with issues of the times, including ethnic unrest, women's liberation, the hippie culture, liberals vs. con-

servatives, and politics. The show ran from 1971 to 1979, followed by *Archie Bunker's Place* (1979–1983).

1992

Desi Arnaz (1917–1986) was a bandleader from Cuba who met Lucille Ball in &July of 1940 during filming of a musical, *Too Many Girls*. At a time when fake ethnic humor such as that on *Amos 'n' Andy* was disappearing from television, Arnaz was a hit, with his genuine Spanish dialect and the interethnic marriage portrayed on *I Love Lucy*. After he and Ball divorced in 1960, Arnaz stayed in television, producing such shows as *The Untouchables* and *The Mothers-in-Law*.

Danny Thomas (1912–1991) as a teenager sold candy in a burlesque theater in Toledo, where he watched and learned. In 1932, he performed monologues and dialect stories on a Detroit radio show. His TV credits include the *All Star Revue* (1950–1952), *Make Room for Daddy* (also called *The Danny Thomas Show*) (1953–1964), and *The Danny Thomas Hour* (1967–1968).

1993

Bill Cosby (1937–), a little-known black comedian, was unexpectedly given a starring role in the TV show *I Spy,* which ran from 1965 to 1968. After succeeding in this role, he returned to comedy, with his biggest success coming in the 1980s when *The Cosby Show* was number one in the Nielsen ratings nearly all of its six-year run.

Andy Griffith (1926–) played the role of Sheriff Andy Taylor in *Make Room for Daddy,* produced by Danny Thomas. He became such a well-loved character that *The Andy Griffith Show* was created as a spin-off, becoming more popular than the original. Between 1960 and 1968, Griffith played a small-town sheriff who had both dignity and humor.

1994

Bob Newhart (1929–) is one of the few comedians who has had four shows named after him: *The Bob Newhart Show* in the early 1960s, *The Bob Newhart Show* in the mid-1970s, *Newhart* through the 1980s, and *Bob* in the 1990s. In all the shows, Newhart produced a low-key "reaction" kind of humor, where other characters do the funny things yet he gets the laughs.

1995

Alan Alda (1936–) was a writer, director, and star of *M*A*S*H*, the Korean War story of a military medical unit. A pioneering combination of comedy and drama, the show ran for an incredible 11 years between 1972 and 1983. Alda, whose father was in vaudeville, first performed on stage at age three.

Bill Hanna (1910–) and **Joseph Barbera** (1911–) first teamed up in 1937 to make the animated movie *Puss Gets the Boot*. The studio that they eventually established has created over 2,000 different characters including Fred Flintstone, Yogi Bear, Tom and Jerry, Baba Looey, Scooby-Doo, and the Jetsons.

1996

Dick Van Dyke (1925–) is best known for the show that in the early 1960s bore his name and was called the first adult sitcom. He has had a variety of television shows since and has also acted in several films.

Betty White (1922–) is most recently known for her role on *Golden Girls* (1985–1992), where she gave both wit and charm to the character of an older woman. She has had key roles in television since 1953, most notably her role as "Happy Homemaker" Sue Ann Nivens on *The Mary Tyler Moore Show*, where she won two Emmys. This was followed by her own show and frequent guest appearances on *The Tonight Show* with Johnny Carson.

1997

No humorists were chosen.

1998

Garry Marshall (1934–) wrote jokes for comedians Phil Foster, Joey Bishop, and Jack Paar, and scripts for *The Danny Thomas Show*, *The Lucy Show*, *The Bill Dana Show*, and *The Dick Van Dyke Show*. He adapted *The Odd Couple* for television, and, in January of 1979, set a record that is unlikely to be broken. His shows *Laverne & Shirley* (co-starring his sister, Penny), *Happy Days*, and *Mork & Mindy* were first, second, and third in the Nielsen ratings. *Angie*, one of his less successful shows, was in fifth place.

1999

Carl Reiner (1922–) has won Emmy awards both for his acting and his writing, which he began in 1957 when working with Sid Caesar and later with *The Dick Van Dyke Show*. He and Mel Brooks are famous for their audio recording of *The 2000 Year Old Man*. More recently, he has worked with movies, directing and writing such films as *Oh God!*, *The Jerk*, *Dead Men Don't Wear Plaid*, and *The Man with Two Brains*.

See also CHILDREN'S TELEVISION, LATE-NIGHT TALK SHOWS, SITCOMS

Further reading: Jess Oppenheimer (with Greg Oppenheimer), *Laughs, Luck . . . and Lucy* (1996). *The Media History Project,* http://www.mediahistory.com (June 1999). *TVlink: Film & Television Website Archive,* http://www.timelapse.com/tvlink.html (June 1999).

U

Understatement

Understatement is the representation of something as less than it is. It is the kind of restraint that W. C. Fields was talking about when he observed that real comedy occurs when you expect something to break, but it only bends. In some ways, understatement is the opposite of exaggeration and hyperbole, but humorous understatements are also a form of exaggeration. People are amused by them only when the downplaying is extreme enough to be surprising, as in Woody Allen's observation that "the lion and the lamb shall lie down together, but the lamb won't get much sleep," and in Allen's confession that, although he doesn't believe in an afterlife, he still plans to pack some clean underwear.

Will Rogers was a master at understatement. When he was being taken to the White House to meet President Calvin Coolidge, he was cautioned not to try to be funny because Coolidge had no sense of humor. The undaunted Rogers bet that he could have the President laughing within 20 seconds. When the formal introduction was made, "Mr. president, may I introduce my friend, Mr. Will Rogers," Rogers held out his hand with a questioning look and said, "Pardon me, I didn't quite get the name." Coolidge roared with laughter, and Rogers won his wager.

Garrison Keillor, in reference to his *Prairie Home Companion* stories on National Public Radio, explained in *Time* magazine (Nov. 4, 1985) that "Left to our own devices, we Wobegonians go straight for the small potatoes. Majestic doesn't appeal to us; we like the Grand Canyon better with Clarence and Arlene parked in front of it, smiling."

Because we expect politicians to exaggerate their strengths, people were amused on the eve of the New Hampshire presidential primary election when candidate Eugene McCarthy was asked if he felt a groundswell. He confided that what he felt was "more like a frost heave." His statement was reminiscent of Mark Twain's calm reaction to a mistaken printing of his obituary, "The reports of my death are grossly exaggerated."

Because people have such an inherent fear of death or other bodily harm, it is all the more surprising when such subjects are treated with understatement, as in these one-liners that first appeared as graffiti during the protests of the 1960s:

> Abortion is hard on little babies.
> Death can stunt your growth.
> War is bad for little children and other living things.
> Rape is inconsiderate.

While these understatements were used for purposes of protest or persuasion, in the early 1900s a similar kind of understatement was used for humor in some of the "Little Willie" or "Little Billie" poems playing with the themes of death and destruction.
See also HUMOROUS ESSAYISTS, LANGUAGE PLAY, PARODY, POETRY, SELF-DISPARAGEMENT

Urban Legends

Urban legends are those fascinating and ironic stories, supposedly about actual happenings, that find their way into the public consciousness, mostly by word-of-mouth. Today they are also distributed on the Internet and sometimes as human interest stories in standard news sources. The development of urban legends coincided with the United States changing from a rural to an urban society, with the attendant insecurities that come from having to depend on strangers for food and for one's physical safety. A few stories are about supernatural visitors, but most are about ordinary people and the complexities of human relationships and interactions with the technology that is part of everyday life: automobiles, machinery, sewers, microwave ovens, computers, and medical abnormalities.

In *There Are Alligators in Our Sewers and Other American Credos*, Paul Dickson and Joseph Goulden list these six features of urban legends:

1. They contain a semblance of seemingly supportive detail.
2. The tellers believe them and pass them on as truth.
3. The stories reflect contemporary fears.
4. They gain momentum from repetition, especially when they find their way into the press.
5. Some of the stories have a grain of truth, which adds immeasurably to their persistence.
6. Formal refutation does nothing to deter the popularity of the fables.

Urban legends are also called "FOAF tales" because they are told by a "friend of a friend." Collector Jan Harold Brunvand, a University of Utah folklorist, explains that people often come to him with some of the classic old automobile stories, such as "The Killer in the Backseat" or "The Death Car," and claim to have indisputable evidence of the truth of a particular story. Brunvand replies, "If you know that one of them is true, then please get me the proof; I'd be delighted to have it." Those reporting the stories try hard to remember who told them, and exactly when it was and where they were living at the time that a fine sports car was advertised for sale by a wronged wife at an extraordinarily low price; or when someone was accidentally sold an experimental car with a carburetor that got 200 miles per gallon; or specifically whose house was robbed when the family was lured away by free tickets to a big game. They "always conclude eventually that they cannot unearth any firsthand information on the stories they thought were true or locate anyone else who can vouch for them." Instead, they "have for verification not personal experience, nor even a friend's own experience, but only an unnamed, elusive, but somehow readily trusted anonymous individual, a friend of a friend."

These following outlines illustrate some of the basics plots of many such contemporary legends:

- A man goes to a hotel with a beautiful, sexy woman he met at a party. They make mad, passionate love, after which he falls asleep. When he wakes in the morning, the woman is gone but written in lipstick on the mirror is the message, "Welcome to the World of AIDS!"

- A young college student wins a trip to Hawaii in the middle of the winter. Not wanting to look pale when she gets there, she goes to several sun-tanning salons, where in each one she stays the maximum time allowed. She "cooks" herself from the inside out and now lies dying in a hospital.

- The driver of a cement truck goes past his house at lunch and sees a brand new car in the driveway. He is suspicious that his wife has a male visitor and so sneaks up to the house, only to hear a man's voice. In anger, he backs his truck up to the new car and dumps in his load of cement, only to learn later that his wife had just purchased the new car as a gift for him.

- On a cold and rainy night, a man sees a young woman standing at a bus stop with no coat and no umbrella. He stops and offers her a ride home, which she gratefully accepts. Because the two are so compatible and she lives right on his way, he arranges to pick her up on a regular basis. But after a few evenings she isn't there. He goes to the house where he has been dropping her off and learns that 20 years ago she had been killed by a speeding car at that very bus stop.

- A vacationing husband takes off all his clothes and is relaxing in the back of the camper while his wife takes a turn driving. When she stops suddenly, he unthinkingly jumps out to see what the trouble is. It was just a dog crossing the road, and the wife immediately speeds off not realizing that she has left her naked husband behind.

Urban legends differ from hoaxes or lies, since the people who pass them on honestly believe the events happened. In many instances the stories are cautionary tales. A "Kentucky Fried Rat" story teaches people to examine their food before eating, while the "Killer in the Back Seat" story teaches people to lock their car doors. The sample stories given here warn against having sex with strangers, giving too much emphasis to one's looks, letting one's jealousy run amok, picking up hitchhikers, and going around unclothed.

With urban legends, people don't recognize they are being preached at, because the lessons are hidden beneath irony and the vivid mental pictures inspired by the details of the stories. Author Max Shulman has observed that when readers are moved by one of his stories to say, "I know someone like that," they will laugh. But if what he writes makes them say, "Oh, no, that's me!" they won't laugh. The success of urban legends illustrates his point, because most listeners can easily see the fatal flaw, the little mistake that one of the characters makes. Listeners feel superior; they smile smugly knowing they are too smart to let such a thing happen to them.
See also COMIC ZEITGEISTS, FRONTIER HUMOR, IRONY

V

Vaudeville and Burlesque

Vaudeville and burlesque were the primary forms of American public entertainment during the 1800s up until about 1930, when they were largely replaced by radio and movies. Early on it was not clear which was vaudeville and which was burlesque because the same people performed in both. As time went on vaudeville took the higher road, burlesque, the lower.

In the classical sense, a burlesque is a form of literary or theatrical entertainment that amuses through distortion, exaggeration, and ridicule. Frivolous matters are treated as though grand and portentous, while noble ideas are trivialized. In frontier America, the word *farce*, which literally means "to stuff," was an appropriate description of the "burleycue" shows that were stuffed with clowning, music, slapstick, suggestive jokes, and sexual titillation. In 1866, a burlesque extravaganza, *The Black Crook*, included a line of dancing girls. Two years later Lydia Thompson brought to America a chorus line of "British Blondes," who performed in tights. Sexy women had previously sung and danced in saloons, but as they became "approved" parts of shows, burlesque was branded as "wicked" entertainment, inappropriate for family viewing. Following World War I, striptease acts became the main attraction of burlesque, with the skits and comedy gradually being reduced to little more than filler in between the "real" entertainment.

In contrast, vaudeville, which was also called *variety*, increased its status so that it played in the most prestigious theaters in New York City, reaching a kind of climax in the *Ziegfeld Follies*. Vaudeville's history goes back to the 15th-century Italian commedia dell'arte, with its miming and clowning, dramatic parodies, improvised skits, animal acts, magic tricks, juggling, dancing, and music. The term *vaudeville* is a French word thought to have originated either from *voix de ville* meaning "voice of the village," that is "street songs," or from *vaux de Vire* meaning "valley of Vire," an area in northwest France famous since the 15th century for lighthearted and satirical drinking songs.

While vaudeville shows had some of the characteristics of minstrel shows, they lacked a formalized structure. Most acts were unrelated, which facilitated changes and substitutions as troupes traveled throughout the country. Besides playing in local theaters, vaudeville troupes performed at resorts, where the shows served much the same role for vacationers as do contemporary shows in Las Vegas, Miami Beach, and New York.

Tony Pastor is known as the "father of vaudeville" because of opening the first theater for vaudeville in New York City in 1865. He courted family audiences and put on fast-paced shows with as many as 35 acts. He was in business nearly until his death in 1908. Among the stars he booked were Lillian Russell, Sophie Tucker, George M. Cohan,

Nat C. Goodwin, Gus Williams, and Maggie Cline, who was known as the "Brunnhilde of the Bowery." Vaudeville teams included the Russell Brothers, McIntyre and Heath, and Montgomery and Stone. He also introduced Americans to London music hall artists Jenny Hill, Lottie Collins, and Vesta Tilley.

In 1885, E. F. Albee and B. F. Keith formed a partnership and established a vaudeville chain. They streamlined their shows, featured Gilbert and Sullivan operas, and made dancing chorus lines respectable. And like Ed Sullivan did for his television variety show some 60 years later, they booked the biggest stars of the day regardless of whether they were comedians, singers, dancers, puppeteers, or another type of performer.

By 1913, Albee had made enough money with his chain that he could open The Palace Theatre in New York. It was the most prestigious of several New York vaudeville theaters. These included the Victoria, owned by Oscar Hammerstein I; the Paradise Roof, owned by Willie Hammerstein; the Fifth Avenue, owned by F. F. Proctor; the Orpheum circuit, owned by Martin Beck; and the New York theater chain, owned by Percy G. Williams. These theaters were the training grounds for such stars as George Burns and Gracie Allen, Bud Abbott and Lou Costello, W. C. Fields, the Marx Brothers, and The Three Stooges, all of whom took the talents they developed in vaudeville and used them to shape the new entertainment fields of motion pictures, radio, and even television.

Other vaudeville stars are less well known, especially if they worked prior to the development of film and sound recordings or if they were unable to transfer their skills to the new media. The sampling given here is incomplete, but it illustrates the variety of talents that contributed to a primary form of American entertainment.

Fred Allen (1894–1956), who went on to radio fame with *Allen's Alley*, was advertised in vaudeville as a poor juggler, but one whose "patter whilst Juggling is Very Humorous." Between dropping objects he would slip in such wisecracks as "I know a man who is so deceitful he puts salt on his toupee to make people think he has dandruff."

Fanny Brice (1891–1951) won an amateur singing contest when she was only 14, and when she was 18 began appearing in the *Ziegfeld Follies*, where she did dialect and comic versions of sexy vamps. She was over 40 when she developed her "Baby Snooks" role, which she played on Broadway and on her own radio show. She died in 1951 and so did not get a chance to try her talents on television.

Fanny Brice was among the early performers who established the format that is still followed in variety shows. *Corbis/Bettmann*

Eddie Cantor (1892–1964) performed in blackface, prancing about the stage, clapping his hands, rolling his eyes, and mugging effeminately. As a teenager he did street performing for spare change and after joining the Gus Edwards troupe, where he worked with George Jessel, Sammy Kessler, and Al Lee, got a part in the *Ziegfeld Follies* in 1917. He became one of Broadway's biggest comic stars and then went on to television and movies.

Jimmy Duffy (1888–1939) and **Fred Sweeney** (1896–1954) were hard-drinking performers who carried their genuine drunkenness onto the stage. They were banned from E. F. Albee's vaudeville houses after Duffy told an audience that he and Sweeney were going to "go through the aisles with a baseball bat and beat the bejesus out of you."

Frank Fay (1897–1961) is credited with establishing the role of a comic master of ceremonies. He broke with tradition by coming on stage well dressed in a top hat and tails. He used standard English to speak intimately with the audience and to involve performers in impromptu patter. Ted Healy and Milton Berle are said to have adopted Fay's brash "try-and-stop-me" style, while Jack Benny copied his way of registering chagrin with a withering glare, and Bing Crosby picked up his method of using self-assured put-downs.

Joey Faye (1909–) capitalized on his vaudeville performing days by doing re-creations. In 1975 he produced *That Wonderful World of Burlesque* and later was a cast member of the comedy *Grind*. Through the 1980s, he continued to tour in nostalgic shows where he performed such classic sketches as "Who's on First?" and "Crazy House."

W. C. Fields (1880–1946) was first billed as "Eccentric Juggler," but soon began adding comedy routines in which he was a golf player and a croquet player, and later "a great drunk," who made an art form out of getting his hat and his cane mixed up. Many of the sketches that he created for the *Ziegfeld Follies* were later put into his 1930s movies, which enjoyed a resurgence in popularity during the 1960s when college students discovered his antiestablishment humor.

Irene Franklin (1876–1941) was a redheaded singer whose style was described as a cross between Mae West and one of the Little Rascals. In the early 1900s, she was the most popular woman in vaudeville, but after the death of her musical partner and husband, Burt Green, in 1922, her songs were less funny and she was unable to make the switch to films.

Ted Healy's (1886–1937) story is one of the saddest from vaudeville. He began by doing impressions of Al Jolson and Ed Wynn, but then made it on his own with a style that is said to have influenced Milton Berle. He and his wife, Betty Brown, did comedy sketches that required a support team. He brought in his old childhood friends Moe and Shemp Howard, who were joined by Larry Fine in 1925. The Three Stooges were born, and while their career took off, Healy's fell into a slump and he died after being beaten in a bar brawl.

George Jessel (1898–1981) began his career at the age of 10 when, with the help of his mother, who was a ticket seller at the Imperial Theater, he formed the Imperial Trio with Walter Winchell and Jack Wiener. He then joined Eddie Cantor in a Gus Edwards kid sketch, but had to leave at age 16 because he had outgrown the "cute" stage. From 1953 to 1954, Jessel had his own television variety show, and was again a hit in 1968 with *Here Come the Stars*. He became famous for his "Hello, Mama," routine: "Hello, Mama, this is George. Isn't it nice to have your own phone? What? Nobody calls you? Even before you had the phone, nobody called you either? Say, Mama, how did you like that bird I sent you for your birthday? You cooked it? But Mama, that was a South American parrot! He spoke five languages. He should have said something?"

Bert Lahr (1895–1967) was a vaudeville veteran at age 15 and by age 20 was starring in burlesque shows, including the 1917 *Best Show in Town*, where he sang comic songs and used his catch phrase, "Some fun, ay kid?" He and his wife developed a skit "Lahr and Mercedes—What's the Idea?" which made them famous and led to comic acting. When he was chosen to play the Cowardly Lion in *The Wizard of Oz* in 1939, Lahr had 20 years of experience to put behind his singing of the "Courage" solo.

Flournoy E. Miller (1887–1971) and **Aubrey Lyles** (1884–1932) were among the first African American comedians to try marketing their talents to white audiences. Some people praised them for "avoiding stereo-types," while others missed the comfortable stereotypical comedy. Shortly after the two tried out for a radio show on WGN, the station developed *Amos and Andy,* to be played by white actors. Miller and Lyles protested that they were not hired due to their color and that the station stole two of their catch phrases, "I'se regusted" and "It all depends on the sitch-ation yo' is in."

Moran and Mack (George Searchy [1881–1949], Jack Swor [1883–1965], and Charles Sellers [1887–1935]) were a comedy "duo" whose membership changed as they quarreled with each other. They were white men play-ing in blackface and telling mostly corny gags in slow, African American dialect. The duo was billed as "The Two Black Crows." In the 1920s, they made several hit comedy records and their catch phrase, "Why bring that up?" became part of everyday speech.

Bert Savoy (stage name of Everett McKenzie, 1888–1923) and **Jay Brennan** (1882–1961) were the most famous of several gay perform-ers. Savoy began by working as a female im-personator in mining camps in Montana and Alaska. When he returned to New York in 1913, he teamed with Brennan and the two developed a polished "boy-and-girl" act that was shocking as well as funny. The act came to an end when Savoy and a friend were struck by lightning and killed while walking with two other gay men in Long Beach, New York. The tragedy inspired a raft of anti-gay jokes.

Joe Smith (1884–1981) and **Charlie Dale** (1881–1971) are the comedy team whose story Neil Simon told in his play *The Sun-shine Boys.* The two met in 1898 when they ran into each other on their bicycles. They exchanged such words that a witness to the accident told them they sounded like a com-edy team. They became on-again, off-again friends, and three years later began perform-ing quarrelsome acts. In Simon's play, the plot revolves around attempts to reunite the aging and cranky comedians, who feud be-cause one of them sprays the other with sa-

liva as he makes all those explosive sounds that make audiences laugh.

Eva Tanguay (1878–1947) was a charismatic singer who flaunted her sexiness and quipped, "When I put on tights, my name went up in lights." Her backstage behavior rated news stories so that people came to see her as much for her outrageousness and her costumes as for her singing and dancing, which W. C. Fields described as "assault and battery." Some of her songs were "I May Be a Nut, but I'm Not a Crossword Fan," "I Want Somebody to Go Wild with Me," and "It's All Been Done Before, but Not the Way I Do It."

Sophie Tucker (1884–1966) began her ca-reer singing in minstrel shows, but by the time she reached The Palace in 1914 she was sing-ing boisterous comic numbers such as "Who Paid the Rent for Mrs. Rip Van Winkle When Rip Van Winkle Went Away?" She began surprising audiences by being a comic sexual aggressor singing such songs as "He Hadn't Up Till Yesterday but I Guess He Will To-night." In the chorus she sang, "He may be the slowest man under the sun, but wait till I get him under the moon." She tilled the same ground as Mae West, but wasn't afraid to include sentimental songs and to make fun of herself, especially as she grew older and fatter and gave herself the label of "the last of the red-hot Mamas."

Joe Weber (1867–1942) and **Lew Fields** (1867–1941) were dialect comedians whose most famous routine went "Who vas dat lady I saw you vit?" "Dat vas no lady, dat vas my wife!" They were the first successful team to get laughs from insulting each other. They engaged in slapstick so violent that Weber had to use cork padding and a steel-plated wig to ward off Fields's blows. By 1940, they had been replaced in the public's affection by Abbott and Costello.

Bert Williams (1876–1922) was an African American who was to vaudeville what Jackie Robinson was to baseball. He played in blackface, but in primarily white shows in-cluding various important roles in the *Ziegfeld*

Follies from 1910 to 1919. W. C. Fields called him "the funniest man I ever saw—the saddest man I ever knew." Wiliam's personal unhappiness was well known, but because he appeared in only one film and the sound recordings of his vaudeville performances are of such poor quality, today it is difficult to appreciate his talent. However, reviewers of the time praised his ability to communicate through gesture and facial expression.

Ed Wynn (1886–1966) billed himself as "The Perfect Fool," a role he began playing while still a teenager when he worked with Jack Lewis in a vaudeville sketch called "The Freshman and the Sophomore." His most quotable line was "Rah Rah Rah! Who pays my bills? Ma and Pa!" He and Lewis (sometimes called Win and Lose) rejected the common technique of the straight man swatting his partner after every joke. Wynn made it to The Palace with a sketch in which he played the role of a jester trying to make his king laugh. He would try all of his best stunts with nothing working until he whispers something to the king. When the king roared with laughter, Wynn would shout, "Why didn't you tell me you wanted to hear that kind of a story?" From vaudeville, Wynn went on to star in comedy roles on Broadway, film, and television. Actor Keenan Wynn was his son. *See also* BLACKFACE COMEDY, RADIO, SILENT FILMS, TELEVISION

Further reading: Susan Kattwinkel, *Tony Pastor Presents: Afterpieces from the Vaudeville Stage* (1998).

W

Wit

According to John Simon in *Paradigms Lost*, wit "is aggressive, often destructive (though, one hopes, in a good cause), and almost always directed at others." He contrasts wit with humor, which he says is "basically good natured and often directed toward oneself, if only by subsumption under the heading 'general human foolishness.'" A characteristic of wit is its succinctness and quickness, as displayed in one-liners, nicknames, retorts, cartoons, and jokes and riddles.

Wit can be found in many of the famous lines spoken by William Shakespeare's characters. For example, the line sometimes described as "changing Romeo and Juliet from a comedy to a tragedy" is spoken by the wounded Mercutio when Romeo says, "Courage, man, the hurt cannot be much," and Mercutio responds, "No, 'tis not so deep as a well, nor so wide as a church-door, but 'tis enough, 'twill serve. Ask for me to-morrow, and you shall find me a grave man."

At a different level are many of the witty remarks that appear in books of quotations such as Dorothy Parker's observation that "brevity is the soul of lingerie," and Clifton Fadiman's criticism of Gertrude Stein as being a "past master at making nothing happen very slowly." Longer pieces such as essays, short stories, and novels written with the intent of ridiculing customs or institutions are usually classified as satire, although short excerpts might be considered wit. *Wit* is cognate with *wisdom*, and as has been pointed out, people can pretend to be serious, but they can't pretend to be witty. Respected thinkers and writers known for their wit include Ambrose Bierce, Abraham Lincoln, Henry L. Mencken, Ogden Nash, Dorothy Parker, Will Rogers, Carl Sandburg, George Bernard Shaw, Mark Twain, and Oscar Wilde.

In his celebrated book, *Le rire* (translated in 1911 into the English *Laughter*), French philosopher Henri Bergson made the point that wit, or derisive humor, is a universal corrective for deviancy in the social order. Douglas R. McKay, a professor at the University of Colorado in Colorado Springs, has cited the conflict over the Mormon's practice of polygamy as a compelling illustration of how contemptuous mockery can be used to intimidate and censure. When the Mormons, under the leadership of Brigham Young, emigrated from the midwestern United States to Utah Territory in 1848 there were no laws against polygamy, but the practice of polygamy nevertheless breached social expectations of American culture. Situations such as this, where someone's actions are questionable although not out-and-out illegal, are common settings for the use of wit as a tool of persuasion.

In such cases the creators of the wit communicate and publicize social norms while pointing the public toward the speakers' own opinions. Wit is used in place of force between people of approximately equal status; it isn't effective with people of unequal status because the more powerful can simply demand that the less powerful comply. Although the wit comes after the fact, it is future-oriented because, by ridiculing what someone has done, the creators are trying to convince that individual not to repeat the offensive action, while at the same time discouraging nearby listeners from doing something similar.

McKay says that between 1848 and 1898, throughout the United States and other English-speaking countries where Mormon missionaries were looking for converts, laughter was elicited by such taunting nicknames for Brigham Young as *Bigamy Young, The Great Marrier, The Incestuous Saint, King Brigham, The Mormon Bull, Old Brig, The Puissant Procreator, The Salt Lake Sodomite, The Sultan of the Wasatch*, and *The Tycoon of Utah*. He was called "the husband to a multitude and father to a nation." Nineteenth-century journalist Artemus Ward said of Young that "he loved not wisely, but two-hundred well," and that "he is dreadfully married; he's the most married man I ever saw in my life . . . !" Ward also contributed these one-liners:

- The pretty girls in Utah mostly marry Young.

- Brigham's religion is singular and his wives are plural.
- Out in Utah they practice Bigamy, Trigamy, and Brighamy.
- Brigham got distracted and gave two of his children the same name.

A popular witticism was that "the first principle of Mormonism is that women are a good thing; and the second principle is that you can't have too much of a good thing."

In 1896, when polygamy was outlawed and Utah became the 45th state in the Union, these jokes lost their sting and faded into historical quaintness. While they are no longer needed as a means of communicating disapproval or of persuading the Mormons to change their practices, they serve as a good example of the same kind of wit that contemporary humorists use when criticizing changing social, sexual, religious, and political mores. *See also* JEWISH HUMOR, POLITICS AND HUMOR, PUT-DOWNS AND REJOINDERS, SATIRE, SUPERIORITY AND HOSTILITY

Further reading: Colin Jarman, *The Guinness Book of Poisonous Quotes* (1992). Eileen Mason (ed.), *Great Book of Funny Quotes* (1993). Bob Phillips, *Phillips' Book of Great Thoughts and Funny Sayings* (1993).

BIBLIOGRAPHY

Adams, Scott. *The Dilbert Principle: A Cubicle's-Eye View of Bosses, Meetings, Management Fads and Other Workplace Afflictions*. New York: HarperBusiness, 1996.

Allen, Steve. *"Dumbth": The Lost Art of Thinking with 101 Ways to Reason Better and Improve Your Mind*. 2nd ed. Buffalo, NY: Prometheus, 1998.

Aman, Reinhold. *Maledicta Monitor*. Waukesha, WI: Maledicta Press, 1992.

————, ed. *Talking Dirty: A Bawdy Compendium of Colorful Language, Humorous Insults, and Wicked Jokes*. New York: Carroll and Graf, 1994.

American Association of Museums. *The Official Museum Directory*. New York: Crowell-Collier Education Group, updated regularly.

Ammons, Elizabeth, and Annette White-Parks, eds. *Tricksterism in Turn-of-the-Century American Literature*. Hanover, NH: Tufts University Press of New England, 1994.

Andersson, Lars, and Peter Trudgill. *Bad Language*. Cambridge, MA: Basil Blackwell, 1990.

Andrew, Sheryl L., ed. *Humor and the Law*. Special Issue of *Brigham Young University Law Review* 2 (1992): 479–92.

Anthony, Brian, and Andy Edmonds. *Smile When the Raindrops Fall: The Story of Charley Chase*. Metuchen, NJ: Scarecrow, 1998.

Apte, Mahadev L. *Humor and Laughter: An Anthropological Approach*. Ithaca, NY: Cornell University Press, 1985.

Armitage, Shelley. *Kewpies and Beyond: The World of Rose O'Neill*. Jackson: University Press of Mississippi, 1994.

Armour, Richard. *A Short History of Sex*. New York: McGraw-Hill, 1970.

Attardo, Salvatore. *Linguistic Theories of Humor*. New York: Mouton, 1994.

Attardo, Salvatore, and Victor Raskin. *The General Theory of Verbal Humor*. New York: Mouton, 1993.

Aylesworth, Thomas G. *Great Moments on Television*. New York: Bookthrift 1987.

Bainy, Moses. *Why Do We Laugh and Cry?* West Ryde, Australia: Sunlight Publications, 1993.

Baird, Bil. *The Art of the Puppet*. New York: Macmillan, 1965.

Baker, Russell. *Russell Baker's Book of American Humor*. New York: W. W. Norton, 1993.

Ballesteros, Octavio. *Mexican Proverbs: The Philosophy, Wisdom, and Humor of a People*. Austin, TX: Eakin Press, 1979.

Barnouw, Eric. *Tube of Plenty: The Evolution of American Television*. New York: Oxford University Press, 1975.

Baron, Dennis. *Declining Grammar and Other Essays on the English Vocabulary*. Urbana: National Council of Teachers of English, 1989.

Barreca, Regina, ed. *Last Laughs: Perspectives on Women and Comedy*. New York: Gordon and Breach, 1988.

———, ed. *New Perspectives on Women and Comedy*. Philadelphia: Gordon and Breach, 1992.

———. *Perfect Husbands (and Other Fairy Tales): Demystifying Marriage, Men, and Romance*. New York: Harmony Books, 1993.

———. *They Used to Call Me Snow White . . . but I Drifted: Women's Strategic Use of Humor*. New York: Viking, 1991.

Barrier, Michael, and Martin Williams. *Smithsonian Book of Comic-Book Comics*. New York: Harry N. Abrams, 1981.

Barsoux, Jean-Louis. *Funny Business: Humor, Management and Business Culture*. New York: Cassell, 1993.

Bartel, Roland. *Metaphors and Symbols: Forays into Language*. Urbana: National Council of Teachers of English, 1983.

Baughman, M. Dale. *Baughman's Handbook of Humor in Education*. West Nyack, NY: Parker, 1974.

Bazalgette, Cary, and David Buckingham, eds. *In Front of the Children: Screen Entertainment and Young Audiences*. London: British Film Institute, 1995.

Bean, Annemarie, James V. Hatch, and Brooks McNamara, eds. *Inside the Minstrel Mask/ Readings in Nineteenth-Century Blackface Minstrelsy*. Hanover, NH: Wesleyan University Press of New England, 1996.

Bendazzi, Giannalberto. *Cartoons: One-Hundred Years of Cinema Animation*. Bloomington: Indiana University Press, 1995.

Bennett, Barbara. *Comic Visions, Female Voices: Contemporary Women Novelists and Southern Humor*. Baton Rouge: Louisiana State University Press, 1998.

Bentley, E. Clerihew. *The Complete Clerihews of E. Clerihew Bentley*. New York: Oxford University Press, 1981.

Benton, Mike. *Science Fiction Comics: The Illustrated History*. Dallas: Taylor Publishing, 1992.

Berger, Arthur Asa. *An Anatomy of Humor*. New Brunswick, NJ: Transaction Publishers, 1993.

———. *The Art of Comedy Writing*. New Brunswick, NJ: Transaction Publishers, 1997.

———. *Blind Men and Elephants: Perspectives on Humor*. New Brunswick, NJ: Transaction Publishers, 1995.

———. *The Genius of the Jewish Joke*. Northvale, NJ: Jason Aronson, 1997.

———. *Li'l Abner: A Study in American Satire*. Jackson: University Press of Mississippi, 1994.

Berger, Peter L. *Redeeming Laughter: The Comic Dimension of Human Experience*. Hawthorne, NY: Walter de Gruyter, 1997.

Berger, Thomas. *Little Big Man*. New York: Dial, 1964.

Berry, Lester V., and Melvin Van Den Bark. *The American Thesaurus of Slang*, 2nd ed. New York: Thomas Y. Crowell, 1953.

Black, Stephen A. *James Thurber: His Masquerades: A Critical Study*. New York: Mouton, 1970.

Blackbeard, Bill, ed. *R. F. Outcault's "The Yellow Kid": A Centennial Celebration of the Kid Who Started the Comics*. Northampton, MA: Kitchen Sink Press, 1995.

Blair, Walter, and Hamlin Hill. *America's Humor: From Poor Richard to Doonesbury*. New York: Oxford University Press, 1978.

Blair, Walter, and Raven I. McDavid Jr. *The Mirth of a Nation: America's Great Dialect Humor*. Minneapolis: University of Minnesota Press, 1983.

Blatner, Adam, and Allee Glatner. *The Art of Play: An Adult's Guide to Reclaiming Imagination and Spontaneity*. New York: Human Science Press. 1988.

Block, Arthur. *Murphy's Law Book II: More Reasons Why Things Go Wrong*. Los Angeles: Price-Stern-Sloan, 1980.

Blount, Roy. *Be Sweet: A Conditional Love Story*. New York: Harcourt, 1999.

———. *Roy Blount's Book of Southern Humor*. New York: W. W. Norton, 1994.

Blumenfeld, Esther, and Lynne Alpern. *Humor at Work*. Atlanta: Peachtree, 1994.

Boatright, Mody C. *Folk Laughter on the American Frontier*. New York: Macmillan, 1949.

Bombeck, Erma. *I Want to Grow Hair, I Want to Grow Up, I Want to Go to Boise: Children Surviving Cancer*. New York: Harper and Row, 1989.

Booth, Wayne. *The Rhetoric of Irony*. Chicago: University of Chicago Press, 1974.

Boskin, Joseph. *Humor and Social Change in 20th Century America*. Boston: Boston Public Library, 1979.

———, ed. *The Humor Prism in 20th-Century America*. Detroit: Wayne State University Press, 1997.

———. *Rebellious Laughter: People's Humor in American Culture*. Syracuse, NY: Syracuse University Press, 1997.

———. *Sambo: The Rise and Demise of an American Jester*. New York: Oxford University Press, 1986.

Botkin, B. A. *A Treasury of American Folklore*. New York: Crown Publishers, 1944.

Brack, O. M., ed. *American Humor*. Scottsdale, AZ: Arete, 1977.

Bradley, Ian, ed. *The Complete Annotated Gilbert and Sullivan*. New York: Oxford, 1996.

Brasch, Walter M. *Cartoon Monickers: An Insight into the Animation Industry*. Bowling Green, OH: Bowling Green State University Press, 1983.

Brooks, Charles. *Best Editorial Cartoons of the Year: 1980–1997, 17 vols*. Gretna, LA: Pelican Publishing, 1980–1999.

Brooks, Tim, and Earle Marsh. *The Complete Directory to Prime Time Network TV Shows 1946–Present*. New York: Ballantine, 1979.

Brown, Jerry Elijah. *Roy Blount, Jr*. New York: Twayne, 1990.

Brown, Ronald L., ed. *Juris-Jocular: An Anthology of Modern American Legal Humor*. Littleton, CO: Fred B. Rothman, 1988.

Brunvand, Jan Harold. *The Choking Doberman and Other "New" Urban Legends*. New York: W. W. Norton, 1984.

———. *The Vanishing Hitchhiker: American Urban Legends and Their Meaning*. New York: W. W. Norton, 1981.

Bryson, Bill. *The Mother Tongue: English and How It Got That Way*. New York: William Morrow, 1990.

Buckman, Elcha Shain, ed. *The Handbook of Humor: Clinical Applications in Psychotherapy*. Malabar, FL: Kreiger, 1994.

Budd, Louis J., and Edwin H. Cady, eds. *On Humor: The Best from American Literature*. Durham, NC: Duke University Press, 1992.

Burke, Ruth. *The Games of Poetics: Ludic Criticism and Postmodern Fiction*. New York: Peter Lang, 1994.

Burke, William J. *The Literature of Slang*. New York: New York Public Library, 1965.

Butler, Francelia. *Sharing Literature with Children: A Thematic Anthology*. Prospect Heights, IL: Waveland Press, 1989.

Cader, Michael. *1996 People Entertainment Almanac*. New York: Little-Brown, 1995.

Callahan, Bob, ed. *The New Comics Anthology*. New York: Macmillan, 1991.

Camfield, Gregg. *Necessary Madness: The Humor of Domesticity in Nineteenth-Century American Literature*. New York: Oxford University Press, 1997.

———. *Sentimental Twain, Samuel Clemens in the Maze of Moral Philosophy*. Philadelphia: University of Pennsylvania Press, 1994.

Campbell, Joseph, with Bill Moyers. *The Power of Myth*. New York: Doubleday, 1988.

Campion, Don. *Peter De Vries and Surrealism*. Lewisburg, PA: Bucknell University Press, 1995.

Carrell, Amy. *International Society for Humor Studies Conference Abstracts*. Edmond: University of Central Oklahoma Press, 1997.

Carroll, Noel. *A Philosophy of Mass Art*. New York: Oxford University Press, 1998.

Cart, Michael. *What's So Funny? Wit and Humor in American Children's Literature*. New York: HarperCollins, 1995.

Cerf, Bennett, ed. *An Encyclopedia of Modern American Humor*. Garden City, NY: Doubleday, 1954.

Chambers, Robert. *The Book of Days*. Detroit, MI: Gale Research, 1914.

Chan, Jeffery Paul, Frank Chin, Lawson Fusao Inada, and Shawn Wong. *The Big Aiieeeee!: An Anthology of Chinese American and Japanese American Literature*. New York: Meridian, 1991.

Chapman, Antony J., and Hugh C. Foot, eds. *Humor and Laughter: Theory, Research, and Applications*. New Brunswick, NJ: Transaction, 1996.

————. *It's a Funny Thing, Humour*. New York: Pergamon, 1977.

Chapman, Robert L. *The HarperCollins Reference Library of American Slang*. New York: HarperCollins, 1987.

Charlton, James, ed. *The Writer's Quotation Book: A Literary Companion*. Yonkers, NY: Pushcart Press, 1980.

Charmasson, Henri. *The Name Is the Game: How to Name a Company or Product*. Homewood, IL: Dow Jones-Irwin, 1988.

Charney, Maurice. *Comedy High and Low: An Introduction to the Experience of Comedy*. New York: Oxford University Press, 1978.

Chiaro, Delia. *The Language of Jokes: Analysing Verbal Play*. New York: Routledge, 1992.

Clark, Michael. *The Philosophy of Laughter and Humor*. Albany: State University of New York Press, 1987.

Clark, William Bedford, and W. Craig Turner, eds. *Critical Essays on American Humor*. Boston: G. K. Hall, 1984.

Clarkson, Wensley. *Quentin Tarantino: Shooting from the Hip*. London: Piatkus, 1995.

Clayton, Lawrence, and Kenneth Davis, eds. *Horsing Around: Contemporary Cowboy Humor*. Detroit: Wayne State University Press, 1991.

Clover, Carol J. *Men, Women and Chain Saws*. Princeton, NJ: Princeton University Press, 1992.

Cohen, Hennig, and William B. Dillingham, eds. *Humor of the Old Southwest*. 3rd ed. Athens: University of Georgia Press, 1994.

Cohen, Karl F. *Forbidden Animation: Censored Cartoons and Blacklisted Animators in America*. Jefferson, NC: McFarland, 1997.

Cohen, Martin. *Humorous Dramatic Interpretation*. Chicago, IL: National Textbook Co., 1985.

Cohen, Sarah Blacher. *Comic Relief: Humor in Contemporary American Literature*. Detroit: Wayne State University Press, 1978.

————. *Cynthia Ozick's Comic Art: From Levity to Liturgy*. Bloomington: Indiana University Press, 1994.

————, ed. *From Hester Street to Hollywood: The Jewish American Stage and Screen*. Bloomington: Indiana University Press, 1986.

————. *Jewish Wry: Essays on Jewish Humor*. Detroit: Wayne State University Press, 1987.

————. *Saul Bellow's Enigmatic Laughter*. Urbana: University of Illinois Press, 1974.

Cole, Bruce, and Adelheid Gealt. *Art of the Western World*. New York: Summit Books, 1989.

Collins, Robert A., and Howard D. Pearce. *The Scope of the Fantastic*. Westport, CT: Greenwood Press, 1985.

Colwell, Lynn Hunter. *Erma Bombeck: Writer and Humorist*. Berkeley Heights, NJ: Enslow Publishers, 1992.

Cook, Jonathan A. *Satirical Apocalypse: An Anatomy of Melville's "The Confidence Man."* Westport, CT: Greenwood, 1996.

Cornett, Claudia E. *Learning through Laughter: Humor in the Classroom*. Bloomington, IN: Phi Delta Kappa, 1986.

Corrigan, Robert, ed. *Comedy: Meaning and Form*. New York: Harper and Row, 1981.

Cousins, Norman. *Anatomy of an Illness as Perceived by the Patient: Reflections on Healing and Regeneration*. New York: Norton, 1979.

Covici, Pascal, Jr. *Humor and Revelation in American Literature: The Puritan Connection*. Columbia: University of Missouri Press, 1997.

———. *Mark Twain's Humor*. Dallas: Southern Methodist University Press, 1962.

Craig, David M. *Tilting at Mortality: Narrative Strategies in Joseph Heller's Fiction*. Detroit: Wayne State University Press, 1997.

Crawford, Hubert H. *Crawford's Encyclopedia of Comic Books*. Middle Village, NY: Jonathan David, 1978.

Crosbie, John S. *Crosbie's Dictionary of Riddles*. New York: Harmony Books, 1980.

Culler, Jonathan, ed. *On Puns: The Foundation of Letters*. New York: Basil Blackwell, 1988.

Curry, Jane. *Marietta Holley*. New York: Twayne/Prentice Hall International, 1996.

Daemmrich, Ingrid G. *The Changing Seasons of Humor in Literature*. 2nd ed. Dubuque, IA: Kendall/Hunt, 1995.

Danilov, Victor J. *University and College Museums, Galleries, and Related Facilities: A Descriptive Directory*. Westport, CT: Greenwood Press, 1996.

Davies, Christie. *Ethnic Humor around the World: A Comparative Analysis*. Bloomington: Indiana University Press, 1990.

———. *Jokes and Their Relation to Society*. New York: Mouton, 1998.

Davis, Douglas M., ed. *The World of Black Humor: An Introductory Anthology of Selections and Criticism*. New York: E. P. Dutton, 1979.

Davis, Murray S. *What's So Funny: The Comic Conception of Culture and Society*. Chicago: University of Chicago Press, 1993.

Debenham, Warren. *Laughter on Record: A Comedy Discography*. Metuchen, NJ: The Scarecrow Press, 1988.

Deloria, Vine, Jr. *Custer Died for Your Sins: An Indian Manifesto*. Norman: University of Oklahoma Press, 1988.

DeMuth, James. *Small Town Chicago: The Comic Perspective of Finley Peter Dunne, George Ade, and Ring Lardner*. Port Washington, NY: Kennikat Press, 1980.

Derrida, Jacques. *The Archeology of the Frivolous*. Pittsburgh, PA: Duquesne University, 1980.

De Santis, Christopher C., ed. *Langston Hughes and the Chicago Defender! Essays on Race, Politics, and Culture*. Urbana: University of Illinois Press, 1995.

Dickson, Paul. *Jokes*. New York: Delacorte Press, 1984.

———. *Names*. New York: Delacorte Press, 1986.

———. *The New Official Rules: Maxims for Muddling through to the Twenty-first Century*. Reading, MA: Addison Wessley, 1989.

Dickson Paul, and Joseph Golden. *There Are Alligators in Our Sewers and Other American Credos*. New York: Delacorte, 1983.

Draitser, Emil A. *Taking Penguins to the Movies: Ethnic Humor in Russia*. Detroit: Wayne State University Press, 1998.

Drennan, Robert E., ed. *The Algonquin Wits: A Crackling Collection of Bon Mots, Wisecracks, Epigrams, and Gags*. Secaucus, NJ: Citadel Press, 1983.

Droz, Marilyn, and Lori Ellis. *Laughing While Learning: Using Humor in the Classroom*. Longmont, CO: Sopris West, 1996.

Dudden, Arthur Power, ed. *American Humor*. New York: Oxford University Press, 1989.

Dundes, Alan. *The Blood Libel Legend: A Casebook in Anti-Semitic Folklore*. Madison: University of Wisconsin Press, 1991.

———. *The Cockfight: A Casebook*. Madison: University of Wisconsin Press, 1994.

———. *Cracking Jokes: Studies of Sick Humor Cycles and Stereotypes*. Berkeley, CA: Ten Speed Press, 1987.

Dundes, Alan, and Carl R. Pagter. *Never Try to Teach a Pig to Sing: Still More Urban Folklore from the Paperwork Empire*. Detroit: Wayne State University Press, 1991.

———. *Sometimes the Dragon Wins: Yet More Urban Folklore from the Paperwork Empire*. Syracuse, NY: Syracuse University Press, 1996.

———. *When You're Up to Your Ass in Alligators . . . : More Urban Folklore from the Paperwork Empire*. Detroit: Wayne State University Press, 1987.

———. *Work Hard and You Shall be Rewarded: Urban Folklore from the Paperwork Empire*. Bloomington: Indiana University Press, 1975.

Dundes, Alan, and Alison Dundes Rentein. *Folk Law: Essays in the Theory and Practice of Lex Non Scripta*. New York: Garland, 1994.

Dunkling, Leslie. *The Guinness Book of Names*. 6th ed. New York: Sterling Publishing, 1993.

Dunning, John. *Tune in Yesterday: The Ultimate Encyclopedia of Old Time Radio (1925–1976)*. Englewood Cliffs, NJ: Prentice Hall, 1976.

Eastman, Max. *Enjoyment of Laughter*. New York: Simon and Schuster, 1936.

———. *The Sense of Humor*. New York: Scribner, 1921.

Eckardt, A. Roy. *On the Way to Death: Essays toward a Comic Vision*. New Brunswick, NJ: Transaction, 1996.

———. *Sitting in the Earth and Laughing: A Handbook of Humor*. New Brunswick, NJ: Transaction, 1991.

Ellenbogen, Glenn C. *The Directory of Humor Magazines and Humor Organizations in America (and Canada)*. 3rd ed. New York: Wry Bred Press, 1992.

Elliot, Bob, and Ray Goulding. *The New! Improved! Bob and Ray Book*. New York: Putnam, 1985.

Enck, J. J., E. T. Forter, and A. Whilley, eds. *The Comic in Theory and Practice*. New York: Appleton-Century-Crofts, 1960.

English, Katharine, ed. *Most Popular Web Sites: The Best of the Net from A2Z*. Indianapolis, IN: Lycos Press, 1996.

Erb, Cynthia. *Tracking King Kong: A Hollywood Icon in World Culture*. Detroit, MI: Wayne State University Press, 1998.

Ernst, Gordon E. Jr., ed. *Robert Benchley: An Annotated Bibliography*. Westport, CT: Greenwood, 1995.

Esar, Evan. *Esar's Comic Dictionary*. 4th ed. Garden City, NY: Doubleday, 1983.

———. *The Humor of Humor*. New York: Bramhall House, 1952.

Escher, M. C. *The Graphic Work of M. C. Escher: Introduced and Explained by the Artist*. New York: Ballantine, 1967.

Espy, Willard R. *Have a Word on Me*. New York: Simon and Schuster, 1981.

Estren, Mark. *A History of Underground Comics*. Berkeley, CA: Ronin, 1993.

Everson, William K. *Hollywood Bedlam: Classic Screwball Comedies*. New York: Citadel Press, 1994.

Fahlman, Clyde. *Laughing Nine to Five: The Quest for Humor in the Workplace*. Portland, OR: Steelhead Press, 1997.

Falk, Robert. *American Literature in Parody: A Collection of Parody, Satire, and Literary Burlesque of American Writers Past and Present*. New York: Twayne, 1955.

Falletta, Nicholas. *The Paradoxicon*. New York: John Wiley, 1983.

Farb, Peter. *Word Play: What Happens When People Talk*. New York: Bantam, 1974.

Farrell, Gregory F. *A Funny Thing Happened at the Interview: Wit, Wisdom and War Stories from the Job Hunt*. Gillette, NJ: Edin Books, 1996.

Fedo, Michael. *The Man from Lake Wobegon*. New York: St. Martin's Press, 1987.

Fein, Richard J. *The Dance of Leah: Discovering Yiddish in America*. Rutherford, NJ: Fairleigh Dickinson University Press, 1986.

Feinberg, Leonard. *Introduction to Satire*. Ames: Iowa State University Press, 1967.

———. *The Secret of Humor*. Amsterdam: Rodopi, 1978.

Feldcamp, Fred, ed. *The Decline and Fall of Practically Everybody*. New York: Holt, Rinehart and Winston, 1950.

Feldman, Gilda, and Phil Feldman. *Acronym Soup: A Stirring Guide to Our Newest Word Form*. New York: William Morrow, 1994.

Finney, Gail, ed. *Look Who's Laughing: Gender and Comedy*. Langhorne, PA: Gordon and Breach, 1994.

Flashner, Graham. *Fun with Woody: The Complete Woody Allen Quiz Book*. New York: Henry Holt, 1987.

Fleet, F. R. *A Theory of Wit and Humour*. Port Washington, NY: Kennikat, 1890.

Fletcher, M. D. *Contemporary Political Satire: Narrative Strategies in the Post-Modern Context*. New York: University Press of America, 1987.

Flexner, Stuart Berg. *I Hear America Talking: An Illustrated Treasury of American Words and Phrases*. New York: Van Nostrand Reinhold, 1976.

Flieger, Jerry Aline. *The Purloined Punch Line: Freud's Comic Theory and the Postmodern Text*. Baltimore, MD: Johns Hopkins University Press, 1991.

Foerstel, Herbert N. *Banned in the U.S.A.: A Reference Guide to Book Censorship in Schools and Public Libraries*. Westport, CT: Greenwood Press, 1994.

Foster, Andy, and Steve Furst. *Radio Comedy: 1938–1968: A Guide to 30 Years of Wonderful Wireless*. London: Virgin Press, 1996.

Fowkes, Katherine A. *Giving Up the Ghost: Spirits, Ghosts, and Angels in Mainstream Comedy Films*. Detroit: Wayne State University Press, 1998.

Fowler, Doreen, and Ann J. Abadie, eds. *Faulkner and Humor*. Jackson: University Press of Mississippi, 1986.

Foxx, Redd, and Norma Miller. *The Redd Foxx Encyclopedia of Black Humor*. Pasadena, CA: W. Ritchie Press, 1977.

Franklin, Joe. *Classics of the Silent Screen*. New York: Bramhall House, 1983.

———. *Encyclopedia of Comedians*. Secaucus, NJ: Citadel Press, 1979.

Fromkin, Victoria, and Robert Rodman. *An Introduction to Language.* 6th ed. Harcourt, Brace, Jovanovich, 1998.

Frommer, Harvey. *Sports Roots: The Story behind Nicknames, Expressions, and Terms Born in the World of Sports.* New York: Atheneum, 1979.

Fry, William F. *Sweet Madness: A Study of Humor*. Palo Alto, CA: Pacific Books, 1963.

Fry, William F. with Melanie Allen. *Make 'Em Laugh: Life Studies of Comedy Writers*. Palo Alto, CA: Science and Behavior Books, 1975.

Fry, William F., and Waleed Salameh, eds. *Advances in Humor and Psychotherapy*. Sarasota, FL: Professional Resource Press, 1993.

———. *Handbook of Humor and Psychotherapy*. Sarasota, FL: Professional Resources Exchange, 1987.

Frye, Northrop. *Anatomy of Criticism: Four Essays*. Princeton, NJ: Princeton University Press, 1957.

———. *Spiritus Mundi: Essays on Literature, Myth, and Society*. Bloomington: Indiana University Press, 1976.

Furtounov, Stefan. *Eighth International Biennial of Humour and Satire in the Arts*. Gabrovo, Bulgaria: House of Humor and Satire, 1989.

Gale, Steven H., ed. *Critical Essays on Harold Pinter*. Boston: G. K. Hall, 1990.

——, ed. *Encyclopedia of American Humorists*. New York: Garland, 1988.

——. *S. J. Perelman: An Annotated Bibliography*. New York: Garland, 1985.

——. *S. J. Perelman: A Critical Study*. New York: Greenwood, 1987.

Galligan, E. *The Comic Vision in Literature*. Athens, GA: University of Georgia Press, 1984.

Galloway, David. *The Absurd Hero in American Fiction: Updike, Styron, Bellow, Salinger*. 2nd ed., Austin: University of Texas Press, 1981.

——, ed. *Comedies and Satires: Edgar Allan Poe*. London: Penguin, 1987.

Gardner, Gerald. *Campaign Comedy: Political Humor from Clinton to Kennedy*. Detroit: Wayne State University Press, 1994.

——. *The Mocking of the President: A History of Campaign Humor from Ike to Ronnie*. Detroit: Wayne State University Press, 1988.

Gates, Henry Louis, Jr. *The Signifying Monkey: A Theory of African American Literary Criticism*. New York: Oxford University Press, 1988.

Gehring, Wes D. *Charlie Chaplin: A Bio-Bibliography*. Westport, CT: Greenwood Press, 1983.

——. *Groucho and W. C. Fields: Huckster Comedians*. Jackson: Jackson Press of Mississippi, 1994.

——. *Laurel and Hardy: A Bio-Bibliography*. Westport, CT: Greenwood Press, 1990.

——. *The Marx Brothers: A Bio-Bibliography*. Westport, CT: Greenwood Press, 1987.

——. *"Mr. B" or Comforting Thoughts about the Bison: A Critical Biography of Robert Benchley*. Westport, CT: Greenwood Press, 1992.

——. *Personality Comedians as Genre: Selected Players*. Westport, CT: Greenwood Press, 1997.

——. *Screwball Comedy: A Genre of Madcap Romance*. Westport, CT: Greenwood Press, 1986.

——. *W. C. Fields: A Bio-Bibliography*. Westport, CT: Greenwood Press, 1984.

Geismar, Maxwell. *Ring Lardner and the Portrait of Folly*. New York: Thomas Y. Crowell, 1972.

Geist, Christopher D. *Directory of Popular Culture Collections*. Phoenix, AZ: Oryx Press, 1989.

Gelbart, Larry. *Laughing Matters*. New York: Random House, 1998.

Gerber, Ernst. *The Photo-Journal Guide to Comic Books*. 2 vols. Minden, NV: Gerber, 1989–1990.

——. *The Photo-Journal Guide to Marvel Comics*. 2 Vols. Minden, NV: Gerber, 1991.

Gibson, William M. *Theodore Roosevelt among the Humorists: W. D. Howells, Mark Twain, and Mr. Dooley*. Knoxville: University of Tennessee Press, 1980.

Gifford, Denis. *American Comic Strip Collections, 1884–1939*. Boston: G. K. Hall, 1990.

——. *Encyclopedia of Comic Characters*. Essex, UK: Longman, 1987.

Gilbert, Michael, ed. *The Oxford Book of Legal Anecdotes*. New York: Oxford University Press, 1986.

Gilliatt, Penelope. *To Wit: The Skin and Bones of Comedy*. New York: Charles Scribner's, 1990.

Glasgow, R. D. V. *Madness, Masks, and Laughter*. Teaneck, NJ: Farleigh Dickinson University Press, 1995.

Goldsmith, Marcella Tarozzi. *Nonrepresentational Forms of the Comic*. New York: Peter Lang, 1991.

Goldstein, Jeffrey, and Paul McGhee, eds. *The Psychology of Humor*. New York: Academic Press, 1972.

Goulart, Ron, ed. *Encyclopedia of American Comics*. New York: Facts on File, 1990.

———. *The Great Comic Book Artists*. New York: St. Martin's Press, 1986.

———. *Ron Goulart's Great History of Comic Books*. Chicago: Contemporary Books, 1986.

Gragert, Steven K., ed. *"How To Be Funny" and Other Writings of Will Rogers*. Stillwater: Oklahoma State University Press, 1983.

Gralla, Preston. *How the Internet Works*. Emoryville, CA: Ziff-Davis Press, 1977.

Granfield, Linda. *Circus: An Album*. New York: DK Ink, 1998.

Grauer, Neil A. *Remember Laughter: A Life of James Thurber*. Lincoln: University of Nebraska Press, 1995.

Grawe, Paul H. *Comedy in Space, Time, and the Imagination*. Chicago: Nelson-Hall, 1983.

Green, Stanley. *Encyclopedia of the Musical Theatre*. New York: Da Capo Press, 1976.

Gregory, Dick, with Robert Lipsyte. *Nigger: An Autobiography*. New York: E. P. Dutton, 1986.

Gruner, Charles R. *The Game of Humor: A Comprehensive Theory of Why We Laugh*. New Brunswick, NJ: Transaction Publishers, 1997.

———. *Understanding Laughter: The Workings of Wit and Humor*. Chicago: Nelson-Hall, 1978.

Gurewitch, Morton. *The Ironic Temper and the Comic Imagination*. Detroit: Wayne State University Press, 1994.

Gutwirth, Marcel. *Laughing Matter: An Essay on the Comic*. Ithaca, NY: Cornell University Press, 1993.

Haas, Karl. *Inside Music*. New York: Bantam, Doubleday, Dell, 1984.

Hall, Rich. *Sniglets (Snig'lit)—Any Word That Doesn't Appear in the Dictionary, but Should*. New York: Collier Books, 1984.

Hall, Wade. *"The Truth Is Funny": A Study of Jesse Stuart's Humor*. Terre Haute: Indiana Council of Teachers of English, 1970.

Hanly, Sheila. *Peek-A-Boo! 101 Ways to Make a Baby Smile*. New York: DK Publishers, 1988.

Harper, Donna A. S. *Not So Simple: The "Simple" Stories by Langston Hughes*. Columbia: University of Missouri Press, 1995.

Harrington, Oliver W. *Why I Left America and Other Essays*. Jackson: University Press of Mississippi, 1993.

Harris, Charles B. *Contemporary American Novelists of the Absurd*. New Haven, CT: College and University Press, 1971.

Harris, Jay S., ed. *TV Guide: The First 25 Years*. New York: Simon and Schuster, 1978.

Harris, Sidney. *Can't You Guys Read? Cartoons on Academia*. New Brunswick, NJ: Rutgers University Press, 1991.

———. *So Sue Me! Cartoons on the Law*. New Brunswick, NJ: Rutgers University Press, 1993.

Harvey, Earl, and Jim Harvey. *Still More Funny Laws*. New York: New American Library, 1987.

Harvey, Robert C. *The Art of the Funnies: An Aesthetic History*. Jackson: University Press of Mississippi, 1994.

Haskell, Molly. *From Reverence to Rape: The Treatment of Women in the Movies*. Hamondsworth, UK: Penguin, 1974.

Hatch, Jane M. *The American Book of Days*. New York: Wilson, 1978.

Hauge, Ron, and Sean Kelly. *Nicknames*. New York: Macmillan, 1987.

Hauptman, Don. *Cruel and Unusual Puns*. New York: Bantam, Doubleday, Dell, 1991.

Hawes, David S., ed. *The Best of Kin Hubbard: Abe Martin's Sayings and Wisecracks, Abe's Neighbors, His Almanack, Comic Drawings*. Bloomington: Indiana University Press, 1995.

Helitzer, Melvin. *Comedy Techniques for Writers and Performers: How to Think Funny, Write Funny, Act Funny, and Get Paid for It*. Athens, OH: Lawhead Press, 1984.

Henisch, Heinz K., and Bridget A. Henisch. *Positive Pleasures: Early Photography and Humor*. University Park: Pennsylvania State University Press, 1998.

Henkle, Roger B. *Comedy and Culture*. Princeton, NJ: Princeton University Press, 1980.

Hennessy, Brendan. *The Gothic Novel*. Harlow, UK: Longman, 1978.

Henning, Charles. *The Wit and Wisdom of Politics*. Golden, CO: Fulcrum, 1989.

Hentoff, Nat. *Free Speech for Me—But Not for Thee: How the American Left and Right Relentlessly Censor Each Other*. New York: HarperCollins, 1992.

Herzberg, M. J., and L. Mones. *Humor of America*. New York: Appleton-Century-Crofts, 1945.

Highet, Gilbert. *The Anatomy of Satire*. Princeton, NJ: Princeton University Press, 1962.

Hill, Deborah J. *School Days, Fun Days: Creative Ways to Teach Humor Skills in the Classroom*. Springfield, IL: Charles C. Thomas, 1993.

Hill, Hamlin, ed. *Essays on American Humor: Blair through the Ages*. Madison: University of Wisconsin Press, 1993.

Hill, Hamlin, and Walter Blair. *America's Humor*. New York: Oxford University Press, 1978.

Hirsch, Foster. *Love, Sex, Death, and the Meaning of Life: The Films of Woody Allen*. New York: McGraw-Hill, 1981.

Hixson, Vivian Scott. *He Looks Too Happy to Be an Assistant Professor*. Columbia: University of Missouri Press, 1996.

Hoff, Syd. *Editorial and Political Cartooning: From the Earliest Times to the Present*. New York: Stravon Educational Press, 1927.

Hofstadter, Douglas R. *Godel, Escher, Bach: An Eternal Golden Braid*. New York: Basic Books, 1979.

Holman, C. Hugh, and William Harmon. *A Handbook to Literature*. 6th ed. New York: Macmillan, 1992.

Hook, J. N. *All Those Wonderful Names: A Potpourri of People, Places, and Things*. New York: Wiley, 1991.

Horn, Maurice, ed. *World Encyclopedia of Cartoons*. Detroit: Gale Research, 1980.

——, ed. *World Encyclopedia of Comics*. New York: Chelsea House, 1976.

Horowitz, Susan. *Queens of Comedy: Lucille Ball, Phyllis Diller, Carol Burnett, Joan Rivers, and the New Generation of Funny Women*. New York: Gordon and Breach, 1997.

Hoyle, Susan M., and Carolyn Temple Adger, eds. *Kids Talk: Strategic Language Use in Later Childhood*. New York: Oxford, 1998.

Huck, Charlotte S., Susan Hepler, and Janet Hickman. *Children's Literature in the Elementary School*. 5th ed. New York: Harcourt, Brace, Jovanovich, 1993.

Hughes, Robert. *American Visions: The Epic History of Art in America*. New York: Knopf, 1997.

Hulstijn, J., and A. Nijholt, eds. *Twente Workshop on Language Technology 12: Automatic Interpretation and Generation of Verbal Humor*. Twente, Netherlands: University of Twente Department of Computer Science, 1996.

Hutcheon, Linda. *A Theory of Parody: The Teachings of Twentieth-Century Art Forms*. New York: Methuen, 1985.

Hyatt, Wesley. *The Encyclopedia of Daytime Television*. New York: Watson-Guptill, 1997.

Hyers, Conrad M. *And God Created Laughter: The Bible as Divine Comedy*. Atlanta: John Knox Press, 1987.

——. *The Spirituality of Comedy: Comic Heroism in a Tragic World*. New Brunswick, NJ: Transaction, 1996.

Hynes, William J., and William G. Doty, eds. *Mythical Trickster Figures: Contours, Contexts, and Criticisms*. Tuscaloosa: University of Alabama Press, 1993.

Inge, M. Thomas. *American Humor*. New York: Oxford University Press, 1978.

——. *Anything Can Happen in a Comic Strip: Centennial Reflections on an American Art Form*. Jackson: University of Mississippi Press, 1995.

——. *Comics as Culture*. Jackson: University Press of Mississippi, 1990.

———. *Dark Laughter: The Satiric Art of Oliver W. Harrington*. Jackson: University Press of Mississippi, 1993.

———. *The Frontier Humorists: Critical Views*. New York: Archon, 1975.

———. *Handbook of American Popular Literature*. Westport, CT: Greenwood Press, 1988

———. *Perspectives on American Culture: Essays on Humor, Literature, and the Popular Arts*. Cornwall, CT: Locust Hill Press, 1994.

Jacobus, Lee A. *The Bedford Introduction to Drama*. 3rd ed. New York: St. Martin's Press, 1997.

Jarvik, Lawrence. *PBS: Behind the Screen*. Rockline, CA: Forum, 1997.

Jenkins, Ron. *Subversive Laughter: The Liberating Power of Comedy*. New York: Free Press, 1994.

Johansen, Ruthann Knechel. *The Narrative Secret of Flannery O'Connor: The Trickster as Interpreter*. Notre Dame, IN: University of Notre Dame, 1994.

Johnson, Kim "Howard." *Life before and after Monty Python: The Solo Flights of the Flying Circus*. New York: St. Martin's Press, 1993.

Johnson, Spencer. *The Value of Humor: The Story of Will Rogers*. New York: Oak Tree, 1976.

Jones, Gerard. *Honey, I'm Home! Sitcoms: Selling the American Dream*. New York: Grove Weidenfield, 1992.

Jones, Richard Glyn, ed. *The Fish Is Loaded! Surreal and Bizarre Humour*. New York: Citadel, 1991.

Jouris, David. *All Over the Map: An Extraordinary Atlas of the United States*. Berkeley, CA: Ten Speed Press, 1994.

Jurich, Marilyn. *Scheherazade's Sisters: Trickster Heroines and Their Stories in World Literature*. Westport, CN: Greenwood, 1998.

Karnick, Kristine Brunovska, and Henry Jenkins, ed. *Classical Hollywood Comedy*. London, UK: Routledge, 1995.

Karolyi, Otto. *Modern American Music from Charles Ives to the Minimalists*. Cranbury, NJ: Fairleigh Dickinson, 1996.

Karvoski, Ed. *A Funny Time to Be Gay*. New York: Fireside, 1997.

Kattwinkel, Susan. *Tony Pastor Presents: Afterpieces from the Vaudeville Stage*. Westport, CN: Greenwood, 1998.

Kaufman, Will. *The Comedian as Confidence Man: Studies in Irony Fatigue*. Detroit: Wayne State University Press, 1997.

Keillor, Garrison. *ME by Jimmy (Big Boy) Valente as told to Garrison Keillor*. New York: Penguin Viking, 1999.

———. *A Voice of America*. Jackson: University Press of Mississippi, 1991.

Kelly, Fred C. *George Ade: Warmhearted Satirist*. Indianapolis, IN: Bobbs-Merrill, 1947.

Keough, William. *Punchlines: The Violence of American Humor*. New York: Paragon House, 1966.

Kesterson, David B., ed. *The New Yorker from 1925–1950*, Special issue of *Studies in American Humor* NS3.1 (1984).

Kharpertian, Theodore D. *A Hand to Turn the Time: The Menippean Satires of Thomas Pynchon*. London: Associated University Press, 1990.

Kiley, Frederick, and Walter McDonald. *A "Catch-22" Casebook*. New York: Thomas Y. Crowell, 1973.

Kiley, Frederick, and J. M. Shuttleworth, eds. *Satire: From Aesop to Buchwald*. New York: Odyssey/Bobbs-Merrill, 1971.

King, Norman. *Here's Erma! The Bombecking of America*. Chicago: Caroline House, 1982.

Klaus, Carl H., Miriam Gilbert, and Bradford S. Field Jr. *Stages of Drama: Classical to Contemporary Theater*. 3rd ed. New York: Wiley, 1995.

Klein, Allen. *The Courage to Laugh: Humor, Hope, and Healing in the Face of Death and Dying*. New York: Tarcher Putnam, 1998.

Klinkowitz, Jerome, and Donald Lawler, eds. *Vonnegut in America*. New York: Delta, 1977.

Koestler, Arthur. *The Act of Creation*. New York: Macmillan, 1964.

Koller, Marvin R. *Humor and Society: Explorations in the Sociology of Humor*. Houston: Cap and Gown Press, 1988.

Kominsky-Crumb, Alice, and Diane Noonin, eds. *Twisted Sisters*. New York: Penguin, 1990.

Kurtzman, Harvey. *From Aargh! to Zap!; Harvey Kurtzman's Visual History of the Comics*. New York: Prentice Hall Press, 1991.

Kushner, Malcolm. *The Light Touch: How to Use Humor for Business Success*. New York: Simon and Schuster, 1990.

Kumove, Shirley. *More Words, More Arrows: A Further Collection of Yiddish Folk Sayings*. Detroit: Wayne State University Press, 1999.

Lahr, John. *Astonish Me: Adventures in Contemporary Theater*. New York: Viking Press, 1973.

Lakoff, George, and Mark Johnson. *Metaphors We Live By*. Chicago: University of Chicago Press, 1982.

Lancy, David, and Allan Tindall, eds. *The Study of Play: Problems and Prospects*. West Point, NY: Leisure Press, 1977.

Latta, Robert L. *The Basic Humor Process: A Cognitive-Shift Theory and the Case against Incongruity*. New York: Mouton, 1998.

Lauter, Paul, ed. *Theories of Comedy*. Garden City, NY: Doubleday, 1964.

Lazarus, A. L., ed. *The Best of George Ade*. Bloomington: Indiana University Press, 1985.

LeMaster, J. R., and James D. Wilson, eds. *The Mark Twain Encyclopedia*. New York: Garland, 1993.

Leach, Maria, ed. *The Ultimate Insult*. New York: Carroll and Graf, 1996.

Leacock, Stephen, ed. *The Greatest Pages of American Humor*. New York: Doubleday, 1936.

———. *Humour and Humanity*. New York: Henry Holt, 1938.

Lear, Norman. *The Wit and Wisdom of Archie Bunker*. New York: Popular Press, 1971.

Lederer, Richard. *Anguished English: An Anthology of Accidental Assaults upon Our Language*. New York: Delacorte Press, 1987.

———. *Get Thee to a Punnery*. New York: Laurel, 1988.

———. *Literary Trivia: Fun and Games for Book Lovers*. New York: Vintage/Random House, 1994.

———. *Nothing Risqué, Nothing Gained*. Chicago: Chicago Review Press, 1995.

———. *Pun and Games*. Chicago: Chicago Review Press, 1996.

Lee, Judith Yaross. *Garrison Keillor: A Voice of America*. Jackson: University Press of Mississippi, 1991.

Lent, John A., ed. *Animation, Caricature, and Gag and Political Cartoons in the United States and Canada: An International Bibliography*. Westport, CT: Greenwood Press, 1994.

———, ed. *Comic Books and Comic Strips in the United States: An International Bibliography*. Westport, CT: Greenwood Press, 1994.

Levine, Jacob. *Motivation in Humor*. New York: Atherton Press, 1969.

Levine, John, and Margaret Levine Young. *The Internet for Dummies*. 3rd ed. San Mateo, CA: IDG Books, 1997.

Levy, Barbara. *Ladies Laughing: Wit as Control in Contemporary American Women Writers*. New York: Gordon and Breach, 1997.

Lewis, Gerald E. *How to Talk Yankee*. Thorndike, ME: Thorndike Press, 1979.

Lewis, Paul. *Comic Effects: Interdisciplinary Approaches to Humor in Literature*. Albany: State University of New York Press, 1989.

Lhamon, W. T. *Raising Cain: Blackface Performance from Jim Crow to Hip Hop*. Cambridge, MA: Harvard University Press, 1998.

Lim, Shirley Geok-lin, ed. *Approaches to Teaching Kingston's* The Woman Warrior. New York: Modern Language Association, 1991.

Lincoln, Kenneth. *Indi'n Humor: Bicultural Play in Native America*. New York: Oxford University Press, 1993.

Linderman, Frank B. *Indian Old-Man Stories: More Sparks from War Eagle's Lodge-Fire*. Lincoln: University of Nebraska Press, 1996.

———. *Indian Why Stories: Sparks from War Eagle's Lodge-Fire*. Lincoln: University of Nebraska Press, 1996.

Lindvall, Terry. *Surprised by Laughter*. Nashville, TN: T. Nelson, 1996.

Lipman, Steve. *Laughter in Hell: The Use of Humor during the Holocaust*. North Vale, NJ: Jason Aronson, 1991.

Lipson, Eden Ross. *The New York Times Parent's Guide to the Best Books for Children*. 2nd ed. New York: Random House, 1991

Loeschke, Maravene Sheppard. *All About Mime: Understanding and Performing the Expressive Silence*. Englewood Cliffs, NJ: Prentice Hall, 1982.

Lorenz, Lee. *The Art of the New Yorker, 1925–1995*. New York: Knopf/Random House, 1995.

Lott, Eric. *Love and Theft: Blackface Minstrelsy and the American Working Class*. New York: Oxford University Press, 1993.

Lowe, John, ed. *Melus: Special Issue on Ethnic Humor* 21:4. Los Angeles: Quarterly of the Society for the Study of Multi-Ethnic Literature of the United States, 1996.

Lowery, Burling, ed. *Twentieth-Century Parody*. New York: Harcourt, 1960.

Lurie, Alison. *Don't Tell the Grown-Ups: Subversive Children's Literature*. Boston: Little-Brown, 1990.

Lyman, Darryl. *The Jewish Comedy Catalog*. New York: Jonathan David, 1989.

Lynn, Kenneth, ed. *The Comic Tradition in America: An Anthology of American Humor*, New York: Norton. 1968.

McCrum, Robert, William Cran, and Robert MacNeil. *The Story of English*. 2nd ed. New York: Penguin, 1992.

MacDonald, Dwight, ed. *Parodies: An Anthology from Chaucer to Beerbohm—And After*. New York: Random House, 1960.

MacDonald, J. Fred. *Blacks on White TV: Afro-Americans in Television since 1948*. Chicago, IL: Nelson-Hall, 1983.

———. *Don't Touch That Dial! Radio Programming in American Life, 1920–1960*. Chicago: Nelson-Hall, 1979.

McDowell, John Holmes. *Children's Riddling*. Bloomington: Indiana University Press, 1979.

McFadden, George. *Discovering the Comic*. Princeton, NJ: Princeton University Press, 1982.

McGhee, Paul E. *How to Develop Your Sense of Humor: An 8-Step Humor Development Training Program*. Dubuque, IA: Kendall/Hunt, 1994.

———. *Humor and Children's Development: A Guide to Practical Applications*. New York: Haworth, 1989.

———. *Humor Log for the 8-Step Humor Development Training Program*. Dubuque, IA: Kendall/Hunt, 1994.

———. *The Laughter Remedy: Health, Healing, and the Amuse System*. Randolph, NJ: The Laughter Remedy Publishers, 1991.

McGhee, Paul E., and Jeffrey Goldstein, eds. *Handbook of Humor Research, Volume I: Basic Issues* and *Volume II: Applied Studies*. New York: Springer-Verlag, 1983.

MacHale, Desmond. *Comic Sections: The Book of Mathematical Jokes, Humour, Wit, and Wisdom*. Dublin, Ireland: Boole Press, 1993.

MacHovec, Frank J. *Humor: Theory, History, Applications*. Springfield, IL: Charles C. Thomas, 1988.

McKeldin, Caroline. *Japanese Jive: Wacky and Wonderful Products from Japan*. New York: Tengu Books, 1993.

McLean, Albert F., Jr. *American Vaudeville as Ritual*. Lexington: University of Kentucky Press, 1965.

Macaulay, David. *Great Moments in Architecture*. Boston: Houghton, Mifflin, 1978.

Maltin, Leonard. *Leonard Maltin's 1998 Movie and Video Guide*. New York: Signet, 1997.

——. *Of Mice and Magic: A History of American Animated Cartoons*. 2nd ed. New York: Penguin, 1987.

Mamchak, P. Susan, and Steven R. Mamchak. *Encyclopedia of School Humor: Icebreakers, Classics, Stories, Puns and Roasts for All Occasions*. West Nyack, NY: Parker, 1987.

Manning, Frank, ed. *The World of Play*. West Point, NY: Leisure Press, 1983.

Manser, Martin. *Melba Toast, Bowie's Knife, and Caesar's Wife: A Dictionary of Eponyms*. New York: Avon, 1988.

Marc, David. *Comic Visions: Television Comedy and American Culture*. 2nd ed. Boston, MA: Unwin Hyman, 1997.

Marling, Karal Ann, ed. *Designing Disney's Theme Parks: The Architecture of Reassurance*. Montreal: Canadian Center for Architecture/Flammarion, 1997.

Marquis, Don. *Archyology: The Long Lost Tales of Archy and Mehitabel*. Hanover, NH: University Press of New England, 1996.

Marsh, Dave, and James Bernard. *The New Book of Rock Lists*. New York: Simon and Schuster, 1994.

Martin, Ben. *Marcel Marceau: Master of Mime*. New York: Grosset and Dunlap, 1978.

Martin, Mich, and Marsha Porter. *Video Movie Guide: 1998*. New York: Ballantine, 1997.

Masinton, Charles G. *J. P. Donleavy: The Style of His Sadness and Humor*. Bowling Green, OH: Popular Press, 1975.

Masson, Thomas L. *Our American Humorists*. New York: Ayer, 1977.

Meade, Marion. *Buster Keaton: Cut to the Chase*. New York: HarperCollins, 1995.

Meglin, Nick. *The Art of Humorous Illustration*. New York: Watson-Guptil, 1981.

Michael, Paul, ed. *The Great American Movie Book*. Englewood Cliffs, NJ: Prentice Hall, 1980.

Miller, Will. *Teletherapy—Why We Watch: Killing the Gilligan Within*. New York: Simon and Schuster, 1996.

Mintz, Lawrence E., ed. *Humor in America: A Research Guide to Genres and Topics*. Westport, CT: Greenwood Press, 1988.

Montanaro, Ann R. *Pop-Up and Movable Books: A Bibliography*. Metuchen, NJ: Scarecrow Press, 1993.

Montanaro, Tony, with Karen Hurll Montanaro. *Mime Spoken Here: The Performer's Portable Workshop*. Gardner, ME: Tilbury House, 1995.

Mordden, Ethan. *Better Foot Forward: The History of American Musical Theatre*. New York: Grossman Publishers, 1976.

Morreall, John. *Comedy, Tragedy, and Religion*. Albany: State University of New York Press, 1999.

——. *Humor Works*. Amherst, MA: HRD Press, Inc., 1997.

——, ed. *The Philosophy of Laughter and Humor*. Albany: State University of New York Press, 1987.

——. *Taking Laughter Seriously*. Albany: State University of New York Press, 1983.

Morris, Linda A., ed. *American Women Humorists: Critical Essays*. New York: Garland, 1994.

Mott, Frank Luther. *History of American Magazines*. 5 vols. Cambridge, MA: Harvard University Press, 1938–1965.

Muir, Frank. *Oxford Book of Humorous Prose: From William Caxton to P. G. Wodehouse, a Conducted Tour by Frank Muir*. New York: Oxford University Press, 1990.

Mulkay, M. *On Humor: Its Nature and Its Place in Modern Society*. New York: Basil Blackwell/Polity Press, 1988.

Nagel, James, ed. *Critical Essays on "Catch-22."* Encino, CA: Dickenson Publishing Co., 1974.

Nahemow, Lucille, Kathleen A. McCluskey-Fawcett, and Paul E. McGhee, eds. *Humor and Aging*. Orlando, FL: Academic Press, 1986.

Naremore, James. *More Than Night: Film Noir in Its Contexts*. Berkeley: University of California Press, 1998.

Nash, Walter. *The Language of Humor*. New York: Longman, 1985.

Nelson, Roy Paul. *Comic Art and Caricature*. Chicago: Contemporary Books, 1978.

Nelson, T. G. A. *Comedy*. Oxford, UK: Oxford University Press, 1990.

Néret, Gilles. *Salvador Dali*. Köln, Germany: Benedikt Taschen, 1994.

Newlin, Keith. *Hard-Boiled Burlesque: Raymond Chandler's Comic Style*. Madison, WI: Brownstone Books, 1984.

Nichols, Mary P. *Reconstructing Woody: Art, Love, and Life in the Films of Woody Allen*. Totowa, NJ, 1998.

Nilsen, Don L. F. *Humor in American Literature: A Selected Annotated Bibliography*. New York: Garland, 1992.

———. *Humor in British Literature: From the Middle Ages to the Restoration: A Reference Guide*. Westport, CT: Greenwood Press, 1997.

———. *Humor in Eighteenth- and Nineteenth-Century British Literature: A Reference Guide*. Westport, CT: Greenwood Press, 1998.

———. *Humor in Irish Literature: A Reference Guide*. Westport, CT: Greenwood Press, 1996.

———. *Humor in Twentieth-Century British Literature: A Reference Guide*. Westport, CT: Greenwood Press, 1999.

———. *Humor Scholarship: A Research Bibliography*. Westport, CT: Greenwood Press, 1993.

Nilsen, Don L. F., and Alleen Pace Nilsen. *Language Play: An Introduction to Linguistics*. Rowley, MA: Newbury House, 1978.

Norrick, Neal R. *Conversational Joking: Humor in Everyday Talk*. Bloomington: Indiana University Press, 1993.

Novak, William, and Moshe Waldoks, eds. *The Big Book of Jewish Humor*. New York: Harper and Row, 1981.

———. *The Big Book of New American Humor: The Best of the Past 25 Years*. New York: Harper Perennial, 1990.

O'Neill, Patrick. *The Comedy of Entropy: Humour, Narrative, Reading*. Toronto: University of Toronto Press, 1990.

Olalquiaga, Celeste. *The Artificial Kingdom: The Experience of Kitsch*. New York: Pantheon, 1998.

Oldham, Gabriella. *Keaton's Silent Shorts: Beyond the Laughter*. Carbondale: Southern Illinois University Press, 1996.

Olsen, Lance. *Circus of the Mind in Motion: Postmodernism and the Comic Vision*. Detroit: Wayne State University Press, 1990.

Oppenheimer, Jess. *Laughs, Luck . . . and Lucy*. Syracuse, NY: Syracuse University Press, 1996.

Oring, Elliott. *Jokes and Their Relations*. Lexington: University Press of Kentucky, 1992.

Owen, Rob. *Gen X TV: The Brady Bunch to Melrose Place*. Syracuse, NY: Syracuse University Press, 1997.

Page, Tim, ed. *Dawn Powell at Her Best*, New York: Steerforth. 1994.

Palmer, Jerry. *Taking Humour Seriously*. London: Routledge, 1994.

Paquet, Marcel. *René Magritte*. Köln, Germany: Benedikt Taschen, 1994.

Partridge, Eric, and Paul Beale. *Shorter Slang Dictionary*. New York: Routledge, 1993.

Paul, William. *Laughing Screaming: Modern Hollywood Horror and Comedy*. New York: Columbia University Press, 1994.

Paulos, John Allen. *Mathematics and Humor*. Chicago: University of Chicago Press, 1980.

———. *I Think, Therefore I Laugh: An Alternative Approach to Philosophy*. New York: Columbia University Press, 1985.

Paulson, Ronald, ed. *Satire: Modern Essays in Criticism*. Englewood Cliffs, NJ: Prentice-Hall, 1971.

Paulson, Terry L. *Making Humor Work: Take Your Job Seriously and Yourself Lightly*. Los Altos, CA, 1989.

Peck, Abe. *Uncovering the Sixties: The Life and Times of the Underground Press*. New York: Pantheon, 1991.

Perret, Gene. *Become a Richer Writer: Shift Your Writing Career into High Gear*. Cincinnati, OH: Writer's Digest Books, 1997.

Pilling, Jayne, and J. Libbey, eds. *A Reader in Animation Studies*. Bloomington: Indiana University Press, 1997.

Pollard, Arthur. *Satire*. London: Methuen, 1970.

Potter, Stephen. *Sense of Humour*. New York: Henry Holt, 1954.

Powell, Dawn. Ed. by Tim Page. *The Diaries of Dawn Powell*. South Royalton, VT: Steerforth, 1995.

Praeger, Charles. *20th-Century Humor*. New York: Viking Press, 1978.

Pratt, Alan R. Ed. *Black Humor: Critical Essays*. New York: Garland, 1993.

Preminger, Alex. *Princeton Encyclopedia of Poetry and Poetics*. Princeton, NJ: Princeton University Press, 1965.

Pughe, Thomas. *Comic Sense: Reading Robert Coover, Stanley Elkin, Philip Roth*. Basel, Germany: Birkhauser Verlag, 1994.

Purdie, Susan. *Comedy: The Mastery of Discourse*. London: Harvestrer Wheatsheaf, 1993.

Radaway, Janice, ed. *American Humor*. Special issue of *American Quarterly* 37.1 (1985).

Raskin, Victor. *Semantic Mechanisms of Humor*. Dordrecht, Netherlands: D. Reidel, 1985.

Rasky, Harry. *Tennessee Williams: A Portrait in Laughter and Lamentation*. New York: Dodd Mead, 1986.

Raymond, Eric S. *The New Hacker's Dictionary*. 2nd ed. Cambridge, MA: MIT Press, 1993.

Read, Allen Walker. *Classic American Graffiti*. Waukesha, WI: Maledicta Press, 1988.

Reaves, Wendy Wick. *Celebrity Caricature in America*. New Haven, CT: Yale University Press, 1998.

Redfern, Walter. *Puns*. New York: Basil Blackwell, 1984.

Reed, John Shelton, ed. *Southern Humor Issue*. *Southern Cultures* 1.4 (Summer 1995). Durham, NC: Duke University Press, 1995.

Remy, Tristan. Trans. by Bernard Sahlins. *Clown Scenes*. Portland, OR: Ivan-R-Dee, 1996.

Reynolds, Richard. *Super Heroes: A Modern Mythology*. Jackson: University Press of Mississippi, 1994.

Richler, Mordecai, ed. *The Best of Modern Humor*. New York: Alfred A. Knopf, 1983.

Richter, Mischa, and Harald Bakken. *The Cartoonist's Muse: A Guide to Generating and Developing Creative Ideas*. Chicago: Contemporary Books, 1992.

Riggs, Robert, Patricia Murrell, and Joanne Cutting. *Sexual Harassment in Higher Education: From Conflict to Community*. Washington, DC: George Washington University Press, 1993.

Robinson, David. *From Peep Show to Palace: The Birth of American Film*. New York: Columbia University Press, 1996.

Robinson, Jerry. *The Comics: An Illustrated History of Comic Strip Art*. New York: Putnam, 1974.

Rodriguez, Clara E., ed. *Latin Looks: Images of Latinas and Latinos in the U.S. Media*. Boulder, CO: Westview, 1997.

Rogin, Michael. *Blackface, White Noise: Jewish Immigrants in the Hollywood Melting Pot*. Berkeley: University of California Press, 1996.

Rollins, Peter C. *Will Rogers: A Bio-Bibliography*. Westport, CT: Greenwood, 1984.

Room, Adrian. *Trade Name Origins*. Boston: Routledge, Kegan, and Paul, 1982.

Rosa, Alfred, and Paul Eschholz. *Language Awareness*. 7th ed. New York: St. Martin's Press, 1997.

Ross, Bob. *Laugh, Lead and Profit: Building Productive Workplaces with Humor*. San Diego: 1989.

Rosten, Leo. *The Joys of Yiddish*. New York: McGraw-Hill, 1968.

Rourke, Constance. *American Humor: A Study of the National Character*. Tallahassee: Florida State University Press, 1931.

Rowen, Beth, ed. *1998 A & E Entertainment Almanac from Information Please*. Boston: Houghton Mifflin, 1997.

Rubin, Louis D., Jr., ed. *The Comic Imagination in American Literature*. New Brunswick, NJ: Rutgers University Press, 1983.

Ruch, Willibald. *The Sense of Humor: Explorations of a Personality Characteristic*. New York: Mouton, 1998.

Russ, Hume R. *How to Write Jokes in 20 Funny Lessons*. Somerville, NJ: Fun-E Productions, 1990.

Rutter, Jason. *The Social Faces of Humour: Practices and Issues*. Hampshire: Gower Press, 1984.

Sacks, Sheldon. *On Metaphor*. Chicago: University of Chicago Press, 1979.

Safer, Elaine B. *The Contemporary American Comic Epic: The Novels of Barth, Pynchon, Gaddis, and Kesey*. Detroit: Wayne State University Press, 1988.

Safian, Louis A., ed. *The Giant Book of Insults*. Secaucus, NJ: Castle Books, 1967.

Safire, William. *On Language*. New York: Avon, 1980.

Sampson, Henry T. *Blacks in Black and White: A Source Book on Black Films*. 2nd ed. Metuchen, NJ: Scarecrow, 1995.

Sanders, Barry. *Sudden Glory: Laughter as Subversive History*. Boston: Beacon, 1995.

Sandler, Kevin S., ed. *Reading the Rabbit: Explorations in Warner Brothers Animation*. New Brunswick, NJ: Rutgers University Press, 1998.

Sanfedele, Ann. *Sign Language: A Photograph Album of Visual Puns*. New York: Citadel Press, 1992.

Schaaf, Barbara, ed. *Mr. Dooley: Finley Peter Dunne*. Springfield, IL: Lincoln-Herndon, 1988.

Schaub, Thomas H. *Pynchon: The Voice of Ambiguity*. Urbana: University of Illinios Press, 1981.

Schiff, James A. *John Updike Revisited*. New York: Twayne/Prentice Hall, 1998.

Schmitz, Neil. *Of Huck and Alice: Humorous Writing in American Literature*. Minneapolis: University of Minnesota Press, 1983.

Schoenstein, Ralph. *You Can't be Serious: Writing and Living American Humor*. New York: St. Martin's Press, 1990.

Scholl, Peter A. *Garrison Keillor*. New York: Twayne, 1993.

Schulz, Max F. *Black Humor Fiction of the Sixties*. Athens: Ohio University Press, 1973.

Schutz, Charles J. *Political Humor: From Aristophanes to Sam Ervin*. Rutherford, NJ: Fairleigh Dickinson University Press, 1977.

Scott, Randall W. *Comic Books and Strips; An Information Sourcebook*. Phoenix: Oryx Press, 1988.

———. *Comics Librarianship; A Handbook*. Jefferson, NC: McFarland, 1990.

Secrest, Meryle. *Stephen Sondheim: A Life*. New York: Knopf, 1998.

Segel, Harold B. *Pinocchio's Progeny: Puppets, Marionettes, Automatons, and Robots in Modernist and Avant-garde Drama*. Baltimore, MD: Johns Hopkins University Press, 1995.

Sevilla, Charles M. *Disorder in the Court: Great Fractured Moments in Courtroom History*. New York: W. W. Norton, 1992.

Seward, Samuel S., Jr. *The Paradox of the Ludicrous*. Stanford, CA: Stanford University Press, 1930.

Shafer, Harry T., and Angie Papadakis. *The Howls of Justice*. San Diego: Harcourt, Brace, Jovanovich, 1988.

Shalit, Gene, ed. *Laughing Matters: A Celebration of American Humor*. Garden City, NY: Doubleday, 1987.

Shepard, Richmond. *Mime: The Technique of Silence*. New York: Drama Book Specialists, 1971.

Sherzer, Dina, and Joel Sherzer, eds. *Humor and Comedy in Puppetry: Celebration in Popular Culture*. Bowling Green, OH: Bowling Green State University Press, 1987.

Shloss, Carol. *Flannery O'Connor's Dark Comedies*. Baton Rouge: Louisiana State University Press, 1980.

Siegel, David. *Creating Killer Web Sites*. Indianapolis, IN: Hayden Books, 1996.

Sikov, Ed. *On Sunset Boulevard: The Life and Times of Billy Wilder*. New York: Hyperion, 1998.

Simon, John. *Paradigms Lost: Reflections on Literacy and Its Decline*. New York: C. N. Potter/Crown, 1980.

Simon, Neil. *The Comedy of Neil Simon*. New York: Avon, 1971.

Simon, Richard Keller. *The Labyrinth of the Comic: Theory and Practice from Fielding to Freud*. Tallahassee: Florida State University Press, 1985.

Sklar, Robert. *Movie-Made America: A Cultural History of American Movies*. 2nd ed. New York: Vintage, 1994.

Sloane, David E. E., ed. *American Humor Magazines and Comic Periodicals*. Westport, CT: Greenwood Press, 1987.

———. *The Literary Humor of the Urban Northeast 1830–1890*. Baton Rouge: Louisiana State University Press, 1983.

———. *Mark Twain as a Literary Comedian*. Baton Rouge: Louisiana State University Press, 1979.

———, ed. *New Directions in American Humor*. Birmingham: University of Alabama Press, 1998.

Smith, John M., and Tim Cawkwell, eds. *The World Encyclopedia of the Film*. New York: Galahad Books, 1972.

Smith, Ronald L. *The Comedy Quote Dictionary*. New York: Doubleday, 1992.

———. *Who's Who in Comedy: Comedians, Comics and Clowns from Vaudeville to Today's Stand-Ups*. New York: Facts on File, 1992.

Smitherman, Geneva. *Talkin and Testifyin: The Language of Black America*. Detroit: Wayne State University Press, 1977.

Sobel, Bernard. *A Pictorial History of Burlesque*. New York: Bonanza Books, 1956.

Sobkowiak, Wlodzimierz. *Metaphonology of English Paronomastic Puns*. Frankfurt, Germany: Peter Lang, 1991.

Sochen, June, ed. *Women's Comic Visions*. Detroit: Wayne State University Press, 1991.

Sonnichsen, C. L. *The Laughing West: Humorous Western Fiction, Past and Present*. Athens: Ohio University Press, 1988.

Soukhanov, Anne H. *Word Watch: The Stories behind the Words of Our Lives*. New York: Henry Holt, 1995.

Spalding, Henry D. *Encyclopedia of Jewish Humor: From Biblical Times to the Modern Age*. New York: Jonathan David, 1969.

———. *Joys of Jewish Humor*. New York: Jonathan David, 1985.

Staake, Bob. *The Complete Book of Caricature*. Cincinnati, OH: North Light Books, 1991.

Staake, Bob, and Roseann Shaughnessy, eds. *Humor and Cartoon Markets*. Cincinnati, OH: Writer's Digest, 1993.

Staples, Shirley. *Male-Female Comedy Teams in American Vaudeville, 1865–1932*. Ann Arbor, MI: UMI Research Press, 1984.

Sterling, Bryan, and Frances N. Sterling. *Will Rogers Treasury: Reflections and Observations*. New York: Bonanza, 1982.

Stone, Laurie. *Laughing in the Dark: A Decade of Subversive Comedy*. New York: Ecco, 1997.

Sullivan, Frank, ed. *The Time of Laughter*. Boston: Little, Brown, and Company, 1967.

Swann, Brian, and Arnold Krupat, eds. *I Tell You Now: Autobiographical Essays by Native American Writers*. Lincoln: University of Nebraska, 1987.

Sypher, Wylie, ed. *Comedy*. Baltimore, MD: Johns Hopkins University Press, 1956.

Taylor, Mary-Agnes. *Humor in Children's Literature*. Special issue of *Studies in American Humor* NS5.4 (1986–1987): 223–98.

Tennant, Rich, and John Barry. *The Unofficial I Hate Computers Book*. New York: Hayden Books, 1984.

Terban, Marvin. *Dictionary of Idioms, Phrases and Expressions*. New York: Scholastic, 1996.

Terrace, Vincent. *Television Character and Story Facts*. Jefferson, NC: McFarland and Co., 1993.

Terry, Robert W. *Authentic Leadership: Courage in Action*. San Francisco: Jossey-Bass Publishers, 1993.

Thomas, Jeannie B. *Featherless Chickens, Laughing Women, and Serious Stories*. Charlottesville: University Press of Virginia, 1997.

Thompson, Don, and Dick Lupoff, eds. *The Comic-Book Book*. New Rochelle, NY: Arlington House, 1973.

Thurber, James. *The Years with Ross*. Boston: Little-Brown, 1959.

Tigges, Wim, ed. *An Anatomy of Literary Nonsense*. Amsterdam: Rodopi, 1988.

———, ed. *Explorations in the Field of Nonsense*. Amsterdam: Rodopi, 1987.

Tillman, Albert. *Pop-Up! Pop-Up!: Pop-Up Books: Their History, How to Collect Them, and How Much They're Worth*. Eastsound, WA: Paper-Jam Publishing, 1997.

Tilton, John W. *Cosmic Satire in the Contemporary Novel*. Lewisburg, PA: Bucknell University Press, 1977.

Tittler, Jonathan. *Narrative Irony in the Contemporary Spanish-American Novel*. Ithaca, NY: Cornell University Press, 1984

Toll, Robert C. *Blacking Up: The Minstrel Show in Nineteenth-Century America*. New York: Oxford University Press, 1974.

Toombs, Sarah Eleanor. *James Thurber: An Annotated Bibliography of Criticism*. New York: Garland, 1987.

Towson, John H. *Clowns*. New York: Hawthorn, Books, 1976.

Trachtenberg, Stanley, ed. *Dictionary of Literary Biography, Volume 11: American Humorists, 1800–1950, Part 1: A-L* and *Part 2: M-Z*. Detroit: Bruccoli Clark/Gale Research, 1982.

Tracy, Anne B. *The Gothic Novel: 1790–1830*. Lexington: University Press of Kentucky, 1981.

Truesdell, Bill, ed. *Directory of Unique Museums*. Kalamazoo, MI: Creative Communications, 1985.

Twain, Mark. *The War Prayer*. New York: Harper and Row, 1951.

Udall, Morris K. *Too Funny to be President*. New York: Henry Holt, 1988.

Upton, Dell. *Architecture in the United States*. New York: Oxford, 1998.

Veron, Enid, ed. *Humor in America*. New York: Harcourt, Brace, Jovanovich, 1976.

Vickers, Scott B. *Native American Identities: From Stereotype to Archetype in Art and Literature*. Albuquerque: University of New Mexico Press, 1998.

Vogler, Christopher. *The Writer's Journey: Mythic Structure for Storytellers and Screenwriters*. Studio City, CA: Michael Wiese, 1992.

Walker, John. *Halliwell's Film and Video Guide: 1998*. New York: HarperCollins, 1998.

Walker, Nancy A. *The Disobedient Writer: Women and Narrative Tradition*. Austin: University of Texas Press, 1995.

———. *Feminist Alternatives: Irony and Fantasy in the Contemporary Novel by Women*. Jackson: University Press of Mississippi, 1990.

———. *Humor in America*. Special issue of *Open Places* 38–39 (1985): 1–222.

———. *The Tradition of Women's Humor in America*. Huntington Beach, CA: American Studies Publishing Company, 1984.

———. *A Very Serious Thing: Women's Humor and American Culture*. Minneapolis: University of Minnesota Press, 1988.

———. *What's So Funny? Humor in American Culture*. Wilmington, DE: Scholar Resources, Inc., 1998.

Walker, Nancy A., and Zita Dresner. *Redressing the Balance: American Women's Literary Humor from Colonial Times to the 1980s*. Jackson: University Press of Mississippi, 1988.

Wallace, Ronald. *God Be With the Clown: Humor in American Poetry*. Columbia: University of Missouri Press, 1984.

———. *The Last Laugh: Form and Affirmation in the Contemporary American Comic Novel*. Columbia: University of Missouri Press, 1979.

———. *No Harm in Smiling: Vladimir Nabokov's "Lolita."* Columbia: University of Missouri Press, 1979.

Watkins, Mel. *On the Real Side: Laughing, Lying, and Signifying*. New York: Simon and Schuster, 1994.

Weales, Gerald. *Canned Goods as Caviar: American Film Comedy of the 1930s*. Chicago: University of Chicago Press, 1985.

Weber, Brom, ed. *Thomas Berger*. Two special issues of *Studies in American Humor* NS2.1, NS2.2 (1983).

———. *Sherwood Anderson*. Minneapolis: University of Minnesota Press, 1964.

Wechsler, Robert. *Columbus à la Mode: Parodies of Contemporary American Writers*. North Haven, CT: Catbird Press, 1993.

———, ed. *Here We Are: The Humorists' Guide to the United States*. North Haven, CT: Catbird Press, 1991.

Weisenberger, Steven. *Fables of Subversion! Satire and the American Novel: 1930–1980*. Athens: University of Georgia Press, 1995.

Weiss, Helen S., and M. Jerry Weiss, eds. *Woody Allen*. Bantam, 1977.

Wells, Carolyn. *Folly for the Wise*. Indianapolis: Bobbs Merrill, 1904.

Wentworth, Harold, and Stuart Berg Flexner, eds. *Dictionary of American Slang*. New York: Thomas Y. Crowell, 1975.

Wernblad, Annette. *Brooklyn Is Not Expanding: Woody Allen's Comic Universe*. Cranbury, NJ: Associated University Presses, 1992.

Wertham, Arthur Frank. *Radio Comedy*. New York: Oxford University Press, 1979.

———. *The Seduction of the Innocent*. Port Washington, NY: Kennikat Press, 1954.

White, David Manning, and Robert H. Abell. *The Funnies: An American Idiom*. London: Collier-Macmillan, 1963.

White, E. B., and Katharine S. White. *A Subtreasury of American Humor*. New York: Coward-McCann, 1941.

Whitton, Blair. *Paper Toys of the World*. Cumberland, MD: Hobby House Press, 1986.

Wickberg, Daniel. *The Sense of Humor: Self and Laughter in Modern America*. Ithaca, NY: Cornell University Press, 1998.

Wiget, Andrew, ed. *Dictionary of Native American Literature*. New York: Garland, 1994.

Willeford, William. *The Fool and His Scepter: A Study in Clowns and Jesters and Their Audience*. Evanston, IL: Northwestern University Press, 1969.

Williams, John Alfred. *If I Stop I'll Die: The Comedy and Tragedy of Richard Pryor*. New York: Thunder's Mouth Press, 1991.

Williams, Kenny J., and Bernard Duffey, eds. *Chicago's Public Wits: A Chapter in the American Comic Spirit*. Baton Rouge: Louisiana State University Press, 1983.

Winokur, Mark. *American Laughter: Immigrants, Ethnicity, and 1930s Hollywood Film Comedy*. New York: St. Martin's Press, 1996.

Wittke, Carl. *Tambo and Bones: A History of the American Minstrel Stage*. New York: Greenwood Press, 1930.

Wolfenstein, Martha. *Children's Humor: A Psychological Analysis*. Bloomington: Indiana University Press, 1954.

Wood, Art. *Great Cartoonists and Their Art*. Gretna, LA: Pelican, 1987.

Wooten, Patty. *Compassionate Laughter: Jest for Your Health*. Salt Lake City, UT: Commune-A-Key Publishing, 1996.

Yacowar, Maurice. *Loser Take All: The Comic Art of Woody Allen*. New York: Frederick Ungar, 1982.

———. *Method in Madness: The Comic Art of Mel Brooks*. New York: St. Martin's, 1981.

Yan, Gao. *The Art of Parody: Maxine Hong Kingston's Use of Chinese Sources*. New York: Peter Lang, 1996.

Yates, Norris W. *The American Humorist: Conscience of the Twentieth Century*. Ames: Iowa State University Press, 1964.

Ziv, Avner, ed. *Jewish Humor*. Tel Aviv: Papyrus, 1986.

———, ed. *National Styles of Humor*. Westport, CT: Greenwood Press, 1988.

Zurier, Rebecca, Robert W. Snyder, and Virginia M. Mecklenburg. *Metropolitan Lives: The Ashcan Artists and Their New York*. New York: National Museum of American Art/W. W. Norton, 1995.

INDEX

by John Lewis

Index

Index

Index

Index

Index

Index

Slade, Bernard, 106, 114
Slang, **283–84**. *See also* Language play
Slaughterhouse-Five, 37, 49, 124, 275
Sleepless in Seattle, 154, 206
A Slipping Down Life, 124
Sloane, David E. E., 6, 194
Slouching toward Kalamazoo, 121
Smackout, 248
A Small Book of Grave Humor, 226
Smiley, Jane, 123
Smirnoff, Yakov, 115, 287, 288
Smith, Bob, 131–32, 133
Smith, "Buffalo" Bob, 72, 241
Smith, Jack, 132
Smith, Joe, 307
Smith, Lane, 70
Smith, Patti, 194
Smith, Roger, 235
Smith, Ronald L., 82, 137
Smith, Seba, 52, 101, 251
Smith, Senator Margaret Chase, 136
Smith, Will, 18
Smith, William Kennedy, 113
Smithson, Robert, 42
Smithsonian Magazine, 209
Smoke Signals, 28–29
Smokey and the Bandit, 204
Smothers Brothers, 15, 65, 85, 244
The Smothers Brothers Comedy Hour, 115, 221, 259, 296
Smothers, Dick. *See* Smothers Brothers
Smothers, Tom. *See* Smothers Brothers
The Smurfs, 72
Sneaky People, 120
Snicker, 223
Snoop Doggy Dog, 214
Snow White and the Seven Dwarfs, 33
Soap, 16
Social Studies, 155
Sojourner, Maddi, 166–67
Some Like it Hot, 206, 270
Something BIG Has Been Here, 71
Something Happened, 121
Sometimes A Great Notion: A Novel, 121
Sondheim, Stephen, 213
Song of the South, 33
The Sonny and Cher Comedy Hour, 244, 296, 297
Sons of the Desert, 198
Sophie's Choice, 261
The Sorcerer, 213
Soto, Gary, 225
The Sound and the Fury, 121
The Sound of Music, 211
Soupy Sales, 286
Soupy Sales Show, 73

South Park, 35–36
Southern, Terry, 46, 195
Space Station Seventh Grade, 66
Spaceballs, 53, 204
Spafford, Eugene, 151
Spalding, Henry, 173
Special effects in humorous movies, 203–4
spell #7, 110
Spice World, 206
Spider-Man, 87–88, 93
Spiegel, Fritz, 226
Spiegelman, Art, 90, 195
Spielberg, Steven, 11, 31
Spike and Mike's…Festival of Animation, 36
Spinelli, Jerry, 66, 68
Spiral Jetty, 42
The Spirit, 87
Splash, 203
Spooner, William A., 9
Sports language, **284–86**, 295
Sports mascots, 78
Springer, Jerry, 18
Spy, 194, 197, 198
Spy vs. Spy, 195
St. Louis Post-Dispatch, 61
Stage names, 12–13, 284–86
Stageberg, Norman, 26
Stalag 17, 37
Stallone, Sylvester, 207
Stand-up comedy, **287–91**
  body humor and, 53–56
  gay and lesbian humor and, 130–34
  gender humor and, 136–38
  Hispanic humor and, 147–48
  impersonations and, 160–62
  musical comedians and, 214–18
Stanford, M.D., 143
Stanwyck, Barbara, 270
Stapleton, Jean, 281
Star Trek television series, 99
Star Wars movies, 53, 99, 203
Stars and Stripes newsletter, 61
"The State of Humor in the States", 227
Stay Free!, 222
Steamboat Bill Jr., 277
Steamboat Willie, 33
Steaming to Bamboola: The World of a Tramp Freighter, 153
Stebbins, Robert A., 104
Steig, William, 69, 70
Stein, Gertrude, 220, 224
Stein, Jill, 144
Steinbeck, John, 123
Stengel, Casey, 9
Stepin Fetchit, 15
Stereotyping, **291–92**
  African American humor and, 14
  American Indian Humor and, 27

blackface comedy and, 50
ethnic humor and, 117
gender and humor and, 134
Hispanic humor and, 146
Stern, Howard, 2–3, 65, 249
Sterngold, James, 271
Steve Canyon, 93, 95
Stevens, James, 128
Stevenson, Adlai, 233
Stewart, Jimmy, 203, 204
Stewart, Jon, 174, 253, 289
Still Talking, 81
Still the Official Lawyer's Handbook, 187
Stine, R.L., 66, 71, 141
The Stinky Cheese Man: And Other Fairly Stupid Tales, 70, 264
Stir Crazy, 205
Stoker, Bram, 139
Stone, Laurie, 17, 132, 133
Stoopnagle and Budd, 247
Stoppard, Tom, 110
The Stories of Bernard Malamud, 122
The Story of English, 132
The Story of the Three Little Pigs, 264
Storyteller, 30
Streep, Meryl, 261
Streisand, Barbra, 286
Stringbean (David Akeman), 287
Stromquist, Eric, 58
The Strong Man, 277
Struthers, Sally, 281
Stuart Little, 70, 157
Stuck Rubber Baby, 90
Studer, Debra, 188
Studies in American Humor, 3
The Stupids Die, 68
The Stupids Have a Ball, 68
The Stupids Step Out, 68
A Subtreasury of American Humor, 157
Suddenly Susan, 271
Suicide in B-flat, 110
Sullivan, Arthur, 213
Sullivan, Ed, 298
Summer Switch, 69
Sunday Newspaper Parody, 155
The Sunday Times, 197
The Sunshine Boys, 205, 307
Superiority and hostility, **292–94**.
  See also Black humor
  children's literature and, 68
  sports language and, 284–86
  wit and, 309–10
Superman, 87, 93
Supernatural in humorous movies, 204
The Surprise Symphony, 211
Surrell, Matt, 129
Surrounded Islands, 42
Suspects, 120
Swain, Mack, 56

Index

Index

Alleen Pace Nilsen is professor of English at Arizona State University and the editor of the International Society for Humor Studies (ISHS) Newsletter. She is also a recipient of the Lifetime Achievement Award for Scholarship and Service from the ISHS. She is the author of *Literature for Today's Young Adults*, *Presenting M. E. Kerr*, and *Language Play: An Introduction to Linguistics* in addition to many humor related articles. In addition, Dr. Nilsen is a founding member of the ISHS and a former president of the American Humor Studies Association.

Don L. F. Nilsen is professor of English at Arizona State University and executive secretary for the International Society for Humor Studies (ISHS). He is the author of many books about humor including *Humor in Eighteenth- and Nineteenth-Century British Literature: A Reference Guide*; *Humor Scholarship: A Research Bibliography*; *Humor in American Literature: A Selected Annotated Bibliography*; *Language Play: An Introduction to Linguistics*; and *English Adverbials*. He has also edited several books on humor including *Humor and Translation* and a series of six *World Humor and Irony Membership Serial Yearbook (WHIMSY)* titles. Dr. Nilsen has also been recognized *by Contemporary Authors*, *International Who's Who in Education*, and *2,000 Notable American Men*.